Jennifer Kyrnin

Julie Meloni

Sams **Teach Yourself**

HTML, CSS, and JavaScript

Third Edition

All in One

Pearson

Sams Teach Yourself HTML, CSS, and JavaScript All in One, Third Edition

Copyright © 2019 by Pearson Education, Inc.

ISBN-13: 978-0-672-33808-3

ISBN-10: 0-672-33808-4

Library of Congress Control Number: 2018953965

01 18

Trademarks

All terms mentioned in this book that are known to be trademarks or service marks have been appropriately capitalized. Pearson cannot attest to the accuracy of this information. Use of a term in this book should not be regarded as affecting the validity of any trademark or service mark.

Warning and Disclaimer

Every effort has been made to make this book as complete and as accurate as possible, but no warranty or fitness is implied. The information provided is on an "as is" basis. The author and the publisher shall have neither liability nor responsibility to any person or entity with respect to any loss or damages arising from the information contained in this book or from the use of the CD or programs accompanying it.

Special Sales

For information about buying this title in bulk quantities, or for special sales opportunities (which may include electronic versions; custom cover designs; and content particular to your business, training goals, marketing focus, or branding interests), please contact our corporate sales department at corpsales@pearsoned.com or (800) 382-3419.

For government sales inquiries, please contact governmentsales@pearsoned.com.

For questions about sales outside the U.S., please contact intlcs@pearson.com.

Editor-in-Chief
Mark Taub

Editor
Mark Taber

Managing Editor
Sandra Schroeder

Senior Project Editor
Lori Lyons

Copy Editor
Kitty Wilson

Project Manager
Suganya Karuppasamy

Indexer
Ken Johnson

Proofreader
Abigail Manheim

Technical Editor
Julie Meloni

Editorial Assistant
Cindy Teeters

Cover Designer
Chuti Prasertsith

Compositor
codemantra

Contents at a Glance

Part V: Getting Started with Dynamic Sites

Part VI: Advanced Website Functionality and Management

Table of Contents

Part VI: Advanced Website Functionality and Management

About the Authors

Jennifer Kyrnin consults professionally on web design and web development. She has built and maintained websites of all sizes, from small single-page sites to large million-page database-driven sites for international audiences. She has taught HTML, XML, and web design online since 1997 and is the author of *Sams Teach Yourself HTML5 Mobile Application Development*, *Sams Teach Yourself Responsive Web Design*, and *Sams Teach Yourself Bootstrap*.

Julie Meloni is a software development manager and technical consultant living in Washington, DC. She has written several books and articles on web-based programming languages and database topics, including the bestselling *Sams Teach Yourself PHP, MySQL, and Apache All in One*.

Dedication

To Mark and Jaryth. As usual, you inspired me and kept me writing.

Acknowledgments

I would like to thank Mark Taber for thinking of me when this new edition came out. I couldn't have had a good-looking book without Kitty Wilson, my extraordinary copy editor. Any errors are not her fault. And thanks also go to Julie Meloni for believing that I could take over her book effectively. I hope I live up to her reputation.

Accessing the Free Web Edition

Your purchase of this book in any format, print or electronic, includes access to the corresponding Web Edition, which provides several special features to help you learn:

- ▶ The complete text of the book online

- ▶ Interactive quizzes and exercises to test your understanding of the material

- ▶ Updates and corrections as they become available

The Web Edition can be viewed on all types of computers and mobile devices with any modern web browser that supports HTML5.

To get access to the Web Edition of *Sams Teach Yourself HTML, CSS, and JavaScript All in One*, Third Edition, all you need to do is register this book:

1. Go to www.informit.com/register.

2. Sign in or create a new account.

3. Enter the ISBN: **9780672338083**.

4. Answer the questions as proof of purchase.

The Web Edition will appear under the Digital Purchases tab on your Account page.

Click the Launch link to access the product.

Reader Services

Register your copy of *Sams Teach Yourself HTML, CSS, and JavaScript All in One* at informit.com for convenient access to downloads, updates, and corrections as they become available. To start the registration process, go to informit.com/register and log in or create an account.* Enter the product ISBN, 9780672338083, and click Submit. Once the process is complete, you will find any available bonus content under Registered Products.

*Be sure to check the box that you would like to hear from us in order to receive exclusive discounts on future editions of this product.

LESSON 1
Understanding How the Web Works

What You'll Learn in This Lesson:

▶ A very brief history of the World Wide Web

▶ What is meant by the term *web page* and why this term doesn't always reflect all the content involved

▶ How content gets from your personal computer to someone else's web browser

▶ How to select a web hosting provider

▶ How different web browsers and device types can affect your content

▶ How to transfer files to your web server by using FTP

▶ Where files should be placed on a web server

▶ How to distribute web content without a web server

▶ How to use other publishing methods, such as blogs

▶ Tips for testing the appearance and functionality of web content

Before you learn the intricacies of HTML (Hypertext Markup Language), CSS (Cascading Style Sheets), and JavaScript, it is important to gain a solid understanding of the technologies that help transform these plain-text files to the rich multimedia displays you see on your computer or handheld device when browsing the World Wide Web.

For example, a file containing HTML and CSS is useless without a web browser to view it, and no one besides yourself will see your content unless a web server is involved. Web servers make your content available to others, who, in turn, use their web browsers and other devices to navigate to an address and wait for the server to send information to them. You will be intimately involved in this publishing process because you must create files and then put them on a server to make them available in the first place, and you must ensure that your content will appear to the end user as you intended, whether the user has a screen the size of a watch face or a billboard.

A Brief History of HTML and the World Wide Web

Once upon a time, back when there weren't any footprints on the Moon, some farsighted folks decided to see whether they could connect several major computer networks. We'll spare you the names and stories (there are plenty of both), but the eventual result was the "mother of all networks," which we now call the Internet.

Until 1990, accessing information through the Internet was a rather technical affair. It was so hard, in fact, that even Ph.D.-holding physicists were often frustrated when trying to swap data. One such physicist, the now-famous (and knighted) Sir Tim Berners-Lee, cooked up a way to easily cross-reference text on the Internet through hypertext links.

This wasn't a new idea, but his simple Hypertext Markup Language (HTML) managed to thrive while more ambitious hypertext projects floundered. *Hypertext* originally meant text stored in electronic form with cross-reference links between pages. It is now a broader term that refers to just about any object (text, images, files, and so on) that can be linked to other objects. *Hypertext Markup Language* is a language for describing how text, graphics, and files containing other information are organized and linked.

By 1993, only 100 or so computers throughout the world were equipped to serve up HTML pages. Those interlinked pages were dubbed the *World Wide Web* (*WWW*), and several web browser programs had been written to enable people to view web pages. Because of the growing popularity of the Web, a few programmers soon wrote web browsers that could view graphical images along with text. From that point forward, the continued development of web browser software and the standardization of HTML has led us to the world we live in today, one in which more than a billion websites serve billions of text and multimedia files.

NOTE

For more information on the history of the World Wide Web, see the Wikipedia article on this topic: http://en.wikipedia.org/wiki/History_of_the_Web.

These few paragraphs provide a very brief history of what has been a remarkable period. Today's college students have never known a time in which the World Wide Web didn't exist, and the idea of always-on information and ubiquitous computing will shape all aspects of our lives moving forward. Instead of seeing web content creation and management as a set of skills possessed by only a few technically oriented folks (okay, call them geeks, if you will), by the end of these lessons, you will see that these are skills that anyone can master, regardless of inherent geekiness.

Creating Web Content

You might have noticed the use of the term *web content* rather than *web pages*; that was intentional. Although we talk of "visiting a web page," what we really mean is something like "looking at all the text and the images at one address on our computer." The text that we read and the images that we see are rendered by our web browsers, which are given certain instructions found in individual files.

Those files contain text that is *marked up* with, or surrounded by, HTML codes that tell the browser the structure of the text—as a heading, as a paragraph, as a quotation, and so on. Some HTML markup tells the browser to display an image or video file rather than plain text, which brings us back to this point: Different types of content are sent to your web browser, so simply saying *web page* doesn't begin to cover it. Here we use the term *web content* instead, to cover the full range of text, image, audio, video, and other media found online.

Other files contain CSS that tells the browser how a page should look—bold text, with a blue border, red color, and so on. CSS defines how the browser should display the content structure that is defined in the HTML.

In addition, JavaScript tells the browser how a page should interact with the user—changing colors when clicked, making a sound when the page loads, and so on. Whereas HTML describes the structure and CSS the design, JavaScript defines the behavior of the content, or how it responds to different conditions.

In later lessons, you'll learn the basics of linking to or creating the various types of multimedia web content found in websites. You will also learn how to style that content with CSS and how to make it interactive with JavaScript. All you need to remember at this point is that *you* are in control of the content a user sees when visiting your website. Beginning with the file that contains text to display or codes that tell the server to send a graphic along to the user's web browser, you have to plan, design, and implement all the pieces that will eventually make up your web presence. As you will learn throughout these lessons, it is not a difficult process as long as you understand all the little steps along the way.

In its most fundamental form, web content begins with a simple text file containing HTML markup. In these lessons, you'll learn about and compose standards-compliant HTML5 markup. You will then learn how to decorate it with CSS and modern style properties and how to affect the page behavior with unobtrusive JavaScript and modern JavaScript frameworks. One of the many benefits of writing modern, standards-compliant code is that, in the future, you will not have to worry about having to go back to your code to fundamentally alter it. Instead, your code will (likely) always work for as long as web browsers adhere to standards (hopefully a long time), and your code will work on any device that runs a standards-compliant browser (hopefully most of them).

Understanding Web Content Delivery

Several processes occur, in many different locations, to eventually produce web content that you can see. These processes occur very quickly—on the order of milliseconds—and occur behind the scenes. In other words, although we might think all we are doing is opening a web browser, typing in a web address, and instantaneously seeing the content we requested, technology in the background is working hard on our behalf. Figure 1.1 shows the basic interaction between a browser and a server.

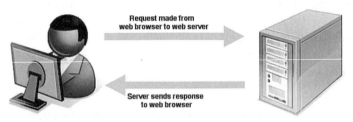

FIGURE 1.1
A browser request and a server response.

However, the process involves several steps—and potentially several trips between the browser and the server—before you see the entire content of the site you requested.

Suppose you want to do a Google search, so you dutifully type **www.google.com** in the address bar or select the Google bookmark from your bookmarks list. Almost immediately, your browser shows you something like what's shown in Figure 1.2.

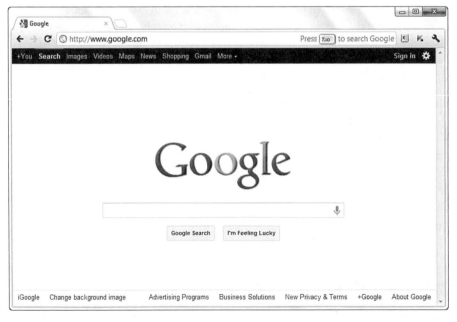

FIGURE 1.2
Visiting www.google.com.

Figure 1.2 shows a website that contains text plus one image (the Google logo). A simple version of the processes that occurred to retrieve that text and image from a web server and display it on your screen follows:

1. Your web browser sends a request for the `index.html` file located at the http://www.google.com address. The `index.html` file does not have to be part of the address that you type in the address bar; you'll learn more about the `index.html` file further along in this lesson.

2. After receiving the request for a specific file, the web server process looks in its directory contents for the specific file, opens it, and sends the content of that file back to your web browser.

3. The web browser receives the content of the `index.html` file, which is text marked up with HTML codes, and renders the content based on these HTML codes. While rendering the content, the browser happens upon the HTML code for the Google logo, which you can see in Figure 1.2. The HTML code looks something like this:

```
<img alt="Google" src="/images/srpr/logo4w.png"
     width="275" height="95">
```

   The `<img>` tag provides attributes that tell the browser the file source location (`src`), alternate text (`alt`), width (`width`), and height (`height`) necessary to display the logo. (You'll learn more about attributes throughout later lessons.)

4. The browser looks at the `src` attribute in the `<img>` tag to find the source location. In this case, the image `logo4w.png` can be found in the `images` directory at the same web address (www.google.com) from which the browser retrieved the HTML file.

5. The browser requests the file at the web address http://www.google.com/images/srpr/logo4w.png.

6. The web server interprets that request, finds the file, and sends the contents of that file to the web browser that requested it.

7. The web browser displays the image on your monitor.

As you can see in the description of the web content delivery process, web browsers do more than simply act as picture frames through which you can view content. Browsers assemble the web content components and arrange those parts according to the HTML commands in the file.

It is possible to view web content locally—that is, on your own hard drive—without the need for a web server. The process of content retrieval and display is the same as the process listed in the previous steps, in that a browser looks for and interprets the codes and content of an HTML file. However, the trip is shorter: The browser looks for files on your own computer's hard drive rather than on a remote machine. A web server would be needed to interpret any server-based programming language embedded in the files, but that is beyond the scope of these lessons. In fact, you could work through all the lessons without having a web server to call your own, but then nobody but you could view your masterpieces.

Selecting a Web Hosting Provider

Despite my just telling you that you can work through all these lessons without having a web server, having a web server is the recommended method for continuing. Don't worry; obtaining a hosting provider is usually a quick, painless, and relatively inexpensive process. In fact, you can get your own domain name and a year of web hosting for just slightly more than the cost of the lessons you are reading now.

If you type **web hosting provider** in your search engine of choice, you will get millions of hits and an endless list of sponsored search results (also known as *ads*). Even if you are looking at a managed list of hosting providers, it can be overwhelming—especially if all you are looking for is a place to host a simple website for yourself or your company or organization.

You'll want to narrow your search when looking for a provider and choose one that best meets your needs. Some selection criteria for a web hosting provider follow:

- ▶ **Reliability/server "uptime"**—If you have an online presence, you want to make sure people can actually get there consistently.

- ▶ **Customer service**—Look for multiple methods for contacting customer service (phone, email, chat), as well as online documentation for common issues.

- ▶ **Server space**—Does the hosting package include enough server space to hold all the multimedia files (images, audio, video) you plan to include in your website (if any)?

- ▶ **Bandwidth**—Does the hosting package include enough bandwidth that all the people visiting your site and downloading files can do so without your having to pay extra?

- ▶ **Domain name purchase and management**—Does the package include a custom domain name, or must you purchase and maintain your domain name separately from your hosting account?

- ▶ **Price**—Do not overpay for hosting. You will see a wide range of prices offered and should immediately wonder, "What's the difference?" Often the difference has little to do with the quality of the service and everything to do with company overhead and what the company thinks it can get away with charging people. A good rule of thumb is that if you are paying more than $75 per year for a basic hosting package and domain name, you are probably paying too much.

Here are three reliable web hosting providers whose basic packages contain plenty of server space and bandwidth (as well as domain names and extra benefits) at a relatively low cost:

NOTE

The authors have used all these providers (and then some) over the years and have no problem recommending any of them. Julie predominantly uses DailyRazor as a web hosting provider, especially for advanced development environments, while Jennifer tends to use Bluehost.

▸ **A Small Orange (www.asmallorange.com)**—The Tiny and Small shared hosting packages are perfect starting places for a new web content publisher.

▸ **DailyRazor (www.dailyrazor.com)**—Its website hosting package is full featured and reliable.

▸ **Bluehost (www.bluehost.com)**—The Basic shared hosting package is suitable for many personal and small business websites.

If you don't go with any of these web hosting providers, you can at least use their basic package descriptions as a guideline as you shop around.

One feature of a good hosting provider is that it provides a "control panel" for you to manage aspects of your account. Figure 1.3 shows the control panel for a hosting account at DailyRazor. Many web hosting providers offer this particular control panel software (called cPanel) or another control panel that is similar in design—with clearly labeled icons leading to tasks you can perform to configure and manage your account.

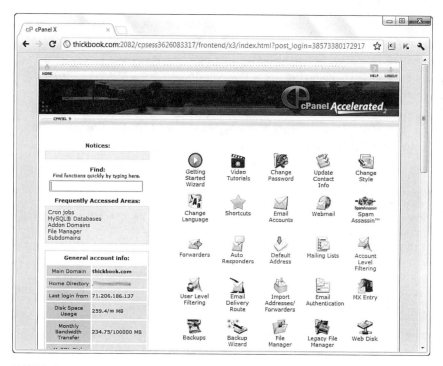

FIGURE 1.3
A sample control panel.

You might never need to use your control panel, but having it available to you simplifies the installation of databases and other software, the viewing of web statistics, and the addition of email addresses (among many other features). If you can follow instructions, you can manage your own web server—no special training required.

Testing with Multiple Web Browsers and Devices

Now that we've just discussed the process of web content delivery and the acquisition of a web server, it might seem a little strange to step back and talk about testing your websites with multiple web browsers and devices. However, before you go off and learn all about creating websites with HTML and CSS, do so with this very important statement in mind: Every visitor to your website will potentially use hardware and software configurations that are different from your own, including their device types (desktop, laptop, tablet, phone), operating systems (Windows, Mac, Android, iOS), screen resolutions, browser types, browser window sizes, and connection speeds. Remember that you cannot control any aspect of what your visitors use when they view your site. So just as you're setting up your web hosting environment and getting ready to work, think about downloading several web browsers so that you have a local test suite of tools available to you. Let us explain why this is important.

Although all web browsers process and handle information in the same general way, some specific differences among them result in things not always looking the same in different browsers. Even users of the same version of the same web browser can alter how a page appears by choosing different display options and/or changing the size of their viewing windows. All the major web browsers allow users to override the background colors and fonts the web page author specifies with those of their own choosing. Screen resolution, window size, and optional toolbars can also change how much of a page someone sees when it first appears on their screens. You can ensure only that you write standards-compliant HTML and CSS.

NOTE

In Part IV, "Responsive Web Design," you'll learn about the concept of responsive web design, in which the design of a site shifts and changes automatically depending on the user's behavior and viewing environment (screen size, device, and so on).

Do not, under any circumstances, spend hours on end designing something that looks perfect only on your own computer—unless you are willing to be disappointed when you look at it on your friend's computer, on the computer in the coffee shop down the street, or on your iPhone.

You should always test your websites with as many of these web browsers as possible:

- Apple Safari (https://www.apple.com/safari/) for Mac
- Google Chrome (https://www.google.com/chrome/) for Mac, Windows, and Linux/UNIX

▶ Mozilla Firefox (https://www.mozilla.com/firefox/) for Mac, Windows, and Linux/UNIX

▶ Microsoft Edge (https://www.microsoft.com/edge/) for Windows

▶ Opera (https://www.opera.com) for Mac, Windows, and Linux/UNIX

Now that you have a development environment set up, or at least some idea of the type you'd like to set up in the future, let's move on to creating a test file.

Creating a Sample File

Before you actually create a file, take a look at Listing 1.1. This listing represents a simple piece of web content—a few lines of HTML that print `"Hello World! Welcome to My Web Server."` in large bold letters on two lines centered within the browser window. You'll learn more about the HTML and CSS used within this file as you read future lessons.

LISTING 1.1 Our Sample HTML File

```
<!doctype html>
<html lang="en">
  <head>
    <meta charset="utf-8">
    <title>Hello World!</title>
  </head>
  <body>
    <h1 style="text-align: center;">Hello World!<br>
      Welcome to My Web Server.</h1>
  </body>
</html>
```

To make use of this content, open a text editor of your choice, such as Notepad (on Windows) or TextEdit (on a Mac). Do not use WordPad, Microsoft Word, or other full-featured word processing software because those programs create different sorts of files from the plain-text files we use for web content.

Most web designers don't use Notepad or TextEdit for writing web pages. Instead, they use editors designed specifically for the purpose. These editors give you more features to make it easy to write and design web pages. The following are some of the most popular editors:

▶ **Coda** (https://panic.com/coda/)—A text editor for Mac made specifically for editing web pages.

▶ **HTML-Kit** (https://www.htmlkit.com)—A popular text editor for Windows. The older versions are free.

- **Komodo Edit** (https://www.activestate.com/komodo-edit)—A free, open-source version of the popular Komodo IDE. It runs on Windows, Mac, and Linux.

- **Notepad++** (https://notepad-plus-plus.org)—A free, open-source editor for Windows.

- **Sublime Text** (https://sublimetext.com)—A popular editor for all platforms that also has a healthy ecosystem of free plug-ins.

Once you've decided on the editor you want to use, type the content that you see in Listing 1.1 and then save the file, using `sample.html` as the filename. The `.html` extension tells the web server that your file is written in HTML. When the file contents are sent to the web browser that requests it, the browser will also know that it is HTML and will render it appropriately.

Now that you have a sample HTML file to use—and hopefully somewhere to put it, such as a web hosting account—let's get to publishing your web content.

Using FTP to Transfer Files

As you've learned so far, you have to put your web content on a web server to make it accessible to others. This process typically occurs by using *File Transfer Protocol* (*FTP*). To use FTP, you need an FTP client—a program used to transfer files from your computer to a web server.

FTP clients require three pieces of information to connect to your web server; this information will have been sent to you by your hosting provider after you set up your account:

- The hostname, or address, to which you will connect

- Your account username

- Your account password

When you have this information, you are ready to use an FTP client to transfer content to your web server.

Selecting an FTP Client

All FTP clients generally use the same type of interface. Figure 1.4 shows an example of FireFTP, which is an FTP client used with the Firefox web browser. The directory listing of the local machine (your computer) appears on the left of the screen, and the directory listing of the remote machine (the web server) appears on the right. Typically, you see right arrow and left arrow buttons, as shown in Figure 1.4. The right arrow sends selected files from your computer to your web server; the left arrow sends files from the web server to your computer. Many FTP clients also enable you to simply select files and then drag and drop them to the target machines.

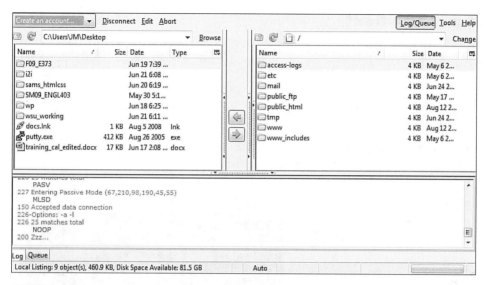

FIGURE 1.4
The FireFTP interface.

NOTE

Many web editing programs include a built-in FTP client. If you are planning on using a web editing program, find out if it does before you download (or purchase) another FTP client.

Many FTP clients are freely available to you, but you can also transfer files via the web-based File Manager tool that is likely part of your web server's control panel. However, that method of file transfer typically introduces more steps into the process and isn't nearly as streamlined (or simple) as the process of installing an FTP client on your own machine.

Here are some popular free FTP clients:

▸ **Classic FTP** (https://www.nchsoftware.com/classic/) for Mac and Windows

▸ **Cyberduck** (https://cyberduck.io) for Mac

▸ **FileZilla** (https://filezilla-project.org) for all platforms

▸ **Transmit** (https://panic.com/transmit) for Mac

When you have selected an FTP client and installed it on your computer, you are ready to upload and download files from your web server. In the next section, you'll see how this process works, using the sample file from Listing 1.1.

Using an FTP Client

The following steps show how to use Transmit to connect to your web server and transfer a file. However, all FTP clients use similar interfaces, so if you understand the following steps, you should be able to use any FTP client.

Remember that you first need the hostname, the account username, and the account password. When you have them, follow these steps:

1. Start the Transmit program and click the FTP tab. You are prompted to fill out information for the site to which you want to connect, as shown in Figure 1.5.

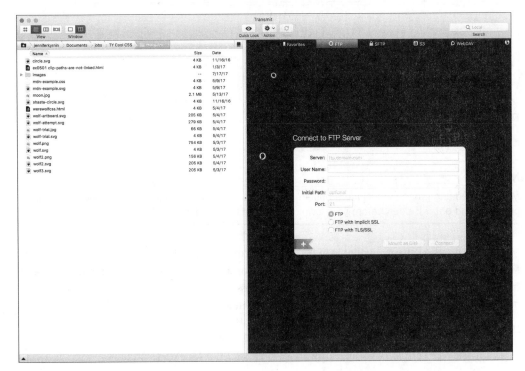

FIGURE 1.5
Connecting to a new site in Transmit.

2. Fill in each of the items shown in Figure 1.5, as described here:

▶ The Server is the FTP address of the web server to which you need to send your web pages. Your hosting provider will have given you this address. It probably is *yourdomain*.com, but check the information you received when you signed up for service.

▶ Complete the User Name field and the Password field using the information your hosting provider gave you.

▸ Leave the Initial Path field blank for now. You learn more about this later in the lesson.

▸ Leave the Port field set to 21 and choose **FTP** unless your hosting provider specified to use SSL or TLS/SSL.

▸ When you're finished with the settings, click Connect to go to the FTP server. You can click the plus icon if you want to add this server to your favorites.

You now see a countdown timer in the lower right, indicating that Transmit is attempting to connect to the web server. Upon successful connection, you see an interface like the one in Figure 1.6, showing the contents of the local directory on the left and the contents of your web server on the right.

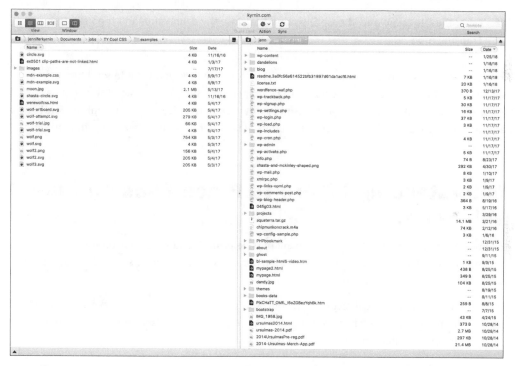

FIGURE 1.6
A successful connection to a remote web server via Transmit.

You are now *almost* ready to transfer files to your web server. All that remains is to change directories to what is called the *document root* of your web server. The document root of your web server is the directory that is designated as the top-level directory for your web content—the starting point of the directory structure, which you'll learn more about later in this lesson. Often, this directory is named `public_html`, www (because www has been created as an alias for `public_html`), or `htdocs`. You do not have to create this directory; your hosting provider will have created it for you.

3. Double-click the document root directory name to open it. The display shown on the right of the FTP client interface changes to show the contents of this directory. (It will probably be empty at this point, unless your web hosting provider has put placeholder files in that directory on your behalf.)

4. The goal is to transfer the `sample.html` file you created earlier from your computer to the web server, so find the file in the directory listing on the left of the FTP client interface (navigate if you have to).

5. Click the file and drag it to the right side of the window to send the file to the web server. (Alternatively, you can double-click the file to transfer it.) When the file transfer completes, the right side of the client interface refreshes to show you that the file has made it to its destination.

6. Go to the File menu and choose Disconnect to close the connection and then exit the Transmit program.

These steps are conceptually similar to the steps you take anytime you want to send files to your web server via FTP. You can also use your FTP client to create subdirectories on the remote web server. To create a subdirectory using Transmit, right-click in the directory you want the folder to be in and choose New Folder. Different FTP clients have different interface options for achieving the same goal.

Understanding Where to Place Files on the Web Server

An important aspect of maintaining web content is determining how you will organize that content—not only for the user to find but also for you to maintain on your server. Putting files in directories helps you manage those files.

How you name and organize directories on your web server and whether you develop rules for file maintenance are completely up to you. Maintaining a well-organized server makes your management of its content more efficient in the long run.

Basic File Management

As you browse the Web, you might have noticed that URLs change as you navigate through websites. For instance, if you're looking at a company's website and you click on graphical navigation leading to the company's products or services, the URL probably changes from

http://www.*companyname*.com/

to

http://www.*companyname*.com/products/

or

http://www.*companyname*.com/services/

In the preceding section, we used the term *document root* without really explaining what that is all about. The document root of a web server is essentially the trailing slash in the full URL. For instance, if your domain is *yourdomain*.com and your URL is http://www.*yourdomain*.com/, the document root is the directory represented by the trailing slash (/). The document root is the starting point of the directory structure you create on your web server; it is the place where the web server begins looking for files requested by the web browser.

If you put the `sample.html` file in your document root as previously directed, you will be able to access it via a web browser at the following URL:

http://www.*yourdomain*.com/sample.html

If you entered this URL into your web browser, you would see the rendered `sample.html` file, as shown in Figure 1.7.

FIGURE 1.7
The `sample.html` file, accessed via a web browser.

However, if you created a new directory within the document root and put the `sample.html` file in that directory, the file would be accessed at this URL:

http://www.*yourdomain*.com/newdirectory/sample.html

If you put the `sample.html` file in the directory you originally saw upon connecting to your server—that is, if you did *not* change directories and place the file in the document root—the `sample.html` file would not be accessible from your web server at any URL. The file would still be on the machine that you know as your web server, but because the file is not in the document root—where the server software knows to start looking for files—it will never be accessible to anyone via a web browser.

The bottom line? Always navigate to the document root of your web server before you start transferring files. And if your FTP client allows, change the default starting directory to your document root, just to be extra careful.

This is especially true with graphics and other multimedia files. A common directory on web servers is called `images`, where, as you can imagine, all the image assets are placed for retrieval. Other popular directories include `css` for style sheet files (if you are using more than one) and `js` for external JavaScript files. Alternatively, if you know that you will have an area on your website where visitors can download many types of files, you might simply call that directory `downloads`.

Whether it's a ZIP file containing your art portfolio or an Excel spreadsheet with sales numbers, it's often useful to publish files on the Internet that aren't simply web pages. To make available on the Web a file that isn't an HTML file, just upload the file to your website as if it *were* an HTML file, following the instructions earlier in this lesson for uploading. After the file is uploaded to the web server, you can create a link to it (as you'll learn in Lesson 7, "Using External and Internal Links"). In other words, your web server can serve much more than HTML.

Here's a sample of the HTML code that you will learn more about later in these lessons. The following code would be used for a file named `artfolio.zip`, located in the `downloads` directory of your website, and with link text that reads `Download my art portfolio!`:

```
<a href="/downloads/artfolio.zip">Download my art portfolio!</a>
```

Using an Index Page

When you think of an index, you probably think of the section in the back of a book that tells where to look for various keywords and topics. The index file in a web server directory can serve a similar purpose—if you design it that way. In fact, that's where the name originates.

The `index.html` file (or just *index file*, as it's usually referred to) is the name you give to the page you want people to see as the default file when they navigate to a specific directory in your website.

Another function of the index page is that users who visit a directory on your site that has an index page but who do not specify that page will still land on the main page for that section of your site—or for the site itself.

For instance, you can type either of the following URLs and land on Apple's iPhone informational page:

> http://www.apple.com/iphone/
>
> http://www.apple.com/iphone/index.html

If there were no `index.html` page in the `iphone` directory, the results would depend on the configuration of the web server. If the server is configured to disallow directory browsing, the user would see a "Directory Listing Denied" message when attempting to access the URL without a specified page name. However, if the server is configured to allow directory browsing, the user would see a list of the files in that directory.

Your hosting provider will already have determined these server configuration options. If your hosting provider enables you to modify server settings via a control panel, you can change these settings so that your server responds to requests based on your own requirements.

Not only is the index file used in subdirectories, but it's used in the top-level directory (or document root) of your website as well. The first page of your website—or *home page* or *main page*, or however you like to refer to the web content you want users to see when they first visit your domain—should be named `index.html` and placed in the document root of your web server. This ensures that when users type **http://www.*yourdomain*.com/** into their web browsers, the server responds with the content you intended them to see (instead of "Directory Listing Denied" or some other unintended consequence).

Distributing Content Without a Web Server

Publishing HTML and multimedia files online is obviously the primary reason to learn HTML and create web content. However, there are also situations in which other forms of publishing may be useful? For example, you might want to distribute CD-ROMs, DVD-ROMs, or USB drives at a trade show with marketing materials designed as web content—that is, hyperlinked text viewable through a web browser but without a web server involved. You might also want to include HTML-based instructional manuals on removable media for students at a training seminar. These are just two examples of how HTML pages can be used in publishing scenarios that don't involve the Internet.

This process is called creating *local* sites; even though no web server is involved, these bundles of hypertext content are still called *sites*. The *local* term comes into play because your files are accessed locally and not remotely (via a web server).

Publishing Content Locally

Let's assume that you need to create a local site that you want to distribute on a USB drive. Even the cheapest USB drives hold so much data these days—and basic hypertext files are quite small— that you can distribute an entire site *and a fully functioning web browser* all on one little drive.

NOTE

Distributing a web browser isn't required when you are creating and distributing a local site, although it's a nice touch. You can reasonably assume that users have their own web browsers and will open the `index.html` file in a directory to start browsing the hyperlinked content. However, if you want to distribute a web browser on the USB drive, go to https://portableapps.com/ and look for Portable Firefox or Portable Chrome.

You can think of the directory structure of your USB drive just as you would the directory structure of your web server. The top level of the USB drive directory structure can be your document root. Or if you are distributing a web browser along with the content, you might have two directories— for example, one named `browser` and one named `content`. In that case, the `content` directory would be your document root. Within the document root, you could have additional subfolders in which you place content and other multimedia assets.

It's as important to maintain good organization with a local site as it is with a remote website so that you avoid broken links in your HTML files. You'll learn more about the specifics of linking files in Lesson 7.

Publishing Content on a Blog

You might have a blog hosted by a third party, such as WordPress, Tumblr, or Blogger, and thus have already published content without having a dedicated web server or even knowing any HTML. These services offer *visual editors* in addition to *source editors*, meaning that you can type your words and add presentational formatting such as bold, italics, or font colors without knowing the HTML for these actions. The content becomes actual HTML when you click the Publish button in these editors.

However, with the knowledge you will acquire from these lessons, your blogging will be enhanced because you will be able to use the source editor for your blog post content and blog templates, and this will afford you more control over the look and feel of that content. These actions occur differently from the process you learned for creating an HTML file and uploading it via FTP to your own dedicated web server, but we would be remiss if we did not note that blogging is, in fact, a form of web publishing.

Tips for Testing Web Content

Whenever you transfer files to your web server or place them on removable media for local browsing, you should test every page thoroughly. The following list helps you ensure that your web content behaves the way you expect. Note that some of the terms might be unfamiliar to you at this point, but come back to this list as you progress through these lessons and create larger projects:

▶ Before you transfer your files, test them locally on your machine to ensure that the links work and the content reflects the visual design you intended. After you transfer the pages to a web server or removable device, test them all again.

▶ Perform these tests with as many browsers and devices as you can—Chrome, Firefox, Microsoft Edge, Opera, and Safari is a good list—and on both Mac and Windows platforms, as well as mobile devices like phones and tablets. If possible, check at low resolution (800 × 600) and high resolution (1920 × 1080).

▶ Turn off auto image loading in your web browser before you start testing so that you can see what each page looks like without the graphics. Check your alt text and then turn image loading back on to load the graphics and carefully review the page again.

▶ Use your browser's font size settings to look at each page in various font sizes to ensure that your layout doesn't fall to pieces if users override your font specifications with their own.

▶ Wait for each page to completely finish loading and then scroll all the way down to make sure all images appear where they should.

▶ Time how long it takes each page to load. Use a tool like Google Page Speed (https://developers.google.com/speed/) to make sure it isn't too slow. Slow pages annoy users and can get your site penalized by search engines.

If your pages pass all those tests, you can rest easy: Your site is ready for public viewing.

Summary

This lesson introduced you to the concept of using HTML to mark up text files to produce web content. You learned that HTML generates the structure, while CSS creates the look, and JavaScript controls the behavior of the pages. You also learned that there is more to web content than just the "page"; web content also includes image, audio, and video files. All this content lives on a web server—a remote machine often far from your own computer. On your computer or other device, you use a web browser to request, retrieve, and eventually display web content onscreen.

You learned the criteria to consider when determining whether a web hosting provider fits your needs. After you have selected a web hosting provider, you can begin to transfer files to your web server by using an FTP client, which you also learned how to do. You also learned a bit about web server directory structures and file management, as well as the very important purpose of the index.html file in a given web server directory. In addition, you learned that you can distribute web content on removable media, and you learned how to go about structuring the files and directories to achieve the goal of viewing content without using a remote web server.

Finally, you learned the importance of testing your work in multiple browsers after you've placed it on a web server. Writing valid, standards-compliant HTML and CSS helps ensure that your site looks reasonably similar for all visitors, but you still shouldn't design without receiving input from potential users outside your development team; it is *especially* important to get input from others when you are a design team of one!

Q&A

Q. I've looked at the HTML source of some web pages on the Internet, and it looks frighteningly difficult to learn. Do I have to think like a computer programmer to learn this stuff?

A. Although complex HTML pages can indeed look daunting, learning HTML is much easier than learning actual software programming languages (such as C++ or Java). HTML is a markup language rather than a programming language; you mark up text so that the browser can render the text a certain way. It requires a completely different set of thought processes than developing a computer program. You really don't need any experience or skill as a computer programmer to be a web content author.

Q. Running all the tests you recommend would take longer than creating my pages! Can't I get away with less testing?

A. If your pages aren't intended to make money or provide an important service, it's probably not a big deal if they look funny to some users or produce errors once in a while. In that case, just test each page with a couple different browsers and call it a day. However, if you need to project a professional image, there is no substitute for rigorous testing.

Q. Seriously, who cares how I organize my web content?

A. Believe it or not, the organization of your web content does matter to search engines and potential visitors to your site. But overall, having an organized web server directory structure helps you keep track of content that you are likely to update frequently. For instance, if you have a dedicated directory for images or multimedia, you know exactly where to look for a file you want to update—no need to hunt through directories containing other content.

Workshop

The Workshop contains quiz questions and exercises to help you solidify your understanding of the material covered.

Quiz

1. How many files would you need to store on a web server to produce a single web page with some text and two images on it?

2. How many requests to the server would a browser make to display a web page with some text and two images on it?

3. What are some of the features to look for in a web hosting provider?

4. How many browsers should you use to test your web pages?

5. What type of editor should you use to create web pages?

6. What three pieces of information do you need in order to connect to your web server via FTP?

7. What is the document root?

8. Is it possible to publish web pages to a USB drive?

9. What is the purpose of the `index.html` file?

10. Does your website have to include a directory structure?

Answers

1. You would need three: one for the web page itself, which includes the text and the HTML markup, and one for each of the two images.

2. There would be three requests to the server: one for the HTML itself and one for each of the two images.

3. Look for reliability, customer service, web space and bandwidth, domain name service, site-management extras, and price.

4. You should test your website in as many browsers and on as many devices as possible.

5. You should use a text editor such as Notepad or TextEdit. You can also use an editor specifically for writing HTML, such as Komodo Edit or Coda.

6. You need the hostname, your account username, and your account password.

7. The document root is the top-level directory on a web server—the trailing slash after the domain name.

8. Yes. This is called publishing content locally.

9. The `index.html` file is typically the default file for a directory in a web server. It enables users to access http://www.*yourdomain*.com/*somedirectory*/ without using a trailing filename and still end up in the appropriate place.

10. No. Using a directory structure for file organization is completely up to you, although using one is highly recommended because it simplifies content maintenance.

Exercises

▶ Get your web hosting in order: Are you going to move through the lessons by viewing files locally on your own computer, or are you going to use a web hosting provider? Note that most web hosting providers will have you up and running the same day you purchase your hosting plan. Name three possible hosting providers.

▶ If you are using an external hosting provider, then use your FTP client to create a subdirectory within the document root of your website. Paste the contents of the `sample.html` file into another file named `index.html`, change the text between the `<title>` and `</title>` tags to something new, and change the text between the `<h1>` and `</h1>` tags to something new. Save the file and upload it to the new subdirectory. Use your web browser to navigate to the new directory on your web server and ensure that the content in the `index.html` file appears. Then, using your FTP client, delete the `index.html` file from the remote subdirectory. Return to that URL with your web browser, reload the page, and see how the server responds without the `index.html` file in place. Name two FTP clients.

▶ Using the same set of files created in the preceding exercise, place these files on a removable media device—a CD-ROM or a USB drive, for example. Use your browser to navigate this local version of your sample website and think about the instructions you would have to distribute with this removable media so that others could use it.

LESSON 2
Structuring an HTML Document

What You'll Learn in This Lesson:

▶ How to create a simple web page in HTML

▶ How to include all the HTML tags that every web page must have

▶ How to organize a page with paragraphs and line breaks

▶ How to organize your content with headings

▶ How to use the semantic elements of HTML5

▶ How to use semantic tags to indicate header and footer content

▶ How to use semantic tags to indicate navigational and secondary content

▶ How to use semantic tags to better structure body content

In the first lesson, you got a basic idea of the process behind creating web content and viewing it online (or locally, if you do not yet have a web hosting provider). In this lesson, we get down to the business of explaining the various elements that must appear in an HTML file so that it is displayed appropriately in your web browser.

In general, this lesson provides a summary of HTML basics and gives some practical tips to help you make the most of your time as a web page developer. You'll begin to dive a bit deeper into the theory behind it all as you learn about the HTML5 elements that enable you to enhance the semantics—the meaning—of the information that you provide in your marked-up text. You'll take a closer look at six elements that are fundamental to solid semantic structuring of your documents: `<header>`, `<section>`, `<article>`, `<nav>`, `<aside>`, and `<footer>`.

Throughout the remainder of these lessons, you will see these tags used appropriately in the code samples, so this lesson makes sure that you have a good grasp of their meaning before you continue.

Getting Prepared

Here's a review of what you need to do before you're ready to move on in this lesson:

1. **Get a computer.** We used a Mac computer to test the sample web content and capture the figures shown in these lessons, but you can use any Windows, Mac, or Linux/UNIX machine to create and view your web content. You can even use a tablet or smartphone, but that is more difficult. For the purposes of these lessons, it's best to get a computer or laptop.

2. **Get a connection to the Internet.** Whether you have a dial-up, wireless, or broadband connection doesn't matter for the creation and viewing of your web content, but the faster the connection, the better for the overall experience. The Internet service provider (ISP), school, or business that provides your Internet connection can help you with the details of setting it up properly. In addition, many public spaces such as coffee shops, bookstores, and libraries offer free wireless Internet service that you can use if you have a laptop computer with Wi-Fi network support.

3. **Get web browser software.** This is the software your computer needs in order to retrieve and display web content. As you learned in the first lesson, the most popular browsers (in alphabetical order) are Apple Safari, Google Chrome, Microsoft Edge, Mozilla Firefox, and Opera. It's a good idea to install several of these browsers so that you can experiment and make sure your content looks consistent across them all; you can't make assumptions about the browsers other people are using.

4. **Explore!** Use a web browser to look around the Internet for websites that are similar in content or appearance to those you'd like to create. Note what frustrates you about some pages, what attracts you and keeps you reading others, and what makes you come back to some pages over and over again. If a particular topic interests you, consider searching for it using a popular search engine such as Google (www.google.com) or Bing (www.bing.com).

CAUTION

Although all web browsers process and handle information in the same general way, some specific differences among them mean that things do not always look the same in different browsers. Be sure to check your web pages in multiple browsers to make sure they look reasonably consistent.

This is doubly true for mobile devices. More and more people use mobile devices such as phones and tablets to access web pages, and the browsers on those devices can display your pages in surprising ways. Always test your pages in as many different devices and screen sizes as possible, along with the different web browsers.

NOTE

As discussed in the first lesson, if you plan to put your web content on the Internet (as opposed to publishing it on CD-ROM or a local intranet), you need to transfer it to a computer that is connected to the Internet 24 hours a day. The same company or school that provides you with Internet access might also provide web space; if not, you might need to pay a hosting provider for the service.

Getting Started with a Simple Web Page

In the first lesson, you learned that a web page is just a text file that is marked up by (or surrounded by) HTML codes that tell the browser how to display the text. To create these text files, use a text editor such as Notepad (on Windows), TextEdit (on a Mac), or any of the other suggested editors; do not use WordPad, Microsoft Word, or other full-featured word-processing software because those create different sorts of files from the plain-text files we use for web content.

CAUTION

We reiterate this point because it is very important to both the outcome and the learning process itself: Do not create your first HTML file with Microsoft Word or any other HTML-compatible word processor; most of these programs attempt to rewrite your HTML for you in strange ways, potentially leaving you totally confused. The same holds true when you use Microsoft Word and "Save As" HTML: You are likely to get a verbose and noncompliant file full of HTML that will not validate and will cause you headaches to edit.

In addition, we recommend that you *not* use a graphical, what-you-see-is-what-you-get (WYSIWYG) editor, such Adobe Dreamweaver. You'll likely find it easier and more educational to start with a simple text editor while you're starting to learn HTML.

NOTE

As mentioned in the first lesson, most professional web developers use a web page editor designed specifically for building web pages and web applications. We prefer to use Coda (for Mac) but Komodo Edit (https://www.activestate.com/komodo-edit) is a free editor that has a lot of useful features for writing HTML, CSS, and JavaScript. And it's available for Windows, Mac, and Linux/UNIX. These are both text editors and do not have the drawbacks of WYSIWYG editors that are mentioned in the previous Caution.

Before you begin working, you should start with some text that you want to put on a web page:

1. Find (or write) a few paragraphs of text about yourself, your family, your company, your softball team, or some other subject in which you're interested.

2. Save this text as plain, standard ASCII text. Notepad (on Windows) and most other simple text editors automatically save files as plain text, but if you're using another program, you might need to choose this file type as an option (after selecting File, Save As).

CAUTION

If you've chosen to use TextEdit on a Mac computer, you need to go into the Preferences dialog box and choose Plain Text in the New Document pane. It's also a good idea to turn off smart copy/ paste, smart quotes, and smart dashes so that your web page files are written correctly.

As you go through this lesson, you will add HTML markup (called *tags*) to the text file, thus making it into web content.

When you save files containing HTML tags, always give them a name ending in `.html`. This is important; if you forget to type the `.html` at the end of the filename when you save the file, most text editors will give it some other extension (such as `.txt`). If that happens, you might not be able to find the file when you try to look at it with a web browser; if you find it, it certainly won't display properly. In other words, web browsers expect a web page file to have the file extension `.html` and to be in plain-text format.

When visiting websites, you might also encounter pages with the file extension `.htm`, which is an acceptable file extension to use. You might find other file extensions used on the Web, such as `.jsp` (Java Server Pages), `.asp` (Microsoft Active Server Pages), or `.php` (PHP: Hypertext Preprocessor), but these file types use server-side technologies that are beyond the scope of HTML and these lessons. However, those files also contain HTML in addition to the programming language. The programming code in those files is compiled on the server side, and all you would see if you viewed the source in a web browser would be the HTML output. If you looked at the source files, you would likely see some intricate weaving of programming and markup codes.

Listing 2.1 shows an example of text you can type and save to create a simple HTML page. If you opened this file with Chrome, you would see the page shown in Figure 2.1. Every web page you create must include a `<!doctype>` declaration, as well as `<html></html>`, `<head></head>`, `<title></title>`, and `<body></body>` tag pairs.

LISTING 2.1   The `<html>`, `<head>`, `<title>`, and `<body>` Tags

```
<!doctype html>
<html lang="en">
  <head>
    <meta charset="utf-8">
    <title>The First Web Page</title>
  </head>
  <body>
    <p>
      In the beginning, Tim created the HyperText Markup Language.
      The Internet was without form and void, and text was upon the
      face of the monitor and the Hands of Tim were moving over the
      face of the keyboard. And Tim said, Let there be links; and
      there were links. And Tim saw that the links were good; and
      Tim separated the links from the text. Tim called the links
```

```
      Anchors, and the text He called Other Stuff. And the whole
      thing together was the first Web Page.
    </p>
  </body>
</html>
```

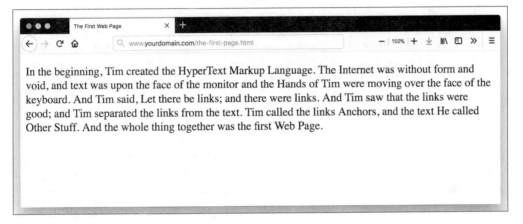

FIGURE 2.1
When you save the text in Listing 2.1 as an HTML file and view it with a web browser, only the actual title and body text are displayed.

In Listing 2.1, as in every HTML page, the words starting with < and ending with > are actually coded commands. These coded commands are called *HTML tags* because they "tag" pieces of text and tell the web browser what kind of text it is. This allows the web browser to display the text appropriately. HTML tags can be written in uppercase, lowercase, or a combination of both. But best practices say you should use all lowercase letters for your tags.

The first line in the document is the document type declaration; you are *declaring* that it is html (specifically, HTML5) because html is the value used to declare a document as HTML5 in the <!doctype> tag. We have written this tag in all lowercase, but many people write it <!DOCTYPE> to differentiate it from the actual HTML in the document.

Creating and Viewing a Basic Web Page

Before you learn the meaning of the HTML tags used in Listing 2.1, you might want to see exactly how we went about creating and viewing the document itself. Follow these steps:

1. Type all the text in Listing 2.1, including the HTML tags, in Windows Notepad (or use TextEdit on a Mac or another text editor of your choice).

2. Select File, Save As. Be sure to select plain text (or ASCII text) as the file type.

3. Name the file `firstpage.html`.

4. Choose the folder on your hard drive where you want to keep your web pages—and remember which folder you choose! Click the Save or OK button to save the file.

5. Now start your favorite web browser. (Leave your text editor running, too, so you can easily switch between viewing and editing your page.)

   In Microsoft Edge, select File, Open and click Browse. If you're using Firefox or Safari, select File, Open File. Navigate to the appropriate folder and select the `firstpage.html` file. Some browsers and operating systems also enable you to drag and drop the `firstpage.html` file onto the browser window to view it.

   Voilà! You should see the page shown in Figure 2.1.

If you have obtained a web hosting account, you could use FTP at this point to transfer the `firstpage.html` file to the web server. In fact, from this lesson forward, the instructions assume that you have a hosting provider and are comfortable sending files back and forth via FTP; if that is not the case, you should review the first lesson before moving on. Alternatively, if you are consciously choosing to work with files locally (without a web host), be prepared to adjust the instructions to suit your particular needs (such as ignoring the instructions "transfer the files" and "type in the URL").

NOTE

You don't need to be connected to the Internet to view a web page stored on your own computer. By default, your web browser tries to connect to the Internet every time you start it, which makes sense most of the time. However, this can be a hassle if you're developing pages locally on your hard drive (offline), and you keep getting errors about a page not being found. If you have a full-time web connection via a LAN, a cable modem, Wi-Fi, or DSL, this is a moot point because the browser will never complain about being offline. Otherwise, the appropriate action depends on your breed of browser; check the options under your browser's Tools menu.

HTML Tags Every Web Page Must Have

The time has come for the secret language of HTML tags to be revealed to you. When you understand this language, you will have creative powers far beyond those of other humans. Don't tell the other humans, but it's really pretty easy.

The first line of code is the document type declaration; in HTML5, this is simply

```
<!doctype html>
```

This declaration identifies the document as being HTML5, which then ensures that web browsers know what to expect and prepare in order to render content in HTML5.

Many HTML tags have two parts: an *opening tag*, which indicates where a piece of text begins, and a *closing tag*, which indicates where the piece of text ends. A closing tag starts with a / (forward slash) just after the < symbol.

Another type of tag is the *empty tag*, which is different in that it doesn't include a pair of matching opening and closing tags. Instead, an empty tag consists of a single tag that starts with < and can end with / just before the > symbol. Although the ending slash is no longer explicitly required in HTML5, it does aid in compatibility with XHTML: If you have a pile of old XHTML in your website, it will not break while you're in the process of upgrading it. In these lessons, we will be leaving the / out of empty tags unless there is an explicit need for it.

Following is a quick summary of these three tags, just to make sure you understand the role each plays:

- ▶ An *opening tag* is an HTML tag that indicates the start of an HTML command; the text affected by the command appears after the opening tag. Opening tags always begin with < and end with >, as in <html>.

- ▶ A *closing tag* is an HTML tag that indicates the end of an HTML command; the text affected by the command appears before the closing tag. Closing tags always begin with </ and end with >, as in </html>.

- ▶ An *empty tag* is an HTML tag that issues an HTML command without enclosing any text in the page. Empty tags always begin with < and end with > and have no closing tag, as in <meta>. Some designers add a closing /> to empty tags, as in <meta />, but this is not required in HTML5.

NOTE

You no doubt noticed in Listing 2.1 that there is some extra code associated with the <html> tag. This code consists of the language attribute (lang), which is used to specify additional information related to the tag. In this case, it specifies that the language of the text within the HTML is English. If you are writing in a different language, replace the en (for English) with the language identifier relevant to you. The <meta> tag also has an attribute (charset) with a value (utf-8).

For example, the <body> tag in Listing 2.1 tells the web browser where the actual body content of the page begins, and </body> indicates where it ends. Everything between the <body> and </body> tags appears in the main display area of the web browser window, as shown in Figure 2.1.

The very top of the browser window (refer to Figure 2.1) shows title text, which is any text that is located between <title> and </title>. The title text also identifies the page on the browser's Bookmarks or Favorites menu, depending on which browser you use. It's important to provide titles for your pages so that visitors to the page can properly bookmark them for future reference; search engines also use titles to provide links to search results.

You define the character set used by the page with the tag `<meta charset="utf-8">`. This tag defines the character set the page will be written in—in this case UTF-8. This tag should always come right after the opening `<head>` tag in your HTML documents. Without it, your pages could become vulnerable to hackers. Most of the web pages you will create in these lessons would be secure without this line, but it's a good habit to always include it. Then when you start creating web applications that could be vulnerable, you won't forget it.

You will use the `<body>` and `<title>` tag pairs in every HTML page you create because every web page needs a title and body text. You will also use the `<html>` and `<head>` tag pairs, which are the other two tags shown in Listing 2.1. Putting `<html>` at the very beginning of a document simply indicates that the document is a web page. The `</html>` at the end indicates the end of the web page.

NOTE

Most web browsers attempt to display anything that appears after the opening `<body>` tag—even if it comes after the closing `</html>` tag. Don't assume that you can hide content by placing it outside the `<html>` tag pair. You will learn how to hide content from being displayed in later lessons.

Within a page, there is a head section and a body section. Each section is identified by `<head>` and `<body>` tags. The idea is that information in the head of the page somehow describes the page but isn't actually displayed by a web browser. Information placed in the body, however, is displayed by a web browser. The `<head>` tag always appears near the beginning of the HTML code for a page, just after the opening `<html>` tag.

NOTE

You might find it convenient to create and save a bare-bones page (also known as a *skeleton* page, or *template*) with just the `doctype`, character set and opening and closing `<html>`, `<head>`, `<title>`, and `<body>` tags, similar to the document in Listing 2.1. You can then open that document as a starting point whenever you want to make a new web page and save yourself the trouble of typing all those obligatory tags every time.

The `<title>` tag pair used to identify the title of a page appears within the head of the page, which means it is placed after the opening `<head>` tag and before the closing `</head>` tag. In the upcoming lessons, you'll learn about some other advanced header information that can go between `<head>` and `</head>`, such as style sheet rules for formatting the page.

The `<p>` tag in Listing 2.1 encloses a paragraph of text. You should enclose your chunks of text in the appropriate container elements whenever possible; you'll learn more about container elements in future lessons.

Organizing a Page with Paragraphs and Line Breaks

When a web browser displays HTML pages, it pays no attention to line endings or the number of spaces between words. For example, the top version of the poem in Figure 2.2 appears with a single space after each word, even though that's not how it's entered in Listing 2.2. This is because extra whitespace in HTML code is automatically reduced to a single space. In addition, when the text reaches the edge of the browser window, it automatically wraps to the next line, no matter where the line breaks were in the original HTML file.

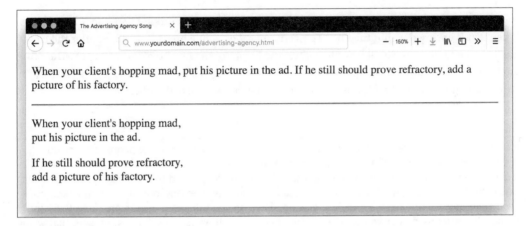

FIGURE 2.2
When the HTML in Listing 2.2 is viewed as a web page, line and paragraph breaks appear only where there are <br> and <p> tags.

LISTING 2.2   HTML Containing Paragraph and Line Breaks

```
<!doctype html>
<html lang="en">
  <head>
    <meta charset="utf-8">
    <title>The Advertising Agency Song</title>
  </head>
  <body>
    <p>
      When your client's    hopping mad,
      put his picture in the ad.

      If he still should    prove refractory,
      add a picture of his factory.
    </p>
```

```
<hr>
<p>
  When your client's hopping mad,<br>
  put his picture in the ad.
</p>
<p>
  If he still should prove refractory,<br>
  add a picture of his factory.
</p>
</body>
</html>
```

You must use HTML tags if you want to control where line and paragraph breaks actually appear. When text is enclosed within the <p></p> container tags, a line break is assumed after the closing tag. In later lessons, you'll learn to control the height of the line break by using CSS. The <br> tag forces a line break within a paragraph. Unlike the other tags you've seen so far, <br> doesn't require a closing </br> tag; this is one of those empty tags discussed earlier.

NOTE

If a closing slash isn't required for empty elements, you might ask why many people still include it. One reason is that over the years, closing tags went from being not required, to required, to not required (again), and many people are used to using the perfectly valid but no longer required closing slash. Another reason is that because that middle period was relatively long, a *lot* of code editors, code generators, and templates use the closing slash, so you will see it used more often than not. It doesn't matter which way you choose to write because both ways are valid; just be sure that whatever coding style you follow, you are consistent in its use.

The poem in Listing 2.2 and Figure 2.2 shows the <br> and <p> tags used to separate the lines and verses of an advertising agency song. You might have also noticed the <hr> tag in the listing, which causes a horizontal line (or "rule," in design terminology) to appear on the page (refer to Figure 2.2). Inserting a horizontal rule with the <hr> tag also causes a line break, even if you don't include a <br> tag along with it. Like <br>, the <hr> horizontal rule tag is an empty tag and, therefore, never gets a closing </hr> tag.

NOTE

In HTML5 it is no longer required to including the closing </p> tag on your paragraphs. The closing tag is assumed based on the appearance of another opening <p> tag or other block-level element. But just as with the closing slash in empty tags, many people prefer to include the closing </p> on their paragraphs. It doesn't matter which way you choose to write your paragraphs because both ways are valid. In these lessons, we close the paragraphs so that we have a visual reminder in the HTML of where any applied styles should end.

Formatting Text in HTML

Try your hand at formatting a passage of text as proper HTML:

1. Add `<html><head><meta charset="utf-8"><title>`*My Title*`</title>` `</head><body>` to the beginning of the text (using your own title for your page instead of *My Title*). Also include the document type declaration at the top of the page that takes care of meeting the requirements of standard HTML.

2. Add `</body></html>` to the very end of the text.

3. Add a `<p>` tag at the beginning of each paragraph and a `</p>` tag at the end of each paragraph.

4. Use `<br>` tags anywhere you want single-spaced line breaks.

5. Use `<hr>` to draw horizontal rules separating major sections of text or wherever you'd like to see a line across the page.

6. Save the file as *mypage*`.html` (using your own filename instead of *mypage*).

CAUTION
___

If you are using a word processor to create the web page, be sure to save the HTML file in plain-text or ASCII format. But as we've reiterated several times, you should really be using a text editor such as Notepad or TextEdit or a web page editor such as Komodo Edit or Coda.
___

7. Open the file in a web browser to see your web content. (Send the file via FTP to your web hosting account, if you have one.)

8. If something doesn't look right, go back to the text editor to make corrections and save the file again (and send it to your web hosting account, if applicable). Click Reload/Refresh in the browser to see the changes you made.

Organizing Your Content with Headings

When you browse web pages on the Internet, you'll notice that many of them have a heading at the top that appears larger and bolder than the rest of the text. Listing 2.3 is sample code and text for a simple web page containing an example of a heading as compared to normal paragraph text. Any text between the `<h1>` and `</h1>` tags will appear as a large heading. In addition, `<h2>` and `<h3>` and so on, as far down as `<h6>`, make progressively smaller headings.

LISTING 2.3 Heading Tags

```
<!doctype html>
<html lang="en">
  <head>
    <meta charset="utf-8">
    <title>My Widgets</title>
  </head>
  <body>
    <h1>My Widgets</h1>
    <p>My widgets are the best in the land. Continue reading to
    learn more about my widgets.</p>

    <h2>Widget Features</h2>
    <p>If I had any features to discuss,  you can bet I'd do
    it here.</p>

    <h3>Pricing</h3>
    <p>Here, I would talk about my widget pricing.</p>

    <h3>Comparisons</h3>
    <p>Here, I would talk about how my widgets compare to my
    competitor's widgets.</p>
  </body>
</html>
```

NOTE

By now, you've probably caught on to the fact that HTML code is often indented by its author to reveal the relationships between different parts of the HTML document, as well as for simple ease of reading. This indentation is entirely optional; you could just as easily run all the tags together with no spaces or line breaks, and they would still look fine when viewed in a browser. You will often see this condensed style used on pages that have been optimized for speed. The indentations are for you and other human editors so that you can quickly look at a page full of code and understand how it fits together. Indenting your code is another good web design habit and ultimately makes your pages easier to maintain, both for yourself and for anyone else who might pick up where you leave off.

As you can see in Figure 2.3, the HTML that creates headings couldn't be simpler. In this example, the phrase "My Widgets" is prominently displayed using the <h1> tag. To create the first (level 1) heading, just put an <h1> tag at the beginning and an </h1> tag at the end of the text you want to use as a heading. For a second-level (level 2) heading—for information that is of lesser importance than the title—use the <h2> and </h2> tags around your text. For content that should appear even less prominently than a level 2 heading, use the <h3> and </h3> tags around your text.

NOTE

Most people think of the heading tags in terms of how large or small they are: The level 1 headings are bigger than level 2, which are bigger than level 3, and so on. But it's better to think of them as you might an outline of a page. The level 1 heading defines the entire page. Level 2 headings define sections within the page. Level 3 headings define areas within the level 2 sections. You can go even deeper with level 4, 5, and 6 headings as well. These use the <h4>, <h5>, and <h6> tags, respectively. By thinking of what the HTML represents, rather than just what it looks like on the page, you will be prepared to make them look however you want with CSS. And you will learn how to use CSS for just this purpose in later lessons.

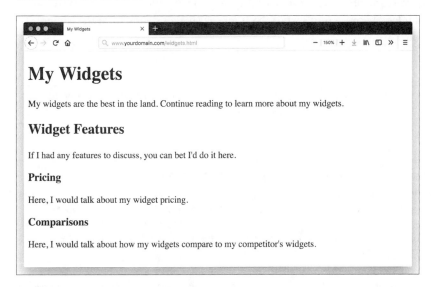

FIGURE 2.3
Using three levels of headings shows the hierarchy of content on this sample product page.

However, bear in mind that your headings should follow a content hierarchy; use only one level 1 heading, have one (or more) level 2 headings after the level 1 heading, use level 3 headings directly after level 2 headings, and so on. Do not fall into the trap of assigning headings to content just to make that content display a certain way. Instead, ensure that you are categorizing your content appropriately (as a main heading, a secondary heading, and so on), while using display styles to make that text render a particular way in a web browser.

Theoretically, you can also use <h4>, <h5>, and <h6> tags to make progressively less important headings, but these aren't used very often. Web browsers seldom show a significant difference between these headings and the <h3> headings anyway—although you can control that with your own CSS—and content usually isn't displayed in such a manner that you'd need six levels of headings to show the content hierarchy.

It's important to remember the difference between a *title* and a *heading*. These two words are often interchangeable in day-to-day English, but when you're talking HTML, `<title>` gives the entire page an identifying name that isn't displayed on the page itself; it's displayed only on the browser window's title bar and in bookmarks and sometimes search engine results. The heading tags, on the other hand, are displayed on the page and often have some type of visual emphasis outside CSS. There can be only one `<title>` per page, and it must appear within the `<head>` and `</head>` tags; on the other hand, you can have as many `<h1>`, `<h2>`, and `<h3>` headings as you want, in any order that suits your fancy. However, as we mentioned before, you should use the heading tags to keep tight control over content hierarchy; do not use headings as a way to achieve a particular look because that's what CSS is for. HTML tags define what the content *is* rather than how it looks.

CAUTION
___
Don't forget that anything placed in the head of a web page is not intended to be viewed on the page, whereas everything in the body of the page *is* intended for viewing.

___

Peeking at Other Designers' Pages

Given the visual and sometimes audio pizzazz present in many popular web pages, you probably realize that the simple pages described in this lesson are only the tip of the HTML iceberg. Now that you know the basics, you might surprise yourself with how much of the rest you can pick up just by looking at other people's pages on the Internet. You can see the HTML for any page by right-clicking and selecting View Source in any web browser.

Don't worry if you aren't yet able to decipher what some HTML tags do or exactly how to use them yourself. You'll find out about all those things in future lessons. However, sneaking a preview now will show you the tags that you do know in action and give you a taste of what you'll soon be able to do with your web pages.

___

Understanding Semantic Elements

HTML5 includes tags that enable you to describe the semantics—the meaning—of the information that you provide in your marked-up text. Instead of simply using HTML as a presentation language, as was the practice in the very early days when `<b>` for bold and `<i>` for italic was the norm, modern HTML has as one of its goals the separation of presentation, meaning, and behavior. While using CSS to provide guidelines for presentation, composers of HTML can provide meaningful names within their markup for individual elements—not only through the use of IDs and class names (which you'll learn about in subsequent lessons) but also through the use of semantic elements.

Some of the semantic elements available in HTML5 follow:

▶ **<header></header>**—This might seem counterintuitive, but you can use multiple <header> tags within a single page. The <header> tag should be used as a container for introductory information, so it might appear only once in your page (likely at the top)—but you also might use it several times if your page content is broken into sections. Any container element can have a <header> element; just make sure that you're using it to include introductory information about the element it is contained within.

▶ **<footer></footer>**—The <footer> tag is used to contain additional information about its containing element (page or section), such as copyright and author information or links to related resources. Just as with the <header> tag, you can define footers in any section of the page, as well as for the page as a whole.

▶ **<nav></nav>**—If your site has navigational elements, such as links to other sections within a site or even within the page itself, these links go in a <nav> tag. A <nav> tag typically is found in the first instance of a <header> tag, just because people tend to put navigation at the top and consider it introductory information, but that is not a requirement. You can put your <nav> element anywhere (as long as it includes navigation), and you can have as many on a page as you need.

▶ **<section></section>**—The <section> tag contains anything that relates thematically; it can also contain a <header> tag for introductory information and possibly a <footer> tag for other related information. You can think of a <section> as carrying more meaning than a standard <p> (paragraph) or <div> (division) tag, which typically conveys no meaning at all; the use of <section> conveys a relationship between the content elements it contains.

▶ **<article></article>**—An <article> tag is like a <section> tag, in that it can contain a <header>, a <footer>, and other container elements such as paragraphs and divisions. But the additional meaning carried with the <article> tag is that it is, well, like an article in a newspaper or some other publication. Use this tag around blog posts, news articles, reviews, and other items that fit this description. One key difference between an <article> and a <section> is that an <article> is a standalone body of work, whereas a <section> is a thematic grouping of information.

▶ **<aside></aside>**—Use the <aside> tag to indicate secondary information; if the <aside> tag is within a <section> or an <article>, the relationship will be to those containers; otherwise, the secondary relationship will be to the overall page or site itself. It might make sense to think of the <aside> as a sidebar—either for all the content on the page or for an article or other thematic container of information.

These semantic elements will become clearer as you practice using them. In general, using semantic elements is a good idea because they provide additional meaning for not only you and other designers and programmers reading and working with your markup but also for machines.

Web browsers and screen readers will respond to your semantic elements by using these elements to determine the structure of your document; screen readers will report a deeper meaning to users, thus increasing the accessibility of your material. But for the most part, browsers do not change how a semantic element is displayed on a page. As we've mentioned previously, this is part of the design and is controlled by CSS.

One of the best ways to understand the HTML5 semantic elements is to see them in action, but that can be a little difficult when the primary purpose of these elements is to provide *meaning* rather than design. That's not to say that you can't add design to these elements; you most certainly can, and you will in later lessons. But the "action" of the semantic elements is to hold content and provide meaning through doing so, as in Figure 2.4, which shows a common use of semantic elements for a basic web page.

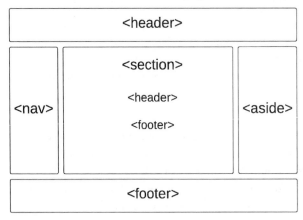

FIGURE 2.4
Showing basic semantic elements in a web page.

Initially, you might think, "Of *course*, that makes total sense, with the header at the top and the footer at the bottom" and feel quite good about yourself for understanding semantic elements at first glance—and you should! A second glance should then raise some questions: What if you want your navigation to be horizontal under your header? Does an aside have to be (literally) on the side? What if you don't want any asides? What's with the use of <header> and <footer> again within the main body section? And that's just to name a few! Another question you might ask is where the <article> element fits in; it isn't shown in this example but is part of this lesson.

This is the time when conceptualizing the page—and specifically the page *you* want to create—comes into play. If you understand the content you want to mark up and you understand that you can use any, all, or none of the semantic elements and still create a valid HTML document, then you can begin to organize the content of your page in the way that makes the most sense for it and for you (and, hopefully, for your readers).

NOTE

Although you do not need to use semantic elements to create a valid HTML document, even a minimal set is recommended so that web browsers and screen readers can determine the structure of your document. Screen readers are capable of reporting a deeper meaning to users, thus increasing the accessibility of your material.

(If this note were marked up in an HTML document, it would use the `<aside>` element.)

Let's take a look at the elements used in Figure 2.4 before moving on to a second example and then a deeper exploration of the individual elements themselves. In Figure 2.4, you see a `<header>` at the top of the page and a `<footer>` at the bottom—straightforward, as already mentioned. The use of a `<nav>` element on the left side of the page matches a common display area for navigation, and the `<aside>` element on the right side of the page matches a common display area for secondary notes, pull quotes, helper text, and "for more information" links about the content. In Figure 2.5, you'll see some of these elements shifted around, so don't worry; Figure 2.4 is not some immutable example of semantic markup.

Something you might be surprised to see in Figure 2.5 is the `<header>` and `<footer>` inside the `<section>` element. In Figure 2.4, you see a `<header>` at the top of the page and a `<footer>` at the bottom—straightforward, as already mentioned. The use of a `<nav>` element on the left side of the page matches the content that comes after it, and the `<header>` element itself does not convey any level in a document outline. Therefore, you can use as many `<header>` elements as you need to mark up your content appropriately; a `<header>` at the beginning of the page might contain introductory information about the page as a whole, and a `<header>` element within the `<section>` element might just as easily and appropriately contain introductory information about the content within it. The same is true for the multiple appearances of the `<footer>` element in this example.

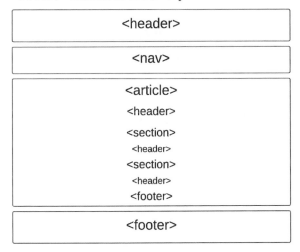

FIGURE 2.5
Using nested semantic elements to add more meaning to the content.

Let's move on to Figure 2.5, which shifts around the <nav> element and also introduces use of the <article> element.

In Figure 2.5, the <header> and <nav> elements at the beginning of the page and the <footer> element at the bottom of the page should make perfect sense to you. And, although we haven't talked about the <article> element yet, if you think about it as a container element that has sections (that use the <section> tag, even!), with each of those sections having its own heading, then the chunk of semantic elements in the middle of the figure should make sense, too.

As you can see, there's no single way to conceptualize page content; you should, however, be able to conceptualize each individual page's content.

If you marked up some content in the structure shown in Figure 2.5, it might look like the markup in Listing 2.4.

LISTING 2.4 Semantic Markup of Basic Content

```
<!doctype html>
<html lang="en">
  <head>
    <meta charset="utf-8">
    <title>Semantic Example</title>
  </head>
  <body>
    <header>
        <h1>SITE OR PAGE LOGO GOES HERE</h1>
    </header>
    <nav>
        SITE OR PAGE NAVIGATION GOES HERE.
    </nav>
    <article>
      <header>
          <h2>Article Heading</h2>
      </header>
      <section>
        <header>
            <h3>Section 1 Heading</h3>
        </header>
        <p>Section 1 content here.</p>
      </section>
      <section>
        <header>
            <h3>Section 2 Heading</h3>
        </header>
        <p>Section 2 content here.</p>
      </section>
      <footer>
```

```
        <p>Article footer goes here.</p>
      </footer>
    </article>
    <footer>
        SITE OR PAGE FOOTER HERE
    </footer>
  </body>
</html>
```

If you opened this HTML document in your web browser, you would see something like what's shown in Figure 2.6—a completely unstyled document but one that has semantic meaning (even if no one can "see" it).

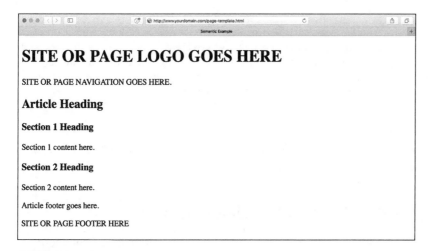

FIGURE 2.6
The output of Listing 2.4.

Just because there is no visible styling doesn't mean the meaning is lost; as noted earlier in this section, machines can interpret the structure of the document as provided for through the semantic elements. You can see the outline of this basic document in Figure 2.7, which shows the output of this file after examination by the HTML5 Outliner tool, available at http://gsnedders. html5.org/outliner/.

FIGURE 2.7
The outline of this document follows the semantic markup.

NOTE

Using the HTML5 Outliner tool is a good way to check that you've created your headers, footers, and sections; if you examine your document and see "untitled section" anywhere, and those untitled sections do not match up with a `<nav>` or an `<aside>` element (which have more relaxed guidelines about containing headers), then you have some additional work to do.

Now that you've seen some examples of conceptualizing the information represented in your documents, you're better prepared to start marking up those documents. The sections that follow take a look at the semantic elements individually.

Using `<header>` in Multiple Ways

At the most basic level, the `<header>` element contains introductory information. That information might take the form of an actual `<h1>` (or other level) element, or it might simply be a logo image or text contained within a `<p>` or `<div>` element. The *meaning* of the content should be introductory in nature, to warrant its inclusion within a `<header></header>` tag pair.

NOTE

Information in the `<header>` element does not have to come first in the section it is introducing. That is the most common place to see it, but it can be displayed anywhere on your page that makes sense. The display location is defined by the CSS.

As you've seen in the examples so far in this lesson, a common placement of a `<header>` element is at the beginning of a page. When it's used in this way, containing a logo or an `<h1>`-level title makes sense, such as here:

```
<header>
    <img src="acmewidgets.jpg" alt="ACME Widgets LLC">
</header>
```

Or even this:

```
<header>
    <img src="acmewidgets.jpg" alt="ACME Widgets LLC">
    <h1>The finest widgets are made here!</h1>
</header>
```

Both of these snippets are valid uses of `<header>` because the information contained within them is introductory to the page overall.

As you've also seen in this lesson, you are not limited to only one `<header>`. You can go crazy with `<header>` elements, as long as they are acting as containers for introductory information. Listing 2.4 showed the use of `<header>` elements for several `<section>` elements within an `<article>`, and this is a perfectly valid use of the element:

```
<section>
    <header>
        <h3>Section 1 Heading</h3>
    </header>
    <p>Section 1 content here.</p>
</section>
<section>
    <header>
        <h3>Section 2 Heading</h3>
    </header>
    <p>Section 2 content here.</p>
</section>
```

The `<header>` element can contain any other element in the flow content category (one of the HTML5 content models) of which it is also a member. This means that a `<header>` *could* contain a `<section>` element, if you wanted, and be perfectly valid markup. However, when you are conceptualizing your content, think about whether that sort of nesting makes sense before you go off and do it.

NOTE

In general, *flow content* elements are elements that contain text, images, or other multimedia embedded content; HTML elements fall into multiple categories.

If you want to learn more about the categorization of elements into content models, see http://www.w3.org/TR/2011/WD-html5-20110525/content-models.html.

The only exceptions to the permitted content within `<header>` are that the `<header>` element cannot contain *other* `<header>` elements, and it cannot contain a `<footer>` element. Similarly, the `<header>` element cannot be contained within an `<address>` or a `<footer>` element.

Understanding the `<section>` Element

The `<section>` element has a simple definition: It is "a generic section of a document" that is also "a thematic grouping of content, typically with a heading." That sounds pretty simple to us and probably does to you as well. So you might be surprised to find that if you type **difference between section and article in HTML5** in your search engine of choice, you'll find tens of thousands of entries talking about the differences because the definitions trip people up all the time. We first discuss the `<section>` element and then cover the `<article>` element—and hopefully avoid any of the misunderstandings that seem to plague new web developers.

In Listing 2.4, you saw a straightforward example of using `<section>` within an `<article>` (repeated here); in this example, you can easily imagine that the `<section>` elements contain a "thematic grouping of content," which is supported by the fact that they each have a heading:

```
<article>
    <header>
        <h2>Article Heading</h2>
    </header>
    <section>
        <header>
            <h3>Section 1 Heading</h3>
        </header>
        <p>Section 1 content here.</p>
    </section>
    <section>
        <header>
            <h3>Section 2 Heading</h3>
        </header>
        <p>Section 2 content here.</p>
    </section>
    <footer>
        <p>Article footer goes here.</p>
    </footer>
</article>
```

But here's an example of a perfectly valid use of `<section>` with no `<article>` element in sight:

```
<section>
    <header>
        <h1>Super Heading</h1>
    </header>
    <p>Super content!</p>
</section>
```

So what's a developer to do? Let's say you have some generic content that you know you want to divide into sections with their own headings. In that case, use <section>. If you need to only *visually* delineate chunks of content (such as with paragraph breaks) that do not require additional headings, then <section> isn't for you; use <p> or <div> instead.

Because the <section> element can contain any other flow content element and can be contained within any other flow content element (except the <address> element), it's easy to see why, without other limitations and with generic guidelines for use, the <section> element is sometimes misunderstood.

Using <article>

We believe that a lot of the misunderstanding regarding the use of <section> versus <article> has to do with the name of the <article> element. When we think of an article, we think specifically about an article in a newspaper or a magazine. We don't naturally think "any standalone body of work," which is how the <article> element is commonly defined. The HTML5 recommended specification defines it as "a complete, or self-contained, composition in a document, page, application, or site and that is, in principle, independently distributable or reusable," such as "a forum post, a magazine or newspaper article, a blog entry, a user-submitted comment, an interactive widget or gadget, or any other independent item of content."

In other words, an <article> element could be used to contain the entire page of a website (whether or not it is an article in a publication), an actual article in a publication, a blog post anywhere and everywhere, part of a threaded discussion in a forum, or a comment on a blog post, or it could be used as a container that displays the current weather in your city. It's no wonder there are tens of thousands of results for a search on "difference between section and article in HTML5."

A good rule of thumb when you're trying to figure out when to use <article> and when to use <section> is simply to answer the following question: Does this content make sense on its own? If so, then no matter what the content seems to be to you (for example, a static web page, not an article in the *New York Times*), start by using the <article> element. If you find yourself breaking it up, do so in <section> elements. And if you find yourself thinking that your "article" is, in fact, part of a greater whole, then change the <article> tags to <section> tags, find the beginning of the document, and surround it from there with the more appropriately placed <article> tag at a higher level.

Implementing the <nav> Element

The <nav> element seems so simple (<nav> implies *navigation*), and it ultimately is—but it is often used incorrectly. In this section, you'll learn some basic uses and also some incorrect uses to avoid. If your site has any navigational elements at all, either sitewide or within a long page of content, you have a valid use for the <nav> element.

For that sitewide navigation, you typically find a <nav> element within the primary <header> element. If you want your navigational content to be introductory (and omnipresent in your template), you can easily make a case for your primary <nav> element to appear within the primary <header>, though you are not required to have it there. It is more important that your HTML be valid (as is <nav> outside a <header>) than that your <header> element contain everything allowed in it. A <nav> element can appear within any flow content, and it can also contain any flow content.

The following code snippet shows the main navigational links of a website, placed within a <header> element:

```html
<header>
    <img src="acmewidgets.jpg" alt="ACME Widgets LLC">
    <h1>The finest widgets are made here!</h1>
    <nav>
        <ul>
            <li><a href="#">About Us</a></li>
            <li><a href="#">Products</a></li>
            <li><a href="#">Support</a></li>
            <li><a href="#">Press</a></li>
        </ul>
    </nav>
</header>
```

You are not limited to a single <nav> element in your documents, which is good for site developers who create templates that include both primary *and* secondary navigation. For example, you might see horizontal primary navigation at the top of a page (often contained within a <header> element) and then vertical navigation in the left column of a page, representing the secondary pages within the main section. In that case, you simply use a second <nav> element, not contained within the <header>, placed and styled differently to delineate the two types visually in addition to semantically.

Remember that the <nav> element is used for *major* navigational content; primary and secondary navigation both count, as does the inclusion of tables of contents within a page. For good and useful semantic use of the <nav> element, do not simply apply it to every link that allows a user to navigate anywhere. Note that we said "good and useful" semantic use, not necessarily "valid" use; it's true that you could apply <nav> to any list of links, and it would be valid according to the HTML specification because links are flow content. But it wouldn't be particularly *useful* to surround a list of links to social media sharing tools with the <nav> element as it wouldn't add accurate or useful meaning.

When to Use `<aside>`

As you'll have guessed based on the number of notes and sidebars in these lessons, we're big fans of the type of content that is most appropriately marked up within the `<aside>` element. The `<aside>` element is meant to contain any content that is tangentially related to the content around it—additional explanation, links to related resources, pull quotes, helper text, and so on. You might think of the `<aside>` element as a sidebar, but be careful not to think of it only as a *visual* sidebar or a column on the side of a page where you can stick anything and everything you want, whether or not it's related to the content or site at hand.

In Figure 2.8, you can see how content in an `<aside>` is used to create a *pull quote*, or a content excerpt that is specifically set aside to call attention to it. The `<aside>`, in this case, is used to highlight an important section of the text, but it could also be used to define a term or link to related documents.

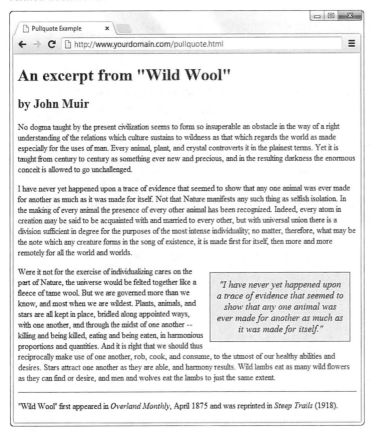

FIGURE 2.8
Using `<aside>` to create meaningful pull quotes.

When determining whether to use the `<aside>` element, think about the content you want to add. Is it related directly to the content in which the `<aside>` would be contained, but not absolutely critical to understanding the content, such as a definition of terms used in an article or a list of related links for the article? If your answer is an easy yes, that's great! Use `<aside>` to your heart's content. If you're thinking of including an `<aside>` outside a containing element that is itself full of content, just make sure that the content of the `<aside>` is reasonably related to your site overall and that you're not just using the `<aside>` element for visual effect.

Using `<footer>` Effectively

The counterpart to the `<header>` element, the `<footer>` element contains additional information about its containing element. The most common use of the `<footer>` element is to contain copyright information at the bottom of a page, as shown here:

```
<footer>
    <p>&copy; 2014 Acme Widgets, LLC. All Rights Reserved.</p>
</footer>
```

Much like the `<header>` element, the `<footer>` element can contain any other element in the flow content category of which it is also a member, with the exception of *other* `<footer>` or `<header>` elements. In addition, a `<footer>` element cannot be contained within an `<address>` element, but a `<footer>` element can contain an `<address>` element; in fact, a `<footer>` element is a common location for an `<address>` element to reside.

Placing useful `<address>` content within a `<footer>` element is one of the most effective uses of the `<footer>` element (not to mention the `<address>` element) because it provides specific contextual information about the page or section of the page to which it refers. The following snippet shows a use of `<address>` within `<footer>`:

```
<footer>
    <p>&copy; 2014-2018 Acme Widgets, LLC. All Rights Reserved.</p>
    <p>Copyright Issues? Contact:</p>
        <address>
        Our Lawyer<br>
        123 Main Street<br>
        Somewhere, CA 95128<br>
        <a href="mailto:lawyer@richperson.com">lawyer@richperson.com</a>
        </address>
</footer>
```

As with the `<header>` element, you are not limited to only one `<footer>`, and these elements don't all have to be displayed below the content they are modifying. You can use as many `<footer>` elements as you need, as long as they are containers for additional information about the containing element. Listing 2.4 shows the use of `<footer>` elements for both the page and an `<article>`, both of which are valid.

Summary

This lesson introduced the basics of what web pages are and how they work. You learned that coded HTML commands are included in a text file, and you saw that typing HTML text yourself is better than using a graphical editor that creates HTML commands for you—especially when you're learning HTML.

You were introduced to the most basic and important HTML tags. By adding these coded commands to any plain-text document, you can quickly transform it into a bona fide web page. You learned that the first step in creating a web page is to put a few obligatory HTML tags at the beginning and end, including adding a title for the page. You can then mark where paragraphs and lines end and add horizontal rules and headings, if you want them. You also got a taste of some of the semantic tags in HTML5, which are used to provide additional meaning by delineating the types of content your pages contain (not just the content itself). Table 2.1 summarizes all the tags introduced in this lesson.

TABLE 2.1 HTML Tags Covered in Lesson 2

Tag	Function
`<html>`...`</html>`	Encloses the entire HTML document.
`<head>`...`</head>`	Encloses the head of the HTML document. Used within the `<html>` tag pair.
`<meta charset="utf-8">`	Defines the character set for the document as UTF-8. Used within the `<head>` tag pair, immediately after the opening `<head>` tag.
`<title>`...`</title>`	Indicates the title of the document. Used within the `<head>` tag pair.
`<body>`...`</body>`	Encloses the body of the HTML document. Used within the `<html>` tag pair.
`<p>`...`</p>`	Encloses a paragraph; skips a line between paragraphs.
` `	Indicates a line break.
`<hr>`	Displays a horizontal rule.
`<h1>`...`</h1>`	Encloses a first-level heading.
`<h2>`...`</h2>`	Encloses a second-level heading.
`<h3>`...`</h3>`	Encloses a third-level heading.
`<h4>`...`</h4>`	Encloses a fourth-level heading (seldom used).

Tag	Function
<h5>...</h5>	Encloses a fifth-level heading (seldom used).
<h6>...</h6>	Encloses a sixth-level heading (seldom used).
<header>...</header>	Contains introductory information.
<footer>...</footer>	Contains supplementary material for its containing element (commonly a copyright notice or author information).
<nav>...</nav>	Contains navigational elements.
<section>...</section>	Contains thematically similar content, such as a chapter of a book or a section of a page.
<article>...</article>	Contains content that is a standalone body of work, such as a news article.
<aside>...</aside>	Contains secondary information for its containing element.
<address>...</address>	Contains address information related to its nearest <article> or <body> element, often contained within a <footer> element.

Q&A

Q. I've created a web page, but when I open the file in my web browser, I see all the text, including the HTML tags. Sometimes I even see weird gobbledygook characters at the top of the page. What did I do wrong?

A. You didn't save the file as plain text. Try saving the file again, being careful to save it as Text Only or ASCII Text. If you can't quite figure out how to get your word processor to do that, don't stress. Just type your HTML files in Notepad or TextEdit instead, and everything should work just fine. Also, always make sure that the filename of your web page ends in .html or .htm. Some text editors will add .txt after you save, giving you a filename that is something like filename.html.txt. If this happens, you should rename the file, removing the .txt extension.

Q. Do I have to use semantic markup at all? Didn't you say throughout this lesson that pages are valid with or without it?

A. True, none of these elements is required for a valid HTML document. You don't have to use any of them, but I urge you to think beyond the use of markup for visual display only and think about it for semantic meaning as well. Visual display is meaningless to screen readers, but semantic elements convey a ton of information to these applications.

Q. I'm still completely befuddled about when to use `<section>` and when to use `<aside>`. Can you make it clearer?

A. We don't blame you. There's a resource available at the HTML5 Doctor website that is one of the best we've seen to help eliminate the confusion. It's a flowchart for HTML5 sectioning, found at http://html5doctor.com/downloads/h5d-sectioning-flowchart.png. This flowchart asks the right questions about your content and helps you determine the correct container element to use.

Workshop

The Workshop contains quiz questions and exercises to help you solidify your understanding of the material covered.

Quiz

1. What six tags does every HTML page require?

2. Why is the `<meta charset>` tag important, and where should it be placed in an HTML document?

3. What HTML tags and text do you use to produce the following body content:

   ▶ A heading with the words `We are Proud to Present...`

   ▶ A secondary heading with the one word `Orbit`

   ▶ A heading of lesser importance with the words `The Geometric Juggler`

4. What code would you use to create a complete HTML web page with the title `Foo Bar`, a heading at the top that reads `Happy Hour at the Foo Bar`, and then the words `Come on down!` in regular type? Try to use some of the semantic elements you just learned.

5. Which of the semantic elements discussed in this lesson is appropriate for containing the definition of a word used in an article?

6. What makes an element semantic?

7. Do you have to use an `<h1>`, `<h2>`, `<h3>`, `<h4>`, `<h5>`, or `<h6>` element within a `<header>` element?

8. Where must the contents of the `<footer>` for the document appear on the page?

9. How many different `<nav>` elements can you have in a single page?

10. What types of things might be enclosed in an `<article>` element?

Answers

1. Every HTML page requires <html>, <head>, <title>, and <body> (along with their clos-ing tags, </html>, </head>, </title>, and </body>), plus <!doctype html> on the very first line and <meta charset> after the opening <head> tag. Technically, the <!doctype html> is not a tag, but rather a declaration, so if you said there were only five required tags, you'd be correct.

2. The <meta charset> tag defines the character set that the page uses, and it should always come immediately after the opening <head> tag in your document.

3. The code within the body would look like this:

```
<h1>We are Proud to Present...</h1>
<h2>Orbit</h2>
<h3>The Geometric Juggler</h3>
```

4. Your code could look like this:

```
<!doctype html>
<html lang="en">
  <head>
    <meta charset="utf-8">
    <title>Foo Bar</title>
  </head>
  <body>
    <header>
      <h1>Happy Hour at the Foo Bar</h1>
    </header>
    <section>
      <p>Come on Down!</p>
    </section>
  </body>
</html>
```

5. The <aside> element is appropriate for this.

6. A semantic element is an HTML element that describes the meaning of the information contained in that element.

7. No. The <header> element can contain any other flow content besides another <header> element or a <footer> element. However, a heading element (<h1> through <h6>) is not required in a <header> element.

8. The contents of the `<footer>` tag can appear wherever it makes sense to have it appear on the page. While most designers place footer content at the end or bottom of the page, there is no requirement that it be displayed there.

9. You can have as many `<nav>` elements as you need. The trick is to "need" only a few (perhaps for primary and secondary navigation only); otherwise, the meaning is lost.

10. The `<article>` element encloses any content that is complete or self-contained and is independently distributable or reusable. This could include a blog entry, a magazine or newspaper article, a forum post, a user-submitted comment, an interactive widget, or any other independent item of content.

Exercises

▶ Even if your main goal in reading these lessons is to create web content for your business, you might want to make a personal web page just for practice. Type a few paragraphs to introduce yourself to the world and use the HTML tags you learned in this lesson to make them into a web page.

▶ Throughout the lessons, you'll be following along with the code examples and making pages of your own. Take a moment now to set up a basic document template containing the document type declaration and tags for the core HTML document structure. That way, you can be ready to copy and paste that information whenever you need it.

▶ Building off a single page template, create a few more related pieces of content. Remember that some of your pages might contain `<article>` elements with no sections, but others might contain `<section>` elements with `<header>` and `<footer>` elements as well.

LESSON 3
Understanding Cascading Style Sheets

What You'll Learn in This Lesson:

▶ How to create a basic style sheet
▶ How to use style classes
▶ How to use style IDs
▶ How to construct internal style sheets and inline styles

In the preceding lesson, you learned the basics of HTML, including how to set up a basic HTML template for all your web content. In this lesson, you'll learn how to fine-tune the display of your web content by using *Cascading Style Sheets (CSS)*.

The concept behind style sheets is simple: You create a style sheet document that specifies the fonts, colors, spacing, and other characteristics that establish a unique look for a website. You then link every page that should have that look to the style sheet instead of specifying all those styles repeatedly in each separate document. Then, when you decide to change your official corporate typeface or color scheme, you can modify all your web pages at once just by changing one or two entries in your style sheet; you don't have to change them in all your static web files. So, *a style sheet* is a grouping of formatting instructions that control the appearance of several HTML pages at once.

Style sheets enable you to set a great number of formatting characteristics, including exact typeface controls, letter and line spacing, and margins and page borders, to name just a few. Style sheets also enable you to specify sizes and other measurements in familiar units, such as inches, millimeters, points, and picas. In addition, you can use style sheets to precisely position graphics and text anywhere on a web page, either at specific coordinates or relative to other items on the page.

In short, style sheets bring a sophisticated level of display to the Web. And they do so, if you'll pardon the expression, with style.

How CSS Works

The technology behind style sheets is called CSS, or Cascading Style Sheets. CSS is a language that defines style constructs such as fonts, colors, and positioning, which describe how information on a web page is formatted and displayed. CSS styles can be stored directly in an HTML web page or in a separate style sheet file. Either way, style sheets contain style rules that apply styles to elements of a given type. When used externally, style sheet rules are placed in an external style sheet document with the file extension `.css`.

A *style rule* is a formatting instruction that can be applied to an element on a web page, such as a paragraph of text or a link. A style rule consists of one or more style properties and their associated values. An *internal style sheet* is placed directly within a web page, whereas an *external style sheet* exists in a separate document and is linked to a web page via a special tag; you'll learn more about this tag in a moment.

The *cascading* part of the name CSS refers to the manner in which style sheet rules are applied to elements in an HTML document. More specifically, styles in a CSS style sheet form a hierarchy in which more specific styles override more general styles. It is the responsibility of CSS to determine the precedence of style rules according to this hierarchy, which establishes a cascading effect. If that sounds a bit confusing, just think of the cascading mechanism in CSS as being similar to genetic inheritance, in which general traits are passed from parents to a child, but more specific traits are entirely unique to the child. Base style rules are applied throughout a style sheet but can be overridden by more specific style rules.

NOTE

You might notice that we use the term *element* a fair amount in this lesson (and we also do in the rest of the course). An *element* is simply a piece of information (content) in a web page, such as an image, a paragraph, or a link. Tags are used to mark up elements, and you can think of an element as a tag, complete with descriptive information (attributes, text, images, and so on) within the tag.

A quick example should clear things up. Take a look at the following code to see whether you can tell what's going on with the color of the text:

```
<div style="color:green;">
  This text is green.
  <p style="color:blue;">This text is blue.</p>
  <p>This text is still green.</p>
</div>
```

In this example, the color green is applied to the <div> tag via the color style property. Therefore, the text in the <div> tag is colored green. Because both <p> tags are children of the

`<div>` tag, the green text style cascades down to them. However, the first `<p>` tag overrides the color style and changes it to blue. The end result is that the first line (not surrounded by a paragraph tag) is green, the first official paragraph is blue, and the second official paragraph retains the cascaded green color.

If you made it through that description on your own and came out on the other end unscathed, congratulations—that's half the battle. Understanding CSS isn't difficult, and the more you practice, the more it will become clear. The real trick is developing an aesthetic design sense that you can then apply to your online presence through CSS.

Like many other web technologies, CSS has evolved over the years. The original version of CSS, known as *Cascading Style Sheets Level 1* (*CSS1*), was created in 1996. The later CSS2 standard, created in 1998, is still in use today. The latest version of CSS is CSS3, and it builds on the strong foundation laid by its predecessors but adds advanced functionality to enhance the online experience. Modern web browsers support all of CSS2 and a majority of CSS3. Throughout this series of lessons, you'll learn core CSS, including new elements of CSS3 that are applicable to the basic design and functionality that this text covers. So, when we talk about CSS, we're referring to CSS3.

You can find a complete reference guide to CSS at www.w3.org/Style/CSS/. The rest of this lesson explains the basics of putting CSS to good use.

A Basic Style Sheet

Despite their intimidating power, style sheets are simple to create. Consider the web pages shown in Figures 3.1 and 3.2. These pages share several visual properties that can be put into a common style sheet:

- ▶ They use a large, bold Verdana font for the headings and a normal-size and -weight Verdana font for the body text.

- ▶ They use an image named `logo.gif` floating within the content and on the right side of the page.

- ▶ All text is black except for subheadings, which are purple.

- ▶ They have margins on the left side and at the top.

- ▶ They include vertical space between lines of text.

- ▶ They include a footer that is centered and in small print.

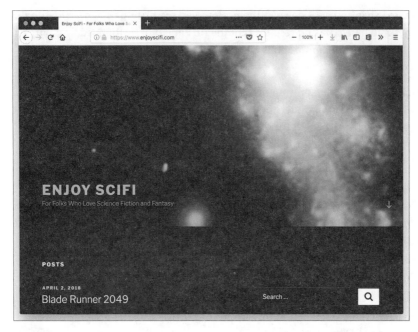

FIGURE 3.1
This page uses a style sheet to fine-tune the appearance and spacing of the text and images.

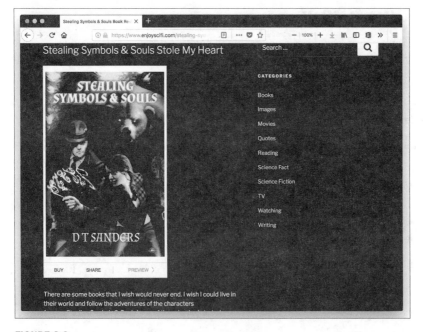

FIGURE 3.2
This page uses the same style sheet as the one in Figure 3.1, thus maintaining a consistent look and feel.

Listing 3.1 shows CSS used in a style sheet to specify these types of properties.

LISTING 3.1   A Single External Style Sheet

```
body {
  font-size: 10pt;
  font-family: Verdana, Geneva, Arial, Helvetica, sans-serif;
  color: black;
  line-height: 14pt;
  padding-left: 5pt;
  padding-right: 5pt;
  padding-top: 5pt;
}

h1 {
  font: 14pt Verdana, Geneva, Arial, Helvetica, sans-serif;
  font-weight: bold;
  line-height: 20pt;
}

p.subheader {
  font-weight: bold;
  color: #593d87;
}

img {
  padding: 3pt;
  float: right;
}

a {
  text-decoration: none;
}

a:link, a:visited {
  color: #8094d6;
}

a:hover, a:active {
  color: #FF9933;
}

footer {
  font-size: 9pt;
  font-style: italic;
  line-height: 12pt;
  text-align: center;
  padding-top: 30pt;
}
```

This might initially appear to be a lot of code, but if you look closely, you'll see that there isn't a lot of information on each line of code. It's fairly standard to place each individual style rule on its own line to help make style sheets more readable, but that is a personal preference; you could put all the rules on one line as long as you kept using the semicolon to separate each rule; you'll learn more on this in a bit. Speaking of code readability, perhaps the first thing you noticed about this style sheet code is that it doesn't look anything like normal HTML code. CSS uses a syntax all its own to specify style sheets.

Of course, the listing includes some familiar HTML tags (although not all tags require an entry in the style sheet). As you might guess, body, h1, p, img, a, and footer in the style sheet refer to the corresponding tags in the HTML documents to which the style sheet will be applied. These are called the *selectors*. The curly braces after each tag name describe how all content within that tag should appear—using the *style rules*.

In this case, the style sheet says that all body text should be rendered at a size of 10 points, in the Verdana font (if possible), and with the color black, with 14 points between lines. If the user does not have the Verdana font installed, the list of fonts in the style sheet represents the order in which the browser should search for fonts to use: Geneva, then Arial, and then Helvetica. If the user has none of those fonts, the browser uses whatever default sans-serif font is available. In addition, the page should have left, right, and top padding of 5 points each.

Any text within an <h1> tag should be rendered in boldface Verdana at a size of 14 points. Moving on, any paragraph that uses only the <p> tag inherits all the styles indicated by the body element. However, if the <p> tag uses a special class named subheader, the text appears bold and in the color #593d87 (a purple color).

The pt after each measurement in Listing 3.1 means *points* (there are 72 points in an inch). If you prefer, you can specify any style sheet measurement in inches (in), centimeters (cm), pixels (px), or "widths of a letter *m*," which are called ems (em) or rems (rem). There are also units for sizes relative to the width of the number 0 (ch), relative to 1% of the viewport width or height (vw or vh), and relative to the container (%). Length measurements in CSS are defined as fixed or relative. Fixed lengths—such as inches, pixels, or points—do not change size, while relative lengths—such as ems, ch, or percentages—can change.

NOTE

In CSS, the rem measurement is sized relative to the width of the letter *m*, but it is relative to the initial font size rather than any changed font sizes that might apply. Best practices recommend that you use relative font sizes (such as rem or em) rather than fixed font sizes (such as inches or points) so that your designs scale more gracefully. Whether you choose rem or em depends mostly on whether you need your type to scale across the whole page (use rem) or you need more explicit control over sections of the document (use em).

You might have noticed that each style rule in the listing ends with a semicolon (;). Semicolons are used to separate style rules from each other. It is therefore customary to end each style rule with a semicolon so that you can easily add another style rule after it. Review the remainder of the style sheet in Listing 3.1 to see the presentation formatting applied to additional tags. Don't worry: You'll learn more about each of these types of entries throughout the lessons in this course.

NOTE
___

Bear in mind that 10pt is a small font size. Not everyone viewing your page will find such a small font size legible or easy to read. You can specify font sizes as large or small as you like with style sheets, although some older display devices and printers do not correctly handle fonts larger than 200 points. Always test your pages in as many browsers and devices as possible.

___

To link this style sheet to HTML documents, include a `<link>` tag in the `<head>` section of each document. Listing 3.2 shows HTML code for a page that contains the following `<link>` tag:

```
<link rel="stylesheet" href="styles.css">
```

This assumes that the style sheet is stored under the name `styles.css` in the same folder as the HTML document. As long as the web browser supports style sheets—and all modern browsers do—the properties specified in the style sheet will apply to the content in the page without the need for any special HTML formatting code. This meets one of the goals of HTML, which is to provide a separation between the content in a web page and the specific formatting required to display that content.

LISTING 3.2   HTML Code for a Page Using an External Style Sheet

```
<!doctype html>
<html lang="en">
  <head>
    <meta charset="utf-8">
    <title>About BAWSI</title>
    <link rel="stylesheet" href="styles.css">
  </head>
  <body>
    <section>
      <header>
        <h1>About BAWSI</h1>
      </header>

      <p><img src="logo.gif" alt="BAWSI logo">The Bay Area Women's
      Sports Initiative (BAWSI) is a public benefit, nonprofit
      corporation with a mission to create programs and
      partnerships through which women athletes bring health, hope
      and wholeness to our community. Founded in 2005 by Olympic
```

```
         and World Cup soccer stars Brandi Chastain and Julie Foudy
         and Marlene Bjornsrud, former general manager of the San Jose
         CyberRays women's professional soccer team, BAWSI provides a
         meaningful path for women athletes to become a more visible
         and valued part of the Bay Area sports culture.</p>

         <p class="subheader">BAWSI's History</p>

         <p>The concept of BAWSI was inspired by one of the most
         spectacular achievements in women's sports history and born out
         of one its biggest disappointments...</p>

         <p><a href="secondpage.html">[continue reading]</a></p>
      </section>

      <footer>
        Copyright &copy; 2005-2013 BAWSI (www.bawsi.org).
        All rights reserved.  Used with permission.
      </footer>
   </body>
</html>
```

NOTE

In most web browsers, you can view the style rules in a style sheet by right-clicking on the page and choosing Inspect or Inspect Element. There you see the HTML and the specific styles associated with the highlighted element. You can even make temporary edits to see how the page might change. To edit your own style sheets, just use a text editor; most designers use the same editor for CSS that they use for HTML.

The code in Listing 3.2 is interesting because it contains no style formatting of any kind. In other words, nothing in the HTML code dictates how the text and images are to be displayed—no colors, no fonts, nothing. Yet the page is carefully formatted and rendered to the screen, thanks to the link to the external style sheet, `styles.css`. The real benefit to this approach is that you can easily create a site with multiple pages that maintains a consistent look and feel. And you have the benefit of isolating the visual style of the page to a single document (the style sheet) so that one change impacts all pages.

NOTE

Not every browser's support of CSS is flawless. If you want to find out what the support is for a specific CSS property (or HTML tag or other web technology), take a look at the website CanIUse (www.caniuse.com).

Creating a Style Sheet of Your Own

Starting from scratch, create a new text document called `mystyles.css` and add some style rules for the following basic HTML tags: <body>, <p>, <h1>, and <h2>. After creating your style sheet, make a new HTML file that contains these basic tags. Play around with different style rules and see for yourself how simple it is to change entire blocks of text in paragraphs with one simple change in a style sheet file.

A CSS Style Primer

You now have a basic knowledge of CSS style sheets and how they are based on style rules that describe the appearance of information in web pages. The next few sections of this lesson provide a quick overview of some of the most important style properties and enable you to get started using CSS in your own style sheets.

CSS includes various style properties that are used to control fonts, colors, alignment, and margins, among other things. The style properties in CSS can be generally grouped into two major categories:

▶ **Layout properties**—Properties that affect the positioning of elements on a web page, such as margins, padding, and alignment

▶ **Formatting properties**—Properties that affect the visual display of elements in a website, such as the font type, size, and color

Basic Layout Properties

CSS layout properties determine how content is placed on a web page. One of the most important layout properties is the `display` property, which describes how an element is displayed with respect to other elements. The `display` property has five basic values:

▶ `block`—The element is displayed on a new line, as in a new paragraph.

▶ `list-item`—The element is displayed on a new line with a list-item mark (bullet) next to it.

▶ `inline`—The element is displayed inline with the current paragraph.

▶ `inline-block`—The element is displayed as a block-level element inline with surrounding block elements.

▶ `none`—The element is not displayed; it is hidden.

NOTE

The display property relies on a concept known as *relative positioning*, which means that elements are positioned relative to the location of other elements on a page. CSS also supports *absolute positioning*, which enables you to place an element at an exact location on a page, independent of other elements. You'll learn more about both of these types of positioning in Lesson 10, "Understanding the CSS Box Model and Positioning."

Understanding the display property is easier if you visualize each element on a web page occupying a rectangular area when displayed; the display property controls the manner in which this rectangular area is displayed. For example, the block value results in the element being placed on a new line by itself, whereas the inline value places the element next to the content just before it. The inline-block value treats the element as a block but positions it next to the content just before it, and the img tag is the most commonly used inline-block element. The display property is one of the few style properties that can be applied in most style rules. Following is an example of how to set the display property:

```
display:block;
```

NOTE

The display property has several other values, including table, flex, and grid, and their inline counterparts inline-table, inline-flex, and inline-grid. These values, which offer powerful layout and display functionality, are covered in more detail in Lesson 12, "Creating Layouts Using Modern CSS Techniques."

You control the dimensions of the rectangular area for an element with the width and height properties. As with many other size-related CSS properties, width and height property values can be specified in several different units of measurement:

- in—Inches
- cm—Centimeters
- em—Ems
- mm—Millimeters
- %—Percentage
- px—Pixels
- pt—Points
- rem—Rems

You can mix and match units any way you like within a style sheet, but it's generally a good idea to be consistent across a set of similar style properties. For example, you might want to stick with rems for font properties and percentages for dimensions. Following is an example of setting the width of an element using pixel units:

```
width: 200px;
```

Basic Formatting Properties

CSS formatting properties are used to control the appearance of content on a web page, as opposed to controlling the physical positioning of the content. One of the most popular formatting properties is the border property, which establishes a visible boundary around an element with a box or partial box. Note that a border is always present in that space is always left for it, but the border does not appear in a way that you can see unless you give it properties that make it visible (such as a color). The following border properties provide a means of describing the borders of an element:

- ▸ border-width—The width of the border edge
- ▸ border-color—The color of the border edge
- ▸ border-style—The style of the border edge
- ▸ border-left—The left side of the border
- ▸ border-right—The right side of the border
- ▸ border-top—The top of the border
- ▸ border-bottom—The bottom of the border
- ▸ border—All the border sides

The border-width property establishes the width of the border edge. It is often expressed in pixels, as the following code demonstrates:

```
border-width:5px;
```

Not surprisingly, the border-color and border-style properties set the border color and style. Following are examples of how these two properties are set:

```
border-color:blue;
border-style:dotted;
```

The border-style property can be set to any of the following basic values:

- ▸ solid—A single-line border
- ▸ double—A double-line border

- ▸ `dashed`—A dashed border

- ▸ `dotted`—A dotted border

- ▸ `groove`—A border with a groove appearance

- ▸ `ridge`—A border with a ridge appearance

- ▸ `inset`—A border with an inset appearance

- ▸ `outset`—A border with an outset appearance

- ▸ `none`—No border

- ▸ `hidden`—Effectively the same as `none`

You'll learn about some more advanced border tricks later in this course.

The default value of the `border-style` property is `none`, which is why elements don't have a border *unless* you set the `border-style` property to a different style. Although `solid` is the most common border style, you will also see the other styles in use.

The `border-left`, `border-right`, `border-top`, and `border-bottom` properties enable you to set the border for each side of an element individually. If you want a border to appear the same on all four sides, you can use the single `border` property by itself, which expects the following styles, separated by spaces: `border-width`, `border-style`, and `border-color`. Following is an example of using the `border` property to set a border that consists of two (`double`) red lines that are a total of 10 pixels in width:

```
border:10px double red;
```

You can also adjust the curve of the boxes by changing the border radius with these properties:

- ▸ `border-top-left-radius`—The top-left corner radius

- ▸ `border-top-right-radius`—The top-right corner radius

- ▸ `border-bottom-left-radius`—The bottom-left corner radius

- ▸ `border-bottom-right-radius`—The bottom-right corner radius

- ▸ `border-radius`—The radius for all four corners

The `border-radius` properties take one or two values. These values define the two radii of a quarter ellipse that describes the shape of the corner. The first value is the horizontal radius and the second the vertical. If there is only one value, it is used for both. This property rounds the corners of both the border and any background placed on the element. Following is an example of using the `border-radius` property set to `1rem`:

```
border-radius: 1rem;
```

Whereas the color of an element's border is set with the `border-color` property, the color of the inner region of an element is set using the `color` and `background-color` properties. The `color` property sets the color of text in an element (foreground), and the `background-color` property sets the color of the background behind the text. Following is an example of setting both color properties to predefined colors:

```
color:black;
background-color:orange;
```

You can also assign custom colors to these properties by specifying the colors in hexadecimal (covered in more detail in Lesson 8, "Working with Colors, Images, and Multimedia") or as RGB (red, green, blue) decimal values:

```
background-color:#999999;
color:rgb(0,0,255);
```

You can even set the transparency of the colors with the RGBa (red, green, blue, alpha channel) decimal values:

```
background-color:rgba(0,0,0,0.8);
color:rgba(0,0,255,1.0);
```

You can also control the alignment and indentation of web page content without too much trouble. This is accomplished with the `text-align` and `text-indent` properties, as the following code demonstrates:

```
text-align:center;
text-indent:12px;
```

NOTE

The `text-align` property applies to the contents of a block-level element, not to the element itself. If you want to center a block element (or an inline-block element, such as an image) you need to use other methods, as discussed in Lesson 9, "Working with Margins, Padding, Alignment, and Floating."

When you have an element properly aligned and indented, you might be interested in setting its font. The following basic font properties set the various parameters associated with fonts (and you'll learn about some more advanced font usage in Lesson 6, "Working with Fonts, Text Blocks, Lists, and Tables"):

- ▶ `font-family`—The typeface of the font
- ▶ `font-size`—The size of the font
- ▶ `font-style`—The style of the font (`normal` or `italic`)
- ▶ `font-weight`—The weight of the font (`normal`, `lighter`, `bold`, `bolder`, and so on)

The `font-family` property specifies a prioritized list of typeface names. A prioritized list is used instead of a single value to provide alternatives in case a font isn't available on a given system. If the typeface has multiple words, such as "Times New Roman," you should surround the name with quotation marks. The `font-size` property specifies the size of the font, using a unit of measurement. Finally, the `font-style` property sets the style of the font, and the `font-weight` property sets the weight of the font. Following is an example of setting these font properties:

```
font-family: Arial, "Gill Sans", sans-serif;
font-size: 1.2rem;
font-style: italic;
font-weight: normal;
```

Now that you know a whole lot more about style properties and how they work, look at Listing 3.1 again and see whether it makes a bit more sense. Here's a recap of the style properties used in that style sheet, which you can use as a guide for understanding how it works:

▶ `font`—Lets you set many font properties at once. You can specify a list of font names separated by commas; if the first one is not available, the next is tried, and so on. You can also include the words `bold` and/or `italic` and a font size. Alternatively, you can set each of these font properties separately with `font-family`, `font-size`, `font-weight`, and `font-style`.

▶ `line-height`—Is also known in the publishing world as *leading*. This sets the height of each line of text. `line-height` is usually defined in the same units as `font`.

▶ `color`—Sets the text color using the standard color names or hexadecimal color codes (see Lesson 8 for more details).

▶ `text-decoration`—Is useful for turning off link underlining; simply set it to `none`. The values of `underline`, `overline`, and `line-through` are also supported. Lesson 7, "Using External and Internal Links," covers applying styles to links in more detail.

▶ `text-align`—Aligns text (`left`, `right`, or `center`) or justifies the text (`justify`).

▶ `padding`—Adds padding to the left, right, top, and bottom of an element; this padding can be in measurement units or a percentage of the page width. Use `padding-left` and `padding-right` if you want to add padding to the left and right of the element independently. Use `padding-top` or `padding-bottom` to add padding to the top or bottom of the element, as appropriate. You'll learn more about these style properties in Lessons 9 and 10.

Using Style Classes

This is a "teach yourself" course, so you don't have to go to a single class to learn how to give your pages great style—although you *do* need to learn what a style class is. Whenever you want some of the text on your pages to look different from the other text, you can create what amounts to a custom-built HTML tag. Each type of specially formatted text you define is called a *style class*. A *style class* is a custom set of formatting specifications that can be applied to any element in a web page.

Before you examine a style class, we need to take a quick step back and clarify some CSS terminology. First, a CSS *style property* is a specific style to which you can assign a value, such as `color` or `font-size`. You associate a style property and its respective value with elements on a web page by using a selector. A *selector* is used to identify tags on a page to which you apply styles. Following is an example of a selector, a property, and a value all included in a basic style rule:

```
h1 { font: 36pt Courier; }
```

In this code, `h1` is the selector, `font` is the style property, and `36pt Courier` is the value. The selector is important because it means that the font setting will be applied to all `h1` elements in the web page. But what if you want to differentiate between some of the `h1` elements? The answer lies in style classes.

Suppose you want two different kinds of <h1> headings for use in your documents. You create a style class for each one by putting the following CSS code in a style sheet:

```
h1.silly { font: 36pt Comic Sans; }
h1.serious { font: 36pt Arial; }
```

Notice that these selectors include a period (.) after `h1`, followed by a descriptive class name. To choose between the two style classes, use the `class` attribute, like this:

```
<h1 class="silly">Marvin's Munchies Inc.</h1>
<p>Text about Marvin's Munchies goes here.</p>
```

Or you could use this:

```
<h1 class="serious">MMI Investor Information</h1>
<p>Text for business investors goes here.</p>
```

When referencing a style class in HTML code, simply specify the class name in the `class` attribute of an element. In the preceding example, the words `Marvin's Munchies Inc.` would appear in a 36-point Comic Sans font, assuming that you included a <link> to the style sheet at the top of the web page and that the user has the Comic Sans font installed. The words `MMI Investor Information` would appear in the 36-point Arial font instead. You can see another example of classes in action in Listing 3.2; look for the `subheader` <p> class.

What if you want to create a style class that can be applied to any element instead of just headings or some other particular tag? In your CSS, simply use a period (.) followed by any style class name you make up and any style rules you choose. That class can specify any number of font, spacing, and margin settings all at once. Wherever you want to apply your custom tag in a page, just use an HTML tag plus the `class` attribute, followed by the class name you created.

For example, the style sheet in Listing 3.1 includes the following style class specification:

```
p.subheader {
  font-weight: bold;
  color:#593d87;
}
```

This style class is applied in Listing 3.2 with the following tag:

```
<p class="subheader">
```

NOTE

You might have noticed a change in the coding style when a style rule includes multiple properties. For style rules with a single style, you commonly see the property placed on the same line as the rule, like this:

```
p.subheader { font-weight: bold; }
```

However, when a style rule contains multiple style properties, it's much easier to read and understand the code if you list the properties one per line, like this:

```
p.subheader {
  font-weight: bold;
  color:#593d87;
}
```

Everything between that tag and the closing </p> tag in Listing 3.2 appears in bold purple text.

What makes style classes so valuable is that they isolate style code from web pages, enabling you to focus your HTML code on the actual content in a page rather than on how it is going to appear on the screen. Then you can determine how the content is rendered to the screen by fine-tuning the style sheet. You might be surprised by how a relatively small amount of code in a style sheet can have significant effects across an entire website. Style classes make your pages much easier to maintain and manipulate.

Using Style IDs

When you create custom style classes, you can use those classes as many times as you like; they are not unique. However, in some instances, you want precise control over unique elements for layout or formatting purposes (or both). In such instances, look to IDs instead of classes.

A *style ID* is a custom set of formatting specifications that can be applied to only one element in a web page. You can use IDs across a set of pages—but only once within each page.

For example, suppose you have a title within the body of all your pages. Each page has only one title, but each page includes one instance of that title. Following is an example of a selector with an ID indicated, plus a property and a value:

```
p#title {font: 24pt Verdana, Geneva, Arial, sans-serif}
```

Notice that this selector includes a hash tag, or pound sign (#), after p, followed by a descriptive ID name. When referencing a style ID in HTML code, simply specify the ID name in the id attribute of an element, like so:

```
<p id="title">Some Title Goes Here</p>
```

Everything between the opening and closing <p> tags will appear in 24-point Verdana text—but only once on any given page. You often see style IDs used to define specific parts of a page for layout purposes, such as a header area, footer area, main body area, and so on. These types of areas in a page appear only once per page, so using an ID rather than a class is the appropriate choice.

Internal Style Sheets and Inline Styles

In some situations, you want to specify styles that will be used in only one web page. You can enclose a style sheet between <style> and </style> tags and include it directly in an HTML document. Style sheets used in this manner must appear in the <head> of an HTML document. No <link> tag is needed, and you cannot refer to that style sheet from any other page (unless you copy it into the beginning of that document, too). This kind of style sheet is known as an internal style sheet, as you learned earlier in the lesson.

NOTE

In many web pages, you see the attribute type="text/css" on the <style> tag. This used to be required for valid HTML, but most modern browsers assume that is the type unless otherwise specified. So, in HTML5, that attribute is no longer required.

Listing 3.3 shows an example of how you might specify an internal style sheet.

LISTING 3.3   A Web Page with an Internal Style Sheet

```
<!doctype html>
<html lang="en">
  <head>
    <meta charset="utf-8">
    <title>Some Page</title>
    <style>
      footer {
        font-size: 9pt;
```

```
        line-height: 12pt;
        text-align: center;
      }
    </style>
  </head>
  <body>
  ...
  <footer>
  Copyright 2018 Acme Products, Inc.
  </footer>
  </body>
</html>
```

In Listing 3.3, the `footer` style class is specified in an internal style sheet that appears in the head of the page. The style class is now available for use within the body of this page. In fact, it is used in the body of the page to style the copyright notice.

Internal style sheets are handy if you want to create a style rule that is used multiple times within a single page. However, in some instances, you might need to apply a unique style to one particular element. This calls for an inline style rule, which enables you to specify a style for only a small part of a page, such as an individual element. For example, you can create and apply a style rule within a `<p>`, `<div>`, or `<span>` tag via the `style` attribute. This type of style is known as an *inline style* because it is specified right there in the middle of the HTML code.

NOTE

The `<span>` and `</span>` tags are dummy tags that do nothing in and of themselves except specify a range of content to apply any `style` attributes that you add. The only difference between `<div>` and `<span>` is that `<div>` is a block element and, therefore, forces a line break, whereas `<span>` doesn't. Therefore, you should use `<span>` to modify the style of any portion of text that is to appear in the middle of a sentence or paragraph without any line break.

Here's how a sample `style` attribute might look:

```
<p style="color:green;">
   This text is green, but <span style="color:red;">this text
   is red.</span>
   Back to green again, but...
</p>
<p>
   ...now the green is over, and we're back to the default color
   for this page.
</p>
```

This code makes use of the `<span>` tag to show how to apply the `color` style property in an inline style rule. In fact, both the `<p>` tag and the `<span>` tag in this example use the `color` property as an inline style. It is important to understand that the `color:red;` style property overrides the `color:green;` style property for the text between the `<span>` and `</span>` tags. Then in the second paragraph, neither of the `color` styles applies because this completely new paragraph adheres to the default color of the entire page.

CAUTION

Using inline styles isn't considered a best practice when used beyond page-level debugging or the process of trying out new things in a controlled setting. The best practice of all is having your pages link to a centrally maintained style sheet so that changes are immediately reflected in all pages that use it.

Validating Your Style Sheets

Just as it is important to validate your HTML or XHTML markup, it is important to validate style sheets. You can find a specific validation tool for CSS at https://jigsaw.w3.org/css-validator/. You can point the tool to a web address, upload a file, or paste content into the form field provided. The ultimate goal is a result like the one in Figure 3.3: `valid`!

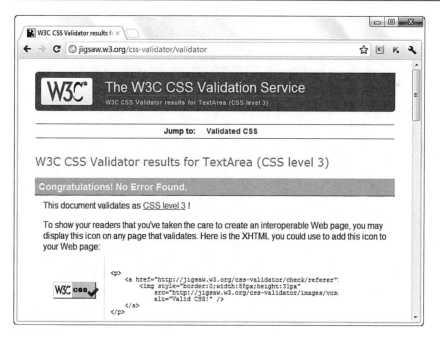

FIGURE 3.3
The W3C CSS Validator shows there are no errors in the style sheet contents of Listing 3.1.

Summary

In this lesson, you learned that a style sheet can control the appearance of many HTML pages at once. It can also give you extremely precise control over the typography, spacing, and positioning of HTML elements. You also learned that, by adding a style attribute to almost any HTML tag, you can control the style of any part of an HTML page without referring to a separate style sheet document.

You learned about three main approaches to including style sheets in your website: a separate style sheet file with the extension .css that is linked to in the <head> of your documents, a collection of style rules placed in the <head> of the document within the <style> tag, and rules placed directly in an HTML tag via the style attribute (although the latter is not a best practice for long-term use).

Table 3.1 summarizes the tags discussed in this lesson. Refer to the CSS style sheet standards at www.w3c.org for details on what options can be included after the <style> tag or the style attribute.

TABLE 3.1 HTML Tags and Attributes Covered in Lesson 3

Tag	Attributes	Function
<style>...</style>		Allows an internal style sheet to be included within a document. Used between <head> and </head>.
	type="contenttype"	The Internet content type. No longer required for HTML5.
<link>		Links to an external style sheet (or other document type). Used in the <head> section of the document.
	href="url"	The address of the style sheet.
	type="contenttype"	The Internet content type. No longer required for HTML5.
	rel="stylesheet"	The link type.
<span>...</span>		Does nothing except provide a place to put style or other attributes. (Similar to <div>...</div>, but does not cause a line break.)
	style="style"	Includes inline style specifications. (Can be used in <span>, <div>, <body>, and most other HTML tags.)

Q&A

Q. Say that I link a style sheet to my page that says all text should be blue, but there's a `<span style="font-color:red;">` tag in the page somewhere. Will that text display as blue or red?

A. Red. Local inline styles always take precedence over external style sheets. Any style specifications you put between `<style>` and `</style>` tags at the top of a page also take precedence over external style sheets (but not over inline styles later in the same page). This is the cascading effect of style sheets mentioned earlier in the lesson. You can think of cascading style effects as starting with an external style sheet, which is overridden by an internal style sheet, which is overridden by inline styles.

Q. Can I link more than one style sheet to a single page?

A. Sure. For example, you might have a sheet for formatting (text, fonts, colors, and so on) and another one for layout (margins, padding, alignment, and so on); you just need to include a `<link>` for each one. Technically, the CSS standard requires web browsers to give the user the option to choose between style sheets when multiple sheets are presented via multiple `<link>` tags. However, in practice, all major web browsers simply include every style sheet unless it has a `rel="alternate"` attribute. Best practices recommend that you limit the number of style sheets you link to. This results in fewer calls to the server and, therefore, faster page load times.

Workshop

The Workshop contains quiz questions and exercises to help you solidify your understanding of the material covered.

Quiz

1. What code would you use to create a style sheet to specify 30-point blue Arial headings and all other text in 10-point blue Times Roman (or the default browser font)?

2. If you saved the style sheet you made for Question 1 as `corporate.css`, how would you apply it to a web page named `intro.html`?

3. How many different ways are there to ensure that style rules can be applied to your content?

4. How do you connect all your website pages to the style sheet named `mystyles.css`?

5. In the following HTML, what color would the text "To come to the aid of their country" be?

```
<div style="color:purple;">
  Now is the time
  <p style="color:orange;">for all good people</p>
  <p>To come to the aid of their country.</p>
</div>
```

6. What does the `display: block;` property do?

7. What does the term `px` mean?

8. What does the style `border-right: dashed red 2px;` do?

9. What does the style `border-radius: 1em 1.5em;` do?

10. What does the style rule `.main { color: purple; }` do?

NOTE

Just a reminder for those of you reading these words in the print or e-book edition of this book: If you go to **www.informit.com/register** and register this book (using ISBN 9780672338083), you can receive free access to an online Web Edition that not only contains the complete text of this book but also features an interactive version of this quiz.

Answers

1. Your style sheet would include the following:

```
h1 { font: 30pt blue Arial; }
body { font: 10pt blue "Times New Roman"; }
```

2. Put the following tag between the <head> and </head> tags of the `intro.html` document:

```
<link rel="stylesheet" href="corporate.css">
```

3. Three: externally, internally, and inline.

4. To connect all your website pages to the style sheet named `mystyles.css`, use the following:

```
<link href="mystyles.css" rel="stylesheet">
```

5. It would be purple.

6. It displays the element on a new line.

7. It is a unit of measure—pixels.

8. It puts a right-side border on the element that is dashed, red, and 2 pixels wide.

9. It rounds the corners of the element with a 1-em horizontal radius and a 1.5-em vertical radius.

10. It sets everything with the class `main` to have a purple text color.

Exercises

▶ Using the style sheet you created earlier in this lesson, add some style classes to your style sheet. To see the fruits of your labor, apply those classes to the HTML page you created as well. Use classes with your \<h1> and \<p> tags to get a feel for things.

▶ Develop a standard style sheet for your website and link it to all your pages. (Use internal style sheets and/or inline styles for pages that need to deviate from it.) If you work for a corporation, chances are it has already developed font and style specifications for printed materials. Get a copy of those specifications and follow them for company web pages, too.

▶ Be sure to explore the official style sheet specs at www.w3.org/Style/CSS/ and try some of the more esoteric style properties not covered in this lesson.

LESSON 4
Understanding JavaScript

What You'll Learn in This Lesson:

- ▶ What web scripting is and what it's good for
- ▶ How scripting and programming are different (and similar)
- ▶ What JavaScript is and where it came from
- ▶ How to include JavaScript commands in a web page
- ▶ What JavaScript can do for your web pages
- ▶ Beginning and ending scripts
- ▶ Formatting JavaScript statements
- ▶ How a script can display a result
- ▶ Including a script within a web document
- ▶ Testing a script in a browser
- ▶ Modifying a script
- ▶ Dealing with errors in scripts
- ▶ Moving scripts into separate files

The World Wide Web (WWW) began as a text-only medium; the first browsers didn't even support images within web pages. The Web has come a long way since those early days. Today's websites include a wealth of visual and interactive features in addition to useful content: graphics, sounds, animation, and video. Using web scripting languages, such as JavaScript, is one of the easiest ways to spice up a web page and to interact with users in new ways.

The first part of this lesson introduces the concept of web scripting and the JavaScript language. As the lesson moves ahead, you'll learn how to include JavaScript commands directly in your HTML documents and how your scripts will be executed when the page is viewed in a browser. You will work with a simple script, edit it, and test it in your browser, all the while learning the basic tasks involved in creating and using JavaScript scripts.

Learning Web Scripting Basics

You already know how to use two types of computer languages: HTML and CSS. You use HTML tags to describe how you want your document formatted. Then you use CSS to describe how you want the document displayed, and the browser shows the decorated content to the user. But because HTML and CSS are simple text-based languages, they can't respond to the user, make decisions, or automate repetitive tasks. Interactive tasks such as these require a more sophisticated language: a programming language or a *scripting* language.

Although many programming languages are complex, scripting languages are generally simple. They have a simple syntax, can perform tasks with a minimum of commands, and are easy to learn. JavaScript is a web scripting language that enables you to combine scripting with HTML and CSS to create interactive web pages.

Scripts and Programs

A movie or a play follows a script—a list of actions (or lines) for the actors to perform. A web script provides the same type of instructions for the web browser. A script in JavaScript can range from a single line to a full-scale application. (In either case, JavaScript scripts usually run within a browser.)

Some programming languages must be *compiled*, or translated, into machine code before they can be executed. JavaScript, on the other hand, is an *interpreted* language: The browser executes each line of script as it comes to it.

There is one main advantage to interpreted languages: Writing or changing a script is very simple. Changing a JavaScript script is as easy as changing a typical HTML document, and the change is enacted as soon as you reload the document in the browser.

NOTE
***
Interpreted languages have disadvantages, too: They can't execute really quickly, so they're not ideally suited for complicated work, such as graphics, and they require the interpreter (in JavaScript's case, usually a browser) in order to work.
***

Introducing JavaScript

JavaScript was developed in 1995 by Netscape Communications Corporation, the maker of the long-defunct Netscape web browser. JavaScript was the first web scripting language to be supported by browsers, and it is still by far the most popular.

NOTE
A bit of history: JavaScript was originally called LiveScript, and it was first introduced in Netscape Navigator 2.0 in 1995. It was soon renamed JavaScript to indicate a marketing relationship with Sun's Java language, although there is no other relationship, structurally or otherwise, between Java and JavaScript.

JavaScript is almost as easy to learn as HTML, and it can be included directly in HTML documents. Here are a few of the things you can do with JavaScript:

- ▶ Display messages to the user as part of a web page, in the browser's status line, or in alert boxes

- ▶ Validate the contents of a form and make calculations (for example, by having an order form automatically display a running total as you enter item quantities)

- ▶ Animate images or create images that change when you move the mouse over them

- ▶ Create ad banners that interact with the user rather than simply displaying a graphic

- ▶ Detect what browser is in use or what features the browser has and perform advanced functions only on browsers that support them

- ▶ Detect installed plug-ins and notify the user if a plug-in is required

- ▶ Modify all or part of a web page without requiring the user to reload it

- ▶ Display or interact with data retrieved from a remote server

You can do all this and more with JavaScript, including creating entire applications. We'll explore the uses of JavaScript throughout these lessons.

How JavaScript Fits into a Web Page

By using the `<script>` tag, as shown in Listing 4.1, you can add a short script (in this case, just one line) to a web document. The `<script>` tag tells the browser to start treating the text as a script, and the closing `</script>` tag tells the browser to return to HTML mode. In most cases, you can't use JavaScript statements in an HTML document except within `<script>` tags. The exception is event handlers, described later in this lesson.

LISTING 4.1 A Simple HTML Document with a Simple Script

```
<!doctype html>
<html lang="en">
  <head>
    <meta charset="utf-8">
    <title>The American Eggplant Society</title>
  </head>
```

```
<body>
  <h1>The American Eggplant Society</h1>
  <p>Welcome to our site. Unfortunately, it is still
  under construction.</p>
  <p>We last worked on it on this date:
  <script>
  <!-- // Hide the script from old browsers
  document.write(document.lastModified);
  // Stop hiding the script -->
  </script>
  </p>
</body>
</html>
```

JavaScript's document.write statement, which you'll learn more about later, sends output as part of the web document. In this case, it displays the modification date of the document, as shown in Figure 4.1.

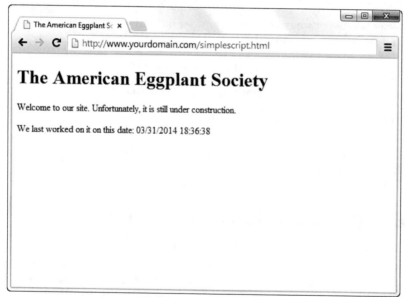

FIGURE 4.1
Using document.write to display a last-modified date.

In this example, we placed the script within the body of the HTML document. There are actually four places where you might use scripts:

▶ **In the body of the page**—In this case, the script's output is displayed as part of the HTML document when the browser loads the page.

▶ **In the header of the page, between the** `<head>` **tags**—Scripts in the header should not be used to create output within the `<head>` section of an HTML document, since that would likely result in poorly formed and invalid HTML documents, but these scripts can be referred to by other scripts here and elsewhere. The `<head>` section is often used for functions—groups of JavaScript statements that can be used as a single unit. You will learn more about functions in Lesson 20, "Getting Started with JavaScript Programming."

▶ **Within an HTML tag, such as** `<body>` **or** `<form>`—This is called an *event handler*, and it enables the script to work with HTML elements. When using JavaScript in event handlers, you don't need to use the `<script>` tag. You'll learn more about event handlers in Lesson 20.

▶ **In a separate file entirely**—JavaScript supports the use of files with the `.js` extension containing scripts; these can be included by specifying a file in the `<script>` tag. While using the `.js` extension is a convention, scripts can actually have any file extension, or none.

As you'll learn in Lesson 25, "JavaScript Best Practices," the best place to put JavaScript is inside the `<body>` tag, just before the closing `</body>` tag. This ensures that JavaScript is the last thing to load and so doesn't disrupt the speed of the rest of the page displaying.

Using Separate JavaScript Files

When you create more complicated scripts, you'll quickly find that your HTML documents become large and confusing. To avoid this problem, you can use one or more external JavaScript files. These are files with the `.js` extension that contain JavaScript statements.

External scripts are supported by all modern browsers. To use an external script, you specify its filename in the `<script>` tag, as shown here:

```
<script src="filename.js"></script>
```

NOTE

The `type` attribute used to be required. But in HTML5 it can be left out if the script referenced is JavaScript.

Because in this case you'll be placing the JavaScript statements in a separate file, you don't need anything between the opening and closing `<script>` tags; in fact, anything between them will be ignored by the browser.

You can create the `.js` file by using the same text editor you use to write HTML and CSS. This file should contain one or more JavaScript commands and only JavaScript; it should not include `<script>` tags, other HTML tags, CSS, or HTML comments. Save the `.js` file in the same directory as the HTML documents that refer to it.

NOTE

External JavaScript files have a distinct advantage: You can link to the same .js file from two or more HTML documents. The browser stores this file in its cache, which can reduce the time it takes your web pages to display. But remember that every linked file requires an additional request to the server. So try to keep all your scripts in as few files as you can.

Understanding JavaScript Events

Many of the useful things you can do with JavaScript involve interacting with the user, and that means responding to *events*—for example, a link or a button being clicked. You can define event handlers within HTML tags to tell the browser how to respond to an event. For example, Listing 4.2 defines a button that displays a message when clicked.

LISTING 4.2 A Simple Event Handler

```
<!doctype html>
<html lang="en">
  <head>
    <meta charset="utf-8">
    <title>Event Test</title>
  </head>
  <body>
    <h1>Event Test</h1>
    <button type="button"
            onclick="alert('You clicked the button.')">
            Click Me!</button>
  </body>
</html>
```

In various places throughout these lessons, you'll learn more about JavaScript's event model and how to create simple and complex event handlers.

Exploring JavaScript's Capabilities

If you've spent any time browsing the Web, you've undoubtedly seen lots of examples of JavaScript in action. The following sections provide some brief descriptions of typical applications for JavaScript, all of which you'll explore in later lessons.

Improving Navigation

Some of the most common uses of JavaScript are in navigation systems for websites. You can use JavaScript to create a navigation tool—for example, a drop-down menu to select the next page to read or a submenu that pops up when you hover over a navigation link.

When it's done right, this kind of JavaScript interactivity can make a site easier to use, even for browsers that don't support JavaScript.

Validating Forms

Form validation is another common use of JavaScript, although the form validation features of HTML5 have stolen a lot of JavaScript's thunder here as well. A simple script can read values the user types into a form and make sure they're in the right format, such as with zip codes, phone numbers, and email addresses. This type of client-side validation enables users to fix common errors without waiting for a response from the web server, telling them that their form submission was invalid. You'll learn how to work with form data in Lesson 27, "Working with Web-Based Forms."

Special Effects

One of the earliest and most annoying uses of JavaScript was to create attention-getting special effects—for example, scrolling a message in the browser's status line or flashing the background color of a page.

These techniques have fortunately fallen out of style, but thanks to the W3C DOM and the latest browsers, some more impressive effects are possible with JavaScript—for example, creating objects that can be dragged and dropped on a page or creating fading transitions between images in a slideshow. Some developers have HTML5, CSS3, and JavaScript working in tandem to create fully functioning interactive games.

Remote Scripting (AJAX)

For a long time, the biggest limitation of JavaScript was that there was no way for it to communicate with a web server. For example, you could use JavaScript to verify that a phone number had the right number of digits but not to look up the user's location in a database based on the number.

Now that most browsers support some of JavaScript's advanced features, this is no longer the case. Your scripts can get data from a server without loading a page, or they can send data back to be saved. These features are collectively known as AJAX (Asynchronous JavaScript and XML), or *remote scripting*.

Displaying Time with JavaScript

One common use of JavaScript is to display dates and times in the browser, and that's where we'll start putting some scripting pieces together. Because JavaScript runs on the browser, the times it displays will be in the user's current time zone. However, you can also use JavaScript to calculate "universal" (UTC) time.

NOTE

UTC, which stands for Universal Time (Coordinated), is the atomic time standard based on the old GMT (Greenwich Mean Time) standard. This is the time at the prime meridian, which runs through Greenwich, London, England.

Your script, like most other JavaScript programs, begins with the HTML `<script>` tag. As you learned earlier in this lesson, you use the `<script>` and `</script>` tags to enclose a script within the HTML document.

CAUTION

Remember to include only valid JavaScript statements between the starting and ending `<script>` tags. If the browser finds anything except valid JavaScript statements within the `<script>` tags, it will display a JavaScript error message. You should use the comment indicator (`//`) in front of any lines that are not JavaScript.

To begin creating the script, open your favorite text editor and type the beginning and ending `<script>` tags, as shown here:

```
<script></script>
```

In this script, you'll use JavaScript to determine the local and UTC times and then display them in the browser. Fortunately, all the hard parts, such as converting between date formats, are built in to the JavaScript interpreter; this is one of the reasons that displaying dates and times is a good starting place for beginners.

Storing Data in Variables

To begin the script, you will use a *variable* to store the current date. You will learn more about variables in Lesson 22, "Using JavaScript Variables, Strings, and Arrays," but for now just understand that a *variable* is a container that can hold a value—a number, some text, or, in this case, a date.

To start writing the script, add the following line after the first `<script>` tag, making sure to use the same combination of uppercase and lowercase letters in your version because JavaScript commands and variable names are case sensitive:

```
now = new Date();
```

This statement creates a variable called now and stores the current date and time in it. This statement and the others you will use in this script use JavaScript's built-in `Date` object, which enables you to conveniently handle dates and times. You'll learn more about working with dates in Lesson 22.

NOTE
_____
Notice the semicolon at the end of the code snippet creating a variable called now. This semicolon tells the browser that it has reached the end of a statement. Semicolons are optional, but using them helps you avoid some common errors. We'll use them throughout these lessons for clarity.
_____

Calculating the Results

Internally, JavaScript stores dates as the number of milliseconds since January 1, 1970. Fortunately, JavaScript includes a number of functions to convert dates and times in various ways, so you don't have to figure out how to convert milliseconds to days, dates, or times.

To continue your script, add the following two statements before the final `</script>` tag:

```
localtime = now.toString();
utctime = now.toGMTString();
```

These statements create two new variables: `localtime`, containing the current time and date in a nice readable format, and `utctime`, containing the UTC equivalent.

NOTE
_____
The `localtime` and `utctime` variables store a piece of text, such as January 1, 2001 12:00 PM. In programming parlance, a piece of text is called a *string*.
_____

Creating Output

You now have two variables—`localtime` and `utctime`—which contain the results you want from your script. Of course, these variables don't do you much good unless you can see them. JavaScript includes several ways to display information, and one of the simplest is by using the `document.write` statement.

The `document.write` statement displays a text string, a number, or anything else you throw at it. Because your JavaScript program will be used within a web page, the output will be displayed as part of the page. To display the result, add these statements before the final `</script>` tag:

```
document.write("<p><strong>Local time:</strong> " + localtime + "</p>");
document.write("<p><strong>UTC time:</strong> " + utctime + "</p>");
```

These statements tell the browser to add some text to the web page containing your script. The output will include some brief strings introducing the results and the contents of the `localtime` and `utctime` variables.

Notice the HTML elements, such as `<p>` and `<strong>`, within the quotation marks; because JavaScript's output appears within a web page, it needs to be formatted using HTML.

NOTE

Notice the plus signs (+) used between the text and variables in the `document.write()` code snippets. In this case, each plus sign tells the browser to combine the values into one string of text. If you use the plus sign between two numbers that aren't in quotes, they are added together.

Adding the Script to a Web Page

You should now have a complete script that calculates a result and displays it. Your script should match Listing 4.3.

LISTING 4.3   The Complete Date and Time Script

```
<script>
  now = new Date();
  localtime = now.toString();
  utctime = now.toGMTString();
  document.write("<p><strong>Local time:</strong> " + localtime + "</p>");
  document.write("<p><strong>UTC time:</strong> " + utctime + "</p>");
</script>
```

To use your script, you need to add it to an HTML document. If you use the general template you've seen in the lessons so far, you should end up with something like Listing 4.4.

LISTING 4.4   The Date and Time Script in an HTML Document

```
<!doctype html>
<html lang="en">
  <head>
    <meta charset="utf-8">
    <title>Displaying Times and Dates</title>
  </head>
  <body>
    <h1>Current Date and Time</h1>
    <script>
      now = new Date();
      localtime = now.toString();
      utctime = now.toGMTString();
      document.write("<p><strong>Local time:</strong> "
          + localtime + "</p>");
      document.write("<p><strong>UTC time:</strong> " + utctime
          + "</p>");
    </script>
  </body>
</html>
```

Now that you have a complete HTML document, save it with an `.html` extension.

Testing the Script

To test your script, you simply need to load the HTML document you created in a web browser. If you typed the script correctly, your browser should display the result of the script, as shown in Figure 4.2. (Of course, your result won't be the same as mine, but it should be the same as the setting of your computer's clock.)

FIGURE 4.2
Using JavaScript to display the date and time.

NOTE

With Internet Explorer, depending on your security settings, the script might not execute, and your browser might display a security warning. In this case, follow your browser's instructions to allow your script to run. (This happens because the default security settings allow JavaScript in online documents but not in local files.)

Modifying the Script

Although the current script does indeed display the current date and time, its display isn't nearly as attractive as the clock on your wall or desk. To remedy that situation, you can use some additional JavaScript features and a bit of HTML to display a large clock.

To display a large clock, you need the hours, minutes, and seconds in separate variables. Once again, JavaScript has built-in functions to do most of the work:

```
hours = now.getHours();
mins = now.getMinutes();
secs = now.getSeconds();
```

These statements load the hours, mins, and secs variables with the components of the time using JavaScript's built-in date functions.

After the hours, minutes, and seconds are in separate variables, you can create document. write statements to display them:

```
document.write("<p><strong>");
document.write(hours + ":" + mins + ":" + secs);
document.write("</p></strong>");
```

The first statement displays an HTML <h2> header tag to display the clock as a second-level header element. The second statement displays the `hours`, `mins`, and `secs` variables, separated by colons, and the third adds the closing </h2> tag.

You can add the preceding statements to the original date and time script to add the large clock display. Listing 4.5 shows the complete modified version of the script.

LISTING 4.5   The Date and Time Script with a Large Clock Display

```
<!doctype html>
<html lang="en">
  <head>
    <meta charset="utf-8">
    <title>Displaying Times and Dates</title>
  </head>
  <body>
    <h1>Current Date and Time</h1>
    <script>
      now = new Date();
      localtime = now.toString();
      utctime = now.toGMTString();
      document.write("<p><strong>Local time:</strong> "
          + localtime + "</p>");
      document.write("<p><strong>UTC time:</strong> "
          + utctime + "</p>");
      hours = now.getHours();
      mins = now.getMinutes();
      secs = now.getSeconds();
      document.write("<h2>");
      document.write(hours + ":" + mins + ":" + secs);
      document.write("</h2>");
    </script>
  </body>
</html>
```

Now that you have modified the script, save the HTML file and open the modified file in your browser. If you left the browser running, you can simply use the Reload button to load the new version of the script. Try it and verify that the same time is displayed in both the upper portion of the window and the new large clock. Figure 4.3 shows the results.

FIGURE 4.3
Displaying the modified date and time script.

NOTE

The time formatting produced by this script isn't perfect: Hours after noon are in 24-hour time, and there are no leading zeros, so 12:04 is displayed as 12:4. See Lesson 22 for solutions to these issues.

Dealing with JavaScript Errors

As you develop more complex JavaScript applications, you're going to run into errors from time to time. JavaScript errors are usually caused by mistyped JavaScript statements.

To see an example of a JavaScript error message, you can modify the statement you added in the preceding section. In this example, we use a common error: omitting one of the parentheses. Change the last `document.write` statement in Listing 4.5 to read

```
document.write("</h2>";
```

Save your HTML document again and load the document into the browser. Depending on the browser version you're using, one of two things will happen: Either an error message will be displayed, or the script will simply fail to execute.

If an error message is displayed, you're halfway to fixing the problem by adding the missing parenthesis. If no error was displayed, you should configure your browser to display error messages so that you can diagnose future problems:

▶ In Firefox, you can select Tools, Web Developer, Web Console. The console displays the error message you created in this example, as shown in Figure 4.4.

▶ In Chrome, from the options menu (three horizontal dots on the right side of the browser bar) select More Tools, Developer Tools. A console displays in the bottom of the browser window. Choose the console tab if it's not selected.

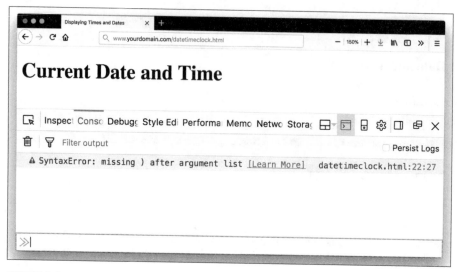

FIGURE 4.4
Showing an error in the JavaScript console in Firefox.

The error you get in this case, `SyntaxError: missing ) after argument list`, points to line 22. In this case, clicking the name of the document takes you directly to the highlighted line containing the error, as shown in Figure 4.5.

```
 1  <!doctype html>
 2  <html lang="en">
 3    <head>
 4      <meta charset="utf-8">
 5      <title>Displaying Times and Dates</title>
 6    </head>
 7    <body>
 8      <h1>Current Date and Time</h1>
 9      <script>
10        now = new Date();
11        localtime = now.toString();
12        utctime = now.toGMTString();
13        document.write("<p><strong>Local time:</strong> "
14          + localtime + "</p>");
15        document.write("<p><strong>UTC time:</strong> " + utctime
16          + "</p>");
17        hours = now.getHours();
18        mins = now.getMinutes();
19        secs = now.getSeconds();
20        document.write("<h2>");
21        document.write(hours + ":" + mins + ":" + secs);
22        document.write("</h2>";
23      </script>
24    </body>
25  </html>
26
```

FIGURE 4.5
Firefox helpfully points out the offending line.

Most modern browsers contain JavaScript debugging tools such as the one you just witnessed. You'll learn more about this in the next lesson.

Summary

During this lesson, you've learned what web scripting is and what JavaScript is. You've also learned how to insert a script into an HTML document or refer to an external JavaScript file, what sorts of things JavaScript can do, and how JavaScript differs from other web languages. You also wrote a simple JavaScript program and tested it using a web browser. You also learned how to modify and test scripts, and you saw what happens when a JavaScript program runs into an error.

In the process of writing this script, you have used some of JavaScript's basic features: variables, the document.write statement, and functions for working with dates and times.

Now that you've learned a bit of JavaScript syntax, you're ready to continue on to learn all sorts of things about web development before settling in to writing interactive websites using client-side scripting.

Q&A

Q. Do I need to test my JavaScript on more than one browser?

A. In an ideal world, any script you write that follows the standards for JavaScript will work in all browsers, and 98% of the time (give or take) that's true in the real world. But browsers do have their quirks, and you should test your scripts in Chrome, Internet Explorer, and Firefox, as well as mobile devices running iOS and Android—at a minimum.

Q. If I plan to learn PHP, Ruby, or some other server-side programming language anyway, will I have any use for JavaScript?

A. Certainly. JavaScript is the ideal language for many parts of a web-based application, such as basic interactivity. Although PHP, Ruby, and other server-side languages have their uses, they can't interact directly with the user on the client side.

Q. When I try to run my script, the browser displays the actual script in the browser window instead of executing it. What did I do wrong?

A. This is most likely caused by one of three errors. First, you might be missing the beginning or ending `<script>` tags. Check them and, if you use the `type` attribute, verify that it reads `type="text/javascript"`. Second, your file might have been saved with a `.txt` extension, causing the browser to treat it as a text file. Rename it to have the extension `.htm` or `.html` to fix the problem. Third, make sure your browser supports JavaScript and ensure that it is not disabled in the preferences.

Q. Why are the `<strong>` and `<p>` tags allowed in the statements to print the time? I thought HTML tags aren't allowed within the `<script>` tags.

A. Because these tags are inside quotation marks, they are considered a valid part of the script. The script's output, including any HTML tags, is interpreted and displayed by the browser. You can use other HTML tags within quotation marks to add formatting, such as the `<h2>` tags you added for the large clock display.

Workshop

The workshop contains quiz questions and exercises to help you solidify your understanding of the material covered.

Quiz

1. When a user views a page containing a JavaScript program, which machine actually executes the script?

    a. The user's machine running a web browser

    b. The web server

    c. A central machine deep within Netscape's corporate offices

    d. A dedicated JavaScript server

2. What software do you use to create and edit JavaScript programs?

    a. A browser

    b. A text editor

    c. A pencil and a piece of paper

    d. A JavaScript editor

3. What are variables used for in JavaScript programs?

    a. Storing numbers, dates, or other values

    b. Varying randomly

    c. Causing high-school algebra flashbacks

    d. Changing the output of the script

4. What should appear at the very end of a JavaScript script embedded in an HTML file?

    a. The `<script>` tag

    b. The `</javascript>` tag

    c. The END statement

    d. The `</script>` tag

5. Which of these is not something you can do with JavaScript?

    a. Detect the features of the browser in use

    b. Modify part of a page without requiring a page refresh

    c. Write data to the remote server

    d. Interact with data from a remote server

6. Where can you place scripts?

   a. In the body of a page

   b. Within an HTML tag

   c. In a separate file

   d. All of the above

7. What do you use to include a separate script file in a page?

   a. `<link src="filename.js">`

   b. `<script src="filename.js"></script>`

   c. `<javascript src="filename.js">`

   d. `<include src="filename.js"></include>`

8. Which of these is an event handler?

   a. `<button>`

   b. `type="button"`

   c. `onclick="alert('You clicked the button.')"`

   d. `</button>`

9. What does the line `now = new Date();` do in JavaScript?

   a. It creates a variable called now and stores the current date in it.

   b. It creates a variable called new and stores the current date in it.

   c. It displays the current time.

   d. Nothing; it's not valid JavaScript.

10. Correct this line of JavaScript:

```
document.write("<p><strong>Dinner Time:</strong> " + localtime + "</p>");
```

   a.
```
document.write("<p><strong>Dinner Time:</strong> "
+ localtime + "</p>");
```

   b.
```
document.write("<p><strong>Dinner Time:</strong> "
+ localtime + "</p>');
```

   c.
```
document.write("<p><strong>Dinner Time:</strong> "
+ localtime + "</p>;
```

   d. The line is correct as written.

NOTE

Just a reminder for those of you reading these words in the print or e-book edition of this book: If you go to **www.informit.com/register** and register this book (using ISBN 9780672338083), you can receive free access to an online Web Edition that not only contains the complete text of this book but also features an interactive version of this quiz.

Answers

1. **a.** JavaScript programs execute in the web browser. (There is actually a server-side version of JavaScript, but that's another story.)

2. **b.** You can use any text editor to create scripts.

3. **a.** Variables are used to store numbers, dates, or other values.

4. **d.** Your script should end with the `</script>` tag.

5. **c.** JavaScript can never write data to the remote server due to security concerns.

6. **d.** JavaScript can be added in the body, a tag, or in a separate file.

7. **b.** Use the line `<script src="filename.js"></script>`.

8. **c.** The `onclick` attribute and its value are the click event handler.

9. **a.** It creates a variable called now and stores the current date in it.

10. **a.** The final quotation mark is missing.

Exercises

▶ Add a millisecond field to the large clock. You can use the `getMilliseconds` function, which works just like `getSeconds` but returns milliseconds.

▶ Modify the script to display the time, including milliseconds, twice. Notice whether any time passes between the two time displays when you load the page.

LESSON 5
Validating and Debugging Your Code

What You'll Learn in This Lesson:

▶ How to validate your HTML and CSS

▶ How to use Developer Tools to debug HTML and CSS

▶ How to use the JavaScript Console to debug JavaScript

It doesn't matter if you're a beginner or a seasoned expert—bugs happen. Bugs are a fact of life for developers of all skill levels, and we would even venture to say that if your code doesn't contain errors at some point during its creation, then you're just not trying hard enough. So don't worry about the bugs; just worry about identifying and fixing them before clients or customers experience their side effects.

In this lesson, you'll learn about how to validate and debug your HTML and CSS as you develop it, as well as how to use some handy tools built directly into your web browser to identify and debug issues with your JavaScript.

Validating Your Web Content

In the first lesson of this series, I discussed ways to test the web pages you create; one very important way to test your pages is to *validate* them. Think of it this way: It's one thing to design and draw a beautiful set of house plans, but it's quite another for an architect to stamp it as a safe structure suitable for construction. Validating your web pages is a similar process; in this case, however, the architect is a web-based application, not a person.

In brief, validation is the process of testing your pages with a special application that searches for errors and makes sure the pages adhere to the current HTML and CSS standards. Validation is simple. In fact, the standards body responsible for developing web standards, the World Wide Web Consortium (W3C), offers an online validation tool you can use, at https://validator.w3.org. Figure 5.1 shows the options for using the W3C Markup Validation Service.

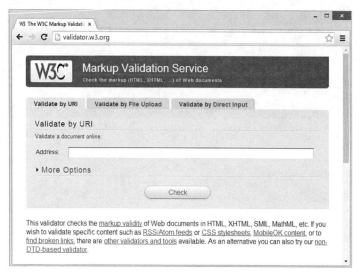

FIGURE 5.1
The W3C Markup Validation Service enables you to validate an HTML document to ensure that it has been coded accurately.

If you've already published a page online, you can use the Validate by URI tab. Use the Validate by File Upload tab to validate files stored on your local computer file system. The Validate by Direct Input tab enables you to paste the contents of a file from your text editor. If all goes well, your page will get a passing report, like the one shown in Figure 5.2, which validates a code listing from Lesson 2, "Structuring an HTML Document."

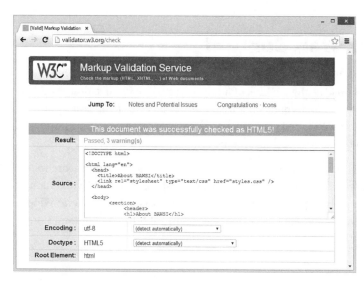

FIGURE 5.2
If a page passes the W3C Markup Validation Service, you know that the code is ready for prime time.

The W3C also provides a tool to validate CSS; visit https://jigsaw.w3.org/css-validator/ and enter a URL or upload a file using the options provided. If the W3C Markup or CSS Validation Service encounters an error, it provides specific details (including the line numbers of the offending code). Figure 5.3 shows an example of an error report; in this instance we have purposely used the CSS property `padding-up`—a property that does not exist—instead of `padding-top`.

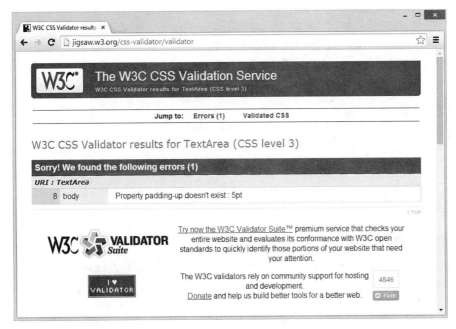

FIGURE 5.3
The W3C CSS Validation Service, like the W3C Markup Validation Service, provides useful error reports.

Using basic validation services is a great way to hunt down problems and rid your HTML and CSS of invalid code, such as incorrectly named CSS properties and mismatched HTML tags. Validation not only informs you when your pages are constructed properly but also assists you in finding and fixing problems in the code before you publish pages for the world to see.

Debugging HTML and CSS Using Developer Tools

You can extend your debugging efforts beyond basic validation by using more advanced tools that are built into most major browsers. Figures 5.4, 5.5, and 5.6 show what some of the major browsers look like with Developer Tools turned on; in each figure you'll notice some consistencies in the names and functionalities of certain tools.

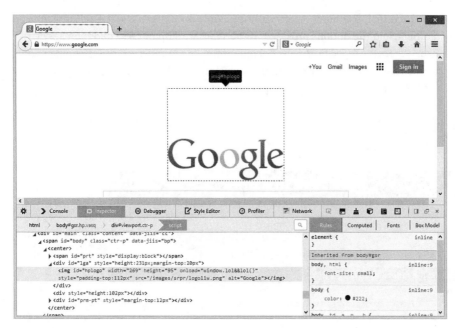

FIGURE 5.4
Inspecting an element containing the Google logo using Developer Tools in Firefox.

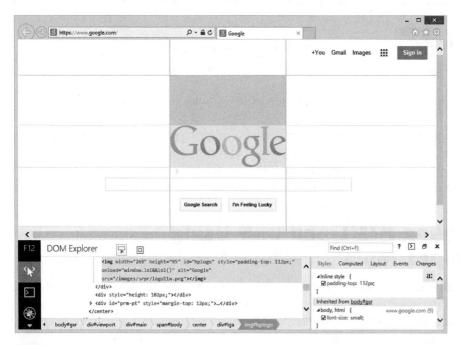

FIGURE 5.5
Inspecting an element containing the Google logo using Developer Tools in Microsoft Internet Explorer.

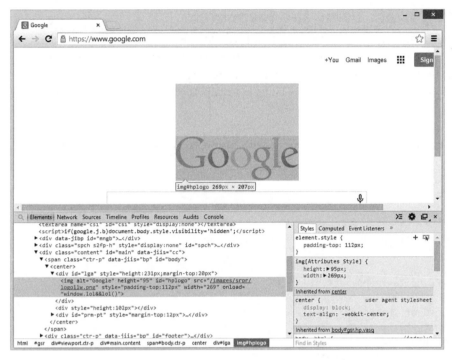

FIGURE 5.6
Inspecting an element containing the Google logo using Developer Tools in Chrome.

Although the examples we'll go through in this section use the Chrome Developer Tools, you can see similarities in all the Developer Tools shown previously (and in other browsers, such as Safari). In this specific case, the ability to inspect an element is present in all three sets of tools. When you are selecting an element on the screen with your mouse, the additional window panels in Developer Tools show the exact HTML used to render that element, as well as the style rules currently applied to that element.

This functionality of the inspector is quite useful because it provides a visual way to see the relationship between the node in the DOM tree and the rendered web page; in addition, note the use of breadcrumbs in each set of tools, which shows the hierarchy of nodes from the root html node down to the img node (with the ID value of #hplogo). This use of breadcrumbs serves to further assist your understanding of where a rendered visual element appears within the DOM (and not just on your screen).

The next few sections take you through some practical applications of using these tools.

Debugging HTML Using the Inspector

To illustrate how to use the inspector to debug HTML, consider the code in Listing 5.1, which is just a basic HTML document containing a list of movies, where the word "Favorite" in the heading is supposed to be italic. However, if you look at the rendered version in Figure 5.7, you'll see some problems: *Everything* is italic, and there is no bullet in front of the first list item. These problems are caused by just two characters in all the text.

LISTING 5.1   A Simple HTML Document with Some HTML Syntax Errors Illustrated in Figure 5.7

```
<!doctype html>
<html lang="en">
  <head>
    <meta charset="utf-8">
    <title>Favorite Movies</title>
  </head>
  <body>
    <h1><i>Favorite<i> Movies</h1>
    <ul>
      <ll>Lord of the Rings</li>
      <li>Harry Potter</li>
      <li>Narnia</li>
      <li>Hot Lead and Cold Feet</li>
    </ul>
  </body>
</html>
```

FIGURE 5.7
This web page has two problems: only the word "Favorite" should be italic, and there is no bullet in front of the first list item.

Follow along with these steps to find and fix the HTML syntax problems using the inspector in Developer Tools:

1. Add the code in Listing 5.1 to a new file, save the document, and then open it in your favorite modern browser (Chrome, Firefox, Safari, or Edge). You can keep the document on your local machine or put it on your web server; it doesn't matter for this example, as long as you can open the file in your web browser.

2. Right-click the screen and choose Inspect Element. You should see something like what's shown in Figure 5.8, with the Elements tab preselected.

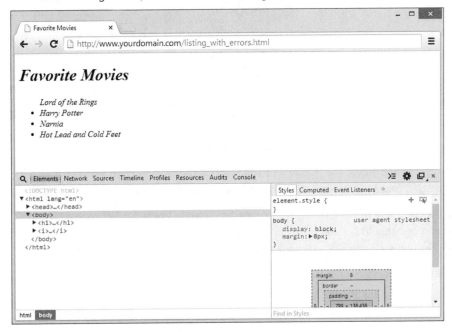

FIGURE 5.8
The Elements tab is selected by default.

3. Click on the arrows in the Elements panel to expand the <h1> tag, as shown in Figure 5.9. Notice there's an <i> element under the <h1> element, and there is also another <i></i> tag pair. That isn't right: You remember (and can see in your source file) that you didn't put <i> elements all over your code, so why do they appear? Well, if you look closely at the Elements panel and then the source code, you will notice that there is a missing / that would make the second instance of the <i> tag the closing </i> tag that you want. This means the browser is rendering (and the inspector is showing) what appear to be <i> </i> elements around every single element in your code because the first <i> element was never closed; the rendering engine is interpreting that all of these phantom <i> elements are present.

FIGURE 5.9
This HTML inspector shows more `<i>` elements in the DOM than are in your source code.

4. In your source file, change the second `<i>` tag to a closing `</i>` tag and save the document. Put it on your web server if that's where you originally placed it.

5. Refresh the document in the browser. Notice that, as shown in Figure 5.10, the word "Favorite" is now italic, as it should be, and all the phantom `<i>` elements are gone from the inspector; however, the bullet point is still missing from the first list item in the browser's display.

FIGURE 5.10
This web page now has only one problem: no bullet point on the first list item.

6. Go back to the Elements panel and expand the `<ul>` element and then the `<ll>`, as shown in Figure 5.11. Notice that instead of a set of four appropriately opened and closed `<li>` elements under the `<ul>` element, there is an open `<ll>` tag followed by three `<li>` elements within it, and then a closing `</li>` tag. Although we haven't covered the HTML list item tags yet (we do that in the next lesson), you can probably deduce that because the three lines with opening and closing `<li>` tags show bullets, and in the source code the `<ll>` element is closed by an `</li>` tag, the opening tag should be an `<li>` tag.

FIGURE 5.11
Viewing the DOM reveals that the browser sees an `<ll>` tag under the `<ul>` tag, not a set of `<li>` tags.

7. In your source file, change the `<ll>` tag to a `<li>` tag and save the document. Put it on your web server if that's where you originally placed it.

8. Reload the web page in the browser. It is now displayed properly, as shown in Figure 5.12.

FIGURE 5.12
Chrome now displays the web page formatted as intended.

Although going through all the steps as you just did shows you some ways in which the inspector can be used to help spot issues, you might wonder just how much more efficient and helpful that process actually is compared to just using a validator. After all, the issues seen earlier were purely validation errors and would have easily been caught by using the W3C Validator you learned about previously. Figure 5.13 shows some of the validation errors present in the original listing.

FIGURE 5.13
The W3C Validator clearly shows errors.

NOTE

When you use a validator, it's best to review the problems in the order in which they appear. Often, fixing one error will cause a lot of the following errors listed to disappear. For example, fixing the first "Unclosed element i" error in Figure 5.13 will fix the second one as well. It will also fix the "End tag h1 seen..." error. It is often a good idea to fix one error and revalidate to see what happens.

It's true that a validator will more quickly identify pure syntax issues and that using the inspector requires you to have the knowledge and experience to see the issue straightaway if it's presented in a different context rather than the raw source code. We recommend that beginners run their code through a validator first, but seeing alternative views of the DOM rendering is quite useful for an ongoing learning process.

Debugging CSS Using the Inspector

Everything you just learned about debugging HTML with the inspector is also true when it comes to CSS: You can use Developer Tools to uncover issues with style definitions and inheritance. These built-in tools become especially useful when you are working with more advanced development, such as when you are using JavaScript to modify the CSS of particular elements beyond their original state in the source code, but they can still be useful in the beginning stages of your development.

The steps in this section go through a brief example of using the inspector when working with CSS—specifically, some ill-formed yet valid CSS, as shown in Listing 5.2. Although you're encountering this lesson (and therefore these examples) very early in your development process, we are quite certain that within a few lessons, you'll remember the steps you've learned here and will be using Developer Tools to enhance your debugging and development throughout the rest of the course.

LISTING 5.2   Valid HTML and CSS That Doesn't Display Nicely

```
<!doctype html>
<html lang="en">
  <head>
    <meta charset="utf-8">
    <style>
    #container {
      margin: 30px;
      padding: 5px;
      width: 300px;
              }

    #tabs {
      padding: 0px;
      width: 50px;
              }
```

```
#content {
  border: 1px solid #000000;
  height: 100px;
  width: 300px;
  clear: both;
}
span {
  margin: 5px;
  width: 100px;
  background-color: #C0C0C0;
  font-weight: bold;
  border-color: #C0C0C0;
  border: 1px solid #000000;
  border-radius: 5px 5px 0px 0px;
  padding: 3px;
  float: left;
  text-align: center;
}

span:hover {
  background-color: #3030FF;
  color: #FFFFFF;
  cursor: pointer;
}

p {
  font-weight: bold;
  text-align: center;
}
    </style>
    <title>Sample Page</title>
  </head>
  <body>
    <div id="container">
      <div id="tabs">
        <span>Name/Title</span>
        <span>Contact Info</span>
        <span>Biography</span>
      </div>

      <div id="content">
        <p>Jimbo Jones</p>
        <p>Rabble-Rouser</p>
      </div>
    </div>
  </body>
</html>
```

If you run this HTML and CSS through a validator, it will produce no errors because it is valid HTML and CSS. However, as you can see in Figure 5.14, it's just not right. The tabs are supposed to align across the top of the box that contains text. If we could get past this initial layout issue, a user would be able to click on the tabs, and the contents in the box would change. But we can't move forward and make that happen until this initial display works as we intend it to work. This is a classic example of a debugging problem in HTML and CSS—it's not wrong (invalid), but it just isn't right (displaying the way we want it to).

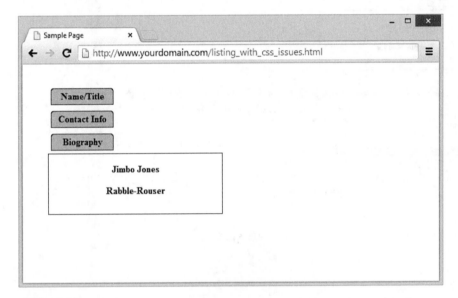

FIGURE 5.14
The result of valid HTML and CSS that needs some additional debugging to look better.

Follow along with these steps to uncover and fix some of the issues using the inspector:

1. Add the code in Listing 5.2 to a new file, save the document, and then open it in your web browser. You can keep the document on your local machine or put it on your web server; it doesn't matter for this example, as long as you can open the file in your web browser.

2. Right-click the page and choose Inspect Element to open Developer Tools.

3. Click on the arrows in the Elements panel to expand the <div> element with the ID "container" and then the <div> element with the ID "tabs". Click on the <div> element with the ID "tabs" so that it is highlighted on your screen, as shown in Figure 5.15. The width of this particular <div> will be shown; in this case, it is 50 pixels wide. This should lead you to wonder if the width of this particular <div>, which is less than the width of any of the <span> elements within it (click on one to see that they are 100 pixels wide)—let alone all three of them—is causing an issue with your layout.

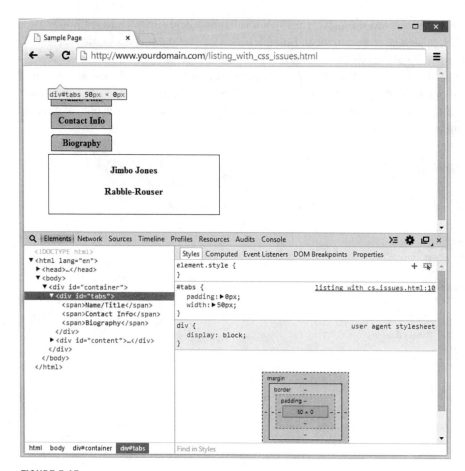

FIGURE 5.15
The selected <div> element is only 50 pixels wide.

4. Following your instincts from the preceding step, click on the <div> element with the ID "container" so that it is highlighted on your screen and so that the style is given focus in the style panel. Note that the width of this particular <div> element is 300 pixels.

5. In the Elements panel, again click on the <div> element with the ID "tabs" so that its styles are in focus in the style panel. Within the style panel, double-click on the width value so that the field becomes editable and change that value to be 300px, as shown in Figure 5.16.

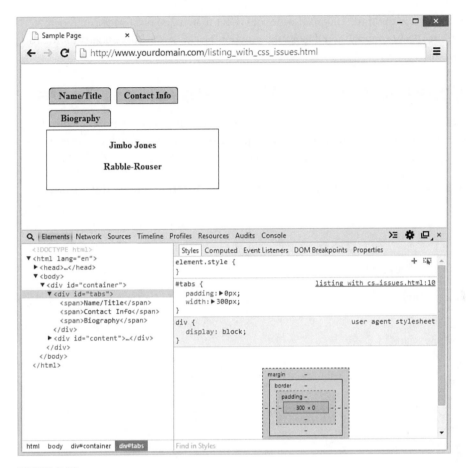

FIGURE 5.16
The layout changes immediately, although it still isn't correct.

Without making any changes to the underlying source code, either locally or on your web server, you can use the inspector as a sort of editor to review possible changes to HTML and CSS. Although the code in this example is still far from looking "good," you can continue to make changes on your own and see how the display reacts. You might have better results after working through later lessons, but even without detailed knowledge of alignment, margins, and padding, you can experience a sort of trial-and-error debugging without having to commit changes in your code.

NOTE
_____

You can use the inspector within Developer Tools for more than just your own code. You can turn on Developer Tools and look at the source code of any page and get a sense of how the page is constructed—and you can change HTML and CSS values to see how these changes affect the display, just as you did here.

Are you wondering why the three 100-pixel-wide tabs don't fit in a 300-pixel-wide container? It has to do with the CSS box model. You'll learn more about that in Lesson 10, "Understanding the CSS Box Model and Positioning."

Debugging JavaScript Using Developer Tools

Developer Tools within most major browsers can help you debug your JavaScript, from catching basic syntax errors in the Console to working through advanced debugging steps using the Sources panel and all that it contains. As we go through the tools in this section, we'll use the code in Listing 5.3.

LISTING 5.3   A Simple HTML Document with a Few Different JavaScript Errors

```
<!doctype html>
<html lang="en">
  <head>
    <meta charset="utf-8">
    <title>Sample Page</title>

    <script src="http://code.jquery.com/jquery-latest.min.js"></script>

    <script>
    function incCount(){
      var count = 0;
      count += 1;
      return count;
    }

    function countIt(){
      $("#counter").html(incCount);
    }
    </script>

    <style>
    button {
      background-color: #0066AA;
      color: #FFFFFF;
      font-weight: bold;
      border: 2px solid, #C0C0C0;
      width: 100px;
    }
    </style>
  </head>

  <body>
    <button onclick="countit()">Click Me</button>
    <div id="counter"></div>
  </body>
</html>
```

If you add the code in Listing 5.3 to a new file, save the document, and then open it in a web browser from either your local machine or your server, you'll see the completely unassuming little button shown in Figure 5.17.

FIGURE 5.17
Showing the initial output of Listing 5.3.

However, if you follow along with these steps, you'll soon uncover issues with this code by using the Console:

1. Right-click on the web page and choose Inspect Element.

2. Switch to the Console panel by clicking the Console tab in Developer Tools.

3. Click the Click Me button that has been rendered by the browser. You should see an error like the one shown in Figure 5.18, which indicates there is an error in the code.

FIGURE 5.18
The Console shows where there is a syntax error in the code.

4. Click on the link that will take you to the precise line in the file that contains the error (in this instance, the link is `listing_with_js_errors.html:32`), and you see that the JavaScript function being called is `countit()`, whereas the function was originally defined in line 15 as `countIt()`. As you learned in the preceding lesson, JavaScript is case sensitive.

If you correct the underlying source file by using `countIt()` in line 32 instead of `countit()` and then reload the document and click the Click Me button, you will no longer see an error in the Console. However, as you'll soon see, there are more issues with this document.

In the `<head>` section of the document is a link to a JavaScript library (jQuery, actually) that is stored externally, as well as some JavaScript code that defines two functions. The `<body>` section includes a `<button>` tag with an `onclick` event to invoke the `countIt()` JavaScript function, as well as a `<div>` element that is used to display the string containing the current count of the number of times the button has been clicked. That's all fine and dandy, except that if you actually click the Click Me button more than once, the number will not increase past 1, and no error will be present in the Console. This situation calls for more advanced debugging.

NOTE

Always do more than one test on your web pages. In the JavaScript in Listing 5.3, fixing the first error makes the page appear to work. But if you click the button only one time, you'll never realize that there is a problem on subsequent clicks. Whenever you deal with interaction on your web pages, you should test at least three times in each browser/device on which you want your pages to work.

Taking a Closer Look at the Sources Panel

The Sources panel (Debug panel in Firefox and Debugger in Safari) contains a set of tools that enable you to pause, resume, and step through code that is loaded in the web browser. By setting breakpoints, you can watch individual sections of your code execute, which is especially helpful when you are trying to track down issues that are unrelated to basic syntax (which the Console will helpfully display without intervention on your part).

With the code in Listing 5.3 loaded into your browser and Developer Tools enabled, click on the Sources tab to see the Sources panel and its related tools. It should look something like what's shown in Figure 5.19.

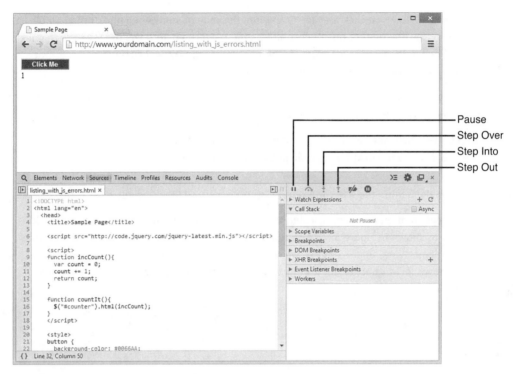

FIGURE 5.19
Showing the Sources panel in Chrome Developer Tools, along with some important tools for this example.

NOTE
_____

For a thorough understanding of all the icons in the Sources panel, see https://developers.google
.com/web/tools/chrome-devtools/. There are similar pages for Firefox (https://developer.mozilla.org/
en-US/docs/Tools/Debugger), Safari (https://developer.apple.com/safari/tools/), and Edge
(https://docs.microsoft.com/en-us/microsoft-edge/devtools-guide/debugger).
_____

To debug the script, we'll focus on setting breakpoints and stepping through the code using the
tools highlighted in Figure 5.19. But first, some explanations of terms:

▸ **Breakpoints**—Breakpoints enable you to specify where you would like to stop the JavaScript
from executing. When you set a breakpoint, the browser stops executing and breaks into the
debugger before it executes that line of code. This enables you to see the state of the code
at that specific point. You set a breakpoint by clicking on a line number in the code listing,
and you remove a breakpoint by clicking the line number again; breakpoints are indicated
by a highlighted blue arrow icon. The Breakpoints tab shows a list of breakpoints that have
been set. You can disable a breakpoint by unchecking the check box next to it.

▶ **Step Over**—When you click the Step Over icon, the code advances one line. If the line of code is to execute another function, that function is executed, and you are taken to the next line of code in the current function. If a breakpoint is encountered when stepping over a function, the browser stops executing at that location in the script.

▶ **Step Into**—When you click the Step Into icon, the code advances one line. If the line of code is to execute another function, you are taken to the first line of code in that function.

▶ **Step Out**—When you click the Step Out icon, the current function finishes executing, and you are taken to the next line of code in the calling function.

Now, let's start debugging the script in Listing 5.3 and see why it won't advance the count past 1:

1. Set a breakpoint on line 10 by clicking to the left of the line number. A blue arrow should appear, as shown in Figure 5.20. Also note that the Scope Variables section of the rightmost pane is open. We've opened this so we can watch how the value of count changes as the script moves forward. After all, it's this value that is the problem, since it's not changing after the first click.

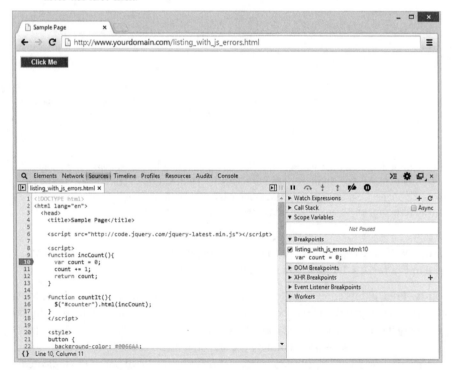

FIGURE 5.20
A breakpoint is set on line 10 of the script.

2. Now click the button on the web page. You should see a yellow arrow appear in the body of the web page, indicating that the script is paused in the debugger, and line 10 in the code listing will be highlighted. In the script, line 11 is the first line of the incCount() function; the incCount() function is supposed to determine the value of the counter string, represented by the variable count. In the Scope Variables area, you should see that the value of count is currently undefined.

3. Click the Step Over icon. In the Scope Variables area, you should see the value of count go to 0 because the value has been defined with a starting number of 0.

4. Click the Step Over icon again. Now the value of count is 1, as expected, changed by the count += 1; line, which says "take the current value of count and increment it by one."

5. Click the Step Out icon four times to step out of this function and the jQuery functions in between. Notice that the value on the web page has gone to 1.

6. Click the Continue or Resume icon (the Pause icon will change to a Continue icon or Resume in Firefox as soon as the script is started) to allow the script to complete. So far, so good.

7. Click the button in the web page again. The debugger should activate again and be stopped in the same location as in step 2. Notice that the value of count is undefined again, when common sense (but not our code) says it should be 1.

8. Click the Step Over icon; count changes to 0. Click Step Over again, and count changes to 1. As the button is clicked, count is reset to undefined, set to 0, and then incremented to 1. This is not the desired behavior.

9. To fix the problem, return to the source code and switch lines 10 and 11 so that the definition of count happens before the definition of the function that uses it (incCount()). This change defines the variable count and sets the value only once when the script is loaded and before the function is defined.

If you load the newly debugged file, you'll find that the counter increments as expected. You may need to remove the breakpoint if it isn't removed automatically. Listing 5.4 shows the corrected JavaScript.

LISTING 5.4   Corrected Script

```
var count = 0;
function incCount(){
  count += 1;
  return count;
}

function countIt(){
  $("#counter").html(incCount);
}
```

This section has provided a basic example that is simple enough to easily follow and that helps you get used to how the debugger works. Keep in mind these basic steps to set breakpoints and watch the variables as you step through the code.

Summary

In this lesson you learned various ways to validate and debug issues in your HTML, CSS, and JavaScript. You learned how to use the inspector within Developer Tools in your browser to see the HTML elements and CSS styles and properties that the browser has rendered while loading a web page. In addition, you learned the basics of reviewing JavaScript syntax errors in the Console and setting breakpoints and systematically stepping through the code to debug more complex problems.

The methods you learned in this lesson will be very helpful to you as you finish this course, not to mention in future projects, because they will save a lot of time and frustration with simple validation and syntax errors that always seem to creep into code, no matter how experienced you are.

Q&A

Q. I've seen web pages that don't have a `<!doctype>` tag at the beginning, yet they look just fine. How is that possible?

A. Many web browsers forgive you if you forget to include the `<!doctype>` tag and display the page anyway by using their best guess as to which standard to follow. However, it's a good idea to include a proper `<!doctype>` tag not only because you want your pages to be bona fide valid HTML pages that conform to the latest web standards but also because if you don't, and the browser applies a default standard that doesn't include the tags you've used in the code, the display will look incorrect.

Q. Developer Tools seems really rich. What else can I debug with these tools?

A. You're right: There are a lot of elements of Developer Tools in Chrome that aren't covered here, and there are also many idiosyncrasies of the other major browsers' implementations of Developer Tools. In general, you can use Developer Tools to debug values stored in cookies, the status of external resources used by your script (whether they are found/not found, whether they are slow to load, and so on), and the amount of memory used by the page and its scripts, among other things.

Workshop

The Workshop contains quiz questions and exercises to help you solidify your understanding of the material covered.

Quiz

1. Using Chrome Developer Tools, how would you find the current value of the `background-color` CSS property for a specific `<div>` tag in a document?

2. Using a debugger, how do you stop code execution on a specific line of code?

3. Which section of Chrome Developer Tools enables you to see the value of a variable as a script is stepped through?

4. What web languages can you validate with a W3C validator?

5. What browsers have Developer Tools?

6. What is a way to debug broken HTML code?

7. When is using the Developer Tools inspector particularly useful?

8. What happens when you change a style value (or add a style rule) in the CSS inspector?

9. What does the Step Over command do in a web page debugger?

10. How do you set a breakpoint in Developer Tools?

NOTE

Just a reminder for those of you reading these words in the print or e-book edition of this book: If you go to www.informit.com/register and register this book (using ISBN 9780672338083), you can receive free access to an online Web Edition that not only contains the complete text of this book but also features an interactive version of this quiz.

Answers

1. Click on the Elements tab to open the Elements panel and then select the specific `<div>` you're interested in. The current style values will appear in the rightmost panel.

2. You can stop script execution on a particular line by setting a breakpoint. This is true with most debugging tools and is not specific to Chrome Developer Tools.

3. The Scope Variables section of the Sources panel enables you to see the values of variables used in a script.

4. This lesson mentions an HTML validator and a CSS validator from the W3C. The W3C also offers other validation services, such as link checking, RSS and Atom feed checking, and even mobile content checking.

5. Nearly every modern desktop browser has some form of Developer Tools built in. This lesson mentions tools in Chrome, Firefox, Safari, and Internet Explorer. There are also developer tools in Edge and Opera.

6. You can use an HTML validator to find the error or use Developer Tools in a browser to view the code. Or you can go through your HTML line-by-line.

7. The inspector in Developer Tools is particularly useful when you're working with JavaScript that modifies CSS beyond the original state in the HTML.

8. The web page will change to reflect the new CSS rule, but that rule will not be applied outside the current page. If you do not add the changes to the CSS file, they will not be applied permanently to the web page.

9. The Step Over command advances the JavaScript code one line.

10. To set a breakpoint, click on the line number where you want the breakpoint. A blue arrow then appears on that line and sets the breakpoint. To turn it off, click the line number again. To disable it temporarily, uncheck the check box next to the breakpoint in the Breakpoints tab.

Exercises

▶ Continue debugging Listing 5.2 until the elements line up in ways that look appealing to you. Since you haven't explicitly learned these skills yet, we'll give you a hint: Try modifying values for widths and values for padding in the CSS.

▶ Use Console logging to output specific strings at different points throughout your script. You can log to the Console by inserting code like the following in your JavaScript and then review these strings in the Console panel as the script executes:

```
console.log("Some string.");
```

Working with Fonts, Text Blocks, Lists, and Tables

What You'll Learn in This Lesson:

- ▶ How to use boldface, italic, and special text formatting
- ▶ How to tweak the font
- ▶ How to use special characters
- ▶ How to align text on a page
- ▶ How to use the three types of HTML lists
- ▶ How to nest lists within lists
- ▶ How to create simple tables
- ▶ How to control the size of tables
- ▶ How to align content and span rows and columns within tables
- ▶ How to use CSS columns

In the early days of the Web, text was displayed in only one font and one size. However, a combination of HTML and CSS now makes it possible to control the appearance of text (typeface, size, color) and how it is aligned and displayed on a web page. In this lesson you'll learn how to change the visual display of the font—its font family (the typeface), size, and weight—and how to incorporate boldface, italic, superscripts, subscripts, and strikethrough text into your pages. You will also learn how to change typefaces and font sizes and how to use web fonts.

Then, after becoming conversant in these textual aspects, you'll learn the basics of text alignment and some other text tips and tricks, such as the use of lists. Because lists are very common, HTML provides tags that automatically indent text and add numbers, bullets, or other symbols in front of each listed item. You'll learn how to format different types of lists.

In this lesson, you'll learn how to build HTML tables that you can use to control the spacing, layout, and appearance of tabular data in your web content. Although you can achieve similar results using CSS, there are definitely times when using a table is the best way to present information in rows and columns. You'll also see in this lesson how designers had to use tables for page layout in the past—and how to avoid ever doing that in the future.

Finally, you'll learn a new technique for displaying large blocks of text—CSS columns. You'll find out how to create newspaper-style columns out of your content and how to make the columns look nice on the page.

NOTE

When viewing other designers' web content, you might notice methods of marking up text that are different from those this series teaches. Some telltale signs of the old way of formatting text include the use of the `<b></b>` tag pair to indicate when a word should be bolded, the `<i></i>` tag pair to indicate when a word should be in italics, and the `<font></font>` tag pair to specify font family, size, and other attributes. However, this method is being phased out of HTML, and CSS is considerably more powerful.

▼ TRY IT YOURSELF

Preparing Sample Text

You can make the most of learning how to style text throughout this lesson if you have some sample text that you can use to display different fonts and colors and that you can indent, center, or otherwise manipulate. It doesn't really matter what type of text you use because there are so many stylistic possibilities to try that they would never appear all on the same web page anyway (unless you wanted to drive your visitors batty). Take this opportunity to get a feel for how text-level changes can affect the appearance of your content.

▶ If the text you'll be using is from a word processing or database program, be sure to save it to a new file in plain-text or ASCII format. You can then add the appropriate HTML tags and style attributes to format it as you go through this lesson.

▶ Any text will do but try to find (or type) some text you want to put onto a web page. The text from a company brochure or from your résumé might be a good choice.

▶ Any type of outline, bullet points from a presentation, numbered steps, glossary, or list of textual information from a database will serve as good material to work with.

▶ Before you use the code introduced in this lesson to format the body text, add the set of skeleton HTML tags you've used in previous lessons (at least the `<!doctype>`, `<html>`, `<head>`, `<title>`, and `<body>` tags).

Working with Special Characters

Before we rush headlong into font changes, let's talk for a minute about special characters in fonts. Most fonts include special characters for European languages, such as the accented *é* in *café*. You'll also find a few mathematical symbols and special punctuation marks, such as the circular • bullet.

You can insert these special characters at any point in an HTML document by using the appropriate codes (see Table 6.1). You'll find an even more extensive list of codes for multiple character sets at the following URL:

https://www.webstandards.org/learn/reference/charts/entities/namedentities/

HTML uses a special code known as a *character entity* to represent special characters such as © and ®. Character entities are always specified starting with & and ending with ; . Table 6.1 lists the most commonly used character entities, although HTML supports many more.

Table 6.1 includes codes for the angle brackets, quotation marks, and ampersand. You must use those codes if you want these symbols to appear on your pages; otherwise, the web browser interprets them as HTML commands.

Listing 6.1 and Figure 6.1 show several of the symbols from Table 6.1 in use.

For example, you can produce the word *café* by using either of the following:

```
caf&eacute;
caf&#233;
```

NOTE

One of the reasons it's a good idea to use the line `<meta charset="utf-8">` in your HTML is because it reduces the need for these special character codes. By setting your character set to UTF-8, you tell the browser to expect these characters without any special encoding. In other words, in a UTF-8 web page, you can write `<h1>My Café</h1>` instead of `<h1>My Caf&eacute;</h1>`, and it will display correctly.

You should still use encodings for characters that are used in HTML, such as `&lt;` for <, `&gt;` for >, and `&amp;` for &. This ensures that the browser knows that these characters are part of the text and not HTML.

TABLE 6.1 Commonly Used English-Language Special Characters

Character	Numeric Code	Code Name	Description
"	&#34;	&quot;	Quotation mark
&	&#38;	&amp;	Ampersand
<	&#60;	&lt;	Less than
>	&#62;	&gt;	Greater than
¢	&#162;	&cent;	Cents sign
£	&#163;	&pound;	Pound sterling
¦	&#166;	&brvbar;	Broken vertical bar
§	&#167;	&sect;	Section sign
©	&#169;	&copy;	Copyright

Character	Numeric Code	Code Name	Description
®	`&#174;`	`&reg;`	Registered trademark
°	`&#176;`	`&deg;`	Degree sign
±	`&#177;`	`&plusmn;`	plus or minus
^{2}	`&#178;`	`&sup2;`	Superscripted two
^{3}	`&#179;`	`&sup3;`	Superscripted three
·	`&#183;`	`&middot;`	Middle dot
^{1}	`&#185;`	`&sup1;`	Superscripted one
¼	`&#188;`	`&frac14;`	Fraction one-fourth
½	`&#189;`	`&frac12;`	Fraction one-half
¾	`&#190;`	`&frac34;`	Fraction three-fourths
Æ	`&#198;`	`&AElig;`	Capital AE ligature
æ	`&#230;`	`&aelig;`	Small ae ligature
É	`&#201;`	`&Eacute;`	Accented capital E
é	`&#233;`	`&eacute;`	Accented lowercase e
×	`&#215;`	`&times;`	Multiplication sign
÷	`&#247;`	`&divide;`	Division sign

Although you can specify character entities by number, each symbol also has a mnemonic name that is often easier to remember.

NOTE

Looking for the copyright (©) and registered trademark (®) symbols? Those codes are `&copy;` and `&reg;`, respectively.

To create an unregistered trademark (™) symbol, use `&trade;`.

LISTING 6.1 Special Character Codes

```
<!doctype html>
<html lang="en">
  <head>
    <meta charset="utf-8">
    <title>Punctuation Lines</title>
    <style>
    section {
      margin-bottom: 20px;
    }
    </style>
  </head>
```

```
<body>
  <section>
    Q: What should you do when a British banker picks a fight
    with you?<br>
    A: &pound; some &cent;&cent; into him.
  </section>
  <section>
    Q: What do you call it when a judge takes part of a law
    off the books?<br>
    A: &sect; violence.
  </section>
  <section>
    Q: What did the football coach get from the locker room
    vending machine in the middle of the game?<br>
    A: A &frac14; back at &frac12; time.
  </section>
  <section>
    Q: How hot did it get when the police detective interrogated
    the mathematician?<br>
    A: x&sup3;&deg;
  </section>
  <section>
    Q: What does a punctilious plagiarist do?<br>
    A: &copy;
  </section>
</body>
</html>
```

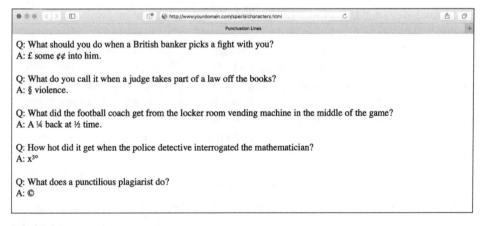

FIGURE 6.1
This is how the HTML page in Listing 6.1 looks in most web browsers.

Boldface, Italic, and Special Text Formatting

Way back in the age of the typewriter, we were content with a plain-text display and with using an occasional underline to show emphasis. Today, **boldface** and *italic* text have become de rigueur in all paper communication. Naturally, you can add bold and italic text to your web content as well. Several tags and style rules make text formatting possible.

NOTE

Although you should use styles wherever possible to affect presentation, an alternative to using style rules when it comes to bold and italic text is to use the `<strong></strong>` and `<em></em>` tag pairs. The `<strong>` tag does the same thing as the `<b>` tag in most browsers, whereas the `<em>` tag acts just like the tag `<i>`, formatting text as italic. Of course, you can style these tags however you'd like, but those are the defaults.

The `<strong>` and `<em>` tags are considered an improvement over `<b>` and `<i>` because they imply only that the text should receive special emphasis; they don't dictate exactly how that effect should be achieved. In other words, a browser doesn't necessarily have to interpret `<strong>` as meaning bold or `<em>` as meaning italic. This makes `<strong>` and `<em>` more fitting in HTML5 because they add meaning to text along with affecting how the text should be displayed.

The old-school approach to adding bold and italic formatting to text—discussed briefly here because invariably you will see it in the source code of many older websites, if you choose to look— involves the `<b></b>` and `<i></i>` tag pairs. For boldface text, you wrap the `<b>` and `</b>` tags around your text. Similarly, to make any text appear in italics, you enclose it in `<i>` and `</i>` tags. Although this approach still works fine in browsers, it isn't as flexible or powerful as the CSS style rules for text formatting and should be avoided.

Part III, "Advanced Web Page Design with CSS," covers CSS style rules in more depth, but a little foreshadowing is appropriate here just so that you understand some basic text formatting options. The `font-weight` style rule enables you to set the weight, or boldness, of a font by using a style rule. Standard settings for `font-weight` include `normal`, `bold`, `bolder`, and `lighter` (with `normal` being the default). Italic text is controlled via the `font-style` rule, which you can set to `normal`, `italic`, or `oblique`. You can specify style rules together as well if you want to apply more than one rule, as the following example demonstrates:

```
<p style="font-weight:bold; font-style:italic;">This paragraph is bold and
italic!</p>
```

In this example, both style rules are specified in the `style` attribute of the `<p>` tag. The key to using multiple style rules is that they must be separated by a semicolon (;).

You aren't limited to using font styles in paragraphs, however. The following code shows how to italicize text in a bulleted list:

```
<ul>
  <li style="font-style:italic;">Important Stuff</li>
  <li style="font-style:italic;">Critical Information</li>
  <li style="font-style:italic;">Highly Sensitive Material</li>
  <li>Nothing All That Useful</li>
</ul>
```

You can also use the `font-weight` style rule within headings, but a heavier font usually doesn't have an effect on headings because they are already bold by default.

Although using CSS enables you to apply richer formatting, there are a few HTML5 tags that are good for adding special formatting to text when you don't necessarily need to be as specific as CSS enables you to be. Following are some of these tags:

- `<sup></sup>`—Superscript text

- `<sub></sub>`—Subscript text

- `<em></em>`—Emphasized (typically italic) text

- `<strong></strong>`—Strong (typically boldface) text

- `<pre></pre>`—Monospaced text, preserving spaces and line breaks

Listing 6.2 and Figure 6.2 demonstrate each of these tags in action.

CAUTION

In the past, a `<u>` tag was useful in creating underlined text, but you don't want to use it now, for a couple of reasons. First, users expect underlined text to be a link, so they might get confused if you underline text that isn't a link. Second, the `<u>` tag is *obsolete*, which means that it has been phased out of the HTML language (as has the `<strike>` tag). Both tags are still supported in web browsers and likely will be for quite a while, but using CSS is the preferred approach to creating underlined and strikethrough text.

LISTING 6.2   Special Formatting Tags

```
<!doctype html>
<html lang="en">
  <head>
    <meta charset="utf-8">
    <title>The Miracle Product</title>
  </head>
```

```
<body>
  <p>
    New <sup>Super</sup><strong>Strength</strong> H<sub>2</sub>0
    <em>plus</em> will knock out any stain.<br>Look for new
    <sup>Super</sup><strong>Strength</strong>
    H<sub>2</sub>0 <em>plus</em> in a stream near you.
  </p>
  <pre>
    NUTRITION INFORMATION (void where prohibited)
                    Calories   Grams    USRDA
                    /Serving   of Fat   Moisture
        Regular        3         4        100%
        Unleaded       3         2        100%
        Organic        2         3         99%
        Sugar Free     0         1        110%
  </pre>
</body>
</html>
```

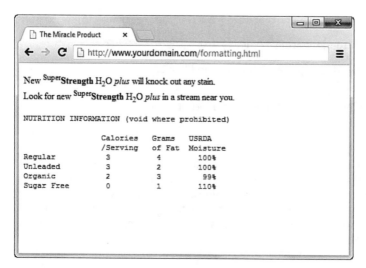

FIGURE 6.2
Here's what the character formatting from Listing 6.2 looks like.

The `<pre>` tag causes text to appear in a monospaced font—and it does something else unique and useful. As you learned in Lesson 2, "Structuring an HTML Document," multiple spaces and line breaks are normally ignored in HTML files, but `<pre>` causes exact spacing and line breaks to be preserved. For example, without `<pre>`, the text at the end of Figure 6.2 would look like the following:

```
calories grams usrda /serving of fat moisture regular
3 4 100% unleaded 3 2 100% organic 2 3 99% sugar free 0 1 110%
```

Even if you added <br> tags at the end of every line, the columns wouldn't line up properly. However, when you put <pre> at the beginning and </pre> at the end, the columns line up properly because the exact spaces are kept; no <br> tags are needed. The <pre> tag gives you a quick and easy way to preserve the alignment of any monospaced text files you might want to transfer to a web page with minimum effort.

CSS provides you with more robust methods for lining up text (and doing anything with text, actually), and you'll learn more about them throughout Part III.

Tweaking the Font

Sometimes you want a bit more control over the size and appearance of your text than just some boldface or italic. Before we get into the appropriate way to tinker with the font using CSS, let's briefly look at how things were done *before* CSS; you might still find examples of this method when you look at the source code for other websites. Remember, just because these older methods are in use doesn't mean you should follow suit.

Before style sheets entered the picture, the now-phased-out <font> tag was used to control the fonts in web page text.

NOTE
We cannot stress enough that the <font> tag is not to be used! It is mentioned here for illustrative and historical purposes only.

For example, the following HTML was once used to change the size and color of some text on a page:

```
<font size="5" color="purple">This text will be big and purple.</font>
```

As you can see, the size and color attributes of the <font> tag made it possible to alter the font of the text without too much effort. Although this approach worked fine, it was replaced with a far superior approach to font formatting, thanks to CSS style rules. Following are a few of the main style rules used to control fonts:

- font-family—Sets the family (typeface) of the font
- font-size—Sets the size of the font
- color—Sets the color of the font

NOTE

You'll learn more about controlling the color of the text on your pages in Lesson 8, "Working with Colors, Images, and Multimedia." That lesson also shows how to create your own custom colors and how to control the color of text links.

The font-family style rule enables you to set the typeface used to display text. You can and usually should specify more than one value for this style (separated by commas) so that if the first font isn't available on a user's system, the browser can try alternatives.

Providing alternative font families is important because each user potentially has a different set of fonts installed, at least beyond a core set of common basic fonts (Arial, Times New Roman, and so forth). By providing a list of alternative fonts, you have a better chance of your pages gracefully falling back on a known font when your ideal font isn't found.

Following is an example of the font-family style used to set the typeface for a paragraph of text:

```
<p style="font-family:arial, sans-serif, 'times roman';">
```

This example has several interesting parts. First, arial is specified as the primary font. Capitalization does not affect the font family, so arial is no different from Arial or ARIAL. Another interesting point about this code is that single quotes are used around the times roman font name because it has a space in it. However, because 'times roman' appears after the generic specification of sans-serif, it is unlikely that 'times roman' would be used. Because sans-serif is in the second position, it says to the browser "if Arial is not on this machine, use the default sans-serif font." Every browser has a default serif font, sans-serif font, cursive font, monospace font, and fantasy font. However, they may not look anything like what you would expect, so it's best to define a list of two or three specific font families and then place the generic family name last.

The font-size and color style rules are also commonly used to control the size and color of fonts. The font-size style can be set to a predefined size (such as small, medium, or large), or you can set it to a specific point size (such as 12pt or 14pt). The color style can be set to a predefined color (such as white, black, blue, red, or green), or you can set it to a specific hexadecimal color (such as #ffb499). Following is a better version of the previous paragraph example, and with the font size and color specified:

```
<p style="font-family:arial, 'times roman', sans-serif;
          font-size:14pt; color:green;">
```

NOTE

You'll learn about hexadecimal colors in Lesson 8. For now, just understand that the color style rule enables you to specify exact colors beyond just using color names such as green, blue, orange, and so forth.

The sample web content in Listing 6.3 and shown in Figure 6.3 uses some font style rules to create the beginning of a basic online résumé.

LISTING 6.3   Using Font Style Rules to Create a Basic Résumé

```
<!doctype html>
<html lang="en">
  <head>
    <meta charset="utf-8">
    <title>R&eacute;sum&eacute; for Jane Doe</title>
    <style>
      body {
        font-family: Verdana, sans-serif;
        font-size: 12px;
      }
      header {
        text-align: center;
      }
      h1 {
        font-family:Georgia, serif;
        font-size: 28px;
        text-align: center;
      }
      p.contactinfo {
        font-size: 14px;
      }
      p.categorylabel {
        font-size: 12px;
        font-weight: bold;
        text-transform: uppercase;
      }
      div.indented {
        margin-left: 25px;
      }
    </style>
  </head>
  <body>
    <header>
      <h1>Jane Doe</h1>
      <p class="contactinfo">1234 Main Street, Sometown,
      CA 93829<br>
      tel: 555-555-1212, e-mail: jane@doe.com</p>
    </header>
    <section>
      <p class="categorylabel">Summary of Qualifications</p>
      <ul>
        <li>Highly skilled and dedicated professional offering a
        solid background in whatever it is you need.</li>
```

```
      <li>Provide comprehensive direction for whatever it is
      that will get me a job.</li>
      <li>Computer proficient in a wide range of industry-related
      computer programs and equipment. Any industry.</li>
    </ul>
  </section>
  <section>
    <p class="categorylabel">Professional Experience</p>
    <div class="indented">
      <p><strong>Operations Manager,
      Super Awesome Company, Some City, CA [Sept 2002 -
      present]</strong></p>
      <ul>
        <li>Direct all departmental operations</li>
        <li>Coordinate work with internal and external
        resources</li>
        <li>Generally in charge of everything</li>
      </ul>
      <p><strong>Project Manager,
      Less Awesome Company, Some City, CA [May 2000 - Sept
      2002]</strong></p>
      <ul>
        <li>Direct all departmental operations</li>
        <li>Coordinate work with internal and external
        resources</li>
        <li>Generally in charge of everything</li>
      </ul>
    </div>
  </section>
  <section>
    <p class="categorylabel">Education</p>
    <ul>
      <li>MBA, MyState University, May 2002</li>
      <li>B.A, Business Administration, MyState University,
      May 2000</li>
    </ul>
  </section>
  <section>
    <p class="categorylabel">References</p>
    <ul>
      <li>Available upon request.</li>
    </ul>
  </section>
  </body>
</html>
```

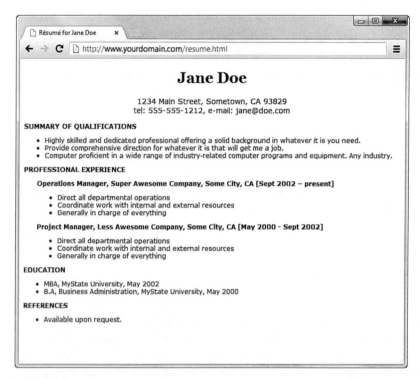

FIGURE 6.3
Here's what the code used in Listing 6.3 looks like.

Using CSS, which organizes sets of styles into classes—as you learned in Lesson 3, "Understanding Cascading Style Sheets"—you can see how text formatting is applied to different areas of this content. If you look closely at the definition of the `div.indented` class, you will see the use of the `margin-left` style. This style, which you will learn more about in Part III, applies a certain amount of space (25 pixels, in this example) to the left of the element. That space accounts for the indentation shown in Figure 6.3.

Using Web Fonts

In the preceding section, you saw uses of font families that we're pretty sure reside on everyone's computers. That is, you can be assured that most computers would render Arial or Times New Roman or have a go-to default serif font and sans-serif font, if that's what your style sheet calls for. But with the inclusion of the `@font-face` feature in CSS3, you can wield even greater design power over the content you place online.

In brief, the `@font-face` rule enables you to define fonts for use in your HTML5 markup so that they are displayed to users regardless of whether they have those fonts installed on their computers (and chances are incredibly great that users do not have your selected fancy font on their own computer). The definition of the font can be local (to your web server, if you care to include font files there) or remote (in case you link to locations where many fonts are stored).

In your style sheet, to define a new font for use throughout your page(s), you can simply use the following structure:

```
@font-face {
    font-family: 'some_name_goes_here';
    src: url('some_location_of_the_font_file');
}
```

After it's defined, you can refer to the `font-family` as you would anywhere else in your style sheet, such as here:

```
h1 {
  font-family: 'some_name_goes_here';
  font-size: 28px;
  text-align: center;
}
```

But where do you get fonts? You can obtain fonts from many locations—some free, others not. A widely popular location is Google Fonts (www.google.com/fonts), not only because the fonts are free but also because Google is widely recognized as providing a stable platform, which is important if your web typography relies on a font that's sitting on someone else's web server. Some other reliable pay sites for obtaining fonts are Adobe Typekit (https://typekit.com) and Fontspring (www.fontspring.com). Pay sites aren't necessarily bad—artists have to make money, too. We have used Typekit, but we also use Google Fonts for many projects.

Let's take a look at modifying the code in Listing 6.3 to include a font from Google Fonts for the h1 element. If you go to www.google.com/fonts and select a font you like, Google gives you code to include in your HTML and CSS. We've selected a font called Cherry Swash, and Google has advised us to include the following in our HTML template, in the <head> section:

```
<link href="http://fonts.googleapis.com/css?family=Cherry+Swash:400,700"
      rel="stylesheet">
```

NOTE

If you look at the file at the Google link location, you can see that it is Google's `@font-face` definition, already done for you. Specifically, it says this:

```
@font-face {
  font-family: 'Cherry Swash';
  font-style: normal;
  font-weight: 400;
  src: local('Cherry Swash'), local('CherrySwash-Regular'),
url(http://themes.googleusercontent.com/static/fonts/cherryswash/v1/
```

```
HqOk7C7J1TZ5i3L-ejFOvnhCUOGz7vYGh680lGh-uXM.woff) format('woff');
}
@font-face {
  font-family: 'Cherry Swash';
  font-style: normal;
  font-weight: 700;
  src: local('Cherry Swash Bold'), local('CherrySwash-Bold'),
url(http://themes.googleusercontent.com/static/fonts/cherryswash/v1/
-CfyMyQqfucZPQNBOnvYyHl4twXkwp3_u9ZoePkT564.woff) format('woff');
}
```

Now that the code knows where to look for the font, you just refer to it:

```
h1 {
  font-family:'Cherry Swash';
  font-size:28px;
  text-align:center;
}
```

Figure 6.4 shows the new résumé with the web font in use.

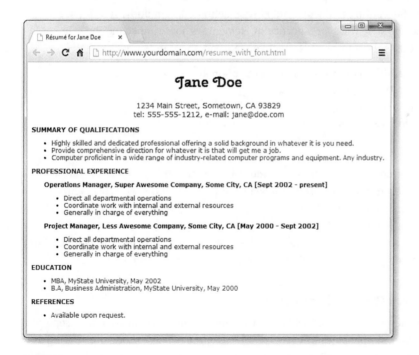

FIGURE 6.4
The résumé, using Cherry Swash as the font in the heading.

Aligning Text on a Page

It's easy to take for granted the fact that most paragraphs are automatically aligned to the left when you're reading information on the Web. However, there certainly are situations in which you might choose to align content to the right or justify the text. HTML gives you the option to align a single HTML block-level element, such as text contained within a <p></p> or <div> </div> tag pair. Before we get into the details of aligning block elements, however, let's briefly look at how attributes work.

Using Style, Class, and ID Attributes

Attributes provide additional information related to an HTML tag. *Attributes* are special code words used inside an HTML tag to control exactly what the tag does. They are very important in even the simplest bit of web content, so it's important that you are comfortable using them.

Attributes invoke the use of styles, classes, or IDs that are applied to particular tags. If you define a particular class or ID in a style sheet—as you learned to do in Lesson 3—then you can invoke that class or ID by using class="someclass" or id="someid" within the tag itself. When the browser renders the content for display, it looks to the style sheet to determine exactly how the content will appear, according to the associated style definitions. Similarly, you can use the style attribute to include style rules for a particular element without connecting the element to an actual style sheet; this is the inline style format you learned about in Lesson 3.

In the following example, each paragraph could be left-aligned:

```
<p style="text-align: left;">Text goes here.</p>
<p class="leftAlignStyle">Text goes here.</p>
<p id="firstLeftAlign">Text goes here.</p>
```

In the first paragraph, the style appears directly in the style attribute. This is useful for debugging or for short-term formatting tests—but not so much for ongoing maintenance of your web content. In the second paragraph, the paragraph will be left-aligned if the style sheet entry for the .leftAlignStyle class includes the text-align statement; remember that using a class means other tags can reuse the class. Similarly, the third paragraph will be left-aligned if the style sheet entry for the #firstLeftAlign id includes the text-align statement; remember that using an id means these styles can be applied to only the one identified tag.

Aligning Block-Level Elements

To align text in a block-level element such as <p> to the right margin without creating a separate class or ID in a style sheet, simply place style="text-align:right;" inside the <p> tag at the beginning of the paragraph (or define it in a class or an ID). Similarly, to center the text in the element, use <p style="text-align:center;">. To align text in a paragraph to the left, use <p style="text-align:left;">.

The `text-align` part of the `style` attribute is referred to as a *style rule*, which means it sets a particular style aspect of an HTML element. You can use many style rules to carefully control the formatting of web content.

The `text-align` style rule is not reserved for just the <p> tag. In fact, you can use the `text-align` style rule with any block-level element, including semantic elements such as <section> and <header>, as well as <h1>, <h2>, the other heading-level tags, and the <div> tag, among others. The <div> tag is especially handy because it can encompass other block-level elements and thus allows you to control the alignment of large portions of your web content all at once. The *div* in the <div> tag is for *division*.

Listing 6.4 demonstrates the `style` attribute and `text-align` style rule with different block-level elements. Figure 6.5 displays the results.

LISTING 6.4 The `text-align` Style Rule Used with the `style` Attribute
_____

```
<!doctype html>
<html lang="en">
  <head>
    <meta charset="utf-8">
    <title>Bohemia</title>
  </head>
  <body>
    <section style="text-align:center;">
      <header>
        <h1>Bohemia</h1>
        <h2>by Dorothy Parker</h2>
      </header>
    </section>
    <section>
      <p style="text-align:left;">
      Authors and actors and artists and such<br>
      Never know nothing, and never know much.<br>
      Sculptors and singers and those of their kidney<br>
      Tell their affairs from Seattle to Sydney.
      </p>
```

```
    <p style="text-align:center;">
    Playwrights and poets and such horses' necks<br>
    Start off from anywhere, end up at sex.<br>
    Diarists, critics, and similar roe<br>
    Never say nothing, and never say no.
    </p>
    <p style="text-align:right;">
    People Who Do Things exceed my endurance;<br>
    God, for a man that solicits insurance!
    </p>
  </section>
 </body>
</html>
```

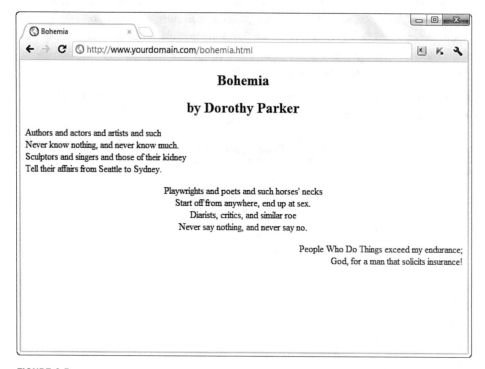

FIGURE 6.5
The results of using the text alignment in Listing 6.4.

The use of `<section style="text-align:center;">` ensures that the content area, including the two headings, is centered. However, the inline styles applied to the individual paragraphs within the `<section>` override the setting and ensure that the text of the first paragraph is left-aligned, the second paragraph is centered, and the third paragraph is right-aligned.

The `text-align` property also allows you to justify text so that both the right and left margins are straight. This can cause strange gaps between words on a line but is another way to align your text blocks. Just write `text-align:justify;` for your style rule.

The Three Types of HTML Lists

For clarity, it's often useful to present information on a web page as a list of items. There are three basic types of HTML lists:

► **Ordered list**—An indented list that has numbers or letters before each list item. The ordered list begins with the `<ol>` tag and ends with a closing `</ol>` tag. List items are enclosed in the `<li></li>` tag pair, and line breaks appear automatically at each opening `<li>` tag. The entire list is indented.

► **Unordered list**—An indented list that has a bullet or another symbol before each list item. The unordered list begins with the `<ul>` tag and closes with `</ul>`. As with the ordered list, its list items are enclosed in the `<li></li>` tag pair. A line break and symbol appear at each opening `<li>` tag, and the entire list is indented.

► **Definition list**—A list of terms and their meanings. This type of list, which has no special number, letter, or symbol before each item, begins with `<dl>` and ends with `</dl>`. The `<dt></dt>` tag pair encloses each term, and the `<dd></dd>` tag pair encloses each definition. Line breaks and indentations appear automatically.

These three types of lists are shown in Figure 6.6, and Listing 6.5 reveals the HTML used to construct them.

LISTING 6.5 Unordered Lists, Ordered Lists, and Definition Lists

```
<!doctype html>
<html lang="en">
  <head>
    <meta charset="utf-8">
    <title>How to Be Proper</title>
  </head>
  <body>
    <article>
      <header>
        <h1>How to Be Proper</h1>
      </header>
      <section>
        <header>
          <h1>Basic Etiquette for a Gentleman Greeting a
          Lady Acquaintance</h1>
        </header>
```

```
    <ul>
      <li>Wait for her acknowledging bow before tipping your
      hat.</li>
      <li>Use the hand farthest from her to raise the hat.</li>
      <li>Walk with her if she expresses a wish to converse;
      never make a lady stand talking in the street.</li>
      <li>When walking, the lady must always have the wall.</li>
    </ul>
  </section>
  <section>
    <header>
      <h1>Recourse for a Lady Toward Unpleasant Men Who Persist
      in Bowing</h1>
    </header>
    <ol>
      <li>A simple stare of iciness should suffice in most
      instances.</li>
      <li>A cold bow discourages familiarity without offering
      insult.</li>
      <li>As a last resort: "Sir, I have not the honour of your
      acquaintance."</li>
    </ol>
  </section>
  <section>
    <header>
      <h1>Proper Address of Royalty</h1>
    </header>
    <dl>
      <dt>Your Majesty</dt>
      <dd>To the king or queen.</dd>
      <dt>Your Royal Highness</dt>
      <dd>To the monarch's spouse, children, and siblings.</dd>
      <dt>Your Highness</dt>
      <dd>To nephews, nieces, and cousins of the sovereign.</dd>
    </dl>
  </section>
  </article>
  </body>
</html>
```

Note the use of semantic elements (<article>, <section>, and <header>) in Listing 6.5 to provide a better sense of the content outline, including how the chunks of text relate to one another. Each of these elements could have its own styles applied, which would provide further visual separation of the elements.

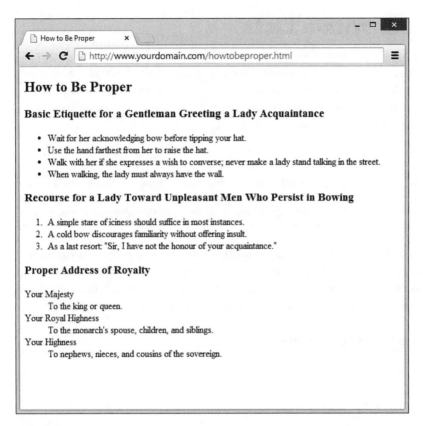

FIGURE 6.6
The three basic types of HTML lists.

NOTE

Remember that different web browsers can display web content quite differently. The HTML standard doesn't specify exactly how web browsers should format lists, so users with older web browsers might not see exactly the same indentation you see. You can use CSS to gain precise control over list items, and you will learn about this later in this lesson.

CAUTION

Although definition lists are officially supposed to be used for defining terms, many web page authors use them anywhere they'd like to see some indentation. In practice, you can indent any text simply by putting `<dl><dd>` at the beginning of it and `</dd></dl>` at the end and skipping over the `<dt></dt>` tag pair. This is a bad habit to get into, as it reduces your control over the design and implies a semantic meaning to those indented areas that shouldn't be there. Instead, you should use CSS to indent content.

Placing Lists Within Lists

Lists placed within lists are called *nested lists*. It used to be common to see designers use nested lists to indent content quickly. Because of the level of control you have over the display of your items when using CSS, there is no need to use nested lists to achieve the visual appearance of indentation. Reserve your use of nested lists for when the content warrants it. In other words, use nested lists to show a hierarchy of information, such as in Listing 6.6.

NOTE

Nesting refers to a tag that appears entirely within another tag. Nested tags are also referred to as *child tags* of the (parent) tag that contains them. It is a common (but not required) coding practice to indent nested tags in the HTML code so that you can easily see their relationship to the parent tag.

Ordered and unordered lists can be nested inside one another, down to as many levels as you want. In Listing 6.6, a complex indented outline is constructed from several unordered lists. Notice in Figure 6.7 that the web browser automatically uses a different type of bullet for each of the first three levels of indentation, which makes the list very easy to read. This is common in modern browsers.

LISTING 6.6   Using Lists to Build Outlines

```
<!doctype html>
<html lang="en">
  <head>
    <meta charset="utf-8">
    <title>Vertebrates</title>
  </head>
  <body>
    <section>
      <header>
        <h1>Vertebrates</h1>
      </header>
      <ul>
        <li><strong>Fish</strong>
          <ul>
            <li>Barramundi</li>
            <li>Kissing Gourami</li>
            <li>Mummichog</li>
          </ul>
        </li>
        <li><strong>Amphibians</strong>
          <ul>
            <li>Anura
            <ul>
              <li>Goliath Frog</li>
              <li>Poison Dart Frog</li>
```

```
        <li>Purple Frog</li>
        </ul>
      </li>
      <li>Caudata
        <ul>
          <li>Hellbender</li>
          <li>Mudpuppy</li>
        </ul>
      </li>
      </ul>
    </li>
    <li><strong>Reptiles</strong>
      <ul>
        <li>Nile Crocodile</li>
        <li>King Cobra</li>
        <li>Common Snapping Turtle</li>
      </ul>
    </li>
    </ul>
  </section>
</body>
</html>
```

FIGURE 6.7
Multilevel unordered lists are neatly indented and bulleted for improved readability.

As Figure 6.7 shows, a web browser normally uses a solid disc for the first-level bullet, a hollow circle for the second-level bullet, and a solid square for all deeper levels. However, you can explicitly choose which type of bullet to use for any level by using <ul `style="list-style-type:disc;">`, <ul `style="list-style-type:circle;">`, or <ul `style="list-style-type:square;">` instead of <ul>, either inline or in a specific style sheet.

You can even change the bullet for any single point within an unordered list by using the `list-style-type` style rule in the <li> tag. For example, the following code displays a hollow circle in front of the words *extra* and *super* and a solid square in front of the word *special*:

```
<ul style="list-style-type:circle;">
  <li>extra</li>
  <li>super</li>
  <li style="list-style-type:square;">special</li>
</ul>
```

The `list-style-type` style rule also works with ordered lists, but instead of choosing a type of bullet, you choose the type of numbers or letters to place in front of each item. Listing 6.7 shows how to use Roman numerals (`list-style-type:upper-roman;`), capital letters (`list-style-type:upper-alpha;`), lowercase letters (`list-style-type:lower-alpha;`), and ordinary numbers (`list-style-type:decimal;`) in a multilevel list. Figure 6.8 shows the resulting outline, which is nicely formatted.

Although Listing 6.7 uses the `list-style-type` style rule only with the <ol> tag, you can also use it for specific <li> tags within a list (though it's hard to imagine a situation when you would want to do this). You can also explicitly specify ordinary numbering with `list-style-type:decimal;`, and you can make lowercase Roman numerals with `list-style-type:lower-roman;`.

LISTING 6.7 Using the `list-style-type` Style Rule with the `style` Attribute in Multitiered Lists

```
<!doctype html>
<html lang="en">
  <head>
    <meta charset="utf-8">
    <title>Advice from the Golf Guru</title>
  </head>
  <body>
    <article>
      <header>
        <h1>How to Win at Golf</h1>
      </header>
      <ol style="list-style-type:upper-roman;">
        <li><strong>Training</strong>
          <ol>
```

```
  <li>Mental prep
    <ol style="list-style-type:upper-alpha;">
      <li>Watch golf on TV religiously</li>
      <li>Get that computer game with Tiger whatsisname</li>
      <li>Rent "personal victory" subliminal tapes</li>
    </ol>
  </li>
  <li>Equipment
    <ol style="list-style-type:upper-alpha;">
      <li>Make sure your putter has a pro autograph on it</li>
      <li>Pick up a bargain bag of tees-n-balls at Costco</li>
    </ol>
  </li>
  <li>Diet
    <ol style="list-style-type:upper-alpha;">
      <li>Avoid junk food
        <ol style="list-style-type:lower-alpha;">
          <li>No hotdogs</li>
        </ol>
      </li>
      <li>Drink wine and mixed drinks only, no beer</li>
    </ol>
  </li>
  </ol>
</li>
<li><strong>Pre-game</strong>
  <ol>
    <li>Dress
      <ol style="list-style-type:upper-alpha;">
        <li>Put on shorts, even if it's freezing</li>
        <li>Buy a new hat if you lost last time</li>
      </ol>
    </li>
    <li>Location and Scheduling
      <ol style="list-style-type:upper-alpha;">
        <li>Select a course where your spouse or boss won't
        find you</li>
        <li>To save on fees, play where your buddy works</li>
      </ol>
    </li>
    <li>Opponent
      <ol style="list-style-type:upper-alpha;">
        <li>Look for: overconfidence, inexperience</li>
        <li>Buy opponent as many pre-game drinks as possible</li>
      </ol>
    </li>
  </ol>
</li>
```

```
    <li><strong>On the Course</strong>
      <ol>
        <li>Tee off first, then develop severe hayfever</li>
        <li>Drive cart over opponent's ball to degrade
        aerodynamics</li>
        <li>Say "fore" just before ball makes contact with
        opponent</li>
        <li>Always replace divots when putting</li>
        <li>Water cooler holes are a good time to correct any
        errors in ball placement</li>
      </ol>
    </li>
  </ol>
 </article>
</body>
</html>
```

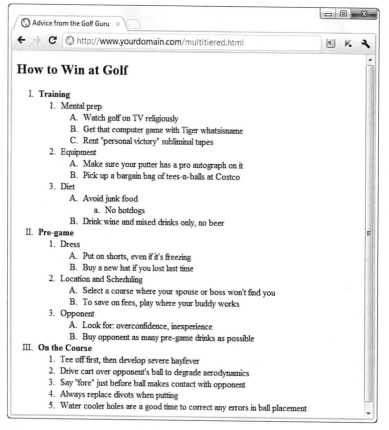

FIGURE 6.8
A well-formatted outline can make almost any plan look more plausible.

Creating a Simple Table

Another method for controlling the layout of information within your web pages is to display that information within a table. A table consists of rows of information with individual cells inside. To make a table, you have to start with a `<table>` tag. Of course, you end a table with the `</table>` tag. CSS contains numerous properties that enable you to modify a table, such as the various border properties you learned about in previous lessons.

With the `<table>` tag in place, you next need the `<tr>` tag. The `<tr>` tag creates a table row, which contains one or more cells of information before the closing `</tr>`. To create these individual cells, use the `<td>` tag (`<td>` stands for *table data*). Place the table information between the `<td>` and `</td>` tags. A *cell* is a rectangular region that can contain any text, images, and HTML tags. Each row in a table consists of at least one cell. Multiple cells within a row form columns in a table.

One more basic tag is involved in building tables. The `<th>` tag works exactly like a `<td>` tag, except that `<th>` indicates that the cell is part of the heading of the table. Most web browsers automatically render the text in `<th>` cells as centered and boldface, as you can see with Chrome in Figure 6.9. However, if your browser does not automatically render this element with a built-in style, you have an element that you can style using CSS without using a class to differentiate among types of table data elements.

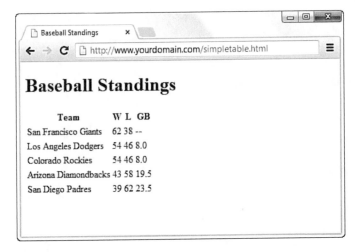

FIGURE 6.9
The code in Listing 6.8 creates a table with four columns and six rows.

You can create as many cells as you want, but each row in a table should have the same number of columns as the other rows. The HTML code in Listing 6.8 creates a simple table using only the four table tags mentioned thus far.

LISTING 6.8 Creating Tables with the `<table>`, `<tr>`, `<td>`, and `<th>` Tags

```
<!doctype html>
<html lang="en">
  <head>
    <meta charset="utf-8">
    <title>Baseball Standings</title>
  </head>
  <body>
  <h1>Baseball Standings</h1>
    <table>
      <tr>
        <th>Team</th>
        <th>W</th>
        <th>L</th>
        <th>GB</th>
      </tr>
      <tr>
        <td>San Francisco Giants</td>
        <td>54</td>
        <td>46</td>
        <td>8.0</td>
      </tr>
      <tr>
        <td>Los Angeles Dodgers</td>
        <td>62</td>
        <td>38</td>
        <td>—</td>
      </tr>
      <tr>
        <td>Colorado Rockies</td>
        <td>54</td>
        <td>46</td>
        <td>8.0</td>
      </tr>
      <tr>
        <td>Arizona Diamondbacks</td>
        <td>43</td>
        <td>58</td>
        <td>19.5</td>
      </tr>
      <tr>
        <td>San Diego Padres</td>
        <td>39</td>
        <td>62</td>
        <td>23.5</td>
      </tr>
    </table>
  </body>
</html>
```

NOTE
You might find your HTML tables easier to read (and less prone to time-wasting errors) if you use spaces to indent <tr> and <td> tags, as shown in Listing 6.8. Remember that browsers ignore spaces when rendering HTML, so the layout of your code has no effect on the layout of the table that people will see.

The table in the example contains baseball standings, which are perfect for arranging in rows and columns—but the table is a little plain. For instance, this example doesn't even have any borders! You'll learn to jazz things up a bit in just a moment. The headings in the table show the Team, Wins (W), Losses (L), and Games Behind (GB) in the standings.

You can add the following style sheet entries to add a basic border around the table and its cells:

```
table, tr, th, td {
    border: 1px solid black;
    border-collapse: collapse;
    padding: 3px;
}
```

You might wonder why you have to specify these styles for all four elements used to create the table instead of just the overall table element itself. Basically, this is because a table is made up of its elements, and each element can have these styles applied. To emphasize this point, the following figures demonstrate how the table would look with various elements styled and unstyled.

Figure 6.10 shows the output of the styles just listed. The border-collapse property, with the value collapse, makes all the borders of the <table>, <tr>, and <th> or <td> elements collapse into one shared border. The padding adds a little breathing room to the content of the cells.

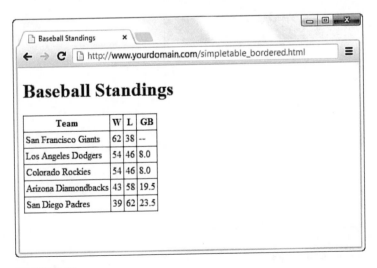

FIGURE 6.10
Adding some CSS styles to the table, including the use of border-collapse.

In Figure 6.11, you can see what the table would look like without the `border-collapse` property specified. (The default value then takes effect, in this case `separate`, for separate borders.)

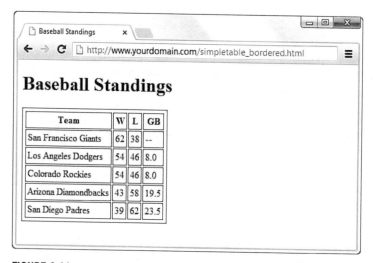

FIGURE 6.11
Removing the `border-collapse` property causes borders to appear for all the elements.

In Figure 6.12, you can see what the table would look like if you did not specify any of the previous styles for the `<th>` and `<td>` elements. Note the lack of border denoting the columns.

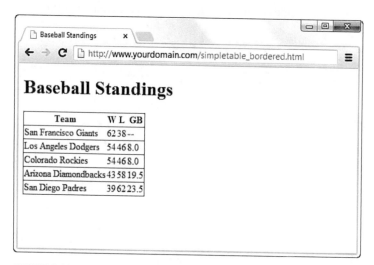

FIGURE 6.12
Removing the styles for the `<th>` and `<td>` elements.

NOTE

You can use three other useful but not required table-related tags when creating simple tables:

▶ `<thead></thead>`—Wrap your header rows in this element to add more meaning to the grouping and also allow these header rows to be printed across all pages (if your table is that long). You can then style the `<thead>` element as well as or instead of individual `<th>` cells.

▶ `<tfoot></tfoot>`—Much as with the `<thead>` element, use this to wrap your footer rows (if you have any) to add more meaning to the grouping and style it as a whole. An example of a footer row might be a summation of the data presented in the columns, such as financial totals. To be valid, your `<tfoot>` rows should be listed in the HTML of the table before the `<tbody>` rows, but the browser will render them after the `<tbody>` rows. This ensures that, in long tables, the footer data displays while the rest of the table is loading.

▶ `<tbody></tbody>`—Wrap the rows that make up the "body" of this table (everything besides the header and the footer rows) in this element to add more meaning to the grouping. You can also style the `<tbody>` element as a whole as well as or instead of styling individual `<td>` cells.

Controlling Table Sizes

When a table width is not specified, the size of a table and its individual cells automatically expand to fit the data you place into it. This is different from other HTML elements, like `<div>` and `<p>`, which stretch to fit the width of their container. However, you can control the width of the entire table by defining the `width` CSS property for the `<table>` element; you can also define the width of each cell through the `width` CSS property assigned to the `<td>` elements. The `width` property can be specified as any length measure, such as pixels, ems, or percentages.

To make the first cell of a table 20% of the total table width and the second cell 80% of the table width, you use the following property definitions:

```
<table style="width:100%;">
  <tr>
    <td style="width:20%;">skinny cell</td>
    <td style="width:80%;">fat cell</td>
  </tr>
</table>
```

Notice that the table is sized to 100%, which ensures that it fills the entire width of the browser window. When you use percentages instead of fixed pixel sizes, the table resizes automatically to fit any size browser window while maintaining the aesthetic balance you're seeking. In this case, the two cells within the table are automatically resized to 20% and 80% of the total table width, respectively.

In Listing 6.9, the simple table from Listing 6.8 (plus the border-related styles) is expanded to show very precise control over table cell widths. (In addition, the border-related styles have been added.)

LISTING 6.9 Specifying Table Cell Widths

```
<!doctype html>
<html lang="en">
  <head>
    <meta charset="utf-8">
    <title>Baseball Standings</title>
    <style>
      table, tr, th, td {
          border: 1px solid black;
          border-collapse: collapse;
          padding: 3px;
      }
    </style>
  </head>
  <body>
    <h1>Baseball Standings</h1>
    <table>
      <tr>
        <th style="width: 200px;">Team</th>
        <th style="width: 25px;">W</th>
        <th style="width: 25px;">L</th>
        <th style="width: 25px;">GB</th>
      </tr>
      <tr>
        <td>San Francisco Giants</td>
        <td>62</td>
        <td>38</td>
        <td>--</td>
      </tr>
      <tr>
        <td>Los Angeles Dodgers</td>
        <td>54</td>
        <td>46</td>
        <td>8.0</td>
      </tr>
      <tr>
        <td>Colorado Rockies</td>
        <td>54</td>
        <td>46</td>
        <td>8.0</td>
      </tr>
      <tr>
        <td>Arizona Diamondbacks</td>
        <td>43</td>
        <td>58</td>
        <td>19.5</td>
      </tr>
```

```
      <tr>
        <td>San Diego Padres</td>
        <td>39</td>
        <td>62</td>
        <td>23.5</td>
      </tr>
    </table>
  </body>
</html>
```

You can see the consistent column widths in Figure 6.13.

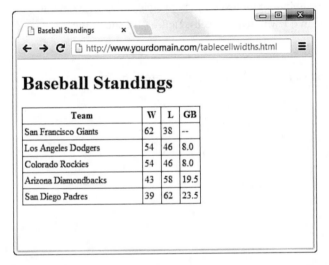

FIGURE 6.13
The code in Listing 6.9 creates a table with four columns and six rows, with specific widths used for each column.

The addition of a specific width style for each `<th>` element in the first row defines the widths of the columns. The first column is defined as 200px wide, and the second, third, and fourth columns are each 25px wide. In Figure 6.13, you can see whitespace after the text in the first column, indicating that the specified width is indeed greater than the column width would have been had the table been allowed to render without explicit width indicators.

Also note that these widths are not repeated in the `<td>` elements in subsequent rows. Technically, you need to define the widths in only the first row; the remaining rows will follow suit because they are all part of the same table. However, if you had used another formatting style (such as a style to change font size or color), you would've had to repeat that style for each element that should have those display properties.

Alignment and Spanning Within Tables

By default, anything you place inside a table cell is aligned to the left and vertically centered. All the figures so far in this lesson have shown this default alignment. However, you can align the contents of table cells both horizontally and vertically with the `text-align` and `vertical-align` style properties.

You can apply these alignment attributes to any `<tr>`, `<td>`, or `<th>` tag. Alignment attributes assigned to a `<tr>` tag apply to all cells in that row. Depending on the size of your table, you can save yourself some time and effort by applying these attributes at the `<tr>` level and not in each `<td>` or `<th>` tag.

The HTML code in Listing 6.10 uses a combination of text alignment styles to apply a default alignment to a row, but it is overridden in a few individual cells. Figure 6.14 shows the result of the code in Listing 6.10.

LISTING 6.10 Alignment, Cell Spacing, Borders, and Background Colors in Tables

```
<!doctype html>
<html lang="en">
  <head>
    <meta charset="utf-8">
    <title>Dandelions</title>
    <style>
    table {
        border: 2px solid black;
        border-collapse: collapse;
        padding: 3px;
        width: 100%;
    }

    tr, th, td {
        border: 2px solid black;
        border-collapse: collapse;
        padding: 3px;
    }
    thead {
        background-color: #ff0000;
        color: #ffffff;
    }
    .aligntop {
        vertical-align:top;
    }
    .description {
        font-size: 14px;
        font-weight: bold;
```

```
        vertical-align: middle;
        text-align: center;
      }
      .size {
        text-align: center;
      }
    </style>
  </head>
  <body>
    <h1>Things to Fear</h1>
    <table>
      <thead>
        <tr>
          <th colspan="2">Description</th>
          <th>Color</th>
          <th>Size</th>
        </tr>
      </thead>
      <tbody>
        <tr class="aligntop">
          <td><img src="flower.jpg" alt="Flower"></td>
          <td class="description">Flower</td>
          <td>Yellow</td>
          <td class="size">1-2 inches</td>
        </tr>
        <tr class="aligntop">
          <td><img src="seeds.jpg" alt="Seeds"></td>
          <td class="description">Seeds</td>
          <td>White</td>
          <td class="size">1-2 inches</td>
        </tr>
        <tr class="aligntop">
          <td><img src="leaves.jpg" alt="Leaves"></td>
          <td class="description">Leaves</td>
          <td>Green</td>
          <td class="weight">3-4 inches</td>
        </tr>
      </tbody>
    </table>
  </body>
</html>
```

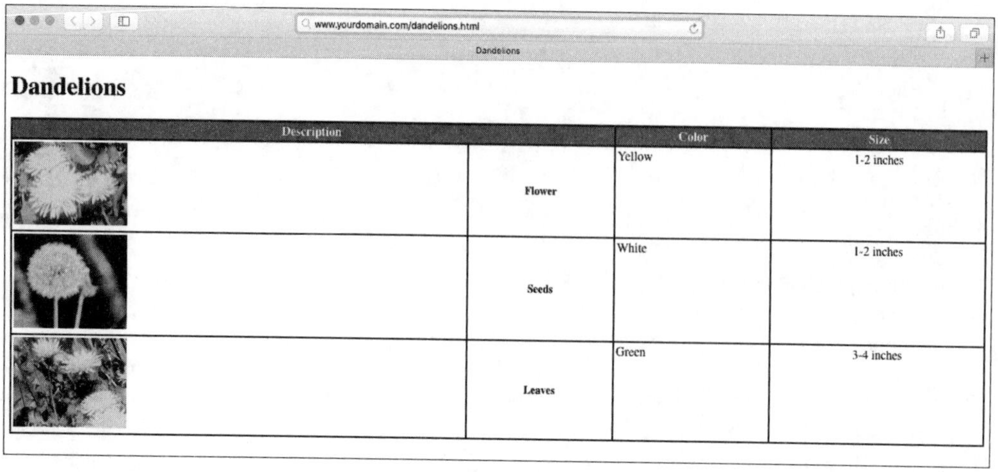

FIGURE 6.14
The code in Listing 6.10 shows the use of the `colspan` attribute and some alignment styles.

Following are some of the most commonly used `vertical-align` style property values: `top`, `middle`, `bottom`, `text-top`, `text-bottom`, and `baseline` (for text). These property values give you plenty of flexibility in aligning table data vertically.

NOTE

Keeping the structure of rows and columns organized in your mind can be the most difficult part of creating tables with cells that span multiple columns or rows. The tiniest error can often throw the whole thing into disarray. You can save yourself time and frustration by sketching complicated tables on paper before you start writing the HTML to implement them.

Spanning is the process of forcing a cell to stretch across more than one row or column of a table. The `colspan` attribute causes a cell to span multiple columns; `rowspan` has the same effect on rows.

At the top of Figure 6.14, a single cell (`Description`) spans two columns. This is accomplished with the `colspan` attribute in the `<th>` tag for that cell. As you might guess, you can also use the `rowspan` attribute to create a cell that spans more than one row.

In addition, text styles are defined in the style sheet and applied to the cells in the Description column to create bold text that is both vertically aligned to the middle and horizontally aligned to the center of the cell.

A few tricks in Listing 6.10 haven't been explained yet. You can give an entire table—and each individual row or cell in a table—its own background, distinct from any background you might use on the web page itself. You can do this by placing the `background-color` or `background-image` style in the `<table>`, `<tr>`, `<td>`, `<th>`, `<thead>`, `<tbody>`, or `<tfoot>` tags (or assigning the value in the style sheet for these elements), exactly as you would in the `<body>` tag. In Listing 6.10, only the top row has a background color; the style sheet defines the `<thead>` element as having a red background and white text in the cells in that row.

NOTE

You often see alternating row colors in a table. For instance, one row might have a gray background, and the next row might have a white background. Alternating the row colors helps users read the content of a table more clearly, and it is especially helpful if the table is large. You can do this automatically with CSS, as you'll learn in Lesson 13, "Taking Control of Backgrounds and Borders."

Similar to the `background-color` style property is the `background-image` property (not shown in this example), which is used to set an image for a table background. If you wanted to set the image `leaves.gif` as the background for a table, you would use `background-image:url(leaves.gif);` in the style sheet entry for the `<table>` element. Notice that the image file is placed within parentheses and preceded by the word `url`, which indicates that you are describing where the image file is located.

Tweaking tables goes beyond just using style properties. As Listing 6.10 shows, you can control the space around the content of the cell, within its borders, by applying some padding to the cell. If you want to add some space between the borders of the cells themselves, you can use the `border-spacing` CSS property, which enables you to define the horizontal and vertical spacing, like so:

```
border-spacing: 2px 4px;
```

In the example, spacing is defined as 2 pixels of space between the horizontal borders and 4 pixels of space between the vertical borders. If you use only one value, the value is applied to all four borders.

Page Layout with Tables

At the beginning of this lesson, we indicated that designers have used tables for page layout, as well as to display tabular information. You will still find many examples of table-based layouts if you peek at another designer's source code. This method of design grew out of inconsistencies in browser support for CSS in the mid-1990s to early 2000s. Because all browsers supported tables, and in generally the same way, web designers latched on to the table-based method of content layout to achieve the same visual page display across all browsers. However, now that support for CSS is relatively similar across all major browsers, designers can follow the long-standing standards-based recommendation *not* to use tables for page layout.

NOTE

HTML5 has changed the recommendation again. Using tables for layout is still not a good idea, but as long as you define the containing table as a layout table with either a `border="0"` or `role="presentation"` attribute on the table, you will be in alignment with the recommendation. But it's still not a good idea to use tables for layout. In Lesson 12, "Creating Layouts Using Modern CSS Techniques," you'll learn several CSS alternatives that work much better than tables.

The World Wide Web Consortium (W3C), the standards body that oversees the future of the web, has long promoted using style sheets as the proper way to lay out pages (instead of using tables). Style sheets are ultimately much more powerful than tables, which is why the bulk of these lessons teach you how to use style sheets for page layout.

The main reasons for avoiding using tables for layout include these:

▶ **Mixing presentation with content**—One goal of CSS and standards-compliant web design is to separate the presentation layer from the content layer.

▶ **Creating unnecessarily difficult redesigns**—To change a table-based layout, you have to change the table-based layout on every single page of your site (unless it is part of a complicated, dynamically driven site, in which case you have to undo all the dynamic pieces and remake them).

▶ **Addressing accessibility issues**—Screen reading software looks to tables for content and often tries to read layout tables as content tables.

▶ **Rendering on mobile devices**—Table layouts are often not flexible enough to scale downward to small screens (see Lesson 17, "Designing for Mobile Devices").

Using CSS Columns

If you have a large amount of text-only information, you might want to present it much like a physical newspaper does: in columns. Over 100 years of research have shown a correlation between the length of a line and reading speed. There is a "sweet spot," or optimum length of a line that allows for a quick and enjoyable reading experience. The continued presence of this sweet spot—lines that are around 4 inches long—is why physical newspapers still present information in columns.

If you have a lot of information to present to readers, or if you simply want to mimic the aesthetic of a newspaper layout, you can use CSS columns. True, you could also use a table, because tables are made of rows and columns, but the preceding section explained some of the reasons to avoid a table-based layout. Also, columns aren't just for text; you can put anything you want into defined columns, such as advertisements or related text in a sidebar.

In Figure 6.15, you can see a basic use of CSS columns to define a traditional newspaper-type layout. Listing 6.11 shows the code to create this three-column layout.

FIGURE 6.15
The code in Listing 6.11 shows a three-column layout.

LISTING 6.11   Alignment, Cell Spacing, Borders, and Background Colors in Tables

```
<!doctype html>
<html lang="en">
  <head>
    <meta charset="utf-8">
    <title>Breaking News!</title>
    <style>
    article {
        column-count: 3;
        column-gap: 21px;
    }
```

```
    h1 {
       text-align: center;
       column-span: all;
    }
    p {
       margin-top: 0px;
       margin-bottom: 12px;
    }
    footer {
       column-span: all;
    }
  </style>
 </head>
 <body>
   <article>
     <header>
       <h1>Breaking News!</h1>
     </header>
     <p>Breaking news, also known as a special report or news
     bulletin, is a current issue that broadcasters feel warrants
     the interruption of scheduled programming and/or current news
     in order to report its details. Its use is also assigned to
     the most significant story of the moment or a story that is
     being covered live. It could be a story that is simply of wide
     interest to viewers and has little impact otherwise. Many
     times, breaking news is used after the news network has
     already reported on this story. When a story has not been
     reported on previously, the graphic and phrase "Just In" is
     sometimes used instead.</p>
     <p>In early coverage of a breaking story, details are commonly
     sketchy, usually due to the limited information available at the
     time. For example, during the Sago Mine disaster, initial reports
     were that all twelve miners were found alive, but news
     organizations later found only one actually survived.</p>
     <p>Another criticism has been the diluting of the importance of
     breaking news by the need of 24-hour news channels to fill time,
     applying the title to soft news stories of questionable importance
     and urgency, for example car chases. Others question whether the
     use of the term is excessive, citing occasions when the term is
     used even though scheduled programming is not interrupted.</p>
     <footer>
       <em>Text courtesy of Wikipedia:
       http://en.wikipedia.org/wiki/Breaking_news</em>
     </footer>
   </article>
 </body>
</html>
```

The code in Listing 6.11 is from a fake news article, and we've used the `<article>` element to hold all the content. Inside the `<article>` element is a `<header>` element that contains the "Breaking News!" heading (at the `<h1>` level), followed by three paragraphs of text and a `<footer>` element. All the styling is handled in the style sheet at the beginning of the listing; styles are provided for four of the elements just named: `<article>`, `<h1>`, `<p>`, and `<footer>`.

In the style sheet, we're applying the primary definition of the columns within the `<article>` element. We've used `column-count` to define three columns, and we've used `column-gap` to define the space between the columns as 21 pixels wide. Next, we've added a definition for the `<h1>` element, first to make the text align in the center of the page and second to ensure that the text spans all the columns. We've applied the same `column-span` property to the entry for the `<footer>` element for the same reason.

After the entry for the `<h1>` element, we added some specific margins to the `<p>` element— namely, a top margin of 0 pixels and a bottom margin of 12 pixels. We could have left well enough alone and just allowed the `<p>` elements to display as the default style, but that would have created a margin at the top of each paragraph. "What's the big deal?" you might ask, because it looks as though we've manually added space between the paragraphs anyway—and that's true. However, we added the space *after* each paragraph and took away the space *before* each paragraph so that the first column doesn't begin with a space and thus cause the tops of the three columns to misalign.

NOTE

You will sometimes see related entries with `-webkit`, `-o`, `-ms`, and `-moz` prefixes, such as `-webkit-column-count: 2;`. These are added to style sheets when a property is not fully supported by browsers. The `-webkit` prefix is for Chrome and Safari (and their mobile counterparts Android and iOS), `-o` is for Opera, `-ms` is for Microsoft Edge and Internet Explorer, and `-moz` is for Firefox. While you can use these prefixes for CSS columns, browser support is basically universal now, so the prefixes are necessary only if you need to support older browser versions. A good site to reference what prefixes you might need is www.caniuse.com.

You can even add vertical lines between columns, as shown in Figure 6.16. The style sheet entries we added to achieve this appearance are shown here:

```
column-rule-width: 1px;
column-rule-style: solid;
column-rule-color: #000;
```

Note that these style sheet entries look remarkably similar to the ones you use to define borders (which you will learn about in Lesson 13).

FIGURE 6.16
The code in Listing 6.11, with the addition of vertical lines between the columns.

You will learn more about how to use CSS columns for responsive layouts in Lesson 17.

Summary

In this lesson, you learned how to make text appear as boldface or italic and how to code superscripts, subscripts, special symbols, and accented letters. You saw how to control the size, color, and typeface of any section of text on a web page, including how to use web fonts for more interesting typefaces. You also learned that attributes are used to specify options and special behavior for many HTML tags, and you learned to use the `style` attribute with CSS style rules to affect the appearance of text. You also learned how to create and combine three basic types of HTML lists: ordered lists, unordered lists, and definition lists. Lists can be placed within other lists to create outlines and other complex arrangements of text.

Finally, you learned to arrange text and images into organized rows and columns called tables. You learned the basic tags for creating tables and several CSS properties for controlling the alignment, spacing, and appearance of tables. You also learned that tables should not be used for layout purposes but that you can achieve a multicolumn layout by using CSS columns.

Table 6.2 summarizes the HTML tags and attributes discussed in this lesson. Don't feel as though you have to memorize all these tags, by the way!

TABLE 6.2 HTML Tags and Attributes Covered in Lesson 6

Tag/Attribute	Function
...	Adds emphasis (usually italic).
...	Adds stronger emphasis (usually bold).
<pre>...</pre>	Indicates preformatted text (with exact line endings and spacing preserved—usually rendered in a monospaced font).
_{...}	Indicates subscript.
^{...}	Indicates superscript.
<div>...</div>	Specifies a region of text to be formatted.
<dl>...</dl>	Indicates a definition list.
<dt>...</dt>	Indicates a definition term, as part of a definition list.
<dd>...</dd>	Specifies the corresponding definition to a definition term, as part of a definition list.
<ol>...</ol>	Indicates an ordered (numbered) list.
<ul>...</ul>	Indicates an unordered (bulleted) list.
<li>...</li>	Indicates a list item for use with <ol> or <ul>.
<table>...</table>	Creates a table that can contain any number of rows and columns.
<thead>...</thead>	Defines the header rows of a table.
<tbody>...</tbody>	Defines the body rows of a table.
<tfoot>...</tfoot>	Defines the footer rows of a table.
<tr>...</tr>	Defines a table row containing one or more cells (<td> tags).
<th>...</th>	Defines a table heading cell. (Accepts all the same styles as <td>.)
<td>...</td>	Defines a table data cell.

Attribute	*Function*
style="font-family: typeface;"	Specifies the typeface (family) of the font, which is the name of a font, such as Arial. (Can also be used with <p>, <h1>, <h2>, <h3>, and so on.)
style="font-size:size;"	Specifies the size of the font, which can be set to small, medium, or large, as well as x-small, x-large, and so on. Can also be set to a specific size (such as 12pt or 2em).
style="color:color;"	Changes the color of the text.
style="text-align: alignment;"	Aligns text to center, left, or right. (Can also be used with <p>, <h1>, <h2>, <h3>, and so on.)

Tag/Attribute	Function
Attribute	*Function*
style="list-style-type:*numtype*;"	Indicates the type of numerals used to label the list. Possible values are decimal, lower-roman, upper-roman, lower-alpha, upper-alpha, and none.
style="list-style-type:*bullettype*;"	Indicates the bullet dingbat used to mark list items. Possible values are disc, circle, square, and none.
style="list-style-type:*type*;"	Indicates the type of bullet or number used to label this item. Possible values are disc, circle, square, decimal, lower-roman, upper-roman, lower-alpha, upper-alpha, and none.

Q&A

Q. How do I find out the exact name for a font I have on my computer?

A. On a Windows 10 computer, open the Control Panel and go to the Appearance and Personalization section. Then click the Fonts folder, and you see a list of the fonts on your system. On a Mac, open Font Book in the Applications folder to find a list of the fonts on your system. When specifying fonts in the font-family style rule, use the exact spelling of each font name. Font names are not case sensitive, however.

Q. How do I put Kanji, Arabic, Chinese, and other non-European characters on my pages?

A. First of all, users who need to read these characters on your pages must have the appropriate language fonts installed. If you have your browser set to the UTF-8 character set, you should be able to just type the characters onto your page, just as you do English characters.

You can also use the Character Map program in Windows (or a similar program in other operating systems) to get the numeric codes for the characters in any language font. To find Character Map, click Start, All Programs, Accessories, and then System Tools. (On a Mac, look for the Emoji & Symbols option in the Edit menu of any application.) If the character you want has the code 214, use Ö to place it on a web page. If you cannot find the Character Map program, use your operating system's built-in Help function to find the specific location.

Q. I've seen web pages that use little three-dimensional balls or other special graphics for bullets. How do they do that?

A. That trick is a little bit beyond what this lesson covers. You'll learn how to do this in Lesson 8.

Q. I made a big table, and when I load the page, nothing appears on the page for a long time. Why the wait?

A. Complex tables can take a while to appear on the screen. The web browser has to figure out the size of everything in the table before it can display any part of it. You can speed things up a bit by defining the width and height attributes for every image within a table. Defining specific widths for the <table> and <td> elements also helps. You may want to split extremely large tables into smaller tables, so that they render individually.

Workshop

The workshop contains quiz questions and activities to help you solidify your understanding of the material covered.

Quiz

1. How would you create a paragraph in which the first three words are bold, using styles rather than the <b> or <strong> tags?

2. How would you represent the chemical formula for water?

3. How do you display "© 2018, Webwonks Inc." on a web page?

4. How would you center all the text on a page?

5. How can you create a simple two-column, two-row table with a single-pixel black border outlining the table?

6. Why should you use character codes to write 3 < 6 on a web page?

7. What typeface will be used in most browsers with this style property: `font-family: Geneva, Arial, helvetica, sans-serif;`?

8. What is the CSS command to define a web font?

9. What do you call a list enclosed inside another list?

10. What is the CSS property for creating a three-column newspaper layout on a web page?

NOTE

Just a reminder for those of you reading these words in the print or e-book edition of this book: If you go to **www.informit.com/register** and register this book (using ISBN 9780672338083), you can receive free access to an online Web Edition that not only contains the complete text of this book but also features an interactive version of this quiz.

Answers

1. You can use this code:

   ```
   <p><span style="font-weight: bold;">First three words</span> are bold.</p>
   ```

2. You can use H₂0.

3. You can use either of the following:

   ```
   &copy; 2018, Webwonks Inc.
   &#169; 2018, Webwonks Inc.
   ```

4. If you thought about putting a `<div style="text-align:center;">` immediately after the `<body>` tag at the top of the page and `</div>` just before the `</body>` tag at the end of the page, then you're correct. However, the `text-align` style is also supported directly in the `<body>` tag, which means you can forgo the `<div>` tag and place the `style="text-align:center;"` style directly in the `<body>` tag. Presto, the entire page is centered!

5. Use the following HTML:

```
<table style="border: 1px solid #000000; border-collapse: collapse;">
  <tr>
    <td>Top left...</td>
    <td>Top right...</td>
  </tr>
  <tr>
    <td>Bottom left...</td>
    <td>Bottom right...</td>
  </tr>
</table>
```

6. Because the < character is also the character that starts an HTML tag, by writing 3 < 6, you will ensure that the browser knows to display the less-than sign rather than thinking < is the start of an HTML tag.

7. This will display in most browsers in the typeface Geneva. If the browser doesn't have that font, it will display in Arial, then Helvetica, and then in its default sans-serif font.

8. You use the `@font-face` rule to define the name and source URL of a web font.

9. A list inside another list is called a *nested list*.

10. Use `column-count: 3;` to define a three-column layout on your page.

Exercises

▶ Apply the font-level style attributes you learned about in this lesson to various block-level elements, such as `<p>`, `<div>`, `<ul>`, and `<li>` items. Try nesting your elements to get a feel for how styles do or do not cascade through the content hierarchy.

Use the text alignment style attributes to place blocks of text in various places on your web page. Try nesting your paragraphs and divisions (`<p>` and `<div>`) to get a feel for how styles do or do not cascade through the content hierarchy.

▶ Try producing an ordered list outlining the information you'd like to put on your web pages. This will give you practice formatting HTML lists and also give you a head start on thinking about the issues covered in later lessons.

Using External and Internal Links

- ▶ How to use anchor links
- ▶ How to link between pages on your own site
- ▶ How to link to external content
- ▶ How to link to non-Web documents such as PDF and Word documents
- ▶ How to link to an email address
- ▶ How to use window targeting with your links
- ▶ How to style your links with CSS
- ▶ How to add descriptions to links
- ▶ Best practices for web page links

So far, you have learned how to use HTML tags to create some basic web pages. However, at this point, those pieces of content are islands unto themselves, with no connection to anything else. To turn your work into real web content, you need to connect it to the rest of the Web—or at least to other pages within your own sites.

This lesson shows you how to create hypertext links to content within your own document and how to link to other external documents. In addition, you will learn how to style hypertext links so that they display in the color and decoration you desire—not necessarily the default blue underlined display. You will also learn some of the best practices that designers have learned from over 20 years of linking web pages.

Using Web Addresses

The simplest way to store web content for an individual website is to place all the files in the same folder. When files are stored together like this, you can link to them by simply providing the name of the file in the href attribute of the <a> tag.

NOTE

Before you get too far into this lesson, you might want a refresher on the basics of where to put files on your server and how to manage files within a set of directories. This information is important to understand when creating links in web content. Refer to Lesson 1, "Understanding How the Web Works," specifically the section titled "Understanding Where to Place Files on the Web Server."

An *attribute* is a piece of information associated with a tag that provides further details about the tag. For example, the href attribute of the <a> tag identifies the address of the page or document to which you are linking.

When you have more than a few pages, or when you start to have an organization structure to the content in your site, you should put your files into directories (or *folders*, if you will) whose names reflect the content within them. For example, all your images could be in an images directory, corporate information could be in an about directory, and so on. Regardless of how you organize your documents within your own web server, you can use relative addresses, which include only enough information to find one page from another.

A *relative address* describes the path from one web page to another, as opposed to a full (or *absolute*) Internet address.

As you recall from Lesson 1, the document root of your web server is the directory designated as the top-level directory for your web content. In web addresses, that document root is represented by the forward slash (/). All subsequent levels of directories are separated by the same type of forward slash, as in this example: */directory/subdirectory/subsubdirectory/*.

CAUTION

The forward slash (/) is always used to separate directories in HTML. Don't use the backslash (\), which is normally used in the Windows operating system, to separate your directories. You can remember this by thinking that everything on the web moves *forward*, so use forward slashes.

Suppose you are creating a page named zoo.html in your document root, and you want to include a link to pages named african.html and asian.html in the elephants subdirectory. The links would look like the following:

```
<a href="/elephants/african.html">Learn about African elephants.</a>
<a href="/elephants/asian.html">Learn about Asian elephants.</a>
```

These specific addresses are actually called *relative-root addresses*, in that they are relative addresses that lack the entire domain name, but they are specifically relative to the document root specified by the forward slash.

Using a regular relative address, you can skip the initial forward slash. This type of address allows the links to become relative to whatever directory they are in—whether that is the document root or another directory one or more levels down from the document root. This is what a regular relative address looks like:

```
<a href="elephants/african.html">Learn about African elephants.</a>
<a href="elephants/asian.html">Learn about Asian elephants.</a>
```

Your `african.html` and `asian.html` documents in the `elephants` subdirectory could link back to the main `zoo.html` page in either of these ways:

```
<a href="http://www.yourdomain.com/zoo.html">Return to the zoo.</a>
<a href="/zoo.html">Return to the zoo.</a>
<a href="../zoo.html">Return to the zoo.</a>
```

The first link is an absolute link. With an absolute link, there is *absolutely* no doubt where the link should go because the full URL is provided—domain name included.

The second link is a relative-root link. It is relative to the domain you are currently browsing and, therefore, does not require the protocol type (for example, `http://`) or domain name (for example, `www.yourdomain.com`); the initial forward slash is provided to show that the address begins at the document root.

NOTE

The general rule surrounding relative addressing (`elephants/african.html`) versus absolute addressing (`http://www.takeme2thezoo.com/elephants/african.html`) is that you should use relative addressing when linking to files that are stored together, such as files that are all part of the same website. Use absolute addressing when you're linking to files somewhere else—another computer, another disk drive, or, more commonly, another website on the Internet.

In the third link, the *double dot* (. .) is a special command that indicates the folder that contains the current folder—in other words, the *parent folder*. Anytime you see the double dot, just think to yourself, "Go up a level in the directory structure."

The advantage of relative addressing is that the links will work as long as the pages remain on the same site. If you use relative addressing consistently throughout your web pages, you can move directories of pages to another folder, disk drive, or web server without changing the links.

Relative addresses can span quite complex directory structures, if necessary. Lesson 28, "Organizing and Managing a Website," offers more detailed advice for organizing and linking large numbers of web pages.

Creating a Simple Site Architecture

Hopefully by now you've created a page or two of your own while working through the lessons. Follow these steps to add a few more pages and link them:

1. Use a home page as a main entrance and as a central hub to which all your other pages are connected. If you created a page about yourself or your business, use that page as your home page. You also might like to create a new page now for this purpose.

2. On the home page, put a list of links to the other HTML files you've created (or placeholders for the HTML files you plan to create soon). Be sure that the exact spelling of the filename, including any capitalization, is correct in every link.

NOTE
_____
Most web servers run UNIX or Linux, which are case sensitive, but Windows does not distinguish between cases when you're viewing your pages locally. This means that links to `african.html` and `African.html` will both point to the same page on a Windows machine, but they will point to different pages on the web server. It's best to stick to one case—preferably lowercase—for all your web filenames.
_____

3. On every other page besides the home page, include a link at the bottom (or top) leading back to your home page. This makes navigating around your site simple and easy.

4. You might also want to include a list of links to related or interesting sites, either on your home page or on a separate links page. People often include a list of their friends' personal pages on their own home page. However, businesses should be careful not to lead potential customers away to other sites too quickly, as there's no guarantee that they'll return to your site after leaving, and the other site might not have a link back.

Linking Within a Page Using Anchors

The <a> tag—the tag responsible for hyperlinks on the web—got its name from the word *anchor*, because a link serves as a designation for a spot in a web page. In examples throughout these lessons so far, you've learned how to use the <a> tag to link to somewhere else, but that's only half its usefulness. Let's get started working with anchor links that link to content within the same page.

Identifying Locations in a Page with Anchors

The <a> tag can be used to mark a spot on a page as an anchor, enabling you to create a link that points to that exact spot. Listing 7.1, presented a bit later in this lesson, demonstrates a link to an anchor within a page. To see how such links are made, let's take a quick peek ahead at the first <h1> tag in the listing:

```
<h1 id="top">First Lines of Shakespearean Sonnets</h1>
```

The <a> tag uses the href attribute to specify a hyperlinked target. The <a href> is what you click, and the element with the corresponding id attribute is where you go when you click there. In this example, the <h1> tag is specifying a target, but it is also the headline for that section of the page. The id attribute gives a name, in this case top, to the specific point on the page where the tag occurs. A unique name must be assigned to the id attribute, but it can be placed on any element in the page where you want the link to land.

NOTE

You can use an id attribute on any container element in HTML5, and you can use the <a> tag to point to those elements as anchor links as well. Best practices recommend that you not add extra tags to your document but simply add the id attribute to relevant tags that are already present.

Linking to Anchor Locations

Listing 7.1 shows a site with various anchor points placed throughout a single page. Take a look at the last <a> tag in Listing 7.1 to see an example:

```
<a href="#top">Return to Index.</a>
```

The # symbol means that the word top refers to a named anchor point within the current document rather than to a separate page. When a user clicks Return to Index, the web browser displays the part of the page starting with the tag with the id="top" attribute.

LISTING 7.1 Setting Anchor Points by Using the <a> Tag with an id Attribute

```
<!doctype html>
<html lang="en">
  <head>
    <meta charset="utf-8">
    <title>Alphabetical Shakespeare</title>
  </head>
  <body>
    <article>
      <header>
        <h1 id="top">First Lines of Shakespearean Sonnets</h1>
      </header>
      <p>Don't you just hate when you go a-courting, and you're
      down on one knee about to rattle off a totally romantic
      Shakespearean sonnet, and zap! You space it. <em>"Um... It
      was, uh... I think it started with a B..."</em></p>
      <p>Well, appearest thou no longer the dork. Simply refer to
```

this page, click on the first letter of the sonnet you want, and get an instant reminder of the first line to get you started. <em>"Beshrew that heart that makes my heart to groan..."</em></p>

```
<p style="text-align:center"><strong>Alphabetical Index</strong></p>
<div style="text-align:center">
  <a href="#A">A</a> <a href="#B">B</a> <a href="#C">C</a>
  <a href="#D">D</a> <a href="#E">E</a> <a href="#F">F</a>
  <a href="#G">G</a> <a href="#H">H</a> <a href="#I">I</a>
  <a href="#J">J</a> <a href="#K">K</a> <a href="#L">L</a>
  <a href="#M">M</a> <a href="#N">N</a> <a href="#O">O</a>
  <a href="#P">P</a> <a href="#Q">Q</a> <a href="#R">R</a>
  <a href="#S">S</a> <a href="#T">T</a> <a href="#U">U</a>
  <a href="#V">V</a> <a href="#W">W</a> <a href="#X">X</a>
  <a href="#Y">Y</a> <a href="#Z">Z</a>
</div>
<hr>

<section>
  <header>
    <h1 id="A">A</h1>
  </header>
  <ul>
    <li>A woman's face with nature's own hand painted,</li>
    <li>Accuse me thus, that I have scanted all, </li>
    <li>Against my love shall be as I am now</li>
    <li>Against that time (if ever that time come) </li>
    <li>Ah wherefore with infection should he live, </li>
    <li>Alack what poverty my muse brings forth, </li>
    <li>Alas 'tis true, I have gone here and there, </li>
    <li>As a decrepit father takes delight, </li>
    <li>As an unperfect actor on the stage, </li>
    <li>As fast as thou shalt wane so fast thou grow'st, </li>
  </ul>
  <p><a href="#top">Return to Index.</a></p>
</section>
<hr>
<!-- continue with the alphabet -->
<section>
  <header>
    <h1 id="Z">Z</h1>
  </header>
  <p>(No sonnets start with Z.)</p>
  <p><a href="#top"><em>Return to Index.</em></a></p>
</section>
</article>
</body>
</html>
```

NOTE

Near the end of Listing 7.1 you see the following line:

`<!-- continue with the alphabet -->`

This text (an HTML comment) will appear in your source code but will not be displayed by the browser. You will learn more about commenting your code in Lesson 28.

Each of the `<a href>` links in Listing 7.1 makes an underlined link leading to a corresponding `<a id>` anchor—or it would if all the text were filled in. Only A and Z will work in this example because only the A and Z links have corresponding text to link to, but feel free to fill in the rest on your own! Clicking the letter Z under Alphabetical Index in Figure 7.1, for example, takes you to the part of the page shown in Figure 7.2.

NOTE

In HTML4, anchor names specified via the `id` attribute in a tag have to start with a letter. But HTML5 is less strict. The ID must contain at least one character and no space characters. Best practices suggest that it's best to avoid characters that have meaning in HTML, CSS, JavaScript, and HTTP (the protocol that web servers use to load pages). These include periods (.), colons (:), semicolons (;) pound signs (#), slashes (/), and backslashes (\). We recommend using only numbers and letters from a standard keyboard in your `id` attributes.

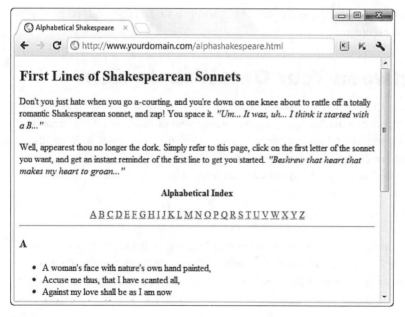

FIGURE 7.1
The `<h1 id>` tags in Listing 7.1 don't appear differently from standard `<h1>` tags. The `<a href>` tags appear as underlined links.

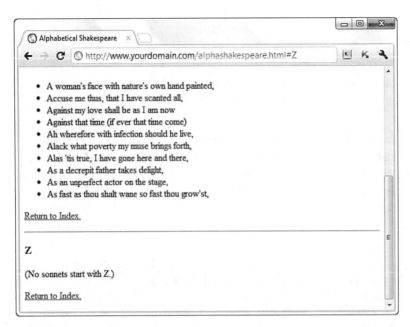

FIGURE 7.2
Clicking the letter Z on the page shown in Figure 7.1 takes you to the appropriate section of the same page.

Having mastered the concept of linking to sections of text within a single page, you will now learn to link other pieces of web content.

Linking Between Your Own Web Content

As you learned earlier in this lesson, you do not need to include http:// before each address specified in the href attribute when linking to content within your domain (or on the same computer, if you are viewing your site locally). When you create a link from one file to another file within the same domain or on the same computer, you don't need to specify a complete Internet address. In fact, if the two files are stored in the same folder, you can simply use the name of the HTML file by itself:

```
<a href="pagetwo.html">Go to Page 2.</a>
```

For example, Listing 7.2 and Figure 7.3 show a quiz page with a link to the answers page shown in Listing 7.3 and Figure 7.4. The answers page contains a link back to the quiz page. Because the page in Listing 7.2 links to another page in the same directory, the filename can be used in place of a complete address.

LISTING 7.2 The `historyanswers.html` File

```
<!doctype html>
<html lang="en">
  <head>
    <meta charset="utf-8">
    <title>History Quiz</title>
  </head>
  <body>
    <section>
      <header>
        <h1>History Quiz</h1>
      </header>
      <p>Complete the following rhymes. (Example: William the
      Conqueror played cruel tricks on the Saxons in... ten
      sixty-six.)</p>
      <ol>
        <li>Columbus sailed the ocean blue in...</li>
        <li>The Spanish Armada met its fate in...</li>
        <li>London burnt like rotten sticks in...</li>
      </ol>
      <p style="text-align: center;">
        <a href="historyanswers.html">Check Your Answers!</a>
      </p>
    </section>
  </body>
</html>
```

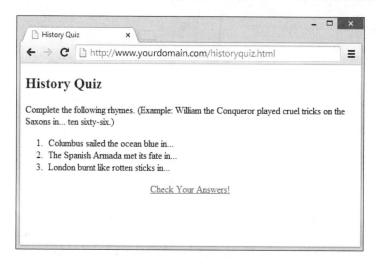

FIGURE 7.3
This is the `historyquiz.html` file listed in Listing 7.2 and referred to by the link in Listing 7.3.

LISTING 7.3 The `historyanswers.html` File That `historyquiz.html` Links To

```
<!doctype html>
<html lang="en">
  <head>
    <meta charset="utf-8">
    <title>History Quiz Answers</title>
  </head>
  <body>
    <section>
      <header>
        <h1>History Quiz Answers</h1>
      </header>
      <ol>
        <li>...fourteen hundred and ninety-two.</li>
        <li>...fifteen hundred and eighty-eight.</li>
        <li>...sixteen hundred and sixty-six.</li>
      </ol>
      <p style="text-align: center;">
        <a href="historyquiz.html">Return to the Questions</a>
      </p>
    </section>
  </body>
</html>
```

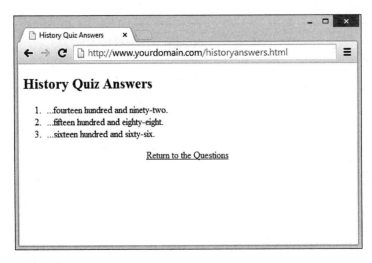

FIGURE 7.4
The Check Your Answers! link in Figure 7.3 takes you to this answers page. The Return to the Questions link takes you back to what's shown in Figure 7.3.

Using filenames instead of complete Internet addresses saves you a lot of typing. More importantly, the links between your pages will work properly no matter where the group of pages is stored. You can test the links while the files are still on your computer's hard drive. You can then move them to a web server, a CD-ROM, a DVD, or a USB drive, and all the links will still work correctly. There is nothing magic about this simplified approach to identifying web pages; it all has to do with web page addressing, as you've already learned.

NOTE

In both Listing 7.2 and Listing 7.3, you'll see the use of the `<section></section>` tag pair around the bulk of the content. You might wonder whether that is entirely necessary—after all, it is the only content on the page. The answer is, no, it isn't entirely necessary. The HTML would validate just fine, and no one looking at this code would be confused by its organization if the `<section></section>` tags were not present. The tags are used here just to make sure you get used to seeing them throughout these code examples and to provide an opportunity to include this note about how you *might* use the `<section></section>` tags at some point in the future. For example, if you were to put both the questions section and the answers section on one page and apply styles and a little bit of JavaScript-based interactivity, you could hide one section (the questions) until the reader clicked a link that would then show the other section (the answers). This action is beyond the scope of these lessons, but it is an example of how the simplest bit of markup can set you up for bigger things later.

Linking to Non-HTML Files

Once you know how to link to an HTML document, you can link to non-HTML documents in the same way. Items like word processing documents and PDF files are examples of other files on the web. To link to them, you just replace the URL in the `href` attribute with the location of the document, as in these examples:

```
<a href="myWordDoc.doc">my word-processed document</a>
<a href="myPDFfile.pdf">my PDF file</a>
```

The first example links to a word processing document (`.doc`), and the second example links to a PDF file (`.pdf`). When these links are clicked, the browser will do one of two things: It will either open the document in the window or it will open a download dialog box that asks the user to download the file.

Sometimes it makes sense to require that a linked document be downloaded to the user's local computer. But web browsers typically try to display as much as they can without downloading, as downloading can be slow, and some operating systems don't allow it. In order to force the browser to open a download dialog box, add the attribute `download` to the link. This is what's called a *Boolean attribute* because it is either on or off. Sometimes you will see them written as having self-referential values, such as `download="download"`. This attribute is new in HTML5 and has good support in all modern browsers except Internet Explorer (but it works in Edge) and iOS Safari.

To force the previous two links to be download links, write the following:

```
<a href="myWordDoc.doc" download>my word-processed document</a>
<a href="myPDFfile.pdf" download>my PDF file</a>
```

Linking to External Web Content

The only difference between linking to pages within your own site and linking to external web content is that when linking outside your site, you need to include the full address to that bit of content. The full address includes the `http://` or `https://` before the domain name and then the full pathname to the file (for example, an HTML file, an image file, a multimedia file, and so on). This is called the *fully qualified domain name* (FQDN).

For example, to include a link to Google from within one of your own web pages, you would use this type of absolute addressing in your <a> link:

```
<a href="https://www.google.com/">Go to Google</a>
```

NOTE
_____

These days, it is more common to see web pages with `https://` as the protocol for the web page URL. This is because more and more servers are using secure SSL certificates to keep their websites secure. You will learn more about this in Lesson 27, "Working with Web-Based Forms."
_____

CAUTION
_____

As you might know, you can leave out the protocol (`http://` or `https://`) at the front of any address when typing it into most web browsers. However, you *cannot* leave out that part when you type an Internet address into an <a `href`> link on a web page.
_____

You can apply what you have learned in previous sections to creating links to named anchors on other pages. Linked anchors are not limited to the same page. You can link to a named anchor on another page by including the address or filename followed by # and the anchor name. For example, the following link would take you to an anchor named `photos` within the `african.html` page inside the `elephants` directory on the (fictional) domain `www.takeme2thezoo.com`:

```
<a href="http://www.takeme2thezoo.com/elephants/african.html#photos">
Check out the African Elephant Photos!</a>
```

If you are linking from another page already on the www.takeme2thezoo.com domain (because you are, in fact, the site maintainer), your link might simply be as follows:

```
<a href="/elephants/african.html#photos">Check out the
African Elephant Photos!</a>
```

The protocol and the domain name would not be necessary in this instance, as you have already learned.

Linking to an Email Address

In addition to linking between pages and between parts of a single page, the <a> tag enables you to link to email addresses. This is the simplest way to enable your web page visitors to talk back to you. Of course, you could just provide visitors with your email address and trust them to type it into whatever email programs they use, but that increases the likelihood for errors. By providing a clickable link to your email address, you make it almost completely effortless for them to send you messages and eliminate the chance for typos.

An HTML link to an email address looks like the following:

```
<a href="mailto:yourusername@yourdomain.com">Send me an
email message.</a>
```

The words Send me an email message will appear just like any other <a> link.

If you want people to see your actual email address (so that they can make note of it or send a message using a different email program), include it both in the href attribute and as part of the message between the <a> and </a> tags, like this:

```
<a href="mailto:you@yourdomain.com">you@yourdomain.com</a>
```

CAUTION

Many spammers use automated tools to harvest email addresses from web pages by looking for mailto links and email addresses. There are ways to try to hide the email address from spammers, but in general if the email address works in the web page, spammers can grab it. So be sure that whatever address you point to has a strong spam filter on it.

In most web browsers, when a user clicks the link, that person gets a window into which he or she can type a message that is immediately sent to the mailto email address—and the email program that person uses to send and receive email will automatically be used.

You can provide some additional information in the link so that the subject and body of the message also have default values. You do this by adding subject and body variables to the mailto link. You separate the variables from the email address with a question mark (?), separate the value from the variable with an equal sign (=), and then separate each of the variable and value pairs with an ampersand (&). You don't have to understand the variable/value terminology at this point. Here is an example of specifying a subject and body for the preceding email example:

```
<a href="mailto:author@somedomain.com?subject=Book Question&body=
When is the next edition coming out?">author@somedomain.com</a>
```

When a user clicks this link, an email message is created with `author@somedomain.com` as the recipient, `Book Question` as the subject of the message, and `When is the next edition coming out?` as the message body.

NOTE

If you want to specify only an email message subject and not the body, you can just leave off the ampersand and the body variable, equal sign, and value text string, as follows:

```
<a href="mailto:author@somedomain.com?subject=Book Question">
author@somedomain.com</a>
```

You can add carbon-copy and blind carbon-copy recipients to the message as well with the `cc` and `bcc` properties, like so:

```
<a href="mailto:author@somedomain.com?subject=
Book Question&cc=coauthor@somedomain.com&
bcc=publisher@somedomain.com">Mail the author</a>
```

This will send the `Book Question` message to author@somedomain.com, cc `coauthor@somedomain.com`, and bcc `publisher@somedomain.com`.

NOTE

If you put an email contact link in the footer of all your web pages, you make it easy for others to contact you; you give them a way to tell you about any problems with the page that your testing might have missed. Use the `<address>` HTML tag to semantically define this email address as the address for the web page.

Opening a Link in a New Browser Window

Now that you have a handle on how to create addresses for links—both internal (within your site) and external (to other sites)—there is one additional method of linking: forcing the user to open links in new windows.

You've no doubt heard of *pop-up windows*, which are browser windows—typically advertising products or services—that are intended to be opened and displayed automatically without the user's approval. Many modern browsers disallow this behavior. However, the concept of opening another window or targeting another location serves a valid purpose in some instances. For example, you might want to present information in a smaller secondary browser window but still allow the user to see the information in the main window. This is often the case when the user is clicking on a link to an animated demo, a movie clip, or some other multimedia element. You might also want to target a new browser window when you are linking to content offsite.

The word *target* is important because this is the name of the attribute used with the <a> tag. The `target` attribute points to a valid browsing context, or "new window to open."

A valid HTML link that opens in a new window is constructed like so:

```
<a href="/some/file.html" target="_blank">Open a Window!</a>
```

The keyword `_blank` is a special target name that tells the browser to open in a new window without a name. The initial underscore (_) is not a typo but is part of the name. You can also give windows names by targeting them with any text designation, such as the following:

```
<a href="/some/file.html" target="newWindow">Open a New Window!</a>
```

In this case, the new window will be called `newWindow`. Any other links you target with that same name will open in that same window.

Remember that forcing a link to open in a new browser window—especially when it's a full-size new window—goes against some principles of usability and accessibility. Best practices recommend that you avoid doing this unless you have no other choice.

Giving Titles to Links

One feature of links that many web designers forget is the `title` attribute. This attribute lets you add to your links descriptions that aren't immediately visible on web pages. For example, this HTML creates a link that reads `Come see my page`:

```
<a href="myPage.html" title="This is the best page on this site">
Come see my page</a>
```

When people view the page, it will display as a standard link, but if they hover over or focus on the link, the browser will display the message `This is the best page on this site`.

Giving title to links is especially useful for people who rely on screen readers, as they can get a little more information about a link before they click on it. You can also use the `title` attribute as a style hook. To reference every link with a `title` attribute you write the following:

```
a[title] { /* put styles here */ }
```

Think of the `title` attribute as a way to give a little more information about a link without taking up space on the page. It's not meant to be a repetition of the link text, as that would be pointless and boring. And it does nothing for search engine visibility, so don't fill it with spammy keyword phrases. Use it to provide more useful information. If you don't have any more useful information, don't use the `title` attribute.

Using CSS to Style Hyperlinks

The default display of a text-based hyperlink on a web page is underlined blue text. You might also have noticed that links you have previously visited appear as underlined purple text; that color is also a default. If you've spent any time at all on the Web, you will also have noticed that not all links are blue or purple—and for that we are all thankful. Using a little CSS and knowledge of the various pseudo-classes for the <a> link, you can make your links look however you want.

NOTE

You can use graphics as links (instead of using text as links) by putting an <img> tag between the opening <a> and closing </a> tags.

A *pseudo-class* is a class that describes styles for elements that apply to certain circumstances, such as various states of user interaction with that element.

For example, these are the common pseudo-classes for the <a> tag:

▶ `a:link`—Describes the style of a hyperlink that has not been visited previously.

▶ `a:visited`—Describes the style of a hyperlink that has been visited previously and is present in the browser's memory.

▶ `a:hover`—Describes the style of a hyperlink as a user's mouse hovers over it (and before it has been clicked).

▶ `a:focus`—Describes the style of a hyperlink as the user activates the link. This is often used on devices where there is no mouse, so clicking is not possible.

▶ `a:active`—Describes the style of a hyperlink that is in the act of being clicked but has not yet been released.

NOTE

It's important to remember to style the `:focus` property because many people today use devices without mice to view web pages. Most people view web pages on tablets and smartphones more often than on computers with mice. And `:focus` is also important for accessibility to people who use the keyboard to navigate the web.

For example, let's say you want to produce a link with the following styles:

- ▶ A font that is bold and Verdana (and not underlined, meaning it has no text decoration)
- ▶ A base color that is light blue
- ▶ The color red when users hover over it, give it focus, or are clicking it
- ▶ The color gray after users have visited it

Your style sheet entries might look like the following:

```
a {
    font-family: Verdana, sans-serif;
    font-weight: bold;
    text-decoration: none;
}
a:link {
    color: #6479A0;
}
a:visited {
    color: #cccccc;
}
a:hover {
    color: #e03a3e;
}
a:focus {
    color: #e03a3e;
}
a:active {
    color: #e03a3e;
}
```

NOTE

The colors in this example are indicated by their hexadecimal values.

Because the sample link will be Verdana bold (and not underlined), regardless of the state it is in, those three property and value pairs can reside in the rule for the a selector. However, because each pseudo-class must have a specific color associated with it, we use a rule for each pseudo-class, as shown in the code example. The pseudo-class inherits the style of the parent rule unless the rule for the pseudo-class specifically overrides that rule. In other words, all the pseudo-classes in the preceding example will be Verdana bold (and not underlined). However, if we used the following rule for the hover pseudo-class, the text would display in Comic Sans when users hover over it (if, in fact, they have the Comic Sans font installed):

```
a:hover {
    font-family: "Comic Sans MS";
    color: #e03a3e;
}
```

In addition, because the `active`, `focus`, and `hover` pseudo-classes use the same font color, you can combine style rules for them:

```
a:hover, a:focus, a:active {
   color: #e03a3e;
}
```

Listing 7.4 puts these code snippets together to produce a page using styled pseudo-classes; Figure 7.5 shows the results of this code.

LISTING 7.4   Using Styles to Display Link Pseudo-classes

```
<!doctype html>
<html lang="en">
  <head>
    <meta charset="utf-8">
    <title>Sample Link Style</title>
    <style>
    a {
      font-family: Verdana, sans-serif;
      font-weight: bold;
      text-decoration: none;
    }
    a:link {
      color: #6479a0;
    }
    a:visited {
       color: #cccccc;
    }
    a:hover, a:active {
       color: #ff0000;
    }
    </style>
  </head>
  <body>
    <h1>Sample Link Style</h1>
    <p><a href="simplelinkstyle.html">The first time you see me,
    I should be a light blue, bold, non-underlined link in
    the Verdana font</a>.</p>
  </body>
</html>
```

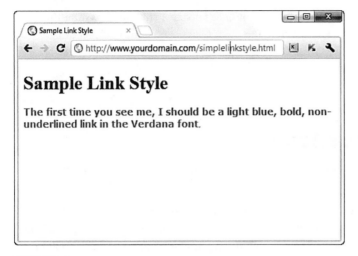

FIGURE 7.5
A link can use particular styles to control the visual display.

If you view the example in your web browser, indeed the link should be a light blue, bold, non-underlined Verdana font. If you hover over the link or click the link without releasing it, it should turn red. If you click and release the link, the page simply reloads because the link points to the file with the same name. However, at that point, the link is in your browser's memory and thus is displayed as a visited link—and it appears gray instead of blue.

You can use CSS to apply a wide range of text-related changes to your links. You can change fonts, sizes, weights, decoration, and so on. Sometimes you might want several sets of link styles in your style sheet. In that case, you can create classes; you aren't limited to working with only one set of styles for the <a> tag. The following example is a set of style sheet rules for a `footerlink` class for links you might want to place in the footer area of a website:

```
a.footerlink {
    font-family: Verdana, sans-serif;
    font-weight: bold;
    font-size: 75%;
    text-decoration: none;
}
a.footerlink:link,
a.footerlink:visited {
    color: #6479a0;
}
a.footerlink:hover,
a.footerlink:active,
a.footerlink:focus {
    color: #e03a3e;
}
```

As you can see in the example that follows, the class name (`footerlink`) appears after the selector name (`a`), separated by a dot, and before the pseudo-class name (`hover`), separated by a colon:

```
selector.class:pseudo-class
a.footerlink:hover
```

Using Links Effectively

Throughout this lesson we've mentioned a few best practices for using links effectively, but there are a few more you should be aware of:

▶ **Make your links stand out**—Links should stand out from the text on the page so that customers know that they can do something with them. You can make your links stand out by changing their color, changing their background color, underlining them (the default in most browsers), making their font larger, making them bold, or in other ways. The important thing is that for links to work, your users must know they are links.

▶ **For links use only link styles**—This is the corollary to the first rule. If your links are to stand out, they must look different from the surrounding text. If you underline links, then you should not underline non-links. The same idea applies to link colors: If you color your links red, then you should not use red for other, non-link text.

▶ **Style visited links**—It's important to let people know when they've been to a page before. Users get frustrated when they end up in a loop of links because the visited links look the same as the unvisited ones. A good rule of thumb is to use a slightly darker shade of the same color you used for the standard links. This provides a visual cue that the links are visited without messing with your design.

▶ **Use descriptive content for link text**—It's tempting to write "Click here" and make just those two words the link, but such links are harder to use. There is nothing about "Click here" that says what the user will get when he or she clicks. It forces the reader to scan the rest of the content to determine whether it's worth clicking, and the more work you make your readers do, the more likely they will be to go to someone else's site. Note that this doesn't mean you can't say "Click here"; just don't have that be the only text that is clickable.

▶ **Add padding to text links**—Padding is the space surrounding links. By adding padding, you ensure that your links are more clickable, even if the words are very small. To add some padding, you could write: `a { padding: 3px; }`. This is especially important for navigation links. You'll learn more about padding in Lesson 9, "Working with Margins, Padding, Alignment, and Floating."

▶ **Link images**—Usability studies have shown that people notice and click on images even when they are not links. So if you have images on your web pages, it makes sense to make them links. At a bare minimum, you should link your logo to your home page, but any other images on you pages should be linked as well.

▶ **Use icons to aid in comprehension**—You can add icons to links to help people quickly see where they go. There are icons for all kinds of things, from social media to file types to entertainment and more.

▶ **Avoid tiny links**—Small links are hard to click and can be nearly impossible to tap on a touchscreen device. The smaller the text, the harder it is for your readers to use. If your site targets seniors, you should use fonts for all your text of at least 12 points.

Summary

The <a> tag is what makes hypertext "hyper." With it, you can create links between pages, as well as links to specific anchor points on any page. This lesson focused on creating and styling simple links to other pages by using either relative or absolute addressing to identify the pages.

You learned that when you're creating links to other people's pages, it's important to include the full Internet address of each page in an <a href> tag. For links between your own pages, include just the filenames and enough directory information to get from one page to another.

You also learned how to create named anchor points within a page and how to create links to a specific anchor. You learned how to link to your email address so that users can easily send messages to you. You also learned how to protect your email address from spammers. Finally, you learned methods for controlling the display of your links by using CSS and some of the best practices for linking based on over 20 years of web design.

Table 7.1 summarizes the <a> tag discussed in this lesson.

TABLE 7.1 HTML Tags and Attributes Covered in Lesson 7

Tag/Attribute	Function
<a>...</a>	With the href attribute, creates a link to another document or anchor. With the id attribute, creates an anchor that can be linked to.
Attributes	*Function*
href="*address*"	Specifies the address of the document or anchor point to link to.
id="*name*"	Specifies the name for this anchor point in the document.

Q&A

Q. What happens if I link to a page on the Internet, and then the person who owns that page deletes or moves it?

A. It depends on how the maintainer of that external page has set up his or her web server. Usually, you will see a `page not found` message (sometimes called a 404 page, referencing the HTTP error code the server delivers) when you click a link that has been moved or deleted. You can still click the Back button to return to your page. As a site maintainer, you can periodically run link-checking programs to ensure that your internal and external links are valid. An example of this is the Link Checker service at https://validator.w3.org/checklink.

Q. One of the internal links on my website works fine on my computer, but when I put the pages on the Internet, the link doesn't work anymore. What's up?

A. These are the most likely culprits:

▶ **Capitalization problems**—On Windows computers, linking to a file named `MyFile.html` with `<a href="myfile.html">` works. On most web servers, the link must be `<a href="MyFile.html">` or you must change the name of the file to `myfile.html`. To make matters worse, some text editors and file transfer programs actually change the capitalization without telling you. The best solution is to stick with all-lowercase filenames for web pages.

▶ **Spaces in filenames**—Most web servers don't allow filenames with spaces. For example, you should never name a web page `my page.html`. Instead, name it `mypage.html` or even `my_page.html` or `my-page.html` (using an underscore or dash instead of a space).

▶ **Local absolute addresses**—If you link to a file using a local absolute address, such as `C:\mywebsite\news.html`, the link won't work when you place the file on the Internet. You should never use local absolute addresses; when this occurs, it is usually an accident caused by a temporary link that was created to test part of a page. So be careful to remove any test links before publishing a page on the Web.

Q. Can I put both `href` and `id` in the same `<a>` tag? Would I want to do this for any reason?

A. You can, and it might save you some typing if you have a named anchor point and a link right next to each other. It's generally better, however, to use the `id` attribute on another element entirely to avoid confusion. Remember that they play very different roles in an HTML document.

Q. What happens if I accidentally misspell the name of an anchor or forget to put the # in front of it?

A. If you link to an anchor name that doesn't exist within a page or if you misspell the anchor name, the link goes to the top of that page. If you write an anchor without a URL or # in front of it, the browser will attempt to take you to a page by the same name, which will usually result in a Page Not Found error.

Workshop

The Workshop contains quiz questions and exercises to help you solidify your understanding of the material covered.

Quiz

1. Your best friend from elementary school finds you on the Internet and says he wants to trade home page links. How do you put a link to his site at www.supercheapsuits.com/~billybob/ on one of your pages?

2. What HTML would you use to make it possible for someone clicking the words "About the Authors" at the top of a page to skip down to a list of credits somewhere else on the page?

3. If your email address is bon@soir.com, how would you make the text "goodnight greeting" into a link that people can click to compose and send you an email message?

4. What attribute can you add to an HTML element to turn it into an anchor?

5. What character do you use to link to an anchor?

6. How do you tell a browser that the link target document should be downloaded rather than loaded in the window?

7. When should you include `http://` in a link?

8. What mail features can you use in a mailto link?

9. When is the best case to force a link to open in a new window?

10. What pseudo-class do you use to style visited links?

NOTE

Just a reminder for those of you reading these words in the print or e-book edition of this book: If you go to **www.informit.com/register** and register this book (using ISBN 9780672338083), you can receive free access to an online Web Edition that not only contains the complete text of this book but also features an interactive version of this quiz.

Answers

1. Put the following on your page:

   ```
   <a href="http://www.supercheapsuits.com/~billybob/">Billy
   Bob's site</a>
   ```

2. Type this at the top of the page:

   ```
   <a href="#credits">About the Authors</a>
   ```

   Type this at the beginning of the credits section:

   ```
   <anytag id="credits">
   ```

3. Type the following on your web page:

   ```
   Send me a <a href="mailto:bon@soir.com">goodnight greeting</a>!
   ```

4. The `id` attribute can be used on any HTML element as an anchor.

5. You use the pound sign (#) to link to a named anchor point on the page.

6. Use the attribute `download` to tell the browser the link target should be downloaded.

7. You should include the `http://` and the rest of the FQDN when you are linking to a page outside the current site.

8. You must point to the email address the message is to. Optional values are `subject`, `body`, `cc`, and `bcc`.

9. You should avoid forcing links to open in a new window at all costs.

10. Use the `a:visited` pseudo-class to style visited links.

Exercises

▶ Create an HTML file consisting of a formatted list of your favorite websites. You might already have these sites bookmarked in your web browser, in which case you can visit them to find the exact URL in the browser's address bar.

▶ If you have created any pages for a website, look through them and consider whether there are any places in the text where you'd like to make it easy for people to contact you. Include a link to your email address there. You can never provide too many opportunities for people to contact you and tell you what they need or what they think about your products—especially if you're running a business.

LESSON 8
Working with Colors, Images, and Multimedia

This lesson covers a lot of topics, but have no fear, for each of these tasks is short and sweet, and this lesson will help you move your web development experience from the white background/ black text examples so far in this series to more interesting (or at least colorful) examples. But that's not to say that dark text on a light background is bad; in fact, it's the most common color combination you'll find online.

Paying attention to color schemes and producing a visually appealing website is important, but you don't have to be an artist by trade to implement high-impact color schemes in your website or to put a few appealing flourishes on what would otherwise be a drab, square world. You don't need to spend hundreds or thousands of dollars on software packages, either, just to manipulate digital photographs or other source graphics you might want to use. The topics in this lesson should help you understand the very basics of color theory and how to modify colors using CSS, as well as how to create images you can use in your website.

NOTE
_____

Although the sample figures in this lesson use a popular and free graphics program for Windows, Mac, and Linux users (GNU Image Manipulation Program [GIMP]), you can apply the knowledge you learn in this lesson to any major Windows or Mac graphics application—although the menus and options will look different, of course.

_____

After you learn to create the graphics themselves, you'll be ready to include them in your website. Beyond just the basics of using the HTML <img> tag to include images for display in a web browser, you'll learn how to provide descriptions of these images (and why). You'll also learn about image placement, including how to use images as backgrounds for different elements. You'll learn how to use image maps, which enable you to use a single image as a link to multiple locations.

Finally, you'll learn a little bit about working with multimedia. The term *multimedia* encompasses everything we see and hear on a web page: audio, video, and animation, as well as static images and text. Although you won't learn how to create any particular audio or video, you will learn how to include such files in your site, through either linking or embedding the content.

Best Practices for Choosing Colors

We can't tell you exactly which colors to use in your website, but we can help you understand certain considerations when selecting colors on your own. The colors you use can greatly influence your visitors; for example, if you are running an e-commerce site, you want to use colors that entice your users to view your catalog and eventually purchase something. If you are creating a text-heavy site, you want to make sure the color scheme helps create easy-to-read text. Overall, you want to make sure you use colors judiciously and with respect.

You might wonder how respect enters into the mix when talking about colors. Remember that the World Wide Web is an international community and that people's interpretations differ. For instance, pink is very popular in Japan but very unpopular in Eastern European countries. Similarly, green is the color of money in the United States, but the vast majority of other countries have multicolored paper bills—"the color of money" thus isn't a single color at all, so the metaphor would be of no value to international visitors.

Besides using culturally sensitive colors, other best practices include the following:

▶ **Use a natural palette of colors**—This doesn't mean you should use earth tones; rather, you should use colors that you would naturally see on a casual stroll around town and avoid ultra-bright colors that can cause eye strain.

▶ **Use accessible color combinations**—Color blindness is not uncommon, and you should avoid using color as the only differentiator for important information. For example, if you need to display a warning, you can change the text or background color, but you should also add an icon or other aid to indicate the problem. For accessibility, you might consider using the Toptal Colorblind Web Page Filter tool at www.toptal.com/designers/colorfilter to see how your site looks to a person with colorblindness.

▶ **Use colors with good contrast, especially for blocks of text**—The reason that black text on a white background is so popular is because it has good contrast and so is easy to read. Avoid using background/foreground color combinations that have too little contrast. You can test the contrast of two colors at https://webaim.org/resources/contrastchecker/.

▶ **Use a small color palette**—You don't need to use 15 colors to achieve your goals. In fact, if your page includes text and images in 15 colors, you might reevaluate the message you're attempting to send. Focus on 3 or 4 main colors, with 1 or 2 complementary colors at most.

▶ **Consider your demographics**—You likely can't control your demographics, so you have to find a middle ground that accommodates everyone. The colors younger people enjoy are not necessarily the same ones older people appreciate, just as there are color biases between men and women and between people from different geographic regions and cultures.

You might now be thinking that your color options are limited. Not so. You simply need to think about the decisions you're making before you make them. A search for "color theory" in the search engine of your choice should give you more food for thought, as will the use of a color wheel.

A *color wheel* is a chart that shows the organization of colors in a circular manner. Its method of display is an attempt to help you visualize the relationships among primary, secondary, and complementary colors. Color schemes are developed from working with the color wheel; understanding color schemes can help you determine the color palette to use consistently throughout your website. For example, knowing something about color relationships will hopefully enable you to avoid using orange text on a light blue background, or bright blue text on a brown background.

Some common color schemes in web design are given here:

▶ **Analogous**—Using colors that are adjacent to each other on the color wheel, such as yellow and green. One color is the dominant color, and its analogous friend enriches the display.

▶ **Complementary**—Using colors that are opposite each other on the color wheel, such as a warm color (red) and a cool color (green).

▶ **Monochromatic**—Using colors that are all the same primary hue. The secondary colors are created by adding white and black to the primary color.

▶ **Triadic**—Using three colors that are equally spaced around the color wheel. The triadic scheme provides balance while still allowing rich color use.

Entire books and courses are devoted to understanding color theory, so continuing the discussion in this lesson would indeed be a tangent. However, if you intend to work in web design and development, you will be served well with a solid understanding of the basics of color theory. Spend some time reading about it; an online search will provide a wealth of information.

In addition, spend some hands-on time with the color wheel. The color scheme designer Paletton, at http://paletton.com, enables you to start with a base color and produce monochromatic, complementary, triadic, tetradic, analogic, and accented analogic color schemes.

Understanding Web Colors

Specifying a background color other than white for a web page is easier than you probably realize. For example, to specify blue as the background color for a page, put `style="background-color:blue;"` inside the <body> tag or in the style sheet rule for the body element. Of course, you can use many colors other than blue. In fact, the W3C standards list 16 colors: aqua, black, blue, fuchsia, gray, green, lime, maroon, navy, olive, purple, red, silver, teal, white, and yellow.

NOTE

The CSS color gray has the U.S. spelling in the standards document. But most web browsers also support grey as an alternate spelling. However, the CSS style properties `color` and `background-color` must be spelled with the U.S. spelling.

Obviously, many more than just those 16 colors are displayed on the Web. In fact, you can use 140 color names with the assurance that all browsers will display these colors similarly. Here's a partial list of the 140 descriptive color names: azure, bisque, cornflowerblue, darksalmon, firebrick, honeydew, lemonchiffon, papayawhip, peachpuff, saddlebrown, thistle, tomato, wheat, and whitesmoke.

NOTE

For a complete list of the 140 descriptive color names, as well as their hexadecimal codes and an example of the color as displayed by your browser, visit www.w3.org/TR/SVG/types.html#ColorKeywords.

But names are subjective. For instance, if you look at the color chart of 140 cross-browser color names, you'll see that you can't distinguish between fuchsia and magenta. The associated RGB color values for those two color, fuchsia and magenta, are also exactly the same: `rgb(255, 0, 255)`. You'll learn about RGB color values in the next section, but for now, know that if you want to be standards compliant and use more than the 16 color names the W3C standards dictate, you should use RGB or hexadecimal color values.

NOTE

Color names are not case sensitive. So `Black`, `black`, and `BLACK` are all black, although most web designers stick with lowercase or mixed case (if they use color names at all; most designers use hexadecimal notation for a more nuanced approach to color use).

Hexadecimal color codes make possible 16 million colors, and most modern computer displays can display all of them. However, be aware that not all computer monitors display colors in the same hues. What might appear as a beautiful light blue background color on your monitor might be more of a purple hue on another user's monitor. Neutral, earth-tone colors (such as medium gray, tan, and ivory) can produce even more unpredictable results on many computer monitors. These colors might even seem to change color on a single monitor, depending on lighting conditions in the room or the time of day.

In addition to changing the background of your pages to a color other than white, you can change the color of text links, including various properties of links (such as the color for when a user hovers over a link versus when the user clicks a link—as you learned in previous lessons). You can also set the background color of container elements (such as paragraphs, sections, block quotes, and table cells), and you can use colors to specify the borders around those elements. You'll see some examples of colors and container elements later in this lesson.

There are plenty of very bad websites, some created by earnest people with no trace of irony whatsoever. However, the World's Worst Website, in Figure 8.1, was purposefully created to show some of the more egregious sins of website design, especially in terms of the use of colors. A screenshot does not do it justice, though (especially in the printed version of this book, which is in black and white), so visit and experience the site for yourself, at www.angelfire.com/super/badwebs/main .htm. For the full effect, make sure to have your sound turned on.

If you search for "bad website examples" in your search engine, you will find many sites that collect examples of bad design and explain just why such a site should be in a Hall of Shame rather than a Hall of Fame. Many sites are considered bad because of their visual displays, and the display begins with color selection. Therefore, understanding colors, including the nuances of their specification and use, is a crucial step in creating a good website.

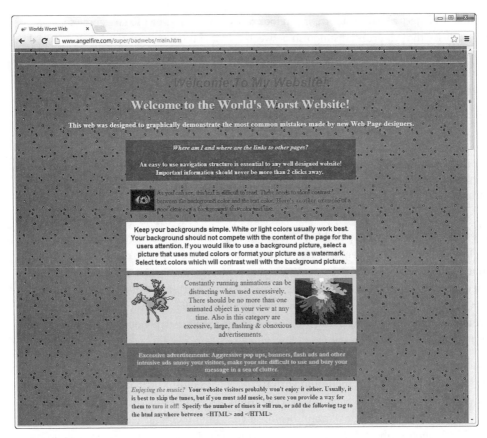

FIGURE 8.1
A partial screenshot of the World's Worst Website.

Using Hexadecimal Values for Colors

To remain standards compliant, as well as to retain precise control over the colors in your website, you can reference colors by their hexadecimal values. The hexadecimal value of a color is an indication of how much red, green, and blue light should be mixed into each color. It works a little bit like Play-Doh: Just mix in the amounts of red, blue, and green you want in order to get the appropriate color.

The hexadecimal color format is *#rrggbb*, in which *rr*, *gg*, and *bb* are two-digit hexadecimal values for the red (*rr*), green (*gg*), and blue (*bb*) components of the color. If you're not familiar with hexadecimal numbers, don't sweat it. Just remember that ff is the maximum, and 00 is the minimum. Use one of the following codes for each component:

- ff means full brightness.
- cc means 80% brightness.

▶ 99 means 60% brightness.

▶ 66 means 40% brightness.

▶ 33 means 20% brightness.

▶ 00 means none of this color component.

For example, bright red is #ff0000, dark green is #003300, bluish-purple is #660099, and medium gray is #999999. To make a page with a red background and dark green text, you could use the following HTML code within inline styles:

```
<body style="background-color:#ff0000; color:#003300;">
```

Although only 6 examples of two-digit hexadecimal values are shown here, there are actually 256 combinations of two-digit hexadecimal values: 0–9 and a–f, paired up. For example, f0 is a possible hex value (decimal value 240), 62 is a possible hex value (decimal value 98), and so on.

As previously discussed, the *rr*, *gg*, and *bb* in the #*rrggbb* hexadecimal color code format stand for the red, green, and blue components of the color. Each of those components has a decimal value ranging from 0 (no color) to 255 (full color).

So white (or #ffffff) translates to a red value of 255, a green value of 255, and a blue value of 255. Similarly, black (#000000) translates to a red value of 0, a green value of 0, and a blue value of 0. True red is #ff0000 (all red, no green, and no blue), true green is #00ff00 (no red, all green, no blue), and true blue is #0000ff (no red, no green, and all blue). All other hexadecimal notations translate to some variation of the 255 possible values for each of the three colors. The cross-browser-compatible color name cornflowerblue is associated with the hexadecimal notation #6495ed—a red value of 100, a green value of 149, and a blue value of 237 (almost all of the available blue values).

When picking colors, either through a graphics program or by finding something online that you like, you might see the color notation in hexadecimal or decimal. If you type "hexadecimal color converter" into your search engine, you will find numerous options to help you convert color values into something you can use in your style sheets.

Using RGB and RGBa Values for Colors

Hexadecimal codes define the red, green, and blue percentages of each color for millions of colors. But you can also define those colors with RGB values. The RGB format is rgb(*red*, *green*, *blue*), where *red*, *green*, and *blue* are values of 0 to 255—just like hexadecimal, but written in base-10 numbers (decimal) rather than base-16 (hexadecimal). You simply need to remember that 255 is the maximum, and 0 is the minimum.

Use the following values in your RGB colors:

- 255 means full brightness.
- 204 means 80% brightness.
- 153 means 60% brightness.
- 102 means 40% brightness.
- 51 means 20% brightness.
- 0 means none of this color component.

To make a page with a red background and dark green text using RGB, you could use the following CSS:

```
background-color:rgb(255,0,0); color:rgb(0,51,0);
```

Every hexadecimal color code has a corresponding RGB code. So white (or #ffffff) is the same as rgb(255,255,255). Black (#000000) is rgb(0,0,0). True red is rgb(255,255,255), true green is rgb(0,255,0), and true blue is rgb(0,0,255). All other hexadecimal notations translate to some variation of the 255 possible values for each of the three colors. The cross-browser-compatible color name cornflowerblue is associated with the hexadecimal notation #6495ed and the RGB notation rgb(100,149,237). There are lots of color conversion apps online.

Designers often use RGB codes because a lot of graphics programs are set up to use RGB. But the better reason to use RGB is RGBa—RGB with alpha transparency. RGBa allows you to set the opaqueness or transparency of a color. The more transparent a color is, the more of the background color will show through.

To define the alpha transparency, you write your RGB color with one extra value: rgba(*red*, *green*, *blue*, *transparency*). The *transparency* value is a number between 0 and 1, representing the transparency percentage. 0 is fully transparent, meaning the background is all you see, 1 is fully opaque meaning the background is completely covered, and 0.5 is 50% transparent.

To make a page with faded cornflowerblue text on a white background, you could use this CSS:

```
body { color: rgba(100,149,237,0.5); }
```

You could then change the transparency to 1 for bold text, to make it stand out more, with this CSS:

```
strong { color: rgba(100,149,237,1); font-weight: normal; }
```

Remember when using RGBa that the color of the foreground depends on the color of the background. While rgba(100,149,237,0.5) is a pale blue on a white background, it is going to look darker on a black background.

Using CSS to Set Background, Text, and Border Colors

When using CSS, it's most common to use color values in three instances: when specifying the background color, the text color, or the border color of elements. In Lesson 7, "Using External and Internal Links," you learned about using colors for various link states, and in this lesson, we focus on basic element display.

Figure 8.2 shows an example of color usage that could very easily go into a web design Hall of Shame. We can't imagine ever using these combinations of colors and styles in a serious website, but it serves here as an example of how color style *could* be applied to various elements. The image printed here will likely not do justice to the horrific colors used (especially if you're reading a printed copy of this book, which is in black and white) so be sure to open the sample file or type up the code in Listing 8.1 and load it in your browser.

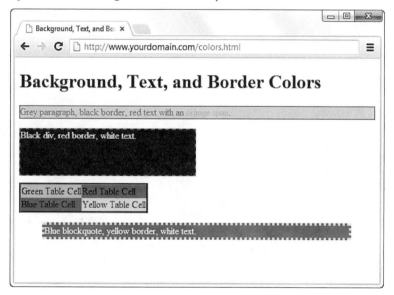

FIGURE 8.2
You can set background, text, and border colors by using CSS.

Listing 8.1 shows the HTML and CSS styles used to produce Figure 8.2.

LISTING 8.1   Using Styles to Produce Background, Text, and Border Colors

```
<!doctype html>
<html lang="en">
  <head>
    <meta charset="utf-8">
    <title>Background, Text, and Border Colors</title>
    <style>
```

```
#uglyparagraph {
    background-color: #cccccc;
    color: #ff0000;
    border:1px solid #000000;
}
.orange {
    color: #ffa500
}
#uglydiv {
    width: 300px;
    height: 75px;
    margin-bottom: 12px;
    background-color: #000000;
    border: 2px dashed #ff0000;
    color: #ffffff;
}
table {
    border: 1px solid #000;
    border-spacing: 2px;
    border-style: outset;
    border-collapse: collapse;
}
.greencell {
    background-color: #00ff00;
}
.redcell {
    background-color: #ff0000;
}
.bluecell {
    background-color: #0000ff;
}
.yellowcell {
    background-color: #ffff00;
}
#uglybq {
    background-color: #0000ff;
    border:4px dotted #ffff00;
    color:#ffffff;
}
    </style>
</head>
<body>
  <h1>Background, Text, and Border Colors</h1>
  <p id="uglyparagraph">Grey paragraph, black border, red text
  with an <span class="orange">orange span</span>.</p>
  <div id="uglydiv">Black div, red border, white text. </div>
  <table>
    <tr>
      <td class="greencell">Green Table Cell</td>
```

```
        <td class="redcell">Red Table Cell</td>
      </tr>
      <tr>
        <td class="bluecell">Blue Table Cell</td>
        <td class="yellowcell">Yellow Table Cell</td>
      </tr>
    </table>
    <blockquote id="uglybq">
      Blue blockquote, yellow border, white text.
    </blockquote>
  </body>
</html>
```

Looking at the styles in Listing 8.1, you should be able to figure out almost everything except some of the border styles. In CSS you can't designate a border as a color without also having a width and type. In the first example in Listing 8.1, for `uglyparagraph`, the border width is `1px`, and the border type is `solid`. In the example for `uglydiv`, the border width is `2px`, and the border type is `dashed`. In the `uglybq` example, the border width is `4px`, and the border type is `dotted`.

When picking colors for your website, remember that a little goes a long way. If you really like a bright and spectacular color, use it as an accent color, not throughout the primary design elements. In addition, remember that light backgrounds with dark text are much easier to read than dark backgrounds with light text.

Choosing Graphics Software

You can use almost any graphics program to create and edit images for your website, from the simple painting or drawing program that typically comes free with your computer's operating system, to an expensive professional program such as Adobe Photoshop. Similarly, if you have a digital camera or scanner attached to your computer, it probably came with some graphics software capable of creating images suitable for online use. Several free image editors also are available for download— or even online as web applications—that deal just with the manipulation of photographic elements.

NOTE
Without a doubt, Adobe Photoshop is the cream of the crop when it comes to image-editing programs. However, it is expensive and quite complex and so may not be a great choice for someone who doesn't have experience working with computer graphics. For more information on Adobe's products, visit the Adobe website, at www.adobe.com. If you are in the market for one of the company's products, you can download a free evaluation version from the site.

If you already have software you think might be good for creating web graphics, try using it to do everything described in these next sections. If your software can't handle some of the tasks covered here, it probably isn't a good tool for web graphics. In that case, download and install GIMP from www.gimp.org. This fully functional graphics program is completely free and can definitely perform the actions shown in this lesson.

Using Images Found Elsewhere

One of the best ways to save time creating graphics and media files for web pages is, of course, to avoid creating them altogether. Grabbing a graphic from any web page is as simple as right-clicking it (or Option+clicking with an Apple mouse) and selecting Save Image As or Save Picture As (depending on the browser). Extracting a background image from a page is just as easy: Right-click it and select Save Background As.

However, you should *never* use images without the explicit permission of the owner, either by asking or by looking for a Creative Commons license. Using images without explicit permission is a copyright violation (and is also distasteful). To learn more about copyrights, we recommend the Copyright Crash Course online tutorial from the University of Texas, at http://guides.lib.utexas.edu/copyright.

You might also want to consider using royalty-free clip art, which doesn't require you to get copyright permission. One good source of copyright-free photos and images is Pixabay (https://pixabay.com). These images are released under Creative Commons CCO, which makes them free to use without permission or attribution, even for commercial purposes. Clipart.com is a popular clip art destination; for a small fee this site gives you access to thousands of stock images.

If GIMP doesn't suit you, consider downloading the evaluation version of CorelDRAW for Windows or Macintosh (www.coreldraw.com) or Acorn for Macintosh (https://flyingmeat.com/acorn/). For photo manipulation only, there are many free options, all with helpful features. Pixlr (https://pixlr.com) is a good option. It is suited for editing images rather than creating them from scratch. These types of programs won't necessarily help you design a banner or button image for your site; however, they can help you work with some supplementary images, and they are powerful enough that they're worth checking out.

The Least You Need to Know About Graphics

Two forces are always at odds when you post graphics and multimedia on the Internet. The users' eyes and ears want all your content to be as detailed and accurate as possible, and they also want information to be displayed immediately. Intricate, colorful graphics mean big file sizes, which increase the transfer time—even over a fast connection. How do you maximize the quality of your presentation while minimizing file size? To make these choices, you need to understand how color and resolution work together to create a subjective sense of quality.

The resolution of an image is the number of individual dots, or pixels, that make up an image (typically 72 dots per inch, or 72dpi). Large, high-resolution images generally take longer to transfer and display than small, low-resolution images. Image dimensions are usually specified as the width times the height of the image, expressed in pixels; a 300×200 image, for example, is 300 pixels wide and 200 pixels high.

NOTE
Several types of image resolution are used, including pixel, spatial, spectral, temporal, and radiometric. You could spend hours just learning about each type—and if you were taking a graphics design class, you might do just that. For now, however, all you need to remember is that large images take longer to download and also use a lot of space in your display. Display size and storage or transfer size are factors to take into consideration when you are designing a website.

You might be surprised to find that resolution isn't the most significant factor in determining an image file's storage size (and transfer time). This is because images used on web pages are always stored and transferred in compressed form. Image compression is the mathematical manipulation that images are put through to squeeze out repetitive patterns. The mathematics of image compression are complex, but the basic idea is that repeating patterns or large areas of the same color can be squeezed out when the image is stored on a disk. This makes the image file much smaller and allows it to be transferred faster over the Internet. The web browser then restores the original appearance of the image when the image is displayed.

In the sections that follow, you'll learn how to create graphics with big visual impact but small file sizes. The techniques you use to accomplish this depend on the contents and purpose of each image. There are as many uses for web graphics as there are web pages, but four types of graphics are by far the most common:

- ▶ Photos of people, products, and places

- ▶ Graphical banners and logos

- ▶ Buttons or icons to indicate actions and provide links

- ▶ Background textures for container elements

Preparing Photographic Images

To put photos on your web pages, you need to convert your print-based photos to digital images or create photos digitally by using a digital camera, such as the camera in your smartphone. In the case of some older models of hardware, you might need to use the custom software that came with your device to transfer images to your hard drive, but in most cases, you should be able to connect your device and then drag and drop files to your hard drive. If you are using a scanner to create digital versions of your print photos, you can control just about any scanner directly from the graphics program of your choice; see your software documentation for details.

NOTE
If you don't have a scanner or digital camera, note that almost all film developers offer the service of transferring photos from 35mm film to a CD-ROM or DVD-ROM for a modest fee. You can then copy the files to your hard drive and use your graphics program to open and modify the image files.

After you transfer the digital image files to your computer, you can use your graphics program to crop, resize, color-correct, and compress to get them ready for use in your website.

Cropping an Image

Because you want web page graphics to be as compact as possible, you usually need to crop your digital photos. When you *crop* a photo, you select the area you want to display and crop away the rest.

▼ TRY IT YOURSELF

Cropping in GIMP

The GIMP toolbox offers quick access to the crop tool and its possible attributes. Find an image file—either a digital image you have taken with your camera and stored on your hard drive or an image you found online. After opening the image in GIMP, perform the following steps to crop it in GIMP:

1. In the GIMP toolbox, click the Crop tool (see Figure 8.3). Depending on the tool you select, you might have additional attributes you can select. For example, Figure 8.3 shows the attributes for the cropping tool (such as the aspect ratio, position, size, and so on).

FIGURE 8.3
Select the Crop tool from the toolbox.

2. In the image you want to crop, draw a box around the selection by clicking the upper-left corner of the portion of the image you want to keep and holding down the left mouse button while you drag down to the lower-right corner. See Figure 8.4.

FIGURE 8.4
Select the area of the image that you want to display. *(Credit: Scott Prokop/Shutterstock)*

3. Click one of the corners of the selection to apply the cropping.

Your graphics program will likely have a different method than the one shown, but the concept is the same: Select the area to keep and then crop out the rest.

Even after your image has been cropped, it might be larger than it needs to be for a web page. For most responsive designs, your images don't need to be more than 2000 pixels wide. This would allow the image to expand up to 2000px on large screens without losing quality. If you never plan on using the image all by itself on a page, you can crop the image smaller, but the larger the starting image is, the more screens it will support.

NOTE

Your graphics software will likely have an omnipresent size display somewhere in the image window itself. In GIMP, you can see the current image size in the window title bar. Other programs might show it in the lower-right corner or the lower-left corner. You might also see the magnification ratio in the window, and you might be able to change it by zooming in or out.

The key to good cropping is to remove unwanted details from the image. One way to do this is with the rule of thirds. Positioning the interesting elements at the top, right, bottom, or left third of the image makes the whole thing more visually interesting. Other cropping rules you can apply include the golden ratio, golden spiral, triangle, and diagonal crops.

Resizing an Image

The exact tool necessary to change an image's size depends on the program you are using. In GIMP, go to the Image menu and click Scale Image to open the Scale Image dialog box (see Figure 8.5).

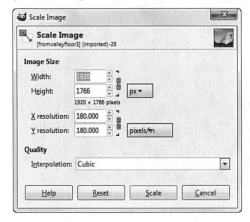

FIGURE 8.5
Use the Scale Image dialog box to change the size of an image.

You'll almost always want to resize using the existing aspect ratio, meaning that when you enter the width you'd like the image to be, the height is calculated automatically (and vice versa) to keep the image from squishing out of shape. In GIMP, the aspect ratio is locked by default, as indicated by the chain link displayed next to the Width and Height options shown in Figure 8.5. Clicking once on the chain unlocks it, enabling you to specify pixel widths and heights of your own choosing—squished or not.

NOTE

As with many other features in GIMP, the Scale Image dialog box appears in front of the window containing the image being resized. This placement enables you to make changes in the dialog box, apply them, and see the results immediately.

In most, if not all, graphics programs, you can also resize an image based on percentages instead of by providing specific pixel dimensions. For example, if an image starts out as 1815×1721 and you don't want to do the math to determine the values necessary to show it as half that size, you can simply select Percent (in this instance, from the drop-down next to the pixel display in Figure 8.5) and change the default setting from 100 to 50. The image then becomes 908 pixels wide by 861 high—and you don't have to do any math to make it so.

CAUTION

You should never resize an image to be larger than what you started with. While most image editors will allow you to enlarge images, they typically don't do a good job of it. This is because enlarging an image beyond the starting image requires that the editor make guesses about what the additional pixels should be. This can result in ugly, blurry images. Instead, you should start with images that are much larger than you think you would ever need and then resize and crop them down to fit your web designs.

Deciding the right size for a web page image can be challenging. You need to always consider download speeds and the size of the device or screen viewing the page, plus the amount of space available in the design for the image. A good rule of thumb is to create images that are slightly larger than the largest width at which they might display. While people do have large 4K monitors, 1920×1080 is the most common large size monitor. So, resizing your images to be no more than 2000 pixels wide will ensure that they look good even on large monitors while keeping the file size small. Later in this lesson you will learn how to use the same image at several sizes for responsive web design.

NOTE

It can be tempting to crop and resize your images down as small as possible, and for best speed you should. But always keep a copy of the original, full-sized file offline or in a backup location. This way, if two years from now you want to resize your website to be larger, you're not limited by the 640×480 images you created for the old design.

Tweaking Image Colors

If you are editing photographic images instead of creating your own graphics, you might need to use some color-correction tools to get photos just right. Like many other image-editing programs, GIMP offers several options for adjusting an image's brightness, contrast, and color balance, as well as a filter to reduce the dreaded red-eye. To remove red-eye using GIMP, go to Filters, click Enhance, and then click Red Eye Removal.

Most of these options are pretty intuitive. If you want an image to be brighter, adjust the brightness. If you want more red in your image, adjust the color balance. In GIMP, the Colors menu gives you access to numerous tools. As with the Scale Image dialog box described in the preceding section, each tool displays a dialog box in the foreground of your workspace. As you adjust the colors, the image reflects those changes. This preview function is a feature included in most image-editing software.

Figure 8.6 shows the Adjust Hue/Lightness/Saturation tool, one of the many tools provided on the Colors menu. As shown in the figure, you can achieve many color-related changes by using various sliders in dialog boxes to adjust the values you are working with. The Preview feature enables you to see what you are doing as you are doing it. The Reset Color button returns the image to its original state without applying any changes.

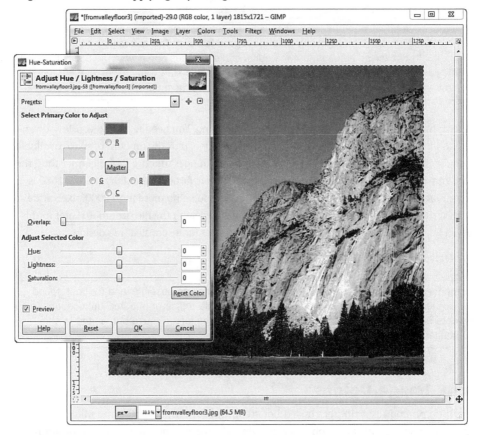

FIGURE 8.6
The Adjust Hue/Lightness/Saturation tool is one of many slider-based color-modification tools available in GIMP. *(Credit: Scott Prokop/Shutterstock)*

Because of the numerous tools available to you, and the preview function available with each tool, a little playful experimentation is the best way to find out what each tool does.

Controlling JPEG Compression

Photographic images on the web work best when saved in the JPEG file format rather than GIF; JPEG enables you to retain the number of colors in the file while still keeping the overall file size to a manageable level. When you're finished adjusting the size and appearance of a photo, select File, Export, and choose JPEG as the file type. Your graphics program will likely provide you with another dialog box for controlling various JPEG options, such as compression.

Figure 8.7 shows the Export Image as JPEG dialog box you see when you export a JPEG in GIMP. You can see here that you can control the compression ratio for saving JPEG files by adjusting the Quality slider between 1 (low quality, small file size) and 100 (high quality, large file size).

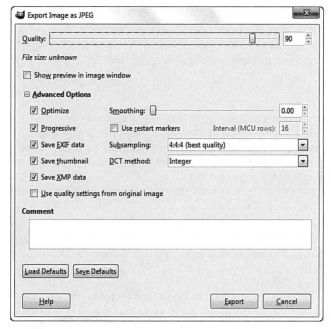

FIGURE 8.7
GIMP enables you to reduce file size while still retaining image quality by saving in the JPEG format.

You might want to experiment a bit to see how various JPEG compression levels affect the quality of your images, but 85% quality (or 15% compression) is generally a good compromise between file size (and, therefore, download speed) and quality for most photographic images. If your site caters more to mobile devices, you should opt for a lower quality/higher compression option to reduce download times.

Creating Banners and Buttons

Graphics that you create from scratch, such as banners and buttons, require you to make considerations uniquely different from those that apply to photographs.

The first decision you need to make when you produce a banner or button is how big it should be. Most people accessing the web now have a computer with a screen that is at least 1024 × 768 pixels in resolution, if not considerably larger. Other popular resolutions are 1440 × 900 and 1366 × 768 pixels.

It's important to design your graphics to fit on mobile devices. In late 2017, the most popular resolution was 360 × 640. While people have larger desktop and laptop screens, they are more and more often viewing web pages on their phones. But in general, you should focus less on the dimensions of your images and more on the file size. An image that is 2000 × 3000 pixels but only 80Kb will load quickly and look great on a mobile device and a desktop screen.

NOTE

For many years, designing for 800 × 600 screen resolution was the norm. Now, people tend to browse web pages on their phones with resolutions as low as 360 × 640. With responsive web design (RWD) you can create designs that support both the small screens and the big ones. You will learn more about RWD in Lesson 16, "Understanding the Importance of Responsive Web Design," and how to do it in Lesson 17, "Designing for Mobile Devices."

Assuming that you target a maximum resolution of 1920 × 1080 pixels, full-size banners and title graphics should be no more than 2000 pixels wide. This gives the images space to be slightly larger than the browser window or smaller, depending on the needs of the design and the device viewing it.

To create a new image in GIMP, go to File and choose New. The Create a New Image dialog box displays (see Figure 8.8). If you aren't sure how big the image needs to be, just accept the default size of 640 × 480. Or you can choose one of the other predetermined sizes in the Template dropdown, such as Web Banner Common 468 × 60 or Web Banner Huge 728 × 90. Those two settings are conservative, yet perfectly acceptable, interpretations of "common" and "huge" for banners. In this dialog box, you can also enter your own width and height for the new image.

For the image's background color, you should usually choose white to match the background that most web browsers use for web pages (although, as you learned previously, that color can be changed). When you know that you'll be creating a page with a background other than white, you can choose a different background color for your image. Or you might want to create an image with no background at all, in which case you select Transparency as the background color. When the final, Web-ready image includes a transparent background, the web page (and its background color) behind the image is allowed to show through. In GIMP, select the background color for your new image by opening Advanced Options in the Create a New Image dialog box.

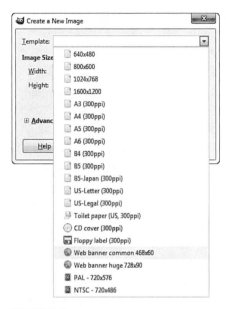

FIGURE 8.8
You must decide on the size of an image before you start working on it, but you can always resize it later.

After you enter the width and height of the image in pixels and click OK, you are faced with a blank canvas—an intimidating sight if you're as art-phobic as most of us! However, so many image-creation tutorials (not to mention entire books) are available to lead you through the process that we're comfortable leaving you to your own creative devices. This section is all about introducing you to the things you want to keep in mind when creating graphics for use in your sites. This section does not necessarily teach you exactly how to do it because being comfortable with the tool *you* choose is the first step to mastering it.

Optimizing Images by Reducing or Removing Colors

It's easy to get hung up on the dimensions of images as you create them, but it's more important to focus on the file size. More and more people use mobile devices such as smartphones to view the web, and bandwidth limits and charges make large images annoyingly slow to load at best. By optimizing your images as much as possible, you make your pages more mobile friendly. And they will load more quickly on desktops and laptops, too.

One of the most effective ways to reduce the size of an image—and, therefore, its download time—is to reduce the number of colors used in the image. This can drastically reduce the visual quality of some photographic images, but it works great for most banners, buttons, and other icons.

You'll be glad to know that there is a special file format for images with a limited number of colors, the Graphics Interchange Format (GIF). When you save or export an image as a GIF, you might be prompted to flatten layers or reduce the number of colors by converting to an indexed image because those are requirements for GIFs; check your software's Help file regarding layers and indexed colors for a full understanding of what you might need to do.

Remember that the GIF image format is designed for images that contain areas of solid colors, such as web page titles and other illustrated graphics; the GIF format is not ideal for photographs; use JPEG or PNG files for photos instead.

PNG (pronounced "ping") is a useful file format that is supported in all major web browsers. Whereas the GIF image format enables you to specify a single transparent color, which means the background of the web page will show through those areas of an image, the PNG format takes things a step further, enabling you to specify varying degrees of transparency.

You might have seen websites that use background colors or images in their container elements but that also have images present in the foreground that allow the background to show through parts of the foreground graphics. In these cases, the images in the foreground have portions that are transparent so that the images themselves—which are always on a rectangular canvas—do not show the areas of the canvas where the design does not occur. You often want to use these types of partially transparent images to make graphics look good over any background color or background image you have in place.

To make part of an image transparent, the image must be saved in the GIF or PNG file format. As mentioned previously in this lesson, most graphics programs that support the GIF format enable you to specify one color to be transparent, whereas PNG images allow for a range of transparency. Largely because of this transparency range, the PNG format is superior to GIF. All the latest web browsers already support PNG images.

The process of creating a transparent image depends on the type of image you are creating (GIF or PNG) and the graphics software you are using to create it. For instructions, look in your graphics program's Help files or type "transparent images with [*your program here*]" into your search engine.

Creating Tiled Background Images

You can use any GIF, JPEG, or PNG image as a background tile within a container element, but before you go off and create a tiled background, especially a highly patterned tiled background, ask yourself what that tiled background adds to the overall look and feel of your website. More importantly, ask yourself whether the text of the site can be read easily when placed over that pattern.

Think about the websites you frequent every day and consider the fact that few sites use tiled, heavily patterned backgrounds on their entire pages. If you restrict your browsing to websites for companies, products, sports teams, or other sites in which information (primarily text) is privileged, the number of sites with tiled, heavily patterned backgrounds decreases even further. The web affords everyone the right of individuality in design, but if you are creating a site for your business, you might want to avoid using a highly patterned background with contrasting colored text.

If you do use a tiled background image for your entire site, remember that tiled images look best when you can't tell they're tiled images. In other words, you know you have a good image when the top edge of a background tile matches seamlessly with the bottom edge and the left edge matches with the right.

Figures 8.9 and 8.10 show background tiles in use, both with seamless backgrounds but with varying degrees of effectiveness.

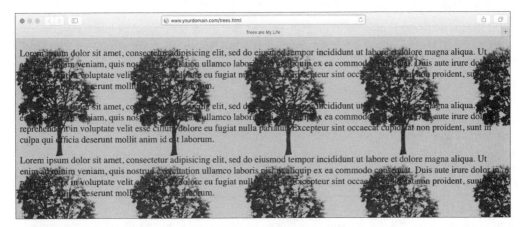

FIGURE 8.9
This is an example of a seamless background image in which you can tell the background is tiled because you can see several identical shapes.

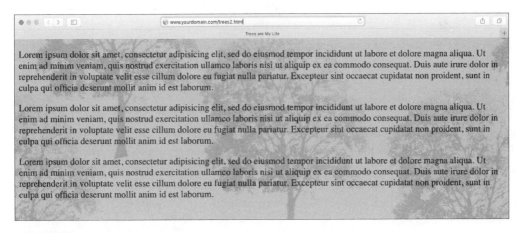

FIGURE 8.10
This is another example of a seamless background image, but you can't tell that it's tiled.

Later in this lesson, you'll learn how to place background images within container elements. Despite our warnings so far in this section, background images can be powerful weapons in your design arsenal—just not when heavily patterned. You can find some great (and freely available) examples of background images—often referred to as *textures*—at the Subtle Patterns website (www.toptal.com/designers/subtlepatterns/).

Placing Images on a Web Page

To get started with image placement on your website, first move the image file into the same folder as the HTML file or into a directory named `images` (which you might want to use for easy organization).

NOTE

It doesn't matter to the web server, web browser, or end user just where you put your images, as long as you know where they are and use the correct paths in your HTML code.

We prefer to put all our images in a separate `images` directory or in a subdirectory of a generic `assets` directory (such as `assets/images`) so that all the images or other assets, such as multimedia and JavaScript files, are neatly organized.

In this first example, let's assume you have placed an image called `myimage.gif` in the same directory as the HTML file you want to use to display it. To display it, insert the following HTML tag at the point in the text where you want the image to appear, using the name of your image file instead of `myimage.gif`:

```
<img src="myimage.gif" alt="My Image">
```

If your image file were in the `images` directory below the document root, you would use the following code, which you can see now contains the full path to `myimage.gif` in the `images` directory:

```
<img src="/images/myimage.gif" alt="My Image">
```

Both the `src` and the `alt` attributes of the `<img>` tag are required for valid HTML web pages. The `src` attribute identifies the image file, and the `alt` attribute enables you to specify descriptive text about the image. The `alt` attribute is intended to serve as an alternative to the image if a user is unable to view the image either because it is unavailable or because the user is using a text-only browser or screen reader. You'll read more on the `alt` attribute later, in the section "Describing Images with Text."

NOTE
The <img> tag is one of the HTML tags that also supports a title attribute; you can use this attribute to describe an image, much like the alt attribute. But while the alt attribute is intended to describe the image, the title provides additional information about the image. You might see the title attribute being used, but please do not use it in place of an alt attribute; doing so will limit your site's usefulness on many types of devices. And if you don't include the alt attribute, your HTML will not be valid.

As an example of how to use the <img> tag, Listing 8.2 inserts an image at the top of the page, before a paragraph of text. Whenever a web browser displays the HTML file in Listing 8.2, it automatically retrieves and displays the image file, as shown in Figure 8.11.

LISTING 8.2   Using the <img> Tag to Place Images on a Web Page

```
<!doctype html>
<html lang="en">
  <head>
    <meta charset="utf-8">
    <title>A Spectacular Yosemite View</title>
  </head>
  <body>
    <section>
      <header>
        <h1>A Spectacular Yosemite View</h1>
      </header>
      <img src="hd.jpg" alt="Half Dome">
      <p><strong>Half Dome</strong> is a granite dome in Yosemite
        National Park, located in northeastern Mariposa County,
        California, at the eastern end of Yosemite Valley. The
        granite crest rises  more than 4,737 ft (1,444 m) above the
        valley floor.</p>
      <p>This particular view is of Half Dome as seen from Washburn
        Point.</p>
    </section>
  </body>
</html>
```

If you guessed that img refers to "image," you're right. Likewise, src refers to "source," or a reference to the location of the image file. As discussed in the first few lessons, an image is always stored in a file separate from the text of your web page (your HTML file), even though it appears to be part of the same page when viewed in a browser.

FIGURE 8.11
When a web browser displays the HTML shown in Listing 8.2, it renders the hd.jpg image.
(Credit: Bernhard Richter/Shutterstock)

NOTE

You can include an image from any website within your own pages. In those cases, the image is retrieved from the other page's web server whenever your page is displayed. Although you could do this, you shouldn't! Not only is it bad manners (and probably a copyright violation) because you are using the other person's bandwidth for your own personal gain, but it also can make your pages display more slowly. In addition, you have no way of controlling when the image might be changed or deleted.

If you are granted permission to republish an image from another web page, always transfer a copy of that image to your computer and use a local file reference, such as `<img src="myimage.jpg">` instead of `<img src="http://www.otherserver.com/theirimage.jpg">`. This advice is not applicable, however, when you host your images—such as photographs—at a service specifically meant as an image repository, such as Flickr (www.flickr.com). Services such as Flickr provide you with a URL for each image, and each URL includes Flickr's domain in the address. The same is true if you want to link to images you have taken with mobile applications such as Instagram; these types of services also provide you with a full URL to an image that you can then link to in your own website.

As with the `<a>` tag used for hyperlinks, you can specify any complete Internet address as the location of an image file in the `src` attribute of the `<img>` tag. You can also use relative addresses, such as `/images/birdy.jpg` or `../smiley.gif`.

Describing Images with Text

The `<img>` tag in Listing 8.2 includes a short text description—in this case, `alt="Half Dome"`. The `alt` stands for *alternate text*, which is the message that appears in place of the image itself if it does not load. An image might not load if its address is incorrect, if the Internet connection is very slow and the data has not yet transferred, or if the user is using a text-only browser or screen reader. Figure 8.12 shows one example of `alt` text used in place of an image. Each web browser renders `alt` text differently, but the information is still provided when it is part of your HTML document.

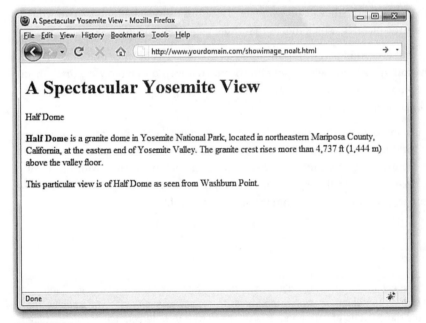

FIGURE 8.12
Users will see `alt` messages when images do not appear.

Even when graphics have fully loaded and are visible in the web browser, the `alt` message might appear in a little box (known as a *tooltip*) whenever the mouse pointer passes over an image. The `alt` message also helps any user who is visually impaired (or is using a voice-based interface to read the web page).

You must include a suitable `alt` attribute in every `<img>` tag on your web pages, keeping in mind the variety of situations in which people might see that message. A very brief description of the image is usually best, but web page authors sometimes put short advertising messages, keyword phrases for SEO, or subtle humor in their `alt` messages; too much humor and not enough information is frowned upon as being not all that useful. And search engines may view too many keywords as SEO spam. For small or unimportant images, it's tempting to omit the `alt` message altogether, but the `alt` attribute is a required attribute of the `<img>` tag. If you omit it, it doesn't mean your page won't display properly, but it does mean you'll be in violation of HTML standards. We recommend assigning an empty text message to `alt` if you absolutely don't need it (`alt=""`), which is sometimes the case with small or decorative images.

Specifying Image Height and Width

Because text moves over the Internet much faster than graphics, most web browsers end up displaying the text on a page before they display images. This gives users something to read while they're waiting to see the pictures, which makes the whole page seem to load faster.

You can make sure that everything on your page appears as quickly as possible and in the right places by explicitly stating each image's height and width. That way, a web browser can immediately and accurately make room for each image as it lays out the page and while it waits for the images to finish transferring.

For each image you want to include in your site, you can use your graphics program to determine its exact height and width in pixels. You might also be able to find these image properties by using system tools. For example, in Windows, you can see an image's height and width by right-clicking the image, selecting Properties, and then selecting Details. When you know the height and width of an image, you can include its dimensions in the CSS, like this:

```
<img src="myimage.gif" alt="Fancy Pic" style="width:200px;height:100px;">
```

NOTE

The height and width specified for an image don't have to match the image's actual height and width. A web browser tries to squish or stretch the image to display whatever size you specify. The best way to adjust the dimensions of your images is to set `width` to a percentage of the container and `height` to `auto`, as shown here:

```
style="width:100%; height:auto;"
```

This ensures that the image will fit in the design width and the aspect ratio will remain the same as the original size.

Just as with other design elements such as background color or font size, you should not specify the exact dimensions of images in the HTML. Instead, you should set the width and height by using CSS style sheets. You can use any measurement you want for the width and height, but to ensure that the image doesn't look bad, it's best to set one of the dimensions to auto.

> **NOTE**
>
> HTML5 has introduced the <picture> element and the srcset and sizes attributes. The <picture> element lets designers control which image should be displayed to which browser. And the srcset and sizes attributes define multiple image resources for browsers of different sizes. These will be discussed in more detail in Lesson 17. These new features are well supported in modern browsers and give designers more options for images.

Aligning Images

Just as you can align text on a page, you can align images on a page by using special attributes. You can align images both horizontally and vertically with respect to text and other images that surround them.

Horizontal Image Alignment

As discussed in Lesson 6, "Working with Fonts, Text Blocks, Lists, and Tables," you can use the text-align CSS property to align content within an element as centered, aligned with the right margin, or aligned with the left margin. These style settings affect both text and images, and they can be used in any block element, such as <p>.

Like text, images are normally lined up with the left margin unless another alignment setting indicates that they should be centered or right-justified. In other words, left is the default value of the text-align CSS property.

You can also wrap text around images by applying the float CSS property to the <img> tag.

In Listing 8.3, <img style="float:left;"> aligns the first image to the left and wraps text around the right side of it, as you might expect. Similarly, <img style="float:right;"> aligns the second image to the right and wraps text around the left side of it. Figure 8.13 shows how these images align on a web page. There is no concept of floating an image to the center because there would be no way to determine how to wrap text on each side of it.

LISTING 8.3 Using float Style Properties to Align Images on a Web Page

```
<!doctype html>
<html lang="en">
  <head>
    <meta charset="utf-8">
    <title>More Spectacular Yosemite Views</title>
  </head>
```

```
<body>
  <section>
    <header>
      <h1>More Spectacular Yosemite Views</h1>
    </header>
    <p><img src="elcap_sm.jpg" alt="El Capitan"
    style="float:left;padding:12px;width:100px;height:75px;"><strong>El
    Capitan</strong> is a 3,000-foot (910 m) vertical rock formation
    in Yosemite National Park, located on the north side of Yosemite
    Valley, near its western end. The granite monolith is one of the
    world's favorite challenges for rock climbers. The formation was
    named "El Capitan" by the Mariposa Battalion when it explored the
    valley in 1851.</p>
    <p><img src="tunnelview_sm.jpg" alt="Tunnel View"
    style="float:right;padding:12px;width:100px;height:80px;"><strong>Tunnel
    View</strong> is a viewpoint on State Route 41 located directly east
    of the Wawona Tunnel as one enters Yosemite Valley from the south.
    The view looks east into Yosemite Valley including the southwest face
    of El Capitan, Half Dome, and Bridalveil Falls. This is, to many, the
    first views of the popular attractions in Yosemite.</p>
  </section>
</body>
</html>
```

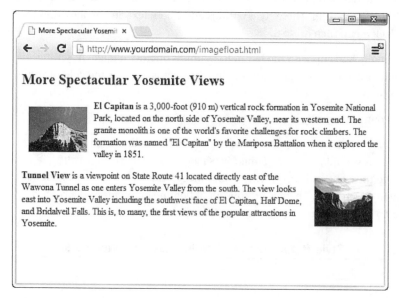

FIGURE 8.13
Showing the image alignment from Listing 8.3.

NOTE

Notice the addition of padding in the `style` attribute for both `<img>` tags used in Listing 8.3. This padding provides some breathing room between the image and the text—12 pixels on all four sides of the image. You'll learn more about padding in Lesson 9, "Working with Margins, Padding, Alignment, and Floating."

Vertical Image Alignment

Sometimes you want to insert a small image in the middle of a line of text, or you want to put a single line of text next to an image as a caption. In either case, having some control over how the text and images line up vertically would be handy. Should the bottom of the image line up with the bottom of the letters, or should the text and images all be arranged so that their middles line up? You can choose between these and several other options:

▶ To line up the top of an image with the top of the tallest image or letter on the same line, use this:

```
<img style="vertical-align:text-top;">
```

▶ To line up the bottom of an image with the bottom of the text, use this:

```
<img style="vertical-align:text-bottom;">
```

▶ To line up the middle of an image with the overall vertical center of everything on the line, use this:

```
<img style="vertical-align:middle;">
```

▶ To line up the bottom of an image with the baseline of the text, use this:

```
<img style="vertical-align:baseline;">
```

NOTE

The `vertical-align` CSS property also supports the values `top` and `bottom`, which can align images with the overall top or bottom of a line of elements, regardless of any text on the line.

All four of these options are used in Listing 8.4 and displayed in Figure 8.14. Four thumbnail images are now listed vertically down the page, and descriptive text appears next to each image. Various settings for the `vertical-align` CSS property are used to align each image and its relevant text. This is certainly not the most beautiful page, but it should help make the various alignments clear.

LISTING 8.4 Using `vertical-align` Styles to Align Text with Images

```
<!doctype html>
<html lang="en">
  <head>
    <meta charset="utf-8">
    <title>Small But Mighty Spectacular Yosemite Views</title>
  </head>
  <body>
    <section>
      <header>
        <h1>Small But Mighty Yosemite Views</h1>
      </header>
      <p><img src="elcap_sm.jpg" alt="El Capitan"
      style="width:100px;height:75px;vertical-align:text-top;"><strong>El
      Capitan</strong> is a 3,000-foot (910 m) vertical rock formation
      in Yosemite National Park.</p>
      <p><img src="tunnelview_sm.jpg" alt="Tunnel View"
      style="width:100px;height:80px;vertical-align:text-bottom;">
      <strong>Tunnel View</strong> looks east into Yosemite Valley.</p>
      <p><img src="upperyosefalls_sm.jpg" alt="Upper Yosemite Falls"
      style="width:87px;height:100px;vertical-align:middle;"><strong>Upper
      Yosemite Falls</strong> are 1,430 ft and are among the twenty highest
      waterfalls in the world. </p>
      <p><img src="hangingrock_sm.jpg" alt="Hanging Rock"
      style="width:100px;height:75px;vertical-align:baseline;">
      <strong>Hanging Rock</strong>, off Glacier Point, used to be a popular
      spot for people to, well, hang from. Crazy people.</p>
    </section>
  </body>
</html>
```

NOTE

If you don't assign any `vertical-align` CSS property in an `<img>` tag or class used with an `<img>` tag, the bottom of the image will line up with the baseline of any text next to it. This means you never have to use `vertical-align:baseline;` because it is assumed by default. However, if you specify a margin for an image and intend for the alignment to be a bit more exact in relationship to the text, you might want to explicitly set the `vertical-align` property to `text-bottom`.

FIGURE 8.14
Showing the vertical image alignment options used in Listing 8.4.

Turning Images into Links

You probably noticed in Figure 8.11 that the image on the page is quite large. This is fine in this particular example, but it isn't ideal when you're trying to present multiple images. It makes more sense to create smaller image thumbnails that link to larger versions of each image. Then you can arrange the thumbnails on the page so that visitors can easily see all the written content, even if they see only a smaller version of the actual (larger) image. Using thumbnails is one of the many ways you can use image links to spice up your pages.

To turn any image into a clickable link to another page or image, you can use the <a> tag that you learned about in Lesson 7 to make text links. Listing 8.5 contains the code to display thumbnails of images within text, with those thumbnails linking to larger versions of the images. To ensure that the user knows to click the thumbnails, the image and some helper text are enclosed in a <div>, as shown in Figure 8.15.

LISTING 8.5   Using Thumbnails for Effective Image Links

```
<!doctype html>
<html lang="en">
  <head>
    <meta charset="utf-8">
    <title>More Spectacular Yosemite Views</title>
    <style>
    div.imageleft {
      float: left;
      text-align: center;
      font-size: 10px;
      font-style: italic;
    }
    div.imageright {
      float: right;
      text-align: center;
      font-size: 10px;
      font-style: italic;
    }
    img {
      padding: 6px;
      border: none;
    }
    </style>
  </head>
  <body>
    <section>
      <header>
        <h1>More Spectacular Yosemite Views</h1>
      </header>
      <div class="imageleft">
        <a href="http://www.flickr.com/photos/nofancyname/614253439/"><img
        src="elcap_sm.jpg" alt="El Capitan"
        style="width:100px; height:75px;"></a>
        <br>click image to enlarge
      </div>
      <p><strong>El Capitan</strong> is a 3,000-foot (910 m) vertical rock
      formation in Yosemite National Park, located on the north side of
      Yosemite Valley, near its western end. The granite monolith is one
      of the world's favorite challenges for rock climbers. The formation
      was named "El Capitan" by the Mariposa Battalion when it explored
      the valley in 1851.</p>
      <div class="imageright">
        <a href="http://www.flickr.com/photos/nofancyname/614287355/"><img
        src="tunnelview_sm.jpg" alt="Tunnel View"
        style="width:100px; height:80px;"></a>
        <br>click image to enlarge
```

```
    </div>
    <p><strong>Tunnel View</strong> is a viewpoint on State Route 41
    located directly east of the Wawona Tunnel as one enters Yosemite
    Valley from the south. The view looks east into Yosemite Valley
    including the southwest face of El Capitan, Half Dome, and
    Bridalveil Falls. This is, to many, the first views of the
    popular attractions in Yosemite.</p>
  </section>
 </body>
</html>
```

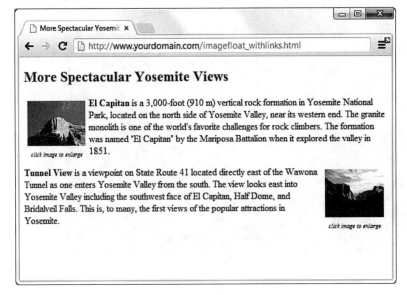

FIGURE 8.15
Using thumbnails as links improves the layout of a page that uses large images.

The code in Listing 8.5 uses additional styles that are explained in more detail in other lessons, but you should be able to figure out the basics:

▶ The <a> tags link these particular images to larger versions, which, in this case, are stored on an external server (at Flickr).

▶ The <div> tags, and their styles, are used to align those sets of graphics and caption text (and also include some padding).

Unless instructed otherwise, web browsers display a colored border around the edge of each image link. As with text links, the rectangle usually appears blue for links that haven't been visited recently and purple for links that have been visited recently—unless you specify different-colored links in your style sheet. Because you seldom, if ever, want this unsightly line around your linked images, you should usually include `style="border:none;"` in any `<img>` tag within a link. In this instance, the `border:none` style is made part of the style sheet entry for the `img` element because we use the same styles twice.

When you click one of the thumbnail images on the sample page shown, the link opens in the browser, as shown in Figure 8.16.

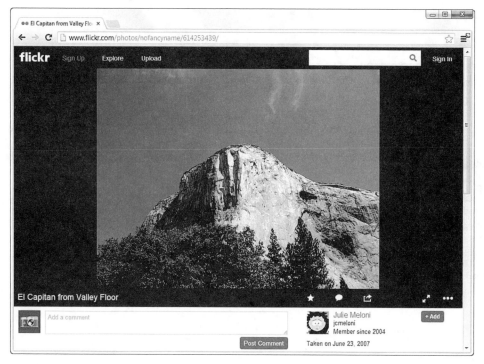

FIGURE 8.16
Clicking a linked thumbnail image opens the target of the link.

Using Background Images

As you learned earlier in this lesson, you can use background images to act as a sort of wallpaper in a container element so that the text or other images appear on top of this underlying design.

The basic CSS properties that work together to create a background are listed here:

> ▶ `background-color`—Specifies the background color of the element. Although it is not image related, it is part of the set of background-related properties. If an image is transparent or does not load, the user will see the background color instead.

> ▶ `background-image`—Specifies the image to use as the background of the element, using the following syntax: `url('imagename.gif')`.

▶ background-repeat—Specifies how the image should repeat, both horizontally and vertically. By default (without specifying anything), background images repeat both horizontally and vertically. Other options are repeat (same as default), repeat-x (horizontal), repeat-y (vertical), and no-repeat (only one appearance of the graphic).

▶ background-position—Specifies where the image should be initially placed, relative to its container. Options include top-left, top-center, top-right, center-left, center-center, center-right, bottom-left, bottom-center, bottom-right, and specific pixel and percentage placements.

When specifying a background image, you can put all these specifications together into the background property, like so:

```
body {
    background: #ffffff url('imagename.gif') no-repeat top right;
}
```

In the preceding style sheet entry, the body element of the web page will be white and will include a graphic named imagename.gif at the top right. Another use for the background property is to create custom bullets for your unordered lists. To use images as bullets, first define the style for the <ul> tag as shown here:

```
ul {
  list-style-type: none;
  padding-left: 0;
  margin-left: 0;
}
```

Next, change the declaration for the <li> tag to this:

```
li {
  background: url(mybullet.gif) left center no-repeat
}
```

Make sure that mybullet.gif (or whatever you name your graphic) is on the web server and accessible; in this case, all unordered list items will show your custom image instead of the standard filled-disc bullet.

We return to the specific use of background properties in Part III, "Advanced Web Page Design with CSS," when using CSS for overall page layouts.

Using Image Maps

Sometimes you want to use an image as navigation—but beyond the simple button-based or link-based navigation that you often see in websites. For example, perhaps you have a website with medical information, and you want to show an image of the human body that links to pages that provide information about various body parts. Or you might have a website that provides a world map that users can click to access information about countries. You can divide an image into regions that link to different documents, depending on where users click within that image. This is called an *image map*, and any image can be made into an image map.

Why Image Maps Aren't Always Necessary

The first point to know about image maps is that you probably won't need to use them except in very special cases. It's almost always easier and more efficient to use several ordinary images that are placed directly next to one another and provide a separate link for each image.

For example, Figure 8.17 shows a web page that displays 12 different corporate logos; this example is a common type of web page in the business world, in which you give a little free advertisement to your partners. You *could* present these logos as one large image and create an image map that provides links to each of the 12 companies. Users could click each logo in the image to visit each company's site. But every time you wanted to add a new logo to the image map, you would have to modify the entire image and remap the hotspots—which would not be a good use of anyone's time. In such a case, when an image map is not warranted, you simply display the images on the page as in this example by using 12 separate images (1 for each company) and having each image include a link to the particular company.

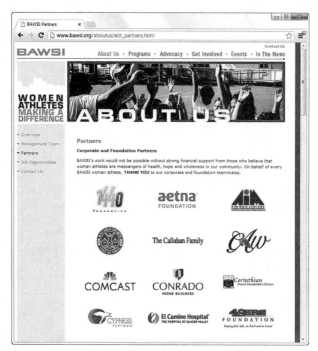

FIGURE 8.17
A web page with 12 different logos; this could be presented as a single image map or divided into 12 separate pieces.

Using an image map is the best choice for an image that has numerous parts, is oddly arranged, or has a design that is itself too complicated to divide into separate images. Figure 8.18 shows an image that is best suited as an image map—a public domain image provided by the U.S. CIA of the standard time zones of the world.

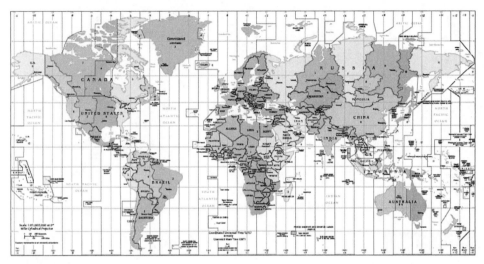

FIGURE 8.18
This image wouldn't respond well to being sliced up into perfectly equal parts; better make it an image map.

Mapping Regions Within an Image

To create any type of image map, you need to figure out the numeric pixel coordinates of each region within the image that you want to turn into a clickable link. These clickable links are also known as *areas*. Your graphics program might provide you with an easy way to find these coordinates. Or you might want to use a standalone image mapping tool such as Mapedit (https://boutell.com/mapedit/) or an online image map maker such as the one at www.image-maps.com. In addition to helping you map the coordinates, these tools provide the HTML code necessary to make the maps work.

Using an image mapping tool is often as simple as using your mouse to draw a rectangle (or a custom shape) around the area you want to be a link. Figure 8.19 shows the result of one of these rectangular selections, as well as the interface for adding the URL and the title or alternate text for this link. Several pieces of information are necessary for creating the HTML for your image map: coordinates, target URL, and alternate text for the link.

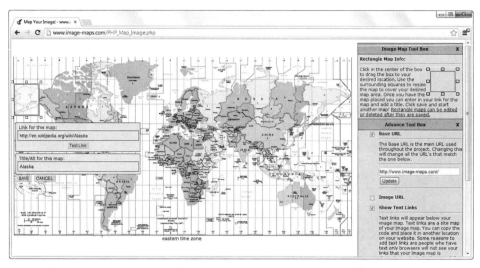

FIGURE 8.19
Using an image mapping tool to create linked areas of a single graphic.

▼ TRY IT YOURSELF

Creating Your Own Image Map

You're more likely to remember how to make image maps if you get an image of your own and turn it into an image map as you continue with this lesson:

▶ For starters, it's easiest to choose a fairly large image that is visually divided into roughly rectangular regions.

▶ If you don't have a suitable image handy, use your favorite graphics program to make one. Perhaps use a single photograph showing several people. You can use each person as an area of the image map.

▶ Try a few different image mapping tools to determine which one you like best. Start with standalone software such as Mapedit (https://boutell.com/mapedit/) and move to the online image map maker at www.image-maps.com. There are others; use the search engine of your choice to find variations on the image map software theme. (Some web editors and graphic editors can make image maps as well.)

Creating the HTML for an Image Map

If you use an image map generator, it will provide the necessary HTML for creating the image map. However, it is a good idea to understand the parts of the code so that you can check it for accuracy. The following HTML code is required to start any image map:

```
<map name="mapname">
```

Keep in mind that you can use whatever name you want for the name of the <map> tag, although it helps to make it as descriptive as possible. Next, you need an <area> tag for each region of the image. Following is an example of a single <area> tag that was produced by the actions shown in Figure 8.19:

```
<area shape="rect" coords="1,73,74,163"
  href="http://en.wikipedia.org/wiki/Alaska"
  alt="Alaska"    title="Alaska">
```

This <area> tag has five attributes, which you use with every area you describe in an image map:

- shape—Indicates whether the region is a rectangle (shape="rect"), a circle (shape="circle"), or an irregular polygon (shape="poly").

- coords—Gives the exact pixel coordinates for the region. For rectangles, give the x,y coordinates of the upper-left corner followed by the x,y coordinates of the lower-right corner. For circles, give the x,y center point followed by the radius in pixels. For polygons, list the x,y coordinates of all the corners in a connect-the-dots order.

  Here is an example of a mapped polygon (which can get a little crazy looking):

```
<area shape="poly"
coords="233,0,233,20,225,22,225,101,216,121,212,154,212,167,212,
181,222,195,220,209,226,214,226,234,232,252,224,253,223,261,231,
264,232,495,254,497,274,495,275,482,258,463,275,381,270,348,257,
338,266,329,272,313,271,301,258,292,264,284,262,262,272,263,272,
178,290,172,289,162,274,156,274,149,285,151,281,134,272,137,274,3"
href="http://en.wikipedia.org/wiki/Eastern_Time_Zone"
alt="Eastern Time Zone" title="Eastern Time Zone">
```

- href—Specifies the location to which the region links. You can use any address or filename that you would use in an ordinary <a> link tag.

- alt—Enables you to provide a piece of text that describes the shape; as you learned previously, providing this text is important to users browsing with text-only browsers or screen readers.

- title—Ensures that tool tips containing the information are also visible when the user accesses the designated area.

Each distinct clickable region in an image map must be described as a single area, which means that a typical image map consists of a list of areas. After you've coded the <area> tags, you are done defining the image map, so wrap things up with a closing </map> tag.

The last step in creating an image map is wiring it up to the actual map image. The map image is placed on the page using an ordinary <img> tag. However, an extra usemap attribute is coded, like this:

```
<img src="timezonemap.png" usemap="#timezonemap"
  style="border:none; width:977px;height:498px "
  alt="World Timezone Map">
```

When specifying the value of the usemap attribute, use the name you put in the id of the <map> tag (and don't forget the # symbol). Also include the style attribute to specify the height and width of the image and to turn off the border around the image map, which you might or might not elect to keep in image maps of your own.

Listing 8.6 shows the complete code for a sample web page containing the map graphic, its image map, and a few mapped areas.

LISTING 8.6   Defining the Regions of an Image Map with <map> and <area> Tags

```
<!doctype html>
<html lang="en">
  <head>
    <meta charset="utf-8">
    <title>Testing an Image Map</title>
  </head>
  <body>
    <section>
      <header>
        <h1>Testing an Image Map</h1>
      </header>
      <div style="text-align:center;">
        Click on an area to learn more about
        that location or time zone.<br>
        <img src="timezonemap.png" usemap="#timezonemap"
        style="border:none;width:977px;height:498px;"
        alt="World Timezone Map">
      </div>
    </section>
    <map name="timezonemap" id="timezonemap">
      <area shape="poly" coords="233,0,233,20,225,22,225,101,216,121,212,
      154,212,167,212,181,222,195,220,209,226,214,226,234,232,252,224,
      253,223,261,231,264,232,495,254,497,274,495,275,482,258,463,275,
      381,270,348,257,338,266,329,272,313,271,301,258,292,264,
      284,262,262,272,263,272,178,290,172,289,162,274,156,274,
      149,285,151,281,134,272,137,274,3"
      href="http://en.wikipedia.org/wiki/eastern_time_zone"
      alt="Eastern Time Zone" title="Eastern Time Zone">
      <area shape="rect" coords="1,73,74,163 "
```

```
        href="http://en.wikipedia.org/wiki/Alaska"
        alt="Alaska" title="Alaska">
    </map>
  </body>
</html>
```

Figure 8.20 shows the image map from Listing 8.6 in action. When you hover the mouse over an area, the `alt` or `title` text for that area—in this example, `Eastern Time Zone`—is displayed on the image map.

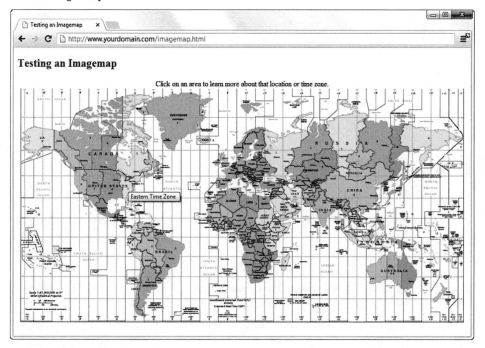

FIGURE 8.20
The image map defined in Listing 8.6, as it displays on the web page.

NOTE

One method of producing mapped images relies solely on CSS, not the HTML <map> tag. You will learn more about this in Lesson 11, "Using CSS to Do More with Lists, Text, and Navigation."

Linking to Multimedia Files

Let's move away from static images for a moment and move into more exciting multimedia such as audio and video. The simplest and most reliable option for incorporating a video or audio file into your website is to simply link it in with an <a> tag, exactly as you would link to another HTML file.

For example, you could use the following line to offer an MOV video of a cute chickadee:

```
<a href="chickadee.mov">View a cute chickadee!</a>
```

When the user clicks the words `View a cute chickadee!`, the `chickadee.mov` QuickTime video file is transferred to his or her computer from your web server. Whichever helper application or plug-in the user has installed automatically starts as soon as the file has finished downloading. If no compatible helper or plug-in can be found, the web browser offers the user a chance to download the appropriate plug-in or save the video on the hard drive for later viewing.

NOTE

In case you're unfamiliar with *helper applications* (*helper apps* for short), they are the external programs that a web browser calls on to display any type of file it can't handle on its own. Generally, the helper application associated with a file type is called on whenever a web browser can't display that type of file on its own.

Plug-ins are a special sort of helper application installed directly into a web browser. They enable you to view multimedia content directly in the browser window. Most browsers have video plugins installed by default.

▼ TRY IT YOURSELF

Create or Find Some Multimedia to Use in Your Website

Before you learn how to place multimedia on your web pages, you need to have some multimedia content.

Creating multimedia of any kind can be a challenging and complicated task. If you're planning to create your own content from scratch, you need far more than these lessons to become the next crackerjack multimedia developer. When you have some content, however, you can use the tips in this lesson to show you how to place your new creations into your web pages.

If you're artistically challenged, you can obtain useful multimedia assets in several alternative ways. Aside from the obvious (such as hiring an artist), here are a few suggestions:

▶ Much of the material on the Internet is free. Of course, it's still a good idea to double-check with the author or current owner of the content; you don't want to be sued for copyright infringement. In addition, various offices of the U.S. government generate content that, by law, belongs to all Americans. (For example, any NASA footage found online is free for your use.)

▶ Many search engines have specific search capabilities for finding multimedia files. As long as you are careful about copyright issues, this can be an easy way to find multimedia related to a specific topic. A simple search for "sample MP4 movie" or "sample audio files" will produce more results than you can handle.

▶ If you are creatively inclined, determine the medium you like most—video production, audio production, or animation, for example. When you have a starting point, look into the various types of software that will enable you to create such artistic masterpieces. Many companies, including Adobe (www.adobe.com) and Apple (www.apple.com), provide multimedia software. One popular tool available for Windows and Macintosh is Camtasia (www.techsmith.com/video-editor.html).

Listing 8.7 contains the code for a web page that uses a simple image link to play a video in Windows Media file format. In addition to the image link, a link is placed within the text to provide context for the user.

LISTING 8.7   Linking an Image to a Windows Media Video

```
<!doctype html>
<html lang="en">
  <head>
    <meta charset="utf-8">
    <title>This Chickadee Thinks It's a Hummingbird!</title>
  </head>

  <body>
    <h1>This Chickadee Thinks It's a Hummingbird!</h1>
    <div style="border-style:none; float:left; padding:12px;">
      <a href="chickadee.wmv"><img src="projector.gif"
        alt="Chickadee Video"></a>
    </div>
    <p>Chickadees have to eat too! But most don't eat hummingbird
      nectar.</p>
    <p>Click <a href="chickadee.wmv">here</a> or on the projector graphic to
      see a movie clip of this chickadee in action.</p>
  </body>
</html>
```

This code simply uses the `projector.gif` GIF image as a link to the `chickadee.wmv` video clip. Figure 8.21 shows the chickadee sample page with the projector image in view. When the image is clicked, the Windows Media Player is invoked and begins to play the movie.

FIGURE 8.21
The `projector.gif` GIF image is used as an image link to a Windows Media file that launches an external helper application. Note that not all computers support WMV files.

To view the video, you need only click the animated projector (or the text link in the paragraph). This action results in the browser either playing the video with the help of a plug-in (if one is found that can play the clip) or deferring to a suitable helper application or downloading the image to the hard drive.

If you change the link from chickadee.wmv (Windows Media) to chickadee.mov (QuickTime), your browser handles the link differently. Instead of launching another program, the QuickTime plug-in enables you to view the movie clip directly in the browser window (see Figure 8.22).

FIGURE 8.22
When you follow the image link, the chickadee.mov QuickTime movie is played using the QuickTime browser plug-in.

NOTE

If your browser has no support for QuickTime, you can download the QuickTime player free from Apple at www.apple.com/quicktime/. Even if you do have QuickTime installed, some browsers play QuickTime movies differently based on whether a plug-in is installed. For example, on my Windows computer, Internet Explorer and Firefox both play QuickTime movies directly in the browser window via a plug-in, whereas Opera launches QuickTime as a helper application.

As you might have guessed, this approach of using a simple link to play multimedia files offers the best backward compatibility because the browser bears all the responsibility of figuring out how to play a multimedia clip. The downside to this is that you don't have much control over how a clip is played, and the clip won't play directly in the context of a page.

Embedding Multimedia Files

HTML5 introduced two new tags for embedding media files in a web page: `<video>` and `<audio>`. These tags are widely supported in both desktop and mobile browsers and are used like the `<img>` tag to embed either video or audio files. These tags also use the `<source>` tag to define the source files for the video or audio to play.

Using the `<video>` Element to Play Video on Web Pages

Embedding a video file into a web page produces a set of software controls that enable the file to be played directly; no secondary window is necessary, and there's no need to navigate away from the page you are on. Following is code to embed a chickadee video using the `<video>` tag:

```
<video controls style="width: 400px; height: auto;"
  src="chickadee.wmv" type="video/x-ms-wmv">
  <p>Your browser does not support HTML5 video.</p>
</video>
```

The `<video>` element contains the fallback text `Your browser does not support HTML5 video.` that is displayed only if the tag doesn't display—much like the `alt` attribute in the `<img>` tag. In most browsers, the video will display, and many designers don't include this alternative text.

That is all you need to embed a video file, but that HTML won't work reliably across computers because the video is embedded as a Windows Media file. You could change the HTML to just point to the MP4 file, you could convert the file to an MP4 file, or you could use the `<source>` tag to define alternatives, like so:

```
<video controls>
  <source src="images/chickadee.wmv" type="video/x-ms-wmv">
  <source src="images/chickadee.mp4" type="video/mp4">
  <p>Your browser does not support HTML5 video.</p>
</video>
```

CAUTION

There are many video codecs and containers out there, including MOV, AVI, Flash, and WMV. But there are only three that work reliably in web pages:

▶ MP4 or H264 has the best support with all modern browsers able to play these files.

▶ WebM is well supported by Firefox and Chrome. It is partially supported in Edge and works with installed codecs for Safari and Internet Explorer.

▶ Ogg or Ogg/Theora is supported by Firefox and Chrome, and it will be supported by Edge, but doesn't have good support in other browsers.

It's best to convert any video files you have to MP4. Search your favorite search engine to find free online converters.

You can see the result of this code in Figure 8.23. The `<source>` element allows you to define as many source files as you need or want. You still have to create and upload those videos, but the browsers will only download and use the one they support. This makes your videos more cross-compatible.

NOTE

There are many different video formats you can use. Most designers use MP4 because it is supported across all modern browsers, including mobile devices. Other formats you might see on web pages include WebM, HEVC, and OggTheora or OggV.

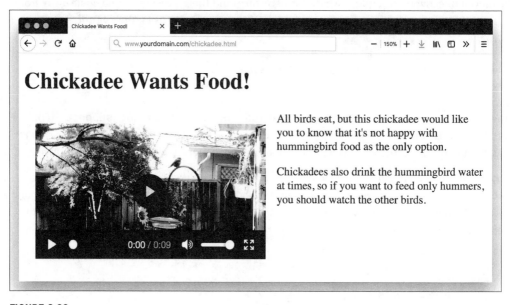

FIGURE 8.23
The `<video>` tag enables you to embed a video clip on a web page.

The `width` and `height` style properties of the `<video>` element determine the size of the embedded player. Some browsers automatically size the embedded player to fit the content if you leave these off, whereas others don't show anything. Play it safe by always defining the dimensions of the video to suit the multimedia content being played. Just as with images, you can set the width to a relative value such as 100% of the container width and then set the height to `auto` so that it isn't distorted.

The other attribute most designers use on the `<video>` tag is `controls`. This tells the browser to display the video with play/pause control buttons. But there are a couple other attributes that can be useful:

- ▶ preload—Has three possible values: none, auto, and metadata. Use none if you do not want to buffer the file, use auto to buffer the file, and use metadata if you want to buffer only the metadata for the file.

- ▶ loop—Tells the browser to start the video from the beginning when it gets to the end.

- ▶ poster—Points to an image file that is shown when the video isn't available, such as when it is still downloading.

- ▶ autoplay—Causes the video to start playing as soon as it is ready.

Listing 8.8 shows the relevant code for the chickadee web page, and you can see the <video> element as it appears in context.

LISTING 8.8   Using a <video> Element to Directly Embed a Video Clip

```
<!doctype html>
<html lang="en">
  <head>
    <meta charset="utf-8">
    <title>Chickadee Wants Food!</title>
    <style>
      video {
        width: 50%; height: auto; float: left; padding: 1rem;
      }
    </style>
  </head>
  <body>
    <h1>Chickadee Wants Food!</h1>
    <video controls>
      <source src="images/chickadee.wmv" type="video/x-ms-wmv">
      <source src="images/chickadee.mp4" type="video/mp4">
      <p>Your browser does not support HTML5 video.</p>
    </video>
    <p>All birds eat, but this chickadee would like you to know
    that it's not happy with hummingbird food as the only option.
    </p>
    <p>Chickadees also drink the hummingbird water at times, so if
    you want to feed only hummers, you should watch the other birds.
    </p>
  </body>
</html>
```

Using the `<audio>` Element for Audio Playback

In the preceding section, you learned about how to embed video files with the HTML5 `<video>` element. The `<audio>` element works in much the same way. You just put the `<audio>` element where you want your player to display, and the browser will include it.

Listing 8.9 shows how to use the `<audio>` element to embed an audio file that will be played by the browser. The `<audio>` element is quite simple and requires only one attribute: `src`, or the location of the resource you want to play. However, as you see in Listing 8.9, you'll probably want to use a few other handy attributes.

LISTING 8.9 Using the `<audio>` Element to Embed and Play an Audio File

```
<!doctype html>
<html lang="en">
  <head>
    <meta charset="utf-8">
    <title>Let's Hear Some Music</title>
  </head>
  <body>
    <h1>Let's Hear Some Music</h1>
    <p>Better yet, let's use the HTML5 &lt;audio&gt; element
    to do so!</p>
    <audio
        src="manhattan_beach.mp3"
        preload="auto"
        controls
        autoplay
        loop>
        <p>Your browser does not support the audio element.</p>
    </audio>
  </body>
</html>
```

NOTE

Notice the inclusion of a message to users inside the `<audio>` element. Although current versions of all major browsers support the `<audio>` element, just as with the `<video>` element, if a user's browser does not support it, that user will instead see the message within the `<p></p>` tags. The message can be any combination of HTML, including links, images, or scripts.

In addition to the `src` attribute, which, in this case, has the value `manhattan_beach.mp3` because that is the name of the audio file we want to play, we're using four other attributes in this `<audio>` element:

- ▶ `preload`—Has three possible values: `none`, `auto`, and `metadata`. Use `none` if you do not want to buffer the file, use `auto` to buffer the file, and use `metadata` if you want to buffer only the metadata for the file.

- ▶ `controls`—If present, shows the controls for the audio player.

- ▶ `autoplay`—If present, plays the file as soon as it loads.

- ▶ `loop`—If present, continues to play the file repeatedly until it is manually stopped.

Figure 8.24 shows the page in Listing 8.9 as rendered by the Chrome web browser.

FIGURE 8.24
Using the `<audio>` element to play a sound file.

In practice, you probably wouldn't want to automatically play and loop a sound file in your website as doing so is typically considered a particularly negative user experience. However, if you *do* automatically play a sound file (please don't!), be sure to include the player controls so that users can immediately turn off the sound.

Just as with videos, you should define the MIME type for the audio files you want to include. Following are the MIME types for several popular audio formats you might want to use in your web pages:

- ▶ WAV audio—`audio/vnd.wave`

- ▶ MP3 audio—`audio/mpeg`

- ▶ MP4 audio—`audio/mp4`

Additional Tips for Using Multimedia

Before you add video, audio, or animations to your website, ask yourself whether you really should do so. When you use these types of multimedia, be sure to do so for a reason. Gratuitous sound and video, just like gratuitous images, can detract from your overall message. Then again, if your message is "Look at the videos I've made" or "Listen to my music and download some songs," then multimedia absolutely must play a role in your website.

Keep a few additional tips in mind:

▶ Don't include multimedia in a page and set it to automatically play when the page loads. Always give users the option to start (and stop) your sound or video. If you're using a video background, make sure the sound is muted or removed; video is distracting, and sound is often more so.

▶ When providing files for direct download, give users a choice of file type. Don't limit yourself to providing multimedia content playable by only one type of player on only one operating system. Use the `<source>` tag to provide multiple options on your embedded media as well.

▶ Multimedia files are larger than typical graphics and text files, which means you need to have the space on your web server to store them, as well as the bandwidth allotment to transfer them to whomever requests them via your website. Check with your hosting provider if you plan to serve more than a few videos on your website; it may have restrictions or offer deals for better hosting of large files.

▶ If your site is entirely audio or video and offers very little by way of text or graphics, understand that a certain segment of your audience won't see or hear what you want to present because of the limitations of their system or bandwidth. Provide these users with additional options to get your information. This is also good for accessibility.

▶ Leverage free online video hosting services, such as YouTube (www.youtube.com). Not only does YouTube provide storage for your video clips, it also gives you the code necessary to embed the video in your own web page.

Summary

In this lesson, you learned a few best practices for color use, and you learned how to use the color wheel to find colors that will complement your text. In addition, you learned about hexadecimal notation for colors—where all colors are expressed in notations related to the amount of red, green, and blue in them—and saw how hexadecimal notation enables you to apply nuanced colors to your elements. You also learned how to add transparency to your colors with the RGBa color model. More importantly, you learned about the three color-related style properties that you can use to apply color to container backgrounds, borders, and text using CSS. In addition, you learned the basics of preparing graphics for use on web pages. You saw that this is a complex topic, and you learned just enough in this lesson to whet your appetite. The examples in this lesson use the popular (and free!) GIMP software package, but feel free to use the graphics software that best suits your needs. Among the actions you learned were how to crop, resize, and tweak image colors, and you also learned about the different file formats. You must keep in mind many considerations when including graphics in your site, including graphic size and resolution, as well as how to use transparency, animated GIFs, and tiled backgrounds.

After creating images, you also learned how to use images in your web pages. You learned how to place them in your pages using the `<img>` tag and how to include a short text message that appears in place of the image as it loads and that also appears whenever users move the mouse pointer over the image. You also learned how to control the horizontal and vertical alignment of each image and how to wrap text around the left or right of an image. To make your pages more interactive, you learned how to use images as links—either by using the `<a>` tag around the images or by creating image maps. Finally, you learned how to embed video and sound in a web page. You learned how to use a simple link to a multimedia file, which is the most broadly supported but least flexible option for playing media content. You then learned how to use the `<video>` and `<source>` elements to embed a media player directly in a web page. You also learned about the `<audio>` element in HTML5, which enables the browser to render audio files. In addition, you got some tips for including multimedia in your pages.

Table 8.1 summarizes the tags and attributes covered in this lesson.

TABLE 8.1 Tags and Attributes Covered in Lesson 8

Tag	Function
`<img>`	Places an image file within the page.
Attribute/Style	*Function*
`style="background-color:color;"`	Sets the background color of an element (such as `<body>`, `<p>`, `<div>`, `<blockquote>`, and other containers).
`style="color:color;"`	Sets the color of text within an element.
`style="border:size type color;"`	Sets the color of the four borders around an element. Border colors cannot be used without also specifying the width and type of the border.
`src="address"`	Gives the address or filename of the image.
`alt="altdescription"`	Gives an alternative description of the image that is displayed in place of the image, primarily for users who can't view the image itself.

Tag	Function
title="*title*"	Specifies a text message that is displayed as an image title, typically in a small pop-up box (tooltip) over the image.
style="width:*length*;"	Specifies the width of the image (in pixels).
style="height:*length*;"	Specifies the height of the image (in pixels).
style="border:*size type color*;"	Gets rid of the border around the image if the image is serving as a link.
style="vertical-align:*alignment*;"	Aligns the image vertically to text-top, top, text-bottom, bottom, middle, or baseline.
style="float:*location*;"	Floats the image to one side so that text can wrap around it. Possible values are left, right, and none (default).

Tag	Function
<map>...</map>	Defines a client-side image map referenced by <img usemap="...">. Includes one or more <area> tags.
<area>	Defines a clickable link within a client-side image map.

Attribute/Style	Function
usemap="*name*"	Defines the name of an image map for client-side image mapping. Used with <map> and <area>.
shape="*value*"	Within the <area> tag, specifies the shape of the clickable area. Valid options for this attribute are rect, poly, and circle.
coords="*values*"	Within the <area> tag, specifies the coordinates of the clickable region within an image. Its meaning and setting vary according to the type of area.
href="*linkurl*"	Within the <area> tag, specifies the URL that should be loaded when the area is clicked.

Tag	Function
<audio>...</ audio >	Plays an audio file natively in the browser.

Attribute/Style	Function
src="*mediaurl*"	Gives the URL of the file to embed.
preload="*preloadtype*"	Tells whether to preload the media file. Options are none, auto, and metadata.
controls	Instructs the browser to show the audio player controls.
autoplay	Instructs the browser to play the file when it has finished loading.

loop	Instructs the browser to play the file until it is explicitly stopped.
Tag	**Function**
<video>...</ video >	Plays a video file natively in the browser.
Attribute/Style	*Function*
src="*mediaurl*"	Gives the URL of the file to embed.
preload="*preloadtype*"	Tells whether to preload the media file. Options are none, auto, and metadata.
style="width:*length*;"	Specifies the width of the embedded object, in pixels.
style="height:*length*;"	Specifies the height of the embedded object, in pixels.
controls	Instructs the browser to show the video player controls.
autoplay	Instructs the browser to play the file when it has finished loading.
loop	Instructs the browser to play the file until it is explicitly stopped.

Q&A

Q. I've produced graphics for printing on paper. Are web page graphics any different?

A. Yes. In fact, many of the rules for print graphics are reversed on the Web. Web page graphics should be low resolution to keep the file size small, whereas print graphics should be the highest resolution possible. White washes out black on computer screens, whereas black bleeds into white on paper. Also, someone might stop a web page from loading when only half the graphics have been downloaded, which isn't a consideration when one is looking at images in print. Try to avoid falling into old habits if you've done a lot of print graphics design.

Q. I used the <img> tag just as you advised, but when I view the page, all I see is a little box with some shapes in it. What's wrong?

A. The broken image icon you're seeing can mean one of two things: Either the web browser couldn't find the image file or the image isn't saved in a format the browser recognizes. To solve these problems, first check to make sure the image is where it is supposed to be. If it is, then open the image in your graphics editor and save it again as a GIF, JPEG, or PNG.

Q. **What happens if I overlap areas on an image map?**

A. You are allowed to overlap areas on an image map. Just keep in mind that, in the determination of which link to follow, one area has precedence over the other area. Precedence is assigned according to which areas are listed first in the image map. For example, the first area in the map has precedence over the second area, which means that a click in the overlapping portion of the areas will link to the first area. If you have an area within an image map that doesn't link to anything (known as a *dead area*), you can use this overlap trick to deliberately prevent this area from linking to anything. To do this, just place the dead area before other areas so that the dead area overlaps them and then set its href attribute to " " (blank).

Q. **I hear a lot about streaming video and audio. What does that mean?**

A. In the past, video and audio files took minutes and sometimes hours to be retrieved through most modems, which severely limited the inclusion of video and audio on web pages. The goal everyone is moving toward is streaming video or audio, which plays while the data is being received. In other words, you don't have to completely download the clip before you can start to watch it or listen to it.

Streaming playback is now widely supported through most media players, in both stand-alone versions and plug-ins. When you embed a media object using the <video> element, you have fine-grained control over the buffering and playback of your multimedia resource, and the underlying media player automatically streams the media clip if the player supports streaming.

For live streaming, most modern browsers support the Media Source Extensions (MSE) specification (www.w3.org/TR/media-source/). This extends the <audio> and <video> elements to let you dynamically change the source files without using plug-ins. This allows for live streaming, splicing, and video editing right from the web page.

Workshop

The Workshop contains quiz questions and exercises to help you solidify your understanding of the material covered.

Quiz

1. How would you give a web page a black background and make all text bright green? Based on what you've learned in this lesson, would you even want to use that color combination?

2. What CSS properties and values would you use to ensure that a paragraph has a white background, orange text, and a 3-pixel-wide dashed green border?

3. If you have a square image of a blue flower on a transparent background, and the background color of the containing element is gray, will your flower image appear on the page as a square or as some other shape?

4. If you have an image called `myimage.png` and you want to align it so that a line of text lines up at the middle of the image, what style property should you use?

5. What's the simplest method to provide access to a video on your website for the widest possible audience?

6. What is the CSS to create a background that is red with 50% transparency?

7. What is a rule for cropping an image effectively?

8. What is the most important aspect of an image for web pages: the dimensions, the file size, the colors, or the content?

9. What are two ways to align images vertically?

10. What element do you use to define a file to play in a `<video>` tag?

NOTE

Just a reminder for those of you reading these words in the print or e-book edition of this book: If you go to **www.informit.com/register** and register this book (using ISBN 9780672338083), you can receive free access to an online Web Edition that not only contains the complete text of this book but also features an interactive version of this quiz.

Answers

1. Although it is highly recommended that you don't do it, you would put the following at the beginning of the web page or use a style rule for the body element:

   ```
   <body style="background-color:#000000; color:#00FF00">
   ```

2. The following properties and values would work:

   ```
   background-color: #ffffff;
   color: #ffa500;
   border: 3px dashed #00ff00;
   ```

3. It will appear as the shape of the flower because the image has a transparent background. The gray background of the containing element will show through.

4. You can use `vertical-align:middle` to ensure that the text lines up at the middle of the image.

5. Just link to it:

   ```
   <a href="myvideo.mov">my video</a>
   ```

6. The `background-color: rgba(255, 0, 0, 0.5);` property uses RGBa to define the red color with 50% alpha transparency.

7. You can apply cropping rules such as the rule of thirds, the golden ratio, the golden spiral, triangle, and diagonal crops.

8. The most important aspect of a web page image is the file size: You want it to download as quickly as possible without sacrificing quality.

9. You can align images vertically to the text top, text bottom, middle, baseline, top, and bottom.

10. You use the `<source>` element to define the file to play. You can also use the `src` attribute on the `<video>` tag itself.

Exercises

▶ Select a base color that you like—perhaps a lovely blue or an earthy tone—and use the Color Scheme Designer at http://paletton.com to come up with a set of colors that you can use in a website. I recommend the tetrad or accented analogic scheme types.

▶ When you have a set of colors—or a few options for sets of colors—create a basic HTML page with an `<h1>` element, a paragraph of text, and perhaps some list items. Use the color-related styles you learned about in this lesson to change the background color of the page and the text of the various block-level elements to see how these sets of colors might work together. See how they interact and determine which colors are best used for containers and which are best used for plain text, header text, and link text.

▶ Practicing any of the image placement methods in this lesson will go a long way toward helping you determine the role that images can, and will, play in the websites you design. Using a few sample images, practice using the `float` style to place images and text in relationship to one another. Remember that the possible values for `float` are `left`, `right`, and `none` (default).

▶ Find some freely available audio and video clips on the web and practice placement within your text by using the HTML5 `<audio>` and `<video>` elements.

Working with Margins, Padding, Alignment, and Floating

What You'll Learn in This Lesson:

▶ How to add margins around elements
▶ How to add padding within elements
▶ How to keep everything aligned
▶ How to use the `float` property

Now that you've learned some of the basics of creating web content, in this lesson you'll learn the nitty-gritty of using CSS to enhance the display of that content. In the lessons that follow, you'll dive in to using CSS to control aspects of your entire web page rather than just individual pieces of text or graphics.

Before you tackle page layout, however, it is important to understand four particular CSS properties individually before putting them all together:

▶ `margin` **and** `padding`—For adding space around elements

▶ `align` **and** `float`—For placing your elements in relationship to others

The examples provided in this lesson are not the most stylish examples of web content ever created, but they are not intended to be. Instead, the examples clearly show just how HTML5 and CSS are working together. Although this lesson is short in terms of page count, the concepts deserve careful reading and hands-on practice. When you master CSS through this and other sections of the course, as well as through ongoing practice of what you've learned, you'll be able to use your own design skills to enhance what can be (and often is) the relatively basic underlying scaffolding.

Using Margins

Style sheet *margins* enable you to add empty space around the *outside* of the rectangular area for an element on a web page. It is important to remember that the `margin` property works with space outside the element.

Following are the style properties for setting margins:

- `margin-top`—Sets the top margin

- `margin-right`—Sets the right margin

- `margin-bottom`—Sets the bottom margin

- `margin-left`—Sets the left margin

- `margin`—Sets the top, right, bottom, and left margins as a single property

You can specify margins by using any of the individual margin properties or by using the `margin` property. Margins can be specified as `auto`, meaning that the browser sets the margins in specific lengths (pixels, points, or ems, among others) or in percentages. If you decide to set a margin as a percentage, keep in mind that the percentage is calculated based on the size of the containing element. So, if you set the `margin-left` property of an element within the body to 25%, the left margin of the element will end up being 25% of the width of the entire page. However, if you set the `margin-left` property of an element within *that* element to 25%, it will be 25% of whatever that original 25% was calculated to be.

The code in Listing 9.1 produces four rectangles on the page, each 250 pixels wide and 100 pixels high, with a 5-pixel solid black border (see Figure 9.1). Each rectangle—or `<div>`, in this case—has a different background color. If you want the margin around each `<div>` to be 15 pixels on all sides, you can use the following:

```
margin-top: 15px;
margin-right: 15px;
margin-bottom: 15px;
margin-left: 15px;
```

NOTE

You can remember the shorthand order in at least two different ways. First, if you think of an element as being a rectangle, start at the top and work your way clockwise around the sides: top side, right side, bottom side, left side. Or you can use a first-letter mnemonic device and remember *TRBL* (pronounced "trouble" or "tribble," if you're a *Star Trek* fan), which also represents a possible state of being in case you forget the order of the margin properties.

Also note that the TRBL order is valid for padding properties and border properties as well.

You can also write that in shorthand, using the `margin` property:

```
margin: 15px 15px 15px 15px;
```

When you use the `margin` property (or `padding` or `border`) and you want all four values to be the same, you can simplify this even further and use the following:

```
margin: 15px;
```

When using shorthand for setting margins, padding, or borders, three approaches apply, which vary based on how many values you use when setting the property:

- ▶ **One value**—The size of all the margins

- ▶ **Two values**—The size of the top/bottom margins and the left/right margins (in that order)

- ▶ **Three values**—The size of the top margin, the left and right margins (they are given the same value), and the bottom margin (in that order)

- ▶ **Four values**—The size of the top, right, bottom, and left margins (in that order)

You might find it easiest to consistently use one value or consistently use all four values, but that's certainly not a requirement.

LISTING 9.1 Simple Code to Produce Four Colored `<div>` Elements with Borders and Margins

```
<!doctype html>
<html lang="en">
  <head>
    <meta charset="utf-8">
    <title>Color Blocks</title>
    <style>
      div {
          width: 250px;
          height: 100px;
          border: 5px solid #000000;
          color: black;
          font-weight: bold;
          text-align: center;
      }
      div#d1 {
          background-color: red;
          margin: 15px;
      }
      div#d2 {
          background-color: green;
          margin: 15px;
      }
      div#d3 {
          background-color: blue;
          margin: 15px;
      }
      div#d4 {
          background-color: yellow;
          margin: 15px;
      }
```

```
    </style>
  </head>
  <body>
    <div id="d1">DIV #1</div>
    <div id="d2">DIV #2</div>
    <div id="d3">DIV #3</div>
    <div id="d4">DIV #4</div>
  </body>
</html>
```

You can see the output of Listing 9.1 in Figure 9.1.

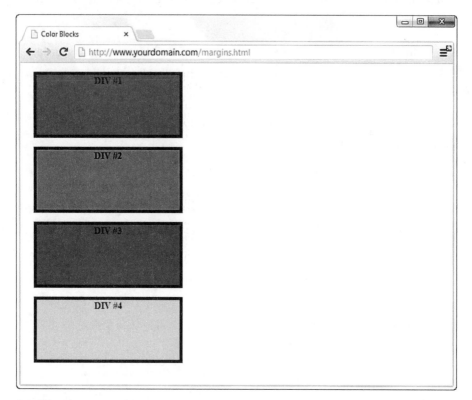

FIGURE 9.1
The basic color blocks sample page shows four color blocks, each with equal margins.

Next, working with just the `margin` property in the style sheet entries in Listing 9.1, let's shift the margins. In this example, you can't really see the right-side margin on any of these `<div>` elements because there's nothing to the right of them, and they're not aligned to the right. With that in mind, you can set `margin-right` to `0px` in all of these. Beyond that, the next set of goals is to produce the following:

- No margin around the first color block
- A left-side margin of 15 pixels, a top margin of 5 pixels, and no bottom margin around the second color block
- A left-side margin of 75 pixels and no top margin or bottom margin around the third color block
- A left-side margin of 250 pixels and a top margin of 25 pixels around the fourth color block

This seems as though it would be straightforward—no margin is being set around the first block. But if there is a margin at the top of the second block, there really *will* be a visible margin between the first and second blocks, even if you do not specify a margin for the first block.

The new style sheet entries for the four named `<div>` elements now look like this:

```
div#d1 {
  background-color: red;
  margin: 0px;
}
div#d2 {
  background-color: green;
  margin: 5px 0px 0px 15px;
}
div#d3 {
  background-color: blue;
  margin: 0px 0px 0px 75px;
}
div#d4 {
  background-color: yellow;
  margin: 25px 0px 0px 250px;
}
```

The result of the code changes (see Figure 9.2) seems random but is actually quite useful for pointing out a few other important points. For example, recall that one of the goals was to produce no margin around the first color block, and you might expect the border of the color block to be flush with the browser window. But as Figure 9.2 shows, there is a clear space between the content of the page and the frame of the browser window.

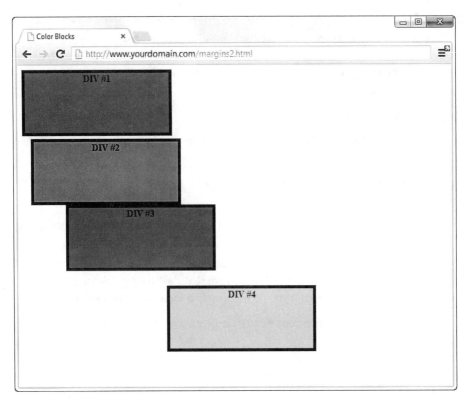

FIGURE 9.2
Modifications to the color blocks sample page display some different margins.

If you were working on element placement—which we get to in the next lesson—this would cause a problem in the layout. To ensure that your placements and margins are counted from a position flush with the browser, you need to address the margin of the <body> element itself. In this case, you add the following to your style sheet:

```
body {
  margin: 0px;
}
```

Another "gotcha" to remember is that if you have two bordered elements stacked on top of each other but no margin between them, the point at which they touch appears to have a double border. You might therefore consider making the top element's border-bottom half the width and then also make the bottom element's border-top half the width. If you do this, the borders appear to be the same width as the other sides when the elements are stacked on top of each other.

In addition, you might think that using a left-side margin of 250 pixels—the width of the <div> elements—would begin the fourth color block where the third color block ended. That is not the case, however, because the third color block has a `margin-left` of 75 pixels. For those elements to be even close to lining up, the `margin-left` value for the fourth `div` would have to be 325 pixels.

Changing the styles to those shown in the following code produces the spacing shown in Figure 9.3:

```
body {
  margin: 0px;
}
div {
  width: 250px;
  height: 100px;
  color: black;
  font-weight: bold;
  text-align: center;
}
div#d1 {
  border: 5px solid #000000;
  background-color: red;
  margin: 0px;
}
div#d2 {
  border-width: 6px 6px 3px 6px;
  border-style: solid;
  border-color: #000000;
  background-color: green;
  margin: 10px 0px 0px 15px;
}
div#d3 {
  border-width: 3px 6px 6px 6px;
  border-style: solid;
  border-color: #000000;
  background-color: blue;
  margin: 0px 0px 0px 15px;
}
div#d4 {
  border: 5px solid #000000;
  background-color: yellow;
  margin: 0px 0px 0px 265px;
}
```

These changes give the <body> element a zero margin, thus ensuring that a `margin-left` value of 25 pixels truly is 25 pixels from the edge of the browser frame. It also shows the second and third color blocks stacked on top of each other, but with modifications to the `border` element so that a double border does not appear. In addition, the fourth color block begins where the third color block ends.

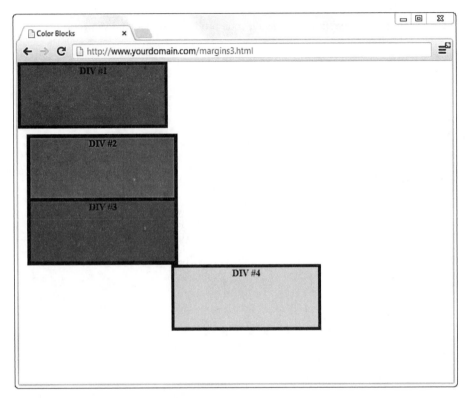

FIGURE 9.3
A third modification to the color blocks pulls items into closer relationship with each other.

As you can see in Figure 9.3, some overlap occurs between the right edge of the third color block and the left edge of the fourth color block. Why is that the case, if the color blocks are 250 pixels wide, the third color block has a `margin-left` value of 15 pixels, and the fourth color block is supposed to have a 265-pixel margin to its left? Well, it does have that 265-pixel margin, but that margin size is not enough because you also have to factor in the 6 pixels of border. Changing the `margin` property for the fourth color block to reflect the following code makes the third and fourth blocks line up according to plan (see Figure 9.4):

```
margin:0px 0px 0px 276px;
```

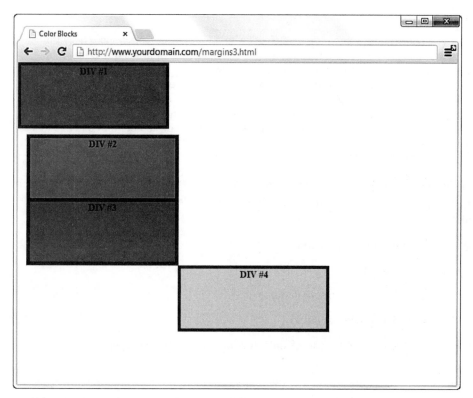

FIGURE 9.4
Changing the margin to allow for 11 pixels of border width.

As shown in these examples, margin specifications are incredibly useful for element placement, but you must use caution when setting these specifications.

Padding Elements

Adding padding is similar to using margins, in that both add extra space to elements. The big difference is where that space is located. Recall that margins are added to the outsides of elements. On the other hand, padding adds space *inside* the rectangular area of an element. Because the padding of an element appears within the element's content area, it assumes the same style as the content of the element, including the background color.

CAUTION

Most designers assume that if you create an element with a width of 50 pixels and a height of 30 pixels and then set the padding to 5 pixels, the remaining content area will be 40 pixels by 20 pixels. But *this is not the default action* in most web browsers or the HTML/CSS specifications. Instead, the width of the content area will be 50 pixels, but the entire box will take up 60 pixels in width (50 + 5 for the left padding + 5 for the right padding). If there are any borders defined, they are added to the total rendered width as well. The height acts the same way. In Lesson 10, "Understanding the CSS Box Model and Positioning," you will learn how to deal with this and make boxes behave as you expect.

You specify the padding of a style rule by using one of the `padding` properties, which work much like the `margin` properties. The following properties are available for use in setting the padding of style rules:

- `padding-top`—Sets the top padding

- `padding-right`—Sets the right padding

- `padding-bottom`—Sets the bottom padding

- `padding-left`—Sets the left padding

- `padding`—Sets the top, right, bottom, and left padding as a single property

As with margins, you can set the padding of style rules by using individual padding properties or the `padding` property. You can also express padding by using either a unit of measurement or a percentage.

Following is an example of how you might set the left and right padding for a style rule so that there are 10 pixels of padding on each side of an element's content:

```
padding-left: 10px;
padding-right: 10px;
```

As with margins, you can set all the padding for an element with a single property (the `padding` property). To set the `padding` property, you can use the same three approaches available for the `margin` property. Following is an example of how you would set the vertical padding (top/bottom) to 12 pixels and the horizontal padding (left/right) to 8 pixels in a style rule:

```
padding: 12px 8px;
```

Following is more explicit code that performs the same task by specifying all four padding values:

```
padding: 12px 8px 12px 8px;
```

In all the figures so far in this lesson, note that the text DIV #1, DIV #2, and so on appears at the top of the colored block, with just a little space between the border and the text. That amount of space hasn't been specified by any padding value, but it appears as a sort of default within the element. Listing 9.2 shows some examples of the specific control you can have over your element padding. All the color blocks are 250 pixels wide and 100 pixels high, have a 5-pixel solid black border, and have 25 pixels of margin (see Figure 9.5). The fun stuff happens within the padding values for each individual <div>.

LISTING 9.2   Simple Code to Produce Four Colored <div> Elements with Borders, Margins, and Padding

```html
<!doctype html>
<html lang="en">
  <head>
    <meta charset="utf-8">
    <title>Color Blocks</title>
    <style>
      body {
        margin: 0px;
      }
      div {
        width: 250px;
        height: 100px;
        border: 5px solid #000000;
        color: black;
        font-weight: bold;
        margin: 25px;
      }
      div#d1 {
        background-color: red;
        text-align: center;
        padding: 15px;
      }
      div#d2 {
        background-color: green;
        text-align: right;
        padding: 25px 50px 6px 6px;
      }
      div#d3 {
        background-color: blue;
        text-align: left;
        padding: 6px 6px 6px 50px;
      }
      div#d4 {
        background-color: yellow;
        text-align: center;
        padding: 50px;
      }
    </style>
  </head>
  <body>
```

```
    <div id="d1">DIV #1</div>
    <div id="d2">DIV #2</div>
    <div id="d3">DIV #3</div>
    <div id="d4">DIV #4</div>
  </body>
</html>
```

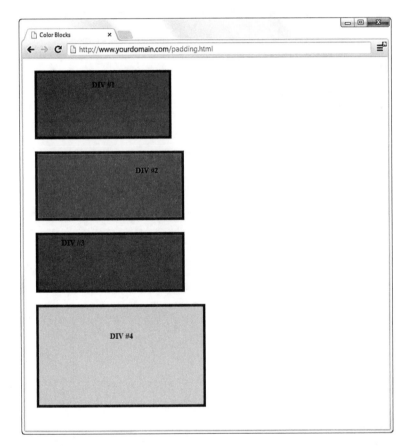

FIGURE 9.5
The basic color blocks sample page shows four color blocks with variable padding.

You should immediately recognize that something is amiss in this example. The color blocks are all supposed to be 250 pixels wide and 100 pixels high. The color blocks in Figure 9.5 are not uniform because the `width` and `height` declarations apply only to the content box. Any padding or border lengths are added to those dimensions in the final rendered display.

If you place the text in a <p> element and give that element a white background (see Figure 9.6), you can see where the padding is in relationship to the text. You will learn about this effect in detail in Lesson 10, as well as how to fix it.

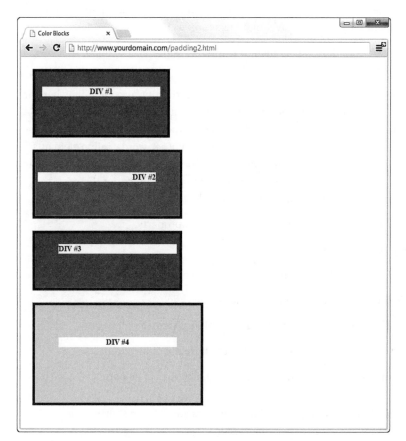

FIGURE 9.6
Showing the padding in relationship to the text.

The greatest number of tweaks or nudges you make in your web design with CSS will have to do with margins and padding. Just remember: Margins are outside the element; padding is inside it.

Keeping Everything Aligned

Because content on a web page doesn't always fill the entire width of the rectangular area in which it is displayed, it is often helpful to control the alignment of the content. Even if text within a rectangular area extends to multiple lines, alignment enters the picture because you might want the text left-justified, right-justified, or centered. Two style properties enable you to control the alignment of elements inside a box: `text-align` and `vertical-align`.

You saw examples of these style properties in action (when aligning images) in Lesson 8, "Working with Colors, Images, and Multimedia," but it doesn't hurt to mention these properties again here because alignment plays a role in overall page design as well.

As a refresher, using `text-align` aligns an element horizontally within its bounding area, and it can be set to `left`, `right`, `center`, or `justify`.

The `vertical-align` property is similar to `text-align` except that it is used to align elements vertically. The `vertical-align` property specifies how an element is aligned with its parent or, in some cases, the current line of elements on the page. "Current line" refers to the vertical placement of elements that appear within the same parent element—in other words, inline elements. If several inline elements appear on the same line, you can set their vertical alignments the same to align them vertically. A good example is a row of images that appear one after the next; the `vertical-align` property enables you to align them vertically.

Following are common values for use with the `vertical-align` property:

- `top`—Aligns the top of an element with the current line
- `middle`—Aligns the middle of an element with the middle of its parent
- `bottom`—Aligns the bottom of an element with the current line
- `text-top`—Aligns the top of an element with the top of its parent
- `baseline`—Aligns the baseline of an element with the baseline of its parent
- `text-bottom`—Aligns the bottom of an element with the bottom of its parent

Alignment works in conjunction with margins, padding, and (as you'll learn shortly) the `float` property to enable you to maintain control over your design.

Centering Blocks of Content

One thing you may have noticed when you were working in the previous section is that centering, especially centering blocks of content, can be challenging. While you can center text and other inline elements (such as links or buttons) with `text-align: center;` getting things like images or text boxes to center is difficult. Many novice web designers fall back on the old and *very* outdated <center> tag. But please: *Don't use the* <center> *tag.*

As we just mentioned, it's old and outdated; it's also been *deprecated*, which means it's been removed from the HTML specification. Browser makers can support it (and other deprecated syntax) if they wish, but they don't have to, and in the future, it may stop working completely. But more importantly, the `<center>` tag does only one thing: It defines the presentation of the contents as centered. It doesn't provide any semantic meaning or otherwise affect the structure of the document. Instead of using the `<center>` tag, you should use CSS.

If you're trying to center an image or a block of content in your design, the easiest way is to change the horizontal (left and right) margins to `auto`, like so:

```
margin-left: auto;
margin-right: auto;
```

You can also use the `margin` shorthand property:

```
margin: 0 auto;
```

This works only on elements that have a width set that is smaller than the current container. If you try to center a `<div>` that does not have the width set, nothing will happen. But if you add a `width` or maximum width value and then the `margin: 0 auto;` style, the browser will automatically add space on the left and right to center it. You will learn other ways to center block elements in Lesson 12, "Creating Layouts Using Modern CSS Techniques."

Understanding the `float` Property

The `float` property is an important tool for understanding a popular type of CSS-based layout and design. Briefly stated, the `float` property allows elements to be moved around in the design so that other elements can wrap around them. You often find `float` used in conjunction with images (as you saw in Lesson 8), but you can—and many designers do—float all sorts of elements in the layout.

Elements float horizontally, not vertically, so you have to concern yourself with just two possible values: `right` and `left`. An element that floats will float as far right or as far left (depending on the value of `float`) as the containing element will allow it. For example, if you have three `<div>` elements with `float` set to `left`, they will all line up to the left of the containing body element. If you have these `<div>` elements within another `<div>`, they will line up to the left of *that* element, even if that element itself is floated to the right.

You can best understand floating by seeing a few examples, so take a look at Listing 9.3. This listing simply defines three rectangular `<div>` elements and floats them next to each other (floating to the left).

LISTING 9.3 Using `float` to Place `<div>` Elements

```
<!doctype html>
<html lang="en">
  <head>
    <meta charset="utf-8">
    <title>Color Blocks</title>
    <style>
      body {
        margin:0px;
      }
      div {
        width: 250px;
        height: 100px;
        border: 5px solid #000000;
        color: black;
        font-weight: bold;
        margin: 25px;
      }
      div#d1 {
        background-color: red;
        float: left;
      }
      div#d2 {
        background-color: green;
        float: left;
      }
      div#d3 {
        background-color: blue;
        float: left;
      }
    </style>
  </head>

  <body>
    <div id="d1">DIV #1</div>
    <div id="d2">DIV #2</div>
    <div id="d3">DIV #3</div>
  </body>
</html>
```

Figure 9.7 shows the resulting page. Already you can see a problem: These three color blocks were supposed to be floated next to each other. Well, actually they *are* floated next to each other, but the browser window is not wide enough to display these three 250-pixel-wide blocks with 25 pixels of margin between them. Because they are floating, the third one simply floats to the next line.

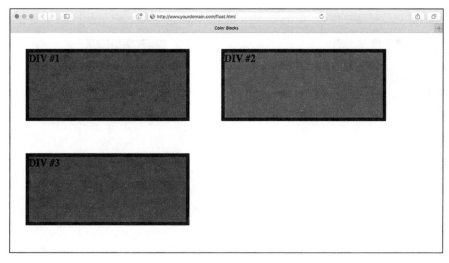

FIGURE 9.7
Using `float` to place the color blocks.

You can imagine that this could be a problem in a specifically designed visual layout, so pay attention to your margins, padding, alignment, and floating while also testing within a target browser window size. Granted, the browser window in Figure 9.7 is a small one to make this point about floating elements moving to the next line when there is no room for them to fit where they should. In other words, if you open the same HTML file with a larger browser window, you might not see the issue; this is why you should always check your sites at different resolutions to see whether a fix is needed. The fix here is to adjust the margins and other size-related properties of your `<div>` elements.

Figure 9.8 shows another interesting possibility when the `float` property is used. This figure shows what happens with just a few changes to the code from Listing 9.3: making the color blocks only 100 pixels wide, reducing the margins to 10px, and changing the `float` alignment of the second color block to `right` (instead of `left`).

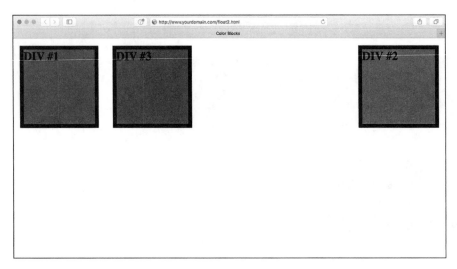

FIGURE 9.8
Using float to place the color blocks.

However, something interesting has happened. The second color block now appears visually as the third color block because it is flush right. The second color block has a float value of right, so it has floated all the way to the right. The first and third color blocks are floating as far to the left as possible, regardless of the way in which the <div> code appears in the HTML, which is as follows:

```
<div id="d1">DIV #1</div>
<div id="d2">DIV #2</div>
<div id="d3">DIV #3</div>
```

Getting used to floating takes a lot of practice, especially when your page has additional elements rather than just a few colored blocks. For example, what happens when you add a basic paragraph to the mix? All elements placed after the floating element then float around that element. To avoid that problem, use the clear property.

The clear property has five possible values: left, right, both, none, and inherit. The most common values are left, right, and both. Specifying clear:left; ensures that no other floating elements are allowed to the left, clear:right; ensures that no other floating elements are allowed to the right, and so on. Using floating and clearing is a learn-by-doing process, so look for more situations in the Workshop at the end of this lesson.

Summary

This lesson introduced you to some of the most fundamental style properties in CSS-based design: `margin`, `padding`, and `float`. You learned how the `margin` property controls space around the outside of elements and how the `padding` property works with space within the elements.

After getting a refresher on the `text-align` and `vertical-align` properties you learned about in a previous lesson, you learned about the `float` property. The `float` property allows for specific placement of elements and additional content around those elements.

Q&A

Q. The examples of margins and padding in this lesson all had to do with boxes and text. Can I apply margins and padding to images as well?

A. Yes, you can apply margins and padding to any block-level element, such as a <p>, a <div>, an <img>, and lists such as <ul> and <ol>, as well as list items (<li>)—just to name a few. You can also apply margins and padding to inline elements, but the results may not be as you expect, so always test your pages in multiple browsers.

Q. Is there a good rule of thumb for when you should use margins versus padding?

A. You need to understand two differences between CSS margins and padding. The first difference is that padding on a link can be clicked or tapped to interact with it, while a margin cannot. Because of this, you should use padding, rather than margins, around links to make them easier to click.

There is also another difference you should be aware of. For block-level elements, the vertical margins will collapse together into a single margin that is equal to the largest individual margin. You saw this in this lesson. In Listing 9.1, each of the <div> elements had a top and bottom margin of 15 pixels, but the vertical space between the elements was not 30 pixels; it was just 15 pixels. If you change one of the elements to have a bottom or top margin of 20 pixels, the space between the elements will grow only 5 pixels. Vertical padding, because it is inside the element, does not collapse. Because vertical padding does not collapse, you should use the `padding` property whenever you want a set amount of space around the element, regardless of where it displays on the page. Otherwise, you should use margins.

Workshop

The Workshop contains quiz questions and exercises to help you solidify your understanding of the material covered.

Quiz

1. To place two `<div>` elements next to each other, but with a 30-pixel margin between them, what entry or entries can you use in the style sheet?

2. Which CSS style property and value are used to ensure that content does not appear to the left of a floating element?

3. What style sheet entry is used to place text within a `<div>` to appear 12 pixels from the top of the element?

4. What is the shorthand property to set the vertical margins to 1rem and the horizontal margins to 2rem?

5. Where is the padding applied to an element?

6. What non-shorthand properties would you use to set the padding of an element to 1 pixel from the top, 2 pixels from the right, and 6 pixels from the left?

7. What property would you use to align text to the vertical middle of the line?

8. What does the `text-align: justify;` property do?

9. How can you position a 50% wide paragraph to line up on the right side of the screen (with the text aligned to the left)?

10. Where would the text YOU ARE HERE display in the following HTML in a 640 × 480 screen?

```
<!doctype html>
<html lang="en">
  <head>
    <meta charset="utf-8">
    <title>Where does the text go?</title>
    <style>
      div {
        width: 100px;
        height: 100px;
        border: solid red 2px;
      }
      p {
        width: 300px;
        text-align: center;
      }
      .left { float: left; }
      .right { float: right; }
    </style>
  </head>
```

```
  <body>
    <div class="left"></div>
    <div class="right"></div>
    <p>YOU ARE HERE</p>
  </body>
</html>
```

NOTE

Just a reminder for those of you reading these words in the print or e-book edition of this book: If you go to **www.informit.com/register** and register this book (using ISBN 9780672338083), you can receive free access to an online Web Edition that not only contains the complete text of this book but also features an interactive version of this quiz.

Answers

1. You can use several entries. The first `<div>` uses the style property `margin-right:15px`. The second `<div>` uses the style property `margin-left:15px`. Or you can assign the full 30 pixels to either `<div>` by using `margin-right` or `margin-left`, as appropriate. In addition, at least the first `<div>` needs to have `float:left` assigned to it.

2. In this instance, use `clear:left`.

3. You would use `padding-top:12px`.

4. You would use `margin: 1rem 2rem;`.

5. The padding is applied inside the element.

6. You would use `padding-top: 1px;`, `padding-right: 2px;`, and `padding-left: 6px;`.

7. You would use `vertical-align: middle;`.

8. It lines up the text so that it is straight on both the right and left edges, with no rag.

9. You would use `p { float: right; }`.

10. The text would appear between the two boxes but closer to the left one.

Exercises

▶ Fully understanding margins, padding, alignment, and floating takes practice. Using your own color blocks code or <div> elements, practice all manner and sorts of spacing and floating before moving on to the next lesson. The next lesson discusses the CSS box model as a whole, which encompasses the individual items discussed in this lesson.

▶ While you're at it, practice applying margins and padding to every block-level element you've learned so far. Get used to putting images within blocks of text and putting margins around the images so that the text does not run right up to the edge of the graphic.

Understanding the CSS Box Model and Positioning

What You'll Learn in This Lesson:

- ▶ How to conceptualize the CSS box model
- ▶ How to change the box model the browser uses
- ▶ How to position your elements
- ▶ How to control the way elements stack up
- ▶ How to manage the flow of text

In the preceding lesson, we mentioned the CSS box model a few times. This lesson begins with a discussion of the box model and explains how the information you learned in the preceding lesson helps you understand this model. It's important to spend some time focusing on and practicing working with the box model because if you have a good handle on how the box model works, you won't tear your hair out when you create a design and then realize that the elements don't line up or that they seem a little "off." You'll know that, in almost all cases, something—the margin, the padding, the border—just needs a little tweaking, or you may need to just check which box model your page is using.

You'll also learn more about CSS positioning, including stacking elements on top of each other in a three-dimensional way (instead of a vertical way). Finally, you'll learn a little more about controlling the flow of text around elements by using the `float` property.

The CSS Box Model

Every element in HTML is considered a "box," whether it is a paragraph, a `<div>`, an image, or something else. Boxes have consistent properties, whether we see them or not and whether the style sheet specifies them or not. They're always present, and as designers, we have to keep their presence in mind when creating a layout.

Figure 10.1 is a diagram of the box model. The box model describes the way in which every HTML block-level element has the potential for a border, padding, and margin and, specifically, how the border, padding, and margin are applied. In other words, all elements have some padding between the content and the border of the element. In addition, the border might or might not be visible, but space for it is there, just as there is a margin between the border of the element and any other content outside the element.

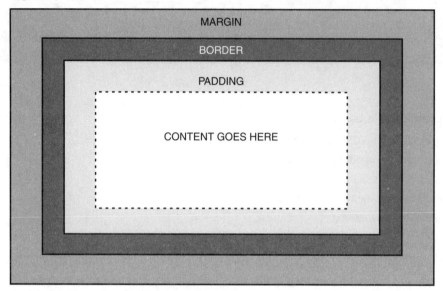

FIGURE 10.1
Every element in HTML is represented by the CSS box model.

Here's yet another explanation of the box model, going from the outside inward:

▶ The *margin* is the area outside the element. It never has color; it is always transparent.

▶ The *border* extends around the element, on the outer edge of any padding. The border can be of several types, widths, and colors.

▶ The *padding* exists around the content and inherits the background color of the content area.

▶ The *content* is surrounded by padding.

Here's where the tricky part comes in: In the default box model, to know the true or rendered height and width of an element, you have to take into account all the elements of the box model. Think back to the example from the preceding lesson: Despite the specific indication that a <div> should be 250 pixels wide and 100 pixels high, that <div> had to grow larger to accommodate the padding in use. If you had added a border, those dimensions would have added to the width and height of the rendered element as well.

You already know how to set the width and height of an element by using the `width` and `height` properties. The following example shows how to define a `<div>` that is 250 pixels wide and 100 pixels high, with a red background and a black single-pixel border:

```css
div {
  width: 250px;
  height: 100px;
  background-color: #ff0000;
  border: 1px solid #000000;
}
```

Figure 10.2 shows this simple `<div>`.

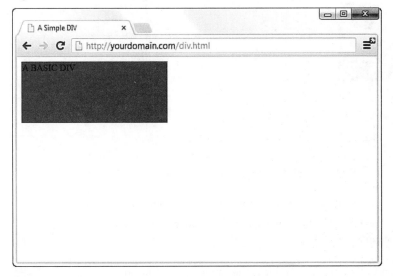

FIGURE 10.2
This is a simple `<div>`.

If we define a second element with these same properties but also add `margin` and `padding` properties of a certain size, we begin to see how the size of the element changes. This is because of the box model.

The second `<div>` is defined as follows, just adding 10 pixels of margin and 10 pixels of padding to the element:

```css
div#d2 {
  width: 250px;
  height: 100px;
  background-color: #ff0000;
  border: 5px solid #000000;
  margin: 10px;
  padding: 10px;
}
```

The second `<div>`, shown in Figure 10.3, is defined as the same height and width as the first one, but the overall height and width of the entire box surrounding the element itself is much larger when margins and padding are put in play.

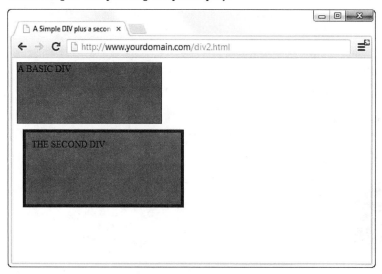

FIGURE 10.3
This is another simple `<div>`, but the box model affects the rendered size of the second `<div>`.

The total *width* the element takes up on the page is the sum of the following:

```
width + padding-left + padding-right + border-left + border-right +
margin-left + margin-right
```

The total *height* the element takes up on the page is the sum of the following:

```
height + padding-top + padding-bottom + border-top + border-bottom +
margin-top + margin-bottom
```

Therefore, the second `<div>` has an actual width of 300 (250 + 10 + 10 + 5 + 5 + 10 + 10) and an actual height of 150 (100 + 10 + 10 + 5 + 5 + 10 + 10).

NOTE

Throughout this course, you've been drilled in the use of the `doctype` declaration, and each bit of sample code includes a `doctype`. Continue this practice not only so that your code validates but because a very specific issue arises with some older versions of Internet Explorer and the CSS box model: If a `doctype` is not defined, some older versions of Internet Explorer manipulate the height and width of your elements in a way you did not intend. This causes browser incompatibility issues with your layout. So, remember to include a `doctype`.

By now, you can begin to see how the box model affects your design. Let's say that you have only 250 pixels of horizontal space, but you'd like 10 pixels of margin, 10 pixels of padding, and 5 pixels of border on all sides. To strike a balance between what you'd like and what you have room to display, you must specify the width of your <div> as only 200 pixels so that 200 + 10 + 10 + 5 + 5 + 10 + 10 adds up to that 250 pixels of available horizontal space.

The mathematics of the model are important as well. In dynamically driven sites or sites in which user interactions drive the client-side display (such as through JavaScript events), your server-side or client-side code could draw and redraw container elements on the fly. In other words, your code will produce the numbers, but you have to provide the boundaries.

NOTE

There is one other set of properties in the CSS box model: the outline properties:

- outline
- outline-width
- outline-style
- outline-color
- outline-offset

The outline properties act just like the border properties except that they do not take up any space in the box model. They also may not be rectangular.

Use these properties if you want to add a visible edge to elements without affecting the layout or changing the box model. Note that outlines do not have rounded corners (with the border-radius property) because they are not borders.

Changing the Box Model

At this point, you are probably wondering what the people who designed the CSS box model were thinking. In most design models, you start out with a given amount of space and work within it to position your elements. But with the default box model, you can stretch out well beyond your given amount of space completely without realizing it.

This is especially true with layouts that use flexible widths such as percentages, rems, or ems. Take this example:

```
div {
  width: 50%;
  height: 300px;
  float: left;
  padding: 0.25rem;
  border: solid 1px aqua;
}
```

If you place two `<div>` elements in your HTML, you would expect them to line up side by side as they both should take up 50%. But they do not. This is because, as you learned in the previous section, the space the elements take up includes the padding, border, and margin. Luckily, CSS3 gives us a tool to change that: the `box-sizing` property.

This property takes one of two values:

▶ `content-box`—The `width` and `height` values are assigned to the content box only, and `padding` and `border` are added afterward. This is the default.

▶ `border-box`—Any defined `padding` and `border` are included inside the assigned `width` and `height` values. This used to be called "quirks mode."

To make the previous example work, just add `box-sizing: border-box;`, and the two `<div>` elements float side by side as expected.

NOTE

The `box-sizing` property does not have a "margin-box" value. If you need to create layouts with variable widths or heights and fixed margins, you need to use a different layout style, such as flexible boxes. You will learn more about these in Lesson 12, "Creating Layouts Using Modern CSS Techniques."

Now that you've been schooled in the way of the box model, keep it in mind throughout the rest of the work you do in these lessons and in your web design. Among other things, it will affect element positioning and content flow, which are the two topics we tackle next.

The Whole Scoop on Positioning

Relative positioning is the default type of positioning HTML uses. You can think of relative positioning as being akin to laying out checkers on a checkerboard: The checkers are arranged from left to right, and when you get to the edge of the board, you move on to the next row. Elements that are styled with the `block` value for the `display` style property are automatically placed on a new row, whereas `inline` elements are placed on the same row, immediately next to the element preceding them. As an example, `<p>` and `<div>` tags are considered block elements, whereas the `<span>` and `<code>` tags are considered inline elements. There is also a third type of element—the `inline-block` element. The `<img>` tag is the most commonly used element of this type. Inline block elements are placed on the same row as other inline elements, but they can have width and height associated with them, whereas inline elements cannot.

The other type of positioning CSS supports is known as *absolute positioning* because it enables you to set the exact position of HTML content on a page. Although absolute positioning gives you the freedom to spell out exactly where an element is to appear, the position is still relative to any parent elements that appear on the page. In other words, absolute positioning enables you to specify the exact location of an element's rectangular area with respect to its parent's area, which is very different from relative positioning.

With the freedom of placing elements anywhere you want on a page, you can run into the problem of overlap, when an element takes up space another element is using. Nothing is stopping you from specifying the absolute locations of the elements so that they overlap. In this case, CSS relies on the z-index of each element to determine which element is on the top and which is on the bottom. You'll learn more about the z-index of elements later in this lesson. For now, let's look at exactly how you control whether a style rule uses relative or absolute positioning.

The type of positioning a particular style rule uses is determined by the `position` property, which can have any of the following four values:

- `relative`—The element is positioned relative to its current position in the document flow.

- `absolute`—The element is positioned based on its container element.

- `fixed`—The element is positioned relative to the browser window.

- `static`—The element is placed as it appears in the normal flow. This is the default.

NOTE
_____

There is also another value, `position: sticky;`, which causes the element to toggle between `relative` and `fixed`, depending on the scroll position. It is `relative` until a scrolling offset position is reached, and then it is `fixed`. You should use this with the `-webkit` browser prefix (`position: -webkit-sticky;`) for widest support.

After specifying the type of positioning, you provide the specific position by using the following properties:

- `left`—The left position offset

- `right`—The right position offset

- `top`—The top position offset

- `bottom`—The bottom position offset

You might think that these position properties make sense only for absolute positioning, but they actually apply to all types of positioning except `static`. With relative positioning, the position of an element is specified as an offset relative to the original position of the element. So, if you set the `left` property of an element to 25px, the left side of the element shifts over 25 pixels from its original (relative) position. An absolute position, on the other hand, is specified relative to the parent of the element to which the style is applied. So, if you set the `left` property of an element to 25px under absolute positioning, the left side of the element appears 25 pixels to the right of the parent element's left edge. On the other hand, using the right property with the same value positions the element so that its *right* side is 25 pixels to the right of the parent's *right* edge.

You cannot set both horizontal or both vertical position properties on the same element. If you set both the left and the right positions (or both top and bottom) on an element, the left and top properties will take precedence in left-to-right documents.

Let's return to the color-blocks example to see how positioning works. In Listing 10.1, the four colored blocks have relative positioning specified. As you can see in Figure 10.4, the blocks are positioned vertically.

LISTING 10.1   Showing Relative Positioning with Four Color Blocks

```
<!doctype html>
<html lang="en">
  <head>
    <meta charset="utf-8">
    <title>Positioning the Color Blocks</title>
    <style>
    div {
      position: relative;
      width: 250px;
      height: 100px;
      border: 5px solid #000;
      color: black;
      font-weight: bold;
      text-align: center;
    }
    div#d1 {
      background-color: red;
    }
    div#d2 {
      background-color: green;
    }
    div#d3 {
      background-color: blue;
    }
    div#d4 {
      background-color: yellow;
    }
    </style>
  </head>
  <body>
    <div id="d1">DIV #1</div>
    <div id="d2">DIV #2</div>
    <div id="d3">DIV #3</div>
```

```
     <div id="d4">DIV #4</div>
   </body>
</html>
```

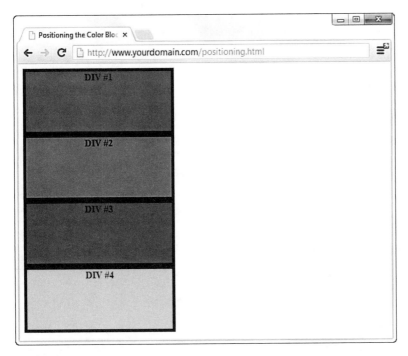

FIGURE 10.4
The colored blocks are positioned vertically, one on top of the other.

The style sheet entry for the `<div>` element sets the `position` style property for the `<div>` element to `relative`. Because the remaining style rules are inherited from the `<div>` style rule, they inherit its relative positioning. In fact, the only difference between the `div` rule and the other `div#d1` through `div#d4` rules is the different background colors.

Notice in Figure 10.4 that the `<div>` elements are displayed one after the next, which is what you would expect with relative positioning. But to make things more interesting, which is what we're here to do, you can change the positioning to absolute and explicitly specify the placement of the blocks. In Listing 10.2, the style sheet entries are changed to use absolute positioning to arrange the color blocks.

LISTING 10.2 Using Absolute Positioning of the Color Blocks

```
<!doctype html>
<html lang="en">
  <head>
```

```html
<meta charset="utf-8">
<title>Positioning the Color Blocks</title>
<style>
div {
    position: absolute;
    width: 250px;
    height: 100px;
    border: 5px solid #000;
    color: black;
    font-weight: bold;
    text-align: center;
}
div#d1 {
    background-color: red;
    left: 0px;
    top: 0px;
}
div#d2 {
    background-color: green;
    left: 75px;
    top: 25px;
}
div#d3 {
    background-color: blue;
    left: 150px;
    top: 50px;
}
div#d4 {
    background-color: yellow;
    left: 225px;
    top: 75px;
}
</style>
</head>
<body>
    <div id="d1">DIV #1</div>
    <div id="d2">DIV #2</div>
    <div id="d3">DIV #3</div>
    <div id="d4">DIV #4</div>
</body>
</html>
```

This style sheet sets the position property to absolute, which is necessary for the style sheet to use absolute positioning. In addition, the left and top properties are set for each of the inherited <div> style rules. However, the position of each of these rules is set so that the elements are displayed overlapping each other, as Figure 10.5 shows.

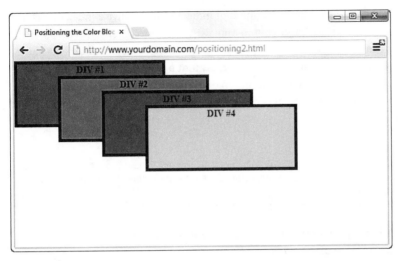

FIGURE 10.5
The color blocks are displayed using absolute positioning.

Now we're talking layout! Figure 10.5 shows how absolute positioning enables you to place elements exactly where you want them. It also reveals how easy it is to arrange elements so that they overlap. You might be curious about how a web browser knows which elements to draw on top when they overlap.

The fixed position places an element inside the browser window and leaves it there. This is often used as a type of watermark on web pages because the element will remain where it is positioned on the page, and other page elements will scroll past it. Other elements will overlap the fixed element, but you can control where the element appears in the stack. The next section covers how you can control stacking order.

Controlling the Way Things Stack Up

In certain situations, you want to carefully control the manner in which elements overlap each other on a web page. The z-index style property enables you to set the order of elements with respect to how they stack on top of each other. The name *z-index* might sound a little strange, but it refers to the notion of a third dimension (z) that points into the computer screen, in addition to the two dimensions that go across (x) and down (y) the screen. Another way to think of the z-index is to consider the relative position of a single magazine within a stack of magazines. A magazine nearer the top of the stack has a higher z-index than a magazine lower in the stack. Similarly, an overlapped element with a higher z-index is displayed on top of an element with a lower z-index.

The z-index property is used to set a numeric value that indicates the relative z-index of a style rule. The number assigned to z-index has meaning only with respect to other style rules in a style sheet, which means that setting the z-index property for a single rule doesn't mean much. On the other hand, if you set z-index for several style rules that apply to overlapped elements, the elements with higher z-index values appear on top of elements with lower z-index values. If you don't set the z-index for an element, it is assumed to have a value of 0 with respect to other elements with set z-index values.

NOTE

Regardless of the z-index value you set for a style rule, an element displayed with the rule will always appear on top of its parent.

Listing 10.3 contains another version of the color-blocks style sheet and HTML that uses z-index settings to alter the natural overlap of elements.

LISTING 10.3   Using z-index to Alter the Display of Elements in the Color-Blocks Sample

```
<!doctype html>
<html lang="en">
  <head>
    <meta charset="utf-8">
    <title>Positioning the Color Blocks</title>
    <style>
    div {
      position: absolute;
      width: 250px;
      height: 100px;
      border: 5px solid #000;
      color: black;
      font-weight: bold;
      text-align: center;
    }
    div#d1 {
      background-color: red;
      left: 0px;
      top: 0px;
      z-index: 0;
    }
    div#d2 {
      background-color: green;
      left: 75px;
      top: 25px;
      z-index: 3;
    }
```

```
  div#d3 {
    background-color: blue;
    left: 150px;
    top: 50px;
    z-index: 2;
  }
  div#d4 {
    background-color: yellow;
    left: 225px;
    top: 75px;
    z-index: 1;
  }
    </style>
  </head>
  <body>
    <div id="d1">DIV #1</div>
    <div id="d2">DIV #2</div>
    <div id="d3">DIV #3</div>
    <div id="d4">DIV #4</div>
  </body>
</html>
```

The only change in this code from what you saw in Listing 10.2 is the addition of the z-index
property in each of the numbered div style classes. Notice that the first numbered div has a
z-index setting of 0, which should make it the lowest element in terms of the z-index, whereas
the second div has the highest z-index. Figure 10.6 shows the color-blocks page as displayed with
this style sheet, which clearly shows how the z-index affects the displayed content and makes it
possible to carefully control the overlap of elements.

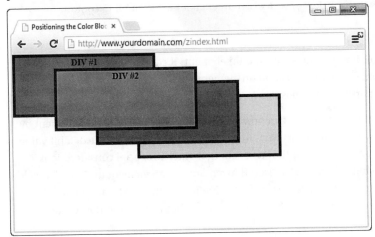

FIGURE 10.6
Using z-index to alter the display of the color blocks.

NOTE

The z-index property can be either positive or negative. So, if you want to force an item to be below another, you would change the z-index to a negative integer such as -1. This allows you to place positioned elements below other elements without explicitly setting the z-index for all of them.

Although the examples show colored blocks that are simple <div> elements, the z-index style property can affect any HTML content, including images.

Managing the Flow of Text

Now that you've seen some examples of placing elements relative to other elements or placing them absolutely, it's time to revisit the flow of content around elements. The conceptual *current line* is an invisible line used to place elements on a page. This line has to do with the flow of elements on a page; it comes into play as elements are arranged next to each other across and down the page. Part of the flow of elements is the flow of text on a page. When you mix text with other elements (such as images), it's important to control how the text flows around those other elements.

You've already seen two of these style properties in Lesson 9, "Working with Margins, Padding, Alignment, and Floating." Following are some style properties that give you control over text flow:

- ▶ float—Determines how text flows around an element

- ▶ clear—Stops the flow of text around an element

- ▶ overflow—Controls the overflow of text when an element is too small to contain all the text

The float property controls how text flows around an element. It can be set to either left or right. These values determine where to position an element with respect to flowing text. So, setting an image's float property to left positions the image to the left of flowing text.

As you learned in the preceding lesson, you can prevent text from flowing next to an element by using the clear property, which you can set to none, left, right, or both. The default value for the clear property is none, indicating that text is to flow with no special considerations for the element. The left value causes text to stop flowing around an element until the left side of the page is free of the element. Likewise, the right value means that text is not to flow around the right side of the element. The both value indicates that text isn't to flow around either side of the element.

The overflow property handles overflow text, which is text that doesn't fit within its rectangular area; this can happen if you set the width and height properties of an element too small. The overflow property can be set to visible, hidden, or scroll. The visible setting automatically enlarges the element so that the overflow text fits within it; this is the default setting for the property. The hidden value leaves the element the same size, allowing the overflow text to remain hidden from view. Perhaps the most interesting value is scroll, which adds scrollbars to the element so that you can move around and see the text.

Summary

This lesson began with an important discussion about the CSS box model and how to calculate the width and height of elements when considering margins, padding, and borders. You also learned how to change the default box model by using the box-sizing property. The lesson continued by tackling absolute positioning of elements, and you learned about positioning using z-index. You then learned about a few nifty style properties that enable you to control the flow of text on a page.

This lesson is brief but chock-full of fundamental information about controlling the design of your site. It is worth rereading and working through the examples so that you have a good foundation for your work.

Q&A

Q. An awful lot of web pages talk about the "box model hack" regarding margins and padding. Are you sure I don't have to use a hack?

A. At the beginning of this lesson, you learned that the HTML and CSS in this lesson (and others) all look the same in the current versions of the major web browsers. This is the product of several years of web developers having to do code hacks and other tricks before modern browsers began handling things according to CSS specifications rather than their own idiosyncrasies. In addition, there is a growing movement to rid Internet users of the *very* old web browsers that necessitated most of these hacks in the first place. So although we wouldn't necessarily advise you to design *only* for the current versions of the major web browsers, we also wouldn't recommend that you spend a ton of time implementing hacks for the older versions of browsers—which fewer than 2% of those on the Internet use, by the way. You should continue to write solid code that validates and adheres to design principles, test your pages in a suite of browsers and devices that best reflect your audience, and release your site to the world.

Q. **How would I determine when to use relative positioning and when to use absolute positioning?**

A. Although there are no set guidelines regarding the use of relative versus absolute positioning, the general idea is that absolute positioning is required only when you want to exert a finer degree of control over how content is positioned. This has to do with the fact that absolute positioning enables you to position content down to the exact pixel, whereas relative positioning is much less predictable in terms of how it positions content. This isn't to say that relative positioning can't do a good job of positioning elements on a page; it just means that absolute positioning is more exact. Of course, this also makes absolute positioning potentially more susceptible to changes in screen size, which you can't really control.

Q. **If I don't specify the z-index of two elements that overlap each other, how do I know which element will appear on top?**

A. If the `z-index` property isn't set for overlapping elements, the element that appears later in the web page will appear on top. The easy way to remember this is to think of a web browser drawing each element on a page as it reads it from the HTML document; elements read later in the document are drawn on top of those that were read earlier.

Workshop

The Workshop contains quiz questions and exercises to help you solidify your understanding of the material covered.

Quiz

1. What's the difference between relative positioning and absolute positioning?

2. Which CSS style property controls the manner in which elements overlap each other?

3. What HTML code could you use to display the words Where would you like to starting exactly at the upper-left corner of the browser window and display the words GO TODAY? in large type exactly 80 pixels down and 20 pixels to the right of the same corner?

4. How do you place an element so that it stays halfway down the browser window and on the right side and doesn't move with scrolling?

5. What is another term for the `border-box` box model?

6. What are the four parts of the box model?

7. What is the default `box-sizing` value?

8. Can you specify both the left and right or both the top and bottom positions in absolute positioning?

9. How can you stop text from flowing around a left floated element?

10. What happens to content that overfills the content area when the `overflow: hidden;` property is set?

NOTE

Just a reminder for those of you reading these words in the print or e-book edition of this book: If you go to **www.informit.com/register** and register this book (using ISBN 9780672338083), you can receive free access to an online Web Edition that not only contains the complete text of this book but also features an interactive version of this quiz.

Answers

1. In relative positioning, content is displayed according to the flow of a page, with each element physically appearing after the element preceding it in the HTML code. Absolute positioning, on the other hand, enables you to set the exact position of content on a page.

2. The `z-index` style property controls the manner in which elements overlap each other.

3. You can use this code:

```
<span style="position:absolute;left:0px;top:0px;">
Where would you like to</span>
<h1 style="position:absolute;left:80px;top:20px;">GO TODAY?</h1>
```

4. Use the following CSS:

```
position: fixed;
top: 50%;
right: 0;
```

5. The `border-box` box model is sometimes called "quirks mode."

6. The four parts of the box model are margin, border, padding, and content.

7. The default `box-sizing` value is `content-box`.

8. No, if you set both, the `left` or `top` statements will have precedence in left-to-right documents.

9. Set the `clear: left;` property.

10. The content disappears from sight on the screen. However, it is still visible in the HTML code.

Exercises

▶ Practice working with the intricacies of the CSS box model by creating a series of elements with different margins, padding, and borders and see how these properties affect their height and width.

▶ Find a group of images that you like and use absolute positioning and maybe even some z-index values to arrange them in a sort of gallery. Try to place your images so that they form a design (such as a square, triangle, or circle).

▶ Add a watermark image to a page with the position: fixed; and z-index properties.

Using CSS to Do More with Lists, Text, and Navigation

What You'll Learn in This Lesson:

- ▶ How the CSS box model affects lists
- ▶ How to customize the list item indicator
- ▶ How to use list items and CSS to create an image map
- ▶ How navigation lists differ from regular lists
- ▶ How to create vertical navigation with CSS
- ▶ How to create horizontal navigation with CSS

In Lesson 6, "Working with Fonts, Text Blocks, Lists, and Tables," you were introduced to three types of HTML lists, and in Lesson 9, "Working with Margins, Padding, Alignment, and Floating," you learned about margins, padding, and alignment of elements. In this lesson, you will learn how margins, padding, and alignment styles can be applied to different types of HTML lists, which will help you produce some powerful design elements purely in HTML and CSS.

Specifically, you will learn how to modify the appearance of list elements—beyond the use of the `list-style-type` property that you learned in Lesson 6—and how to use a CSS-styled list to replace the client-side image maps you learned about in Lesson 8, "Working with Colors, Images, and Multimedia." You will put into practice many of the CSS styles you've learned thus far, and the knowledge you will gain in this lesson will lead directly into using lists for more than just simply presenting a bulleted or numbered set of items. You will learn a few of the many ways to use lists for vertical or horizontal navigation, including how to use lists to create drop-down menus.

The methods explained in this lesson represent a very small subset of the numerous and varied navigation methods you can create using lists. However, the concepts are all similar; different results come from your own creativity and application of these basic concepts. To help you get your creative juices flowing, we will provide pointers to other examples of CSS-based navigation at the end of this lesson.

HTML List Refresher

As you learned in Lesson 6, there are three basic types of HTML lists. Each presents content in a slightly different way, based on its type and the context:

- ▶ **Ordered list**—This type of list is an indented list that displays numbers or letters before each list item. An ordered list is surrounded by `<ol>` and `</ol>` tags, and list items are enclosed in the `<li></li>` tag pair. This list type is often used to display numbered steps or levels of content.

- ▶ **Unordered list**—This type of list is an indented list that displays a bullet or another symbol before each list item. An unordered list is surrounded by `<ul>` and `</ul>` tags, and list items are enclosed in the `<li></li>` tag pair. This list type is often used to provide a visual cue that brief, yet specific, bits of information will follow.

- ▶ **Definition list**—This type of list is often used to display terms and their meanings, thereby providing information hierarchy within the context of the list itself—much like an ordered list but without the numbering. A definition list is surrounded by `<dl>` and `</dl>` tags, with `<dt>` and `</dt>` tags enclosing the term and `<dd>` and `</dd>` tags enclosing the definitions.

When the content warrants it, you can nest your ordered and unordered lists—or place lists within other lists. Nested lists produce a content hierarchy, so reserve their use for when your content actually has a hierarchy you want to display (such as content outlines or tables of contents). Or, as you will learn later in this lesson, you can use nested lists when your site navigation contains sub-navigational elements.

How the CSS Box Model Affects Lists

Specific list-related styles include `list-style-image` (for placement of an image as a list-item marker), `list-style-position` (indicating where to place the list-item marker), and `list-style-type` (the type of list-item marker itself). But while these styles control the structure of the list and list items, you can use `margin`, `padding`, `color`, and `background-color` styles to achieve even more specific displays with your lists.

NOTE
_____

Some older browsers handle margins and padding differently, especially around lists and list items. However, at the time of writing, the HTML and CSS in this and other lessons in this course are displayed identically in current versions of the major web browsers (Apple Safari, Google Chrome, Microsoft Edge, Mozilla Firefox, and Opera). Of course, you should still review your web content in all browsers before you publish it online, but the need for "hacking" style sheets to accommodate the rendering idiosyncrasies of browsers is effectively a thing of the past.
_____

In Lesson 9, you learned that every element has some padding between the content and the border of the element; you also learned there is a margin between the border of the element and any other content. This is true for lists, and when you are styling lists, you must remember that a "list" is actually made up of two elements: the parent list element type (<ul> or <ol>) and the individual list items themselves. Each of these elements has margins and padding that can be affected by a style sheet.

The examples in this lesson show you how different CSS styles affect the visual display of HTML lists and list items. Keep these basic differences in mind as you practice working with lists in this lesson, and you will be able to use lists to achieve advanced visual effects in site navigation.

Listing 11.1 creates a basic list containing three items. In this listing, the unordered list itself (the <ul>) is given a blue background, a black border, and a specific width of 100 pixels, as shown in Figure 11.1. The list items (the individual <li> items) have a gray background and a yellow border. The list item text and indicators (the bullet) are black.

LISTING 11.1   Creating a Basic List with Color and Border Styles

```
<!doctype html>
<html lang="en">
  <head>
    <meta charset="utf-8">
    <title>List Test</title>
    <style>
      ul {
        background-color: #6666ff;
        border: 1px solid #000000;
        width: 100px;
      }
      li {
        background-color: #cccccc;
        border: 1px solid #ffff00;
      }
    </style>
  </head>
  <body>
    <h1>List Test</h1>
    <ul>
      <li>Item #1</li>
      <li>Item #2</li>
      <li>Item #3</li>
    </ul>
  </body>
</html>
```

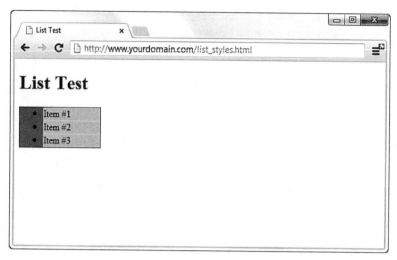

FIGURE 11.1
Styling the list and list items with colors and borders.

As Figure 11.1 shows, the `<ul>` creates a box in which the individual list items are placed. In this example, the entirety of the box has a blue background (`background-color: #6666ff;`). But also note that the individual list items—in this example, they use a gray background (`background-color: #cccccc;`) and a yellow border (`border: 1px solid #000000;`)— do not extend to the left edge of the box created by the `<ul>`.

This is because browsers automatically add a certain amount of padding to the left side of the `<ul>`. Browsers don't add padding to the margin, because that would appear around the out- side of the box. They add padding inside the box and only on the left side. That padding value is approximately 40 pixels.

NOTE

You can test the default `padding-left` value as displayed by different browsers by creating a simple test file such as the one shown in Listing 11.1 and then adding `padding-left: 40px;` to the declaration for the `ul` selector in the style sheet. If you reload the page and the display does not change, you know that your test browser uses 40 pixels as a default value for `padding-left`.

The default left-side padding value remains the same, regardless of the type of list and regardless of what box model you use (see `box-sizing` in Lesson 10, "Understanding the CSS Box Model and Positioning"). If you add the following line to the style sheet, creating a list with no item indicators, you will find that the padding remains the same (see Figure 11.2):

```
list-style-type: none;
```

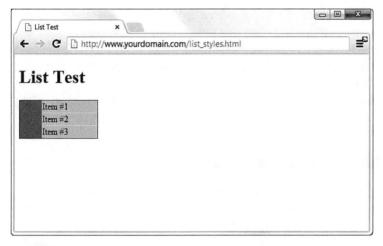

FIGURE 11.2
The default left-side padding remains the same with or without list item indicators.

When you are creating a page layout that includes lists of any type, play around with padding to place the items "just so" on the page. Similarly, just because no default margin is associated with lists doesn't mean you can't assign some to the display; adding `margin` values to the declaration for the `ul` selector provides additional layout control.

But remember that so far, we've worked with only the list definition itself; we haven't worked with the application of styles to the individual list items. In Figures 11.1 and 11.2, the gray background and yellow border of the list item show no default padding or margin. Figure 11.3 shows the different effects created by applying padding or margin values to list items rather than the overall list "box" itself.

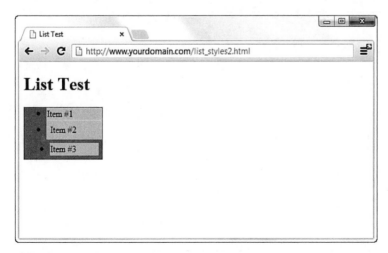

FIGURE 11.3
Different values affect the padding and margins on list items.

The first list item is the base item, with no padding or margin applied to it. The second list item uses a class called `padded`, defined in the style sheet as `padding: 6px;`, and you can see the 6 pixels of padding on all sides (between the content and the yellow border surrounding the element). Note that the placement of the bullet remains the same as the placement of the first list item. The third list item uses a class called `margined`, defined in the style sheet as `margin: 6px;`, to apply 6 pixels of margin around the list item; this margin allows the blue background of the `<ul>` to show through.

Placing List Item Indicators

All this talk of margins and padding raises another issue: the control of list item indicators (when used) and how text should wrap around them (or not). The default value of the `list-style-position` property is `outside`. This placement means that the bullets, numbers, and other indicators are kept to the left of the text, outside the box created by the `<li></li>` tag pair. When text wraps within the list item, it wraps within that box and remains flush left with the left border of the element.

But when the value of `list-style-position` is `inside`, the indicators are inside the box created by the `<li></li>` tag pair. Not only are the list item indicators then indented further (they essentially become part of the text), the text wraps beneath each item indicator.

Figure 11.4 shows an example of both outside and inside list style positions. The only changes between Listing 11.1 and the code used to produce the example in Figure 11.4 (not including the filler text added to Item #2 and Item #3) is that the second list item uses a class called `outside`, defined in the style sheet as `list-style-position: outside;`, and the third list item uses a class called `inside`, defined in the style sheet as `list-style-position: inside;`.

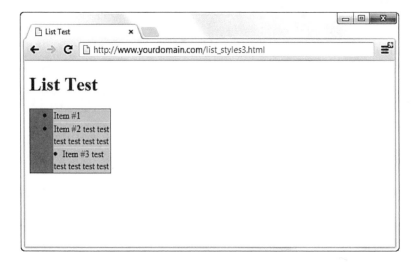

FIGURE 11.4
The difference between outside and inside values for list-style-position.

The additional filler text used for the second list item shows how the text wraps when the width of the list is defined as a value that is too narrow to display all on one line. You could achieve the same result without using `list-style-position: outside;` because that is the default value of `list-style-position` without any explicit statement in the code.

However, you can clearly see the difference when the `inside` position is used. In the third list item, the bullet and the text are both within the gray area bordered by yellow—the list item itself. Margins and padding affect list items differently when the value of `list-style-position` is `inside` (see Figure 11.5).

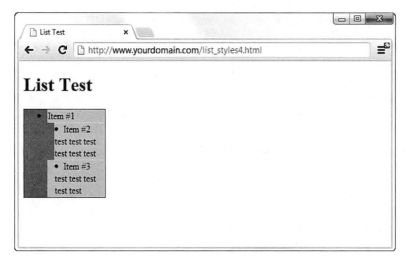

FIGURE 11.5
Margins and padding change the display of items using the `inside` value for `list-style-position`.

In Figure 11.5, the second and third list items both have a `list-style-position` value of `inside`. However, the second list item has a `margin-left` value of 12 pixels (`12px`), and the third list item has a `padding-left` value of 12 pixels. Although both content blocks (list indicator plus the text) show text wrapped around the bullet, and the placement of these blocks within the gray area defining the list item is the same, the affected area is the list item within the list itself.

As you would expect, the list item with the `margin-left` value of 12 pixels displays 12 pixels of blue showing through the transparent margin surrounding the list item. Similarly, the list item with the `padding-left` value of 12 pixels displays 12 pixels of gray background (of the list item) before the content begins. Padding is within the element; the margin is outside the element.

By understanding the way margins and padding affect both list items and the list in which they appear, you can create navigation elements in your website that are pure CSS and do not rely on external images. Later in this lesson, you'll learn how to create both vertical and horizontal navigation menus, as well as menu drop-downs.

NOTE

Remember that you can always use background colors when you're testing your designs to remind yourself which margins and paddings affect what inside lists. Once you've got the settings correct, remove the background colors or change them to fit your design.

Creating Image Maps with List Items and CSS

In Lesson 8 you learned how to create client-side image maps using the <map> element in HTML. Image maps enable you to define an area of an image and assign a link to that area (rather than having to slice an image into pieces, apply links to individual pieces, and stitch the image back together in HTML). However, you can also create an image map purely out of valid HTML and CSS.

The code in Listing 11.2 produces the image map that Figure 11.6 shows. When the code is rendered in a web browser, it simply looks like a web page with an image placed in it. The actions happen when your mouse hovers over a "hot" area, as you can see in Figure 11.6: The thick, dashed yellow border and image alt text show the area the mouse is hovering over, and in the lower left of the browser window, you can see the URL assigned to that hotspot.

LISTING 11.2   Creating an Image Map Using CSS

```
<!doctype html>
<html lang="en">
  <head>
    <meta charset="utf-8">
    <title>CSS Image Map Example</title>
    <style>
    #theImg {
        width: 400px;
        height: 500px;
        background: url(pets-collage.jpg) no-repeat;
        position: relative;
        border: 1px solid #000000;
        margin: 0 auto;
    }
    #theImg ul {
        margin: 0px;
        padding: 0px;
        list-style: none;
    }
    #theImg a {
        position: absolute;
        text-indent: -1000em;
    }
    #theImg a:hover {
        border: 4px dashed #ffff00;
    }
    #mc a {
        top: 0px;
        left: 0px;
```

```
        width: 231px;
        height: 146px;
    }
    #su a {
        top: 0px;
        left: 236px;
        width: 164px;
        height: 250px;
    }
    #st a {
        top: 150px;
        left: 0px;
        width: 231px;
        height: 100px;
    }
    #di a {
        top: 255px;
        left: 0px;
        width: 160px;
        height: 245px;
    }
    #sh a {
        top: 255px;
        left: 165px;
        width: 235px;
        height: 110px;
    }
    #au a {
        top: 370px;
        left: 165px;
        width: 235px;
        height: 130px;
    }
    </style>
</head>
<body>
    <div id="theImg">
        <ul>
            <li id="mc"><a href="[some URL]"
                title="McKinley">McKinley</a></li>
            <li id="su"><a href="[some URL]"
                title="Suni">Suni</a></li>
            <li id="st"><a href="[some URL]"
                title="Stormageddon">Stormageddon</a></li>
            <li id="di"><a href="[some URL]"
                title="Diamond">Diamond</a></li>
            <li id="sh"><a href="[some URL]"
                title="Shasta">Shasta / Inara</a></li>
            <li id="au"><a href="[some URL]"
                title="Auto">Suni / Auto</a></li>
```

```
        </ul>
      </div>
   </body>
</html>
```

FIGURE 11.6
CSS enables you to define hotspots in an image map.

As Listing 11.2 shows, the style sheet has quite a few entries, but the actual HTML is quite short.
List items are used to create several distinct clickable areas; those "areas" are list items that are
assigned a specific height and width and then placed over an image that sits in the background.
If the image is removed from the background of the <div> that surrounds the list, the list items
still exist and are still clickable.

Let's walk through the style sheet so that you understand the pieces that make up this HTML and
CSS image map, which is—at its most basic level—just a list of links.

The list of links is enclosed in a <div> named theImg. In the style sheet, this <div> is defined as
a block element that is 400 pixels wide and 500 pixels high, with a 1-pixel solid black border. The
background of this element is an image named pets-collage.jpg that is placed in one position and does not repeat (background: url ('pets-collage.jpg') no-repeat;). The
next bit of HTML that you see is the beginning of the unordered list (<ul>). In the style sheet, this
unordered list is given margin and padding values of 0 pixels all around and a list-style of
none—list items will not be preceded by any icon.

The list item text itself never appears to the user because of this trick in the style sheet entry for all <a> tags within the <div>:

```
text-indent: -1000em;
```

By indenting the text *negative* 1,000 ems, you can be assured that the text will never appear. It does exist, but it exists in a nonviewable area 1,000 ems to the left of the browser window. In other words, if you raise your left hand and place it to the side of your computer monitor, text-indent:-1000em; places the text somewhere to the left of your pinky finger. But that's what we want because we don't need to see the text link. We just need an area to be defined as a link so that the user's cursor changes as it does when rolling over any link in a website.

When the user's cursor hovers over a list item containing a link, that list item shows a 4-pixel border that is dashed and yellow, thanks to this entry in the style sheet:

```
#theImg a:hover {
    border: 4px dashed #ffff00;
}
```

The list items themselves are then defined and placed in specific positions based on the areas of the image that are supposed to be the clickable areas. For example, the list item with the di ID, for Diamond—the name of the item shown in the figure—has its top-left corner placed 255 pixels from the top of the <div> and 0 pixels in from the left edge of the <div>. This list item is 160 pixels wide and 245 pixels high. Similar style declarations are made for the #mc, #su, #st, #sh, and #au list items so that the linked areas associated with those IDs appear in certain positions relative to the image.

How Navigation Lists Differ from Regular Lists

When we talk about using lists to create navigation elements, we really mean using CSS to display content in the way website visitors expect navigation to look—in short, *different* from simple bulleted or numbered lists. Although it is true that a set of navigation elements is essentially a list of links, those links are typically displayed in a way that makes it clear that users should interact with the content:

▶ The user's mouse cursor will change to indicate that the element is clickable.

▶ The area around the element changes appearance when the mouse hovers over it.

▶ The content area is visually set apart from regular text.

Older methods of creating navigation tended to rely on images—such as graphics with beveled edges and the use of contrasting colors for backgrounds and text—plus client-side programming with JavaScript to handle image swapping based on mouse actions. But using pure CSS to create navigation from list elements produces a more usable, flexible, and search engine–friendly display that is accessible by users using all manner and sorts of devices.

Regardless of the layout of your navigational elements—horizontal or vertical—this lesson discusses two levels of navigation: primary and secondary. *Primary navigation* takes users to the introductory pages of main sections of the site; *secondary navigation* takes users to pages within a certain section of the site.

Creating Vertical Navigation with CSS

Depending on your site architecture—both the display template you have created and the manner in which you have categorized the information in the site—you might find yourself using vertical navigation for either primary navigation or secondary navigation.

For example, suppose you have created a website for your company and the primary sections are About Us, Products, Support, and Press. Within the primary About Us section, you might have several other pages, such as Mission, History, Executive Team, and Contact Us; these other pages are the secondary navigation within the primary About Us section.

Listing 11.3 sets up a basic secondary page with vertical navigation on the side of the page and content in the middle of the page. The links in the side and the links in the content area of the page are basic HTML list elements.

Listing 11.3 and the example shown in Figure 11.7 provide a starting point for showing how CSS enables you to transform two similar HTML structures into two different visual displays (and thus two different contexts).

LISTING 11.3   Basic Page with Vertical Navigation in a List

```
<!doctype html>
<html lang="en">
  <head>
    <meta charset="utf-8">
    <title>About Us</title>
    <style>
      body {
          font: 12pt Verdana, Arial, Georgia, sans-serif;
      }
      nav {
          width: 150px;
          float: left;
```

```
            margin-top: 12px;
            margin-right: 18px;
        }
        section {
            width: 550px;
            float: left;
        }
    </style>
</head>

<body>
    <nav>
      <ul>
        <li><a href="#">Mission</a></li>
        <li><a href="#">History</a></li>
        <li><a href="#">Executive Team</a></li>
        <li><a href="#">Contact Us</a></li>
      </ul>
    </nav>
    <section>
      <header>
        <h1>About Us</h1>
      </header>
      <p>On the introductory pages of main sections, it can be useful
      to repeat the secondary navigation and provide more context,
      such as:</p>
      <ul>
        <li><a href="#">Mission</a>: Learn more about our corporate
        mission and philanthropic efforts.</li>
        <li><a href="#">History</a>: Read about our corporate history
        and learn how we grew to become the largest widget maker
        in the country.</li>
        <li><a href="#">Executive Team</a>: Our team of executives makes
        the company run like a well-oiled machine (also useful for
        making widgets).</li>
        <li><a href="#">Contact Us</a>: Here you can find multiple
        methods for contacting us (and we really do care what you
        have to say).</li>
      </ul>
    </section>
  </body>
</html>
```

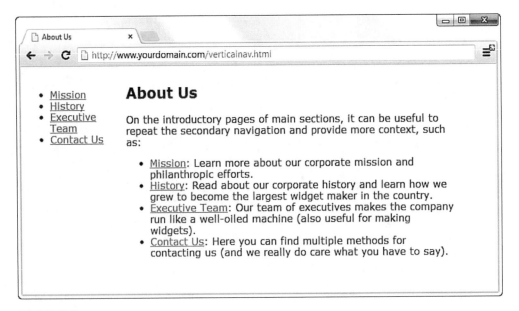

FIGURE 11.7
The starting point: an unstyled list navigation.

The contents of this page are set up in two sections: a <nav> element containing navigation and a single <section> element containing the primary text of the page. The only styles assigned to anything in this basic page are the width, margin, and float values associated with each element. No styles have been applied to the list elements.

To differentiate between the links present in the list in the content area and the links present in the list in the side navigation, add the following styles to the style sheet:

```
nav a {
   text-decoration: none;
}
section a {
   text-decoration: none;
   font-weight: bold;
}
```

These styles simply say that all <a> links in the <nav> have no underline, and all <a> links in the <section> have no underline and are bold. Figure 11.8 shows the difference.

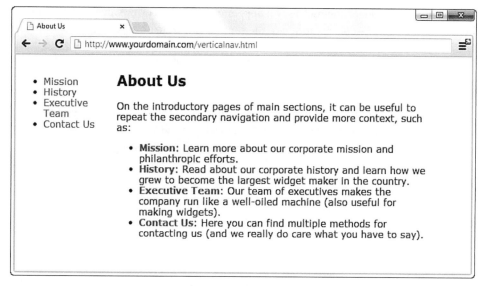

FIGURE 11.8
Differentiating the list elements using CSS.

But to really make the side navigation list look like something special, you have to dig deeper into the style sheet.

Styling the Single-Level Vertical Navigation

The goal with this particular set of navigation elements is simply to present them as a block of links without bullets and with background and text colors that change depending on their link state (regular link, visited link, hovering over the link, or activated link—covered in Lesson 7, "Using External and Internal Links"). The first step in the process is already complete: separating the navigation from the content. We've done that by putting the navigation in a <nav> element.

Next, we need to modify the <ul> that defines the link within the <nav> element. Let's take away the list indicator and ensure that there is no extra margin or padding hanging around besides the top margin. That top margin is used to line up the top of the navigation with the top of the "About Us" header text in the content area of the page:

```
nav ul {
    list-style: none;
    margin: 12px 0px 0px 0px;;
    padding: 0px;
}
```

Because the navigation list items themselves will appear as colored areas, we give each list item a bottom border so that some visual separation of the content can occur:

```
nav li {
   border-bottom: 1px solid #ffffff;
}
```

Now on to building the rest of the list items. The idea is that when the list items simply sit there acting as links, they are a special shade of blue with bold white text (although they are a smaller font size than the body text itself). To achieve that effect, we add the following:

```
nav li a:link, nav li a:visited {
   font-size: 10pt;
   font-weight: bold;
   display: block;
   padding: 3px 0px 3px 3px;
   background-color: #628794;
   color: #ffffff;
}
```

All the styles used previously should be familiar to you, except perhaps for `display: block;` in the style sheet entry. Setting the `display` property to `block` ensures that the entire `<li>` element is in play when a user hovers a mouse over it. Figure 11.9 shows the vertical list menu with these new styles applied to it.

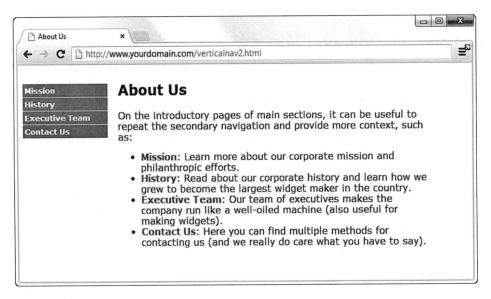

FIGURE 11.9
The vertical list is starting to look like a navigation menu.

When the user's mouse hovers over a navigational list element, the idea is for some visual change to take place so that the user knows that the element is clickable. This is akin to how most software menus change color when a user's cursor hovers over the menu items. In this case, we'll change the background color of the list item and change the text color of the list item so that they are different from the blue and white shown previously:

```
nav li a:hover, nav li a:active {
    font-size: 10pt;
    font-weight: bold;
    display: block;
    padding: 3px 0px 3px 3px;
    background-color: #c1a02e;
    color: #000000;
}
```

Figure 11.10 shows the results of all the stylistic work so far. A few entries in a style sheet have transformed the simple list into a visually differentiated menu.

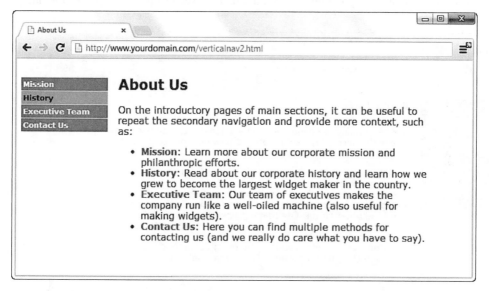

FIGURE 11.10
The list items now change color when the mouse hovers over them.

Styling the Multilevel Vertical Navigation

What if the site architecture calls for another level of navigation that we want users to see at all times? That is represented by nested lists (which you learned about in previous lessons) and more style sheet entries. In this case, assume that there are four navigation elements under the Executive Team link. In the HTML, modify the list as shown here:

```
<ul>
  <li><a href="#">Mission</a></li>
  <li><a href="#">History</a></li>
  <li><a href="#">Executive Team</a>
      <ul>
      <li><a href="#">&raquo; CEO</a>
      <li><a href="#">&raquo; CFO</a>
      <li><a href="#">&raquo; COO</a>
      <li><a href="#">&raquo; Other Minions</a>
      </ul>
  </li>
  <li><a href="#">Contact Us</a></li>
</ul>
```

This code produces a nested list under the Executive Team link (see Figure 11.11). The » HTML entity produces the right-pointing arrows that are displayed before the text in the new links.

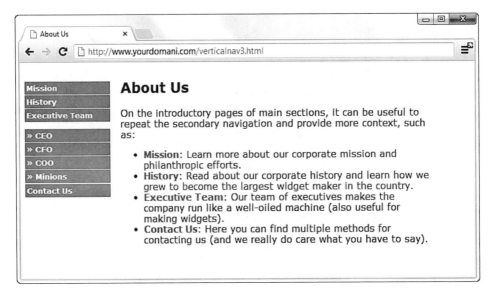

FIGURE 11.11
Creating a nested navigation list (but one that is not yet styled well).

The new items appear as block elements within the list, but the hierarchy of information is not visually represented. To add some sort of visual element that identifies these items as sub-navigational elements attached to the Executive Team link, we modify the style sheet again to add some indentation.

But before doing that, we need to modify some of the other style sheet entries as well. In the preceding section, we added selectors such as nav ul and nav li, which indicate "all <ul> in the

<nav> element" and "all <li> in the <nav> element," respectively. However, we now have two instances of <ul> and another set of <li> elements within the <nav> element, all of which we want to appear different from the original set.

To ensure that both sets of list items are styled appropriately, make sure that the style sheet selectors clearly indicate the hierarchy of the lists. To do that, use entries such as nav ul and nav ul li for the first level of lists and use nav ul ul and nav ul ul li for the second level of lists. Listing 11.4 shows the new version of style sheet entries and the HTML that produces the menu shown in Figure 11.12.

LISTING 11.4   Multilevel Vertical Navigation in a List

```
<!doctype html>
<html lang="en">
  <head>
    <meta charset="utf-8">
    <title>About Us</title>
    <style>
      body {
          font: 12pt Verdana, Arial, Georgia, sans-serif;
      }
      nav {
          width: 150px;
          float: left;
          margin-top: 12px;
          margin-right: 18px;
      }
      section {
          width: 550px;
          float: left;
      }
      nav a {
          text-decoration: none;
      }
      section a {
          text-decoration: none;
          font-weight: bold;
      }
      nav ul {
          list-style: none;
          margin: 12px 0px 0px 0px;
          padding: 0px;
      }
      nav ul li {
          border-bottom: 1px solid #ffffff;
      }
      nav ul li a:link, nav ul li a:visited {
          font-size: 10pt;
          font-weight: bold;
```

```
        display: block;
        padding: 3px 0px 3px 3px;
        background-color: #628794;
        color: #ffffff;
      }
      nav ul li a:hover, nav ul li a:active {
        font-size: 10pt;
        font-weight: bold;
        display: block;
        padding: 3px 0px 3px 3px;
        background-color: #c1a02e;
        color: #000000;
      }
      nav ul ul {
        margin: 0px;
        padding: 0px;
      }
      nav ul ul li {
        border-bottom: none;
      }
      nav ul ul li a:link, nav ul ul li a:visited {
        font-size: 8pt;
        font-weight: bold;
        display: block;
        padding: 3px 0px 3px 18px;
        background-color: #628794;
        color: #ffffff;
      }
      nav ul ul li a:hover, nav ul ul li a:active {
        font-size: 8pt;
        font-weight: bold;
        display: block;
        padding: 3px 0px 3px 18px;
        background-color: #c1a02e;
        color: #000000;
      }
    </style>
  </head>
  <body>
    <nav>
      <ul>
        <li><a href="#">Mission</a></li>
        <li><a href="#">History</a></li>
        <li><a href="#">Executive Team</a>
        <ul>
          <li><a href="#">&raquo; CEO</a></li>
          <li><a href="#">&raquo; CFO</a></li>
          <li><a href="#">&raquo; COO</a></li>
          <li><a href="#">&raquo; Other Minions</a></li>
        </ul></li>
```

```
      <li><a href="#">Contact Us</a></li>
    </ul>
  </nav>
  <section>
    <header>
      <h1>About Us</h1>
    </header>
    <p>On the introductory pages of main sections, it can be useful
    to repeat the secondary navigation and provide more context,
    such as:</p>
    <ul>
      <li><a href="#">Mission</a>: Learn more about our corporate
      mission and philanthropic efforts.</li>
      <li><a href="#">History</a>: Read about our corporate history
      and learn how we grew to become the largest widget maker
      in the country.</li>
      <li><a href="#">Executive Team</a>: Our team of executives makes
      the company run like a well-oiled machine (also useful for
      making widgets).</li>
      <li><a href="#">Contact Us</a>: Here you can find multiple
      methods for contacting us (and we really do care what you
      have to say.)</li>
    </ul>
  </section>
</body>
</html>
```

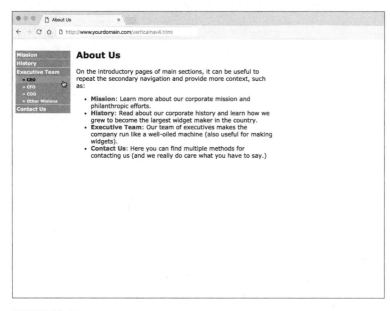

FIGURE 11.12
Creating two levels of vertical navigation using CSS.

The different ways of styling vertical navigation are limited only by your creativity. You can use colors, margins, padding, background images, and any other valid CSS to produce vertical navigation that is quite flexible and easily modified. If you type **CSS vertical navigation** in your search engine, you will find thousands of examples—and they are all based on the simple principles you've learned in this lesson.

Creating Horizontal Navigation with CSS

The lessons on navigation began with vertical navigation because the concept of converting a list into navigation is easier to grasp when the navigation still looks like a list of items that you might write vertically on a piece of paper, like a grocery list. When creating horizontal navigation, you still use HTML list elements, but instead of a vertical display achieved by using the `inline` value of the `display` property for both the `<ul>` and the `<li>` elements, use the block value of the `display` property. It really is as simple as that.

Listing 11.5 shows a starting point for a page featuring horizontal navigation. The page contains a `<header>` element for a logo and navigation and a `<section>` element for content. Within the `<header>` element, a `<div>` containing a logo is floated next to a `<nav>` element containing the navigational links. The list that appears in the `<nav>` element has a display property value of `inline` for both the list and the list items. You can see these elements and their placement in Figure 11.13.

LISTING 11.5 Basic Horizontal Navigation from a List

```
<!doctype html>
<html lang="en">
  <head>
    <meta charset="utf-8">
    <title>ACME Widgets LLC</title>
    <style>
      body {
          font: 12pt Verdana, Arial, Georgia, sans-serif;
      }
      header {
          width: auto;
      }
      #logo {
          float: left;
      }
      nav {
          float: left;
      }
```

```
      nav ul {
         list-style: none;
         display: inline;
      }
      nav li {
         display: inline;
      }
      section {
         width: auto;
         float: left;
         clear: left;
      }
      section a {
         text-decoration: none;
         font-weight: bold;
      }
   </style>
</head>
<body>
   <header>
      <div id="logo">
         <img src="acmewidgets.jpg" alt="ACME Widgets LLC">
      </div>
      <nav>
         <ul>
           <li><a href="#">About Us</a></li>
           <li><a href="#">Products</a></li>
           <li><a href="#">Support</a></li>
           <li><a href="#">Press</a></li>
         </ul>
      </nav>
   </header>
   <section>
      <p><strong>ACME Widgets LLC</strong> is the greatest widget-maker
      in all the land.</p>
      <p>Don't believe us? Read on...</p>
      <ul>
        <li><a href="#">About Us</a>: We are pretty great.</li>
        <li><a href="#">Products</a>: Our products are the best.</li>
        <li><a href="#">Support</a>: It is unlikely you will need support,
        but we provide it anyway.</li>
        <li><a href="#">Press</a>: Read what others are saying (about how
        great we are).</li>
      </ul>
   </section>
</body>
</html>
```

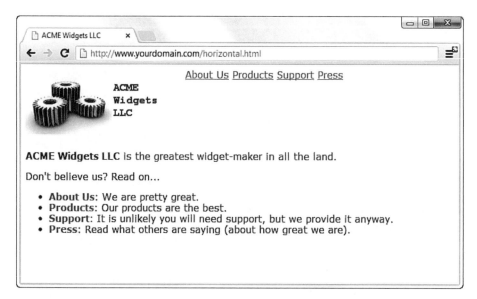

FIGURE 11.13
Creating functional—but not necessarily beautiful—horizontal navigation using inline list elements.
(Credit: Kjpargeter/Shutterstock)

Modifying the display of this list occurs purely through CSS; the structure of the content within the HTML itself is already set. To achieve the desired display, use the following CSS:

```
nav {
    float:left;
    margin: 85px 0px 0px 0px;
    width: 400px;
    background-color: #628794;
    border: 1px solid black;
}
```

First, the <nav> element is modified to be a particular width, it displays a background color and border, and uses a top margin of 85 pixels (so that it displays near the bottom of the logo).

The definition for the <ul> remains the same as in Listing 11.5 except for the changes in margin and padding:

```
nav ul {
    margin: 0px;
    padding: 0px;
    list-style: none;
    display: inline;
}
```

The definition for the <li> remains the same as in Listing 11.5 except that it has been given a line-height value of 1.8em:

```
nav li {
```

```
    display: inline;
    line-height: 1.8em;
}
```

The link styles are similar to those used in the vertical navigation; these entries have different padding values, but the colors and font sizes remain the same:

```
nav ul li a:link, nav ul li a:visited {
    font-size: 10pt;
    font-weight: bold;
    text-decoration: none;
    padding: 7px 10px 7px 10px;
    background-color: #628794;
    color: #ffffff;
}
nav ul li a:hover, nav ul li a:active {
    font-size: 10pt;
    font-weight: bold;
    text-decoration: none;
    padding: 7px 10px 7px 10px;
    background-color: #c6a648;
    color: #000000;
}
```

Putting these styles together produces the display shown in Figure 11.14.

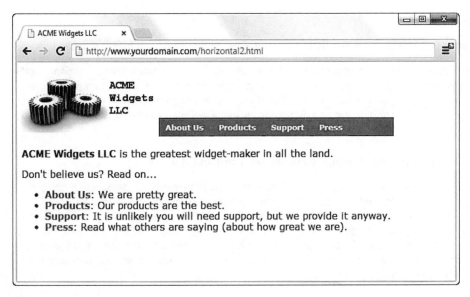

FIGURE 11.14
Creating horizontal navigation with some style. *(Credit: Kjpargeter/Shutterstock)*

When the user rolls over the navigation elements, the background and text colors change in the same way they did when the user hovered the mouse over the vertical navigation menu earlier in this lesson. Also, just as with the vertical navigation menu, you can use nested lists to produce drop-down functionality in your horizontal menu. Try it yourself!

Summary

This lesson began with examples of how lists and list elements are affected by padding and margin styles. You first learned about the default padding associated with lists and how to control that padding. Next, you learned how to modify padding and margin values and how to place the list item indicator either inside the list item or outside it, so you could begin to think about how styles and lists can affect your overall site design. Finally, you learned how to leverage lists and list elements to create a pure HTML and CSS image map, thus reducing the need for slicing up linked images or using the <map> element.

After learning to "think outside the (list) box," if you will, you learned how to use unordered lists to produce horizontal or vertical navigation within your website. By using CSS instead of graphics, you have more flexibility in both the display and maintenance of your site. In this lesson, you learned that with a few entries in your style sheet, you can turn plain underlined text links into areas with borders and background colors and other text styles. In addition, you learned how to present nested lists within menus.

Q&A

Q. Creating CSS image maps seems like a lot of work. Is the <map> element so bad?

A. The <map> element isn't at all bad, and it is valid HTML5. The determination of coordinates used in client-side image maps can be difficult, however, especially without graphics software or software intended for the creation of client-side image maps. The CSS version gives you more options for defining and displaying clickable areas, only one of which you've seen here.

Q. Can I use graphics in the navigation menus as a custom list indicator?

A. Yes. You can use graphics within the HTML text of the list item or as background images within the <li> element. You can style your navigation elements just as you style any other list element. The only differences between an HTML unordered list and a CSS-based horizontal or vertical navigation list is that you are calling it that, and you are using the unordered list for a specific purpose outside the body of the text. Also, you style the list to show the user that it is indeed something different—and you can do that with small graphics to accentuate your lists.

Q. **Where can I find more examples of what I can do with lists?**

A. The last time we checked, typing **CSS navigation** in a search engine returned approximately 88 million results. Here are a few starting places:

A List Apart's CSS articles, at www.alistapart.com/topics/css/, Maxdesign's CSS Listamatic, at http://css.maxdesign.com.au/listamatic/, and Vitaly Friedman's CSS Showcase, at www.alvit.de/css-showcase/.

Workshop

The workshop contains quiz questions and activities to help you solidify your understanding of the material covered.

Quiz

1. What is the difference between the `inside` and `outside` values for `list-style-position`? Which is the default value?

2. Does a `list-style` with a value of `none` produce a structured list, either ordered or unordered?

3. When creating list-based navigation, how many levels of nested lists can you use?

4. When creating a navigation list of any type, can the pseudo-classes for the `a` selector have the same values?

5. What style do most browsers apply to <ul> and <ol> elements by default?

6. What is a good way to test the margins and paddings on lists?

7. How do you hide list contents when creating an image map from a list of links?

8. Where is the image in an image map that is built using a list?

9. In what way does a navigation list differ from a regular list?

10. What is the one thing you need to do to create a horizontal list?

NOTE

Just a reminder for those of you reading these words in the print or e-book edition of this book: If you go to **www.informit.com/register** and register this book (using ISBN 9780672338083), you can receive free access to an online Web Edition that not only contains the complete text of this book but also features an interactive version of this quiz.

Answers

1. The `list-style-position` value `inside` places the list item indicator inside the block created by the list item. The value `outside` places the list item indicator outside the block. With `inside`, content wraps beneath the list item indicator. The default value is `outside`.

2. Yes. The only difference is that no list item indicator is present before the content within the list item.

3. Technically, you can nest your lists as deeply as you want to. But from a usability stand-point, there is a limit to the number of levels that you would *want* to use to nest your lists. Three levels is typically the limit. More than that, and you run the risk of creating a poorly organized site or simply giving users more options than they need to see at all times.

4. Sure, but then you run the risk of users not realizing that your beautiful menus are indeed menus (because no visual display would occur for a mouse action).

5. Most browsers apply a left padding of 40 pixels to lists, written `padding-left: 40px;`.

6. Use CSS to color the background of the lists and list items.

7. Use `text-indent:-1000em;` to push the text off the screen to the left.

8. The image is a background on the list element itself.

9. A navigation list makes it clear that the users should interact with it by changing the cursor, changing the area around the element, and setting it apart from the regular content.

10. To create a horizontal list, set the display property to `inline` on the `<ul>` and `<li>` elements.

Exercises

▶ Find an image and try your hand at mapping areas using the technique shown in this lesson. Select an image that has areas in which you could use hotspots or clickable areas leading to other web pages on your site or to someone else's site. Then create the HTML and CSS to define the clickable areas and the URLs to which they should lead.

▶ Using the techniques shown for a multilevel vertical list, add sub-navigation items to the vertical list created at the end of the lesson.

▶ Look at the numerous examples of CSS-based navigation used in websites and find some tricky-looking actions. Using the View Source function of your web browser, look at the CSS used by these sites, and try to implement something similar for yourself.

LESSON 12
Creating Layouts Using Modern CSS Techniques

What You'll Learn in This Lesson:

▶ How fixed layouts work

▶ How liquid layouts work

▶ How to create a fixed/liquid hybrid layout

▶ How to create CSS flexible box layouts

▶ How to use CSS grid layouts

So far, you've learned a lot about styling web content, from font sizes and colors to images, block elements, lists, and more. But what we haven't yet discussed is a high-level overview of page layout. *Page layout* is how a whole web page looks to the viewer. Most beginning web designers think of this as a static feature and have a goal of creating web pages that look identical in every web browser and device that views it. But that's only one way to design web pages, and it's not a very good way.

There are two basic types of layouts: fixed and liquid. But it's also possible to use a combination of the two, with some elements fixed and others liquid. In this lesson, you'll first learn about the characteristics of these two types of layouts and see a few examples of websites that use them. You'll then see a basic template that combines elements of both types of layouts, using an older style of web design.

Modern CSS gives you more tools for building web page layouts, and in this lesson you will learn how to design pages using the CSS Flexible Box Layout module and the CSS Grid Layout module.

Ultimately, the type of layout you choose is up to you; it's hard to go wrong as long as your sites follow HTML and CSS standards.

Finding Examples of Layouts You Like

A good place for examples of liquid layouts is the WordPress Theme Directory, at https://wordpress.org/themes/. WordPress began as a blogging platform but in recent years has seen an increase in use as a nonblog content or site-management tool. The WordPress Theme Directory shows hundreds of examples of both fixed-width and liquid layouts that give you ideas, if not all the code, for what you can create. Even though you are not working with a WordPress blog or site as part of the exercises in these lessons, the Theme Directory is a place where you can see and interact with many variations on designs.

Spend some time looking at the WordPress examples and perhaps CSS Zen Garden as well, at www.csszengarden.com. This will help you get a feel for the types of layouts you like without being swayed by the content in the layout.

Once you have found some layouts you like, you can use the techniques you learn in this lesson to re-create them on your website.

Getting Ready to Do Page Layout

In the previous lessons, you have learned how to build HTML and CSS web pages, but in order to create effective layouts, you need to be very clear about the following things:

▸ **CSS box model**—If you don't feel completely comfortable with margins, padding, borders, and content boxes, you should take another look at Lesson 9, "Working with Margins, Padding, Alignment, and Floating" and Lesson 10, "Understanding the CSS Box Model and Positioning." These two lessons are the basis of most page layout techniques and are particularly important for building the fixed and liquid layouts in the first few sections of this lesson.

▸ **Progressive enhancement**—Progressive enhancement is the idea that you should start by creating web pages with the minimum required to work, and then you can enhance them with design and interactivity elements. To do this, you need to focus your attention on exactly what each page on your site needs to do. That one thing is what needs to be visible, functional, and accessible—no matter what. Once you have that element, you can add CSS styles to make it look good and JavaScript scripts to make it interactive, but these steps should never get in the way of the primary purpose of that page.

▸ **Separation of structure from design and interactivity**—Your goal should be to create web pages where the HTML holds only the structure and content, the CSS holds only the design, and the JavaScript holds only the interactivity.

The Importance of Putting Mobile Devices First

One aspect of web page layout that many designers forget is that most people are not viewing their web pages the way the designers are viewing them. Most designers use large computer monitors (sometimes multiple monitors) with web browsers that, if not maximized, are at least filling up a lot of space. For example, my default browser is currently open to around 1500px by 900px, and I'm using it on a 5120×2880 display, so I could make it much larger.

However, according to StatCounter, as of this writing, the most popular resolution worldwide is 360×640, with 23% share. And even in the United States, while the most popular resolution is 1920×1080, it accounts for only 10.4% of users, and smaller resolutions like 360×640 and 375×667 are right behind, at 10.2% and 9.8% of users, respectively. Using mobile devices is becoming a more and more popular way to consume web content, and your pages should reflect that.

In the previous section, you learned about progressive enhancement, and it is critical that your page layouts use this technique with regard to mobile devices. You should design your pages for the smallest devices first and then add enhancements for larger and larger screens.

CAUTION

It may be easy to ignore this advice, as designing for small screens can be tedious, and your pages may seem ugly. But if you rely on search engines for any of your traffic, you will need to keep this in mind. Google and other search engines are starting to give sites that function well on mobile devices priority over sites that do not.

In this lesson, you'll learn about specific layout techniques that may not be mobile friendly or that may not put mobile design first. But you need to know how to do them so that you can implement mobile first techniques. You will learn more about how to make your designs more mobile friendly in Part IV, "Responsive Web Design."

Understanding Fixed Layouts

A fixed layout, or fixed-width layout, is just what it sounds like: a layout in which the body of the page is set to a specific width. That width is typically controlled by a master "wrapper" element that contains all the content. The `width` property of a wrapper element, such as a `<div>`, is set in the style sheet entry if the `<div>` was given an ID value such as `main` or `wrapper` (although the name is up to you).

NOTE

If you have been paying attention, you may realize that the minute you give an HTML element an ID such as `wrapper`, you are moving the design of the page into the HTML instead of keeping it in the CSS. One way to evaluate this is to ask yourself the question "Does the meaning or function of this element's ID change if the layout changes?" If the answer is yes, then you've given it an ID that is more design than structure. It's better to use a more semantic ID, such as `main`, which tells the browser that the contained content is the main part of the page. Then, if the layout changes, that content will still be the main part of the page, although it might be in a different location in the layout.

When creating a fixed-width layout, the most important decision is determining the minimum screen resolution to accommodate. The best way to decide how to set a fixed-width layout is to look at the stats for the visitors to your website. If the majority of your viewers use a small screen such as 800 × 600, then your layout should reflect that. But if you don't have stats from your site because it is new or for some other reason, you can use a service like StatCounter (http://gs.statcounter.com/screen-resolution-stats/) to get a more generic view.

For many years, 800 × 600 was the "lowest common denominator" for web designers, resulting in a typical fixed width of approximately 760 pixels. However, the percentage of people using 800 × 600 screen resolution for nonmobile browsers is now less than 1%. Many web designers now consider 1280 × 800 the minimum screen resolution, so if they create fixed-width layouts, the fixed width typically is somewhere between 1100 and 1200 pixels.

CAUTION

Remember that the web browser window contains non-viewable areas, including the scrollbar. So, if you are targeting a 1280-pixel-wide screen resolution, you really can't use all 1280 of those pixels.

A main reason for creating a fixed-width layout is so that you can have precise control over the appearance of the content area. However, if users visit your fixed-width site with smaller or much larger screen resolutions than the resolution you had in mind while you designed it, they will encounter scrollbars (if their resolution is smaller) or a large amount of empty space (if their resolution is greater). Finding fixed-width layouts is difficult among the most popular websites these days because site designers know they need to cater to the largest possible audience (and therefore make no assumptions about browser size). However, fixed-width layouts still have wide adoption, especially by site administrators using content management systems with strict templates.

The following figures show one such site, for San Jose State University. University websites commonly use a strict template and content management system, so this was an easy example to find. It has a wrapper element fixed at 960 pixels wide. In Figure 12.1, the browser window is a shade under 900 pixels wide. On the right side of the image, important content is cut off (and at the bottom of the figure, a horizontal scrollbar displays in the browser).

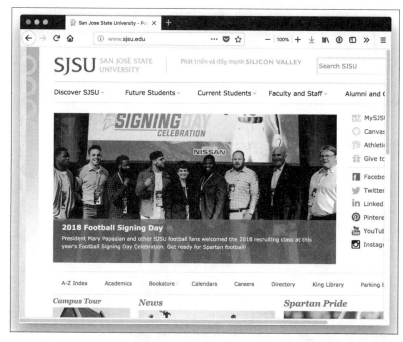

FIGURE 12.1
A fixed-width example with a smaller screen size (note the horizontal scrollbar).

Figure 12.2 shows how this site looks when the browser window is more than 1500 pixels wide: You see a lot of empty space (or "real estate") on both sides of the main body content, which some consider aesthetically displeasing.

FIGURE 12.2
A fixed-width example with a larger screen size.

In addition to deciding whether to create a fixed-width layout in the first place, you need to determine whether to place the fixed-width content flush left or centered. Placing the content flush left produces extra space on the right side only; centering the content area creates extra space on both sides. However, centering at least provides balance, whereas a flush-left design could end up looking like a small rectangle shoved in the corner of the browser, depending on the size and resolution of a user's monitor.

Understanding Liquid Layouts

A liquid layout—also called a *fluid* layout—is a layout in which the body of the page does not use a specified width in pixels, although it might be enclosed in a master wrapper element that uses a percentage width. The idea behind a liquid layout is that it can be perfectly usable and still retain the overall design aesthetic, even if the user has a very small or very wide screen.

Figures 12.3, 12.4, and 12.5 show three examples of a liquid layout in action.

FIGURE 12.3
A liquid layout viewed in a relatively small screen.

FIGURE 12.4
A liquid layout viewed in a very small screen.

FIGURE 12.5
A liquid layout viewed in a wide screen.

In Figure 12.3, the browser window is approximately 770 pixels wide. This example shows a reasonable minimum screen width before a horizontal scrollbar appears. In fact, the scrollbar does not appear until the browser is 735 pixels wide. On the other hand, Figure 12.4 shows a very small browser window (less than 600 pixels wide).

In Figure 12.4, you can see a horizontal scrollbar; in the header area of the page content, the logo graphic is beginning to take over the text and appear on top of it. But the bulk of the page is still quite usable. The informational content on the left side of the page is still legible and is sharing the available space with the input form on the right side.

Figure 12.5 shows how this same page looks in a very wide screen. In Figure 12.5, the browser window is approximately 1330 pixels wide. There is plenty of room for all the content on the page to spread out. This liquid layout is achieved because all the design elements have a percentage width specified instead of a fixed width. This way, the layout makes use of all the available browser real estate.

The liquid layout approach might seem like the best approach at first glance; after all, who wouldn't want to take advantage of all the screen real estate available? But there's a fine line between taking advantage of space and not allowing the content to breathe. Too much content is overwhelming; not enough content in an open space is underwhelming. Plus, if the screen gets too wide, the text will be much harder to read.

A purely liquid layout can be quite impressive, but it requires a significant amount of testing to ensure that it is usable in a wide range of browsers at varying screen resolutions. You might not have the time and effort available to produce such a design; in that case, a reasonable compromise is a fixed/liquid hybrid layout, or a fully responsive design, as we'll discuss later on.

Creating a Fixed/Liquid Hybrid Layout

A fixed/liquid hybrid layout contains elements of both types of layouts. For example, you could have a fluid layout that includes fixed-width content areas either within the body area or as anchor elements (such as a left-side column or as a top navigation strip). You can even create a fixed content area that acts like a frame, in which a content area remains fixed even as users scroll through the content.

Starting with a Basic Layout Structure

In this example, you'll learn to create a template that is liquid but with two fixed-width columns, one on each side of the main body area (which is a third column, if you think about it, only much wider than the others). The template also has a delineated header and footer area. Listing 12.1 shows the basic HTML structure for this layout.

LISTING 12.1 Basic Fixed/Liquid Hybrid Layout Structure

```
<!doctype html>
<html lang="en">
  <head>
    <meta charset="utf-8">
    <title>Sample Layout</title>
    <link href="layout.css" rel="stylesheet">
  </head>
  <body>
    <header>HEADER</header>
    <section id="main">
      <article id="main_content">CONTENT</article>
      <aside id="secondary_content">LEFT SIDE</aside>
      <aside id="tertiary_content">RIGHT SIDE</aside>
    </section>
    <footer>FOOTER</footer>
  </body>
</html>
```

First, note that the style sheet for this layout is linked to with the <link> tag instead of included in the template. A template is used for more than one page, and you want to be able to control the display elements of the template in the most organized way possible. This means you need to change the definitions of those elements in only one place—the style sheet.

Next, notice that the basic HTML is just that: extremely basic. Truth be told, this basic HTML structure can be used for a fixed layout, a liquid layout, or the fixed/liquid hybrid in this example because all the actual styling that makes a layout fixed, liquid, or hybrid happens in the style sheet.

Even the IDs on the elements say nothing about where the content should live in the layout; they just provide semantic information about the content itself. Right now the secondary_content <aside> element is being displayed on the left side (according to the content itself), but there is no reason you couldn't move it to the right side or below the footer or anywhere else on the page you wanted to put it.

With the HTML structure in Listing 12.1, you actually have an identification of the content areas you want to include in your site. This planning is crucial to any development; you have to know what you want to include before you can think about the type of layout you are going to use, let alone the specific styles that will be applied to that layout.

At this stage, the `layout.css` file includes only this entry:

```
body {
    margin:0;
    padding:0;
}
```

If you look at the HTML in Listing 12.1 and say to yourself, "But those elements will just stack on top of each other without any styles," you are correct. As shown in Figure 12.6, there is no layout to speak of.

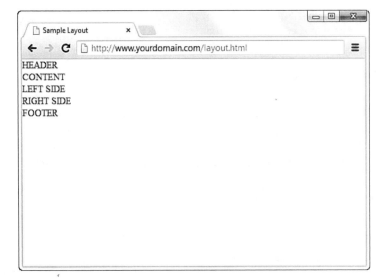

FIGURE 12.6
A basic HTML template with no styles applied to the container elements.

Defining Two Columns in a Fixed/Liquid Hybrid Layout

Because this layout is supposed to be liquid, we know that whatever we put in the header and footer areas will extend the width of the browser window, regardless of how narrow or wide the window might be.

Adding the following code to the style sheet gives the header and footer area each a width of 100% as well as the same background color and text color:

```
header, footer {
    float: left;
    width: 100%;
```

```
  background-color: #7152f4;
  color: #ffffff;
}
```

Now things get a little trickier. We have to define the two fixed columns on either side of the page, plus the column in the middle. In the HTML we're using here, note that a `<section>` element, called `main`, surrounds all the columns. This element is defined in the style sheet as follows:

```
#main {
  float: left;
  padding-left: 200px;
  padding-right: 125px;
}
```

The two padding definitions essentially reserve space for the two fixed-width columns on the left and right of the page. The column on the left will be 200 pixels wide, the column on the right will be 125 pixels wide, and each will have a different background color. But we also have to position the items relative to where they would be placed if the HTML remained unstyled (refer to Figure 12.6). This means adding `position: relative;` to the style sheet entries for each of these columns.

But in the case of the `secondary_content` `<aside>`, we also indicate that we want the rightmost margin edge to be 200 pixels in from the edge. (This is in addition to the column being defined as 200 pixels wide.) We also want the margin on the left side to be a full negative margin; this will pull it into place (as you will soon see). The `tertiary_content` `<aside>` does not include a value for `right`, but it does include a negative margin on the right side:

```
#secondary_content {
  position: relative;
  float: left;
  width: 200px;
  background-color: #52f471;
  right: 200px;
  margin-left: -100%;
}
#tertiary_content {
  position: relative;
  float: left;
  width: 125px;
  background-color: #f452d5;
  margin-right: -125px;
}
```

At this point, let's also define the content area so that it has a white background, takes up 100% of the available area, and floats to the left relative to its position:

```
#main_content {
  position: relative;
  float: left;
  background-color: #ffffff;
  width: 100%;
}
```

At this point, the basic layout should look something like Figure 12.7, with the areas clearly delineated.

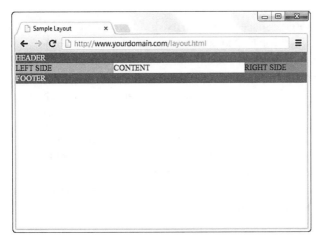

FIGURE 12.7
A basic HTML template after some styles have been put in place.

However, there's a problem with this template if the window is resized below a certain width. Because the left column is 200 pixels wide and the right column is 125 pixels wide, and you want at least *some* text in the content area, you can imagine that this page will break if the window is only 350 to 400 pixels wide. There is also an issue if the browser is too wide. We address these issues in the next section.

Setting the Minimum and Maximum Width of a Layout

Although users won't likely visit your site with a desktop browser that displays less than 400 pixels wide, many people might view it on a small mobile phone that size. You can extrapolate and apply this information broadly: Even in fixed/liquid hybrid sites, at some point, your layout will break down unless you do something to prevent that outcome.

One of those "somethings" is to use the `min-width` CSS property. The `min-width` property sets the minimum width of an element, not including padding, borders, or margins. Figure 12.8 shows what happens when `min-width` is applied to the `<body>` element.

FIGURE 12.8
The basic HTML template resized to under 400 pixels, with a minimum width applied.

Figure 12.8 shows a small portion of the right column after the screen has been scrolled to the right, but the point is that the layout does not break apart when resized below a minimum width. In this case, the minimum width is 525 pixels:

```
body {
  margin: 0;
  padding: 0;
  min-width: 525px;
}
```

The horizontal scrollbar appears in this example because the browser window itself is less than 500 pixels wide. The scrollbar disappears when the window is slightly larger than 525 pixels wide.

You can use the `max-width` CSS property in the same way to ensure that elements of the page with percentage widths don't get too wide. This property lets the element expand up to a point and then stop.

Handling Column Height in a Fixed/Liquid Hybrid Layout

This example is all well and good except for one problem: It has no content. When content is added to the various elements, more problems arise. As Figure 12.9 shows, the columns become as tall as necessary for the content they contain.

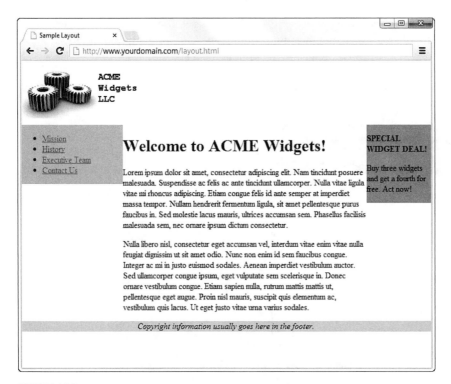

FIGURE 12.9
Columns are only as tall as their contents. *(Credit: Kjpargeter/Shutterstock)*

NOTE

In Figure 12.9, we have moved beyond the basic layout example. So, we also took the liberty of removing the background and text color properties for the header and footer, which is why the example no longer shows white text on a very dark background. In addition, we've centered the text in the <footer> element, which now has a light gray background.

Because you cannot count on a user's browser being a specific height or the content always being the same length, you might think this poses a problem with the fixed/liquid hybrid layout. Not so. If you think a little outside the box, you can apply a few more styles to bring all the pieces together.

First, add the following declarations in the style sheet entries for the secondary_content, tertiary_content, and main_content IDs:

```
margin-bottom: -2000px;
padding-bottom: 2000px;
```

These declarations add a ridiculous amount of padding and assign a too-large margin to the bottom of all three elements. You must also add `position:relative;` to the footer element definitions in the style sheet so that the footer is visible despite this padding.

At this point, the page looks as shown in Figure 12.10, which is still not what we want but is closer.

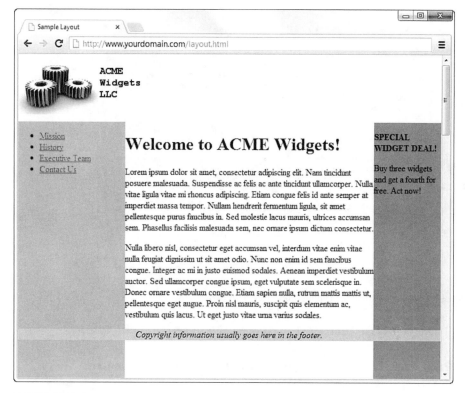

FIGURE 12.10
The columns now extend to the bottom of the page, despite the amount of content in the columns.
(Credit: Kjpargeter/Shutterstock)

To clip off the bottom of the columns, add the following to the style sheet for the `main` ID:

```
overflow: hidden;
```

Figure 12.11 shows the final result: a fixed-width/liquid hybrid layout with the necessary column spacing. Here we took the liberty of styling the navigational links and adjusting the margin around the welcome message. You can see the complete style sheet in Listing 12.3.

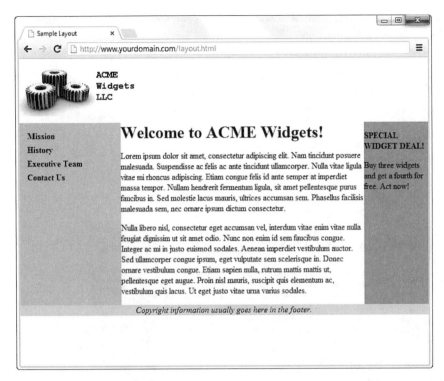

FIGURE 12.11
Congratulations! It's a fixed-width/liquid hybrid layout. *(Credit: Kjpargeter/Shutterstock)*

The full HTML code appears in Listing 12.2, and Listing 12.3 shows the final style sheet.

LISTING 12.2 Basic Fixed/Liquid Hybrid Layout Structure (with Content)

```
<!doctype html>
<html lang="en">
  <head>
    <meta charset="utf-8">
    <title>Sample Layout</title>
    <link href="layout.css" rel="stylesheet">
  </head>
  <body>
    <header>
      <img src="acmewidgets.jpg" alt="ACME Widgets LLC">
    </header>
    <section id="main">
      <article id="main_content">
        <h1>Welcome to ACME Widgets!</h1>
        <p>Lorem ipsum dolor sit amet, consectetur adipiscing elit.
        Nam tincidunt posuere malesuada. Suspendisse ac felis ac ante
        tincidunt ullamcorper. Nulla vitae ligula vitae mi rhoncus
```

adipiscing. Etiam congue felis id ante semper at imperdiet
massa tempor. Nullam hendrerit fermentum ligula, sit amet
pellentesque purus faucibus in. Sed molestie lacus mauris,
ultrices accumsan sem. Phasellus facilisis malesuada sem, nec
ornare ipsum dictum consectetur.</p>
<p>Nulla libero nisl, consectetur eget accumsan vel, interdum
vitae enim vitae nulla feugiat dignissim ut sit amet odio.
Nunc non enim id sem faucibus congue. Integer ac mi in justo
euismod sodales. Aenean imperdiet vestibulum auctor. Sed
ullamcorper congue ipsum, eget vulputate sem scelerisque in.
Donec ornare vestibulum congue. Etiam sapien nulla, rutrum
mattis ut, pellentesque eget augue. Proin nisl mauris,
suscipit quis elementum ac, vestibulum quis lacus. Ut eget
justo vitae urna varius sodales. </p>
    </article>
    <aside id="secondary_content">
      <ul>
        <li><a href="#">Mission</a></li>
        <li><a href="#">History</a></li>
        <li><a href="#">Executive Team</a></li>
        <li><a href="#">Contact Us</a></li>
      </ul>
    </aside>
    <aside id="tertiary_content">
      <p><strong>SPECIAL WIDGET DEAL!</strong></p>
      <p>Buy three widgets and get a fourth for free. Act now!</p>
    </aside>
  </section>
  <footer>Copyright information usually goes here in the
  footer.</footer>
 </body>
</html>

LISTING 12.3   Full Style Sheet for the Fixed/Liquid Hybrid Layout

```
body {
  margin:0;
  padding:0;
  min-width: 525px;
}
header {
  float: left;
  width: 100%;
}
footer {
  position:relative;
  float: left;
  width: 100%;
```

```css
    background-color: #cccccc;
    text-align:center;
    font-style: italic;
}
#main {
    float: left;
    padding-left: 200px;
    padding-right: 125px;
    overflow: hidden;
}
#secondary_content {
    position: relative;
    float: left;
    width: 200px;
    background-color: #52f471;
    right: 200px;
    margin-left: -100%;
    margin-bottom: -2000px;
    padding-bottom: 2000px;

}
#tertiary_content {
    position: relative;
    float: left;
    width: 125px;
    background-color: #f452d5;
    margin-right: -125px;
    margin-bottom: -2000px;
    padding-bottom: 2000px;

}
#main_content {
    position: relative;
    float: left;
    background-color: #ffffff;
    width: 100%;
    margin-bottom: -2000px;
    padding-bottom: 2000px;

}
h1 {
    margin: 0;
}
#secondary_content ul {
    list-style: none;
    margin: 12px 0px 0px 12px;
    padding: 0px;
}
```

```
#secondary_content li a:link, #secondary_content li a:visited {
  font-size: 12pt;
  font-weight: bold;
  padding: 3px 0px 3px 3px;
  color: #000000;
  text-decoration: none;
  display: block;
}
#secondary_content li a:hover, #secondary_content li a:active {
  font-size: 12pt;
  font-weight: bold;
  padding: 3px 0px 3px 3px;
  color: #ffffff;
  text-decoration: none;
  display: block;
}
```

Using Modern CSS Layout Techniques

In the previous sections, you learned how web designers used to build web page layouts—methods that many designers still use. But CSS3 offers several new ways to handle web page layout, and most modern browsers support them without much trouble. These are the three that are most commonly used:

▶ **CSS table**—CSS properties that change the display of page elements to tables, table rows, and table columns.

▶ **CSS flexible box layout**—CSS properties that make it easier to lay out, align, and distribute space among elements in a container.

▶ **CSS grid layout**—A grid-based layout system with rows and columns.

These CSS layout systems all start with the display property. Before CSS3, the display property took the values inline, block, and none. This meant you could change how elements were displayed in the normal flow or hide them completely. CSS3 added a number of new values, including list-item, to indicate that the element was a list item, and inline-block, to indicate that the element was like an <img> element with characteristics of inline and block elements. In the next few sections, you will learn about more values of the display property that help with layout.

How to Use CSS display: table;

Unlike HTML tables, the CSS display: table; property is not a structural table in HTML. This means you can convert any element into a table and use it to build your layout.

There are several table options on the `display` property:

- `table`—Behaves like a `<table>` element
- `inline-table`—Behaves like a `<table>` element that is rendered inline
- `table-row`—Behaves like a table row (`<tr>`) element
- `table-cell`—Behaves like a table cell (`<td>`) element
- `table-column`—Behaves like a `<col>` element
- `table-caption`—Behaves like a `<caption>` element
- `table-row-group`—Behaves like a `<tbody>` element
- `table-header-group`—Behaves like a `<thead>` element
- `table-footer-group`—Behaves like a `<tfoot>` element
- `table-column-group`—Behaves like a `<colgroup>` element

NOTE
Some people are concerned about using CSS table styles for layout because they learned that you should never use tables for layout. However, despite the name, CSS table properties are not HTML table tags. The issues with accessibility are mitigated when you use CSS table styles because the HTML can be structured in a way that is accessible, regardless of the layout.

By using CSS tables, you can create layouts similar to how web designers might have created them using actual tables back in the "bad old days." For example, you can take the HTML you used in Listing 12.2 and change the CSS to create a similar three-column layout.

First, define the `main` `<section>` as a table and give it 100% width:

```
#main {
  width: 100%;
  display: table;
}
```

This tells the browsers that this element contains table content and should display like a table.

Then define the three content areas as table cells:

```
#main_content, #secondary_content, #tertiary_content {
  display: table-cell;
}
```

If you set the background colors and other styles so that you end up with the CSS in Listing 12.4, the page will look as shown in Figure 12.12.

LISTING 12.4   Three-Column Layout with `display: table;`

```css
#main {
  width: 100%;
  display: table;
}
#main_content, #secondary_content, #tertiary_content {
  display: table-cell;
}
footer {
  width: 100%;
  background-color: #cccccc;
  text-align:center;
  font-style: italic;
}
#secondary_content { width: 200px; background-color: #52f471; }
#tertiary_content { width: 125px; background-color: #f452d5; }
#secondary_content ul {
  list-style: none;
  margin: 12px 0px 0px 12px;
  padding: 0px;
}
#secondary_content li a:link, #secondary_content li a:visited {
  font-size: 12pt;
  font-weight: bold;
  padding: 3px 0px 3px 3px;
  color: #000000;
  text-decoration: none;
  display: block;
}
#secondary_content li a:hover, #secondary_content li a:active {
  font-size: 12pt;
  font-weight: bold;
  padding: 3px 0px 3px 3px;
  color: #ffffff;
  text-decoration: none;
  display: block;
}
```

One thing you will notice is that the `secondary_content` column is now in the middle of the three columns. This is because that is where it is located in the HTML source. One of the drawbacks to this layout method is that to change the positions of different elements, you need to change the actual HTML. But as you will see in the next sections, CSS3 has answers for this, too.

FIGURE 12.12
Creating a layout with `display: table;`. *(Credit: Kjpargeter/Shutterstock)*

▼ TRY IT YOURSELF

Using CSS `display: table;` **to Vertically Align Content**

One thing that the `display: table-*;` properties do that can be really useful is allow you to center content vertically in the space. This is because table cells have vertical alignment.

To center content vertically in the space, simply add the `display: table-cell;` property to an element with an explicit height and then set `vertical-align` to `middle`.

Understanding the CSS Flexible Box Layout Module

The CSS Flexible Box module gives you a way to position elements that display on a line in a container. The container can alter the dimensions of the elements inside it to best fit the available free space. A flexible box container, or flex container, will expand items to fill available free space or shrink them to prevent overflow in smaller spaces.

NOTE

While you can use the flexible box layout for any web page, this model is best suited for application components and small-scale layouts. If you are designing a full website or other larger-scale project, you should use the grid layout model, described later in this lesson.

Normal layout in web pages is based on block and inline elements interacting with one another in the *normal flow*. Normal flow in web page designs travels from left to right (or right to left on pages with RTL formatting), filling the width of the available space and then moving down the document until all the content is available on the page. With flexible box layout, items in the layout can be placed on the page in a more flexible fashion. If the designer wants the items to stack vertically from top to bottom, the box can accommodate that. This layout is, as its name promises, flexible.

Building a Flexible Box Container

The first thing you need when creating a flexible layout is a container element. This is the element that holds all the items that will be laid out on the page. You define a flex container with the display property:

```
.container {
  display: flex;
}
```

This enables a flex context for all of the direct children of the container.

Once you have defined the container, you need to determine in what direction the elements in the container are going to flow. For this you use the flex-direction property with one of these values:

▶ row—The flex items flow left to right in ltr layouts and right to left in rtl layouts. This is the default.

▶ row-reverse—The items flow right to left in ltr layouts and left to right in rtl layouts. This is the opposite of row.

▶ column—Items flow from top to bottom in a column.

▶ column-reverse—Items flow from bottom to top in a column. This is the opposite of column.

Once you have the flow direction, you need to consider how the items will wrap when they come to a boundary. By default, flex items try to fit onto one line. But you can change this with the `flex-wrap` property and these values:

- ▸ `nowrap`— All flex items are on one line (horizontal or vertical). This is the default.

- ▸ `wrap`—Flex items wrap to multiple lines from top to bottom.

- ▸ `wrap-reverse`—Flex items wrap to multiple lines from bottom to top. This is the opposite of `wrap`.

You can define both the flex direction and wrap with the `flex-flow` shorthand property:

```
flex-flow: flex-direction || flex-wrap;
```

The last three properties you need to know for your flex containers are `justify-content`, `align-items`, and `align-content`. These properties control how the items will be displayed within the container.

The `justify-content` property defines how the items will be spaced if there is more room in the container than the items take up. You can distribute the extra free space so that it is between or around the items. These are the possible values:

- ▸ `flex-start`—The items are placed at the start of the container, and any extra space is placed after all the items. This is the default.

- ▸ `flex-end`—This is the same as `flex-start`, only instead of placing the extra space at the end, you place it at the beginning and push all the items to the end.

- ▸ `center`—The items are placed in the center of the container, and extra free space is placed evenly at the start and end.

- ▸ `space-between`—The items are evenly distributed in the line, with the first item right at the start and the last placed right at the end. Extra space is distributed evenly between all the items.

- ▸ `space-around`—The items are placed evenly on the line, with equal space all around them. This spacing does not appear equal, however, as inner items will have twice as much space between them as the first and last items will have on the outer edges.

Figure 12.13 shows how the different `justify-content` values look.

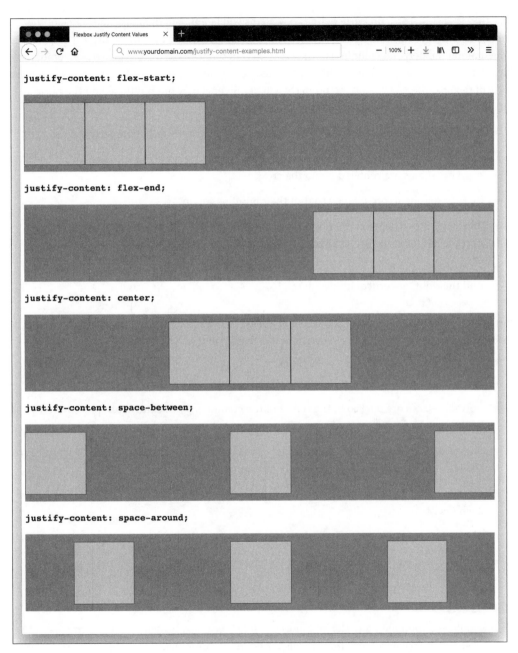

FIGURE 12.13
Using the justify-content property.

The `justify-content` property defines how items will be laid out along the main line of the container (either horizontally or vertically). But you can also define how the items will be positioned along the perpendicular line of the container. In other words, if you have a horizontal flexbox, the `align-items` will define how the items are positioned on the vertical axis. If you have a vertical flexbox, the `align-items` property will define how they are positioned on the horizontal axis. This property has the following possible values:

- ▶ `stretch`—The items should stretch to fill the whole container while respecting `min-width` and `max-width` rules. This is the default.

- ▶ `center`—Items are centered along the cross axis.

- ▶ `baseline`—Items are aligned so that their baselines align.

- ▶ `flex-start`—The items are positioned at the start of the element (the top for horizontal and the left for vertical `ltr` layouts).

- ▶ `flex-end`—The items are positioned at the end of the element (the bottom for horizontal and the right for vertical ltr layouts).

If there are multiple lines in your container, you need to use the `align-content` property to determine how any extra space between lines will be distributed. This property can have the following values:

- ▶ `stretch`—Lines stretch to take up the remaining space. This is the default.

- ▶ `center`—Lines are packed in the center of the container, with extra space placed evenly before and after.

- ▶ `space-between`—The first line is placed at the start of the container, and the last line is at the end, and remaining lines are evenly distributed between them.

- ▶ `space-around`—The lines are evenly distributed, with extra space placed before and after each line.

- ▶ `flex-start`—Lines are pushed to the start of the container, with extra space placed after.

- ▶ `flex-end`—Lines are pushed to the end of the container, with extra space placed first.

Modifying Flex Items

Once you have a container, any element placed inside if is a flexbox item. But there are several things you can do to control how they are displayed in the container.

Normally, flexbox items appear on the page in the same order in which they appear in the HTML, but with the `order` property, you can change that. This property takes an integer. The lower the number (including negative numbers) the closer to the start the item will appear. If items have the same `order` value, they will be ordered the way they appear in the HTML source. (This helps solve the problem shown in Figure 12.12.) Starting with the CSS from Listing 12.4, change the `#main` element to `display: flex;` and remove the `display: table-cell;` from the content blocks. This gives you a layout just like the layout shown in Figure 12.12, but now you can reorder the columns. Change the order of the columns with the CSS like so:

```
#secondary_content {
  order: -1;
}
```

This simple CSS places the `#secondary_content` lowest in the list order, so it comes first. The other two columns display in the order in which they are listed in the HTML because we did not specify an order for them. Listing 12.5 shows the CSS we used to get the layout in Figure 12.14. We used exactly the same HTML as in Listing 12.2.

LISTING 12.5 Changing the Order of the Layout Columns with a Flexible Box Layout

```
#main {
  width: 100%;
  display: flex;
}
#secondary_content {
  order: -1;
}
footer {
  width: 100%;
  background-color: #cccccc;
  text-align:center;
  font-style: italic;
}
#secondary_content { width: 200px; background-color: #52f471; }
#tertiary_content { width: 125px; background-color: #f452d5; }
#secondary_content ul {
  list-style: none;
  margin: 12px 0px 0px 12px;
  padding: 0px;
}
#secondary_content li a:link, #secondary_content li a:visited {
  font-size: 12pt;
  font-weight: bold;
  padding: 3px 0px 3px 3px;
  color: #000000;
  text-decoration: none;
  display: block;
}
```

```
#secondary_content li a:hover, #secondary_content li a:active {
  font-size: 12pt;
  font-weight: bold;
  padding: 3px 0px 3px 3px;
  color: #ffffff;
  text-decoration: none;
  display: block;
}
```

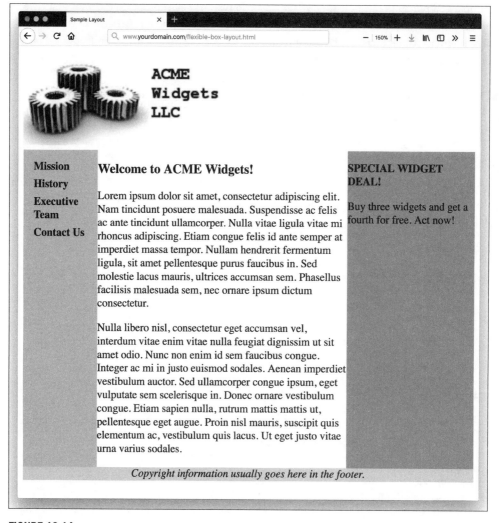

FIGURE 12.14
Getting the desired layout with flexible boxes. *(Credit: Kjpargeter/Shutterstock)*

NOTE
_____

If the order feature of flexible box layouts does not excite you, I don't know what will. Because of the order property, you can create designs for all sorts of layouts that rely on databased entries of content. Normally, you would have to program the order of display into the database functionality itself, but now you can control it with CSS. Now, if you are selling shoes and want to highlight a certain style by displaying it first, you can just change the order in the CSS—no database programming or server-side scripting required.

_____

The Flexible Box Layout module is very complicated and hard to use, and there are a lot more features to it, but it can be very useful in certain situations. There are lots of places you can learn more about CSS flexible boxes, but one fun online game is Flexbox Zombies (https://flexboxzombies.com). It's long but worth it.

Understanding CSS Grid Layout Module

You may not be familiar with the CSS Grid Layout module, but chances are if you've done any web design, you have used grids. Most web pages are built using some form of invisible grid. If you use tables for layout, you are using a grid. And the three-column layout used in the previous sections is also laid out on a grid.

With the CSS3 Grid Layout module, you can define any container element as a grid with specific row and column sizes and then place your child elements into the grid. Just as with flexible box layouts, the order of items in the HTML doesn't matter. Once they are in the grid, you can place them wherever you want. Just as with flexible boxes, the grid layout system has full support in modern browsers. Only Internet Explorer 11 requires a prefix (-ms), for example display: -ms-grid;.

To use the CSS Grid Layout system, you define a container element as display: grid; and then define your columns and rows with the grid-template-columns and grid-template-rows properties. Once you have defined the grid, you place the child elements into the grid with grid-template-areas and the grid-area property.

Working with the Grid Container

The first thing you do when creating a grid layout is to define the container element as a grid. You do this in the same way as with flex boxes, with the display property. There are three possible values for grids:

- ▶ grid—Generates a block-level grid

- ▶ inline-grid—Generates an inline grid

- ▶ subgrid—With nested grids, indicates that the nested grid should take the sizes of its rows and columns from the parent grid rather than requiring the designer to specify new ones.

Then you define the grid columns and rows with the `grid-template-columns` and `grid-template-rows` properties, both of which use space-separated lists of values.

The best way to think about grids created in the CSS Grid Layout module is to imagine that you're creating your grid in text form right in the CSS. The values of the `grid-template-columns/rows` properties represent the track size, and the space between them represents the grid line. One way to build it is to write your CSS so it represents the grid, like so:

```
                        /*  column1   column 2   column 3   column 4 */
grid-template-columns:  100px      auto       100px      200px;
grid-template-rows:
  /* row 1 */           100px
  /* row 2 */           300px
  /* row 3 */           100px;
```

The browser will ignore the whitespace, but you can immediately see that this grid will be 4 × 3 (that is, four columns by three rows).

NOTE

One useful feature of the CSS grid system is that it adds a new unit of measure—`fr`. This refers to the free space inside the container. The browser first removes any space taken by non-flexible items and then divides up the remaining space among the elements with `fr` units. For example, you might have a three-column layout with a 15% left column and the remaining columns taking up three-quarters and one-quarter of the remaining available space. This is written like so:

```
grid-template-columns: 15% 3fr 1fr;
```

While you can define your columns and rows with spacing and comments as described previously, an easier way is to use the `grid-template-areas` property. To use this property, you need to name the different items with the `grid-area` property. For example, you might name your layout elements like this:

```
header { grid-area: header; }
footer { grid-area: footer; }
section { grid-area: main; }
aside { grid-area: sidebar; }
nav { grid-area: navigation; }
```

Then you define your layout grid with the `grid-template-areas` property. You reference the names of a grid area in the cell in which you want them to display. If you repeat it, the content will span those columns or rows. And a period is an empty cell in the layout.

To replicate the three-column layout from the beginning of this lesson, first we apply the style sheet to the HTML from Listing 12.2. In it, we define the `#main` section as the grid container:

```
#main {
  display: grid;
}
```

Then we name the grid elements with the `grid-area` property:

```
#main_content {
  grid-area: main_content;
}
#secondary_content {
  grid-area: secondary_content;
  background-color: #52f471;
}
#tertiary_content {
  grid-area: tertiary_content;
  background-color: #f452d5;
}
```

Here we removed all the `width` styles as those will be defined in the grid itself. Next, we add the columns and rows to the `#main` element:

```
grid-template-columns: 200px auto 125px;
grid-template-rows: auto;
```

And then we lay out the design with `grid-template-areas`. Remember that the names of the areas should be in quotation marks:

```
grid-template-areas:
  "secondary_content main_content tertiary_content";
```

Listing 12.6 shows the full CSS for this example, and Figure 12.15 shows the result.

LISTING 12.6   Using the CSS Grid Module to Lay Out a Web Page

```
#main {
  display: grid;
  grid-template-columns: 200px auto 125px;
  grid-template-rows: auto;
  grid-template-areas:
    "secondary_content main_content tertiary_content";
}
#main_content {
  grid-area: main_content;
}
footer {
  background-color: #cccccc;
  text-align:center;
  font-style: italic;
}
#secondary_content {
  grid-area: secondary_content;
  background-color: #52f471;
}
```

```css
#tertiary_content {
  grid-area: tertiary_content;
  background-color: #f452d5;
}
#secondary_content ul {
  list-style: none;
  margin: 12px 0px 0px 12px;
  padding: 0px;
}
#secondary_content li a:link, #secondary_content li a:visited {
  font-size: 12pt;
  font-weight: bold;
  padding: 3px 0px 3px 3px;
  color: #000000;
  text-decoration: none;
  display: block;
}
#secondary_content li a:hover, #secondary_content li a:active {
  font-size: 12pt;
  font-weight: bold;
  padding: 3px 0px 3px 3px;
  color: #ffffff;
  text-decoration: none;
  display: block;
}
```

CAUTION

When you turn a container element into a grid container, the grid elements are only the immediate children of that container. In the examples in this lesson, the container is the main <section> element. If you turned the <body> element in these examples into the container, then the grid items would be the <header>, <section>, and <footer> elements because these are the first children of the <body> element.

Like the Flexible Boxes module, the CSS Grid module has a lot more to it than this lesson could cover. You can do things like name grid lines, control how "extra" items fit in the layout, span rows and columns, and more. One site we find useful for understanding how CSS Grid works is Grid by Example (https://gridbyexample.com/examples/), but there are many other excellent tutorials as well—just search for **CSS Grid Layout**.

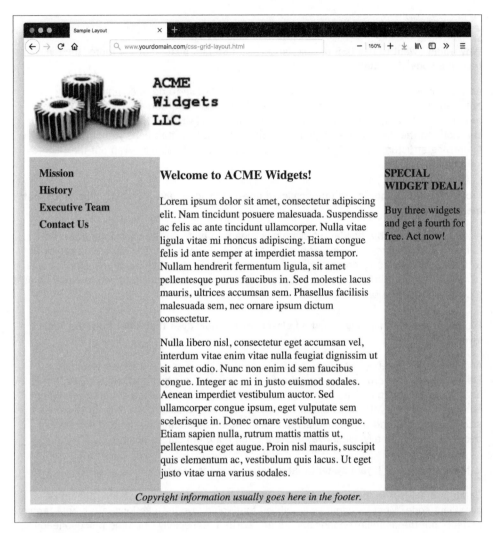

FIGURE 12.15
Creating the same layout as before with the CSS Grid module. *(Credit: Kjpargeter/Shutterstock)*

Summary

In this lesson, you learned about the three main types of layouts: fixed, liquid, and a fixed/liquid hybrid. In the middle of the lesson, an extended example walked you through the process of creating a fixed/liquid hybrid layout in which the HTML and CSS all validate properly. Then you saw how to create a similar layout by using modern CSS layout, with flexible boxes and grids. In this lesson, you learned that the most important part of creating a layout is figuring out the sections of content you think you might need to account for in the design.

Q&A

Q. Why would I want to use CSS flexible boxes or a CSS grid instead of the more "tried and true" methods of layout?

A. As with many other areas of web design, what you choose to do is completely up to you, but the new CSS flexible box and grid methods give you a lot more flexibility to change the layout right within the CSS, without changing the HTML at all. This means that you can work on the design of a page and even create multiple iterations without affecting the underlying structure. If the first layout you try doesn't work, simply swap out the CSS to something else.

Q. I read that flexible boxes are often called a *one-dimensional layout system*. What does that mean?

A. At its core, the flexible box layout system is meant to allow you to control the layout of items in a single direction—either horizontally or vertically. While flex box items can flow to a second line or column, the primary intention was for the singular dimension. In comparison, the CSS grid layout defines both rows *and* columns and allows you to place items anywhere within the predefined grid.

Q. I've heard about something called an *elastic layout*. How does that differ from the liquid layout?

A. An *elastic layout* is a layout whose content areas resize when the user resizes the text. Elastic layouts use ems, which are inherently proportional to text and font size. An em is a typographical unit of measurement equal to the point size of the current font. When ems are used in an elastic layout, if a user forces the text size to increase or decrease in size by using Ctrl and the mouse scroll wheel, the areas containing the text increase or decrease proportionally. Elastic layouts are often quite difficult to achieve.

Q. Is there one type of layout system that is better than the others?

A. *Better* is a subjective term; the goal of these lessons is to help you create standards-compliant code. Most designers will tell you that liquid layouts take longer to create (and perfect), but the usability enhancements are worth it, especially when the process leads to a responsive design. Grid and flexible box layouts give you more options in terms of controlling the content display, but because they are so new, many designers are not yet comfortable using them. In general, most designers avoid fixed layout designs because they are not responsive and can be difficult for mobile users to navigate. You'll learn more about how to build responsive websites in Part IV.

Workshop

The Workshop contains quiz questions and activities to help you solidify your understanding of the material covered.

Quiz

1. Which is the best layout to use, in general: fixed, liquid, or hybrid?

2. Can you position a fixed layout anywhere on the page?

3. What does `min-width` do?

4. Which would be better to use to display a group of products for sale: a CSS grid or flexible boxes layout?

5. Why is it important to consider mobile devices when creating your design?

6. Which is a better ID on an element: `container` or `primary`?

7. If you are targeting an audience with a standard browser size of 800 × 600 pixels, what should be the maximum fixed width in pixels, and why?

8. How do you define a container as a table?

9. Name three modern CSS layout techniques.

10. What does `display: inline-grid;` do?

NOTE

Just a reminder for those of you reading these words in the print or e-book edition of this book: If you go to **www.informit.com/register** and register this book (using ISBN 9780672338083), you can receive free access to an online Web Edition that not only contains the complete text of this book but also features an interactive version of this quiz.

Answers

1. This is a trick question; there is no "best" layout. What is best depends on the content and the needs of the audience. Note that we ultimately lean toward responsive grid layouts as the "best" and recommend against using fixed layouts except in very limited situations.

2. Sure. Although most fixed layouts are flush left or centered, you can assign a fixed position on an x,y axis and could place a `<div>` that contains all the other layout `<div>` elements.

3. The `min-width` property sets the minimum width of an element, not including padding, borders, or margins.

4. Flexible boxes were designed specifically for this type of layout, where there is a series of objects (the products for sale) that need to be displayed neatly within a container.

5. More and more people are accessing web pages primarily on their mobile devices, and if your layout is hard to read on such a device, they won't stick around.

6. The ID `primary` is better because it doesn't define a part of the layout but rather defines that the included content is primary.

7. It should be no more than 780 pixels or so, to account for the non-viewable areas of the browser.

8. Use the `display: table;` property.

9. The three modern layout techniques discussed in this lesson are CSS tables, flexible boxes, and grid layouts.

10. It indicates that the container is a grid that should be displayed inline with the surrounding content.

Exercises

▶ Figure 12.15 shows the finished CSS grid layout, but a few areas could stand to be improved. For example, there isn't any space around the text in the right-side column, there aren't any margins between the body text and either column, the footer strip is a little sparse, and so on. Take some time to fix these design elements.

▶ Figure 12.14 shows the finished flexible boxes layout, but there are problems with it as well. In addition to the issues mentioned above, the columns aren't necessarily the right size, and the colors are hard on the eyes. Use what you learned in this lesson to modify this layout to better reflect your design skills. Don't edit the HTML; do this just with CSS.

Taking Control of Backgrounds and Borders

What You'll Learn in This Lesson:

▸ How to layer backgrounds

▸ How to use gradients as backgrounds

▸ How to use CSS properties to create "zebra-stripe" tables automatically

▸ How to create rounded corners on elements

▸ How to use images as borders

▸ How outlines are different from borders

In earlier lessons you learned how to add basic borders and backgrounds to your elements, but there is much more you can do to dress up modern web pages. In many ways, CSS backgrounds define modern designs. In this lesson you will learn how to layer background images on your elements and use gradients that are created by the CSS itself as backgrounds.

And borders are just as critical. Every element has a border, even if it isn't visible. In this lesson you will learn how to adjust the borders of your elements to make your designs more interesting. You'll learn how to create rounded corners as well as how to use images as borders. Plus, you'll learn a little more about the CSS outline property and how it differs from borders.

Reviewing Background and Border Basics

In order to go into more depth with borders and backgrounds, you need to be sure you know the basics.

background is a shorthand property that allows you to define a number of background properties at the same time. With this property, you can set the following properties:

▸ background-image—The image used as a background

▸ background-position—Where the image should be placed on the element, written as a length, a percentage, or a keyword (top, bottom, center, right, and left)

▸ background-size—The size of the image in the element, either as the width, the width and height, or a keyword (cover or contain)

- ▶ `background-repeat`—Whether and how the image should tile in the element, using one of the values `repeat`, `repeat-x`, `repeat-y`, `no-repeat`, `space`, or `round`

- ▶ `background-origin`—Where the background image should start tiling; possible values are `border-box`, `padding-box`, and `content-box`

- ▶ `background-clip`—How the background should display beyond the element's content or padding; possible values are `border-box`, `padding-box`, or `content-box`

- ▶ `background-attachment`—How the background should move relative to the viewport; possible values are `scroll`, `fixed`, or `local`

- ▶ `background-color`—The color of the background, using a color keyword or color code

You don't need to include the properties in the order shown here, but best practices recommend using this order to keep your CSS clear. Some properties, like `background-position` and `background-size`, can be left out. Many designers use the `background` property with just one or two elements, as in these examples:

```
background: #dfdfdf;
background: url('paper.png') #dfdfdf;
```

You can apply the `background` property to any HTML element.

The `border` property is a shorthand property for setting `border-width`, `border-style`, and `border-color`, like so:

```
border: border-width border-style border-color;
```

For the `border-width` and `border-color` properties, you can use 10 different border style keywords:

- ▶ `solid`—Draws a solid, continuous line (This is the default.)

- ▶ `none`—Draws no border line

- ▶ `hidden`—Draws a border line but does not display it

- ▶ `dashed`—Draws a line of dashes

- ▶ `dotted`—Draws a line of dots

- ▶ `double`—Draws two lines around the element, taking up the full border width

- ▶ `groove`—Adds a bevel to make the element appear pressed into the page

- ▶ `ridge`—Adds a bevel to make the element appear raised above the page

- ▶ `inset`—Adds a slight bevel to make the element appear slightly depressed

- ▶ `outset`—Adds a slight bevel to make the element appear slightly raised

Using Multiple Borders and Backgrounds

When you're working with borders and backgrounds, it's easy to forget that you aren't stuck with just one. You can style all four borders of an element in different ways, and you can even layer multiple backgrounds, one on top of the other, to create different effects.

NOTE

Putting more than one border around one element is not currently supported in CSS. However, you can fake it by using pseudo-elements, using the `outline` property, using the `box-shadow` property, or changing the `background-clip` property. You can learn more about how to do this online by searching for **multiple borders with CSS** in your favorite search engine.

While it's most common to use just the `border` property to style all four borders of an element exactly the same, this isn't your only option. There are four other shorthand properties that work in the same way but each applies to only one side of the element: `border-top`, `border-right`, `border-bottom`, and `border-left`. For example, if you wanted to style all four borders differently, you would write CSS for all four sides, like so:

```
border-top: 2px solid red;
border-right: 2px dashed aqua;
border-bottom: 5px dashed red;
border-left: 5px solid aqua;
```

But it's not common to see an element that needs vastly different borders on all four sides. Instead, you might see an element that needs three borders the same, with the fourth different. You can write your CSS with the four border properties separated out, or you can use the cascade to your advantage. To do this, define all the borders the same and then follow that with the one different one:

```
border: 2px solid aqua;
border-bottom: 5px dashed red;
```

Using multiple backgrounds on the same element is a little different. With CSS3 you can now stack border images on your elements to create a layered effect. This is especially useful if your images have transparent or clipped areas that allow images or color below to show through. You specify multiple backgrounds in a comma-separated list, where each item is a background layer. The order of the items correlates with the order of the layers: The first item is the top layer and on down through the backgrounds.

NOTE

One of the issues designers most commonly face when using multiple backgrounds is determining the order to place them in the CSS. We can't count how many times we have carefully created designs only to have one of the backgrounds not show up or appear cut off because we forgot where it belonged in the layer list. *Just remember that the layer that is on top comes first.*

To create an element with multiple backgrounds, we need multiple images. Figure 13.1 shows an image of a howling wolf and a picture of the moon.

FIGURE 13.1
Two separate images to be combined into a background. *(Credit: claudiodivizia/123RF)*

Both of these images have transparent areas and solid color areas, so they will work well as layered backgrounds. We also need to add an element to place the background on. The `background` property can be placed on any block-level HTML element, so we can add a `<div>` with the class `box` to the HTML:

```
<div class="box"></div>
```

Because the `<div>` element currently has no content, we need to set the height and width so the background will show up:

```
.box {
  width: 500px;
  height: 400px;
}
```

Then we can add the first background image:

```
background: url(images/wolf.svg)
```

Remember that this image will be on top, and any other images will be layered below it.

We can position this background image in the middle of the `<div>` and at the bottom so it looks like the wolf is howling at the moon:

```
background: url(images/wolf.svg) center bottom
```

Then, to make sure it doesn't look bad, we can set the image to fill up the element with the `cover` and `no-repeat` keywords:

```
background: url(images/wolf.svg) center bottom / cover no-repeat
```

To add the second background image, we add a comma and then the second image URL:

```
background: url(images/wolf.svg) center bottom / cover no-repeat,
            url(images/moon.png)
```

We need to put the moon at the top right and make it 45% of the element, and we also need to make sure it displays only once (and be sure to include the closing semicolon):

```
background: url(images/wolf.svg) center bottom / cover no-repeat,
            url(images/moon.png) right top / 45% no-repeat;
```

After taking all these steps, the code should look like the code in Listing 13.1, which creates the image shown in Figure 13.2.

LISTING 13.1   Adding Multiple Backgrounds

```
<!doctype html>
<html lang="en">
  <head>
    <meta charset="utf-8">
    <title>Layering Backgrounds on an Element</title>
    <style>
      .box {
        margin: 0 auto;
        width: 500px;
        height: 400px;
        background: url(images/wolf.svg) center bottom /
                                        cover no-repeat,
                   url(images/moon.png) right top / 45% no-repeat;
      }
    </style>
  </head>
  <body>
  <div class="box"></div>
  </body>
</html>
```

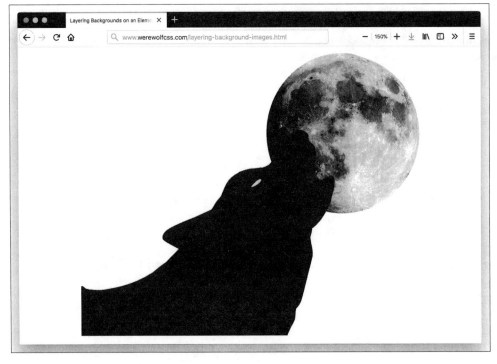

FIGURE 13.2
Multiple background images on one element. *(Credit: claudiodivizia/123RF)*

One of the best reasons for using multiple backgrounds on your web pages is so that you can modify the backgrounds programmatically. For example, we could modify the background in Figure 13.2 with a script so that at different times of day, the moon image is in a different location on the element. With only one background image, we'd have to create multiple images for the different times. But by layering multiple background images, we just need to move the moon picture with the CSS.

Using Forgotten Background Properties

There are several background properties in CSS that designers forget about or hardly ever use. But if you use these properties, you'll have more control over how the backgrounds display and more tools for animation and interactivity in your web pages.

Choosing How to Place the Background

Background images are placed on boxes, and boxes on web pages are affected by the box model. The box model defines the margins, border, padding, and content area of a box, as you learned in Lesson 10, "Understanding the CSS Box Model and Positioning." But when you place a background on that box, where does it go? The default placement of a background is behind the content and right up to the border, covering the padding.

The `background-clip` property lets you change what parts of the box the background covers. These are your choices:

▶ `border-box`—This extends the background all the way under the border. If your border is transparent, the background will show through it.

▶ `padding-box`—This clips the background within the padding area but leaves the border with no background.

▶ `content-box`—This clips the background to the content area only. The padding and border will have no background.

As with all other CSS properties, you can also use the values `initial`, `inherit`, and `unset` on the `background-clip` property. These values set the background to the default or initial state, the same as the parent element, and remove settings, respectively.

There is another property you can use to adjust how the image displays in the background: the `background-origin` property. This property might seem like it does the same thing as `background-clip`, but it is slightly different. It determines the positioning area of the background. The `background-clip` property specifies whether the background will extend under the border or padding of the element. The `background-origin` property uses the same three values: `border-box`, `padding-box`, and `content-box`.

Another way to think about the difference between these two properties is that background-origin defines where the background image starts, and background-clip defines where the background image ends.

If you have multiple backgrounds, you can set the background-clip and background-origin for all of them by separating the values with commas. Just as with multiple backgrounds, the first value is for the top layer and down through the list.

Changing the Background Size

When the background-size property made it to browsers, we were in heaven. Finally, there was a way to adjust the size of a background in an element without having to get out a graphics program. But while you don't need to edit the graphics, background sizes are complex. There are four ways to define the background-size:

- ▶ Using keywords
- ▶ Using one value
- ▶ Using two values
- ▶ Using multiple values

Using background-size **Keywords**

There are three keywords you can use with background-size: auto, cover, and contain. The auto keyword sets the background to be the size it would normally be. cover sets the background image to cover the entire container. The image might be stretched or cropped, but the entire box will have a background. contain resizes the image to fit the entire thing within the box. This means that small images will be stretched to fit, and large images will be shrunk. But if there is extra space (and the background-repeat property allows it), the background will be tiled.

Using background-size **Values**

You can specify the exact size of a background image by putting in one or two length values. When you use one length, that number is assumed to be the width of the background, and the height is set to auto. When you use two numbers, the first is the width, and the second is the height. You can use any CSS length values, including pixels, percentages, rems/ems, lengths (centimeters, inches, and so on), and viewport relative units, such as vw and vh.

If you have multiple backgrounds layered on an element, you can set their sizes by separating the values with commas:

```
background-size: 400px 400px, cover;
```

Positioning Your Background Image

Once you have your background image sized so that it fits the element, you will probably want to have more control over the placement than just the upper-left corner. The `background-position` property lets you define where the background will be drawn relative to the upper-left corner of the element. You can use the keywords `top`, `bottom`, `right`, `left`, and `center`. Or you can use two percentage or length values. One value moves the background right, and two values move it to the right and down.

But what if you want to position your background based on the right or bottom edges? There are two ways to do this: Use `background-position` with edge offsets or use `calc()`.

To use edge offsets, you first indicate which edge you want to offset from: `top`, `bottom`, `right`, or `left`. You follow that with a length value. Here is an example:

```
background-position: top 2rem right 1rem;
```

This four-value syntax is well supported in all modern browsers. But if you don't know the exact length of an element—for example, in a responsive design—then using the `calc()` as a value would make more sense. Describing how `calc()` works is beyond the scope of this book, but you can search for more information in any search engine.

Changing the Scrolling of Backgrounds

On most web pages, the backgrounds are set to scroll with the browser window. When a customer scrolls down, the background moves up, along with the rest of the content. But with the `background-attachment` property, you can change how this works. And with the popularity of parallax designs, this is a useful property to know.

These are the values for the `background-attachment` property:

- `scroll`
- `fixed`
- `local`

Most designers are familiar with the first two: `scroll` and `fixed`. A background set to scroll will scroll with the main view (usually the browser window) but will remain fixed inside the local view (usually a container element). A background that is fixed will stay where it is no matter what. The third value, `local`, was created to allow you to scroll the background with both the main view and the local view.

The easiest way to understand this is to follow along as we build a page with different background attachments. First we create three `<div>` elements that will have the different attachments:

```
<div class="inner"><h1>scroll</h1></div>
<div class="inner"><h1>fixed</h1></div>
<div class="inner"><h1>local</h1></div>
```

Then we surround each of those `<div>` elements with another `<div>` and set the classes to scroll, fixed, and local:

```
<div class="scroll">
  <div class="inner"><h1>scroll</h1></div>
</div>
<div class="fixed">
  <div class="inner"><h1>fixed</h1></div>
</div>
<div class="local">
  <div class="inner"><h1>local</h1></div>
</div>
```

We then add a paragraph at the bottom of the document with the class addscrollbar to deal with larger browsers:

```
<p class="addscrollbar"></p>
```

We need to style all the `<div>` elements with a height of 300px, a width of 60%, a maximum width of 500px, a margin of 1rem on top and bottom and centered, and hidden horizontal overflow and a scrollbar for the vertical overflow. We can add styles to the inner `<div>` elements: 100% width, 600px height, and hidden vertical overflow. We can also add a 50rem margin to the .addscrollbar element:

```
div {
  height: 300px;
  width: 60%;
  max-width: 500px;
  margin: 1rem auto;
  overflow-x: hidden;
  overflow-y: scroll;
}
.inner {
  width: 100%;
  height: 600px;
  overflow-y: hidden;
}
.addscrollbar { margin-bottom: 50rem; }
```

In order to affect the attachment, you need a background image on the .scroll, .fixed, and .local elements. We can use LoremPixel (http://lorempixel.com) or another random image generator for the images, as shown here:

```
.scroll, .fixed, .local {
  background-image: url('http://lorempixel.com/600/400/nature/');
}
```

Then we set background-attachment on the .scroll, .fixed, and .local elements to
scroll, fixed, and local respectively:

```
.scroll { background-attachment: scroll; }
.fixed { background-attachment: fixed; }
.local { background-attachment: local; }
```

If you load this page in a browser, as you scroll, the backgrounds may or may not scroll with you.
Notice how the different values affect whether the background scrolls with the main browser
scrollbar or the element scrollbar or both. Listing 13.2 shows the complete HTML and CSS for this
example.

LISTING 13.2   **The Difference Between** background-attachment **Values**

```
<!doctype html>
<html lang="en">
  <head>
    <meta charset="utf-8">
    <title>Learning the Difference Between background-attachment
          Values</title>
    <style>
div {
  height: 300px;
  width: 60%;
  max-width: 500px;
  margin: 1rem auto;
  overflow-x: hidden;
  overflow-y: scroll;
}
.scroll, .fixed, .local {
  background-image: url('http://lorempixel.com/600/400/nature/');
}
.scroll {
  background-attachment: scroll;
}
.fixed {
  background-attachment: fixed;
}
.local {
  background-attachment: local;
}
.inner { width: 100%; height: 600px; overflow-y: hidden; }
.addscrollbar { margin-bottom: 50rem; }
    </style>
  </head>
```

```
<body>
  <div class="scroll">
    <div class="inner"><h1>scroll</h1></div>
  </div>
  <div class="fixed">
    <div class="inner"><h1>fixed</h1></div>
  </div>
  <div class="local">
    <div class="inner"><h1>local</h1></div>
  </div>
  <p class="addscrollbar"></p>
</body>
</html>
```

Alternating Background Colors

When you build tables, especially large ones with a lot of data, coloring the background of the rows can make them much easier to read. To do this, you don't use a background-* CSS property but rather the :nth-child() pseudo-class.

In the past, designers would sometimes create a class in their CSS with a background color and then add that class to every other row in a table. But with the :nth-child() pseudo-class, you can select one or more elements based on the order in which they appear in the source HTML. This means that if the table has 10 body rows today and 13 tomorrow, you don't have to go in and edit the class on every row. The CSS will update automatically.

The :nth-child() selector takes an attribute in the parentheses. This attribute can be one of the following:

▶ **A single integer**—Selects just that one element, such as the fourth row in a table, like so: tr:nth-child(4)

▶ even—Selects only the even-numbered elements

▶ odd—Selects only the odd-numbered elements

▶ **A formula**—Selects the elements that match the formula an+b, where a is an integer, n is the literal letter *n*, + is an operator that may be either + or -, and b is another integer

To create zebra-stripe tables, you can just use the even or odd keywords, like so:

tbody tr:nth-child(odd) { background-color: #dfdfdf; }

This tells the browser to examine every row inside the <tbody> element and add a gray background to the first row, third row, fifth row, and so on.

The real power in using the `:nth-child` selector is with the formula. It allows you to make complicated selections, such as these:

- **Every other element, starting with the fifth one**—`:nth-child(2n+5)`
- **Every sixth element, starting with the second one**—`:nth-child(6n+2)`

You can also use other pseudo-class selectors to select specific elements in your DOM tree, including the following:

- `:nth-of-type()`—Selects based on the element type, such as `<p>`, `<li>`, `<tr>`, and so on.
- `:nth-last-child()`—Selects just like `:nth-child()` but starting at the bottom of the parent element and selecting up the DOM tree
- `:nth-last-of-type()`—Selects based on type but works up from the bottom of the DOM tree

For a useful tester you can use to try out different formulas to see how they work, visit http://lea.verou.me/demos/nth.html.

Using Gradients as Backgrounds

Gradients have been popular on the web for as long as we've had images on web pages. Adding them used to be very difficult. You had to be willing to use gigantic images with lots of colors and very little compression. If you didn't you'd end up with blocky color swaths with bands striping down your page. Sites with smooth gradients were guaranteed to load more slowly. Most designers just left them out completely. Now the combination of modern CSS and modern browsers allows web designers to create beautiful gradients without any images at all.

CAUTION

This may seem counterintuitive, but when you add gradients to your backgrounds, you add them as background images with the `background-image` or the `background` shorthand property. You can use these properties as a fallback for older browsers that don't support gradients. Simply define both the `background-image` with the gradient and the `background-color` with a default color. Browsers that support gradients then place the gradient above the background color, and older browsers just display the color and ignore the gradient.

There are two types of gradients: linear and radial.

Creating Linear Gradients

Linear gradients are gradients that change color along a straight line. They can move horizontally from left to right, vertically from top to bottom, or across any diagonal angle you choose. The default is vertical, or top to bottom. You set a linear gradient by using the `linear-gradient()` expression, with a comma-separated list of colors inside the parentheses. For example, you can create a gradient from pink (`#ff00d5`) to green (`rgba(39, 164, 0, 0.5)`) to blue like so:

```
background-image:
  linear-gradient( #ff00d5, rgba(39, 164, 0, 0.5), blue );
```

The colors can be any color values that are valid in CSS, including named colors, RGBa, hexadecimal, HSL (hue, saturation, and lightness), and so on. You need at least two colors to create a gradient.

After you define your colors, you can indicate where you want them to start. This is called a *color stop*. If you don't include any color stops, the gradient will be applied evenly across the space. Add the color stops after each color value but before the comma separating the next color, like so:

```
background-image:
  linear-gradient(
    red,
    green 35%
  );
```

You add the location of the color stop as a length notation after the color.

If you want to change the direction of the gradient, you add a parameter that is the word `to` and the direction before the colors. The following are some examples:

▶ `to right`—The gradient moves from left to right.

▶ `to left`—The gradient moves from right to left.

▶ `to top`—The gradient moves from bottom to top.

▶ `to top left`—The gradient moves from the bottom-right corner diagonally up to the top-left corner.

▶ `45deg`—The gradient moves along a 45° angle with `0deg` being completely vertical and `90deg` being horizontal and equivalent to `to right`.

Linear gradients can make very nice-looking backgrounds, and they don't add a lot of download time to a page.

Building Radial Gradients

Radial gradients are similar to linear gradients. They take two or more colors and fade from one to the next. But whereas linear gradients fade down a line, radial gradients start at a single point and emanate outward. A default radial gradient starts in exactly the center of the element and moves outward to the edge. It is written just like a linear gradient but with the expression `radial-gradient()`. A basic radial gradient fading from light blue in the center (#9ad6e9) to yellow is written thus:

```
background-image: radial-gradient(
  #9ad6e9,
  yellow
);
```

A gradient makes an ellipse by default unless you place it on a square element. Figure 13.3 shows the same gradient on `<div>` elements of two different shapes. Listing 13.3 shows the HTML and CSS for this figure.

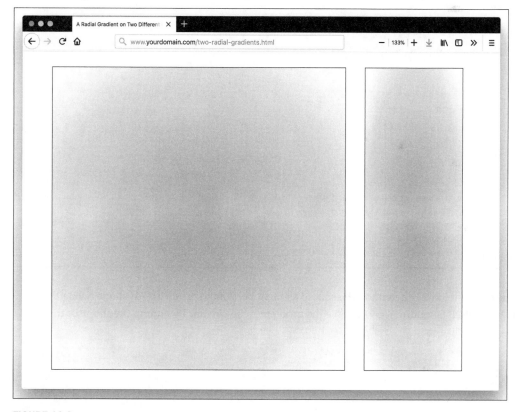

FIGURE 13.3
A radial gradient on two different elements.

LISTING 13.3   A Radial Gradient on Two Different Elements

```
<!doctype html>
<html lang="en">
  <head>
    <meta charset="utf-8">
    <title>A Radial Gradient on Two Different Elements</title>
    <style>
      .container {
        width: 45rem;
        margin: 0 auto;
      }
      .grad { background-image: radial-gradient(
        orange,
        white);
        border: solid 1px black;
        margin: 1rem;
        float: left;
      }
      .one {
        width: 30rem;
        height: 30rem;
      }
      .two {
        width: 10rem;
        height: 30rem;
      }
    </style>
  </head>
  <body>
    <div class="container">
      <div class="grad one"></div>
      <div class="grad two"></div>
    </div>
  </body>
</html>
```

The gradient looks different on the square element because it has a circular shape, while the element itself is square. You can force the gradient to be circular by adding the shape at the beginning, like so:

```
background-image: radial-gradient(
 circle,
 #9ad6e9,
 yellow
);
```

Otherwise, the default value is `ellipse`.

You can also adjust the size of the ellipse by defining a size, using the following values:

▶ `closest-side`—The gradient shape is sized to meet the side closest to the center.

▶ `closest-corner`—The gradient shape is sized to meet the corner closest to the center.

▶ `farthest-side`—The gradient shape is sized to meet the side of the element farthest from the center.

▶ `farthest-corner`—The gradient shape is sized to meet the corner of the element that is farthest from the center.

One way to think of the keywords is to add them to this sentence: "I want my radial gradient to start at the center point and fade to the ____, filling in the rest of the element accordingly." Add them to the first parameter, as in this example:

```
circle closest-side,
```

CAUTION

Early drafts of the CSS specification included two other keywords for defining radial gradients: `contain` and `cover`. These were intended to act as synonyms for `closest-side` and `farthest-corner`, respectively. They were subsequently removed from the specification, and most modern browsers have removed support for them (if they ever did support them). Use the `closest-side` and `farthest-corner` keywords instead.

If you want the placement of the center of your gradient to be more precise, you can use the `at` keyword along with positioning keywords or values. These are the keywords you can use:

▶ `left`

▶ `center`

▶ `right`

▶ `top`

▶ `bottom`

The following example shows how to use the `at` keyword and parameters:

```
circle at bottom right,
```

You can also use exact positions in lengths or percentages for the distance from the top and the left side of the element. For example, Figure 13.4 displays two gradients placed next to one another. One has an origin at the bottom left and the other at the bottom right. Listing 13.4 shows the CSS used to create this effect.

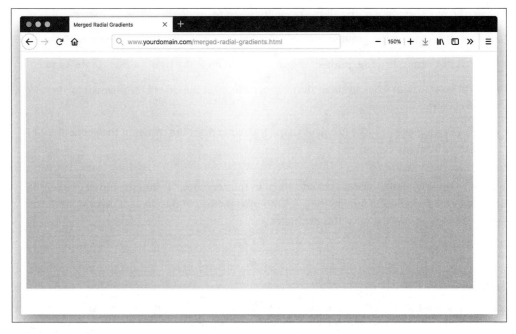

FIGURE 13.4
Radial gradients create an interesting effect.

LISTING 13.4   Two Radial Gradients Create an Interesting Effect

```
.one {
  background-image: radial-gradient(
    at bottom left,
    orange,
    white
  );
}
.two {
  background-image: radial-gradient(
    at bottom right,
    orange,
    white
  );
}
```

And just as with linear gradients, with radial gradients you can define color stops to identify exactly where you want the colors to change. For example, this is a three-color circular gradient centered in the lower-right portion of the element:

```
.gradient {
  background-image: radial-gradient(
```

```
    circle at 70% 64%,
    orange,
    #25b25d 18%,
    gray 77%
  );
}
```

Rounding the Corners of HTML Elements

As you've learned in earlier lessons, HTML elements are all rectangular blocks, and this can make web pages look very boxy and rigid. But with the border-radius properties, you can make the corners as round or square as you like. Simply define the amount of curve you want for the corners, like so:

```
border-radius: 1rem;
```

NOTE

An easy way to remember the style property border-radius is to imagine there is a circle in each corner of your element. The radius of that circle determines the size of the curve.

As long as there is a color change of some sort, the rounded corner will be visible and will curve all four corners of the element. Listing 13.5 shows three <div> elements with rounded corners that are identical except that the first one has a background color, the second has a border, and the third has a background image. Figure 13.5 shows how this would look.

LISTING 13.5　Three <div> Elements with Rounded Corners

```
<!doctype html>
<html lang="en">
  <head>
    <meta charset="utf-8">
    <title>Three DIVs with Rounded Corners</title>
    <style>
      div {
        border-radius: 1rem;
        width: 10rem;
        height: 15rem;
        float: left;
        margin: 1rem;
        box-sizing: border-box;
      }
      .one { background-color: aqua; }
      .two { border: solid 0.25rem aqua; }
```

```
    .three { background: url(images/mckinley.jpg)
        center top / cover no-repeat; }
   </style>
  </head>
  <body>
    <div class="one"></div>
    <div class="two"></div>
    <div class="three"></div>
  </body>
</html>
```

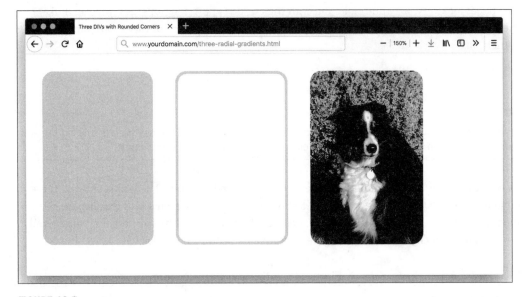

FIGURE 13.5
Three <div> elements with rounded corners.

With the border-radius property you can set all four corners at once, or you can set them to different values. This property can take between one and four values.

You can use one value to set all four corners the same. If you use two values, you set first the top-left and bottom-right corners to the first value and then set the top-right and bottom-left corners to the second value. If you use three values, you set the top-right and bottom-left corners to the second value, with the first value setting the top-left corner and the third value setting the bottom-right corner. You can use four values to set all four corners, in this order: top-left corner, top-right corner, bottom-right corner, and bottom-left corner. Consider these examples:

▶ border-radius: 1rem;—All four corners are 1rem radius.

▶ border-radius: 1rem 0.5rem;—The top-left and bottom-right corners are 1rem. The top-right and bottom-left corners are 0.5rem.

▶ `border-radius: 1rem 0.5rem 0.25rem;`—The top-left corner is 1rem. The top-right and bottom-left corners are 0.5rem. The bottom-right corner is 0.25rem.

▶ `border-radius: 1rem 0.75rem 0.5rem 0.25rem;`—The top-left corner is 1rem. The top-right corner is 0.75rem. The bottom-right corner is 0.5rem, and the bottom-left corner is 0.25rem.

One fun thing you can do is turn any element into a circle or an ellipse with the `border-radius: 50%;` style property. If the element has equal height and width, it will display as a circle. If the height and width are different, it will display as an ellipse.

Using Images as Borders

Borders can be more than just plain colors. You can do a lot with borders by curving the edges, as you learned in the last section, and also by changing their width and style, as you learned in Lesson 10. However, you can't create every effect you might want with borders.

One thing that many designers look for is a way to frame images with another image. Rather than make a solid-color border surrounding an element, you might want a frame like one you would see around a painting. To do this, you need a picture of the frame.

Defining the Border Image: `border-image-source`

CSS allows you to define any picture as a border by using the `border-image` property. This is a shorthand property that defines several other properties. One such property is the URL of the image that will become the border, which is defined as `border-image-source`. The default value for `border-image-source` is `none`, but if you specify an image URL, then that image will be used as the border for the element, like so:

```
.myBorder {
  border-image-source: url(border.png);
}
```

Clipping the Border Image: `border-image-slice`

The `border-image` property also defines the `border-image-slice` property. In order to create decent borders, you need to tell the browser where each portion of the border will be by slicing the border into nine sections. These sections are illustrated in Figure 13.6.

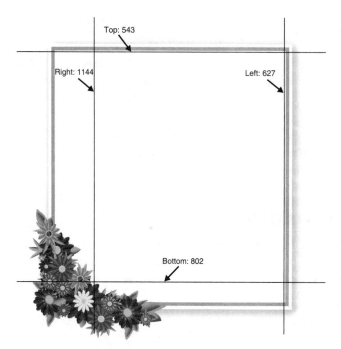

FIGURE 13.6
Slicing an image to use as a border.

The `border-image-slice` property takes up to four positive values, either numbers or percentages, and an optional `fill` keyword. The numbers, which are unitless, measure the coordinates of the slices by pixels on raster images like JPEG or PNG and by coordinates on SVG images. If you use percentages, this is relative to the size of the image itself. The four values measure inward from the top, right, bottom, and left edges of the image:

```
border-image-slice: top right bottom left;
```

This divides the image into nine regions: four corners, four edges, and the center. In most cases, the center is discarded, and only the corners and edges are used for the border.

NOTE

The `border-image-slice` property can have slices that are 0 pixels away from the side. This allows you to create image borders that are applied only to a couple sides of an element rather than all four. For example, if you want to add a border that looks like a ruler, you might place that on only the top or right side of the element. When you slice the border image, the left and bottom sides are zero, and they are not applied to the border.

As mentioned previously, the `border-image-slice` property can also take the keyword `fill`. This tells the browser to keep the middle part of the image and display that section as a background image on the element. You can therefore add a background image with a fancy border to your element and have that border be repeated no matter the size of the element. To use the `fill` keyword, add it after the offsets, like this:

```
border-image-slice: 10 5 8 7 fill;
```

Figure 13.7 shows how a simple image can be sliced and used to fill an element or just create the border. For this image, we used a picture from Pixabay of a series of flowers and sliced it so that only the outer rows and columns are part of the border.

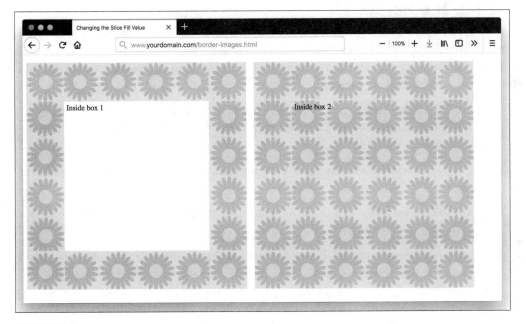

FIGURE 13.7
Using a sliced image for a border and a filled border.

Defining the Border Image Width

One property that is confusing to people when they first start using border images is `border-image-width`. This is different from the slice offsets because it defines the width of the border image regardless of the offset. The initial value is `1`, so if you need the border to be blank on one or more sides, you should specify `border-image-width` for those sides as `0`. Otherwise, if there is a `border` or `border-width` set on the element, that border will display.

This property uses the `top`, `right`, `bottom`, `left` order for the values. You can use percentages relative to the size of the border image area or unitless non-negative numbers that are multiplied by `border-width`.

Extending the Border Image Beyond the Border Edges

If you want your border image to extend past the border box area, you can use the `border-image-outset` property. Border images do not affect the width of the border, and wider borders are inset, covering the padding and even the content area of the element. When you add an outset, this tells the browser to display the border image outset over the element margin.

Making the Border Fit

One thing you'll notice when you start using border images is that they don't fit around every element. Browsers automatically repeat the image as they would with tiled background images to make the border images fit in the space available. There are four ways a browser can do this with the `border-image-repeat` property:

- ▶ `stretch`—The border image is simply stretched to fit the space. If the space is too wide, that slice will be increased, and if it's too narrow, the slice will be compressed. This is the default value.

- ▶ `repeat`—This keyword tiles the image to fill the area. If necessary, the tiles will be cut to fit the space.

- ▶ `round`—This keyword tiles the image to fill the area, but the image is resized and scaled to fit so that tiles are not divided or cut.

- ▶ `space`—This keyword tiles the image to fill the area, but if whole tiles cannot be used, space is inserted around the tiles to create an even fit. This keyword may not be supported by Chrome, Android, or Opera browsers. However, when we tested it in Chrome, it appeared to work.

Figure 13.8 shows the `border-image-repeat` property on four elements. For this figure, we cropped the flower border image so that it was only nine flowers (a 3 × 3 grid) and resized it to be 100 × 100 pixels. If you use a border image that is larger than the elements you're bordering, you can get unexpected results, especially with the `round` and `space` keywords. The former can end up looking identical to `stretch`, while the latter is simply blank because there isn't enough space in the slice to include the whole thing.

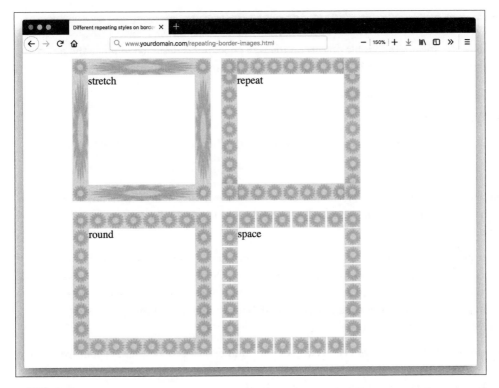

FIGURE 13.8
Different repeating styles on border images.

CAUTION

Most novice web designers think that the `border-image` and related properties should allow you to create a repeating border around the element without slicing the image at all. But that is not how these properties work. In order to create a repeating image, you need to create a 9 × 9 grid of the image (you can leave out the central image) and then slice the image with the `border-image-slice` property. Figure 13.9 shows a 9 × 9 grid of flowers that we used to create a repeating flower border in Figure 13.7.

FIGURE 13.9
A 9 × 9 grid of flowers can be used to create a repeating flower border.

Understanding CSS Outlines

An outline is a line around visible objects on the web page that is designed to make the object stand out. According to the W3C, outlines are different from borders in three ways:

- ▶ Outlines do not take up space.

- ▶ Outlines may be non-rectangular.

- ▶ Browsers and other user agents often render outlines on elements when they are in the `:focus` state.

Because outlines don't take up space, they can cover content, are usually drawn outside the element's border, and don't add to the dimensions of the element. They are not part of the box model.

Because outlines may be non-rectangular, they may display differently in different browsers. This is especially true when the outline is applied to an inline element such as <span>. Some browsers follow the actual contours of the letters with the outline, while others treat the inline element as a rectangular box. Both display methods are valid, but you should be aware of these differences when using CSS outline properties.

Another thing that some browsers do is display the outline of links and other elements when they have been focused on but haven't been clicked. This allows users to see what link may be about to be clicked; this is especially important for accessibility.

CAUTION

You should never use `outline: none;` or `outline: 0;` on links or buttons or other elements that receive keyboard focus. Such an outline tells keyboard users which link currently has focus, and without it, they can't navigate your site. If you must remove the outline, then be sure to redefine any `:focus` states with some other way to recognize the state change, such as a color change, font change, or other indicator.

There are five outline properties: `outline-style`, `outline-color`, `outline-width`, `outline-offset`, and `outline`. They work in the same way as the border properties, with `outline` being a shorthand property where you can define `outline-style`, `outline-color`, and `outline-width` all at once, like so:

```
outline: 8px ridge yellow;
```

The `outline-offset` property defines the amount of space between the outline and the edge or border. The default value is 0, and it can take any length value, including negative numbers if you want the outline to be shown above the content or border. Here is an example:

```
outline-offset: .4rem;
```

Summary

In this lesson you learned several advanced techniques for background images and borders. First, you learned how to adjust the four borders on any element and set them all individually to create an element with several different borders. You also learned how to layer multiple backgrounds on one element to create interesting effects. This lesson covered how to position background elements with the `background-clip` property, how to change the size of the background with `background-size`, and how to use the `background-position` and `background-attachment` properties. You also learned about how to use some other lesser-known CSS properties to create a zebra-striped table. In the section on gradients, you learned about both linear and radial gradients. This lesson also covered how to round the corners of elements with the `border-radius` property and how to use images as borders with the `border-image` properties. Finally, you learned about the CSS `outline` properties and how they differ from `border` properties.

Q&A

Q. **What is the best way to create a responsive background image for a web page?**

A. Responsive web pages need to have background images that are large enough to cover big monitors but small enough to download quickly on mobile devices. You have several options for creating a decent background image, including using a small PNG as a repeating background or seamless tile, using flat color or gradients, or using an SVG file that can scale appropriately. You will learn more about responsive web design in Part IV, "Responsive Web Design."

Q. **Are there rules for when you should use an `<img>` tag versus using a background image?**

A. The `<img>` tag is a part of the HTML and as such is part of the content of the page. It can be printed and animated, but it is considered page content that should be rendered in some fashion even if the user agent is not a visual device such as a screen reader.

Background images are part of the background. They generally are not considered content and will be ignored by visual user agents. They are typically used as decoration or enhancement of existing content. Sprites are usually created using background images.

Workshop

The Workshop contains quiz questions and activities to help you solidify your understanding of the material covered.

Quiz

1. What types of HTML elements (such as block or inline) can have background images?

2. What is the keyword for creating a border that makes the element appear pressed into the page?

3. What are two ways you can give an element a red, dotted, 2px border on the top side and a blue, double 10px border on the right and left sides, leaving the bottom side with no border?

4. How do you separate multiple background images in the `background` property when layering them on one element?

5. Where does the background display when `background-clip` is set to `content-box`?

6. What does the selector `li:nth-child(even)` select?

7. What corners are rounded with the CSS style `border-radius: 10px 5px 15px;`?

8. What CSS property defines the URL used as a border image?

9. What does the `fill` keyword do in the `border-image-slice` property?

10. What are the three ways CSS outlines are different from borders?

NOTE

Just a reminder for those of you reading these words in the print or e-book edition of this book: If you go to **www.informit.com/register** and register this book (using ISBN 9780672338083), you can receive free access to an online Web Edition that not only contains the complete text of this book but also features an interactive version of this quiz.

Answers

1. Backgrounds can be applied to any HTML element.

2. The `border-style` keyword `groove` makes the element appear pressed into the page.

3. You can define all four borders separately, like so:

   ```
   border-top: 2px dotted red;
   border-right: 10px double blue;
   border-bottom: none;
   border-left: 10px double blue;
   ```

   Or you can define all four borders the same and then change just the two different ones, like so.:

   ```
   border: 10px double blue;
   border-top: 2px dotted red;
   border-bottom: none;
   ```

4. You use commas to separate the layered background images.

5. The background will display behind the content only. The padding and border will have no background.

6. It selects every even-numbered `<li>` element in the DOM.

7. The top-left corner is 10px, the top-right and bottom-left corners are 5px, and the bottom right is 15px.

8. The `border-image-source` property defines the image source for any border image.

9. It tells the browser to keep the middle part of the image as a background image on the element.

10. They don't take up space, they may be non-rectangular, and browsers often render them when the element is in a `:focus` state.

Exercises

▶ Use what you've learned in this lesson to add a linear gradient to the background of your web page or an element on the page. Remember that gradients work best on elements that have defined dimensions, so be sure to set them in your CSS.

▶ Once you have a gradient on an element, layer an image above it in the background. This is one of the most common ways to use layered backgrounds. Rather than set multiple images, you set the top layer as an image and the bottom layer as a gradient.

LESSON 14
Using CSS Transformations and Transitions

What You'll Learn in This Lesson:

▶ How to transform elements by rotating, scaling, moving, and tilting

▶ How to work with transformations in three dimensions

▶ How to apply multiple transformations to one element

▶ How to do simple animations with the transition property

In this lesson you will start learning how to make your elements literally move on the screen. You will start by learning about two-dimensional transformations: making elements larger and smaller, moving them, rotating them, and even changing the tilt. The transform properties will help you make your elements look more interesting. You will also learn how to transform elements on a three-dimensional plane.

Where this lesson really gets interesting is when you start to animate those elements with the transition properties. You will learn how to make the browser convert your choppy instant changes when you mouse over an element into smooth transitions that slowly change from the starting point to the end point. This lesson requires a lot of hands-on work to really understand the material, so open your editor and get ready to try out the animations yourself.

Understanding CSS 2D Transformations

CSS lets you transform an element in several ways. The following are some of the most commonly used transformation functions:

▶ rotate—Spins the element on the x,y plane

▶ scale—Shrinks or enlarges the element

▶ translate—Places the element in a new position on the screen

▶ skew—Distorts the element along the horizontal axis or along the vertical axis

You accomplish all these transformations by using the transform property and its 11 transformation functions: rotate, scale, scalex, scaley, skew, skewx, skewy, translate, translatex, translatey, and matrix.

Rotating Elements with `translate: rotate();`

To rotate an element, you set the `rotate()` value to a degree from 0deg to 360deg (or −360deg to 0deg). The element will then rotate that many degrees clockwise for positive numbers or counterclockwise for negative numbers.

To try it out, place two `<div>` elements on a page:

```
<div class="one"></div>
<div class="two"></div>
```

Style both elements so that they are visible on the screen:

```
div {
  width: 20rem;
  height: 30rem;
  border: solid 1px black;
  background: linear-gradient(#f5ea70 0%, #ffffff 100%);
  margin: 1rem;
  float: left;
}
```

Finally, add a rotation of 10 degrees to the second one with the class `two`:

```
.two {
  transform: rotate(10deg);
}
```

Figure 14.1 shows how this looks in Firefox. The only thing that is different about the second `<div>` element is the transformation, and yet it displays very differently on screen.

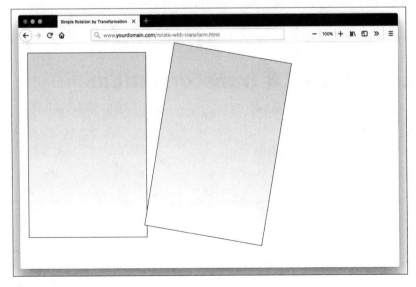

FIGURE 14.1
A simple rotation on a `<div>` element.

Making Elements Larger and Smaller with
transform: scale();

You can transform an element by making it larger or smaller with the `scale()` value. The number inside `scale()` is the *scaling factor*—a number that is multiplied by the element's current size. For example, `1` is the same as no scaling, `0.5` is half the current size, and `3` is three times as large.

The standard use is to apply one value to both the horizontal and vertical dimensions. But you can also use `scalex()` to resize only the horizontal dimension or `scaley()` to resize only the vertical direction. You can also set both values on the `scale()` function by separating them with a comma, like so:

```
transform: scale(horizontal,vertical);
```

CAUTION

When you transform an element, the browser won't change or move the surrounding elements. A transformed element can overlap and even hide other elements on the page.

Changing the size of an element may seem pointless, but it is a good way to give elements more or less emphasis in certain situations. For example, if you want customers to click on a button, you might make that button slightly larger when they hover over it. Listing 14.1 shows how you might achieve that.

LISTING 14.1   Enlarging a Button When in Hover State

```
<!doctype html>
<html lang="en">
  <head>
    <meta charset="utf-8">
    <title>Make the Button Bigger</title>
    <style>
      button {
        font-size: 1.5rem;
        border-radius: 10px;
        border: solid 1px #940c94;
        background: linear-gradient(#cb2ff6 0%, #ffffff 100%);
        padding: 0.25rem;
        margin: 1rem;
      }
      button:hover {
        transform: scale(1.2);
      }
```

```
    </style>
  </head>
  <body>
    <button>Click Me</button>
  </body>
</html>
```

When you hover over the button, it gets a little bit bigger, grabbing attention and encouraging customers to click.

NOTE

Remember that when you transform an element, it affects everything in that element. So if you double the size of a 200 × 200 box with 15px padding with `transform: scale(2);`, it will display as 400 × 400 with 30px padding. The transformation applies to other styles on the element, such as font size, margins, borders, and outlines.

One thing that many designers don't realize about the `transform: scale();` property is that negative values cause an element to scale in a mirror image way. Remember that 1 as the `scale()` value tells the browser to keep the image the same size. So if you want your text to display as mirror writing, you just tell the browser to scale the horizontal to −1, like so:

```
p { transform: scalex(-1); }
```

You can also turn it all upside down with `scaley()`, like so:

```
p { transform: scaley(-1); }
```

This does not hide the text from search engine robots or impact the content in any other way. It just makes the text display backward, which could be fun in some situations.

Moving Elements with `transform: translate();`

The `translate()` function of the `transform` property moves an element from its default position on the page to the defined amount horizontally or vertically. It takes two values separated by a comma, like so:

```
transform: translate(horizontal,vertical);
```

You can move an element on just the horizontal plane with `translatex()` and just on the vertical plane with `translatey()`. Thus, you can move an element 50 pixels to the right and 20 pixels down from where it normally would display on the page like so:

```
transform: translate(50px,20px);
```

You can define an explicit value to move the element with pixels, rems, or other units. But you can also define the amount to move as a percentage of the element's width (`translatex()`) and height (`translatey()`). This comes in handy if you want to center an element both vertically and horizontally.

Start with a simple element that you want centered:

```
<div class="center"><h1>Center Me</h1></div>
```

Give it some styles:

```
div {
  width: 15rem;
  border: solid 1px black;
  padding: 0.25rem 1.2rem;
  background: linear-gradient(#f5ea70 0%, #ffffff 100%);
  text-align: center;
}
```

Using absolute positioning, you can position the element to be halfway down the container and halfway across:

```
.center {
  position: absolute;
  top: 50%;
  left: 50%;
}
```

This places the element with the top-left corner in the center. If you want it truly centered, add a transformation to move it right 50% and up 50%:

```
transform: translate(-50%, -50%);
```

The element now displays in the center both vertically and horizontally.

CAUTION

While using `translate()` to center elements vertically does work, it fails in a couple situations. First, it uses absolute positioning, which can affect the entire layout of a complex page. Second, if the content is too long to fit in the existing viewport, the content is clipped and unreadable. Figure 14.2 demonstrates how this might look.

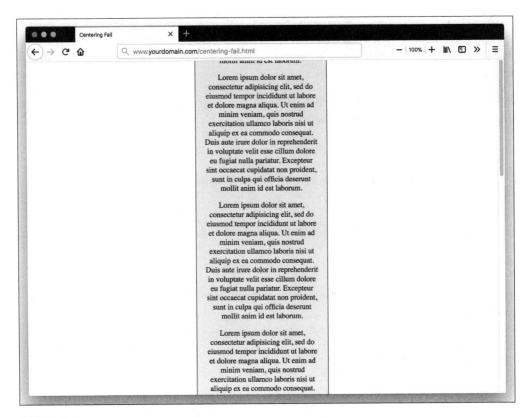

FIGURE 14.2
The vertically centered element is taller than the viewport, so the top is clipped and not visible.

Another way you might use `translate()` in your web pages is on buttons. It is common for buttons on computer operating systems to move a little down and to the left when they are clicked. This is meant to simulate a physical button being pressed. You can accomplish this effect by adding the `translate()` function when a button is active, like so:

```
button:active {
  transform: translate(2px,1px);
}
```

The `translate()` function comes into its own when you start animating your pages with CSS transitions, which are covered later in this lesson. Otherwise, it makes more sense to position elements with the `position` property, covered in Lesson 10, "Understanding the CSS Box Model and Positioning."

Slanting Elements with `transform: skew();`

You can use `transform: skew();` on an element to slant it on the horizontal and vertical axes. Much as with other `transform` functions, you can affect just the horizontal axis with `skewx()`

and just the vertical with skewy(). If you give skew() one value, it defines the slant on the horizontal (skewx()) axis; otherwise, you include the horizontal and vertical values separated by a comma, like so:

```
transform: skew(horizontal,vertical);
```

You define the amount of skew as the number of degrees (between 0 and 360) the element should slant on that axis.

NOTE

You can define the skew and rotation of an element with radians (rad) as well as degrees. Most designers don't use radians as they are more familiar with degree notation. You can also use negative degrees to rotate or tilt the element counterclockwise. So, for example, the value 315deg is the same as -45deg.

Keep in mind that when you transform an element, you are not just changing the container, you're also transforming the contained elements. To understand this, create a <div> with some contents:

```
<div class="one">
  <p>Lorem ipsum dolor sit amet, consectetur adipisicing elit,
     sed do eiusmod tempor incididunt ut labore et dolore magna
     aliqua. Ut enim ad minim veniam, quis nostrud exercitation
     ullamco laboris nisi ut aliquip ex ea commodo consequat.
     Duis aute irure dolor in reprehenderit in voluptate velit
     esse cillum dolore eu fugiat nulla pariatur. Excepteur sint
     occaecat cupidatat non proident, sunt in culpa qui officia
     deserunt mollit anim id est laborum.</p>
</div>
```

Create a second <div> that has a different class on it but has the same contents:

```
<div class="two">
```

Give both <div> elements a background color, such as a gradient, and a narrow width so they don't take up as much space on the screen. You will want to have them stack one above the other. Here is an example:

```
div {
  width: 50%;
  background: linear-gradient(#4138f5 0%, #59c4e4 100%);
  padding: 1rem;
  color: white;
  margin: 0 auto;
}
```

Then transform one of the `<div>` elements to have a slight tilt of around 15 degrees:

```
.two {
  transform: skew(15deg);
}
```

In Figure 14.3, you can see that the second `<div>` and all its contents are tilted. The text is a little harder to read, and the linear gradient moves down the element on an angle as well.

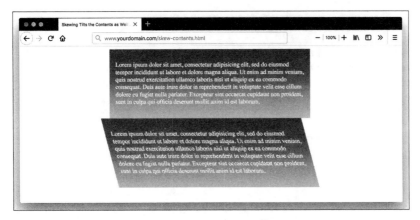

FIGURE 14.3
The `transform: skew();` property tilts the contents as well as the container element it's applied to.

Notice that the element automatically tilts along exactly the center line, horizontal or vertical. You can adjust where the tilt is applied by using the `transform-origin` property. The default is `transform-origin: 50% 50%;`, but you can set it to any horizontal (the first value) and vertical (the second value) values you want, including keywords like `top`, `bottom`, `left`, and `right`. Figure 14.4 uses `transform: skew();` and background gradients to create a shape that looks like a paper folded in three places.

FIGURE 14.4
Having fun with `transform: skew()` and background gradients.

The HTML for Figure 14.4 is four `<div>` elements, and the CSS in Listing 14.2 changes the transform origin for the two inner elements and adds skew to tilt them on the screen.

LISTING 14.2   CSS for Creating a Folded Paper Effect

```
div {
  width: 50%;
  height: 3rem;
  background: linear-gradient(#4138f5 0%, #59c4e4 100%);
  padding: 1rem;
  color: white;
  margin: 0 auto;
  text-align: center;
}
.two {
  background: linear-gradient(#59c4e4 0%, #4138f5 100%);
  transform-origin: top right;
  transform: skew(15deg);
}
.three {
  transform-origin: bottom right;
  transform: skew(345deg);
}
.four {
  background: linear-gradient(#59c4e4 0%, #4138f5 100%);
}
```

Using Multiple Transformations

All the previous examples use just one transformation at a time, but you can use as many as you need, separating each pair of methods with a space. For example, to scale an image and tilt it, you could write CSS like so:

```
img {
  transform: scale(1.2) skew(5deg);
}
```

Or to apply rotation, scaling, translation, and skew to your image, you could write CSS like so:

```
img {
  transform: rotate(30deg) scale(1.2) translate(15px,0) skew(5deg);
}
```

The thing to remember is that the order in which you place the functions in your CSS is the order in which they are applied. Changing the order could change how an element looks on the page.

This mostly applies to `translate()` but could affect other functions, depending on what you do. Test your designs a lot.

NOTE

There is one other transformation method you can use: `transform: matrix();`. This method gives you almost pixel-perfect control over exactly how your elements are transformed. Understanding it requires a lot of math, but tools—such as CSS Transform Generator (http://angrytools.com/css-generator/transform/)—are available to build matrices for you.

Transforming Elements in Three Dimensions

All the properties discussed to this point in the lesson apply to elements in two-dimensional space. But the CSS `transform` function can also affect elements in three dimensions. There are 3D versions of most of the `transform` functions, including the following:

► `rotatex()`, `rotatey()`, **and** `rotate3d(x, y, z, angle)`—Allows you to define a point in 3D space around which to rotate the element.

► `scale3d(x, y, z)` **and** `scalez()`—Resizes the element in three dimensions.

► `translate3d(x, y, z)` **and** `translatez()`—Moves the element in three dimensions.

The trick to transforming an element in three dimensions is to define the perspective from which the third dimension is viewed. The best way to do this is to set the `perspective` property on the parent element. The value of this property determines the intensity of the effect; for example, further away makes the effect less intense than up close. You can use any length value as the perspective, like so:

```
perspective: 40cm;
```

Another thing to keep in mind is that without perspective, elements that have been transformed on the three-dimensional plane will look no different from elements skewed or otherwise transformed in two dimensions. In order for your 3D transformations to be apparent, you need to have some frame of reference. Figure 14.5 demonstrates this with a blank container element around each inner element that has been rotated in 3D.

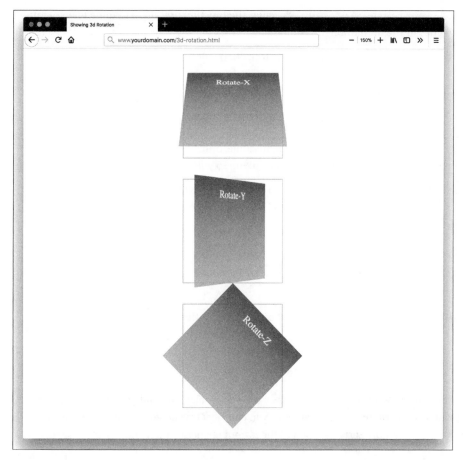

FIGURE 14.5
The outlined squares contain the rotated inner elements.

Working with CSS Transitions

Once you know how to transform elements, you can create simple animations by using the `transition` properties. These properties allow the browser to control an animation, while taking direction from the CSS. The `transition` property is a shorthand property for several other properties:

▶ `transition-property`—Indicates which CSS properties should transition.

▶ `transition-duration`—Defines the amount of time the transition will take.

▶ `transition-timing-function`—Specifies the function used to determine how interme-
diate values in the animation are computed.

▶ `transition-delay`—Defines when the transition will start.

The shorthand notation for the `transition` property is written like so:

```
transition: property duration timing-function delay;
```

The best way to understand transitions is to create some. Still screenshots would only suggest how
these animations would look, so be sure to follow along so you can see the effects in a browser.

First, create a `<div>` element on your page and give it some styles so that it's visible:

```
div {
  width: 10rem;
  height: 10rem;
  background: linear-gradient(#6058ef 0%, #ffffff 100%);
  border: solid 5px #0096ff;
}
```

Then create a new version of the element that appears when the mouse hovers over it:

```
div:hover {
  width: 20rem;
}
```

If you view this in a browser now and hover over the `<div>` element, the `<div>` element will
change instantly from 10rem tall to 20rem. But you can slow this down and animate the change
by using a `transition` property (applied to the parent element rather than to the `:hover`
state):

```
transition: width 2s linear;
```

Now when you mouse over the box, it slowly gets larger over a two-second period. When you
move your mouse off the box, it transitions back at the same speed. You can add multiple properties to transition, with a comma separating each pair. Add the style to the `:hover` state and then
add a second transition, like so:

```
transition: width 2s linear, height 2s ease;
```

Transitions get interesting when you use them with transformations. To see this, change the hover
state on the `<div>` to transform the element to be larger and rotated:

```
div:hover {
  transform: translate(10rem,11rem) scale(2) rotate(45deg);
}
```

These styles move the element 10rem left and 11rem down, make it twice as large, and rotate it 45 degrees. If you don't include a transition, the effect can be jarring at best, and at worst it will not even work. It won't work when the user positions the mouse on the initial location so that it's not hovering over the element in the final location, such as the upper-left corner. When you add a transition, as shown here, the change is less abrupt and lets the user follow along with the mouse when it stops:

```
transition: transform 3s ease-in-out;
```

Listing 14.3 shows the full HTML and CSS for this rotating cube.

LISTING 14.3   A Rotating Cube

```
<!doctype html>
<html lang="en">
  <head>
    <meta charset="utf-8">
    <title>A Rotating Cube</title>
    <style>
      div {
        width: 10rem;
        height: 10rem;
        background: linear-gradient(#6058ef 0%, #ffffff 100%);
        border: solid 5px #0096ff;
        transition: transform 3s ease-in-out;
      }
      div:hover {
        transform: translate(10rem,11rem) scale(2) rotate(45deg);
      }
    </style>
  </head>
  <body>
    <div></div>
  </body>
</html>
```

You can choose nearly any CSS property you want to transition using the `transition-property` property. You can also use the keyword `all` to tell the browser to apply the transition to every property that changes. There are a couple general rules for what you can and cannot transition:

▶ You should transition between absolute values. This means you can, for example, transition from a height of 10% to a height of 30%, but you can't transition from 10rem to auto.

NOTE

The CSS3 specification says that you cannot transition using percentage lengths. But most browsers support that anyway. The specification also says you cannot transition to or from `auto`, but WebKit browsers (Safari and Chrome) support this as well, though sometimes with strange effects. As usual, always test your designs thoroughly.

▶ Adding transitions on pseudo-elements (`::before` and `::after`) doesn't always work, but in the CSS3 specification, if an element has the quality `animatable`, then transitions should work on it, too.

▶ Most browsers don't support transitioning background gradients.

For a list of properties that can be transitioned, see http://oli.jp/2010/css-animatable-properties/. And for a really interesting example of all the ways you can change a very simple element, visit the Animatable site (http://leaverou.github.io/animatable/).

Changing the Timing of a Transition

Once you've set a property to transition, you need to affect the time it takes to transition, how it's going to transition, and when it's going to start. For these effects, you need the `transition-duration`, `transition-timing-function`, and `transition-delay` properties. The `transition-duration` and `transition-delay` properties should be fairly obvious: You set the amount of time—in minutes, seconds, milliseconds, and so on—for the transition to take (`transition-duration`) and for the time until the animation starts (`transition-delay`).

The `transition-timing-function` property is a bit more difficult to understand. This property takes a function that tells the browser how to perform the animation as it transitions the element. It takes the following values:

▶ `ease`—Causes the animation to start slowly, speed up quickly, and then slow down again at the end. This is the default.

▶ `ease-in`—Causes the animation to start slowly and then get up to speed.

▶ `ease-out`—Causes the animation to start at speed and then slow down at the end.

▶ `ease-in-out`—Causes the animation to start slowly, speed up, and then slow down at the end. It's different from `ease` in that it doesn't get up to full speed as quickly.

▶ `linear`—Causes the animation to move at a steady speed the entire time.

You can also define your own custom timing function with the `cubic-bezier()` function. A tool you can use to help build timing functions is the CSS Easing Animation Tool (https://matthewlein.com/tools/ceaser).

NOTE:

The best way to understand the timing functions is to try them out. Try changing the `ease-in-out` value in Listing 14.3 to something else, such as `linear`, and see how the animation changes.

Using JavaScript to Trigger Transitions

Transitions make it easy to add animation to your web pages, but there are some situations where you might want an animation, but there isn't an appropriate CSS selector. For example, CSS has a `:hover` class but doesn't have a `:click` pseudo-class, so if you want to trigger a transition when someone clicks on an element, you need to do it with JavaScript.

One way to do this is to define classes that you can assign when an element is clicked. You would have a class for the element itself and a class for when it's clicked, like so:

```
div {
  width: 10rem;
  height: 10rem;
  background: #ff0000;
  transition: transform 3s linear;
}
div.clicked {
  transform: rotate(230deg);
}
```

Then, using jQuery, which you'll learn more about in Lesson 26, "Using Third-Party JavaScript Libraries and Frameworks," you add and remove the `clicked` class, like so:

```
$(function() {
  $("div").click(function(){
    $(this).toggleClass('clicked');
  });
});
```

You can also do this without a library by using plain JavaScript. Listing 14.4 shows a fully functional version of the script and CSS for this example. (You will learn more about this in Lesson 20, "Getting Started with JavaScript Programming.")

LISTING 14.4   Spinning a Box When You Click It

```
<!doctype html>
<html lang="en">
  <head>
    <meta charset="utf-8">
    <title>Spin Box on Click</title>
    <style>
```

```
   div {
     width: 10rem;
     height: 10rem;
     background: #ff0000;
     transition: transform 3s linear;
   }
   div.clicked {
     transform: rotate(230deg);
   }
 </style>
 <script src="https://ajax.googleapis.com/ajax/
libs/jquery/3.3.1/jquery.min.js"></script>
</head>
<body>
  <div></div>
  <script>
  $(function() {
    $("div").click(function(){
      $(this).toggleClass('clicked');
    });
  });
  </script>
</body>
</html>
```

Summary

This lesson taught you how to add basic animation to web pages by transforming elements and then having the browser transition those transformations slowly and smoothly. In the first section you learned how to use the `transform` property. You learned how to rotate an element around an axis with `rotate()`. Then you learned how to make an element larger or smaller with the `scale()` function. With the `translate()` function, you learned that you could move elements from where they would normally be placed. And the `skew()` function showed you how to tilt elements on the horizontal and vertical axes. But there are also three-dimensional transformations. And in this lesson, you learned how to use the `rotatex()`, `rotatey()`, and `rotate3d(x, y, z, angle)` functions to spin an element around a point in space. You learned that the `scale3d(x, y, z)` and `scalez()` functions resize the element in the three dimensions, and `translate3d(x, y, z)` and `translatez()` move an element in three dimensions. You can't work in 3D without perspective, so this lesson covered the `perspective()` property as well.

This lesson really got interesting when you learned how to animate transformations with the `transition` properties. You learned how to define the properties to transition, how to define the time a transition takes, and how to set a delay for a transition so that it does not start immediately. You also learned about the different timing functions you can use to affect how a transition looks on the screen. This lesson also covered, very briefly, how to kick off a transition with JavaScript; you will learn a lot more about this in future lessons.

Q&A

Q. If I want to transform just a section of a paragraph, such as a code block, is this possible with the `transform` **property?**

A. The transform properties apply only to block-level elements and a few table elements. If you need to transform an inline element such as a <code> block, you should first add the `display: block;` or `display: inline-block;` style to it so that the browser knows that it needs to treat this like a block-level element. Then you can transform it.

Q. If I want to have different transition values for multiple properties, how do I do that?

A. You can separate multiple transitions with commas, like so: `transition: transform 3s linear, background 1s ease;`

This transitions the `transform` property over three seconds in a `linear` fashion, while transitioning the `background` property over one second with the `ease` function.

Workshop

The workshop contains quiz questions and exercises to help you solidify your understanding of the material covered.

Quiz

1. How can you spin an element so that it displays upside down?

2. What would `transform: scale(3);` do to an element?

3. How is using `translate()` different from using CSS positioning?

4. What are two ways to slant an element 5 degrees?

5. What is a style rule you could use to make a paragraph with the class `special` so that it is transformed half as big as normal and slanted 45 degrees counterclockwise?

6. Which value would make a 3D transformation more intense: `perspective: 1m;` or `perspective: 1in;`?

7. How do you move an element 15 pixels on the z-axis?

8. How do you define what feature will change in a transition?

9. What is the correct order for properties in the shorthand `transition` property?

10. Which timing function makes a transition evenly across the entire time period?

NOTE

Just a reminder for those of you reading these words in the print or e-book edition of this book: If you go to **www.informit.com/register** and register this book (using ISBN 9780672338083), you can receive free access to an online Web Edition that not only contains the complete text of this book but also features an interactive version of this quiz.

Answers

1. You can use the `transform: rotate(180deg);` property to turn an element upside down.

2. It would enlarge the element three times the original size while leaving it overlapping the surrounding content.

3. It moves the element from its default position but leaves all the surrounding elements in place.

4. You can use `transform: slant(5deg);` or `transform: slantx(5deg);`.

5. Use this style rule:

```
p.special {
   transform: scale(0.5) skew(-45deg);
}
```

or use this:

```
p.special {
   transform: scale(0.5) skew(320deg);
}
```

6. The closer value looks more intense, so `perspective: 1in;`, at 1 inch away rather than 1 meter, would appear more intense.

7. Use `transform: translatez(15px);` with `perspective: 50px;`. The value of the perspective doesn't matter as much as the fact that it's set.

8. Use `transition-property` to define the CSS properties to transition.

9. They should be written in this order: `transition-property`, `transition-duration`, `transition-timing-function`, and `transition-delay`.

10. The `linear` timing function animates the transition evenly across the time period.

Exercises

▶ Create a simple photo gallery where the images are thrown down on the page haphazardly. Use the CSS `transform` property to change how the images display on the screen. The HTML should be a list of images. The design should be created with CSS.

▶ In Lesson 11, "Using CSS to Do More with Lists, Text, and Navigation," you created a menu where the background and text colors changed when the mouse rolled over them. Go back to that menu and add a transition to the changes.

LESSON 15
Animating with CSS and the Canvas

What You'll Learn in This Lesson:

▶ How to generate a CSS animation

▶ How CSS animations are different from transitions and how they are similar

▶ Creating keyframes to hold and control animations

▶ Using the HTML5 <canvas> element for self-contained animations

In Lesson 14, "Using CSS Transformations and Transitions," you learned how to animate triggered actions on a website. While this is fun and can add some value to web pages, it is not the same as frame-based animation. As you'll learn in this lesson, transitions are just the start of CSS animation.

This lesson takes you beyond the two-frame state of transitions (the beginning frame and the end frame) and teaches you how to add keyframes to the animations. This allows you to add as many state changes as you need and animate between them to create a full animated sequence. You'll learn what keyframes are and how to use them, as well as how to control other aspects of your animations, including the iterations, the direction, and the timing.

This lesson also covers an HTML element, <canvas>, that is often used to create standalone animations with Scalable Vector Graphics (SVG) elements and other elements. You will learn how to draw shapes and text on the canvas as well as add images. You will also be introduced to animating canvas elements.

Understanding CSS Animation

CSS animations let you animate the transformations and transitions you learned in Lesson 14 but in a standalone fashion. You don't need to have some trigger event in your document that starts the animation. CSS animation consists of two things: the styles that are animated and the keyframes that indicate the beginning and end states for each animation style. There are eight animation properties:

- ▶ `animation-delay`—Specifies the delay between when the element is loaded and when the animation starts.

- ▶ `animation-direction`—Determines whether the animation should alternate direction on each sequence or start at the beginning.

- ▶ `animation-duration`—Sets the length of time to complete one cycle of the animation.

- ▶ `animation-iteration-count`—Configures the number of times the animation should repeat. The keyword `infinite` says the animation should repeat forever.

- ▶ `animation-name`—Defines the name of the `@keyframes` rule to use in the animation.

- ▶ `animation-play-state`—Allows the animation to be paused and resumed.

- ▶ `animation-timing-function`—Defines the acceleration curves for the animation to transition through the keyframes.

- ▶ `animation-fill-mode`—Defines the values applied to the animation before and after it executes.

You can combine all these properties in the shorthand `animation` property. The order does not matter.

But in order to use these properties, you need to set up a `@keyframes` rule in your CSS, as you'll learn in the next section.

Defining Keyframes

With a keyframe, you define the state changes for an animation. You define a keyframe in a `@keyframes` rule in the CSS, like so:

```
@keyframes myAnimation {
  from {
    transform: scale(0.5);
    background: red;
  }
  to {
    transform: scale(1);
    background: blue;
  }
}
```

This example defines an animation called `myAnimation`. It will start at half the size of the default element and have a red background color. It will transition to the end state of full size with a blue background color. This animation performs the same changes as a transition rule, but it applies to the element automatically. You don't need to trigger the animation. Listing 15.1 shows how you might apply this animation.

LISTING 15.1   A Simple Animation

```
<!doctype html>
<html lang="en">
  <head>
    <meta charset="utf-8">
    <title>A Simple Animation</title>
    <style>
      div {
        width: 10rem;
        height: 10rem;
        margin: 3rem auto;
        animation: myAnimation 5s infinite;
      }

      @keyframes myAnimation {
        from {
          transform: scale(0.5);
          background: red;
        }
        to {
          transform: scale(1);
          background: blue;
        }
      }
    </style>
  </head>
  <body>
    <div></div>
  </body>
</html>
```

The animation in Listing 15.1 uses the keywords `from` and `to` to define the start and end points of the animation. You can do similar things with transitions. Where animation keyframes really become useful is when you set the frames with percentages, like so:

```
@keyframes {
  0% {
  }
  50% {
  }
  100% {
  }
}
```

If the starting and/or ending states of the animation are the same as the element's default, you can leave off the 0% and 100% styles, like so:

```
@keyframes {
  50% {
  }
}
```

Listing 15.2 shows how you might animate a headline so that it flies in from the top. If you examine the @keyframes rule, you see that the only animation translates the headline off the screen 100 pixels at the beginning (0%). The browser then animates the element to its final position automatically.

LISTING 15.2   Animating a Headline

```
<!doctype html>
<html lang="en">
  <head>
    <meta charset="utf-8">
    <title>Animating a Headline</title>
    <style>
      body {
        background: #efefef;
      }
      h1 {
        font-family: geneva, arial, helvetica, sans-serif;
        font-size: 2rem;
        text-align: center;
        padding: 2rem 0;
        color: red;
        animation: myAnimation 2s;
      }
      @keyframes myAnimation {
        0% {
          transform: translateY(-100px);
        }
      }
    </style>
  </head>
  <body>
    <h1>My Headline</h1>
  </body>
</html>
```

Adjusting Animations

Once you have an animation set up, you can use the CSS `animation` properties to get more control over how it looks. In the previous examples, you saw how to set the animation duration (`animation: myAnimation 2s;`) and how to make the animation loop forever (`animation: myAnimation 5s infinite;`). The animation properties should be fairly familiar to you if you've gone through Lesson 14.

Timing Your Animations

The first property to look at is the `animation-timing-function` property. Just like the equivalent `transition-timing-function` property, this property tells the browser how to accelerate and decelerate the animation along a curve. It takes the same possible values: `ease`, `linear`, `ease-in`, `ease-out`, `ease-in-out`, and `cubic-bezier(P1x,P1y,P2x,P2y)`. The `cubic-bezier()` function takes four values that map to the four points that are part of a Bézier curve: P0, P1, P2, and P3 (see Figure 15.1). P0 is always `0,0`, and P3 is always `1,1`. The other two values define the curve radius points for the beginning and end of the curve.

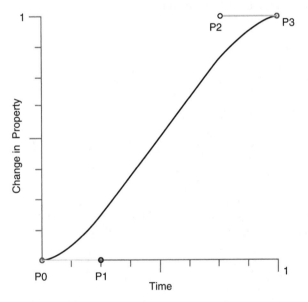

FIGURE 15.1
The points on a Bézier curve.

Each of the standard timing functions has an equivalent `cubic-bezier()` function:

▶ `linear` is the same as `cubic-bezier(0,0,1,1)`

▶ `ease` is the same as `cubic-bezier(0.25,0.1,0.25,1)`

▶ `ease-in` is the same as `cubic-bezier(0.42,0,1,1)`

▶ `ease-out` is the same as `cubic-bezier(0,0,.58,1)`

▶ `ease-in-out` is the same as `cubic-bezier(0.42,0,0.58,1)`

But what makes this function so useful is that you can use it to create your own curves. One popular effect is to make an element bounce at the end. To create this effect, first place a `<div>` on a web page and style it to look like a ball:

```
.ball {
  position: relative;
  left: 75%;
  background-color: #ffb33a;
  width: 20rem;
  height: 20rem;
  border-radius: 10rem;
}
```

Build a `@keyframes` rule to move the ball across the screen horizontally:

```
@keyframes bounce {
  0% {
    left: 0%;
  }
  100% {
    left: 75%;
  }
}
```

Add the bounce animation to the ball:

```
animation: bounce 3s infinite;
```

The animation now uses the default timing function, `ease`. To make it bounce, you need to use something more like `ease-out`. You can see what `ease-out` looks like by adding the timing function to the CSS for the ball:

```
animation-timing-function: ease-out;
```

But this still doesn't look like a bouncing ball. To create a bounce at the end, you need to use a `cubic-bezier()` function. The first point (P1) can be the same as the origin, or `0,0`, but the second point (P2) needs to be higher than the destination point. In this case, let's use the value `0.5, 1.5`:

```
animation-timing-function: cubic-bezier(0, 0, 0.5, 1.5);
```

Listing 15.3 provides the full HTML and CSS for this example. If you try it out in your browser, you'll see a big orange ball start on the left side of the screen and move to the right, before sliding into place on the right side.

LISTING 15.3   Bouncy Ball

```html
<!doctype html>
<html lang="en">
  <head>
    <meta charset="utf-8">
    <title>Bouncy Ball</title>
    <style>
      .ball {
        position: relative;
        left: 75%;
        background-color: #ffb33a;
        width: 20rem;
        height: 20rem;
        border-radius: 10rem;
        animation: bounce 3s;
        animation-timing-function: cubic-bezier(0, 0, 0.5, 1.5);
      }
      @keyframes bounce {
        0% {
          left: 0%;
        }
        100% {
          left: 75%;
        }
      }
    </style>
  </head>
  <body>
    <div class="ball"></div>
  </body>
</html>
```

NOTE

While it's possible to build your own Bézier curves by simply putting in numbers, there is a website that can help you build them more effectively: http://cubic-bezier.com. With this site, you can import curves you're trying out and compare them to standard curves. This site makes creating custom timing functions for both animations and transitions much easier.

You may be wondering why the ball is positioned at 75% left rather than 100% left. When you position the element 100% left, it is placed mostly offscreen. If you want it to be placed up against the left border, without going over, you need to use the CSS `calc()` function. This does a calculation to create the result you want. In this case, you can make the ball end up 100% left but minus its own width (`20rem`), so that it's fully onscreen, like so:

```
left: calc(100% - 20rem);
```

One other way you can affect the timing of your animations is with the `animation-delay` property. This acts exactly like the `transition-delay` property mentioned in Lesson 14. You set a time interval for the browser to wait before starting the animation. This can be any interval, from milliseconds (`ms`), to seconds (`s`), fractions of a second, and so on.

When you set a delay on your animations, you may notice that the animated elements do not behave as you expected them to. This is because animations do not affect the element before the first keyframe is played or after the last one is played. You can change this behavior with the `animation-fill-mode` property, which can take the following values:

- `none`—The animation does not affect the styles of the element either before or after running.

- `forwards`—The animated element keeps the styles set by the last keyframe.

- `backwards`—The element gets the styles set by the first keyframe, including during the `animation-delay`.

- `both`—Both the `forwards` and `backwards` values are applied.

Making an Animation Repeat

The bouncing ball animation is interesting, but if you miss it, you'll never see it because it happens only once. By changing `animation-iteration-count`, you can change how many times the animation repeats. Put in a number to have it repeat a specific number of times or the keyword `infinite` to have it repeat indefinitely, like so:

```
animation-iteration-count: infinite;
```

When you add this line to the bouncing ball animation, there is a jarring point where the animation bounces back to the beginning abruptly. To fix this, you can adjust the `animation-direction` property to `alternate`. This tells the browser to change the direction and run it forward and then backward and then forward on any animation that has an iteration count of 2 or more.

The `animation-direction` property can take four possible values:

- `normal`—Plays the animation from start to finish. This is the default.

- `reverse`—Plays the animation backward, from finish to start.

▶ `alternate`—Plays the animation first from start to finish and then in reverse and so on until the iteration count is reached.

▶ `alternate-reverse`—Plays the animation first from finish to start and then in reverse and so on until the iteration count is reached.

To fix the bouncing ball, add alternation, like so:

```
animation-direction: alternate;
```

The full bouncing ball animation is shown in Listing 15.4. To make the bounce more interesting, we added a bounce to the timing function at the start of the animation.

LISTING 15.4   Improved Bouncy Ball

```html
<!doctype html>
<html lang="en">
  <head>
    <meta charset="utf-8">
    <title>Bouncy Ball</title>
    <style>
      .ball {
        position: relative;
        left: calc(100% - 20rem);
        background-color: #ffb33a;
        width: 20rem;
        height: 20rem;
        border-radius: 10rem;
        animation: bounce 3s;
        animation-timing-function: cubic-bezier(0.5,-0.5, 0.5,1.5);
        animation-iteration-count: infinite;
        animation-direction: alternate;
      }
      @keyframes bounce {
        0% {
          left: 0%;
        }
        100% {
          left: calc(100% - 20rem);
        }
      }
    </style>
  </head>
  <body>
    <div class="ball"></div>
  </body>
</html>
```

CAUTION

As with anything that moves on your web pages, use care with your animations and transitions. Lots of motion, especially repetitive motion, can be annoying and distracting. In most situations, subtle changes are better than larger ones.

Naming and Pausing Your Animations

One thing that many designers forget is that you can pause animations with CSS by using the animation-play-state property. This takes the values paused and running. When an animation is paused, it is not animating, and when it is running, well, it's running. One way to let a user stop an animation is by adding it to a pseudo-class such as :hover, like so:

```
.ball:hover {
  animation-play-state: paused;
}
```

Finally, the last animation property is the animation-name property, which defines the @keyframe rule to use for the animation. This name is a custom identifier for each animation. You can also use the keyword none to turn off the animation.

Using the CSS Canvas

The HTML <canvas> element creates a rectangular region on a web page where you can draw anything you'd like by using JavaScript. You can use it to add images, create slide shows, build games, and display animations.

How to Use the Canvas

When you add the <canvas> element to a document, it creates a blank canvas in the browser. Because the canvas has no width, height, or content, the <canvas> element doesn't display anything on the screen. Most of the time, you will also want to specify a width and height and give your canvas an ID, so you can reference it in your scripts, as in this example:

```
<canvas id="myCanvas" width="350" height="450"></canvas>
```

Of course, if this is all you write, there will simply be a blank 350 × 450-pixel space in your HTML. You can add a border around all canvases in the CSS so you can see them on the page:

```
canvas { border: solid thin black; }
```

NOTE

While most modern browsers support the <canvas> element, you can include fallback content inside this element that displays if the canvas content cannot display. It acts just like fallback content in other HTML5 elements, such as the <video> and <audio> elements.

A canvas gives you a place to draw, add pictures, and bring pictures to life with animation. To draw on the canvas, you need to add some JavaScript. Add a `<script>` element to the bottom of your HTML document, just above the closing `</body>`tag. Inside it, you can define both the canvas and the drawing context, like so:

```
<script>
  var canvas = document.getElementById('myCanvas');
  var context = canvas.getContext('2d');
</script>
```

CAUTION

In order to draw on a `<canvas>` element, you must pass the string 2d to the `getContext()` method. Otherwise, your `<canvas>` element will not display anything. If you draw on a `<canvas>` element and it's blank, ensure that you've set the context first.

Drawing Shapes on the Canvas

It's easy to draw shapes on a canvas. You can draw rectangles, circles, polygons, and lines with just a few lines of JavaScript.

Drawing a Rectangle or Square

To create a filled rectangle or square, you use the function `fillRect()`, like so:

```
context.fillRect(30, 30, 150, 150);
```

The first two values indicate where the rectangle should start drawing. They are the x and y coordinates from the upper-left corner of the canvas. Then you set the width and the height with the last two values. The line above should create a 150 × 150 square at 30 over and 30 down from the upper-left corner of the canvas. The square is black by default, but you can change that by adding a line above the `fillRect()` line that sets the color of the fill, like so:

```
context.fillStyle = "rgb(13, 118, 208)";
```

If you'd rather just draw the outline of a square, you use the function `strokeRect()`, like so:

```
context.strokeRect(35, 35, 150, 150);
```

You can use the `strokeStyle()` method to define the color of the stroke, like so:

```
context.strokeStyle = 'blue';
```

Drawing a Circle

Drawing circles involves using the `arc()` method. To understand how to draw a circle, imagine that you are physically drawing it with a protractor. You set the point of your protractor in the center of the circle, bend the angle so that the pen is at the radius, start drawing at a point, and lift the pen at a second point. You can draw a circle either clockwise or counterclockwise.

You can use the <canvas> element to draw a circle in the same way: Set the x and y coordinates for the center of the circle, the radius, the starting point on the circle (in radians), the ending point on the circle (in radians), and finally the direction of drawing—either clockwise (true) or counterclockwise (false). The syntax for this method is as follows:

```
arc(x, y, radius, startAngle, endAngle, clockwise);
```

NOTE

Arcs in the <canvas> element are measured in radians, not degrees. But because most of us find it easier to think in degrees (12 noon = 0°, 3 o'clock = 90°, and so on), it helps to have a conversion tool. In JavaScript, you can convert degrees to radians with the following expression:

```
var radians = (Math.PI/180)*degrees;
```

The easiest way to draw a circle is to first set the start and end points as variables, like so:

```
var startPoint = (Math.PI/180)*0;
var endPoint = (Math.PI/180)*360;
```

A circle is drawn as a path, so you set your starting point with the beginPath() method and then define the path as a circle with the arc() method:

```
context.beginPath();
context.arc(200,200,100,startPoint,endPoint,true);
```

But you still don't have anything visible on the page while the path is on the canvas until you fill or stroke it with either the fill() method or the stroke() method:

```
context.fill();
```

The fill keeps the same style unless you add a new fillStyle property above the fill() line. If you are stroking the circle, then you need to adjust strokeStyle instead. Listing 15.5 adds a stroked circle to the canvas, and Figure 15.2 shows how it would look.

LISTING 15.5   A Canvas with Squares and a Circle

```
<!doctype html>
<html lang="en">
  <head>
    <meta charset="utf-8">
    <title>A Canvas with Shapes</title>
    <style>
      canvas { border: solid thin black; }
    </style>
```

```
    </head>
    <body>
      <canvas id="myCanvas" width="350" height="450"></canvas>
      <script>
        var canvas = document.getElementById('myCanvas');
        var context = canvas.getContext('2d');
        context.fillStyle = "rgb(13, 118, 208)";
        context.fillRect(30, 30, 150, 150);
        context.strokeStyle = 'blue';
        context.strokeRect(35, 35, 150, 150);

        var startPoint = (Math.PI/180)*0;
        var endPoint = (Math.PI/180)*360;
        context.beginPath();
        context.arc(200,200,100,startPoint,endPoint,true);
        context.fillStyle = "rgba(155, 0, 0, 0.5)";
        context.fill();
        context.strokeStyle = "rgb(255, 0, 0)";
        context.stroke();
      </script>
    </body>
</html>
```

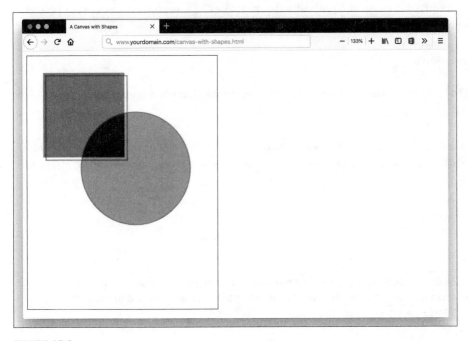

FIGURE 15.2
A canvas with squares and a circle.

Drawing Lines and Polygons

Like circles, lines and polygons are drawn using paths. You can use five methods to draw and use paths:

- ► `beginPath()`—This method creates a path on a canvas.

- ► `closePath()`—This method draws a straight line from the current point to the start. It doesn't do anything when a path is already closed or on a path with only one point.

- ► `stroke()`—This draws an outline of a path.

- ► `fill()`—This fills in the shape of a path.

- ► `moveTo()`—This draws nothing but moves the drawing position to a new location on the canvas.

CAUTION

The first thing you should always do when drawing a path is specify the starting position of the path with the `moveTo()` command. The `<canvas>` element will treat your first construction that way, regardless of what the method actually is, and this will prevent you from getting surprising results.

To draw a line on a canvas, start a path with the `beginPath()` method and move your pointer to the starting point with `moveTo()`, like so:

```
context.beginPath();
context.moveTo(0,0);
```

The `lineTo()` method takes the x and y coordinates for the next point on the line:

```
context.lineTo(60,60);
```

But just as with circles, if you don't stroke or fill the path, nothing will display. The default width of the line is 1 pixel, but you can change that with the `lineWidth` property. Then you stroke the line, like so:

```
context.lineWidth = 15;
context.stroke();
```

NOTE

If you don't close the path and choose to fill the shape, the shape will close automatically, with a straight line from the last point on the path to the first point. You do not need to close the path with the `closePath()` method.

To draw a triangle, you do the same thing as with a line—first begin a new path and move to the starting point:

```
context.beginPath();
context.moveTo(20,30);
```

Then draw a line to the first point on the triangle:

```
context.lineTo(350,100);
```

And a second line to the second point on the triangle:

```
context.lineTo(250,400);
```

If you are not going to stroke the triangle, you don't need to draw the path back to the origin because the fill() method will fill along a straight line to the origin:

```
context.fill();
```

You can create a polygon that is as ornate as you like just by defining the points on the path. Listing 15.6 adds a line and a triangle to the canvas, as shown in Figure 15.3.

LISTING 15.6   Adding More Shapes to the Canvas

```
<!doctype html>
<html lang="en">
  <head>
    <meta charset="utf-8">
    <title>A Canvas with Multiple Shapes</title>
    <style>
      canvas { border: solid thin black; }
    </style>
  </head>
  <body>
    <canvas id="myCanvas" width="350" height="450"></canvas>
    <script>
      var canvas = document.getElementById('myCanvas');
      var context = canvas.getContext('2d');
      context.fillStyle = "rgb(13, 118, 208)";
      context.fillRect(30, 30, 150, 150);
      context.strokeStyle = 'blue';
      context.strokeRect(35, 35, 150, 150);

      var startPoint = (Math.PI/180)*0;
      var endPoint = (Math.PI/180)*360;
      context.beginPath();
      context.arc(200,200,100,startPoint,endPoint,true);
```

```
        context.fillStyle = "rgba(155, 0, 0, 0.5)";
        context.fill();
        context.strokeStyle = "rgb(255, 0, 0)";
        context.stroke();

        context.beginPath();
        context.moveTo(0,0);
        context.lineTo(60,60);
        context.strokeStyle = "black";
        context.lineWidth = 15;
        context.stroke();

        context.beginPath();
        context.moveTo(20,30);
        context.lineTo(350,100);
        context.lineTo(250,400);
        context.fillStyle = "rgba(0, 0, 155, 0.5)";
        context.fill();
    </script>
  </body>
</html>
```

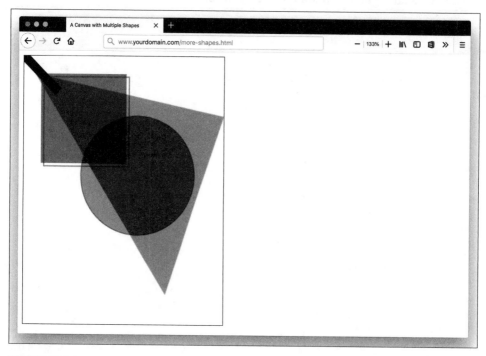

FIGURE 15.3
Adding a triangle to the canvas.

Adding Images to the Canvas

In order to display an image inside a <canvas> element, you need to reference an image object as a source file and then draw the image onto the canvas with the drawImage() method.

You have two choices for the first part: You can access an existing image on the page (in an <img> element), or you can create a new image with JavaScript. To create an image with JavaScript, first you add a new image to the DOM and populate it with the source file, like so:

```
var img = new Image();
img.src = "images/mckinley.jpg";
```

Once the image has loaded, run a function that draws it on the canvas at the x and y coordinates noted in the drawImage() method, like so:

```
img.onload = function() {
  context.drawImage(img, 10,10);
}
```

Listing 15.7 creates a canvas with a photo of a dog named McKinley. But as you see in Figure 15.4, all that is showing is the upper-left corner of the image—no dog to be seen.

LISTING 15.7   Adding an Image to the Canvas

```
<!doctype html>
<html lang="en">
  <head>
    <meta charset="utf-8">
    <title>McKinley on Canvas</title>
    <style>
      #myCanvas {
        width: 800px;
        height: 600px;
        margin: 0 auto;
        display: block;
      }
    </style>
  <body>
    <canvas width="800" height="600" id="myCanvas"></canvas>
    <script>
      var canvas = document.getElementById('myCanvas');
      var context = canvas.getContext('2d');
      var img = new Image();
      img.src = "images/mckinley.jpg";
      img.onload = function() {
        context.drawImage(img, 10,10);
      }
    </script>
  </body>
</html>
```

FIGURE 15.4
Adding an image to a canvas.

You can change the size of the image that is drawn or crop it to fit a certain section by using the `drawImage()` method. To change the size, you include four parameters:

```
context.drawImage(x, y, width, height);
```

The *x* and *y* coordinates specify where you want the image to be placed on the canvas. The *width* and *height* parameters are the new width and height for the image. You can scale the image up or down, but making an image larger often causes a lot of artifacts and makes the image look bad.

You can crop an image by including a clip path on the `drawImage()` method:

```
context.drawImage(clipx, clipy, clipwidth, clipheight, gox, goy, gowidth,
goheight);
```

The parameters in this syntax cover the coordinates to start the crop plus the width and height followed by the placement of the clip on the canvas with the width and height coordinates. Listing 15.8 shows how to add the image twice—first the full 780 × 680 image and then a cropped shot of McKinley's head in the lower left. Figure 15.5 shows what this looks like.

LISTING 15.8 Drawing, Scaling, and Cropping an Image on a Canvas

```
<!doctype html>
<html lang="en">
  <head>
```

```
    <meta charset="utf-8">
    <title>McKinley on Canvas</title>
    <style>
      #myCanvas {
        width: 800px;
        height: 600px;
        margin: 0 auto;
        display: block;
      }
    </style>
  <body>
    <canvas width="800" height="600" id="myCanvas"></canvas>
    <script>
      var canvas = document.getElementById('myCanvas');
      var context = canvas.getContext('2d');
      var img = new Image();
      img.src = "images/mckinley2.jpg";
      img.onload = function() {
        context.drawImage(img, 10,10, 780, 680);
        context.drawImage(img, 842,344,532,594, 0,300,200,200);
      }
    </script>
  </body>
</html>
```

FIGURE 15.5
By scaling and cropping the image, you can now see McKinley, the subject.

Animating the Canvas

After you add things to the canvas, you can move them around. In fact, you already have enough knowledge to create a simple sprite animation. A sprite animation takes a graphic with several images composited together and displays a cropped section of the graphic. You animate it by changing which cropped area is displayed. This type of sprite animation has a big advantage: When the full image is loaded, all the animation parts are loaded.

First, you need to create a sprite image. For example, you can create a second version of the dog's photo with his mouth open and then create a composite image with his mouth open and closed, as in Figure 15.6.

FIGURE 15.6
A sprite file of the dog McKinley.

In this example, both images in the sprite are the same size—1262 × 1209. Creating sprites that are equal in size makes the sprite animation much easier to program.

Because this is going to be a <canvas> animation, add the <canvas> element and create the script with the canvas defined, like so:

```
<canvas id="myCanvas" width="1262" height="1209"></canvas>
<script>
  var canvas = document.getElementById("myCanvas");
  var context = canvas.getContext('2d');
</script>
```

As before, add the image with JavaScript:

```
var mckinleyImage = new Image();
mckinleyImage.src = "images/mckinley-talking-sprite.jpg";
```

The width and height of the single image is 1262×1209, so set those values in JavaScript as variables:

```
var width = 1262;
var height = 1209;
```

Now you need to start thinking about the animation. Sprite animation is similar to framed animation: At a specific interval, the screen switches from one frame (sprite) to the next. So you need to set variables for the number of frames and what frame number you're currently on. Remember that JavaScript counts from zero, so for this animation, there are two sprite images, and the frames variable should be 1. To start with McKinley's mouth open, the currentFrame should be 0:

```
var frames = 1;
var currentFrame = 0;
```

Then you build the image in the <canvas> element. You do this the same way as before, with the drawImage() method. But this time you need to put it inside a function so we can do the animation, as shown here:

```
var draw = function() {
  context.drawImage(
    mckinleyImage,
    width * currentFrame,
    0,
    width,height,
    0,0,
    width,height
  );
};
```

To add the animation, you need to increment currentFrame. But if it's reached the total frames count, then it should reset to 0. Place the following in the draw function below where you drew the image:

```
if (currentFrame == frames) {
   currentFrame = 0;
} else {
   currentFrame++;
}
```

Then you can call the draw function with setInterval() to animate the picture:

```
setInterval(draw, 200);
```

One last thing you may need is a line to clear the canvas between frames. The `<canvas>` element has the method `clearRect`, which clears a rectangular portion of the canvas to make it ready for new drawings. By calling this method and setting it at the position 0,0, with the full canvas width and height, you clear the entire space:

```
context.clearRect(0, 0, width, height);
```

It is best to make this the first line of the `draw` function.

The full code for this animation is in Listing 15.9, and you can see it in action at https://htmljenn.com/mckinley-talking.html.

LISTING 15.9   **The Animated Dog**

```
<!doctype html>
<html lang="en">
  <head>
    <meta charset="utf-8">
    <title>McKinley Has a Lot to Say</title>
    <style>
      canvas {
        transform: scale(0.5) translateY(-600px);
      }
    </style>
  </head>
  <body>
    <canvas id="myCanvas" width="1262" height="1209"></canvas>
    <script>
      var canvas = document.getElementById("myCanvas");
      var context = canvas.getContext('2d');
      var mckinleyImage = new Image();
      mckinleyImage.src = "images/mckinley-talking-sprite.jpg";

      var width = 1262;
      var height = 1209;

      var frames = 1;
      var currentFrame = 0;

      var draw = function() {
        context.clearRect(0, 0, width, height);
        context.drawImage(
          mckinleyImage,
          width * currentFrame,
          0,
```

```
      width,height,
      0,0,
      width,height
    );

    if (currentFrame == frames) {
      currentFrame = 0;
    } else {
      currentFrame++;
    }
  };

  setInterval(draw, 200);
</script>
</body>
</html>
```

Choosing Between CSS Animation and Canvas Animation

At this point in the lesson, you may be wondering why anyone would want to use CSS animation or HTML `<canvas>` animation. They both have strengths and weaknesses, and if you're more familiar with CSS or with JavaScript, you might feel that one is superior to the other. But if you're new to both, they can be equally intimidating. So how do you decide which is better?

There is a widespread belief that CSS animations are faster than JavaScript animations on the canvas. This is because when you use transforms in a 3D context (such as `transform: translate3d();`), the browser uses the GPU and so renders it more quickly. There are 3D methods in JavaScript as well, but most designers forget to use them.

There are some things you can do with JavaScript that you simply cannot do with CSS. For example, you can't seek to a specific spot in a CSS animation, nor can you smoothly reverse midstream. You can't alter the speed or time scale of an animation without creating an entirely new animation.

One aspect of CSS animation that is annoying to most animators is that the keyframes are defined in percentages. But most animators think in terms of time rather than percentages. For example, you might think "The headline needs to fade in for 3 seconds and then bounce once before coming to rest at full opacity 1 second later." How do you define that in percentages? And what if, after you've fiddled with the percentages for a while, the client responds, "It looks great, but the fade needs to be 5 seconds."

One thing we miss in CSS animations is the ability to add multiple control points to the `cubic-bezier()` value. You can do this with JavaScript. You can also add physics-based motion with JavaScript.

We are not saying that you should never use CSS animations. CSS animations are great for basic transitions and rollovers and for adding fun features and games to your sites. You can build very complex games with CSS animations. Plus, if you need to keep all your presentation layer details in the CSS, then CSS animation is what you have to use.

JavaScript animation is harder to learn: It is possible to do a lot more with JavaScript, and the JavaScript you learned in this lesson barely scratches the surface of what you can do.

Summary

This lesson covered how to do animations in two ways: with CSS and with JavaScript on the HTML `<canvas>`. You learned how to create keyframe animation with CSS by defining the `@keyframes` rule and applying it to an element with the `animation` property. You then learned more about timing, looping, and pausing animations.

This lesson also covered the HTML `<canvas>` element, including how to use it to draw shapes like circles, rectangles, and polygons. You also learned how to add images to the canvas and then animate the images with simple sprite animation. Finally, you learned some of the reasons you might choose CSS animation or JavaScript animation.

Q&A

Q. When should I use CSS animations versus CSS transitions?

A. Bear in mind that a CSS transition is an animation, but it's just very limited in scope. If you need an animation that has more than a start state and end state, you should use CSS animations. Also, if you need more granular control over the animation keyframes, then CSS animation is the right tool.

Q. What about SVG animation?

A. Using Scalable Vector Graphics (SVG) animation to create the motion is another way to create animations for your websites. There are many programs you can use to build SVG graphics and animate them. One popular tool to do this is Inkscape (https://inkscape.org/en/).

Workshop

The Workshop contains quiz questions and activities to help you solidify your understanding of the material covered. Try to answer all questions before looking at the "Answers" section that follows.

Quiz

1. What are two ways to create a `@keyframes` rule with a starting state and an ending state?

2. What keyframes are required to create an animation that will change to a new state at 50% and then back to the original state at the end?

3. What property defines how long an animation should play in one iteration?

4. How many points of a Bézier curve are defined in the `cubic-bezier()` value?

5. What is the keyword for the timing function value `cubic-bezier(0,0,1,1)`?

6. How many times will the animation `animation: threeTimes 5s 4;` play?

7. What function can calculate exact values from percentages in CSS properties?

8. What arguments does the `arc()` method take?

9. What method will place an image on the canvas?

10. If the first image on a sprite is 100 × 100, how big can the other images in the sprite be?

NOTE

Just a reminder for those of you reading these words in the print or e-book edition of this book: If you go to **www.informit.com/register** and register this book (using ISBN 9780672338083), you can receive free access to an online Web Edition that not only contains the complete text of this book but also features an interactive version of this quiz.

Answers

1. You can use either this:

```
@keyframes myAnimation {
from { ... }
to { ... }
}
```

or this:

```
@keyframes myAnimation {
0% { ... }
100% { ... }
}
```

2. Only the following is required:

```
@keyframes {
  50% { }
}
```

3. The `animation-duration` property defines how long an animation should play in one iteration.

4. The `cubic-bezier()` value defines the x and y coordinates of two points on a curve.

5. This is a `linear` timing function value.

6. The animation will play four times and then stop.

7. The `calc()` function calculates exact values in CSS.

8. The `arc()` method draws a circle with the x and y coordinates of the center, as well as the starting and ending angles (in radians), and finally the direction to draw the path.

9. The `drawImage()` method draws images that are in the DOM onto the canvas.

10. All the images in a sprite file should be the same size, so they should all be 100 × 100.

Exercises

▶ Add a CSS animation to one of the elements on your web page. Use at least two keyframes and try animating using several different styles.

▶ Put a canvas on your web page with a large image on it. But instead of clipping the image or resizing it to fit, cycle through it with an animation to change what part of the image is displayed every few seconds.

LESSON 16
Understanding the Importance of Responsive Web Design

What You'll Learn in This Lesson:

▶ What is responsive web design (RWD)

▶ Why we need RWD

▶ What is progressive enhancement

▶ How to write HTML that's RWD ready

Until this point in these lessons, you have learned very specific techniques for building web pages. In fact, you could stop right now and have enough knowledge to build and maintain basic websites. But to build truly superior sites, you need to know more theory about web design and how to build sites that provide value to customers.

Responsive design involves looking at how customers interact with websites and attempting to create a site that works best for all customers, *as they arrive on the site*. In this lesson you will learn what responsive web design is and why it's important. You'll learn about the theory of progressive enhancement and how the HTML you write affects whether your pages can be made responsive. But most importantly, you will start down the path of a responsible web designer who creates pages that work well and look great no matter what type of device they are viewed on.

What Is Responsive Web Design?

Responsive web design (RWD) is an approach to web design that considers the customer's device and adapts the design for optimal viewing. RWD helps web designers and site owners by creating an "edit once, display anywhere" website. The web designer builds one page that can then be viewed on a wide-screen desktop or a small-screen cell phone without a change to another site or another page opening. The content on the page moves around in the design to suit the device being used to view the page.

A website that uses responsive design changes the layout of the website depending upon what device is used to view it. But unlike older solutions, RWD does not use scripts or programming to achieve these changes. Instead, RWD uses CSS media queries, which you will learn about in

Lesson 18, "Using Media Queries and Breakpoints," to define fluid grids, variable font sizes, and flexible images. The media queries define what styles will apply to the design, based on the device that being used to view it.

A Short History of RWD

The first web pages were little more than text documents shared between monochrome computers. How the pages looked was secondary to the information they provided. But as color monitors grew less expensive and images were added to HTML, the way the pages looked started to gain importance.

NOTE
_____
You may not realize that computer screens used to be just two colors. But they were not black text on a white background. Often, they were a neon green (for the text) on black.
_____

CSS did not show up until 1996, and it wasn't until 1999 that there was widespread support for it among the browsers. CSS2 didn't gain wide support until the mid-2000s, and it wasn't until CSS3 gained wide support in 2012 that responsive design was really possible.

CSS3 added the media query feature. This allowed web designers to create separate CSS documents for devices with different media features. The most commonly used feature is the browser width. For example, a small smartphone might have a width of 640px, while a widescreen monitor might have a width of more than 4000px. With media queries you can detect the width and build designs to suit the various sizes—without changing the HTML or doing any scripting.

In the mid- to late 2000s, if you visited a website on a mobile device, you were often forced to a "mobile friendly" version of the site. These usually had completely different URLs as well as layouts and even content, and web designers had to build two or more versions of the site. Website owners didn't want to have to maintain two separate sites, so often the mobile site would be left with minimal content, while the primary site business was conducted on the desktop version of the site.

This brought about the theory of "graceful degradation." The idea was that designers could build websites with the coolest new features, but the sites could still operate in a limited capacity, without those features. An alternate theory was the concept of "progressive enhancement." The idea here was that a designer would start with the minimum a site needed to be successful and ensure that all devices could view that. Then, once a site worked, the designer would add new and exciting features for the more modern browsers. This finally led to the design theory most people work from today: Mobile First. Mobile First involves designing a site for mobile devices first and then enhancing it for larger screens and computers. You'll learn more about Mobile First in Lesson 17, "Designing for Mobile Devices."

Why Do We Need Responsive Web Design?

Responsive web design is a combination of many design techniques, including the following:

▶ CSS—especially media queries

▶ Clean, valid HTML code

▶ Progressive enhancement

▶ Feature, device, and browser detection using scripts

▶ Server-side components to produce faster sites

The number of different types of browsers and devices that web designs need to support is constantly growing, and more and more people are using their mobile devices to access the web. Every day new devices come on the market that have limited features. But when a customer browses the web on her refrigerator, she wants to be able to do the same things she can do on her phone or on her laptop. Or if another customer asks Alexa to read the latest article on your site to him, you want your site to be able to handle that.

Responsive web design attempts to respond to the device viewing the page and provide the best experience for that device as possible. As you can see in Figure 16.1, a web page might look very different when displayed on a mobile phone than on a desktop computer, but the content remains the same.

FIGURE 16.1
Desktop and mobile phone versions of the same web page. (Figure to be continued on next page)

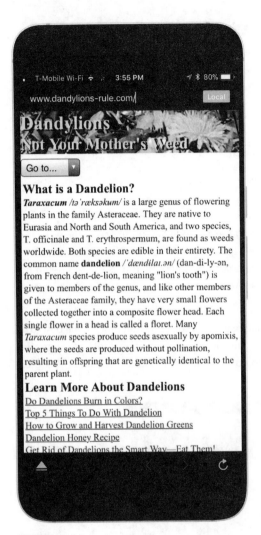

FIGURE 16.1 (continued)

The preceding lessons in this series have taught you how to write clean, valid HTML code and CSS, and you'll learn about media queries in Lesson 18. Progressive enhancement is covered later in this lesson, and you'll learn about scripts and server components to improve your sites in later lessons.

Why Is RWD Important for Mobile Design?

Responsive design is important to mobile customers because it allows them to see the same website as nonmobile customers. Before RWD, web designers would often create entire separate sites for mobile customers, and such a site was invariably a subset of the full site.

RWD allows designers to create sites that work in different devices without having to repost the content multiple times. Worldwide, mobile devices are more popular than computers for viewing the web. And depending upon the market, mobile has overtaken computers in the United States and Europe as well.

RWD lets a designer build a website that doesn't care what device the customer is using. Rather than having to build a site for mobile, a site for desktop, and a site for smart appliances, a designer creates just one site that is flexible enough to support all those devices and more.

In addition, RWD is more future-proof than standard web design. RWD doesn't look at the device but rather looks at the features. For instance, an RWD site that checks for Retina display doesn't care if the device is an Apple iPhone 4S or a Samsung Galaxy S9. It just notices that the screen can handle high-resolution Retina images and displays them.

In 2015, Google and other search engines announced that they were going to start penalizing sites that didn't optimize for mobile customers. One of the best ways to do that is with responsive web design.

What Is Progressive Enhancement?

Progressive enhancement is the process of creating a strong foundation on a website and then adding enhancements to that foundation as browsers and devices can handle them.

Progressive enhancement came as a reaction to graceful degradation. Graceful degradation was a carry-over from software engineering, where the norm was to test for faults and create a system as fault tolerant as possible. In the web design world, graceful degradation turned into an excuse for web designers to create the most amazing website they could on their browser of choice and then pass on whatever scraps they could scrape together to the browsers that weren't as powerful.

The problem was that this whole idea went against the goals of the web as an accessible medium where everyone had access to information, no matter what their situation. As Sir Tim Berners-Lee said in the July 1996 *Technology Review*: "Anyone who slaps a 'this page is best viewed with Browser X' label on a Web page appears to be yearning for the bad old days, before the Web, when you had very little chance of reading a document written on another computer, another word processor, or another network." If you use graceful degradation, that is what you are saying to your customers, even if you don't slap a label on your pages.

But when you switch to a progressive enhancement mindset, you switch your focus away from what browsers and devices your customers use. Instead, you focus on *content*. When you're concerned with building a site with progressive enhancement, your first concern is with the content—what the content is, how it will be manipulated on the site, and where the site will get it.

Progressive enhancement lets you create websites that are inclusive and accessible, which is the ultimate goal of the World Wide Web.

How to Use Progressive Enhancement on a Website

You can add progressive enhancement to a web page fairly quickly. But to do it well across a whole site, you need to think strategically.

Separating Content from Presentation and Functionality

The first thing you should think about when adding progressive enhancement to your site is the content. A website has three layers:

▶ The content stored in the HTML

▶ The presentation defined by CSS

▶ The behavior written in scripts like JavaScript

While it is possible to add CSS and scripts inline in your HTML, the best sites separate them into three different files and maintain strict distinctions between them.

Editing the Content Layer

You should start with the content and the HTML that marks it up. Your HTML should be valid, well formed, and semantic.

Valid HTML means using the most current version of HTML and writing it without deprecated or obsolete elements. The most current version of HTML right now is HTML5.

Well-formed HTML is HTML that is written correctly. Your HTML should have closing tags where required as well as quoted attributes and good nesting. When your HTML isn't written correctly, it can confuse some browsers, and confused browsers don't display web pages correctly. HTML5 doesn't require that all attribute values be quoted, and it allows you to leave off closing tags on elements such as <p> and <li>, but using the quotes and closing tags when you can will keep your HTML cleaner.

Finally, semantic HTML provides information about the content based on the tags that are used. For example, if the content includes a date or time, you can use the <time> element to indicate to the browser that it is a time. The advantage of using semantic HTML is that your content can be used more widely when it's marked up. When you use the <time> element, the user agent can then offer to add the event to a calendar because it knows that it's a date or time. There are many semantic tags.

When you're building HTML for your RWD sites, you should always strive to keep it as clean and clear as possible. The technical term for this is *well formed*. Well-formed HTML has the following characteristics:

- There is a document type declaration at the top of the document.

- Tags should nest correctly, inside to outside, like so:

  `<b><i>text</i></b>`

- Attributes with spaces in their values should be quoted using single or double quotation marks.

- Comments are not allowed inside tags.

- Special characters used in HTML should be escaped, such as an ampersand (&), a less-than sign (<), and a greater than sign (>).

Well formed for XHTML standards involves additional rules, such as always closing every tag and using a closing slash in a singleton tag, including an XML declaration, and quoting every attribute. But if you are using HTML5, the rules are not as strict.

Semantic elements are elements that describe what the content contained *is*. They provide more information to the browser without requiring any extra attributes.

There are a number of HTML elements that are semantic and have been in use for years. The following are several of the semantic elements that are regularly used on web pages:

- **`<abbr>`**—Defines abbreviations and acronyms

- **`<blockquote>`**—Defines a block quotation

- **`<cite>`**—Defines citations, such as for quotations

- **`<code>`**—Defines a code reference

- **`<q>`**—Defines a short inline quotation

There are many more semantic elements in HTML. You can search for **semantic HTML tags** in your favorite search engine to learn about them all.

The other part of clean code is using only the elements and attributes you need—and nothing more. Try to consider what your site needs and limit your HTML to only those elements.

Once the content layer is valid, well formed, and semantic, your web pages will work well even in user agents that don't support CSS or JavaScript, such as screen readers and basic cell phones.

Adjusting How the Content Looks with CSS

Once you have all your content displayed in valid, well-formed, and semantic HTML, you can work with the CSS to adjust how the page looks. As with the content, you want your CSS to be as valid and up to date as it can be to ensure the widest support.

CSS, because of the way it's written, provides a lot of opportunity for progressive enhancement. Some things you should be aware of include the following:

- ▶ **The cascade**—Remember that CSS stands for *Cascading* Style Sheets, and the cascade says that CSS should be evaluated in order, with the last feature taking precedence. There's more to the cascade than that, but when it comes to progressive enhancement, you should use the cascade by putting the most cutting-edge features last, with fallback options above them in the style sheet.

- ▶ **Browser prefixes**—Not all user agents support all the new features of CSS right away, but most provide browser prefixes to give support in the interim. By placing browser-prefixed versions of your style properties first in a style rule, you ensure that the final, official version is supported when possible.

- ▶ **User agents ignoring what they don't recognize**—This means that if a browser sees a property that is new to it, it will ignore it and not change the style at all.

Place your CSS in an external style sheet and make changes there to change your entire site at once.

Adding Interactivity with JavaScript

Interactivity is often the most fun part of a website to work on because it's what makes the site into an application or an entire experience. By adding in the scripts last, you know that your site already works, whether you have the scripts or not. And the best way to add JavaScript is unobtrusively.

There are four rules of unobtrusive JavaScript:

- ▶ The script should be usable without the customer noticing it is there.

- ▶ The script should not generate an error message, *even when it fails.* It should just disappear and not get in the way of the content.

- ▶ The script should never block access to the core content of the page.

- ▶ The script should be maintained in a separate document outside the HTML and CSS.

Unobtrusive JavaScript allows you to add interactivity to your web pages without changing the HTML or CSS. And this means you know the pages already work and look good before you add the interactive elements. Unobtrusive JavaScript is covered in more detail in Lesson 25, "JavaScript Best Practices."

What Are the Benefits of Progressive Enhancement?

The most obvious beneficiaries of progressive enhancement are people who use outdated browsers. In the past, when designers used primarily graceful degradation, outdated browsers would often be given the priority "keep it from crashing," and if that meant removing a majority of the content from those browsers, then that's what happened.

But there are other benefits to using progressive enhancement, such as the following:

- ▶ Basic cell phones can display content in HTML without issue. Because the focus of progressive enhancement is on content, a progressively enhanced website will display content no matter what is viewing it.

- ▶ The same is true for screen readers. These devices handle well-structured HTML and so are more likely to read these pages without a problem.

- ▶ Pages built with progressive enhancement are easier to maintain than their counterparts because the content, design, and functionality are kept separate.

- ▶ Finally, a site built with progressive enhancement is going to get more viewers than one that isn't because the site is not exclusionary in its design.

A progressively enhanced website might not even need any changes to the CSS to be responsive. Depending on how you write the CSS, it can be mobile friendly and not require any extra styling.

Writing HTML for Responsive Web Design

Responsive design doesn't add any new HTML tags or attributes, which makes it easy to learn. You simply write your HTML so that it is well formed, valid, and semantic, as previously mentioned.

You should start with HTML5, the most recent version of HTML, which provides the most assistance to web designers who want to use progressive enhancement and RWD. While you can build RWD sites using other versions of HTML, it's best to stay as up to date as possible. This book uses HTML5 code samples.

Using Tags Every Page Should Contain

There are several HTML tags that every web page should contain:

- ▶ `<!doctype>`
- ▶ `<html>`
- ▶ `<head>`

▶ `<meta charset>`

▶ `<title>`

▶ `<body>`

These tags may not be required for valid HTML, but they provide information about the page to the browser to make them easier to use. These tags are covered in more detail in Lesson 2, "Structuring an HTML Document."

If your web page contains these elements, it contains the minimum HTML required to start building a responsive page. Listing 16.1 provides a standard template you can use for starting any web page. Note that the tags listed above have both starting and ending tags, as well as some attributes.

LISTING 16.1   A Basic HTML Template

```
<!doctype html>
<html>
  <head>
    <meta charset="utf-8">
    <title> </title>
  </head>
  <body>
  </body>
</html>
```

All these elements are covered in Lesson 2.

Writing Tags for Web Content

While the tags in the preceding section are all you need to create a website, the site would be very plain and hard to read. While there are dozens of HTML tags you can use, there are only a few you need to know about to start creating a decent web page:

▶ Headline elements, including `<h1>`, `<h2>`, and `<h3>`

▶ Content elements, such as `<p>` and `<br>`

▶ Links with `<a>`

▶ Semantic elements such as `<strong>` and `<em>`

▶ General container elements such as `<div>` and `<span>`

▶ Multimedia elements such as `<img>`, `<audio>`, and `<video>`

You should also include HTML5 sectioning elements to define the sections of the page. There are many such elements, but these are the most commonly used sectioning elements:

- `<article>`
- `<aside>`
- `<section>`
- `<nav>`
- `<header>`
- `<footer>`

These elements define areas of the content that are commonly found on web pages. A web page typically has a main article that defines the page (`<article>`); there is usually sidebar information for either the article, the page, or the entire site (`<aside>`); navigation is critical (`<nav>`); and many web pages are divided into separate sections with different semantic meanings that don't fall into the above categories (`<section>`).

The `<header>` and `<footer>` tags are not technically sectioning elements, but they are used in a similar fashion. You can add a header or footer to any of the sectioning elements listed above, you can add them to the entire page, or you can add them to both.

Understanding Basic Attributes

Nearly every tag in HTML has attributes. These are keywords that are defined within a tag itself and give the browser more information about that tag. You have already used attributes with the `<img src="">` tag and the `<a href="">` tag. Two other attributes you should be familiar with are `id` and `class`. These attributes, which can be added to any HTML tag in your document, provide additional information about that element.

The `id` attribute is used to give an element a name. The `id` must be unique to the page it is on. But you can give every single tag on your page a unique `id`. This attribute is used to identify the element. You can then link to that element by using the pound sign (#) in your URL followed by the `id` value. For example, if you have the element `<article id="main">`, you add a link to that element by writing `<a href="#main">link to main</a>`.

You can also use the `id` attribute as a hook for styles and scripts such as with the method `getElementById()`. Because it must be unique on the page, you know when you attach a style to that `id`, you will affect only one element. This attribute also makes a style rule that uses it more specific, which means it's more likely to be applied.

Like the id attribute, the class attribute is used to apply styles and scripts to an element. But it does not have to be unique on a page. This means you can apply a class to multiple elements on a page, and any style rules that are written for that class will be applied to all the elements. For instance, say you want some of your <h1> headlines to be red, but others should remain the default color. You could give the red headlines a special class that you would style as red in your CSS: <h1 class="highlight">.

CAUTION

In the class example, we suggested that you might want to make some of your headlines the color red. But in the code, we gave it the class name "highlight". It can be tempting to give your elements classes and IDs that describe exactly what they do, such as <h1 class="red">. But doing so can cause problems in the future. What if two years from now, you decide that all the highlighted headlines need to be colored blue rather than red? The fastest thing to do is simply change the class rule in the CSS so that the font color is blue. But anyone editing the site will look at that rule and think there is an error. The class name is "red" but it changes the color to blue? By giving your elements more generic class and id names, you avoid this problem and keep your code more future-proof.

One of the nicest things about using classes is that you aren't limited to just one. You can include multiple class names on any element to add styles to the element or hook up with your scripts. To add a second class to an element, simply separate the classes with a space, like so:

```
<h1 class="highlight fancy">
```

Validating HTML, CSS, and JavaScript

As you're working through building a site with progressive enhancement and getting ready for responsive web design, you should validate first the HTML and then the CSS and finally the JavaScript.

Validating your HTML is easy and takes only a moment. Simply go to https://validator.w3.org and fill in the URL of the page to be validated. If the page isn't live yet, you can validate it by uploading a file or pasting the HTML in as direct input. If you've been careful, you should see a green line that reads "This document was successfully checked as HTML5!"

Validate CSS the same way, with the Jigsaw validator (https://jigsaw.w3.org/css-validator/). One thing you can check is the vendor extensions, as shown in Figure 16.2. The vendor extensions can give you clues about browser extensions and help you make sure they are correct, along with the standard CSS properties.

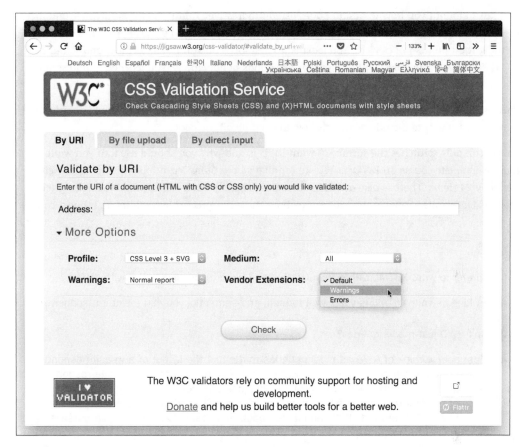

FIGURE 16.2
Validate CSS with the Jigsaw validator.

Validating JavaScript is a little more difficult. There are many online validators you can use. You can also use the web developer tools in modern browsers to make sure your JavaScript works correctly.

Summary

In this lesson you learned a lot more theory of web design than actual coding, but you got a good basis for creating professional web pages that work well on most devices. You learned what responsive web design (RWD) is and the history of web design that brought it about. This lesson explained some of the reasons RWD is important to design, including better content delivery and support for mobile devices.

This lesson taught you how to design pages using progressive enhancement. Progressive enhancement involves determining the most important content on page and ensuring that it is viewable by the largest number of devices. You learned to first focus on valid, well-formed, and semantic HTML. Then you saw how to add styles to make it look good. Finally, you learned to add scripts that add behaviors to the page. But the goal is to keep the core content viewable by all users.

This lesson revisited the keys to writing good HTML to prepare for RWD. You learned about the tags and attributes to include as well as how to validate all the code.

This lesson only scratches the surface of what RWD is and why you should use it. If you want a more complete course on RWD, check out Jennifer's book *Sams Teach Yourself Responsive Web Design in 24 Hours*. There is also a video course based on the book—"Learning Responsive Web Design LiveLessons." You can find out more about these resources at www.html5in24hours.com.

Q&A

Q. I prefer to write XHTML rather than HTML. Can I write responsive pages with XHTML?

A. As long as your XHTML is valid, well formed, and semantic, you can make it responsive.

Q. Isn't RWD just media queries?

A. Most people think of RWD as media queries that affect the layout of a website depending on the width of the device viewing it. But there are other ways to make a site responsive. In Lesson 17 you'll learn some responsive techniques that don't require media queries. And many of the first responsive sites used flexible layouts based on percentages and the `max-width` CSS property that you learned about in Lesson 12, "Creating Layouts Using Modern CSS Techniques."

Workshop

The Workshop contains quiz questions and activities to help you solidify your understanding of the material covered. Try to answer all questions before looking at the "Answers" section that follows.

Quiz

1. True or False: Responsive web design is just a form of progressive enhancement.

2. Is the following HTML well formed?

   ```
   <strong><em>My dog is</strong> big</em>
   ```

3. Is it better to use a `<p>` or a `<div>` tag when marking up a paragraph?

4. Is the `<header>` element semantic?

5. How many versions of a website should you build to create a mobile version and a computer version using modern responsive web design?

6. List four semantic HTML elements that are not also sectioning elements.

7. What language modifies the presentation layer?

8. Where should you store styles and scripts on web pages?

9. What six tags should every web page contain?

10. What web languages should you validate?

NOTE

Just a reminder for those of you reading these words in the print or e-book edition of this book: If you go to **www.informit.com/register** and register this book (using ISBN 9780672338083), you can receive free access to an online Web Edition that not only contains the complete text of this book but also features an interactive version of this quiz.

Answers

1. False. Progressive enhancement is often used in responsive design, but websites that use it do not have to be responsive—and vice versa.

2. No, this is not well formed because the `<strong>` and `<em>` tags do not nest correctly. This is a common error that designers make when they want to close the outermost tag first. Here's how you can correct the HTML:

   `<em><strong>My dog is</strong> big</em>`

3. When you're marking up a paragraph, you should use the `<p>` tag because it defines paragraphs semantically.

4. The `<header>` element is semantic because it describes the content as being the header section of a web page, section, or element.

5. The best websites use just one version of the site for both mobile and desktop computers but make them responsive.

6. There are lots of semantic elements; some commonly used ones include `<abbr>`, `<blockquote>`, `<cite>`, `<code>`, `<q>`, and `<time>`.

7. CSS modifies the presentation layer.

8. Styles and scripts should be stored in external files and linked to in the HTML.

9. Every web page should contain <body>, <!doctype>, <head>, <html>, <meta charset>, and <title>.

10. You should validate your HTML, CSS, and JavaScript as well as any other languages you use on your site.

Exercises

▶ Think about what aspects of your website are not responsive and decide what elements you would change to make it responsive. Consider things like the layout, the font choices, and even colors and backgrounds.

▶ Go through the HTML for the site you are evaluating. Convert it as much as possible to semantic HTML5. Remove unnecessary tags and then validate it with an HTML5 validator. If the validator finds errors, fix them until the page is valid.

LESSON 17
Designing for Mobile Devices

What You'll Learn in This Lesson:

▸ How mobile design differs from standard web design

▸ What the Mobile First design philosophy is

▸ How Mobile First is important to RWD

▸ How to build responsive tables and images for mobile devices

▸ How to use CSS columns to create responsive designs without media queries

According to Statcounter, worldwide mobile usage surpassed desktop usage around October 2016. While desktop computer use still surpasses mobile use in North America, almost 40% of the market share is mobile. And when you include tablets with mobile, that number jumps to closer to 50%. This means that if you're ignoring or downplaying mobile, you're alienating nearly half of a North American audience and a majority of the global audience. Not designing websites for mobile devices is a bad strategy.

In this lesson you will learn all about mobile web design—why to do it, how to do it, and some specific techniques for doing it. Mobile web design isn't the same as responsive web design, but it's an important consideration when you're trying to build a responsive website.

Designing for Mobile Devices

Designing a site for mobile devices is more than just testing on your phone after you've launched the site. The best mobile designs treat mobile devices as if they are just as important as, if not more important than, desktop computers. This is a difficult leap for many web designers to make. After all, they are most likely building their pages on a computer rather than a tablet or phone, and most courses on web design (including, to some extent, this one) focus on computers as the primary design platform.

Understanding Why Mobile Design Is Important

The main reason mobile design is important is because more and more people are using mobile devices to access the web. People access their phones all the time, for everything. If your web page doesn't look good or, even worse, doesn't work on a smartphone, then you can be sure you will lose customers. There is no reason for a customer to stick around trying to fight through a site that is not mobile friendly when there are hundreds of competitors out there.

Another important factor is search engines. If your site receives a significant amount of traffic from search engines, then you should be aware of mobile design. Google started using "mobile-friendliness" as a criterion for ranking in its index in 2015, and other search engine providers followed suit. This means that sites that don't make any effort at optimizing for mobile devices will be penalized in the results.

Luckily, you don't have to guess to find out if Google thinks your web page is mobile friendly. There is a tool at https://search.google.com/test/mobile-friendly that can tell you. Figure 17.1 shows the results for a page that is mobile friendly.

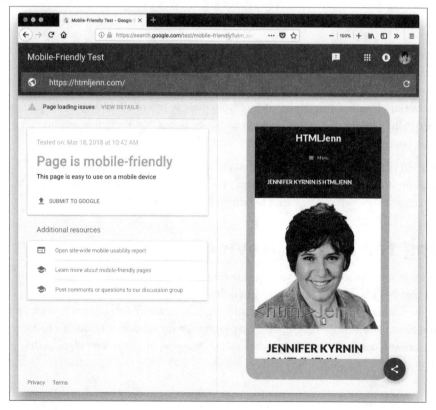

FIGURE 17.1
The HTMLJenn site is mobile friendly, according to Google.

Designing Effective Mobile Interfaces

If you tested your site and it came up as not mobile friendly, you're probably wondering what to do about it. There are a few specific things that Google looks for when assessing a site for mobile friendliness:

- ▸ Using Flash
- ▸ Configuring the viewport
- ▸ Fixed-width designs
- ▸ Image and other box sizes
- ▸ Font sizes
- ▸ Tappable elements

You should also consider several other things about mobile devices when building a mobile-friendly site:

- ▸ Simplifying the layout and the navigation
- ▸ Keeping the download times short
- ▸ Testing on real devices

Flash Is Not Mobile Friendly

Flash and mobile devices don't mix. If your site uses Flash in any way, you have instantly lost all mobile devices, including tablets. In fact, if your customers use Mac computers, they will have to download and install a Flash player to be able to use Flash. While this isn't a total barrier—some customers will do that—the fact is that most will choose the easier path of finding another site that doesn't use Flash.

Instead of using Flash, consider using animation, as discussed in Lesson 15, "Animating with CSS and the Canvas." Dynamic web technologies in HTML5 and CSS3 as well as unobtrusive JavaScript can give you similar experiences to Flash without the drawbacks.

How to Configure the Viewport

The viewport is the window in which web pages are viewed. On mobile devices the viewport is typically the full screen, while on computers it's the browser window, not including the *chrome*—scrollbars, menus, and edges. Some devices have a pixel density of one size and an actual size that differs. For example, the iPhone X ships with screen dimensions 1125×2436, but the device width is 375×812. If you don't set the viewport, your CSS will read the screen as having a width of 1125px, which is as large as the size of a small laptop. If you use media queries based on the width of the screen, your large-screen designs will display instead of your easier-to-read mobile screens. You'll learn more about how to do this in Lesson 18, "Using Media Queries and Breakpoints," but for now just remember that a design intended for a browser window that is around 10 inches wide is not going to be particularly usable on a device that is only around 3 inches wide.

NOTE
This discrepancy in width versus device width is because the device manufacturers make devices with higher and higher pixel densities. In the past, devices had 72 dots per inch. Then the Retina display arrived, placing 2 dots for every 1 dot in a standard display. Newer devices came out with 3 dots per 1 and so on. The number of actual pixels on the screen remained the same, but the amount of data that could be transmitted to those pixels increased.

The fix for this is to set your viewport. And this is easy with the `<meta viewport>` tag, as shown here:

```
<meta name="viewport" content="width=device-width, initial-scale=1">
```

Place this tag in the `<head>` of your documents.

The `width=device-width` rule tells the browser that the page should display using the actual device width as the width rather than using the rendered width. The best value is `device-width` because that sets the width to whatever the current user's device is.

The `initial-scale=1` rule tells the browser that there should be a 1:1 relationship between the device-independent pixels and the CSS pixels. This also allows the page to take advantage of the full landscape width when the device is rotated that way.

Other viewport rules you can assign include `minimum-scale`, `maximum-scale`, and `user-scalable`. You can use these settings to change how much or how little the user can zoom the page, and you can also disable zooming completely.

CAUTION
Using scaling rules other than `initial-scale` is not a good idea because it can interfere with accessibility. You can disable zooming on your web pages by setting `minimum-scale` and `maximum-scale` to be the same as `initial-scale`, or you can set `user-scalable=no`. But if you disable scaling/zooming, you will make your pages very difficult to use for many people.

Avoiding Using Fixed-Width Designs

It is very tempting to use fixed-width designs, as you can set all the elements so they display where and how you want, and you can be sure they will display that way in all browsers. This reflects back to print design, where it was possible to control most variables, so your design looked virtually identical in all situations. But that is not possible on web pages. If you want to use fixed-width designs, you should make sure you have at least two different designs—one for small devices and one for larger ones—and the more designs you have, the more responsive your site will be.

Similarly, while it is possible to set the viewport to a specific width by using the `<meta viewport>` tag, you should not do it. Some designers set the width of the viewport to a specific number of pixels to try to force devices to display the page correctly. But if you do that, Google and other search engines will define your page as not being mobile friendly. Instead, you should set the viewport as mentioned in the previous section and use responsive design techniques to let the page display effectively at different sizes.

Making Sure Your Elements Fit in the Design

One problem that you might see on web pages when they are viewed on mobile is that the images are too big. If an image is set with a specific width and height and those values are not adjusted for mobile devices, then the image might not fit in the window. For example, as mentioned previously, the iPhone X has a CSS width of 375 pixels. This means that, assuming that you've set the viewport correctly, an image that is 400×400 is too large for the window and will force horizontal scrolling to see the right side 25 pixels. This can happen with any block-level element that has absolute values for the dimensions.

To fix this, you should use relative widths and position values, such as percentages or rems. You should also make sure that your images scale with the device so they don't end up running off the edge.

Keeping Font Sizes Legible

One feature of most smartphones is the ability to pinch to zoom. This might be done, for example, to make the text or other elements larger and more legible. The user's ability to pinch to zoom does not give a web designer license to write pages with tiny font sizes that are illegible for most people.

Instead, you should focus on making your pages legible with responsive design. There are several things to consider in making your text legible:

- ▶ Start with a base font size of 16px or larger.
- ▶ Define the sizes of various elements relative to the base font size.
- ▶ Adjust the line height to keep the text vertically legible.
- ▶ Adjust the line length to stay between 8 and 10 words per line.
- ▶ Do not use more than three or four font families and font sizes.

The base font size is the size that the page defaults to if no other rule is defined. Define this with either the * selector to select all elements or the body tag selector to select just the body tag, or define it as both, like so:

```
*, body {
  font-size: 16px;
}
```

Once you have the base font size, you can adjust the internal elements to be larger or smaller with percentage font sizes or rems or ems, like so:

```
h1 {
  font-size: 250%;
}
h2 {
  font-size: 2rem;
}
h3 {
  font-size: 1.8rem;
}
p {
  font-size: 1.2rem;
}
```

CAUTION

Don't be afraid of using larger font sizes for body text. While most web designers have younger, stronger eyes, there are a lot of older people with weaker eyes reading the pages. So, while you might think that 16px is huge, and you might be tempted to decrease the body text size, remember that depending on your site topic, the majority of your users might think that font size is hard to read. Sticking with 16px as the base font size or making the base size larger is a good idea.

The line height or leading is something that many beginning web designers forget about. But if you don't adjust it, your text can appear too far away from headlines or too close together to be readily legible. Leading is defined with the line-height property. It takes a number that is a multiple of the font size. You can also use lengths, but that is often too rigid for good design. The typical line-height is 1.2, but you can change it for different elements, like so:

```
h1, h2, h3 {
  line-height: 0.8;
}
p {
  line-height: 1.1;
}
```

There is no explicit font property to control the line length. Instead, you should adjust the width of the containers to keep the line length legible with the `width` property. As mentioned previously, an ideal line length is between 8 and 10 words or around 70 to 80 characters. When the line length gets longer than that, you should add a breakpoint or change the column width.

The last aspect of font legibility is the number of font changes you have on the page. Multiple font sizes and typefaces make the page more difficult to read. Plus, using multiple web fonts increases the download time. A good rule of thumb is to limit your pages to no more than five different font sizes and typefaces.

Making Links Tappable

Most mobile devices use touch screens, which means that the links need to be tappable. If your links are too small or too close together, they will not be easily tapped. The minimum size that can be tapped easily is around 48px × 48px. So, the first thing you should do is ensure that all links and buttons are at least 48px high and 48px wide. Menu links, such as those in navigation bars, should be tappable across the entire block, not just the text. The best way to create such links is to adjust the `display` property for navigation links, like so.

```
nav a {
  display: block;
}
```

Simplifying Layouts and Navigation Without Sacrificing Content

Designing layouts for mobile devices can be challenging because most web designers use desktop and laptop computers to build their pages. It's easy to add new features and interesting design elements when you have a lot of real estate to work with.

To simplify the layouts, start with the number of columns. The ideal number of columns on most smartphones is one. A single column can be difficult to read on larger screens, but the point of responsive web designs is to first design for the mobile version of the site, such as by making the mobile version of the site one column and then adding columns as the screens get larger.

Similarly, the mobile version of a site should include navigation to the same parts of the site as the desktop version, but it should be simplified. Sub-menus are often difficult to use on mobile devices, so avoiding more than one level of sub-menus is a good idea. Place the navigation as links on the pages themselves or add a second navigation menu below the main content.

Download Speed Is Critical

Mobile web pages should be small. While high-speed Internet is common to homes, mobile devices are often on cellular networks and have data plans with bandwidth limits. And while many of your customers may not have limits, cellular networks—even the fast ones—are slow.

Images are the largest bandwidth hogs on most web pages. When writing for mobile, make sure that your images are as small as possible. Consider these best practices:

▶ Always use JPEG or PNG formats for photographs.

▶ Use GIF or PNG formats for flat-color clip art and illustrations.

▶ Crop images to keep the dimensions as small as possible.

▶ With PNG and GIF images, use a limited palette of colors—as few as possible.

▶ Use the "save for Web" option in image editing programs.

Testing Mobile Web Pages

Testing mobile designs can be challenging because of the many different mobile phones and tablets. When testing, start first with your desktop browser. Modern browsers often have a responsive design mode. Figure 17.2 shows a website in Firefox with Responsive Design Mode turned on.

FIGURE 17.2
Viewing the website Kyrnin.com in responsive design mode in Firefox.

This is a great first step for testing your designs. But for final testing, you should test your mobile designs on mobile devices. You can start by testing on your own devices. It is unlikely that you own dozens of different mobile devices, and you'll want to test on as many devices as possible. There are three ways to test on multiple mobile devices: buy or rent a device, borrow a device, or use a mobile emulator.

You should consider testing on several types of devices, including the following:

- Small flip phones
- iOS phones
- Android phones
- Windows phones
- Smaller tablets on both iOS and Android

Renting a mobile device may be difficult to do, but there are several emulators you can use. The easiest way to emulate your site is the one mentioned previously—using Responsive Design Mode in modern web browsers. But there are several other emulators for specific devices and operating systems:

- **Android Studio**—https://developer.android.com/studio/index.html
- **Apple Xcode Simulator**—https://developer.apple.com/download/
- **BlackBerry 10 Device Simulator**—https://developer.blackberry.com/devzone/develop/simulator/sim_index.html
- **Opera**—https://www.opera.com/
- **Windows Mobile Emulators**—www.microsoft.com/en-us/download/details.aspx?id=9263

There are also online emulators you can use to test live pages, some of which are free and some of which are paid:

- **Cowemo Mobile Phone Emulator**—www.mobilephoneemulator.com
- **Sigos App Experience**—https://appexperience.sigos.com

Understanding Mobile First Design

Traditionally, a web designer first built a website for desktop users and then modified that site for mobile users. Mobile First design turns that formula on its head: It says to build a site for mobile users first and then adjust it to work for desktop users.

Designing for Mobile Devices Before Computers

One of the things many designers forget when building a website is that they are not the customers. You are likely to build a site on a computer, but many of your customers (if not most) will access your site on mobile devices. If you start your design by focusing on mobile, you are immediately changing your focus to a much larger market—worldwide. The global penetration of cell phones is between 89% and 97%. So, if you want your website to be accessible to people all around the world, a Mobile First design strategy is really smart.

How to Use Mobile First

The first thing to do with Mobile First is to create the default design for all your pages for mobile devices. Think about the smallest screen that might be used to view your pages. If you do nothing else for mobile devices, this might just be enough. But there are two other things you can do as well: Concentrate on your content and consider the technologies that mobile devices use.

Changing the Focus to Content

When you design first for mobile devices, you have to focus on the content first. You have to determine what content is the core content for the page because the screen size on a mobile device is much smaller than most desktop computers. (Consider that some people even view web pages on the tiny screens of smart watches.) If you don't know what is the core content or functionality for every page on your site, then your mobile customers won't know either.

One thing you can do is highlight different content for different devices. For instance, a mobile customer might be more interested in the hours and location of a restaurant, while a computer user might want the menus first. It's not that mobile customers don't want the menus, but menus might not be their first focus.

While it's good to highlight different content for different users, you should provide a way for all your users to get to all the content. If you reduce the main navigation or remove links or other elements for mobile users, you need to decide where you're going to put them so that those pages can be found if they are needed.

Experimenting with New Technologies

A lot of new technologies have appeared on mobile devices first or are available only on mobile, including the following:

- Geolocation
- Touch-screen interfaces
- Web storage
- Offline applications
- Mobile web applications

While more of these technologies are appearing on desktop computers, there are still a lot more uses on mobile devices. For example, geolocation isn't terribly useful on a machine that never leaves its current position.

Why Mobile First Works

Mobile First is primarily an implementation of progressive enhancement. You focus on getting the required content and functionality to as many customers as possible and then enhance the site for more diverse devices. There are a lot of different devices out there that can serve web pages, including these:

- ▶ Mobile devices (smartphones, basic cell phones, and tablets)

- ▶ Smart watches

- ▶ Smart speakers and other audio devices (like Amazon Echo, Google Home, and Sonos One)

- ▶ Specialized devices (gaming consoles, e-book readers, televisions, refrigerators, and other items in the Internet of Things)

- ▶ Traditional computing devices (netbooks, laptops, and desktop computers)

NOTE

What Is "The Internet of Things"?

The Internet of Things (IoT) is where an object, an animal, or a person is given a unique identifier and the capability to transmit data over a network without requiring a human to initiate anything. It could be a heart monitor, or a farm animal with an embedded microchip, or even a refrigerator that transmits information on its contents so you know when you're almost out of milk.

The first "thing" in the IoT was a Coke machine at Carnegie Melon University in the 1980s. It was connected to the Internet, and programmers could access its data to determine if there would be a cold drink available—no more getting to the machine only to find that all the root beer is gone!

In addition to this list of common devices in use today, new ones will continue to be invented. By having a Mobile First mindset and using progressive enhancement, you can ensure that any Web-enabled device will have at least basic access to the content and functionality of your website—*no matter what that device is.*

How Mobile First Fails

One of the biggest drawbacks to Mobile First is that it is hard to implement. You start out the design process with a huge barrier—the size you can design for. If you're designing for a smartwatch, for example, you need to make sure your pages look okay on a screen no more than 320 pixels square. For older designers out there, this may feel like a huge step backward: We were designing for 640 × 480 screens in the 1990s, and watches are even smaller than that. Not only are you limited in terms of screen size, you're also limited by the number of design elements you can use, as well as the layouts, the features, the image sizes, and so on.

Mobile First design can move designers into a scarcity mindset. Instead of imagining all the possible things a website can do, they focus on all the things that the mobile devices can't do. It might be that after you start designing for larger-screen devices you figure out something else you could add to the site. But there's nothing stopping you from adding it. Just because you think of a feature for the mobile site while working on the larger site version doesn't mean you can't add it later.

The best solution is to work on your site architecture before you worry about the design—mobile or otherwise. If you have a strong understanding of what pages your site needs, you can create the navigation menus and define the content needed for each page or section. Once you know all that, you're ready to design.

What About Mobile Only Design or Building an App Instead?

Another method of doing web design that is gaining popularity is mobile *only* design. Rather than building a site that will work for both desktop and mobile customers, you focus only on mobile and let the desktop customers fend for themselves.

The benefit of this method is that you have to do a bit less work to create a design that will work effectively than you must do to create a multi-breakpoint responsive web design. You can also customize the content to be 100% mobile friendly.

But most customers are not interested in running just one site optimized for mobile. Chances are they will eventually visit the site from a wide-screen desktop monitor and then be very disappointed by the minimalist style.

However, if 75% or more of your customers are using mobile devices to visit your site, then a mobile-only design makes a lot of sense. In that scenario, it makes sense to worry about desktop customers last or not at all. After all, most desktop browsers will handle any of the designs and scripts that work on mobile browsers.

Some website owners have created mobile apps specifically for their mobile customers. An app can hold onto mobile customers more effectively than a website might. Mobile apps are most useful in certain situations, such as the following:

- ▶ Mobile gaming
- ▶ Personalized content
- ▶ Complex reporting

- With mobile functionality, such as GPS

- Offline access

All of these features can be built into a website, but using an application might make more sense.

Using Responsive Tables and Images

Two aspects of websites that can be difficult to make responsive are tables and images. Data tables are often very big and can thus be very difficult to handle in a responsive design, especially for small devices. Images can be frustrating because they can take up too much space on small screens while being barely visible on larger screens. And they can cause pages to be really slow and take a long time to download.

How to Make Tables Responsive

To make a table responsive, you need to do more than just resize the table. There are several things you need to think about:

- What data is essential to the table and must display on every device?

- How do customers compare the data on the table?

- What are the sizes at which the table no longer displays legibly on the screen?

Mobile First design dictates that you should include the same data in some fashion for even the most limited devices, but you can hide the less crucial information until users need it. So, you need to know what information is most important.

If customers need to compare different rows or columns to each other, such as in a list of features, then your responsive design needs to reflect that. But if the data is in a table to make the information easier to digest, such as a table listing books with their publishing information, then the responsive design doesn't have to make comparing easy.

Finally, you need to consider where the table breaks. You insert *breakpoints* at points where you need to rethink how the table is displayed. You will learn more about breakpoints in Lesson 18.

Once you have considered these issues, you can make decisions about how you want to build your data tables so that they are responsive. There are three ways web designers handle data tables in RWD:

- Resize the cells

- Rearrange the table

- Remove or hide content

Resizing Cells in a Data Table

Resizing cells in a data table is the easiest way to handle tables because it's the way that tables rearrange themselves by default. Listing 17.1 shows the HTML for a simple table. This table has a width of 100%, so it will automatically adjust to the width of the browser.

LISTING 17.1   Basic HTML Table

```
<!doctype html>
<html lang="en">
  <head>
    <meta charset="utf-8">
    <title>Basic HTML Table</title>
    <meta name="viewport"
        content="width=device-width,initial-scale=1">
  </head>
  <body>
    <table width="100%" border="1">
      <thead>
        <tr>
          <th>Name</th>
          <th>URL</th>
          <th>RWD?</th>
          <th>Windows</th>
          <th>Macintosh</th>
        </tr>
      </thead>
      <tbody>
        <tr>
          <td>Adobe Dreamweaver</td>
          <td>http://www.adobe.com/products/dreamweaver.html</td>
          <td>yes</td>
          <td>yes</td>
          <td>yes</td>
        </tr>
        <tr>
          <td>Macaw</td>
          <td>http://macaw.co/</td>
          <td>yes</td>
          <td>yes</td>
          <td>yes</td>
        </tr>
        <tr>
          <td>Coffee Cup Responsive Layout Maker Pro</td>
          <td>http://www.coffeecup.com/responsive-layout-maker-pro/</td>
```

```
         <td>yes</td>
         <td>yes</td>
         <td>yes</td>
       </tr>
       <tr>
         <td>Microsoft Notepad</td>
         <td>http://www.notepad.org/</td>
         <td>no</td>
         <td>yes</td>
         <td>no</td>
       </tr>
       <tr>
         <td>Tummult Hype</td>
         <td>http://tumult.com/hype/</td>
         <td>no</td>
         <td>no</td>
         <td>yes</td>
       </tr>
     </tbody>
   </table>
 </body>
</html>
```

The problem with this table is that when it gets down to really narrow widths, it becomes unreadable. In browsers around 650px wide, the table grows too large for the screen and causes horizontal scrolling. If you reduce the font size from the default 16px to 14px, horizontal scrolling doesn't appear until around 480px.

Rearranging Table Rows and Columns

Another solution to responsive tables is to rearrange how the data is displayed. To use this solution, you need to understand how customers will use the data in the table.

Listing 17.1 shows a table in which information needs to be comparable. Listing 17.2 shows a table where each row of data can stand alone.

LISTING 17.2   Contact Information Table

```
<!doctype html>
<html lang="en">
  <head>
    <meta charset="utf-8">
    <title>Contact Information Table</title>
```

```
    <meta name="viewport"
          content="width=device-width,initial-scale=1">
  </head>
  <body>
    <table width="100%" border="1">
      <thead>
        <tr>
          <th>Name</th>
          <th>Title</th>
          <th>Home Page</th>
          <th>Email</th>
        </tr>
      </thead>
      <tbody>
        <tr>
          <td>Jennifer Kyrnin</td>
          <td>Chief Dandylion Officer</td>
          <td>https://htmljenn.com/</td>
          <td>htmljenn@gmail.com</td>
        </tr>
        <tr>
          <td>McKinley</td>
          <td>Dandelion Observation Officer</td>
          <td>http://responsivewebdesignin24hours.com/mckinley</td>
          <td>mckinley@rwdin24hours.com</td>
        </tr>
        <tr>
          <td>Rambler</td>
          <td>Chief Taste Tester</td>
          <td>http://responsivewebdesignin24hours.com/rambler</td>
          <td>rambler@rwdin24hours.com</td>
        </tr>
      </tbody>
    </table>
  </body>
</html>
```

Because of the URLs, this table breaks the container at around 720px, and because it includes contact information, we don't want to mess with the font size, so we need to adjust how the table displays.

One way to do that is to change the table from a horizontal list of items to a vertical list, with each item displayed individually. Listing 17.3 shows the CSS to display the table, and Figure 17.3 shows what it looks like.

LISTING 17.3   CSS to Rearrange a Table

```
table {
  border-collapse: collapse;
}
table { border: none; }
/* display the whole table as a block */
table, thead, tbody, th, td, tr {
  display: block;
}
/* Hide the headers */
thead tr {
  position: absolute;
  top: -9999px;
  left: -9999px;
}
tr { border: 1px solid #ccc; margin-bottom: 1em; }
tr:nth-of-type(odd) {
  background: #eee;
}
td {
  /* Behave  like a "row" */
  border: none;
  border-bottom: 1px solid #eee;
  position: relative;
  padding-left: 20%;
}
td:before {
  /* Now like a table header */
  position: absolute;
  /* Top/left values mimic padding */
  top: 1px;
  left: 6px;
  width: 45%;
  padding-right: 10px;
  white-space: nowrap;
}
/* Label the data */
td:nth-of-type(1):before { content: "Name"; }
td:nth-of-type(2):before { content: "Title"; }
td:nth-of-type(3):before { content: "Home Page"; }
td:nth-of-type(4):before { content: "Email"; }
```

We found this technique on Chris Coyier's CSS-Tricks site (https://css-tricks.com/responsive-data-tables/). This technique involves turning the table elements (`<table>`, `<tr>`, `<td>`, and so on) into block elements, hiding the `<th>` elements (but not removing them with `display:none;` so that the table is still accessible), and adding a separate line header for each row in the table.

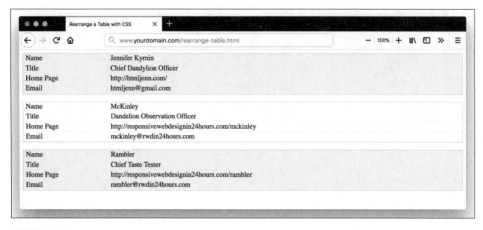

FIGURE 17.3
Rearranging table cells with CSS.

But you're not limited to rearranging the table: You can also change how the data is displayed, such as by changing from a table to a graphic or a chart. As long as the data is available to your mobile customers, displaying a graphical chart instead of a table can work. And you might find that the chart is useful to larger-screen devices as well.

Hiding Table Content

Another option for displaying tables is to hide rows or columns. But to do this, you need to know which items in the table are the most important. You can remove the less important data from the HTML or you can use the `display: none;` CSS property to remove less important data with CSS.

The problem with hiding the data is that some customers will want to see that data, even if it's harder to read on their devices. Most tables break the design because the data is too wide for the layout, and so the entire design must scroll horizontally. But while horizontal scrolling of the entire page is bad, most smartphone users understand what is happening when they see a scroll-bar below a table and can easily scroll from right to left inside that table.

The trick is to use a `<div>` tag around the table and put the scrollbars on it. First, surround the entire table with a `<div>` tag, like so:

```
<div class="responsive">
  <table width="100%" border="1">
    ...
  </table>
</div>
```

Instead of styling the table, you add overflow values to the `<div>` itself, like so:

```
.responsive-table {
  width: 100%;
  margin-bottom: 15px;
```

```
 overflow-y: hidden;
 overflow-x: scroll;
 -ms-overflow-style: -ms-autohiding-scrollbar;
 border: 1px solid #ddd;
 -webkit-overflow-scrolling: touch;
}
```

This causes the table to take up as much room as it needs in order to be legible, with any overflow on the <div> hidden by the scrollbar. Customers can then scroll left or right to see the entire table even on small-screen devices.

How to Make Images Responsive

Many web designers automatically include the width and height of images in the HTML, like so:

```
<img src="my-image.jpg" alt="my image" width="100" height="50">
```

The <img> tag has a src attribute that defines the location of the image, an alt attribute that provides alternative text if the image can't display for some reason, and width and height attributes that define how much space the image should take up in the design.

But if you explicitly set the image height and width in either the HTML or the CSS, the images will remain the same size even if the rest of the design is responsive. And in smaller windows, large images don't work well.

The main problem with many images is that they are too big for mobile screens. The images don't flex with the design. In fact, they are not responsive at all. There are three ways you can deal with images in a responsive web design:

- ▶ Use the images as you always would.
- ▶ Set the image width to something flexible.
- ▶ Change what images are displayed depending device properties.

The first solution has just one advantage: It's easy. The other two solutions are much better because they allow the images to be responsive.

Using Flexible-Width Images

Using flexible-width images is often the best solution for most websites because it's almost as easy as doing nothing and results in images that flex with the browser width. All you need to do is set the width and max-width of your images to 100% and the height to auto, like so:

```
img { width: 100%; max-width: 100%; height: auto; }
```

CAUTION

With most web page editors, when you add an image, the editor automatically includes the width and height attributes on the <img> tag. CSS will override these values, but if you don't set height for your images, you will end up with some really ugly images. Setting height to auto tells the browser to use a height that has the same ratio as the original image.

To use Mobile First, set the img rule in your global style sheet before any media queries, so that it applies to all devices. Then test your design in several browser widths and see what happens. Chances are you'll need to add some container width information so that the images don't blow out the entire browser window in some sizes.

Setting the width so that the images flex with their containers works well, but you will want to upload images that are large so that they look good on large-screen monitors. But the larger you make the images, the longer they will take to download.

Changing the Images Displayed with srcset and sizes

While most responsive solutions are done with CSS, you can create responsive image solutions right in the HTML. The <img> element has two attributes—srcset and sizes—that you can use to define different images to display on different devices.

The srcset attribute is added to the <img> element to define a list of images to use on devices with different pixel densities. For example, as mentioned earlier in this lesson, Retina displays on Apple devices have at least 2 pixels for every 1 pixel on a non-Retina display.

You can define different images to display at different pixel densities in a comma-separated list, like so:

```
<img srcset="images/myImage.jpg 1x,
            images/myImage-2x.jpg 2x,
            images/myImage-3x.jpg 3x"
     src="images/myImage.jpg" alt="My Image">
```

In this example, 1x, 2x, and 3x define the densities at which the preceding image should display. You can define any number of densities with the x descriptor, and you can also use the value hd to select for high-density devices. The src attribute is used in older browsers that don't support the srcset attribute.

But you can also define images based on the device width by using the w descriptor. This describes the width of the image being referenced. You define it in the same way as previously, like so:

```
<img srcset="images/myImage.jpg 100w,
            images/myImage-2x.jpg 200w,
            images/myImage-3x.jpg 400w"
     src="images/myImage.jpg" alt="My Image">
```

Then if you want to change the space the image takes up, you can use the `sizes` attribute. If you have just one size defined, such as `sizes="50vw"`, then the image will take up that much space in all devices—in this case 50% of the viewport window. `sizes` is especially useful when you add media queries to it, like so:

```
sizes="(max-width: 40em) 100vw, 50vw"
```

Media queries are covered in more detail in Lesson 18, but for now, just think of them as a simple `if` statement. In this case, the browser looks at the maximum width of the device, and if it is 40em or less (`(max-width: 40em)`), then the image size should be 100% of the viewport window (`100vw`). Otherwise, it should be 50% of the viewport window (`50vw`).

Use the `srcset` attribute alone when you need multiple versions of the same image at different resolutions, and in this case, use the `x` descriptor. Use `srcset` with `sizes` when you need multiple versions of the image at different sizes, and in this case, use the `w` descriptor.

Changing Images by Using the `<picture>` Element

What if you need to use different images on different devices but want to adjust those images based on resolution as well? For this you need to use the `<picture>` and `<source>` elements. These elements define images in a similar fashion to how you define video and audio with the `<video>` and `<audio>` elements.

You can use the `<picture>` element to contain the different `<source>` elements. Each `<source>` has a media query built into it in the `media` attribute that tells the browser when to use those defined images. In addition, each `<source>` uses a `srcset` attribute (and `sizes` if you want) to define the images for each resolution:

```
<picture>
  <source srcset="images/myImage.jpg 1x,
                  images/myImage-2x.jpg 2x,
                  images/myImage-3x.jpg hd"
          media="(max-width: 30rem)">
  <source srcset="images/myImage.jpg 1x,
                  images/myImage-2x.jpg 2x,
                  images/myImage-3x.jpg hd"
          media="(max-width: 50rem)">
  <img src="images/myImage.jpg" alt="My Image">
</picture>
```

As before, the `src` attribute defines the fallback if the browser doesn't support the `<picture>` and `<source>` tags.

Deciding When to Use Different Images

It's tempting to use different images all over the place, if only to prove that you can. But the best sites adjust the images to suit the design, not the designer. By using pictures that have the same image but are different resolutions, you allow browsers to download the image version that is best for a particular device. This means you can create an image that has a high resolution but small physical size for high-density small screens. Then you can create the same image with a larger physical size (and thus longer download time) for larger screens.

You should create an entirely new image when the size of the device screen makes an image difficult to understand. For example, you might have a photo of a giant vista with a person standing off in the distance. On a large 4k screen, the entire vista would look stunning on the page. But while an iPhone can display the image without a problem, the person standing in the distance might be too small to easily see on the smaller screen. In this case, using HTML or CSS to display a completely different image would make sense. You can zoom in on the subject of the photo to make it more obvious what is important in that image or simply display a completely different image that provides the same information.

Creating Responsive Layouts Without Media Queries

Using media queries is the most common way to create different layouts on devices of different sizes, but one technique that many people overlook is using CSS columns. In Lesson 6, "Working with Fonts, Text Blocks, Lists, and Tables," you learned about how to write CSS columns to create layouts. What you may not have realized is that you can use CSS columns to create responsive layouts.

You can create columns by declaring the column count or the column width. But if you declare both, such as with the `columns` property, you create a column layout that will adjust depending upon the width of the browser.

Listing 17.4 shows some HTML that uses columns.

LISTING 17.4   Responsive Columns Without Media Queries

```
<!doctype html>
<html lang="en">
  <head>
    <meta charset="utf-8">
    <title>A Responsive Column Layout without Media Queries</title>
    <meta name="viewport"
          content="width=device-width,initial-scale=1">
    <style>
      article {
        columns: 2 20rem;
      }
    </style>
```

```
  </head>
  <body>
    <h1>A Responsive Column Layout without Media Queries</h1>
    <article>
      <p>Lorem ipsum dolor sit amet, consectetur adipisicing el</p>
      <p>... additional content here</p>
    </article>
  </body>
</html>
```

At full size, as shown in Figure 17.4, the page displays with two columns that fill the screen. But if the browser is smaller than 20rems in width, the page displays as one column, as shown in Figure 17.5.

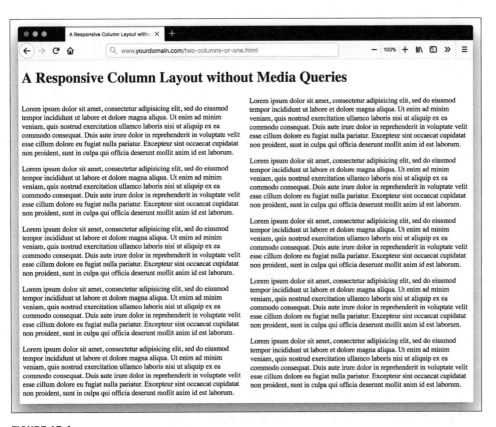

FIGURE 17.4
A page displayed at full size with two columns.

FIGURE 17.5
A page displayed in responsive design mode at 320px wide with one column.

Another responsive feature of this page is that it uses rems for the column width. The rem unit of length depends upon the size of the font on the page. So, if the customer changes the font size in the browser, the layout size will change as well.

It's important to remember that responsive design is more than just media queries. By considering mobile devices and taking the time to design for them, you make your pages responsive.

Alternatives for Mobile Design Besides RWD

RWD is not the only solution for mobile design. There are other things you can do to create mobile websites—and there are good reasons to use them. The most common alternatives are using adaptive design and dynamic serving and using completely separate sites for mobile. Some designers also create an app to run on mobile devices as an alternative to the website.

Why RWD Might Not Be the Answer

Responsive web design can be difficult to do well. It's easy to create a site that is huge and slow to load. This is the opposite of what you want for a mobile site. In most cases, when you use RWD, especially with media queries, the same content, CSS, and scripts are loaded on every device. And this can slow pages excessively.

Another aspect of RWD that is difficult to do well is content management. As mentioned previously, a mobile customer has different goals and desires when viewing a website from a desktop customer. By creating a site that is one-size-fits-all, you make it very difficult for some customers to do what they want to do.

Finally, while most people view web pages in modern, up-to-date browsers and devices, some people don't. And RWD primarily relies on technology that needs modern, up-to-date browsers and devices. On older devices and browsers, a page might load more slowly or possibly not at all.

What Are Adaptive Design and Dynamic Serving?

With *adaptive design*, a designer creates multiple versions of a site to better accommodate the devices viewing it. It can be argued that RWD is a form of adaptive web design because it changes the site depending on the device viewing it. It gets interesting when you use the web server to detect information about the device viewing the page and then deliver the different designs appropriately.

With adaptive design, pages are designed for common screen widths, such as these:

- 320px
- 480px
- 760px
- 960px
- 1200px
- 1600px

As with responsive design, you should start with the smallest screen and move up. Use all the same techniques you've learned to create good websites but adapt the design to best fit the device size.

The second part of adaptive design is the delivery of the pages. This is why it's also called *dynamic serving*. With dynamic serving, the server responds with different HTML, CSS, and JavaScript on the same URL, depending upon the device requesting the page.

Designers commonly make mistakes such as the following when setting up dynamic serving:

- **Blocked content**—You should let all your content—including JavaScript, CSS, and images—be seen by every device and especially by search engine robots. You should also never display a 404 page to only certain devices.
- **Unplayable content**—Some types of media are not playable on various mobile devices, and if you feature that content, you will frustrate many of your customers.

▶ **Incorrect redirects**—One way that dynamic serving is done is by redirecting customers to specific URLs. But if a desktop customer is redirected to mobile, for example, that can be very annoying.

▶ **Links to incorrect pages**—If you have sent a customer to a mobile version of the site, the links should not point to the desktop version.

Using a Separate URL or Domain

Many people consider using a separate domain such as m.*yourdomain*.com for mobile customers to be an old-fashioned way to handle mobile. But it does work. And some very popular sites use mobile domains, including Facebook and Home Depot.

Creating a separate, parallel website for mobile may seem like a lot of work, but if you have a database-driven site with hundreds, thousands, or millions of pages, it can be a lot easier to simply redirect all mobile customers to a different domain.

You should be aware that creating a separate site/domain for your mobile customers could result in a penalty in search engine optimization. Most sites link to the desktop version of a site rather than the mobile one, and when this happens, you lose out on the back links. You also have to create a separate sitemap for the mobile site so that search engines find and index the pages correctly. You'll learn more about search engine optimization in Lesson 28, "Organizing and Managing a Website."

Summary

In this lesson you learned a lot about mobile web design. You learned about how to design effective mobile pages and what design features you should avoid, such as slow-loading pages and images and Flash.

This lesson also covered Mobile First design, where you start with the mobile version of a site design and make sure you have everything there before moving on to larger and larger screens. You learned that your focus should be on content rather than features. But you should stay aware of the technologies that mobile devices use.

This lesson gave you some techniques for making images and tables responsive. You can use what you learned in this lesson along with the media queries you'll learn in Lesson 18 to create tables and images that work well on both mobile and nonmobile screens.

Finally, you learned some techniques for how to build responsive pages without media queries as well as some alternatives to responsive web design. The fact is that RWD is not the best option in all situations, and you can use dynamic serving or a completely separate domain to ensure that mobile users get the features and content they need and want.

Q&A

Q. How can I implement dynamic serving?

A. The most common method is with server-side browser sniffing or device detection. Most corporate websites that use dynamic serving use a service such as DeviceAtlas (https://deviceatlas.com/) or WURFL (http://wurfl.sourceforge.net/). Some people recommend using user-agent strings, but these are ridiculously inaccurate.

Q. Is Mobile First automatically responsive?

A. The short answer is no. Mobile First is a way of thinking of web design. A site can be designed with Mobile First goals but may not be responsive. And a responsive site can be designed without considering mobile customers first.

Workshop

The Workshop contains quiz questions and activities to help you solidify your understanding of the material covered. Try to answer all questions before looking at the "Answers" section that follows.

Quiz

1. What are three things that a mobile-friendly site should consider?

2. What are three things you should always do when building a mobile-friendly site?

3. What is Mobile First design?

4. What should you focus on when designing for mobile devices first?

5. What are some technologies that can primarily be found on mobile devices?

6. What types of situations work well for mobile apps?

7. Why do data tables fail on mobile devices?

8. What are three ways you can adjust data tables to work on smaller screens?

9. What does the `srcset` attribute do for images?

10. What CSS property can make a layout change from three columns to one column, depending on the device width?

NOTE

Just a reminder for those of you reading these words in the print or e-book edition of this book: If you go to **www.informit.com/register** and register this book (using ISBN 9780672338083), you can receive free access to an online Web Edition that not only contains the complete text of this book but also features an interactive version of this quiz.

Answers

1. There are many aspects to mobile-friendly design, but some specifics include not using Flash, configuring the viewport, avoiding fixed-width designs, making elements fit in the design, using legible font sizes, and making links and buttons tappable.

2. You should always create a simple navigation and layout, make the page load as quickly as possible, and test the design on real devices.

3. Mobile First design is a philosophy in which you design for the smallest devices first and make sure that they have everything they need to view and use the site. Then you create the larger versions of the site.

4. You should focus primarily on the content. Consider what content is required to view and use the site and make sure that even the smallest devices can access it.

5. There are lots of mobile-only technologies, including geolocation, touch-screen interfaces, web storage, offline applications, and mobile web applications. Some of these can be used on desktop computers as well.

6. Mobile apps work best for mobile gaming, personalized content, complex reporting, functionality that is only available on mobile devices (for example, GPS), and offline access.

7. The most common reason data tables fail is that they are too wide for the screen. They often contain more information than is readily consumable on a small device.

8. You can change the size of the table cells or contents, rearrange the table, or remove or hide content to make data tables more usable on small screens.

9. The `srcset` attribute defines a list of images to display at different pixel densities.

10. The CSS property `columns` lets you define both the maximum number of columns and the minimum width for those columns. You can create a design that can change from three columns to one column with the style rule `columns: 3 200px;`.

Exercise

▶ Consider the site you are building. Would it benefit from a separate mobile site? Why or why not? What are some of the reasons you might not want to design it with RWD?

LESSON 18

Using Media Queries and Breakpoints

What You'll Learn in This Lesson:

▶ How to write a CSS media query

▶ How to use different media types

▶ How to create media query expressions

▶ Understanding logical keywords in your queries

▶ What CSS breakpoints are

▶ How to define breakpoints

▶ How to find the best breakpoints for your website

For many people, the term *responsive web design* is synonymous with CSS media queries. And while it's possible to have a responsive site without using media queries, using them is the most common way of doing RWD. This lesson will take you through how to write a media query as well as what the different types of queries, keywords, and expressions are.

Breakpoints are the points where media queries adjust the design. Even if you have only one break-point, your web page will respond to the presence of that breakpoint and respond appropriately to user agents that match. In this lesson you will learn what breakpoints are and how to use them. Plus, you'll learn what makes good breakpoints to support a wide variety of devices.

What Is a Media Query?

According to the W3C, a media query is a "logical expression that is either true or false. A media query is true if the media type of the media query matches the media type of the device...." What this is saying is that a web designer can use a media query to define if/then statements based on the characteristics of the device viewing the page.

CSS media types were introduced in the CSS specification in CSS2, and media queries were added in CSS3. Media queries became a full-fledged recommendation in June 2012, but they have been supported by browsers since before 2010. CSS media queries are a stable tool, and web designers should feel confident that modern browsers and user agents support them.

When you are building a media query, you use the @media rule. You then define the media types the rule applies to, as well as the features of that type that you want to focus on. You place these rules right in your CSS style sheet, using the following syntax:

@media *mediaType* and (*mediaFeature*) { }

Using Media Types

There are 10 media types you can test for with CSS media queries:

- all—All media
- braille—Braille and tactile feedback devices
- embossed—Paged braille printers
- handheld—Small-screen low-bandwidth handheld devices
- print—Paged media and documents in print preview mode
- projection—Projected presentations
- screen—Color computer screens
- speech—Speech synthesizers
- tty—Teletypes and media with a fixed-pitch character grid
- tv—Television

CAUTION

The handheld media type was originally used to apply to cell phones and PDAs and other handheld devices, but most cell phone manufacturers wrote their devices to report back a screen media type because they didn't want their customers to be penalized by web designers not wanting to give handheld customers the full experience. So you cannot rely on this media type to detect mobile devices.

The most common media type web designers use is screen because modern cell phones, tablets, and all computer monitors use this designation.

You can use the print media type to create a style sheet for printing web pages. This common way of using media types allows web designers to control how their web pages look when they are printed out.

To create a print style sheet, open a new CSS document for your print styles. Best practices recommend that you do things like remove advertising, change the color of links to the text color, add underlines to links if they are removed, and remove the background colors so they don't print.

You load a style sheet as you would a normal style sheet except that you add the `media` type to your `<link>` element, like so:

```
<link href="print.css" rel="stylesheet" media="print">
```

You can test that the print styles are applied by opening the page in a browser and choosing Print Preview.

You write a print style sheet exactly the way you write any other style sheet. However, because it is a style sheet for print, you can use a few styles you otherwise might ignore, such as `page-break-before`, `page-break-after`, and `page-break-inside`. Because web pages don't have page breaks, these styles aren't used in screen style sheets.

You can set the media type in any style sheet link with the `media` attribute. But most designers leave it off because the default is `all`.

Setting the `media` type in the `<link>` tag is not the best way to define styles for `media` types because it forces the browser to request and load multiple style sheets. The same is true if you use the `@import` rule. Table 18.1 shows how to use the three different methods to include media queries. The first method is in the HTML, and the other two are right in the CSS document.

TABLE 18.1 Three Ways to Add Media Queries

Method	Description
`<link media="type" href="url" rel="stylesheet">`	Use the `media` attribute on a link tag to define media queries as the style sheet is loaded.
`@import url("url") type;`	Include the `media` type in the `@import` command to define media queries when a style sheet is imported.
`@media type { … }`	Include media-specific styles directly in another style sheet to limit the scope of the enclosed styles.

Best practices are to define styles for different media types all in the same style sheet document, using the `@media` rule, like so.

1. Open your style sheet file in a web page editor or text editor.

2. Add the styles you want to apply to all media types at the top of your style sheet. You do not need any media rules to define them.

3. Add the media-specific rules with the `@media` rule. To include a print style sheet, write the following:

```
@media print {
  // put print styles here, such as:
  a:link {
```

```
    color: black;
    text-decoration: underline;
  }
}
```

4. Include as many different media types as you need. Just remember to include all their styles in a separate curly braces block ({   }).

NOTE

Requesting multiple CSS documents with the `<link>` element or `@import` rule will slow down your website. By keeping your media queries all in one CSS document, you reduce the number of requests to the server, and this improves the speed at which your web pages load. For example, if you have three 1KB CSS files you need to load, if you use `@import` or `<link>` tags to include them all, the browser sends three separate requests for each file and has to wait for three responses from the server. If each request and response takes half a second, you've added an extra two seconds to the download time for all three files.

Here's how it would look:

```
request file 1 (.5s)

response file 1 (.5s)

download file 1 (1KB)

request file 2 (.5s)

response file 2 (.5s)

download file 2 (1KB)

request file 3 (.5s)

response file 3 (.5s)

download file 3 (1KB)
```

This gives you a total of the time it takes to download 3KB plus 3 seconds of request and response time. If you combine all three files into one 3KB file, you have the same download time (for 3KB) but only one request and response (1s). Yes, 0.5s is an extremely slow request and response, but even fast response times add up. If you have 10 CSS files, plus another 10 JavaScript files, plus other server requests (images, media, and so on), your site will be slowed down considerably.

Using Media Features

CSS media queries get really interesting when it comes to media features. Rather than limit your designs just to specific media types (screen versus print, for example), media features let you look at the specific features of the media and style your pages accordingly.

There are 13 media features you can test for:

▶ `aspect-ratio`—A ratio of the width of the device to the height

▶ `color`—The number of bits per color component

▶ `color-index`—The number of colors in the device's color input title

▶ `device-aspect-ratio`—The ratio of the device width to the device height

▶ `device-height`—The height of the rendering surface

▶ `device-width`—The width of the rendering surface

▶ `grid`—Whether the device is a grid (such as tty devices or phones with only one font) or bitmap

▶ `height`—The height of the display area

▶ `monochrome`—The number of bits per pixel in monochrome devices; if the device isn't monochrome, the value will be 0

▶ `orientation`—Whether the device is in portrait or landscape mode

▶ `resolution`—The pixel density of the device, in print, which would be the dots per inch (dpi) of the printer

▶ `scan`—The scanning process of TV output devices, such as progressive scanning

▶ `width`—The width of the display area

CAUTION

The `device-width` and `device-height` features are confusing to most web designers at first, as it doesn't seem like there is any difference between them and the related `width` and `height` features, especially on mobile devices. But there is a difference, and it's important. The `width` is the width of the browser window, while `device-width` is the width of the device itself. You can see this most effectively on a computer. When you set a media query with `max-device-width` and then resize the browser, the page will not change, no matter how much you resize. This is because the device width is the computer monitor, and it doesn't change.

This may not seem to matter on mobile devices, but on iOS devices, `device-width` is always the width in portrait mode, *even if the device is in landscape*. On Android devices, however, `device-width` (along with `device-height` and `device-aspect-ratio`) changes when the device is rotated.

Nearly all the media features also have two prefixes you can use to evaluate: `min-` and `max-`. These prefixes evaluate the feature based on whether it is a minimum amount (`min-`) or a maximum amount (`max-`). For example, to set a style sheet to apply to all browsers with at least a width of 320px, you would write the following:

```
@media (min-width: 320px) { ... }
```

And if you wanted to target devices with browsers no wider than 1024px, you would write this:

```
@media (max-width: 1024px) { ... }
```

As you can see, you add the media features to the @media rule with the word and and then enclose your features in parentheses. If you want to get more specific, add more features. For example, to target browsers between 640px and 980px wide, you can write the following:

```
@media (min-width: 640px) and (max-width: 980px) { ... }
```

Notice that none of the expressions just mentioned use a media type. That is because if the media type is left off, it applies to all devices, regardless of type.

Using Media Query Expressions

In order to use media queries effectively, you need to know how to write expressions. In the previous section you learned three basic expressions to target browsers above a certain minimum width, to target browsers below a maximum width, and to target browsers that fall between a minimum width and a maximum width. But you can create much more complicated expressions.

Media query expressions use logical operators to define complex scenarios. These are the operators you can use:

- ▶ **and**—This combines features and types together. The query will match if all elements are present. For example, the following would match a device in landscape mode with a 768px browser window:

  ```
  @media (min-width: 760px) and (orientation: landscape) { ... }
  ```

- ▶ **Comma-separated list**—This is equivalent to the OR logical operator. In a comma-separated list of features or types, if any of them are true, the query will match. For example, this would match both a 480px browser in landscape mode and an 800px browser in portrait mode:

  ```
  @media (min-width: 760px), (orientation: landscape) { ... }
  ```

- ▶ **not**—This negates the entire query. The query will match if the query would normally return false. For example, the following would match a 480px browser that is in portrait mode:

  ```
  @media not (min-width: 760px) and (orientation: landscape) { ... }
  ```

NOTE

The not operator can be confusing to use, but one thing to remember is that it applies only to the entire expression, not individual features. In other words, if you write @media not screen and (max-width:400px), your query will match everything that is both not a screen-based device and that has a width larger than 400px. It helps if you remember to evaluate the not last. So, you write the expression the opposite of what you want and then apply the not operator to the front.

▸ `only`—This prevents browsers that don't support media queries from applying the styles. For example, the following will block extremely old browsers from using the style sheet:

```
@media only screen { ... }
```

Media query expressions are the basis of responsive web design. With them you can define very complex formulas for your style sheets and make sure that the designs look exactly the way you want them to.

What Is a Breakpoint?

A CSS breakpoint is a device feature with a media query declaration assigned to it. They are most commonly based on browser widths, so most designers think of breakpoints as places where the width of the design changes to accommodate different devices.

Most responsive designs have at least one breakpoint that changes the look of the design.

NOTE

Most experts recommend at least two breakpoints so that your site has three versions: one for small mobile devices, one for midsized tablets, and one for desktop computer screens. But for best results, you should use the breakpoints that are right for your website.

Before you decide that you're going to have 10 breakpoints or some other arbitrary number, you need to remember that each additional breakpoint adds to the cost of building and maintaining the website. For each breakpoint in your design, you add one more version of the page to style. In other words, you have to style the page even if you have no breakpoints. When you add one breakpoint, you then have a second version of the page to style, and so on.

How to Define Breakpoints in Your CSS

Defining breakpoints is done with CSS media queries. The most common type of breakpoint is based on the width of the device. Listing 18.1 shows the CSS file for a Mobile First site with three breakpoints: one for every browser (the smallest widths), one for widths between 480px and 1200px (larger smartphones and smaller tablets), and one for widths larger than 1200px.

LISTING 18.1 A Page with Two Breakpoints

```
<!doctype html>
<html lang="en">
  <head>
    <meta charset="utf-8">
    <title>A Page with Two Breakpoints</title>
```

```
<style>
  body {
    color: blue;
    font-family: "Handwriting - Dakota", Papyrus;
  }
  @media all and (min-width:480px) and (max-width:1200px){
    body { color: red; }
  }
  @media screen and (min-width:1201px){
    body { color: green; }
  }
</style>
<meta name="viewport"
      content="width=device-width,initial-scale=1">
</head>
<body>
  <p>Lorem ipsum dolor sit amet, consectetur adipiscing elit.
  Etiam id purus nec eros semper luctus. Proin nisl lectus,
  ullamcorper ultrices leo in, tristique rutrum risus. Morbi
  congue diam tempor lorem semper, congue tempor turpis pretium.
  Nunc eget dui ut lorem auctor ornare. Vivamus lectus purus,
  vehicula eu velit eu, iaculis ultrices dui. Aliquam consectetur
  risus non ligula blandit, et gravida lectus bibendum. Etiam
  laoreet luctus nibh. Nulla sit amet lorem quis arcu accumsan
  mollis.</p>
</body>
</html>
```

Listing 18.1 shows very simple styles that simply change the color of the text depending on the size of the browser—blue for small screens, red for medium-sized screens, and green for large screens. In Figure 18.1 the text is red, and in Figure 18.2 the text is blue.

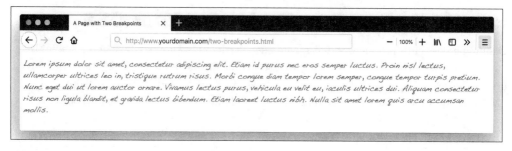

FIGURE 18.1
A page viewed in Firefox at 1024 pixels wide.

FIGURE 18.2
A page viewed in Firefox design mode on a 320px-wide device.

Defining the Styles That Remain the Same for Every Device

When you're writing a style sheet for a responsive website, the first styles you want to define are the ones that are the same no matter what device views them. This is another way of using the Mobile First philosophy. These styles include the following:

▸ Reset styles

▸ Colors

▸ Font families

▸ Background images

While it's certainly possible that you could have designs that use different colors, font families, resets, and background images, depending on the device, most websites like to keep a consistent branding. And by keeping these things the same, you reassure your customers that they are on the same page no matter what device they are using.

Listing 18.2 shows a basic style sheet with some initial styles.

LISTING 18.2   Initial Styles for a Web Page

```
@charset "UTF-8";
/* reset styles here */

/* standard colors */
body { background-color: #fff; color: #000; }
h1, h2 { color: #fbd91f;  /* yellow */ }
h3, h4, h5 { color: #000; }

/* standard fonts */
h1, h2, h3 {
  font-family: Baskerville, "Times New Roman", serif;
}
h1 {
  text-shadow:2px 3px 3px #000000;
  margin-bottom: 0.5em;
}
h2 {
  text-shadow: 2px 2px 0 rgba(0,0,0,.5);
  margin-bottom: 0.5em;
}

/* background image on the header */
header {
  width: 100%;
  padding: 0.5em 0 3em 0.25em;
  background-image: url(images/dandy-header-bg.png);
  background-repeat: no-repeat;
  background-size: cover;
  background-position: 0% 100%;
}
```

While some of the styles set here may be changed for specific devices, this is a good baseline. We set a base font family for our headlines. We gave the document black text and a white background. And we defined a background image for the header. As with any other design, there is always more to do, but this is a start.

Adding Specific Styles for Small Screens

Once you've got your basic styles for any machine in the style sheet, you need to add styles specific to the smallest screens. You should put them below your styles for all devices, but *not inside a media query*. These smallest-screen styles will be overwritten on larger screens by the styles in the media queries because of the CSS cascade.

You should add styles that make your pages as mobile friendly as possible, considering things like the following:

▶ The width of every content element should be 100% to fill the screen.

▶ This means you'll have one column of content.

▶ Lists, especially lists of links, should have a lot of space between list items, to make them easy to read and click.

Listing 18.3 shows some of the styles added at this stage, and Figure 18.3 shows how this might look on a small-screen phone.

LISTING 18.3   CSS Added for Small Screens

```
/* ######## mobile specific styles ######## */
/* headlines */
h1 { font-size: 2em; }
h2 { font-size: 1.5em; }

/* navigation bar */
nav { width: 100%; background-color: #000; color: #fbd91f; }
nav ul { padding-top: 0.15em; padding-bottom: 0.15em; }
nav ul li { margin: 0 0 0.5em 0.2em; }

/* article */
article { width: 100%; padding: 0.25em; }
article img { width: 100%; height: auto; }

/* aside */
aside { width: 100%; }
aside img { width: 100%; height: auto; }
```

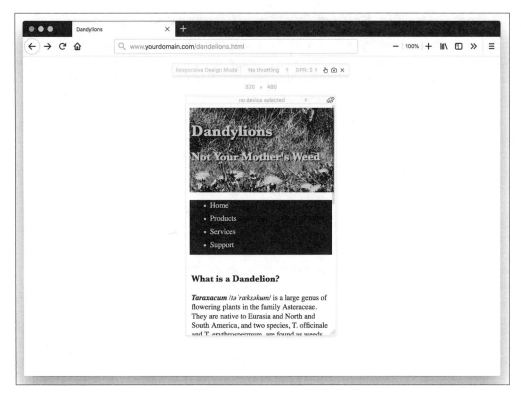

FIGURE 18.3
Viewing a page in Firefox Responsive Design Mode at 320 pixels wide.

Adding Media Queries for Larger Screens

The last thing to add to your style sheet are the media queries with the styles specific to the breakpoints. The Dandylion page shown in Figure 18.3 has two breakpoints: one for medium-sized devices between 481px and 1200px wide and one for large devices with a width bigger than 1201px. Listing 18.4 shows the CSS.

LISTING 18.4 Media Queries in the CSS

```
/* ######## medium sized devices ######## */
@media (min-width: 481px) and (max-width: 1200px) {
}

/* ######## large sized devices ######## */
@media (min-width: 1201px) {
}
```

CAUTION

Remember that these style sheets use the cascade to set initial styles and then overwrite them with styles for other devices later in the document. If you aren't using a WYSIWYG editor or previewing your styles regularly, it can be easy to forget what already has a style. For example, you may set the width of the `article` element to 100%, but in larger screens you wouldn't want that as it would make the text lines too long to read. But if you forget to preview the styles at many different browser widths, you could be surprised at the result.

You need to remember the order of your CSS file. Because of the cascade, whatever styles come last will take precedence over styles that came before. So if you style the `article` element to have 100% width in the first section and then change that to 80% or something else in the medium- or large-sized device media queries, that is the style that will display.

Optimal Breakpoints

RWD beginners commonly wonder what are the best breakpoint numbers. It depends on your customers and your design.

You can use the widths of popular devices to come up with a breakpoint plan that works for your site, but a better solution is to choose breakpoints based on your design. View your site at different widths to see where it breaks. You can use Responsive Design Mode to slowly resize the window until the design breaks. A design is broken when the page is hard to read, content scrolls horizontally, images or text overlaps, or things just look wrong.

Best Practices for Breakpoints

Some of the best practices for choosing the breakpoints include the following:

▶ **Choose breakpoints for the design, not the device**—It's tempting to choose breakpoints for exactly the resolution of the devices you want to support (for example, a `min-width` of 720px to target iPhone 5S devices). But this is a mistake. It's better to choose a width based on where your design starts getting difficult to read or use.

▶ **Keep breakpoints 1px different**—When you use more than one breakpoint, make sure that the second one is exactly 1px wider or narrower than the first one. In other words, if your smallest breakpoint is for browsers with a width of 480px or smaller, then the next breakpoint should have a minimum width of 481px. If you use the same number for each, this can cause browsers that match that width to use the wrong styles.

▶ **Consider device orientation, not just width**—If you have the time and resources, you should consider changing your design based on the orientation of the device and not just the width.

▶ **Don't forget Retina devices**—Pages displayed on Retina displays and other high-pixel-density devices can look bad if your images aren't optimized for them.

Media Queries for Retina Devices

In Lesson 17, "Designing for Mobile Devices" you learned how to use the `srcset` and `sizes` attributes to display different images for different pixel densities. There is also a media query feature that you can use to define styles for high-pixel-density devices. This is the `resolution` feature. You use it just as you do other features, adding the `min-` or `max-` prefixes in your media query. The only browser exception is Safari, which still uses the `-webkit-device-pixel-ratio` feature.

Retina displays have a 2x pixel ratio, so you can define styles for Retina devices with this media query:

```
@media (-webkit-min-device-pixel-ratio: 2), /* Safari and iOS */
       (min-resolution: 192dpi)              /* Others */ {
}
```

You can define higher-density minimum resolutions by changing the dpi you match.

Summary

This lesson introduced you to the meat of responsive web design—media queries with breakpoints. With CSS media queries, you create style sheets that are written explicitly for the devices that you want to define. You can create style sheets only for specific media types or take more granular control with media features. You also learned how to create media query expressions.

You learned what a breakpoint is and how to choose good breakpoints for responsive design. You learned the CSS to create media queries around those breakpoints. And you also learned how to create media queries to detect Retina and other high-pixel-density devices.

Q&A

Q. What's the difference between CSS2 media queries and CSS3 media queries?

A. CSS2 doesn't have media queries, but you can define a style sheet for a specific media type. It wasn't until CSS3 that media queries were developed. Media queries let you define test structures surrounding media types and features that allow only the user agents that fit the query criteria to use the styles.

Q. Why is it important to design for the smallest devices first?

A. Most of the smallest devices are also the least feature rich. In order to build a site using progressive enhancement, you should focus on the minimum you need for the site to work. And that is what you should display to all customers—even those on small-screen devices, as discussed in more detail in Lesson 17, "Designing for Mobile Devices."

Q. Can I use other media features than just the width to set my breakpoints? Why does everyone only seem to use device widths?

A. The width is the easiest type of breakpoint to understand and test. When you use a minimum or maximum width, you can use your web browser to test your designs by simply resizing the browser window. As long as you're browsing on a fairly large screen, you can test nearly any device width. It's a lot harder to test orientation on a desktop computer monitor. But you can use any media feature you need to create the breakpoints that are best for your design.

Workshop

The Workshop contains quiz questions and activities to help you solidify your understanding of the material covered. Try to answer all questions before looking at the "Answers" section that follows.

Quiz

1. What is the official definition of *media query*?

2. What is the syntax of a media query?

3. What are five of the media types?

4. What are five of the media features?

5. What are two of the logical operators?

6. How many breakpoints do you need to create a responsive design?

7. What do best practices suggest as the minimum recommended number of breakpoints?

8. What is the CSS for a breakpoint that catches devices 400px and smaller?

9. What is the CSS for a breakpoint to catch all devices between 800 and 1600px wide?

10. What is the media query to detect Retina devices?

NOTE

Just a reminder for those of you reading these words in the print or e-book edition of this book: If you go to **www.informit.com/register** and register this book (using ISBN 9780672338083), you can receive free access to an online Web Edition that not only contains the complete text of this book but also features an interactive version of this quiz.

Answers

1. According to the W3C, a media query is a "logical expression that is either true or false. A media query is true if the media type of the media query matches the media type of the device."

2. The syntax of a media query looks like this:

   `@media mediaType and (mediaFeature)`

3. The 10 media types are `all`, `braille`, `embossed`, `handheld`, `print`, `projection`, `screen`, `speech`, `tty`, and `tv`.

4. The 13 media features are `aspect-ratio`, `color`, `color-index`, `device-aspect-ratio`, `device-height`, `device-width`, `grid`, `height`, `monochrome`, `orientation`, `resolution`, `scan`, and `width`.

5. The four operators are `and`, comma-separated phrases, `not`, and `only`.

6. A responsive design usually has at least one breakpoint, but it doesn't have to have any.

7. Best practices recommend that you have at least two breakpoints to catch small screens, midsized screens, and large screens.

8. This is the CSS for a breakpoint to catch all devices 400px and smaller:

   `@media screen and (max-width:400px) { }`

9. This is the CSS to catch all devices between 800 and 1600px wide:

   `@media screen and (min-width:800px) and (max-width:1600px) { }`

10. This is the media query to detect Retina devices:

    `@media (-webkit-min-device-pixel-ratio: 2),(min-resolution: 192dpi) { }`

Exercises

▶ Start practicing writing CSS media queries. Look at the site you've been evaluating through the book and decide what types of media features you want to focus on for your styles. For example, decide if you need designs for different widths, different orientations, or different aspect-ratios. Your analytics program can help with this by giving you information about what your current customers are using.

▶ Review the design of the site you're currently working on in Responsive Design Mode. Resize the window to see where the design breaks and decide what breakpoints you want to use for your design. Then create a CSS style sheet with a media query structure to support those breakpoints. Don't forget to add to your style sheet CSS styles that apply to all devices, regardless of device size.

Understanding Dynamic Websites and HTML5 Applications

What You'll Learn in This Lesson:

▶ How to conceptualize different types of dynamic content

▶ How to include JavaScript in your HTML

▶ How to display randomized text with JavaScript

▶ How to change images by using JavaScript and user events

▶ How to begin thinking ahead to putting all the pieces together to create HTML5 applications

The term *dynamic* refers to something active or something that motivates another person to become active. A dynamic website is one that incorporates interactivity into its functionality and design and that also motivates a user to take an action—read more, purchase a product, and so on. In this lesson, you'll learn about the types of interactivity that can make a site dynamic, including information about both server-side and client-side scripting (as well as some practical examples of the latter).

You've had a brief introduction to client-side scripting in Lesson 4, "Understanding JavaScript," and you used a little of it in Lesson 11, "Using CSS to Do More with Lists, Text, and Navigation," when you used event attributes and JavaScript to change the styles of particular elements—which is referred to as manipulating the Document Object Model (DOM). You'll do a bit more of that type of manipulation in this lesson. Specifically, after learning about the different technologies, you'll use JavaScript to display a random quote upon page load, and you'll swap images based on user interaction. Finally, having learned at least the keywords and the basic concepts involved in putting together the HTML, CSS, and JavaScript pieces, you'll be introduced to the possibilities that exist when you're creating HTML5 applications.

Understanding the Different Types of Scripting

In web development, two types of scripting exist: server side and client side. Both types of scripting—which is, in fact, a form of computer programming—are beyond the scope of these lessons. However, they are not *too* far beyond what these lessons cover. Two very useful and popular books in the *Sams Teach Yourself* series are natural extensions to these lessons: *Sams Teach Yourself PHP, MySQL, and JavaScript All in One* (for server-side scripting) and *Sams Teach Yourself JavaScript in 24 Hours* (for client-side scripting).

Server-side scripting refers to scripts that run on the web server, which then sends results to your web browser. If you have ever submitted a form at a website (which includes using a search engine), you have experienced the results of a server-side script. Some popular (and relatively easy-to-learn) server-side scripting languages include the following (to learn more, visit the websites listed):

- ▶ **Perl**—www.perl.org

- ▶ **PHP (PHP: Hypertext Preprocessor)**—www.php.net

- ▶ **Python**—www.python.org

- ▶ **Ruby**—www.ruby-lang.org

On the other hand, *client-side scripting* refers to scripts that run within your web browser; no interaction with a web server is required for the scripts to run. By far the most popular client-side scripting language is *JavaScript*. Recent research has shown that more than 98% of all web browsers have JavaScript enabled. And with the exception of Opera Mini, mobile operating systems support between 90% and 98% of all JavaScript features.

NOTE
_____
Despite its name, JavaScript is not a derivation of or even a close relative of the object-oriented programming language called Java. Released by Sun Microsystems in 1995, Java is closely related to the server-side scripting language JSP. JavaScript was created by Netscape Communications, also in 1995, and given the name to indicate a similarity in appearance to Java but not a direct connection with it.
_____

This lesson and of course the rest of these lessons assume the use of JavaScript for client-side scripting; the coding examples in these lessons are all JavaScript. There are other scripting languages out there, but they are not used by most web developers.

Including JavaScript in HTML

JavaScript code can live in one of two places in your files:

- ▶ In its own file with a .js extension

- ▶ Directly in your HTML files

External files are often used for script libraries (code you can reuse throughout many pages), whereas code that appears directly in the HTML files tends to achieve functionality specific to those individual pages. Regardless of where your JavaScript lives, your browser learns of its existence through the use of the `<script></script>` tag pair.

When you store your JavaScript in external files, it is referenced in this manner:

```
<script src="/path/to/script.js"></script>
```

These `<script></script>` tags are typically placed between the `<head></head>` tags because, strictly speaking, they are not content that belongs in the `<body>` of the page. Instead, the `<script>` tag makes available a set of JavaScript functions or other information that the rest of the page can then use. However, you can also just encapsulate your JavaScript functions or code snippets with the `<script>` tag and place them anywhere in the page, as needed. Listing 19.1 shows an example of a JavaScript snippet placed in the `<body>` of an HTML document.

NOTE

It is best practice to place scripts at the bottom of your page, just before the close of the `<body>` element. This ensures that your pages render without waiting to load the script. However, if you need the script to write content to the page, you need to write that content to the DOM rather than as plain HTML in the JavaScript, as otherwise it would just write that content at the end, which is likely not your intention.

LISTING 19.1   Using JavaScript to Print Some Text

```
<!doctype html>
<html lang="en">
  <head>
    <meta charset="utf-8">
    <title>JavaScript Example</title>
    <meta name="viewport"
          content="width=device-width, initial-scale=1">
  </head>
  <body>
    <h1>JavaScript Example</h1>
    <p>This text is HTML.</p>
    <script>
      <!-- Hide the script from old browsers
      document.write('<p>This text comes from JavaScript.</p>');
      // Stop hiding the script -->
    </script>
    <p>And this text is HTML again.</p>
  </body>
</html>
```

Between the `<script></script>` tags is a single JavaScript command that outputs the following HTML:

```
<p>This text comes from JavaScript.</p>
```

When the browser renders this HTML page, it sees the JavaScript between the `<script>` `</script>` tags, stops for a millisecond to execute the command, and then returns to rendering the output that now includes the HTML output from the JavaScript command. It then continues to render the rest of the HTML in the document. Figure 19.1 shows that this page appears as any other HTML page appears. It's an HTML page, but only a small part of the HTML comes from a JavaScript command.

FIGURE 19.1
The output of a JavaScript snippet looks like any other output.

NOTE

You might have noticed these two lines in Listing 19.1:

```
<!-- Hide the script from old browsers
// Stop hiding the script -->
```

This is an HTML comment. Anything between the `<!--` start and `-->` end will be visible in the source code but will not be rendered by the browser. In this case, JavaScript code is surrounded by HTML comments, on the off chance that your visitor is running a very old web browser or has JavaScript turned off. These days, nearly all browsers use or ignore JavaScript appropriately, but there's no harm in commenting it out for very old browsers or screen readers that do not handle JavaScript at all. You will learn more about comments in Lesson 28, "Organizing and Managing a Website."

Displaying Random Content

You can use JavaScript to display something different each time a page loads. Maybe you have a collection of text or images that you find interesting enough to include in your pages.

Lots of people are suckers for a good quote. You might find it fun to incorporate an ever-changing quote into your web pages. To create a page with a quote that changes each time the page loads, you must first gather all your quotes, along with their respective sources. You then place these quotes into a JavaScript *array*, which is a special type of storage unit in programming languages that is handy for holding lists of items.

After the quotes are loaded into an array, the JavaScript used to pluck out a quote at random is fairly simple (and explained momentarily). You've already seen the snippet that will print the output to your HTML page.

Listing 19.2 contains the complete HTML and JavaScript code for a web page that displays a random quote each time it loads.

LISTING 19.2 A Random-Quote Web Page

```
<!doctype html>
<html lang="en">
  <head>
    <meta charset="utf-8">
    <title>Quotable Quotes</title>
    <script>
      <!-- Hide the script from old browsers
      function getQuote() {
      // Create the arrays
      quotes = new Array(4);
      sources = new Array(4);

      // Initialize the arrays with quotes
      quotes[0] = "When I was a boy of 14, my father was so " +
      "ignorant...but when I got to be 21, I was astonished " +
      "at how much he had learned in 7 years.";
      sources[0] = "Mark Twain";

      quotes[1] = "Everybody is ignorant. Only on different " +
      "subjects.";
      sources[1] = "Will Rogers";

      quotes[2] = "They say such nice things about people at " +
      "their funerals that it makes me sad that I'm going to " +
      "miss mine by just a few days.";
      sources[2] = "Garrison Keillor";
```

```
            quotes[3] = "What's another word for thesaurus?";
            sources[3] = "Steven Wright";

            // Get a random index into the arrays
            i = Math.floor(Math.random() * quotes.length);

            // Write out the quote as HTML
            document.write("<p style='background-color: #ffb6c1' >\"");
            document.write(quotes[i] + "\"");
            document.write("<em>- " + sources[i] + "</em>");
            document.write("</p>");
            }
            // Stop hiding the script -->
        </script>
        <meta name="viewport"
              content="width=device-width, initial-scale=1">
    </head>
    <body>
        <h1>Quotable Quotes</h1>
        <p>Following is a random quotable quote. To see a new quote
        just reload this page.</p>

        <script>
          <!-- Hide the script from old browsers
          getQuote();
          // Stop hiding the script -->
        </script>
    </body>
</html>
```

Although this code looks kind of long, a lot of it consists of just the four quotes available for display on the page.

The large number of lines between the first set of <script></script> tags is creating a function called getQuote(). After a function is defined, it can be called in other places in the same page, as you see later in the code. Note that if the function existed in an external file, the function could be called from all your pages.

If you look closely at the code, you will see some lines like this:

```
// Create the arrays
```

and this:

```
// Initialize the arrays with quotes
```

These are code comments. A developer uses these types of comments to leave notes in the code so that anyone reading it has an idea of what the code is doing in that particular place. After the first comment about creating the arrays, you can see that two arrays are created—one called quotes and one called sources, each containing four elements:

```
quotes = new Array(4);
sources = new Array(4);
```

After the second comment (about initializing the arrays with quotes), four items are added to the arrays. Let's look closely at one of them, the first quote by Mark Twain:

```
quotes[0] = "When I was a boy of 14, my father was so " +
"ignorant...but when I got to be 21, I was astonished at " +
"how much he had learned in 7 years.";
sources[0] = "Mark Twain";
```

You already know that the arrays are named quotes and sources. But the variables to which values are assigned (in this instance) are called quotes[0] and sources[0]. Because quotes and sources are arrays, each item in the array has its own position. When you're using arrays, the first item in the array is not in slot 1; it is in slot 0. In other words, you begin counting at 0 instead of 1, which is typical in programming. (Just file this away as an interesting and useful note for the future...or a good trivia answer.) Therefore, the text of the first quote (a value) is assigned to quotes[0] (a variable). Similarly, the text of the first source is assigned to source[0].

Text strings are enclosed in quotation marks. However, in JavaScript, a line break indicates the end of a command, so the following would cause problems in the code:

```
quotes[0] = "When I was a boy of 14, my father was so
ignorant...but when I got to be 21, I was astonished at
how much he had learned in 7 years.";
```

Therefore, you see that the string is built as a series of strings enclosed in quotation marks, with a plus sign (+) connecting the strings. (This plus sign is called a *concatenation operator*.)

The next chunk of code definitely looks the most like programming. This line is generating a random number and assigning that value to a variable called i:

```
i = Math.floor(Math.random() * quotes.length);
```

But you can't just pick any random number; the purpose of the random number is to determine which of the quotes and sources should be printed, and there are only four quotes. So, this line of JavaScript does the following:

▶ Uses Math.random() to get a random number between 0 and 1. For example, 0.5482749 might be a result of Math.random().

▶ Multiplies the random number by the length of the `quotes` array, which is currently 4; the length of the array is the number of elements in the array. If the random number is 0.5482749 (as shown previously), multiplying that by 4 results in 2.1930996.

▶ Uses `Math.floor()` to round the result down to the nearest whole number. In other words, 2.1930996 turns into 2.

▶ Assigns the variable `i` a value of 2 (for example).

The rest of the function should look familiar, with a few exceptions. First, as you learned earlier this lesson, `document.write()` is used to write HTML that the browser then renders. Next, the strings are separated to clearly indicate when something needs to be handled differently, such as escaping the quotation marks with a backslash when they should be printed literally (`\`) or when the value of a variable is substituted. The actual quote and source that are printed are the ones that match `quotes[i]` and `sources[i]`, where `i` is the number determined by the mathematical functions noted previously.

But the act of simply writing the function doesn't mean that any output will be created. Further on in the HTML, you can see `getQuote();` between two `<script></script>` tags; this is how the function is called. Wherever that function call is made is where the output of the function will be placed. In this example, the output displays below a paragraph that introduces the quotation. This is not the best way to write JavaScript, as it is obtrusive and places behavior and interactivity within the HTML document itself. Later in this lesson, you will learn how to write unobtrusive JavaScript and how to write this script unobtrusively.

Figure 19.2 shows the Quotable Quotes page as it appears when loaded in a web browser. When the page reloads, there is a one in four chance that a different quote will display—it is random, after all!

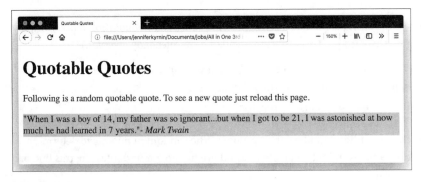

FIGURE 19.2
The Quotable Quotes page displays a random quote each time it is loaded.

Keep in mind that you can easily modify this page to include your own quotes or other text that you want to display randomly. You can also increase the number of quotes available for display by adding more entries in the `quotes` and `sources` arrays in the code. And, of course, you can modify the HTML output and style it however you'd like.

If you use the Quotable Quotes page as a starting point, you can easily alter the script and create your own interesting variation on the idea. And if you make mistakes along the way, so be it. The trick to getting past mistakes in script code is to be patient and carefully analyze the code you've entered. You can always remove code to simplify a script until you get it working and then add new code one piece at a time to make sure each piece works.

Understanding the Document Object Model

As you've read, client-side interactivity using JavaScript typically takes the form of manipulating the Document Object Model in some way. The DOM is the invisible structure of all documents; it is not the HTML structure or the way in which you apply semantic formatting but a sort of overall framework or container. If this description seems vague, that's because it is; the DOM is not a tangible object.

The overall container object is called the `document`. Any container that you create within the document to which you've given an ID can be referenced by that ID. For example, if you have a `<div>` with the ID `wrapper`, then in the DOM that element is referenced as follows:

```
document.wrapper
```

For example, you can change the visibility of a specific element by changing the `style` object associated with it. Similarly, if you wanted to access the `background-color` style of the `<div>` with an ID called `wrapper` (to then do something with it), it would be referred to as follows:

```
document.wrapper.style.background-color
```

To change the value of this style to something else, perhaps based on an interactive user event, use the following to change the color to white:

```
document.wrapper.style.background-color="#ffffff"
```

The DOM is the framework to refer to elements and their associated objects. Obviously, this is a brief overview of something quite complicated, but at least you can now begin to grasp what this document-dot-something business is all about. To learn a lot more about the DOM, visit the World Wide Web Consortium's information about the DOM at www.w3.org/DOM/.

What Is Unobtrusive JavaScript?

Unobtrusive JavaScript is an approach to writing JavaScript scripts. You don't need to use it to create interactive web pages, but best practices recommend that you at least consider it. There are four general rules to unobtrusive JavaScript, developed by the Web Standards Project:

▶ **It should be usable**—JavaScript should work without being noticed by the user. Customers should be able to use it without thinking about it.

▶ **It should be easily degradable**—When an unobtrusive script fails, it should not generate an error message. Instead, it should present the features or silently disappear.

▶ **Make it accessible**—The page should not rely on JavaScript for core functions.

▶ **Keep it separate from structure and style**—JavaScript should be maintained as separate files from the HTML and CSS.

Many of these rules are reminiscent of the Mobile First approach to web design. By using unobtrusive JavaScript, you will ensure that your pages work more effectively on mobile and nonmobile devices.

Using the DOM to Make a Script Unobtrusive

The script in Listing 19.2 is written in the standard style of JavaScript. Several factors prevent this script from being unobtrusive. The most prominent is that the script is not separate from the HTML. The line that reads `getQuote();` must be placed right within the HTML where the quote will be displayed. This means the core functionality of the page—displaying a quotation—is stored only in the JavaScript. If the script fails or if the browser can't load the script, the quote won't be displayed. It also means that the JavaScript is not separated from the HTML.

To make the Quotable Quotes page unobtrusive, you need to make a few changes. The first change is to add an HTML element in the document where the quote will be placed:

`<blockquote id="quote">All cats are black after midnight.</blockquote>`

It doesn't have to be a `<blockquote>`, but as it is a quotation, this seems like the most appropriate HTML element. Notice that there is text inside the `<blockquote>` element: "All cats are black after midnight." This makes the script unobtrusive because if it can't run for some reason, the customer still gets a quotation.

Because the `<blockquote>` element has an ID (`quote`), it can be referenced in the JavaScript:

`blockquote = document.getElementById("quote");`

Then you simply update the contents of that tag with the JavaScript innerHTML property:

```
blockquote.innerHTML = quotes[i];
```

The last thing you need to do is either move the script to an external JavaScript file or place it as the last HTML element on the page before the closing </body> tag. Doing so removes the script from the HTML. Listing 19.3 shows how the entire page looks, including an additional paragraph for the source of each quote that is to be displayed as well.

LISTING 19.3   The Quotable Quotes Page, Made Unobtrusive

```
<!doctype html>
<html lang="en">
  <head>
    <meta charset="utf-8">
    <title>Quotable Quotes - Unobtrusively</title>
    <meta name="viewport"
          content="width=device-width, initial-scale=1">
  </head>
  <body>
    <h1>Quotable Quotes - Unobtrusively</h1>
    <p>Following is a random quotable quote. To see a new quote
    just reload this page.</p>
    <blockquote id="quote">All cats are black after
      midnight.</blockquote>
    <p id="source">Robert A. Heinlein</p>

    <script>
      <!-- Hide the script from old browsers
      function getQuote() {
        // Create the arrays
        quotes = new Array(4);
        sources = new Array(4);

        // get the elements to write to by their ID
        blockquote = document.getElementById("quote");
        source = document.getElementById("source");

        // Initialize the arrays with quotes
        quotes[0] = "When I was a boy of 14, my father was so " +
        "ignorant...but when I got to be 21, I was astonished " +
        "at how much he had learned in 7 years.";
        sources[0] = "Mark Twain";

        quotes[1] = "Everybody is ignorant. Only on different " +
        "subjects.";
        sources[1] = "Will Rogers";
```

```
      quotes[2] = "They say such nice things about people at " +
      "their funerals that it makes me sad that I'm going to " +
      "miss mine by just a few days.";
      sources[2] = "Garrison Keillor";

      quotes[3] = "What's another word for thesaurus?";
      sources[3] = "Steven Wright";

      // Get a random index into the arrays
      i = Math.floor(Math.random() * quotes.length);

      // Write the quote to the DOM
      blockquote.innerHTML = quotes[i];
      source.innerHTML = sources[i];
    }

    getQuote();
    // Stop hiding the script -->
  </script>
 </body>
</html>
```

The unobtrusive version of this script also removes the styles from the quotation, but you can add them by using style sheets, just as you would for any other web page.

Changing Images Based on User Interaction

Lesson 4 introduced you to the concept of user interaction events, such as `onclick`. In that lesson, you invoked changes in window display based on user interaction; in this section, you'll see an example of a visible type of interaction that is both practical and dynamic.

Figure 19.3 shows a page that contains one large image with some text next to it and three small images farther down the page. If you look closely at the list of small images, you might notice that the first small image is, in fact, a smaller version of the large image that is displayed. This is a common display for a type of small gallery, such as one that you might see in an online catalog, in which an item has a description and a few alternate views of the product. Although close-up images of the details of products are important to a potential buyer, using several large images on a page becomes unwieldy from both display and bandwidth points of view, so using this type of gallery view is a popular way to display alternative images. We don't personally have products to sell, but we do have pictures of big trees that we can use as an example, as shown in Figure 19.3.

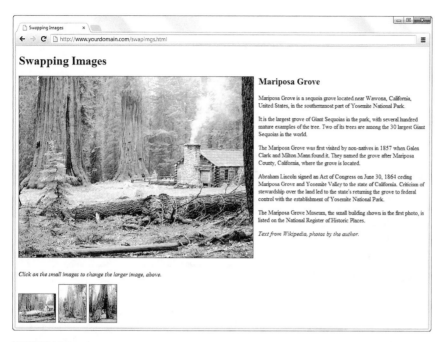

FIGURE 19.3
An informational page with a main image and alternative images ready to click and view.

The large image on the page is called using this `<img>` tag:

```
<img
    id="large_photo"
    style="border: 1px solid black; margin-right: 13px;"
    src="mariposa_large_1.jpg"
    alt="large photo">
```

The `style`, `src`, and `alt` attributes should all make sense to you at this stage of the game. In addition, as you can see, this image is given the ID `large_photo`. Therefore, this image exists in the DOM as `document.images['large_photo']` (an image is referred to by its ID). This is important because a bit of JavaScript functionality enables you to dynamically change the value of `document.images['large_image'].src`, which is the source (`src`) of the image.

The following code snippet creates the third small image in the group of three images shown at the bottom of Figure 19.3. The `onclick` event indicates that when the user clicks on this small image, the value of `document.images['large_image'].src`—the large image slot—is filled with the path to a matching large image:

```
<a href="#"
   onclick="javascript:document.images['large_photo'].src =
   'mariposa_large_1.jpg'">
```

```
<img
  style="border: 1px solid black; margin-right: 3px;"
  src="mariposa_small_1.jpg"
  alt="photo #1"></a>
```

Figure 19.4 shows the same page but not reloaded by the user. The slot for the large image is filled by a different image when the user clicks on one of the other smaller images at the bottom of the page.

FIGURE 19.4
The large image is replaced when the user clicks on a smaller one.

If you've been paying attention, you will realize that this script is not unobtrusive. In fact, the easiest way to determine if a script is unobtrusive is to see if there is JavaScript inside any HTML attributes. In this case, the onclick attribute is holding the JavaScript that makes the page work, and this makes it obtrusive JavaScript.

To make this script unobtrusive, you need to move the JavaScript out of the links and into a separate script file. There are many ways you could do this, but they are beyond the scope of this lesson. One good place to learn more about unobtrusive JavaScript is in the book *Sams Teach Yourself JavaScript in 24 Hours*.

Thinking Ahead to Developing HTML5 Applications

We're not going to lie: There's a pretty big difference between a basic website built with HTML, CSS, and a little JavaScript and a comprehensive application that uses some of the advanced features of HTML5 and the latest JavaScript frameworks. But it's important to your understanding of HTML, the language of the Web, to have some idea of just how far you can extend it—and it's pretty far, as it turns out. Beyond basic markup, HTML5 extends to include APIs (application programming interfaces) for complex applications, beginning with the native integration of audio and video elements, as you learned in previous lessons, and going all the way to built-in offline storage mechanisms that allow full-blown applications to be accessed and run (and data stored on the client side) even without a network connection.

Although HTML5 is incredibly rich, the creation of highly interactive HTML5 websites and applications—including mobile applications—doesn't happen in isolation. Interactivity comes when HTML5 is paired with a client-side language such as JavaScript, which then reaches back into the server and talks to a server-side language (PHP, Ruby, Python, and so on) through a persistent connection called a *web socket*. With this connection open and talking to some server-side code that is (for example) talking to a database or performing some calculation, the browser can relay a bundle of information that is additionally processed by JavaScript and finally rendered in HTML5. Be it a video game, a word processing program, or an email or Twitter client, just to name a few popular types of HTML5 applications, the combination of the advanced features of HTML5 plus JavaScript—and, specifically, the feature-rich JavaScript libraries such as Angular (https://angular.io), jQuery (http://jquery.com), and React (https://reactjs.org)—really makes the opportunities limitless when it comes to application creation. We will go into more detail about these libraries in Lesson 26, "Using Third-Party JavaScript Libraries and Frameworks."

The depth of the technologies involved in HTML5 application creation is beyond the scope of these lessons, but the foundation you should have in standards-compliant HTML5, CSS3, and JavaScript will serve you well if you begin to think outside the box of a basic website. To learn more about HTML5 application creation, take a look at my book *Sams Teach Yourself HTML5 Mobile Application Development in 24 Hours* for an introduction to some of the core features. Throughout these lessons, you get a solid foundation in the basics of HTML5. We are confident that, with additional instruction, you can take the next step and begin to learn and build basic interactions in an HTML5 application.

Summary

In this lesson, you learned about the differences between server-side scripting and client-side scripting, and you learned how to include JavaScript in your HTML files to add a little interactivity to your websites. You also learned how to use the JavaScript `document.write()` method to display random quotes upon page load. Finally, you learned a bit about the Document Object Model and how to write unobtrusive scripts.

By applying the knowledge you've gained from the preceding lesson, you've learned how to use client-side scripting to make images on a web page respond to mouse movements. Although they are simple in their construction, these types of interactions are some of the basic JavaScript-based interactions that form the foundation of web applications. Hopefully this will spur your desire to learn more about server-side programming so that you can give your websites even more complex interactive features, including taking a step into the world of creating HTML5 applications.

Q&A

Q. If I want to use the random-quote script from this lesson, but I want to have a library of a lot of quotes, do I have to put all the quotes in each page?

A. Yes. Each item in the array must be there. This is where you can begin to see a bit of a tipping point between something that can be client side and something that is better dealt with on the server side. If you have a true library of random quotations and only one is presented at any given time, it's probably best to store those items in a database table and use a little piece of server-side scripting to connect to that database, retrieve the text, and print it on the page. Alternatively, you can always continue to carry all the quotes with you in JavaScript, but you should at least put that JavaScript function into a different file that can be maintained separately from the text. Just be aware that the more quotes you have in the JavaScript, the longer your page will take to fully load.

Q. I've seen some online catalogs that display a large image in what looks to be a layer on top of the website content. I can see the regular website content underneath it, but the focus is on the large image. How is that done?

A. This sounds like an effect created by a JavaScript library called Lightbox. The Lightbox library enables you to display an image or a gallery of images in a layer that is placed over your site content. This is a very popular library for showing the details of large images or just a set of images deemed important enough to showcase "above" the content. The library is freely available from its creator, Lokesh Dhakar, at http://lokeshdhakar.com/projects/lightbox/. To install and use it, follow the instructions included with the software; you will be able to integrate it into your site using the knowledge you've gained in the lessons so far.

Workshop

The Workshop contains quiz questions and activities to help you solidify your understanding of the material covered. Try to answer all questions before looking at the "Answers" section that follows.

Quiz

1. You've made a button image and named it `button.gif`. You've also made a simple GIF animation of the button so that it flashes green and white. You've named that GIF `flashing.gif`. What HTML and JavaScript code can you use to make the button flash whenever a user moves the mouse pointer over it and also link to a page named `gohere.html` when a user clicks the button?

a.

```
<a href="gohere.html"
onclick="javascript:document.images['flasher'].src='flashing.gif'"
onhover="javascript:document.images['flasher'].src='button.gif'">
<img src="button.gif" id="flasher" style="border-style:none;"></a>
```

b.

```
<a href="gohere.html"
onmouse="javascript:document.images['flasher'].src='flashing.gif'"
onmouse="javascript:document.images['flasher'].src='button.gif'">
<img src="button.gif" id="flasher" style="border-style:none;"></a>
```

c.

```
<a href="gohere.html"
onmouseover="javascript:document.images['flasher'].src='flashing.gif'"
onmouseout="javascript:document.images['flasher'].src='button.gif'">
<img src="button.gif" id="flasher" style="border-style:none;"></a>
```

d.

```
<a href="gohere.html"
onover="javascript:document.images['flasher'].src='flashing.gif'"
onout="javascript:document.images['flasher'].src='button.gif'">
<img src="button.gif" id="flasher" style="border-style:none;"></a>
```

2. How can you modify the code you wrote for Question 1 so that the button flashes when a user moves the mouse over it and continues flashing even if the user then moves the mouse away from it?

a.

```
<a href="gohere.html"
onmouse="javascript:document.images['flasher'].src='flashing.gif'">
<img src="button.gif" id="flasher" style="border-style:none;"></a>
```

b.

```
<a href="gohere.html"
onmouseover="javascript:document.images['flasher'].src='flashing.gif'">
<img src="button.gif" id="flasher" style="border-style:none;"></a>
```

c.

```
<a href="gohere.html"
onmouseout="javascript:document.images['flasher'].src='button.gif'">
<img src="button.gif" id="flasher" style="border-style:none;"></a>
```

d.

```
<a href="gohere.html"
onover="javascript:document.images['flasher'].src='flashing.gif'">
<img src="button.gif" id="flasher" style="border-style:none;"></a>
```

3. Is the JavaScript in Questions 1 and 2 unobtrusive? Why or why not?

   a. Yes, it is unobtrusive because it works without any errors.

   b. Yes, it is unobtrusive because it uses valid HTML.

   c. No, it is not unobtrusive because it uses the `onmouseover` attribute to place the JavaScript right in the HTML.

   d. No, it is not unobtrusive because it creates a flashing image.

4. What are two examples of server-side scripting languages?

   a. JavaScript and Python

   b. Perl and ActiveX

   c. Perl and Ruby

   d. JavaScript and ActiveX

5. How is JavaScript related to Java?

   a. JavaScript is a sub-set of Java.

   b. JavaScript uses Java methods.

   c. JavaScript is a scripting language for Java.

   d. JavaScript is not related to Java.

6. Where can you store JavaScript?

   a. In the HTML

   b. In a separate file

   c. On a local hard drive

   d. Both A and B

7. If you use a `<script>` tag to store your JavaScript, where is it best to place it in order to create unobtrusive JavaScript?

   a. Right after the `<html>` tag

   b. Right before the `</head>` tag

   c. Right after the `</head>` tag

   d. Right before the `</body>` tag

8. What is the JavaScript to generate a random number?

   a. `Math.random()`

   b. `Math.randomNum()`

   c. `MathRandom()`

   d. `Rand()`

9. What does the `Math.floor()` function do?

   a. Rounds the result down to the nearest whole number

   b. Rounds the result down to the smallest number possible

   c. Rounds the result up to the largest number possible

   d. Rounds the result up to the nearest whole number

10. What does the plus sign mean in the following context?

```
document.write('This is a text string ' + 'that I have created.');
```

   a. The plus sign (+) adds two numbers together.

   b. The plus sign (+) adds the value of two strings together to generate a number.

   c. The plus sign (+) joins a string and a number.

   d. The plus sign (+) joins two strings together.

NOTE

Just a reminder for those of you reading these words in the print or e-book edition of this book: If you go to **www.informit.com/register** and register this book (using ISBN 9780672338083), you can receive free access to an online Web Edition that not only contains the complete text of this book but also features an interactive version of this quiz.

Answers

1. **c.** Your code might look something like this:

```
<a href="gohere.html"
onmouseover="javascript:document.images['flasher'].src='flashing.gif'"
onmouseout="javascript:document.images['flasher'].src='button.gif'">
<img src="button.gif" id="flasher" style="border-style:none;"></a>
```

2. **b.** Your code might look something like this:

```
<a href="gohere.html"
onmouseover="javascript:document.images['flasher'].src='flashing.gif'">
<img src="button.gif" id="flasher" style="border-style:none;"></a>
```

3. **c.** No, it is not unobtrusive because it uses the onmouseover attribute to place the JavaScript right in the HTML.

4. **c.** Some server-side scripting languages include Python, Ruby, PHP, and Perl.

5. **d.** JavaScript is not related to Java. It has a similar name, but that is the only relationship.

6. **d.** JavaScript can be stored in a separate file with a .js extension or directly in the HTML in the <script> tag.

7. **d.** To create unobtrusive JavaScript, you should place all <script> tags as close to the bottom of your document as possible. If you cannot place them directly before the </body> tag, then placing them last in the <head></head> element is acceptable as well.

8. **a.** Math.random() is the JavaScript function used to generate a random number.

9. **a.** The Math.floor() function rounds the result down to the nearest whole number.

10. **d.** The plus sign (+) joins two strings together.

Exercises

▶ Do you have any pages that would look flashier or be easier to understand if the navigation icons or other images changed when the mouse passed over them? If so, try creating some highlighted versions of the images and try modifying your own page by using the information presented in this lesson.

▶ You can display random images—such as graphical banners or advertisements—in the same way you learned to display random content using JavaScript earlier in this lesson. Instead of printing text, just print the <img> tag for the images you want to display.

Getting Started with JavaScript Programming

What You'll Learn in This Lesson:

▶ How and why to organize scripts using functions

▶ What objects are and how JavaScript uses them

▶ How JavaScript can respond to events

▶ How and when to use conditional statements and loops

▶ How browsers execute scripts in the proper order

▶ Basic syntax rules for avoiding JavaScript errors

▶ What JSON is and how it can be used

The preceding lesson reminded you of some of the basic uses of JavaScript and how to include JavaScript in your HTML documents. In this lesson, you'll learn a few more basic JavaScript concepts and script components that you'll use in just about every bit of JavaScript script you write. In addition, you'll learn about JSON (JavaScript Object Notation), which provides a simple structured way to store information that can be used on the client side. Understanding these components will prepare you for the remaining lessons, in which you'll explore specific JavaScript functions and features in greater depth.

Basic Concepts

There are a few basic concepts and terms you'll run into throughout these lessons. In the following sections, you'll learn about the basic building blocks of JavaScript.

Statements

Statements are the basic units of a JavaScript program. A *statement* is a section of code that performs a single action. For example, the following four statements are from the date and time example in Lesson 4, "Understanding JavaScript":

```
now = new Date();
hours = now.getHours();
```

```
mins = now.getMinutes();
secs = now.getSeconds();
```

These statements create a new Date object and then assign the values for the current hour, minutes, and seconds into variables called hours, mins, and secs, respectively. You can then use these variables in your JavaScript code.

Although a statement is typically a single line of JavaScript, it is not a rule that it has to be. It's possible (and fairly common) to break a statement across multiple lines or to include more than one statement in a single line.

A semicolon marks the end of a statement, but you can also omit the semicolon if you start a new line after the statement—if that is your coding style. For example, these are three valid JavaScript statements:

```
hours = now.getHours()
mins = now.getMinutes()
secs = now.getSeconds()
```

CAUTION
While omitting the semicolon is valid, many JavaScript errors are caused by missing semicolons. It's best to get in the habit of always using semicolons at the end of statements to reduce errors.

However, if you combine statements into a single line, you must use semicolons to separate them. For example, the following line is valid:

```
hours = now.getHours(); mins = now.getMinutes(); secs = now.getSeconds();
```

This line is invalid:

```
hours = now.getHours() mins = now.getMinutes() secs = now.getSeconds();
```

Combining Tasks with Functions

A function is a number of JavaScript statements that are treated as a single unit. A statement that uses a function is referred to as a *function call*. For example, you might create a function called alertMe, which produces an alert when called, like so:

```
function alertMe() {
    alert("I am alerting you!");
}
```

When this function is called, a JavaScript alert pops up, and the text "I am alerting you" is displayed in a box, as shown in Figure 20.1.

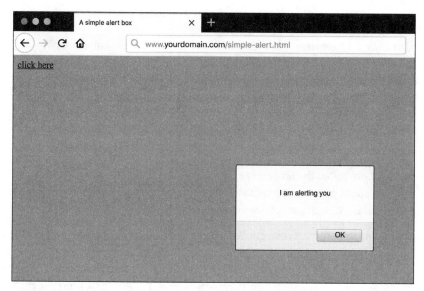

FIGURE 20.1
An alert box on a web page.

A function can take a parameter—an expression inside the parentheses—that tells the function what to do. In addition, a function can return a value to a waiting variable. For example, the following function call prompts the user for a response and stores it in the `text` variable:

```
text = prompt("Enter some text.")
```

Creating your own functions is useful for two main reasons. First, you can separate logical portions of your script to make it easier to understand. Second, and more importantly, you can use the function several times or with different data to avoid repeating script statements.

Variables

If you recall the basic introduction to JavaScript in Lesson 4, you'll remember that a variable is a container that can store a number, a string of text, or another value. For example, the following statement creates a variable called `fred` and assigns it the value 27:

```
var fred = 27;
```

JavaScript variables can contain numbers, text strings, and other values. You'll learn more about variables in much greater detail in Lesson 22, "Using JavaScript Variables, Strings, and Arrays."

Understanding Objects

JavaScript also supports *objects*. Like variables, objects can store data—but they can store two or more pieces of data at once. As you'll learn throughout the JavaScript-specific lessons in this course, using built-in objects and their methods is fundamental to JavaScript; it's one of the ways the language works, by providing a predetermined set of actions you can perform. For example, with the `document.write` functionality you saw in Lesson 19, "Understanding Dynamic Websites and HTML5 Applications," you can use the `write` method of the `document` object to output text to the browser for eventual rendering.

The data stored in an object are called the *properties* of the object. For example, you could use objects to store information about people in an address book. The properties of each person object might include a name, an address, and a telephone number.

You should become intimately familiar with object-related syntax because you will see objects quite a lot, even if you don't build your own. You'll definitely find yourself using built-in objects, and objects will very likely form a large part of any JavaScript libraries you import for use. JavaScript uses periods to separate object names and property names. For example, for a person object called Bob, the properties might include `Bob.address` and `Bob.phone`.

Objects can also include *methods*. A method is a function that works with an object's data. For example, our person object for the address book might include a `display()` method to display the person's information. In JavaScript terminology, the statement `Bob.display()` would display Bob's details.

Don't worry if this sounds confusing. You'll be exploring objects in much more detail later in these lessons. For now, you just need to know the basics. JavaScript supports three kinds of objects:

▶ **Built-in objects**—These objects are built in to the JavaScript language. You've already encountered one of these, `Date`, in Lesson 4. Other built-in objects include `Array` and `String`, which you'll explore in Lesson 22; `Math`, which is also explained in Lesson 22; `Boolean`; `Number`; and `RegExp`.

▶ **DOM (Document Object Model) objects**—These objects represent various components of the browser and the current HTML document. For example, the `alert()` function you used earlier in this lesson is actually a method of the `window` object. You'll explore these in more detail in Lesson 21, "Working with the Document Object Model (DOM)."

▶ **Custom objects**—These are objects you create yourself. For example, you could create a `person` object, as mentioned earlier in this section.

Conditionals

Although you can use event handlers to notify your script (and potentially the user) when something happens, you might need to check certain conditions yourself as your script runs. For example, you might want to validate on your own that a user entered a valid email address in a web form.

JavaScript supports *conditional statements*, which enable you to answer questions. A typical conditional uses the if statement, as in this example:

```
if (count == 1) {
  alert("The countdown has reached 1.");
}
```

This compares the variable count with the constant 1 and displays an alert message to the user if they are the same. It is quite likely you will use one or more conditional statements in most of your scripts, and therefore an entire lesson is devoted to this concept: Lesson 23, "Controlling Flow with Conditions and Loops."

Loops

Another useful feature of JavaScript—and most other programming languages—is the capability to create *loops*, or groups of statements that repeat a certain number of times. For example, these statements display the same alert 10 times, greatly annoying the user:

```
for (i=1; i<=10; i++) {
  alert("Yes, it's yet another alert!");
}
```

The for statement is one of several statements JavaScript uses for loops. Computers are good at performing repetitive tasks like looping. You will use loops in many of your scripts, in much more useful ways than this example, as you'll see in Lesson 23.

Event Handlers

As mentioned in Lesson 4, not all scripts are located within <script> tags. You can also use scripts as *event handlers*. Although this might sound like a complex programming term, it actually means exactly what it says: Event handlers are scripts that handle events. You learned a little bit about events in Lesson 19 but not to the extent you'll read about them in this lesson or in Lesson 24, "Responding to Events and Using Windows."

In real life, an event is something that happens to you. For example, the things you write on your calendar are events, such as *Dentist appointment* or *Fred's birthday*. You also encounter unscheduled events in your life, such as a traffic ticket, an IRS audit, or an unexpected gift from relatives.

Whether events are scheduled or unscheduled, you probably have normal ways of handling them. Your event handlers might include things such as *When Fred's birthday arrives, send him a present* or *When relatives visit unexpectedly, turn out the lights and pretend nobody is home.*

Event handlers in JavaScript are similar: They tell the browser what to do when a certain event occurs. The events JavaScript deals with aren't as exciting as the ones you deal with; they include such events as *When the mouse button is pressed* and *When this page is finished loading.* Nevertheless, they're a very useful part of JavaScript.

Many JavaScript events (such as mouse clicks, which you've seen previously) are caused by the user. Rather than doing things in a set order, your script can respond to the user's actions. Other events don't involve the user directly; for example, an event can be triggered when an HTML document finishes loading.

Each event handler is associated with a particular browser object, and you can specify the event handler in the tag that defines the object. For example, images and text links have an event, onmouseover, that happens when the mouse pointer moves over the object. Here is a typical HTML image tag with an event handler:

```
<img src="button.gif" onmouseover="highlight();">
```

You specify the event handler as an attribute within the HTML tag and include the JavaScript statement to handle the event within the quotation marks. This is an ideal use for functions because function names are short and to the point and can refer to a whole series of statements.

Using an event handler within HTML is fairly easy. Listing 20.1 shows an HTML document that includes a simple event handler.

LISTING 20.1   **An HTML Document with a Simple Event Handler**

```
<!doctype html>
<html lang="en">
  <head>
    <meta charset="utf-8">
    <title>Event Handler Example</title>
    <meta name="viewport"
          content="width=device-width, initial-scale=1">
  </head>
  <body>
    <h1>Event Handler Example</h1>
      <div>
      <a href="http://www.google.com/"
      onclick="alert('A-ha! An Event!');">Go to Google</a>
      </div>
  </body>
</html>
```

The event handler is defined with the following `onclick` attribute within the <a> tag that defines a link:

```
onclick="alert('Aha! An Event!');"
```

This event handler uses the DOM's built-in `alert` method of the `window` object to display a message when you click on the link; after you click OK to dismiss the alert, your browser continues on to the URL. In more complex scripts, you usually define your own functions to act as event handlers. Figure 20.2 shows an example of this in action.

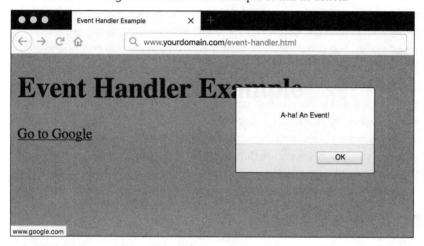

FIGURE 20.2
The browser displays an alert when you click the link.

You'll use other event handlers throughout these lessons, especially in Lesson 24.

NOTE
After you click the OK button to dismiss the alert, the browser follows the link defined in the <a> tag. Your event handler could also stop the browser from following the link, as you will learn in Lesson 24.

As mentioned in earlier lessons, using an attribute on the HTML tag is not unobtrusive. You'll learn how to make event handlers unobtrusively in later lessons.

Which Script Runs First?

You are not limited to a single script within a web document: One or more sets of <script> tags, external JavaScript files, and any number of event handlers can be used within a single document. With all these scripts, you might wonder how the browser knows which to execute first. Fortunately, this is done in a logical fashion:

▶ Sets of `<script>` tags within the `<head>` element of an HTML document are handled first (in the order in which they are written in the HTML), whether they include embedded code or refer to a JavaScript file. Because scripts in the `<head>` element will not create output in the web page, many designers use scripts placed here to define functions for use later.

▶ Sets of `<script>` tags within the `<body>` section of the HTML document are executed after those in the `<head>` section, while the web page loads and displays. If there are two or more scripts, they are executed in the order in which they are written in the HTML.

▶ Event handlers are executed when their events happen. For example, the `onload` event handler is executed when the body of a web page loads. Because the `<head>` section is loaded before any events, you can define functions there and use them in event handlers.

It's important to know that every time the browser encounters a `<script>` tag, it stops concurrent downloading to download and parse just that script. All other HTML tags and elements are *threaded*, which means browsers can download several at a time. This is why it's important to have as few `<script>` tags in your document as possible, and, whenever possible, to load them last in the HTML. Taking these steps helps ensure that everything else on the page loads before the scripts do and thus makes your pages faster.

JavaScript Syntax Rules

JavaScript is a simple language, but you do need to be careful to use its *syntax*—the rules that define how you use the language—correctly. The rest of these lessons cover many aspects of JavaScript syntax, and this lesson discusses a few basic rules that will help you throughout these lessons as well as when you are working on your own.

Case Sensitivity

Almost everything in JavaScript is *case sensitive*, which means you cannot use lowercase and capital letters interchangeably. Here are a few general rules:

▶ JavaScript keywords, such as `for` and `if`, are always lowercase.

▶ Built-in objects, such as `Math` and `Date`, are capitalized.

▶ DOM object names are usually lowercase, but their methods are often a combination of uppercase and lowercase—sometimes called camel case. Usually uppercase letters are used to start all words except for the first one, as in `setAttribute` and `getElementById`.

When in doubt, follow the exact case used in these lessons or another JavaScript reference. If you use the wrong case, the browser will usually display an error message.

Variable, Object, and Function Names

When you define your own variables, objects, or functions, you can choose their names. Names can include uppercase letters, lowercase letters, numbers, and the underscore (_) character. Names must begin with a letter or an underscore.

You can choose whether to use uppercase or lowercase in your variable names, but remember that JavaScript is case sensitive, so, for example, `score`, `Score`, and `SCORE` would be considered three different variables. Be sure to use the same name each time you refer to a variable.

Reserved Words

One more rule applies to variable names: They must not be *reserved words*. These include the words that make up the JavaScript language, such as `if` and `for`, DOM object names such as `window` and `document`, and built-in object names such as `Math` and `Date`.

For a list of JavaScript reserved words, see https://developer.mozilla.org/en-US/docs/Web/JavaScript/Reference/Lexical_grammar#Keywords.

Spacing

JavaScript ignores blank space (which programmers call *whitespace*). You can include spaces and tabs within a line, or blank lines, without causing an error. Blank space often makes a script more readable, so do not hesitate to use it.

Using Comments

JavaScript *comments* enable you to include documentation within your script. Brief documentation is useful if someone else needs to understand the script, or even if you try to understand it when returning to your code after a long break. To include comments in a JavaScript program, begin a line with two slashes, as in this example:

```
//this is a comment.
```

You can also begin a comment with two slashes in the middle of a line, which is useful for documenting a script. In this case, everything on the line after the slashes is treated as a comment, which the browser ignores. For example, the following line is a valid JavaScript statement followed by a comment explaining what is going on in the code:

```
a = a + 1; // add 1 to the value of the variable a
```

JavaScript also supports C-style comments (also used in PHP), which begin with / * and end with * /. These comments can extend across more than one line, as the following example demonstrates:

```
/* This script includes a variety
of features, including this comment. */
```

Because JavaScript statements within a comment are ignored, this type of comment is often used for *commenting out* sections of code. If you have some lines of JavaScript that you want to temporarily take out of the script while you debug it, you can add / * at the beginning of the section and * / at the end.

CAUTION

Because these comments are part of JavaScript syntax, they are valid only inside `<script>` tags or within an external JavaScript file. If you try to use them in an HTML document outside the `<script>` tags, the strings will be rendered by the browser.

Best Practices for JavaScript

Now that you've learned some of the very basic rules for writing valid JavaScript, it's also a good idea to follow a few *best practices*. The following practices are not required, but you'll save yourself and others headaches if you begin to integrate them into your development process:

▶ **Use comments liberally**—Comments make your code easier for others to understand and also easier for you to understand when you edit it later. They are also useful for marking the major divisions of a script.

▶ **Use a semicolon at the end of each statement and use only one statement per line**—Although you learned in this lesson that you do not have to end each statement with a semicolon (if you use a new line), using semicolons and only one statement per line will make your scripts easier to read and also easier to debug.

▶ **Use external JavaScript files whenever possible**—Separating JavaScript into external files helps pages load more quickly and also encourages you to write modular scripts that can be reused.

▶ **Avoid being browser specific**—As you learn more about JavaScript, you'll learn some features that work in only one browser. Avoid such features unless absolutely necessary, and always test your code in more than one browser to ensure that everything works.

▶ **Keep JavaScript optional**—Don't use JavaScript to perform an essential function on your site (for example, for the primary navigation links). Whenever possible, users without JavaScript should be able to use your site, although it might not be quite as attractive or convenient without the JavaScript. This strategy is known as *progressive enhancement*.

There are many more best practices involving more advanced aspects of JavaScript. You'll learn about them not only as you progress through the lessons but also over time as you work with JavaScript and as you collaborate with others on web development projects.

Understanding JSON

Although JSON, or *JavaScript Object Notation*, is not a part of the core JavaScript language, using it is in fact a common way to structure and store information either used by or created by JavaScript-based functionality on the client side. Now is a good time to familiarize yourself with JSON (pronounced "Jason") and some of its uses.

NOTE

JSON formalizes the idea of encoding data in JavaScript. See www.json.org for details and code examples in many languages.

JSON-encoded data is expressed as a sequence of parameter and value pairs, with a colon separating each parameter and its value. These `"parameter"`:`"value"` pairs are separated by commas:

```
"param1":"value1", "param2":"value2", "param3":"value3"
```

Finally, the whole sequence is enclosed in curly braces to form a JSON object. The following example creates a variable called yourJSONObject:

```
var yourJSONObject = {
    "param1":"value1",
    "param2":"value2",
    "param3":"value3"
};
```

JSON objects can have properties and methods accessed directly using the usual dot notation, as shown here:

```
alert(yourJSONObject.param1); // alerts 'value1'
```

More generally, though, JSON has a general-purpose syntax for exchanging data in a string format. It is easy to convert a JSON object into a string through a process known as *serialization*; serialized data is convenient for storage or transmission around networks.

One of the most common uses of JSON these days is as a data interchange format used by application programming interfaces (APIs) and other data feeds that are consumed by a front-end application that uses JavaScript to parse the data. This increased use of JSON in place of other data formats such as XML has come about for several reasons:

- JSON is easy to read—for both people and computers.

- JSON is simple in concept. A JSON object is nothing more than a series of "*parameter*" : "*value*" pairs enclosed by curly braces.

- JSON is largely self-documenting.

- You can create and parse JSON quickly.

- JSON is a subset of JavaScript, which means no special interpreters or other additional packages are necessary.

Summary

In this lesson, you learned about several components of JavaScript programming and syntax, such as functions, objects, event handlers, conditions, and loops. You also learned how to use JavaScript comments to make your script easier to read and looked at a simple example of an event handler. Finally, you were introduced to JSON, a data interchange format that is commonly used by JavaScript-based applications.

Q&A

Q. I've heard the term *object-oriented* applied to languages such as C++ and Java. If JavaScript supports objects, is it an object-oriented language?

A. Yes, although it might not fit some people's strict definition of *object-oriented*. JavaScript objects do not support all the features that languages such as C++ and Java support, although the latest versions of JavaScript have added more object-oriented features.

Q. Having several scripts that execute at different times seems confusing. Why would I want to use event handlers?

A. Using event handlers is the ideal way (and, in JavaScript, the only way) to handle advanced interactions within a web page, such as using buttons, check boxes, and text fields in ways beyond simply completing a form and sending it to a recipient. Rather than write a script that sits and waits for a button to be pushed, you can create an event handler and let the browser do the waiting for you, while allowing the user to continue viewing elements and text on the page.

Workshop

The Workshop contains quiz questions and activities to help you solidify your understanding of the material covered. Try to answer all questions before looking at the "Answers" section that follows.

Quiz

1. A script that executes when the user clicks the mouse button is an example of what?

    a. An object

    b. An event handler

    c. An impossibility

    d. A method

2. Which of the following can a JavaScript function do?

    a. Accept parameters

    b. Return a value

    c. Write data to disk

    d. Both A and B

3. Which of the following is executed first by a browser?

    a. A script in the <head> section

    b. A script in the <body> section

    c. An event handler for a button

    d. A click on a link

4. How many lines make up a valid JavaScript statement?

    a. One

    b. Two

    c. Three

    d. As many as you need

5. How do you separate statements in a script?

    a. A space

    b. A newline

    c. A semicolon

    d. Both B and C

6. How would you write a statement that defines a variable called `myVariable` and assigns it the value 27?

   a. `myVariable 27;`

   b. `var myVariable 27;`

   c. `var myVariable = 27;`

   d. `var myVariable == 27;`

7. When would a script tied to an `onmouseover` attribute run?

   a. When the user clicks the element

   b. When the user taps the element on a touch device

   c. When the mouse hovers over the element

   d. When the mouse leaves the page

8. Is `var Date = "today";` a valid variable statement? Why or why not?

   a. It is not valid because "today" is a string, not a date object.

   b. It is not valid because Date is a built-in object and therefore cannot be used as a variable name.

   c. It is not valid because you assign variables without any operator (=).

   d. It is a valid statement.

9. What are two ways to write JavaScript comments?

   a. Use `//` for single-line comments and `/* */` for multi-line comments.

   b. Use `##` for single-line comments and `// //` for multi-line comments.

   c. Use `;` for single-line comments and `/* */` for multi-line comments.

   d. Use `//` for single-line comments and `&& &&` for multi-line comments.

10. How would you write a JSON variable with two parameter/value pairs?

    a.
    ```
    var myObject = {
      "param1" "value1",
      "param2" "value2"
    };
    ```

    b.
    ```
    var myObject = (
      "param1":"value1",
      "param2":"value2"
    );
    ```

c.
```
var myObject = {
  "param1":"value1",
  "param2":"value2"
};
```

d.
```
var myObject = (
  "param1" "value1",
  "param2" "value2"
);
```

NOTE
_____

Just a reminder for those of you reading these words in the print or e-book edition of this book: If you go to **www.informit.com/register** and register this book (using ISBN 9780672338083), you can receive free access to an online Web Edition that not only contains the complete text of this book but also features an interactive version of this quiz.

_____

Answers

1. b. A script that executes when the user clicks the mouse button is an event handler.

2. d. Functions can both accept parameters and return values.

3. a. Scripts defined in the <head> section of an HTML document are executed first by the browser.

4. a. A statement is just one line of JavaScript code that performs a single action.

5. d. Statements can be separated by a newline character, but it's better to use a semicolon to separate statements.

6. c. The statement is var myVariable = 27;.

7. c. It would run whenever the user hovers over the element with a mouse pointer.

8. b. It is not valid because Date is a built-in object and therefore cannot be used as a variable name.

9. a. You can use // for single-line comments and /* */ for multi-line comments.

10. c. You would write it like this:
```
var myObject = {
  "param1":"value1",
  "param2":"value2"
};
```

Exercises

▶ Examine the date and time script you created in Lesson 4, looking for examples of methods and objects used there.

▶ Add JavaScript comments to the date and time script to make it more clear what each line does. Verify that the script still runs properly.

Working with the Document Object Model (DOM)

What You'll Learn in This Lesson:

▸ How the W3C DOM standard makes dynamic pages easier to control

▸ The basics of the standard DOM objects: `window`, `document`, `history`, and `location`

▸ How to work with DOM nodes, parents, children, and siblings

▸ How to access and use the properties of DOM nodes

▸ How to access and use DOM node methods

▸ How to control element positioning with JavaScript

▸ How to hide and show elements with JavaScript

▸ How to use JavaScript to add and modify text within a page

The preceding lesson introduced you to the basic concepts of programming in JavaScript; this lesson will help you better understand the Document Object Model (DOM), which is the structured framework of a document within a web browser. When using JavaScript objects, methods, and other functionality (in addition to basic HTML), controlling the DOM enables you to develop rich user experiences.

Understanding the Document Object Model

One advantage of JavaScript over plain HTML is that client-side JavaScript scripts can manipulate the web browser and documents (including their contents) right in the browser after the content has been loaded. Your script can load a new page into the browser, work with parts of the browser window and the loaded document, open new windows, and even modify text within the page—all dynamically, without requiring additional requests to a server.

To work with the browser and documents, JavaScript uses the hierarchy of parent and child objects found within the DOM. These objects, which are organized into a treelike structure, represent all the content and components of a web document and the browser that renders it.

NOTE

The DOM is not part of JavaScript or any other programming language. Rather, it's an application programming interface (API) built into the browser.

The objects in the DOM have *properties* that describe the web browser or document, and *methods*, or built-in code that enables you to work with parts of the web browser or document. You'll learn more about these properties and methods and you will practice referencing or using them throughout this lesson.

You've seen DOM object notation already in these lessons, even if it wasn't called out as such. When you refer to a DOM object, you use the parent object name followed by the child object name or names, separated by periods. For example, if you need to refer to a specific image loaded in your web browser, these are child objects of the `document` object. But that `document` object, in turn, is a child of the DOM's `window` object. So, to reference an image called `logo_image`, the DOM object notation would look like this:

```
window.document.logo_image
```

Using `window` Objects

At the top of the browser object hierarchy is the `window` object, which represents a browser window. You've already used at least one method of the `window` object, `alert`, which displays a message in an alert box.

A user might have several windows open at a time, each with its own distinct `window` object, since different documents will presumably be loaded in each window. Even if the same document is loaded into two or more windows, they are considered distinct `window` objects because they are in fact distinct instances of the browser. However, when referencing `window.document` (or just `document`) in your JavaScript, the reference is interpreted to be the window currently in focus— the one actively being used. You'll learn more about windows, including how to reference out-of-focus windows, in Lesson 24, "Responding to Events and Using Windows."

The `window` object is the parent object for all the objects we will be looking at in this lesson. Figure 21.1 shows the `window` section of the DOM object hierarchy and a variety of its objects.

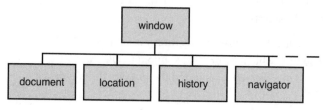

FIGURE 21.1
The `window` section of the DOM object hierarchy and some of its children.

Working with the document Object

Just as it sounds like it would, the document object represents a web document. Web documents are displayed within browser windows, so it shouldn't surprise you to learn that the document object is a child of the window object. Because the window object always represents the current window, as you learned in the preceding section, you can use window.document to refer to the current document. You can also simply refer to document, which automatically refers to the current window.

NOTE

In previous lessons, you've already used the document.write method to display text within a web document. The examples in earlier lessons used only a single window and document, so it was unnecessary to use window.document.write, but this longer syntax would have worked equally well.

In the following sections, you will look at some of the properties and methods of the document object that will be useful in your scripting.

Getting Information About a Document

Several properties of the document object include information about the current document in general:

▶ document.URL—Specifies the document's URL. You (or your code) cannot change the value of this property.

▶ document.title—Refers to the title of the current page, defined by the HTML <title> tag. You can change the value of this property.

▶ document.referrer—Returns the URL of the page the user was viewing before the current page—usually the page with a link to the current page. As with document.URL, you cannot change the value of document.referrer. Note that document.referrer will be blank if a user has directly accessed a given URL directly.

▶ document.lastModified—Indicates the date the document was last modified. This date is sent from the server along with the page.

▶ document.cookie—Enables you to read or set a cookie used within the document.

▶ document.images—Returns a collection of images used in the document.

As an example of a document property, Listing 21.1 shows a short HTML document that displays its last modified date using JavaScript.

LISTING 21.1   Displaying the Last Modified Date

```html
<!doctype html>
<html lang="en">
  <head>
    <meta charset="utf-8">
    <title>Displaying the Last Modified Date</title>
    <meta name="viewport"
          content="width=device-width, initial-scale=1">
  </head>
  <body>
    <h1>Displaying the Last Modified Date</h1>
    <p>This page was last modified on:
    <script>
        document.write(document.lastModified);
    </script>
    </p>
  </body>
</html>
```

Figure 21.2 shows the output of Listing 21.1.

FIGURE 21.2
Viewing the last modified date of a document.

If you use JavaScript to display the value of this document property, you don't have to remember to update the date each time you modify the page, should you choose to expose this information to the user. (You could also use the script to always print the current date instead of the last modified date, but that would be cheating.)

NOTE

You might find that the document.lastModified property doesn't work on your web pages or that it returns the wrong value. The date is received from the web server, and some servers do not maintain modification dates correctly.

Writing Text in a Document

The simplest document object methods are also the ones you use most often. In fact, you've used one of them already in the lessons so far, in very basic examples. The document.write method prints text as part of the HTML in a document window. An alternative statement, document. writeln, also prints text, but it also includes a newline (\n) character at the end. This is handy when you want your text to be the last thing on the line in your source code.

CAUTION

Bear in mind that the browser displays the newline character as a space but doesn't display it on the visible page, except inside a <pre> container. You need to use the <br> tag if you want an actual line break to be shown in the browser.

You can use these methods only within the body of the web page; you can't use these methods to add to a page that has already loaded unless you reload it. You *can* write new content for a document, however, as the next section explains.

NOTE

You can also directly modify the text of a web page by using more advanced features of the DOM, as you'll learn later in this lesson.

The document.write method can be used within a <script> tag in the body of an HTML document. You can also use it in a function, provided that you include a call to the function within the body of the document, as shown in Listing 21.1.

Using Links and Anchors

Another child of the document object is the link object. There can be, and very likely are, multiple link objects in a document. Each link object includes information about a link to another location or to an anchor.

You can access link objects through the links array. Each member of the array is one of the link objects in the current page. A property of the links array, document.links.length, indicates the number of links in the page. You might use the document.links.length property in a script to first determine how many links there are, before performing additional tasks such as dynamically changing the display on a certain number of links.

Each link object (or member of the links array) has a list of properties defining the URL that is ultimately stored in the object. The href property contains the entire URL, and other properties define other, smaller, portions of it. The link object uses the same property names as the location object, defined later in this lesson, so after you commit one set to memory, you will also know the other set.

You can refer to a property by indicating the link number, or position within the array, and property name. For example, the following statement assigns the entire URL of the first link stored in the array to the variable `link1`:

```
var link1 = links[0].href;
```

The `anchor` objects are also children of the `document` object. Each `anchor` object represents an anchor in the current document—a particular location that can be jumped to directly.

As with links, you can access anchors by using an array. For example, with an array called `anchors`, each element of the array is an `anchor` object. The `document.anchors.length` property gives you the number of elements in the `anchors` array. An example of using the `anchors` array to your advantage would be to use JavaScript to loop through all the anchors on a given page to dynamically generate a table of contents at the top of the page.

Accessing Browser History

The `history` object is another child (property) of the `window` object. This object holds information about the locations (URLs) that have been visited before and after the current one, and it includes methods to go to previous or next locations.

The `history` object has one property you can access:

> - **`history.length`**—Keeps track of the length of the history list—in other words, the number of different locations the user has visited.

The `history` object has three methods you can use to move through the history list:

> - **`history.go`**—Opens a URL from the history list. To use this method, specify a positive or negative number in parentheses. For example, `history.go(-2)` is equivalent to clicking the Back button twice.

> - **`history.back`**—Loads the preceding URL in the history list. This is equivalent to clicking the Back button or using `history.go(-1)`.

> - **`history.forward`**—Loads the next URL in the history list, if available. This is equivalent to clicking the Forward button or using `history.go(1)`.

You can use the `back` and `forward` methods of the `history` object to add your own Back and Forward buttons to a web document. The browser already has Back and Forward buttons, of course, but sometimes it is useful to include your own links that serve the same purpose.

Suppose you want to create a script that displays Back and Forward buttons and then use these methods to navigate the browser. Here's the code to create the Back button:

```
<button type="button" onclick="history.back();">Go Back</button>
```

In the preceding snippet, the <button> element defines a button labeled Go Back. The onclick event handler uses the history.back method to go to the preceding page in the browser's history. The code for a Go Forward button is similar:

```
<button type="button" onclick="history.forward();">Go Forward</button>
```

Let's take a look at these buttons in the context of a complete web page. Listing 21.2 shows a complete HTML document, and Figure 21.3 shows a browser's display of this document. After you load this document into a browser, visit other URLs and make sure the Go Back and Go Forward buttons work as expected.

LISTING 21.2 A Web Page That Uses JavaScript to Include Back and Forward Buttons

```
<!doctype html>
<html lang="en">
  <head>
    <meta charset="utf-8">
    <title>Using Custom Go Back and Go Forward Buttons</title>
    <meta name="viewport"
          content="width=device-width, initial-scale=1">
  </head>
  <body>
    <h1>Using Custom Go Back and Go Forward Buttons</h1>
    <p>Buttons on this page allow you to go back or forward in
    your history list.</p>
    <p>These buttons should be the equivalent of the back
    and forward arrow buttons in your browser's toolbar.</p>
    <div>
      <button type="button"
              onclick="history.back();">Go Back</button>
      <button type="button"
              onclick="history.forward();">Go Forward</button>
    </div>
  </body>
</html>
```

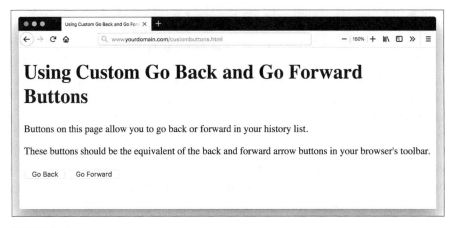

FIGURE 21.3
Showing custom Go Back and Go Forward buttons.

Working with the `location` Object

Another child of the `window` object is the `location` object. This object stores information about the URL currently loaded in the browser window. For example, the following JavaScript statement loads a URL into the current window by assigning a value to the `href` property of this object:

```
window.location.href="http://www.google.com";
```

The `href` property contains the entire URL of the window's current location. Using JavaScript, you can access portions of the URL through various properties of the `location` object. To understand these properties a bit better, consider the following URL:

https://www.google.com:443/search?q=javascript

The following properties represent parts of this URL:

- ▶ `location.protocol`—The protocol part of the URL (`http` in this example)

- ▶ `location.hostname`—The hostname of the URL (`www.google.com` in this example)

- ▶ `location.port`—The port number of the URL (`443` in this example)

- ▶ `location.pathname`—The filename part of the URL (`search` in this example)

- ▶ `location.search`—The query portion of the URL, if any (`q=javascript` in this example)

The following properties can also be used, though they aren't in this example:

- ▶ `location.host`—The hostname of the URL plus the port number (for example, `www.google.com:443`)

▶ `location.hash`—The anchor name used in the URL, if any (for example, www.google.com/#home)

The `link` object, introduced earlier in this lesson, also uses this list of properties for accessing portions of the URL found in the `link` object.

CAUTION

Although the `location.href` property usually contains the same URL as the `document.URL` property described earlier in this lesson. But you can't change the `document.URL` property. Always use `location.href` to load a new page in a given window.

The `location` object has three methods:

▶ `location.assign`—Loads a new document when used as follows:

```
location.assign("https://www.google.com")
```

▶ `location.reload`—Reloads the current document. This is the same as using the Reload button on the browser's toolbar. If you optionally include the `true` parameter when calling this method, the script ignores the browser's cache and forces a reload, whether the document has changed or not.

▶ `location.replace`—Replaces the current location with a new one. This is similar to setting the `location` object's properties yourself. The difference is that the `replace` method does not affect the browser's history. In other words, the Back button can't be used to go to the preceding location. This is useful for splash screens or temporary pages that it would be useless to return to. Remember that most people expect to be able to use the back button, so you should use the `location.replace` method sparingly.

More About the DOM Structure

Previously in this lesson, you learned how some of the most important DOM objects are organized: The `window` object is a parent to the `document` object, and so on. Although these objects were the only ones available in the original conception of the DOM years ago, the modern DOM adds objects under the `document` object for every element of a page.

To better understand the concept of a `document` object for every element, look at the simple HTML document in Listing 21.3. This document has the usual <head> and <body> sections, plus a heading and a single paragraph of text.

LISTING 21.3   A Simple HTML Document

```
<!doctype html>
<html lang="en">
  <head>
    <meta charset="utf-8">
    <title>A Simple HTML Document</title>
    <meta name="viewport"
          content="width=device-width, initial-scale=1">
  </head>
  <body>
    <h1>This is a Level-1 Heading.</h1>
    <p>This is a simple paragraph.</p>
  </body>
</html>
```

Like all other HTML documents, this one is composed of various containers and their contents. The <html> tags form a container that includes the entire document, the <body> tags contain the body of the page, and so on.

In the DOM, each container within the page and its contents are represented by an object. The objects are organized into a treelike structure, with the document object itself at the root of the tree and with individual elements such as the heading and paragraph of text at the leaves of the tree. Figure 21.4 shows a diagram of these relationships.

The following sections examine the structure of the DOM more closely.

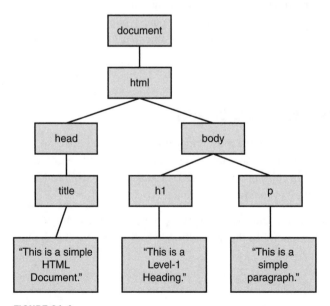

FIGURE 21.4
How the DOM represents an HTML document.

NOTE

Don't worry if this tree structure confuses you right now; just understand that you can assign IDs to elements and refer to them in your JavaScript. Later on, you will see more complicated examples that use this newfound information about how objects are organized in the DOM.

Nodes

Each container or element in a document is called a *node* in the DOM. In the example in Figure 21.4, each of the objects in boxes is a node, and the lines represent the relationships between the nodes.

You will often need to refer to individual nodes in scripts. You can do this by assigning an ID or by navigating the tree using the relationships between the nodes. You will get plenty of practice with nodes as you move forward in these lessons.

Parents and Children

As you have already learned, an object can have a *parent*—an object that contains it—and can also have *children*—objects that it contains. The DOM uses the same terminology as JavaScript in this regard.

In Figure 21.4, the document object is the parent object for the other objects shown, and it does not have a parent itself explicitly listed, although, as you've learned previously, the document object is a child of the window object. The html object is the parent of the head and body objects, and the h1 and p objects are children of the body object.

Text nodes work a bit differently. The actual text in the paragraph is a node in itself and is a child of the p object rather than being a grandchild of the body object. Similarly, the text within the <h1> tags is a child of the h1 object. Don't worry: We'll return to this concept throughout these lessons.

Siblings

The DOM uses another term for organization of objects: *siblings*. As you might expect, this refers to objects that have the same parent—in other words, objects at the same level in the DOM object tree.

In Figure 21.4, the h1 and p objects are siblings because both are children of the body object. Similarly, the head and body objects are siblings under the html object. There's not a lot of practical use in knowing which objects are siblings, but it is offered here as some knowledge that completes the family tree.

Working with DOM Nodes

As you've seen, the DOM organizes objects within a web page into a treelike structure. Each node (object) in this tree can be accessed in JavaScript. In the next sections you will learn how you can use the properties and methods of nodes to manage them.

NOTE

The following sections describe only the most important properties and methods of nodes and those that are supported by current browsers. For a complete list of available properties, see the W3C's DOM specification at www.w3.org/TR/DOM-Level-3-Core/.

Basic Node Properties

Previously, you used the `style` property of nodes to change their style sheet values. Each node also has a number of basic properties that you can examine or set, including the following:

▸ **nodeName**—The name of the node (not the ID). For nodes based on HTML tags, such as <p> or <body>, the name is the tag name: p or body. For the document node, the name is a special code: #document. Similarly, text nodes have the name #text. This is a read-only value.

▸ **nodeType**—An integer describing the node's type, such as 1 for normal HTML tags, 3 for text nodes, and 9 for the document node. This is a read-only value.

▸ **nodeValue**—The actual text contained within a text node. This property returns null for other types of nodes.

▸ **innerHTML**—The HTML content of any node. You can assign a value including HTML tags to this property and change the DOM child objects for a node dynamically.

NOTE

The `innerHTML` property is not a part of the W3C DOM specification. However, it is supported by the major browsers, and using it is often the easiest way to change content in a page. You can also accomplish this in a more standard way by deleting and creating nodes, as described later on. If your web page must be 100% standards compliant, then you should not use `innerHTML`, but in most situations using it is perfectly fine.

Node Relationship Properties

In addition to the basic properties described previously, each node has various properties that describe its relationship to other nodes. These include the following read-only properties:

▸ **firstChild**—The first child object for a node. For nodes that contain text, such as h1 or p, the text node containing the actual text is the first child.

▸ **lastChild**—The node's last child object.

- ▸ **childNodes**—An array that includes all of a node's child nodes. You can use a loop with this array to work with all the nodes under a given node.

- ▸ **previousSibling**—The sibling (node at the same level) previous to the current node.

- ▸ **nextSibling**—The sibling after the current node.

CAUTION

Remember that, like all other JavaScript objects and properties, the node properties and functions described here are case sensitive. Be sure you type them exactly as shown.

Document Methods

The document node itself has several methods you might find useful. You have already used one of them in exercises (getElementById) to refer to DOM objects by their ID properties. The document node's methods include the following:

- ▸ **getElementById(id)**—Returns the element with the specified id attribute.

- ▸ **getElementsByTagName(tag)**—Returns an array of all the elements with a specified tag name. You can use the wildcard * to return an array containing all the nodes in the document.

- ▸ **createTextNode(text)**—Creates a new text node containing the specified text, which you can then add to the document.

- ▸ **createElement(tag)**—Creates a new HTML element for the specified tag. As with createTextNode, you need to add the element to the document after creating it. You can assign content within the element by changing its child objects or the innerHTML property.

Node Methods

Each node within a page has a number of methods available. Which of them are valid depends on the node's position in the page and whether it has parent or child nodes. These methods include the following:

- ▸ **appendChild(new)**—Appends the specified new node after all the object's existing nodes.

- ▸ **insertBefore(new, old)**—Inserts the specified new child node before the specified old child node, which must already exist.

- ▸ **replaceChild(new, old)**—Replaces the specified old child node with a new node.

- ▸ **removeChild(node)**—Removes a child node from the object's set of children.

▶ **hasChildNodes**—Returns the Boolean value `true` if the object has one or more child nodes or `false` if it has none.

▶ **cloneNode**—Creates a copy of an existing node. If a parameter of `true` is supplied, the copy will also include any child nodes of the original node.

Creating Positionable Elements (Layers)

Now that you understand a little more about how the DOM is structured, you should be able to start thinking about how you can control any element in a web page, such as a paragraph or an image. For example, you can use the DOM to change the position, visibility, and other attributes of an element.

Before the W3C DOM and CSS2 standards (remember, we're now on CSS3), you could only reposition *layers*, or special groups of elements defined with a proprietary tag. Although you can now position any element individually, it's still useful to work with groups of elements in many cases.

You can effectively create a layer, or a group of HTML objects that can be controlled as a group, by using the `<div>` container element, which you learned about early in these lessons.

To create a layer with `<div>`, enclose the content of the layer between the `<div>` and `</div>` tags and specify the layer's properties in the `style` attribute of the `<div>` tag. Here's a simple example:

```
<div id="layer1" style="position:absolute; left:100px; top:100px;">
This is the content of the layer.
</div>
```

This code defines a layer with the name `layer1`. This is a movable layer positioned 100 pixels down and 100 pixels to the right of the upper-left corner of the browser window.

NOTE

As you've learned in earlier lessons, you can specify CSS properties such as the `position` property and other layer properties in a `<style>` block, in an external style sheet, or in the `style` attribute of an HTML tag, and you can then control these properties by using JavaScript. The code snippets shown here use properties in the `style` attribute rather than in a `<style>` block just because it is a snippet of an example and not a full code listing.

You've already learned about the positioning properties and seen them in action in Parts II, "Building Blocks of Practical Web Design," and III, "Advanced Web Page Design with CSS," of these lessons. This includes setting object size (such as `height` and `width`) and position (such as `absolute` or `relative`), object visibility, and object background and borders. The remaining examples in this lesson use HTML and CSS much as you've already seen them used but show you JavaScript-based interactions with the DOM in action.

Controlling Positioning with JavaScript

Using the code snippet from the preceding section, in this section you'll see an example of how you can control the positioning attributes of an object by using JavaScript.

Here is our sample layer (a `<div>`):

```
<div id="layer1" style="position:absolute; left:100px; top:100px;">
This is the content of the layer.
</div>
```

To move this layer up or down within the page by using JavaScript, you can change its `style.top` attribute. For example, the following statements move the layer 100 pixels down from its original position:

```
var obj = document.getElementById("layer1");
obj.style.top=200;
```

The `document.getElementById` method returns the object corresponding to the layer's `<div>` tag, and the second statement sets the object's `top` positioning property to 200px; you can also combine these two statements, like so:

```
document.getElementById("layer1").style.top = 200;
```

This simply sets the `style.top` property for the layer without assigning a variable to the layer's object.

NOTE

Some CSS properties, such as `text-indent` and `border-color`, have hyphens in their names. When you use these properties in JavaScript, you need to combine the hyphenated sections and use camel case: `textIndent` and `borderColor`.

Now let's create an HTML document that defines a layer and combine it with a script to allow the layer to be moved, hidden, or shown using buttons. Listing 21.4 shows the HTML document that defines the buttons and the layer. The script itself (`position.js`) follows, in Listing 21.5.

LISTING 21.4   The HTML Document for the Movable Layer Example

```
<!doctype html>
<html lang="en">
  <head>
    <meta charset="utf-8">
    <title>Positioning Elements with JavaScript</title>
    <style>
    #buttons {
        text-align:center;
    }
```

```
    #square {
        position: absolute;
        top: 150px;
        left: 100px;
        width: 200px;
        height: 200px;
        border: 2px solid black;
        padding: 10px;
        background-color: #e0e0e0;
    }
    div {
        padding: 10px;
    }
    </style>
     <meta name="viewport"
           content="width=device-width, initial-scale=1">
    </head>
    <body>
      <h1>Positioning Elements</h1>
      <div id="buttons">
        <button type="button" name="left"
                onclick="pos(-1,0);">Left</button>
        <button type="button" name="right"
                onclick="pos(1,0);">Right</button>
        <button type="button" name="up"
                onclick="pos(0,-1);">Up</button>
        <button type="button" name="down"
                onclick="pos(0,1);">Down</button>
        <button type="button" name="hide"
                onclick="hideSquare();">Hide</button>
        <button type="button" name="show"
                onclick="showSquare();">Show</button>
      </div>
      <hr>
      <div id="square">
        This square is an absolutely positioned layer
        that you can move using the buttons above.
      </div>
     <script src="position.js"></script>
    </body>
</html>
```

In addition to some basic HTML, Listing 21.4 contains the following:

▶ The <style> section is a brief style sheet that defines the properties for the movable layer. It sets the position property to absolute to indicate that it can be positioned at an exact location, sets the initial position in the top and left properties, and sets border and background-color properties to make the layer clearly visible.

▶ The `<button>` tags define six buttons: four to move the layer left, right, up, or down and two to control whether it is visible or hidden.

▶ The `<div>` section defines the layer itself. The `id` attribute is set to the value `"square"`. This `id` is used in the style sheet to refer to the layer and will also be used in your script.

▶ The `<script>` tag right before the `</body>` tag reads a script called `position.js`, which is shown in Listing 21.5.

If you load the HTML into a browser, you should see the buttons and the `"square"` layer, but the buttons won't do anything yet. The script in Listing 21.5 adds the capability to use the actions. When you load the code in Listing 21.4 into your browser, it should look as shown in Figure 21.5.

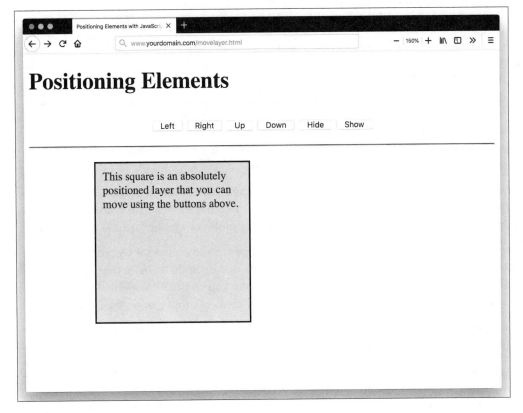

FIGURE 21.5
The movable layer, ready to be moved.

Listing 21.5 shows the JavaScript variables and functions that are called in the HTML in Listing 21.4. This code is expected (by the `<script>` tag) to be in a file called `position.js`.

LISTING 21.5 The Script for the Movable Layer Example

```
var x=100,y=150;
function pos(dx,dy) {
    if (!document.getElementById) return;
    x += 30*dx;
    y += 30*dy;
    obj = document.getElementById("square");
    obj.style.top=y + "px";
    obj.style.left=x + "px";
}
function hideSquare() {
    if (!document.getElementById) return;
    obj = document.getElementById("square");
    obj.style.display="none";
}
function showSquare() {
    if (!document.getElementById) return;
    obj = document.getElementById("square");
    obj.style.display="block";
}
```

The var statement at the beginning of the script defines two variables, x and y, that store the current position of the layer. The pos function is called by the event handlers for all four of the movement buttons.

The parameters of the pos function, dx and dy, tell the script how the layer should move: If dx is negative, a number is subtracted from x, moving the layer to the left. If dx is positive, a number is added to x, moving the layer to the right. Similarly, dy indicates whether to move up or down.

The pos function begins by making sure the getElementById function is supported, so it won't attempt to run in older browsers. It then multiplies dx and dy by 30 (to make the movement more obvious) and applies them to x and y. Finally, it sets the top and left properties to the new position (including the px to indicate the unit of measurement), thus moving the layer.

Two more functions, hideSquare and showSquare, hide or show the layer by setting its display property to "none" (hidden) or "block" (shown).

To use this script, save it as position.js and then load the HTML document in Listing 21.4 into your browser. Figure 21.6 shows this script in action—well, after an action, at least. Figure 21.6 shows the script after the Right button has been clicked four times and the Down button has been clicked five times.

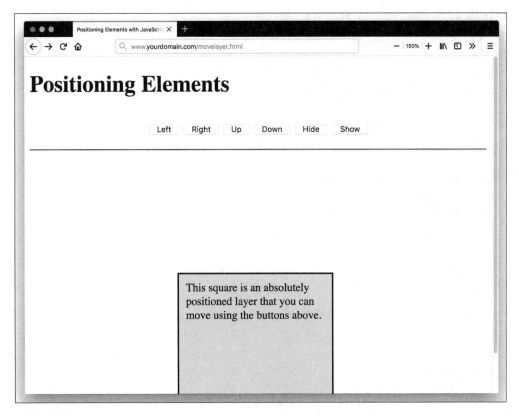

FIGURE 21.6
The movable layer has been moved.

Hiding and Showing Objects

In the preceding example, you saw some functions that can be used to hide or show the "square."
In this section, we'll take a closer look at hiding and showing objects in a page.

As a refresher, objects have a visibility style property that specifies whether they are currently visible within the page:

```
Object.style.visibility="hidden"; // hides an object
Object.style.visibility="visible"; // shows an object
```

Using this property, you can create a script that hides or shows objects in either browser.
Listing 21.6 shows the HTML document for a script that allows two headings to be shown or hidden.

LISTING 21.6   Hiding and Showing Objects

```
<!doctype html>
<html lang="en">
  <head>
    <meta charset="utf-8">
    <title>Hiding or Showing Objects</title>
    <meta name="viewport"
          content="width=device-width, initial-scale=1">
  </head>
  <body>
    <h1 id="heading1">This is the first heading</h1>
    <h1 id="heading2">This is the second heading</h1>
    <p>Using the W3C DOM, you can choose whether to show or hide
    the headings on this page using the checkboxes below.</p>
    <form name="checkboxform">
      <input type="checkbox" name="checkbox1"
             onclick="showHide();" checked>
      <span style="font-weight:bold;">Show first heading</span><br>
      <input type="checkbox" name="checkbox2"
             onclick="showHide();" checked>
      <span style="font-weight:bold;">Show second heading</span><br>
    </form>

    <script>
    function showHide() {
      if (!document.getElementById) return;
      var heading1 = document.getElementById("heading1");
      var heading2 = document.getElementById("heading2");
      var showheading1 = document.checkboxform.checkbox1.checked;
      var showheading2 = document.checkboxform.checkbox2.checked;
      heading1.style.visibility=(showheading1) ? "visible" : "hidden";
      heading2.style.visibility=(showheading2) ? "visible" : "hidden";
    }
    </script>
  </body>
</html>
```

The <h1> tags in this document define headings with the ids heading1 and heading2. Inside the <form> element are two check boxes, one for each of these headings. When a check box is modified (checked or unchecked), the onclick method calls the JavaScript showHide function to perform an action.

The showHide function is defined within the <script> tag at the bottom of the document. This function assigns the objects for the two headings to two variables named heading1 and heading2, using the getElementById method. Next, it assigns the value of the check boxes within the form to the `showheading1` and `showheading2` variables. Finally, the function uses the `style.visibility` attributes to set the visibility of the headings.

NOTE
_____

The lines that set the `visibility` property might look a bit strange. The `?` and `:` characters create *conditional expressions*, a shorthand way of handling `if` statements. You'll learn more about these conditional expressions in Lesson 23, "Controlling Flow with Conditions and Loops."

_____

Figure 21.7 shows this example in action. In the figure, the second heading's check box has been unchecked, so only the first heading is visible.

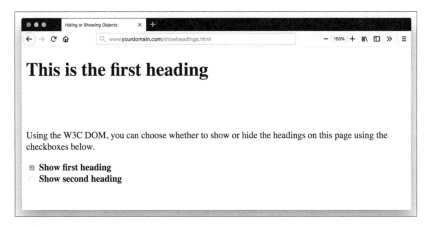

FIGURE 21.7
The text hiding/showing example in action.

Modifying Text in a Page

You can create a simple script to modify the contents of a heading (or any element, for that matter) within a web page. As you learned earlier in this lesson, the `nodeValue` property of a text node contains its actual text, and the text node for a heading is a child of that heading. Thus, this would be how to change the text of a heading with the identifier `heading1`:

```
var heading1 = document.getElementById("heading1");
heading1.firstChild.nodeValue = "New Text Here";
```

This assigns the heading's object to the variable called `heading1`. The `firstChild` property returns the text node that is the only child of the heading, and its `nodeValue` property contains the heading text.

Using this technique, it's easy to create a page that allows the heading to be changed dynamically. Listing 21.7 shows the complete HTML document for a script that does this.

LISTING 21.7 The Complete Text-Modifying Example

```
<!doctype html>
<html lang="en">
  <head>
    <meta charset="utf-8">
    <title>Dynamic Text in JavaScript</title>
    <meta name="viewport"
          content="width=device-width, initial-scale=1">
  </head>
  <body>
    <h1 id="heading1">Dynamic Text in JavaScript</h1>
    <p>Using the W3C DOM, you can dynamically change the
    heading at the top of this page.</p>
    <p>Enter a new title and click the Change! button. </p>

    <form name="changeform">
    <input name="newtitle" size="40">
    <button type="button" onclick="changeTitle();">Change!</button>
    </form>
    <script>
      function changeTitle() {
        if (!document.getElementById) return;
        var newtitle = document.changeform.newtitle.value;
        var heading1 = document.getElementById("heading1");
        heading1.firstChild.nodeValue=newtitle;
      }
    </script>
  </body>
</html>
```

This example defines a form that enables the user to enter a new heading for the page. Clicking the button calls the changeTitle function, defined in the <script> tag at the bottom of the document. This JavaScript function gets the value the user entered in the form and changes the heading's value to the new text by assigning the value of the input to the heading1. firstChild.nodeValue property.

Figure 21.8 shows this page in action after a new title has been entered and the Change! button has been clicked.

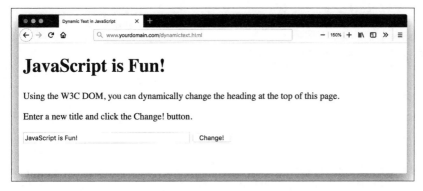

FIGURE 21.8
The heading-modification example in action.

Adding Text to a Page

Next, you can create a script that actually adds text to a page rather than just changing existing text. To do this, you must first create a new text node. This statement creates a new text node with the text "this is a test":

```
var node=document.createTextNode("this is a test");
```

Next, you can add this node to the document. To do this, you use the `appendChild` method. The text can be added to any element that can contain text, but in this example, we will just use a paragraph. The following statement adds the text node defined previously to the paragraph with the identifier `paragraph1`:

```
document.getElementById("paragraph1").appendChild(node);
```

Listing 21.8 shows the HTML document for a complete example that uses this technique, using a form to allow the user to specify text to add to the page.

LISTING 21.8   Adding Text to a Page

```
<!doctype html>
<html lang="en">
  <head>
    <meta charset="utf-8">
    <title>Adding Text to a Page</title>
    <meta name="viewport"
          content="width=device-width, initial-scale=1">
  </head>
  <body>
```

```
<h1 id="heading1">Create Your Own Content</h1>
<p id="paragraph1"> Using the W3C DOM, you can dynamically add
sentences to this paragraph.</p>
<p>Type a sentence and click the Add! button.</p>
<form name="changeform">
  <input name="sentence" size="65">
  <button type="button" onclick="addText();">Add!</button>
</form>

<script>
  function addText() {
    if (!document.getElementById) return;
    var sentence=document.changeform.sentence.value;
    var node=document.createTextNode(" " + sentence);
    document.getElementById("paragraph1").appendChild(node);
    document.changeform.sentence.value="";
  }
</script>
</body>
</html>
```

In this example, the `<p>` element with the `id paragraph1` is the paragraph that will hold the added text. The `<form>` element is a form with a text field called `sentence`, and an Add! button, which calls the `addText` function when clicked. This JavaScript function is defined in the `<script>` tag at the bottom of the document. The `addText` function first assigns text typed in the text field to the `sentence` variable. Next, the script creates a new text node containing the value of the `sentence` variable and appends the new text node to the paragraph.

Load this document into a browser to test it and try adding several sentences by typing them and clicking the Add! button. Figure 21.9 shows this document after several sentences have been added to the paragraph.

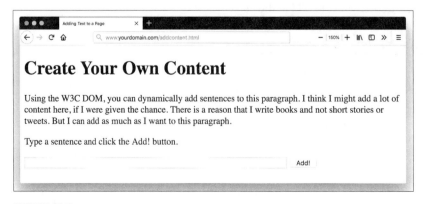

FIGURE 21.9
The text-addition example in action.

Summary

In this lesson, you learned a lot about the Document Object Model (DOM), which creates a hierarchy of web browser and document objects that you can access via JavaScript. You learned how you can use the `document` object to work with documents, and you used the `history` and `location` objects to control the current URL displayed in the browser.

You also learned the methods and properties you can use to manage DOM objects, and you created sample scripts to hide and show elements within a page, modify existing text, and add to existing text. You also learned how to use HTML and CSS to define a positionable layer and how you can use positioning properties dynamically with JavaScript.

This foundational knowledge of the DOM puts you in position (no pun intended) to more effectively work with JavaScript in advanced ways, as you'll learn in the lessons that follow.

Q&A

Q. Can I avoid assigning an `id` attribute to every DOM object I want to handle with a script?

A. Yes. Although the scripts in this lesson typically use the `id` attribute for convenience, you can actually locate any object in the page by using combinations of node properties such as `firstChild` and `nextSibling`. However, keep in mind that any change you make to the HTML can change an element's place in the DOM hierarchy, so the `id` attribute is a reliable recommended way to handle this.

Q. I can use `history` and `document` instead of `window.history` and `window.document`. Can I leave out the `window` object in other cases?

A. Yes. For example, you can use `alert` instead of `window.alert` to display a message. The `window` object contains the current script, so it's treated as a default object. However, be warned that you shouldn't omit the `window` object's name when you're using multiple windows or in an event handler.

Q. Can I change history entries or prevent the user from using the Back and Forward buttons?

A. You can't change the history entries. You also can't prevent the use of the Back and Forward buttons. However, you can use the `location.replace` method to load a series of pages that don't appear in the history. There are a few tricks for preventing the Back button from working properly, but I don't recommend using them as they're the sort of thing that gives JavaScript a bad reputation.

Workshop

The Workshop contains quiz questions and activities to help you solidify your understanding of the material covered. Try to answer all questions before looking at the "Answers" section that follows.

Quiz

1. Which of the following DOM objects never has a parent node?

    a. body

    b. div

    c. document

    d. p

2. Which of the following is the correct syntax to get the DOM object for a heading with the identifier `heading1`?

    a. `document.getElementById("heading1")`

    b. `document.GetElementByID("heading1")`

    c. `document.getElementsById("heading1")`

    d. `documents.getElementsById("heading1")`

3. Which of the following tags can be used to create a layer?

    a. `<layer>`

    b. `<div>`

    c. `<style>`

    d. `<p>`

4. Which property controls an element's left-to-right position?

    a. `left`

    b. `width`

    c. `lrpos`

    d. `position`

5. Which of the following CSS rules would create a heading that is not currently visible in the page?

    a. `h1 {visibility: invisible;}`

    b. `h1 {display: none;}`

    c. `h1 {style: invisible;}`

    d. `h1 {display: invisible;}`

6. What does the `document.URL` property do?

   a. Links to the defined URL

   b. Changes the current URL

   c. Specifies the current URL

   d. Nothing. It is invalid.

7. What is `nodeValue`?

   a. Any non-text content of a node

   b. The function of the node

   c. The method of the node

   d. The text within a node

8. Does the `<body>` tag have a `nodeValue` associated with it?

   a. Yes, the number of nodes attached to it

   b. Yes, the value of the child nodes

   c. Yes, but the value is null

   d. No

9. What method takes a child node out of an object?

   a. `removeNode`

   b. `removeChild`

   c. `deleteChild`

   d. `deleteNode`

10. How can you get the port number for a web page by using JavaScript?

   a. Yes, the number of nodes attached to it

   b. Yes, the value of the child nodes

   c. Yes, but the value is null

   d. No

NOTE

Just a reminder for those of you reading these words in the print or e-book edition of this book: If you go to **www.informit.com/register** and register this book (using ISBN 9780672338083), you can receive free access to an online Web Edition that not only contains the complete text of this book but also features an interactive version of this quiz.

Answers

1. **c.** The `document` object is the root of the DOM object tree and has no parent object.

2. **a.** `getElementById` has a lowercase *g* at the beginning and a lowercase *d* at the end.

3. **b.** The `<div>` tag is one of several container elements that can be used to create position-able layers (but it is the only one in this list that is valid).

4. **a.** The `left` property controls an element's left-to-right position.

5. **b.** The `none` value for the `display` property makes it invisible. The `visibility` property could also be used, but its possible values are `visible` or `hidden`.

6. **c.** It specifies the current document's URL and cannot be changed.

7. **d.** It is the actual text contained within a text node.

8. **c.** Technically, yes, but the value is `null` because it's not a text node.

9. **b.** The `removeChild` method removes a child node from an object.

10. **c.** Use the `location.port` or `location.host` properties to get the port number for a web page.

Exercises

▶ Modify the example in Listing 21.2 to include a Reload button along with the Back and Forward buttons. (This button would trigger the `location.reload` method.)

▶ Modify the positioning example in Listings 21.4 and 21.5 to move the square 1 pixel at a time rather than 30 pixels at a time.

▶ Add a third check box to Listing 21.6 to allow the paragraph of text to be shown or hidden. You need to add an `id` attribute to the `<p>` tag, add a check box to the form, and add the appropriate lines to the script.

LESSON 22
Using JavaScript Variables, Strings, and Arrays

What You'll Learn in This Lesson:

▶ How to name, declare, and assign variables

▶ How to choose whether to use local or global variables

▶ How to convert between different data types

▶ How to create and use `String` objects

▶ How to create and use arrays of numbers and strings

▶ How to define, call, and return values from functions

▶ How to use object properties and values

▶ How to define and use object methods

▶ How to use the `Math` object's methods

▶ How to use `new` and `this` keywords to work with objects

▶ How to use the `Date` object to work with dates

Now that you have learned some of the fundamentals of JavaScript and the DOM, it's time to dig into more details of the JavaScript language.

In this lesson, you'll learn three tools for storing data in JavaScript: *variables*, which store numbers or text; *strings*, which are special variables for working with text; and *arrays*, which are multiple variables you can refer to by number. Variables, strings, and arrays are not the most exciting elements of any programming language when described individually, but as you will see throughout the rest of these lessons, variables, strings, and arrays are fundamental to just about every bit of complex JavaScript that you'll develop.

In this lesson, you'll also learn about two more key JavaScript concepts that you'll use throughout the rest of these lessons (and in your future JavaScript endeavors). You'll learn the details of creating and using functions, which enable you to group any number of statements into a single block. Functions are useful for creating reusable sections of code, and you can create functions that accept parameters and return values for later use.

Whereas functions enable you to group sections of code, objects enable you to group data. You can use objects to combine related data items and functions for working with the data. You'll learn how to define and use objects and their methods and will work specifically with two of the most useful objects built into JavaScript: `Math` and `Date`.

Using Variables

Unless you have skipped over all the JavaScript-related lessons so far, you've already used a few variables. You probably can also figure out how to use a few more without any additional help. Nevertheless, there are some aspects of variables you haven't learned yet, and they are covered in the next few sections.

Choosing Variable Names

As a reminder, *variables* are named containers that can store data (for example, a number, a text string, or an object). As you learned earlier, every variable has a unique name of your choosing. However, there are rules you must follow when choosing a variable name:

▶ Variable names can include letters of the alphabet, both upper- and lowercase. They can also include the digits 0–9 and the underscore (_) character.

▶ Variable names cannot include spaces or any other punctuation characters.

▶ The first character of the variable name must be either a letter or an underscore.

▶ Variable names are case sensitive; for example, `totalnum`, `Totalnum`, and `TotalNum` are interpreted as separate variable names.

▶ There is no official limit on the length of a variable name, but it must fit on one line. Frankly, if your variable names are longer than that—or even longer than 25 or so characters, you might consider a different naming convention.

Using these rules, the following are examples of valid variable names:

```
total_number_of_fish
LastInvoiceNumber
temp1
a
_var39
```

NOTE

You can choose to use either friendly, easy-to-read names or completely cryptic ones. Do yourself a favor: Use longer (but not too long), friendly names whenever possible. Although you might remember the difference between a, b, x, and x1 right now, you might not after spending a few days away from the code, and someone who isn't you most certainly won't understand your cryptic naming convention without some documentation.

Using Local and Global Variables

Some computer languages require you to declare a variable before you use it. JavaScript includes the var keyword, which can be used to declare a variable. In many cases you can omit var, and the variable is still declared the first time you assign a value to it.

To understand where to declare a variable, you need to understand the concept of *scope*. A variable's scope is the area of the script in which that variable can be used. There are two types of variables:

▶ *Global variables* have the entire script (and other scripts in the same HTML document) as their scope. They can be used anywhere, even within functions.

▶ *Local variables* have a single function as their scope. They can be used only within the function they are created in.

To create a global variable, you declare it in the main script, outside any functions. You can use the var keyword to declare the variable, as in this example:

```
var students = 25;
```

This statement declares a variable called students and assigns it the value 25. If this statement is used outside functions, it creates a global variable. The var keyword is optional in this case, so this statement is equivalent to the preceding one:

```
students = 25;
```

Before you get in the habit of omitting the var keyword, be sure you understand exactly when it's required. It's actually a good idea to always use the var keyword; if you always use it, you'll avoid errors and make your script easier to read, and it won't usually cause any trouble.

A local variable belongs to a particular function. Any variable you declare with the var keyword in a function is a local variable. In addition, the variables in the function's parameter list are always local variables.

To create a local variable within a function, you *must* use the var keyword. This forces JavaScript to create a local variable, even if there is a global variable with the same name. However, try to keep your variable names distinct, even if you are using them in different scopes.

You should now understand the difference between local and global variables. If you're still a bit confused, don't worry: If you use the var keyword every time, you'll usually end up with the right type of variable.

Assigning Values to Variables

As you learned in Lesson 4, "Understanding JavaScript," you use the equal sign (=) to assign a value to a variable. For example, this statement assigns the value 40 to the variable `lines`:

```
var lines = 40;
```

You can use any expression to the right of the equal sign, including other variables. For example, earlier you used this syntax to add 1 to a variable:

```
lines = lines + 1;
```

Because incrementing or decrementing variables is quite common, JavaScript includes two types of shorthand for this syntax. The first is the += operator, which enables you to create the following shorter version of the preceding example:

```
lines += 1;
```

Similarly, you can subtract a number from a variable by using the -= operator:

```
lines -= 1;
```

If you still think that's too much to type, JavaScript also includes the increment and decrement operators, ++ and --. This statement adds 1 to the value of `lines`:

```
lines++;
```

Similarly, this statement subtracts 1 from the value of `lines`:

```
lines--;
```

You can alternatively use the ++ or -- operators before a variable name, as in ++`lines`. However, ++`lines` and `lines`++ are not identical. The difference is in when the increment or decrement happens:

▶ If the operator is after the variable name (for example, `lines`++), the increment or decrement happens *after* the current expression is evaluated.

▶ If the operator is before the variable name (for example, ++`lines`), the increment or decrement happens *before* the current expression is evaluated.

This difference is an issue only when you use the variable in an expression and increment or decrement it in the same statement. As an example, suppose you have assigned the `lines` variable the value 40. The following two statements have different effects:

```
alert(lines++);
alert(++lines);
```

The first statement displays an alert with the value 40 and then increments `lines` to 41. The second statement first increments `lines` to 41 and then displays an alert with the value 41.

NOTE

The increment and decrement operators are strictly for your convenience. If it makes more sense to you to stick to `lines = lines + 1`, do it; your script won't suffer.

Understanding Expressions and Operators

An *expression* is a combination of variables and values that the JavaScript interpreter can evaluate to a single value, such as $2 + 2 = 4$. The characters that are used to combine these values, such as + and /, are called *operators*.

NOTE

Along with variables and constant values, expressions can also include function calls that return results.

Using JavaScript Operators

In the basic JavaScript examples so far in these lessons, you've already used some operators, such as the + sign (addition) and the `increment` and `decrement` operators. Table 22.1 lists some of the most important (and common) operators used in JavaScript expressions.

TABLE 22.1 Common JavaScript Operators

Operator	Description	Example
+	Concatenate (combine) strings	`message="this is" + " a test";`
+	Add	`result = 5 + 7;`
−	Subtract	`score = score - 1;`
*	Multiply	`total = quantity * price;`
/	Divide	`average = sum / 4;`
%	Modulo (remainder)	`remainder = sum % 4;`
++	Increment	`tries++;`
--	Decrement	`total--;`

Along with these, there are also many other operators used in conditional statements. You'll learn about them in Lesson 23, "Controlling Flow with Conditions and Loops."

Operator Precedence

When you use more than one operator in an expression, JavaScript uses rules of *operator precedence* to decide how to calculate the value. Table 22.1 lists the operators from lowest to highest precedence, and operators with highest precedence are evaluated first. For example, consider this statement:

```
result = 4 + 5 * 3;
```

If you try to calculate this result, there are two ways to do it. You could multiply 5 * 3 first and then add 4 (result: 19), or you could add 4 + 5 first and then multiply by 3 (result: 27). JavaScript solves this dilemma by following the precedence rules: Because multiplication has a higher precedence than addition, JavaScript first multiplies 5 * 3 and then adds 4, producing a result of 19. Sometimes operator precedence doesn't produce the result you want. For example, consider this statement:

```
result = a + b + c + d / 4;
```

This is an attempt to average four numbers by adding them all together and then dividing by four. However, because JavaScript gives division a higher precedence than addition, it will divide the d variable by 4 before adding the other numbers, producing an incorrect result.

You can control precedence by using parentheses. Here's the working statement to calculate an average:

```
result = (a + b + c + d) / 4;
```

The parentheses ensure that the four variables are added first, and then the sum is divided by four. If you're unsure about operator precedence, you can use parentheses to make sure things work the way you expect and to make your script more readable.

Data Types in JavaScript

In some computer languages, you have to specify the type of data a variable will store (for example, a number or a string). In JavaScript, you don't need to specify a data type in most cases. However, you should know the types of data JavaScript can deal with.

These are the basic JavaScript data types:

▶ **Number**—Examples of numbers are 3, 25, and 1.4142138. JavaScript supports both integers and floating-point numbers.

▶ **Boolean**—Booleans are logical values. A Boolean can have one of two values, `true` or `false`, and is useful for indicating whether a certain condition is true.

▶ **String**—A string, such as `"I am a jelly doughnut"`, consists of one or more characters of text. (Strictly speaking, strings are `String` objects, which you'll learn about later in this lesson.)

▶ **Null**—The null value, represented by the keyword `null`, is the value of an undefined variable. For example, the statement `document.write(fig)` will result in a null value (and an error message) if the variable `fig` has not been previously used or defined.

Although JavaScript keeps track of the data type currently stored in each variable, it doesn't restrict you from changing types midstream. For example, suppose you declare a variable by assigning it a value, like so:

```
var total = 31;
```

This statement declares a variable called `total` and assigns it the value 31. This is a numeric variable. Now suppose you change the value of `total`:

```
total = "albatross";
```

This assigns a string value to `total`, replacing the numeric value. JavaScript will not display an error when this statement executes; it's perfectly valid, although it's probably not a very useful "total."

NOTE

Although this feature of JavaScript is convenient and powerful, it can also make it easy to make a mistake. For example, if the `total` variable is later used in a mathematical calculation, the result would be invalid—but JavaScript does not warn you that you've made this mistake.

Converting Between Data Types

JavaScript handles conversions between data types for you whenever it can. For example, you've already used statements like this:

```
document.write("The total is " + total);
```

This statement prints out the message `"The total is 40"`. Because the `document.write` function works with strings, the JavaScript interpreter automatically converts any nonstrings in the expression (in this case, the value of `total`) to strings before performing the function.

This works equally well with floating-point and Boolean values. However, there are some situations in which it won't work. For example, the following statement will work fine if the value of total is 40:

```
average = total / 3;
```

However, the total variable could also contain a string; in this case, the preceding statement would result in an error.

In some situations, you might end up with a string containing a number and need to convert it to a regular numeric variable. JavaScript includes two functions for this purpose:

▸ **parseInt**—Converts a string to an integer number

▸ **parseFloat**—Converts a string to a floating-point number

Both of these functions will read a number from the beginning of the string and return a numeric version. For example, these statements convert the string "30 angry polar bears" to a number:

```
var stringvar = "30 angry polar bears";
var numvar = parseInt(stringvar);
```

After these statements execute, the numvar variable contains the number 30; the nonnumeric portion of the string is ignored.

NOTE

These functions look for a number of the appropriate type at the beginning of the string. If a valid number is not found, the function returns the special value NaN, meaning *not a number*.

Using String **Objects**

You've already used several strings in the brief JavaScript examples found in previous lessons. Strings store a group of text characters and are named similarly to other variables. As a simple example, this statement assigns the string This is a test to a string variable called stringtest:

```
var stringtest = "This is a test";
```

In the following sections, you'll learn a little more about the String object and see it in action in a full script.

Creating a String Object

JavaScript stores strings as String objects. You usually don't need to worry about this piece of information—that your strings are in fact objects—but it will explain some of the common techniques you'll see for working with strings, which use methods (built-in functions) of the String object.

There are two ways to create a new String object. The first is the one you've already used, and the second way involves using object-oriented syntax. The following two statements create the same string:

```
var stringtest = "This is a test";
stringtest = new String("This is a test");
```

The second statement uses the new keyword, which you use to create objects. This tells the browser to create a new String object containing the text This is a test and assigns it to the variable stringtest.

NOTE

Although you can create a string by using object-oriented syntax, the standard JavaScript syntax is simpler, and there is no difference in the strings created by these two methods.

Assigning a Value

You can assign a value to a string in the same way as any other variable. Both of the examples in the preceding section assigned an initial value to the string. You can also assign a value after the string has already been created. For example, the following statement replaces the contents of the stringtest variable with a new string:

```
var stringtest = "This is only a test.";
```

You can also use the concatenation operator (+) to combine the values of two strings. Listing 22.1 shows a simple example of assigning and combining the values of strings.

LISTING 22.1 Assigning Values to Strings and Combining Them

```
<!doctype html>
<html lang="en">
  <head>
    <meta charset="utf-8">
    <title>String Text</title>
    <meta name="viewport"
          content="width=device-width, initial-scale=1">
  </head>
  <body>
```

```
<h1>String Test</h1>
<script>
  var stringtest1 = "This is a test. ";
  var stringtest2 = "This is only a test.";
  var bothstrings = stringtest1 + stringtest2;
  alert(bothstrings);
</script>
</body>
</html>
```

This script assigns values to two string variables, stringtest1 and stringtest2, and then displays an alert with their combined value (the variable bothstrings). If you load this HTML document in a browser, your output should resemble what's shown in Figure 22.1.

FIGURE 22.1
The output of the string sample script.

In addition to using the + operator to concatenate two strings, you can use the += operator to add text to a string. For example, this statement adds a period to the current contents of a string variable named sentence:

```
sentence += ".";
```

NOTE

The plus sign (+) is also used to add numbers in JavaScript. The browser knows whether to use addition or concatenation based on the type or types of data you use with the plus sign. If you use it between a number and a string, the number is converted to a string and concatenated.

Calculating the Length of a String

From time to time, you might find it useful to know how many characters a string variable contains. You can do this with the length property of String objects, which you can use with any string. To use this property, type the string's name followed by .length.

For example, `stringtest.length` refers to the length of the `stringtest` string. Here is an example of this property:

```
var stringtest = "This is a test.";
document.write(stringtest.length);
```

The first statement assigns the string `This is a test.` to the `stringtest` variable. The second statement displays the length of the string—in this case, 15 characters. The `length` property is a read-only property, so you cannot assign a value to it to change a string's length.

NOTE

Remember that although `stringtest` refers to a string variable, the value of `stringtest.length` is a number and can be used in any numeric expression.

Converting the Case of a String

Two methods of the `String` object enable you to convert the contents of a string to all uppercase or all lowercase:

- ▶ **toUpperCase**—Converts all characters in the string to uppercase
- ▶ **toLowerCase**—Converts all characters in the string to lowercase

For example, the following statement displays the value of the `stringtest` string variable in lowercase:

```
document.write(stringtest.toLowerCase());
```

If this variable contained the text `This Is A Test`, the result would be the following string:

```
this is a test
```

Note that the statement doesn't change the value of the `stringtest` variable. These methods return the upper- or lowercase version of the string, but they don't change the string itself. If you want to change the string's value, you can use a statement like this:

```
stringtest = stringtest.toLowerCase();
```

NOTE

Note that the syntax for these methods is similar to the syntax for the `length` property introduced earlier. The difference is that methods always use parentheses, whereas properties don't. The toUpperCase and toLowerCase methods do not take any parameters, but you still need to use the parentheses.

Working with Substrings

In the short examples so far in this lesson, you've worked only with entire strings. Like most other programming languages, JavaScript also enables you to work with *substrings*, or portions of a string. You can use the `substring` method to retrieve a portion of a string or the `charAt` method to get a single character. These are explained in the following sections.

Using Part of a String

The `substring` method returns a string consisting of a portion of the original string between two index values, which you must specify in parentheses. For example, the following statement displays the fourth through sixth characters of the `stringtest` string:

```
document.write(stringtest.substring(3,6));
```

At this point, you're probably wondering where the 3 and the 6 come from. There are three things you need to understand about using index parameters, regardless of when you're using them:

▸ Indexing starts with 0 for the first character of the string, so the fourth character is actually index 3.

▸ The second index is noninclusive. A second index of 6 includes up to index 5 (the sixth character).

▸ You can specify the two indexes in either order. The smaller one will be assumed to be the first index. In the previous example, (6,3) would produce the same result. Of course, there is rarely a reason to use the reverse order.

As another example, suppose you define a string called `alpha` to hold an uppercase version of the alphabet:

```
var alpha = "ABCDEFGHIJKLMNOPQRSTUVWXYZ";
```

The following are examples of the `substring` method using the `alpha` string:

▸ `alpha.substring(0,4)` returns ABCD.

▸ `alpha.substring(10,12)` returns KL.

▸ `alpha.substring(12,10)` also returns KL. Because 10 is the smaller of the two values, it is used as the first index.

▸ `alpha.substring(6,7)` returns G.

▸ `alpha.substring(24,26)` returns YZ.

- ▶ `alpha.substring(0,26)` returns the entire alphabet.

- ▶ `alpha.substring(6,6)` returns the `null` value, an empty string. This is true whenever the two index values are the same.

Getting a Single Character

Using the `charAt` method is a simple way to grab a single character from a specified position within a string. To use this method, specify the character's index, or position, in parentheses. As you've learned, the index begins at 0 for the first character. Here are a few examples of using the `charAt` method on the `alpha` string:

- ▶ `alpha.charAt(0)` returns A.

- ▶ `alpha.charAt(12)` returns M.

- ▶ `alpha.charAt(25)` returns Z.

- ▶ `alpha.charAt(27)` returns an empty string because there is no character at that position.

Finding a Substring

Another use for substrings is to find a string within another string. One way to do this is with the `indexOf` method. To use this method, add `indexOf` to the string you want to search and specify the string to search for in the parentheses. This example searches for `this` in the `stringtest` string and assigns the result to a variable called `location`:

```
var location = stringtest.indexOf("this");
```

CAUTION

As with most other JavaScript methods and property names, `indexOf` is case sensitive. Make sure you type it exactly as shown here when you use it in scripts.

The value returned in the `location` variable is an index into the string, similar to the first index in the `substring` method. The first character of the string is index 0.

You can specify an optional second parameter in this method to indicate the index value to begin the search. For example, this statement searches for the word `fish` in the `moretext` string, starting with the 20th character:

```
var newlocation = moretext.indexOf("fish",19);
```

NOTE

One use for the second parameter of this method is to search for multiple occurrences of a string. After finding the first occurrence, you search starting with that location for the second one, and so on.

A second method, `lastIndexOf`, works the same way but finds the *last* occurrence of the string. It searches the string backward, starting with the last character. For example, this statement finds the last occurrence of `Fred` in the `names` string:

```
var namelocation = names.lastIndexOf("Fred");
```

As with `indexOf`, you can specify a location to search from as the second parameter. In this case, the string will be searched backward, starting at that location.

Using Numeric Arrays

An *array* is a numbered group of data items that you can treat as a single unit. For example, you might use an array called `scores` to store several scores for a game. Arrays can contain strings, numbers, objects, or other types of data. Each item in an array is called an *element* of the array.

Creating a Numeric Array

Unlike with most other types of JavaScript variables, you typically need to declare an array before you use it. The following example creates an array with four elements:

```
scores = new Array(4);
```

To assign a value to the array, you use an index in brackets. As you've seen earlier in this lesson, an index begins with 0, so the elements of the array in this example would be numbered 0 to 3. These statements assign values to the four elements of the array:

```
scores[0] = 39;
scores[1] = 40;
scores[2] = 100;
scores[3] = 49;
```

You can also declare an array and specify values for elements at the same time. This statement creates the same `scores` array in a single line:

```
scores = new Array(39,40,100,49);
```

You can also use a shorthand syntax to declare an array and specify its contents. Using the following statement is an alternative way to create the `scores` array:

```
scores = [39,40,100,49];
```

CAUTION

Remember to use parentheses when declaring an array with the new keyword, as in a = new Array(3,4,5), and use brackets when declaring an array without new, as in a = [3,4,5]. Otherwise, you'll run into JavaScript errors.

Understanding Array Length

Like strings, arrays have a length property. This property tells the number of elements in the array. If you specified the length when creating the array, this value becomes the length property's value. For example, these statements would print the number 30:

```
scores = new Array(30);
document.write(scores.length);
```

You can declare an array without a specific length and change the length later by assigning values to elements or changing the length property. For example, these statements create a new array and assign values to two of its elements:

```
test = new Array();
test[0]=21;
test[5]=22;
```

In this example, because the largest index number assigned so far is 5, the array has a length property of 6. Remember that elements are numbered starting at 0.

Accessing Array Elements

You can read the contents of an array by using the same notation you used when assigning values. For example, the following statements would display the values of the first three elements of the scores array:

```
scoredisplay = "Scores: " + scores[0] + "," + scores[1] +
   "," + scores[2];

document.write(scoredisplay);
```

NOTE

Looking at this example, you might imagine it would be inconvenient to display all the elements of a large array. This is an ideal job for loops, which enable you to perform the same statements several times with different values. You'll learn all about loops in Lesson 23.

Using String Arrays

So far, you've used arrays of numbers. JavaScript also enables you to use *string arrays*, or arrays of strings. This is a powerful feature that enables you to work with a large number of strings at the same time.

Creating a String Array

You declare a string array in the same way as a numeric array—in fact, JavaScript does not make a distinction between them:

```
names = new Array(30);
```

You can then assign string values to the array elements:

```
names[0] = "John H. Watson";
names[1] = "Sherlock Holmes";
```

As with numeric arrays, you can also specify a string array's contents when you create it. Either of the following statements would create the same string array as the preceding example:

```
names = new Array("John H. Watson", "Sherlock Holmes");
names = ["John H. Watson", "Sherlock Holmes"];
```

You can use string array elements anywhere you would use a string. You can even use the string methods introduced earlier. For example, the following statement prints the first four characters of the first element of the names array, resulting in John:

```
document.write(names[0].substring(0,4));
```

Splitting a String

JavaScript includes a string method called split, which splits a string into its component parts. To use this method, specify the string to split and a character to divide the parts:

```
name = "John Q. Public";
parts = name.split(" ");
```

In this example, the name string contains the name John Q. Public. The split method in the second statement splits the name string at each space, resulting in three strings. These are stored in a string array called parts. After the sample statements execute, the elements of parts contain the following:

- ▸ parts[0] = "John"

- ▸ parts[1] = "Q."

- ▸ parts[2] = "Public"

JavaScript also includes an array method, join, that performs the opposite function. This statement reassembles the parts array into a string:

```
fullname = parts.join(" ");
```

The value in the parentheses specifies a character to separate the parts of the array. In this case, a space is used, resulting in the final string John Q. Public. If you do not specify a character, commas are used.

Sorting a String Array

JavaScript also includes a sort method for arrays, which returns an alphabetically sorted version of the array. For example, the following statements initialize an array of four names and sort it:

```
names[0] = "Public, John Q.";
names[1] = "Doe, Jane";
names[2] = "Duck, Daisy";
names[3] = "Mouse, Mickey";
sortednames = names.sort();
```

The last statement sorts the names array and stores the result in a new array, sortednames.

Sorting a Numeric Array

Because the sort method sorts alphabetically, it won't work with a numeric array—at least not the way you'd expect. If an array contains the numbers 4, 10, 30, and 200, for example, it would sort them as 10, 200, 30, 4—not even close. Fortunately, there's a solution: You can specify a function in the sort method's parameters, and that function is used to compare the numbers. The following code sorts a numeric array correctly:

```
function numbercompare(a,b) {
    return a-b;
}
numbers = new Array(30, 10, 200, 4);
sortednumbers = numbers.sort(numbercompare);
```

This example defines a simple function, numbercompare, that subtracts the two numbers. After you specify this function in the sort method, the array is sorted in the correct numeric order: 4, 10, 30, 200.

NOTE

JavaScript expects the comparison function to return a negative number if a belongs before b, 0 if they are the same, or a positive number if a belongs after b. This is why a-b is all you need for the function to sort numerically.

To gain more experience working with JavaScript's string and array features, you can create a script that enables the user to enter a list of names and displays the list in sorted form. Because this will be a larger script, you should create separate HTML and JavaScript files, as described in Lesson 20,

"Getting Started with JavaScript Programming." First, the sort.html file will contain the HTML structure and form fields for the script to work with. Listing 22.2 shows the HTML document.

LISTING 22.2   The HTML Document for the Sorting Example

```
<!doctype html>
<html lang="en">
  <head>
    <meta charset="utf-8">
    <title>Array Sorting Example</title>
    <meta name="viewport"
          content="width=device-width, initial-scale=1">
  </head>
  <body>
    <h1>Sorting String Arrays</h1>
    <p>Enter two or more names in the field below,
    and the sorted list of names will appear in the
    textarea.</p>
    <form name="theform">
      Name:
      <input name="newname" size="20">
      <input type="button" name="addname" value="Add"
      onclick="SortNames();">
      <br>
      <h2>Sorted Names</h2>
      <textarea cols="60" rows="10" name="sorted">
        The sorted names will appear here.
      </textarea>
    </form>

    <script src="sort.js"></script>
  </body>
</html>
```

Because the script is in a separate document, the <script> tag in this document uses the src attribute to include a JavaScript file called sort.js. This document defines a form named theform, a text field named newname, an addname button, and a <textarea> named sorted. Your script will use these form fields as its user interface.

Listing 22.3 provides the JavaScript necessary for the sorting process.

LISTING 22.3   The JavaScript File for the Sorting Example

```
// initialize the counter and the array
var numbernames=0;
var names = new Array();
function SortNames() {
```

```
   // Get the name from the text field
   thename=document.theform.newname.value;
   // Add the name to the array
   names[numbernames]=thename;
   // Increment the counter
   numbernames++;
   // Sort the array
   names.sort();
   document.theform.sorted.value=names.join("\n");
}
```

The script begins by defining two variables with the var keyword: numbernames is a counter that increments as each name is added, and the names array stores the names.

When you type a name into the text field and click the button, the onclick event handler calls the SortNames function. This function stores the text field value in a variable, thename, and then adds the name to the names array, using numbernames as the index. It then increments numbernames to prepare for the next name.

The final section of the script sorts the names and displays them. First, the sort method is used to sort the names array. Next, the join method is used to combine the names, separating them with line breaks, and display them in the <textarea>.

To test the script, save it as sort.js and then load the sort.html file you created previously into a browser. You can then add some names and test the script. Figure 22.2 shows the result after several names have been sorted.

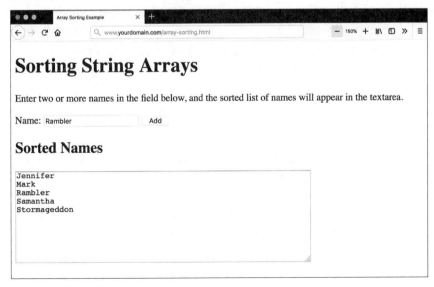

FIGURE 22.2
The output of the name-sorting example.

Using Functions

The scripts you've seen so far have been simple lists of instructions. The browser begins with the first statement after the `<script>` tag and follows each instruction, in order, until it reaches the closing `</script>` tag (or encounters an error).

Although this is a straightforward approach for short scripts, it can be confusing to read a longer script written in this fashion. To make it easier for you to organize your scripts, JavaScript supports functions, which you learned about briefly in Lesson 20. In this section, you will learn how to define and use functions.

Defining a Function

A function is a group of JavaScript statements that can be treated as a single unit. To use a function, you must first define it. Here is a simple example of a function definition:

```
function Greet() {
    alert("Greetings!");
}
```

This snippet defines a function that displays an alert message to the user. It begins with the `function` keyword followed by the name you're giving to the function—in this case, the function's name is `Greet`. Notice the parentheses after the function's name. As you'll learn in short order, the parentheses are not always empty, as they are here.

The first and last lines of the function definition include curly braces (`{ }`). You use these curly braces to enclose all the statements within the function. The browser uses the curly braces to determine where the function begins and ends.

Between the braces is the core JavaScript code of the function. This particular function contains a single line that invokes the `alert` method, which displays an alert message to the user. The message contains the text `"Greetings!"`.

CAUTION

Function names are case sensitive. If you define a function such as `Greet` with a capital letter, be sure you use the identical name when you call the function. If you define the function with the name `Greet` but you attempt to call the function using `greet`, it will not work.

Now, about those parentheses. The current version of the `Greet` function always does the same thing: Each time you use it, it displays the same message in the alert pop-up window.

To make this function more flexible, you can add *parameters*, also known as *arguments*. These are variables that are received by the function each time it is called. For example, you can add a parameter called who that tells the function the name of the person to greet, based on the value of that parameter when the function is called. Here is the modified Greet function:

```
function Greet(who) {
    alert("Greetings, " + who + "!");
}
```

Of course, to actually call this function and see its behavior in action, you need to include it in an HTML document. It used to be common to include all functions in the <head> of the document, but best practices now recommend that you include them at the end of the HTML unless there is some specific reason they need to be positioned higher in the document.

Listing 22.4 shows the Greet function embedded in the header section of an HTML document but not yet called into action.

LISTING 22.4   The Greet Function in an HTML Document

```
<!doctype html>
<html lang="en">
  <head>
    <meta charset="utf-8">
    <title>Functions</title>
    <meta name="viewport"
          content="width=device-width, initial-scale=1">
  </head>
  <body>
    <p>This is the body of the page.</p>

    <script>
      function Greet(who) {
          alert("Greetings, " + who + "!");
      }
    </script>
  </body>
</html>
```

Calling the Function

You have defined a function and placed it in an HTML document. However, if you load Listing 22.4 into a browser, you'll notice that it does absolutely nothing besides display the text "This is the body of the page." This lack of action is because the function is defined—ready to be used—but you haven't used it yet.

Making use of a function is referred to as *calling* the function. To call a function, use the function's name as a statement in a script or as an action associated with an event. To call a function, you need to include the parentheses and the values for the function's parameters, if any. For example, here's a statement that calls the Greet function:

```
Greet("Fred");
```

This tells the JavaScript interpreter to go ahead and start processing the first statement in the Greet function. When you call the function in this manner, with a parameter within the parentheses, you pass the parameter "Fred" to the function. This value of "Fred" is then assigned to the who variable inside the function.

NOTE

A function can have more than one parameter. To define a function with multiple parameters, list a variable name for each parameter, separating the parameters with commas. To call the function, specify values for the parameters, separated by commas.

Listing 22.5 shows a complete HTML document that includes the function definition and a few buttons within the page that call the function as an action associated with an event. To demonstrate the usefulness of functions, we'll call it twice to greet two different people—using two different parameters.

LISTING 22.5   The Complete Function Example

```html
<!doctype html>
<html lang="en">
  <head>
    <meta charset="utf-8">
    <title>Functions</title>
    <meta name="viewport"
          content="width=device-width, initial-scale=1">
  </head>
  <body>
    <h1>Function Example</h1>
    <p>Who are you?</p>
    <button type="button" onclick="Greet('Fred');">I am Fred</button>
    <button type="button" onclick="Greet('Ethel');">I am Ethel</button>

    <script>
      function Greet(who) {
          alert("Greetings, " + who + "!");
      }
    </script>
  </body>
</html>
```

This listing includes two buttons, each of which calls the `Greet` function a bit differently—with a different parameter associated with the call from each button.

Now that you have a script that actually does something, try loading it into a browser. If you click one of the buttons, you should see something like the screen in Figure 22.3, which shows the alert that appears when one of the buttons (I Am Ethel, in this case) is clicked.

FIGURE 22.3
The output of the `Greet` function example, with one button clicked.

Returning a Value

The function you created in the preceding example displays a message to the user in an alert pop-up, but a function can also return a value to the script that called it. This means you can use functions to calculate values. As an example, let's create a function that averages four numbers.

As usual, your function should begin with the `function` keyword, the function's name, and the parameters it accepts. Here we will use the variable names a, b, c, and d for the four numbers to average. Here is the first line of the function:

```
function Average(a,b,c,d) {
```

NOTE

Here we include the opening brace ({) on the first line of the function. This is a common style, but you can also place the brace on the next line or on a line by itself.

Next, the function needs to calculate the average of the four parameters. You can calculate this by adding them and then dividing by the number of parameters (in this case, 4). Thus, here is the next line of the function:

```
var result = (a + b + c + d) / 4;
```

This statement creates a variable called `result` and calculates the value assigned to `result` by adding the four numbers and then dividing by 4. (The parentheses are necessary to tell JavaScript to be absolutely sure to perform the addition before the division.)

To send this result back to the script that called the function, you use the `return` keyword. Here is the last part of the function:

```
return result;
}
```

Listing 22.6 shows the complete `Average` function in an HTML document. This HTML document also includes a small script in the `<body>` section that calls the `Average` function and displays the result.

LISTING 22.6   The `Average` Function in an HTML Document

```
<!doctype html>
<html lang="en">
  <head>
    <meta charset="utf-8">
    <title>Function Example: Average</title>
    <meta name="viewport"
          content="width=device-width, initial-scale=1">
    <script>
      function Average(a,b,c,d)  {
          var result = (a + b + c + d) / 4;
          return result;
      }
    </script>
  </head>
  <body>
    <h1>Function Example: Average</h1>
    <p>The following is the result of the function call.</p>
    <p>
      <script>
        var score = Average(3,4,5,6);
        document.write("The average is: " + score);
      </script>
    </p>
  </body>
</html>
```

The script in Listing 22.6 is an example of a script that won't work if the function is not loaded in the `<head>` of the document. This script is not unobtrusive, as you've learned in previous lessons, but making it unobtrusive would require more advanced JavaScript.

If you open the script in Listing 22.6 in your web browser, you will see the average printed on the screen, courtesy of the `document.write` method, as shown in Figure 22.4.

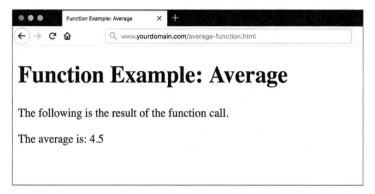

FIGURE 22.4
The output of the `Average` function example.

You can use a variable with the function call, as shown in Listing 22.6. This statement averages the numbers 3, 4, 5, and 6 and stores the result in a variable called `score`:

```
var score = Average(3,4,5,6);
```

NOTE

You can also use the function call directly in an expression. For example, you could use the `alert` statement to display the result of the function `alert(Average(1,2,3,4))`.

Introducing Objects

Earlier in this lesson, you learned how to use variables to represent different kinds of data in JavaScript. JavaScript also supports *objects*, a more complex kind of variable that can store multiple data items and functions. Although a variable can have only one value at a time, an object can contain multiple values, which enables you to group related data items into a single object.

In this lesson, you'll learn how to define and use your own objects. You've already worked with some of them, including the following:

▶ **DOM objects**—These objects enable your scripts to interact with elements of the web browser and web documents. You learned about these in Lesson 21, "Working with the Document Object Model (DOM)."

▶ **Built-in objects**—These include strings and arrays, which you learned about previously in this lesson.

The syntax for working with all three types of objects—DOM objects, built-in objects, and custom objects—is the same, so even if you don't end up creating your own objects, you should have a good understanding of JavaScript's object terminology and syntax.

Creating Objects

When you create an array, you use the following JavaScript statement:

```
scores = new Array(4);
```

The new keyword tells the JavaScript interpreter to use built-in functionality to create an object of the Array type. Objects have one or more *properties*—essentially, properties are variables, with values, that are stored within the object. For example, in Lesson 21, you learned you can use the location.href property to get the URL of the current document because the value (the URL) is assigned to that property, just as a value is assigned to a variable. The href property is one of the properties of the location object in the DOM.

You've also used the length property of String objects, as in the following example:

```
var stringtest = "This is a test.";
document.write(stringtest.length);
```

To reiterate, as with variables, each object property has a *value*. To read a property's value, you simply reference the object name and property name, separated by a period, in any expression. For instance, the example you just saw uses stringtest.length. You can change a property's value by using the = operator, just as you can change the assignment of a value to a variable. The following example sends the browser to a new URL by assigning a new variable to the location.href property:

```
location.href="http://www.google.com/";
```

NOTE

An object can also be a property of another object. This is referred to as a *child object*.

Understanding Methods

Along with properties, each object can have one or more *methods*. These are functions that work with an object's data. For example, as you learned in Lesson 21, the following JavaScript statement reloads the current document:

```
location.reload();
```

When you use the reload method, you're using a method of the location object. Like other functions, methods can accept arguments in parentheses, and they can return values. Each object type in JavaScript has its own list of built-in methods. For example, a list of built-in methods for the Array object can be found at https://developer.mozilla.org/en-US/docs/Web/JavaScript/Reference/Global_Objects/Array/prototype#Methods.

Using Objects to Simplify Scripting

Although JavaScript's variables and arrays provide versatile ways to store data, sometimes you need a more complicated structure, which is when objects are useful. For example, suppose you are creating a script to work with a business card database that contains names, addresses, and phone numbers for various people.

If you were using regular variables, you would need several separate variables for each person in the database: a name variable, an address variable, and so on. This would be very confusing, not to mention quite lengthy to define.

Arrays would improve things—but only slightly. You could have a names array, an addresses array, and a phone number array. Each person in the database would have an entry in each array. This would be more convenient than having many individually named variables, but it is still not perfect.

With objects, you can make the variables that store the database as logical as the physical business cards they are supposed to represent. Each person could be represented by a new `Card` object, which would contain properties for name, address, and phone number. You can even add methods to the object to display or work with the information, which is where the real power of using objects comes into play.

In the following sections, you'll use JavaScript to create a `Card` object and some properties and methods. Later in this lesson, you'll use the `Card` object in a script that will be used to display information for several members of this datastore you've created through the use of objects.

Defining an Object

The first step in creating an object is to name it and its properties. In this case, you should call your object `Card`, and it will have the following properties:

- name
- email
- address
- phone

To use this object in a JavaScript program, you need to create a function to make new instances of the `Card` object. This function is called the *constructor* for an object. Here is the constructor function for the `Card` object:

```
function Card(name,email,address,phone) {
    this.name = name;
    this.email = email;
    this.address = address;
    this.phone = phone;
}
```

The constructor is a simple function that accepts parameters to initialize a new object and assigns them to the corresponding properties. You can think of it like setting up a template for the object. The Card function in particular accepts several parameters from any statement that calls the function and then assigns these parameters as properties of an object. Because the function is called Card, the object created is a Card object.

Notice the this keyword. You'll use it anytime you create an object definition. Use this to refer to the current object—the one that is being created by the function.

Defining an Object Method

Next, you need to create a method to work with the Card object. Because all Card objects will have the same properties, it might be handy to have a function that prints the properties in a neat format. You can call this function printCard.

Your printCard function will be used as a method for Card objects, so you don't need to ask for parameters. Instead, you can use the this keyword again to refer to the current object's properties. Here is a function definition for the printCard function:

```
function printCard() {
    var name_line = "Name: " + this.name + "<br>\n";
    var email_line = "Email: " + this.email + "<br>\n";
    var address_line = "Address: " + this.address + "<br>\n";
    var phone_line = "Phone: " + this.phone + "<hr>\n";
    document.write(name_line, email_line, address_line, phone_line);
}
```

This function simply reads the properties from the current object (this), prints each one with a label string before it, and then creates a new line.

You now have a function that prints a card, but it isn't officially a method of the Card object. The last thing you need to do is make printCard part of the function definition for Card objects. Here is the modified function definition:

```
function Card(name,email,address,phone) {
    this.name = name;
    this.email = email;
    this.address = address;
    this.phone = phone;
    this.printCard = printCard;
}
```

The added statement looks just like another property definition, but it refers to the printCard function. This new method will work as long as printCard has its own function definition elsewhere in the script. (A method is essentially a property that defines a function rather than a simple value.)

NOTE

The previous example uses lowercase names such as `address` for properties and a mixed-case name (`printCard`) for the method. You can use any case for property and method names, but following the convention shown here is one way to make it clear that `printCard` is a method rather than an ordinary property.

Creating an Object Instance

Now you can use the object definition and method you just created. To use an object definition, you use the `new` keyword to create a new object. This is the same keyword you've already used to create `Date` and `Array` objects. The following statement creates a new `Card` object called `tom`:

```
tom = new Card("Tom Jones", "tom@jones.com",
              "123 Elm Street, Sometown ST 77777",
        "555-555-9876");
```

As you can see, creating an object is easy. All you do is call the `Card` function (the object definition) and enter the required attributes in the same order that you defined originally (in this case, the parameters `name`, `email`, `address`, `phone`).

After this statement executes, you will have a new object to hold Tom's information. This new object, now named `tom`, is called an *instance* of the `Card` object. Just as there can be several string variables in a program, there can be several instances of an object you define.

Rather than specify all the information for a card with the `new` keyword, you can assign the properties after the fact. For example, the following script creates an empty `Card` object called `holmes` and then assigns its properties:

```
holmes = new Card();
holmes.name = "Sherlock Holmes";
holmes.email = "sherlock@holmes.com";
holmes.address = "221B Baker Street";
holmes.phone = "555-555-3456";
```

After you've created an instance of the `Card` object, using either of these methods, you can use the `printCard` method to display its information. For example, this statement displays the properties of the `tom` card:

```
tom.printCard();
```

Now you've created a new object to store business cards and a method to print them. As a final demonstration of objects, properties, functions, and methods, you will now use this object in a web page to display data for several cards.

Your script needs to include the function definition for `printCard`, along with the function definition for the `Card` object. You will then create three cards and print them in the body of the document. You will use separate HTML and JavaScript files for this example. Listing 22.7 shows the complete script.

LISTING 22.7   A Sample Script That Uses the `Card` Object

```
// define the functions
function printCard() {
   var name_line = "<strong>Name: </strong>" + this.name + "<br>\n";
   var email_line = "<strong>Email: </strong>" + this.email + "<br>\n";
   var address_line = "<strong>Address: </strong>" + this.address + "<br>\n";
   var phone_line = "<strong>Phone: </strong>" + this.phone + "<hr>\n";
   document.write(name_line, email_line, address_line, phone_line);
}

function Card(name,email,address,phone) {
   this.name = name;
   this.email = email;
   this.address = address;
   this.phone = phone;
   this.printCard = printCard;
}

// Create the objects
var sue = new Card("Sue Suthers",
                   "sue@suthers.com",
                   "123 Elm Street, Yourtown ST 99999",
                   "555-555-9876");
var fred = new Card("Fred Fanboy",
                    "fred@fanboy.com",
                    "233 Oak Lane, Sometown ST 99399",
                    "555-555-4444");
var jimbo = new Card("Jimbo Jones",
                     "jimbo@jones.com",
                     "233 Walnut Circle, Anotherville ST 88999",
                     "555-555-1344");
// Now print them
sue.printCard();
fred.printCard();
jimbo.printCard();
```

Notice that the `printCard` function has been modified slightly to make things look good, with the labels in boldface. To prepare to use this script, save it as `cards.js`. Next, you'll need to include the `cards.js` script in a simple HTML document. Listing 22.8 shows the HTML document for this example.

LISTING 22.8 The HTML File for the Card Object Example

```
<!doctype html>
<html lang="en">
  <head>
    <meta charset="utf-8">
    <title>JavaScript Business Cards</title>
    <meta name="viewport"
          content="width=device-width, initial-scale=1">
  </head>
  <body>
    <h1>JavaScript Business Cards</h1>
    <p>External script output coming up...</p>
    <script src="cards.js"></script>
    <p>External script output has ended.</p>
  </body>
</html>
```

To test the complete script, save this HTML document in the same directory as the cards.js file you created earlier and then load the HTML document into a browser. Figure 22.5 shows how this example looks in a browser.

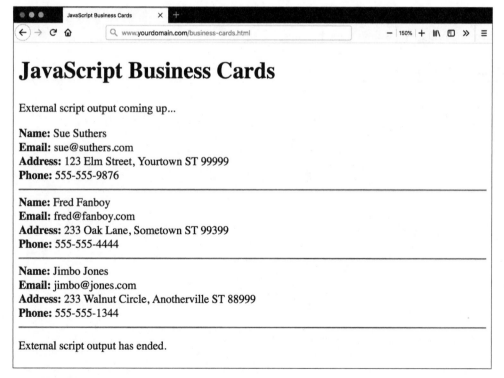

FIGURE 22.5
Displaying the output of the business card example.

Extending Built-in Objects

JavaScript includes a feature that enables you to extend the definitions of built-in objects. For example, if you think the `String` object doesn't quite fit your needs, you can extend it by adding a new property or method. This might be very useful, for example, if you want to create a large script that uses many strings and manipulates those strings in unique ways.

You can add both properties and methods to an existing object by using the `prototype` keyword. (A *prototype* is another name for an object's definition, or constructor function.) The `prototype` keyword enables you to change the definition of an object outside its constructor function.

As an example, you can add a method to the `String` object definition. You will create a method called `heading`, which converts a string into an HTML heading. The following statement defines a string called `myTitle`:

```
var myTitle = "Fred's Home Page";
```

This statement would output the contents of the `myTitle` string as an HTML level 1 heading (`<h1>`):

```
document.write(myTitle.heading(1));
```

Listing 22.9 adds a `heading` method to the `String` object definition that will display the string as a heading and then displays three headings using the new method.

LISTING 22.9   Adding a Method to the `String` Object

```
<!doctype html>
<html lang="en">
  <head>
    <meta charset="utf-8">
    <title>Test of Heading Method</title>
    <meta name="viewport"
          content="width=device-width, initial-scale=1">
  </head>
  <body>
    <script>
      function addHeading(level) {
          var html = "h" + level;
          var text = this.toString();
          var opentag = "<" + html + ">";
          var closetag = "</" + html + ">";
          return opentag + text + closetag;
      }
      String.prototype.heading = addHeading;
      document.write("This is a heading 1".heading(1));
      document.write("This is a heading 2".heading(2));
      document.write("This is a heading 3".heading(3));
```

```
      </script>
    </body>
</html>
```

You need to define the `addHeading` function, which will serve as the new string method. It accepts a number to specify the heading level. The `opentag` and `closetag` variables are used to store the HTML "begin heading tag" and "end heading tag" tags, such as `<h1>` and `</h1>`.

After the function is defined, use the `prototype` keyword to add it as a method of the `String` object. You can then use this method on any `String` object or, in fact, any JavaScript string. This is demonstrated by the last three statements, which display quoted text strings as level 1, 2, and 3 headings.

If you load this document into a browser, it should look something like what's shown in Figure 22.6.

FIGURE 22.6
Displaying the dynamic heading example.

Using the Math Object

The `Math` object is a built-in JavaScript object that includes math constants and functions. You'll never need to create a `Math` object because it exists automatically in any JavaScript program. The `Math` object's properties represent mathematical constants, and its methods are mathematical functions. If you're working with numbers in any way in your JavaScript, the `Math` object will be your new best friend.

Rounding and Truncating

Three of the most useful methods of the Math object enable you to round decimal values up and down:

- ▶ `Math.ceil`—Rounds a number up to the next integer
- ▶ `Math.floor`—Rounds a number down to the next integer
- ▶ `Math.round`—Rounds a number to the nearest integer

All these methods take the number to be rounded as their only parameter. You might notice one thing missing: the capability to round to a decimal place, such as for dollar amounts. Fortunately, you can easily simulate this, as shown in this simple function that rounds numbers to two decimal places:

```
function round(num) {
    return Math.round(num * 100) / 100;
}
```

The function shown here multiplies the value by 100 to move the decimal and then rounds the number to the nearest integer. Finally, the value is divided by 100 to restore the decimal to its original position.

Generating Random Numbers

One of the most commonly used methods of the Math object is the Math.random method, which generates a random number. This method doesn't require any parameters. The number it returns is a random decimal number between zero and one.

You'll usually want a random number between one and some predetermined value. You can generate such a number by using a general-purpose random number function. The following function generates random numbers between one and the parameter you send it:

```
function rand(num) {
    return Math.floor(Math.random() * num) + 1;
}
```

This function multiplies a random number by the value specified in the num parameter and then converts it to an integer between one and the number by using the Math.floor method.

Other Math Methods

The Math object includes many methods beyond those you've looked at here. For example, Math.sin and Math.cos calculate sines and cosines. The Math object also includes properties for various mathematical constants, such as Math.PI. You can see a list of all the built-in methods you can use with the `Math` object at https://developer.mozilla.org/en-US/docs/Web/JavaScript/Reference/Global_Objects/Math#Methods.

Working with `Math` Methods

The `Math.random` method generates a random number between 0 and 1. However, it's essentially impossible for a computer to generate a *truly* random number. (It's also hard for a human being to do so, which is why dice were invented.) Today's computers do reasonably well at generating random numbers, but just how good is JavaScript's `Math.random` function? One way to test it is to generate many random numbers and calculate the average of all of them.

In theory, the average of all generated numbers should be somewhere near .5, or halfway between 0 and 1. The more random values you generate, the closer the average should get to this middle ground. To really do this test, you can create a script that tests JavaScript's random number function by generating 5,000 random numbers and calculating their average.

This example will use a `for` loop, which you'll learn more about in the next lesson, but this is a simple enough example that you should be able to follow along. In this case, the `for` loop will generate the random numbers. You'll be surprised how fast JavaScript can do this.

To begin your script, initialize a variable called `total`. This variable will store a running total of all the random values, so it's important that it starts at 0, like so:

```
var total = 0;
```

Next, begin a loop that will execute 5,000 times. Use a `for` loop because you want it to execute for a fixed number of times (in this case 5,000):

```
for (i=1; i<=5000; i++) {
```

Within the `for` loop, you need to create a random number and add its value to the `total` variable. Here are the statements that do this and continue with the next iteration of the loop:

```
    var num = Math.random();
    total += num;
}
```

Depending on the speed of your computer, it might take a few seconds to generate those 5,000 random numbers. Just to be sure something is happening, you can have the script display a status message after each 1,000 numbers:

```
if (i % 1000 == 0) {
    document.write("Generated " + i + " numbers...<br>");
}
```

NOTE

The % symbol in the previous code is the *modulo* operator, which gives you the remainder after dividing one number by another. In this case it is used to find even multiples of 1,000.

The final part of your script calculates the average by dividing the value of the `total` variable by 5,000. It also rounds the average to three decimal places, for fun:

```
var average = total / 5000;
average = Math.round(average * 1000) / 1000;
document.write("<h2>Average of 5000 numbers is: " + average + "</h2>");
```

To test this script and see just how random the numbers are, combine the complete script with an HTML document and `<script>` tags. Listing 22.10 shows the complete random number testing script.

LISTING 22.10   A Script to Test JavaScript's Random Number Function

```
<!doctype html>
<html lang="en">
  <head>
    <meta charset="utf-8">
    <title>Math Example</title>
    <meta name="viewport"
          content="width=device-width, initial-scale=1">
  </head>
  <body>
    <h1>Math Example</h1>
    <p>How random are JavaScript's random numbers?<br>
    Let's generate 5000 of them and find out.</p>
    <script>
      var total = 0;
      for (i=1; i<=5000; i++) {
        var num = Math.random();
        total += num;
        if (i % 1000 == 0) {
          document.write("Generated " + i + " numbers...<br>");
        }
      }
      var average = total / 5000;
      average = Math.round(average * 1000) / 1000;
      document.write("<h2>Average of 5000 numbers is: " +
                      average + "</h2>");
    </script>
  </body>
</html>
```

To test the script, load the HTML document into a browser. After a short delay, you should see a result. If it's close to .5, the numbers are reasonably random. My result was .502, as shown in Figure 22.7. If you reload the page, you'll likely get different results, but they should all be around .5.

NOTE

The average used here is called an *arithmetic mean*. This type of average isn't a perfect way to test randomness. Actually, all it tests is the distribution of the numbers above and below .5. For example, if the numbers turned out to be 2,500 .4s and 2,500 .6s, the average would be a perfect .5—but the numbers wouldn't be very random. (Thankfully, JavaScript's random numbers don't have this problem.)

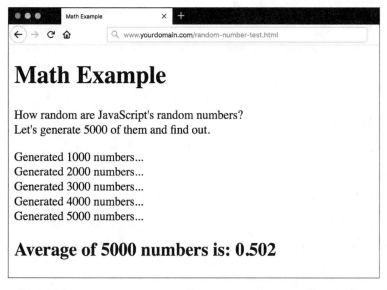

FIGURE 22.7
The random number testing script in action.

Working with Dates

The `Date` object is a built-in JavaScript object that enables you to work more easily with dates and times. You can create a `Date` object anytime you need to store a date and use the `Date` object's methods to work with the date.

You encountered one example of a `Date` object in Lesson 4 with the time and date script. The `Date` object has no properties of its own. To set or obtain values from a `Date` object, use the methods described in the next section.

NOTE
_____

JavaScript dates are stored as the number of milliseconds since midnight on January 1, 1970. This date is called the *epoch*. Dates before 1970 weren't allowed in early versions but are now represented by negative numbers.

_____

Creating a Date Object

You can create a Date object by using the new keyword. You can also optionally specify the date to store in the object when you create it. You can use any of the following formats:

```
birthday = new Date();
birthday = new Date("November 1, 2014 08:00:00");
birthday = new Date(11,1, 2014);
birthday = new Date(11,1,2014, 8, 0, 0);
```

You can choose any of these formats, depending on which values you want to set. If you use no parameters, as in the first example, the current date is stored in the object. You can then set the values by using the set methods, described in the next section.

Setting Date Values

Various set methods enable you to set components of a Date object to values:

▶ **setDate**—Sets the day of the month.

▶ **setMonth**—Sets the month, from 0 for January to 11 for December

▶ **setFullYear**—Sets the year

▶ **setTime**—Sets the time (and the date) by specifying the number of milliseconds since January 1, 1970

▶ **setHours, setMinutes, and setSeconds**—Set the time

As an example, the following statement sets the year of a Date object called holiday to 2018:

```
holiday.setFullYear(2018);
```

Reading Date Values

You can use the get methods to get values from a Date object. This is the only way to obtain these values because they are not available as properties. Here are the available get methods for dates:

▶ **getDate**—Gets the day of the month

▶ **getMonth**—Gets the month

- **getFullYear**—Gets the four-digit year

- **getTime**—Gets the time (and the date) as the number of milliseconds since January 1, 1970

- **getHours, getMinutes, getSeconds, and getMilliseconds**—Get the components of the time

---

NOTE

Along with setFullYear and getFullYear, which require four-digit years, JavaScript includes the setYear and getYear methods, which use two-digit year values.

Working with Time Zones

Finally, a few functions are available to help your Date objects work with local time values and time zones:

- **getTimeZoneOffset**—Gives you the local time zone's offset from UTC (Coordinated Universal Time, based on the old Greenwich Mean Time standard). In this case, *local* refers to the location of the browser. (Of course, this works only if the user has set his or her system clock accurately.)

- **toUTCString**—Converts the date object's time value to text, using UTC.

- **toLocalString**—Converts the date object's time value to text, using local time.

Along with these basic functions, JavaScript includes UTC versions of several of the functions described previously. These are identical to the regular commands but work with UTC instead of local time:

- **getUTCDate**—Gets the day of the month in UTC time

- **getUTCDay**—Gets the day of the week in UTC time

- **getUTCFullYear**—Gets the four-digit year in UTC time

- **getUTCMonth**—Returns the month of the year in UTC time

- **getUTCHours, getUTCMinutes, getUTCSeconds, and getUTCMilliseconds**—Return the components of the time in UTC

- **setUTCDate, setUTCFullYear, setUTCMonth, setUTCHours, setUTCMinutes, setUTCSeconds, and setUTCMilliseconds**—Set the time in UTC

Converting Between Date Formats

Two special methods of the `Date` object enable you to convert between date formats:

▶ `Date.parse`—Converts a date string, such as `March 1, 2018`, to a `Date` object (the number of milliseconds since 1/1/1970)

▶ `Date.UTC`—Converts a `Date` object value (the number of milliseconds) to a UTC (GMT) time

Instead of using these methods with a `Date` object you have created, you use them with the built-in object `Date`.

Summary

In this lesson, we focused on variables and how JavaScript handles them. You've learned how to name variables, how to declare them, and the differences between local and global variables. You also explored the data types supported by JavaScript and how to convert between them.

You learned about JavaScript's more complex variable types—strings and arrays—and looked at features that enable you to perform operations on them, such as converting strings to uppercase and sorting arrays.

You learned several important features of JavaScript in this lesson. First, you learned how to use functions to group JavaScript statements and how to call functions and use the values they return. Next, you learned about JavaScript's object-oriented features—defining objects with constructors, creating object instances, and working with properties, property values, and methods.

As an example of these object-oriented features, you looked more closely at the `Math` and `Date` built-in JavaScript objects and learned more than you ever wanted to know about random numbers.

Q&A

Q. What is the importance of the `var` keyword? Should I always use it to declare variables?

A. You only need to use `var` to define a local variable in a function. However, if you're unsure at all, it's always safe to use `var`. Using it consistently will help you keep your scripts organized and error free.

Q. Is there any reason I would want to use the `var` keyword to create a local variable with the same name as a global one?

A. Not on purpose. The main reason to use `var` is to avoid conflicts with global variables you might not know about. For example, you might add a global variable in the future, or you might add another script to the page that uses a similar variable name. This is more of an issue with large, complex scripts.

Q. What good are Boolean variables?

A. Often in scripts you'll need a variable to indicate whether something has happened—for example, whether a phone number the user has entered is in the right format. Boolean variables are ideal for this; they're also useful in working with conditions, as you'll see in Lesson 23.

Q. Can I store other types of data in an array? For example, can I have an array of dates?

A. Absolutely. JavaScript enables you to store any data type in an array.

Q. Many objects in JavaScript, such as DOM objects, include parent and child objects. Can I include child objects in my custom object definitions?

A. Yes. Just create a constructor function for the child object and then add a property to the parent object that corresponds to it. For example, if you created a `Nicknames` object to store several nicknames for a person in the card file example, you could add it as a child object in the `Card` object's constructor: `this.nick = new Nicknames();`.

Q. Can I create an array of custom objects?

A. Yes. First, create the object definition as usual and define an array with the required number of elements. Then assign a new object to each array element (for example, `cardarray[1] = new Card();`). You can use a loop, as described in the next lesson, to assign objects to an entire array at once.

Q. Can I modify all properties of objects?

A. With custom objects, yes—but this varies with built-in objects and DOM objects. For example, you can use the `length` property to find the length of a string, but it is a *read-only property* and cannot be modified.

Workshop

The Workshop contains quiz questions and activities to help you solidify your understanding of the material covered. Try to answer all questions before looking at the "Answers" section that follows.

Quiz

1. Which of the following is *not* a valid JavaScript variable name?

   a. 2names

   b. first_and_last_names

   c. FirstAndLast

2. If the statement `var fig=2` appears in a function, which type of variable does it declare?

    a. A global variable

    b. A local variable

    c. A constant variable

3. If the string `test` contains the value The eagle has landed., what would be the value of `test.length`?

    a. 4

    b. 21

    c. The

4. Using the same sample string, which of these statements would return the word `eagle`?

    a. `test.substring(4,9)`

    b. `test.substring(5,9)`

    c. `test.substring("eagle")`

5. What will be the result of the JavaScript expression `31 + " angry polar bears"`?

    a. An error message

    b. 32

    c. `"31 angry polar bears"`

6. What JavaScript keyword is used to create an instance of an object?

    a. `object`

    b. `new`

    c. `instance`

7. What is the meaning of the `this` keyword in JavaScript?

    a. It refers to the current object.

    b. It refers to the current script.

    c. It has no meaning.

8. Which of the following objects *cannot* be used with the new keyword?

    a. `Date`

    b. `Math`

    c. `String`

9. How does JavaScript store dates in a `Date` object?

    a. The number of milliseconds since January 1, 1970

    b. The number of days since January 1, 1900

    c. The number of seconds since Netscape's public stock offering

10. What is the range of random numbers generated by the `Math.random` function?

    a. Between 1 and 100

    b. Between 1 and the number of milliseconds since January 1, 1970

    c. Between 0 and 1

NOTE

Just a reminder for those of you reading these words in the print or e-book edition of this book: If you go to **www.informit.com/register** and register this book (using ISBN 9780672338083), you can receive free access to an online Web Edition that not only contains the complete text of this book but also features an interactive version of this quiz.

Answers

1. **a.** 2names is an invalid JavaScript variable name because it begins with a number. The others are valid, although they're probably not ideal choices for names.

2. **b.** Because the variable is declared in a function, it is a local variable. The `var` keyword ensures that a local variable is created.

3. **b.** The length of the string is 21 characters.

4. **a.** The correct statement is `test.substring(4,9)`. Remember that the indexes start with 0 and that the second index is noninclusive.

5. **c.** JavaScript converts the whole expression to the string `"31 angry polar bears"`. (We mean no offense to polar bears, who are seldom angry and are rarely seen in groups this large.)

6. **b.** The new keyword creates an object instance.

7. **a.** The `this` keyword refers to the current object.

8. **b.** The `Math` object is static; you can't create a `Math` object.

9. **a.** Dates are stored as the number of milliseconds since January 1, 1970.

10. **c.** JavaScript's random numbers are between 0 and 1.

Exercises

▶ Modify the sorting example in Listing 22.3 to convert the names to all uppercase and display a numbered list of names in the `<textarea>`.

▶ Modify the definition of the `Card` object to include a property called `personal_notes` to store your own notes about the person. Modify the object definition and `printCard` function in Listings 22.7 and 22.8 to include this property.

▶ Modify the random number script in Listing 22.10 to run three times to calculate a total of 15,000 random numbers and then display a separate total for each set of 5,000 numbers. (Hint: You'll need to use another `for` loop that encloses most of the script.)

Controlling Flow with Conditions and Loops

What You'll Learn in This Lesson:

- ▸ How to test conditions with the `if` statement
- ▸ How to use comparison operators to compare values
- ▸ How to use logical operators to combine conditions
- ▸ How to use alternative conditions with `else`
- ▸ How to create expressions with conditional operators
- ▸ How to test for multiple conditions
- ▸ How to perform repeated statements with the `for` loop
- ▸ How to use `while` and `do...while` loops
- ▸ How to create infinite loops (and why you shouldn't)
- ▸ How to escape from loops and continue loops
- ▸ How to loop through an array's properties

Statements in a JavaScript program generally execute in the order in which they appear, one after the other. Because this order isn't always practical, most programming languages provide *flow control* statements that let you control the order in which code is executed. Functions, which you learned about in the preceding lesson, are one type of flow control; although a function might be defined first thing in your code, its statements can be executed anywhere in the script.

In this lesson, you'll look at two other types of flow control in JavaScript: conditions, which allow a choice of different options depending on values that are tested, and loops, which allow statements to repeat based on certain conditions.

The `if` Statement

One of the most important features of a computer language is the capability to test and compare values and to perform different actions based on the results of the test or the values that are present. This allows your scripts to behave differently based on the values of variables or based on input from the user.

The if statement is the main conditional statement in JavaScript. This statement means much the same in JavaScript as it does in English. For example, here is a typical conditional statement in English:

If the phone rings, answer it.

This statement consists of two parts: a condition (*If the phone rings*) and an action (*answer it*). The if statement in JavaScript works much the same way. Here is an example of a basic if statement:

```
if (a == 1) alert("I found a 1!");
```

This statement includes a condition (if a equals 1) and an action (display a message). This statement checks the variable a and, if it has a value of 1, displays an alert message. Otherwise, it does nothing.

If you use an if statement all on one line, as in the preceding example, you can use only a single statement as the action. However, you can also use multiple statements for the action by enclosing the entire if statement in curly braces ({ }), as shown here:

```
if (a == 1) {
    alert("I found a 1!");
    a = 0;
}
```

This block of statements checks the variable a once again. If the value of the variable matches 1, it displays a message and sets a to 0.

It's up to you, as a matter of personal style, whether you use the curly braces for single statements within flow control structures. Some people find it easier to read if all the flow control structures are clearly delineated through the use of curly braces no matter their length, and other developers are perfectly happy using a mix of single-line conditional statements and statements within braces. It doesn't really matter which you use; just try to use them consistently for easier ongoing maintenance.

Conditional Operators

The action part of an if statement can include any of the JavaScript statements you've already learned (and those you haven't, for that matter), but the condition part of the statement uses its own syntax. This is called a *conditional expression*.

A conditional expression usually includes two values to be compared (in the preceding example, the values a and 1). These values can be variables, constants, or even expressions in themselves.

Either side of the conditional expression can be a variable, a constant, or an expression. You can compare a variable and a value or compare two variables. (You can also compare two constants, but there's usually no reason to do this.)

Between the two values to be compared is a *conditional operator*. This operator tells JavaScript how to compare the two values. For instance, the == operator that you saw in the preceding section is used to test whether the two values are equal.

Various conditional operators are available:

▶ ==—Is equal to

▶ !=—Is not equal to

▶ <—Is less than

▶ >—Is greater than

▶ >=—Is greater than or equal to

▶ <=—Is less than or equal to

CAUTION
Be sure not to confuse the equality operator (==) with the assignment operator (=), even though they both might be read or referred to as "equals." Remember to use = when *assigning* a value to a variable and == when *comparing* values. Confusing these two is one of the most common mistakes in programming (JavaScript or otherwise).

Combining Conditions with Logical Operators

Often, you'll want to check a variable for more than one possible value or check more than one variable at once. JavaScript includes *logical operators*, also known as Boolean operators, for this purpose. For example, the following two statements check different conditions and use the same action:

```
if (phone == "") alert("error!");
if (email == "") alert("error!");
```

Using a logical operator, you can combine them into a single statement:

```
if ((phone == "") || (email == "")) alert("Something Is Missing!");
```

This statement uses the logical OR operator (||) to combine the conditions. Translated to English, this would be, "If the phone number is blank or the email address is blank, display an error message."

An additional logical operator is the AND operator, &&. Consider this statement:

```
if ((phone == "") && (email == "")) alert("Both Values Are Missing!");
```

In this case, the error message will be displayed only if *both* the email address and phone number variables are blank.

NOTE

If the JavaScript interpreter discovers the answer to a conditional expression before reaching the end, it does not evaluate the rest of the condition. For example, if the first of two conditions separated by the | | operator is true, the second is not evaluated because the condition (one or the other) has already been met. You can therefore use operators to improve the speed of your scripts.

A third logical operator is the exclamation point (!), which means NOT. It can be used to invert an expression—in other words, make a true expression false and a false expression true. For example, here's a statement that uses the NOT operator:

```
if (!phone == "") alert("phone is OK");
```

In this statement, the ! (NOT) operator inverts the condition, so the action of the `if` statement is executed only if the phone number variable is *not* blank. You could also use the != (NOT EQUAL) operator to simplify this statement:

```
if (phone != "") alert("phone is OK");
```

Both of the preceding statements will alert you if the phone variable has a value assigned to it (that is, if it is not blank or `null`).

NOTE

Logical operators are powerful, but it's easy to accidentally create an impossible condition with them. For example, the condition ((a < 10) && (a > 20)) might look correct at first glance. However, if you read it out loud, you get "If a is less than 10 and a is greater than 20"—which is an impossibility in our universe. In this case, OR (| |) should have been used to make a meaningful condition.

The else Keyword

An additional feature of the `if` statement is the `else` keyword. Much like its English-language counterpart, `else` tells the JavaScript interpreter what to do if the condition in the `if` statement isn't met. The following is a simple example of the `else` keyword in action:

```
if (a == 1) {
    alert("Found a 1!");
    a = 0;
```

```
} else {
   alert("Incorrect value: " + a);
}
```

This snippet displays a message and resets the variable a if the condition is met. If the condition is *not* met (if a is not 1), a different message is displayed, courtesy of the else statement.

NOTE

Like the if statement, else can be followed either by a single action statement or by a number of statements, enclosed in braces.

Using Shorthand Conditional Expressions

In addition to the if statement, JavaScript provides a shorthand type of conditional expression that you can use to make quick decisions. This uses a peculiar syntax that is also found in other languages, such as C. A conditional expression looks like this:

```
variable = (condition) ? (value if true) : (value if false);
```

This construction ends up assigning one of two values to the variable: one value if the condition is true, and another value if it is false. Here is an example of a conditional expression:

```
value = (a == 1) ? 1 : 0;
```

This statement might look confusing, but it is equivalent to the following if statement:

```
if (a == 1) {
   value = 1;
} else {
   value = 0;
}
```

In other words, the value directly after the question mark (?) will be used if the condition is true, and the value directly after the colon (:) will be used if the condition is false. The colon and what follows represents the else portion of the statement, were it written as an if...else statement and, like the else portion of the if statement, it is optional.

These shorthand expressions can be used anywhere JavaScript expects a value. They provide a quick way to make simple decisions about values. As an example, here's a quick way to display a grammatically correct message about a variable:

```
document.write("Found " + counter +
    ((counter == 1) ? " word." : " words."));
```

This prints the message Found 1 word if the counter variable has a value of 1 and Found 2 words if its value is 2 or greater.

You might, in fact, find that conditional expressions are not quicker or easier for you to use, and that is perfectly fine. You should, however, know what they look like and how to read them in case you encounter them in someone else's code in the future.

Testing Multiple Conditions with if and else

You now have all the pieces necessary to create a script using if and else statements to control flow. In Lesson 4, "Understanding JavaScript," you created a simple script that displays the current date and time. You'll use that knowledge here as you create a script that uses conditions to display a greeting that depends on the time: "Good morning," "Good afternoon," "Good evening," or "Good day." To accomplish this task, you can use a combination of several if statements, like so:

```
if (hour_of_day < 10) {
    document.write("Good morning.");
} else if ((hour_of_day >= 14) && (hour_of_day <= 17)) {
    document.write("Good afternoon.");
} else if (hour_of_day >= 17) {
    document.write("Good evening.");
} else {
    document.write("Good day.");
}
```

The first statement checks the hour_of_day variable for a value less than 10. In other words, it checks whether the current time is before 10:00 a.m. If so, it displays the greeting "Good morning."

The second statement checks whether the time is between 2:00 p.m. and 5:00 p.m. and, if so, displays "Good afternoon." This statement uses else if to indicate that this condition will be tested only if the preceding one failed; if it's morning, there's no need to check whether it's afternoon. Similarly, the third statement checks for times after 5:00 p.m. and displays "Good evening."

The final statement uses a simple else, meaning it will be executed if none of the previous conditions matched. This covers the times between 10:00 a.m. and 2:00 p.m. (neglected by the other statements) and displays "Good day."

The HTML File

To try the time and greeting example in a browser, you need an HTML file. In this case, you can keep the JavaScript code separate. Listing 23.1 is the complete HTML file. Save it as timegreet.html but don't load it into the browser until you've prepared the JavaScript file in the next section.

LISTING 23.1 The HTML File for the Time and Greeting Example

```
<!doctype html>
<html lang="en">
  <head>
    <meta charset="utf-8">
    <title>Time Greet Example</title>
    <meta name="viewport"
          content="width=device-width, initial-scale=1">
  </head>
  <body>
    <h1>Current Date and Time</h1>
    <script src="timegreet.js"></script>
  </body>
</html>
```

The JavaScript File

Listing 23.2 shows the complete JavaScript file for the time and greeting example. This uses the built-in `Date` object functions to find the current date and store it in `hour_of_day`, `minute_of_hour`, and `seconds_of_minute` variables, as you learned in the last lesson. Next, `document.write` statements display the current time, and the `if` and `else` statements, introduced earlier, display an appropriate greeting.

LISTING 23.2 A Script to Display the Current Time and a Greeting

```
// Get the current date
now = new Date();

// Split into hours, minutes, seconds
hour_of_day = now.getHours();
minute_of_hour = now.getMinutes();
seconds_of_minute = now.getSeconds();

// Display the time
document.write("<h2>");
document.write(hour_of_day + ":" + minute_of_hour +
               ":" + seconds_of_minute);
document.write("</h2>");

// Display a greeting
// open the paragraph
document.write("<p>");
```

```
// change the greetings
if  (hour_of_day < 10)  {
    document.write("Good morning.");
}  else if ((hour_of_day >= 14) && (hour_of_day <= 17)) {
    document.write("Good afternoon.");
}  else if (hour_of_day >= 17)  {
    document.write("Good evening.");
}  else  {
    document.write("Good day.");
}
// close the paragraph
document.write("</p>");
```

To try this example, save this file as `timegreet.js` and then load the `timegreet.html` file
into your browser. Figure 23.1 shows the results of this script.

FIGURE 23.1
The output of the time and greeting example.

Using Multiple Conditions with `switch`

In Listing 23.2, you used several `if...else` statements in a row to test for different conditions.
Here is another example of this technique:

```
if (button=="next") {
    window.location="next.html";
} else if (button=="previous") {
    window.location="previous.html";
} else if (button=="home") {
    window.location="home.html";
} else if (button=="back") {
    window.location="menu.html";
}
```

Although using this construction is a logical way of doing things, this method can get messy if each if statement has its own block of code with several statements in it. As an alternative, JavaScript includes the switch statement, which enables you to combine several tests of the same variable or expression into a single block of statements. The following shows the same example converted to use switch:

```
switch(button) {
    case "next":
        window.location="next.html";
        break;
    case "previous":
        window.location="previous.html";
        break;
    case "home":
        window.location="home.html";
        break;
    case "back":
        window.location="menu.html";
        break;
    default:
        window.alert("Wrong button.");
}
```

The switch statement has several components:

▶ **The initial switch statement**—This statement includes the value to test (in this case, button) in parentheses.

▶ **Braces ({ and })**—Braces enclose the contents of the switch statement, much as with a function or an if statement.

▶ **One or more case statements**—Each of these statements specifies a value to compare with the value specified in the switch statement. If the values match, the statements after the case statement are executed. Otherwise, the next case is tried.

▶ **The break statement**—This statement is used to end each case to skip to the end of the switch. If break is not included, statements in multiple cases might be executed, whether or not they match.

▶ **The default case**—Optionally, the default case can be included and followed by one or more statements that are executed if none of the other cases were matched.

NOTE

You can use multiple statements after each case statement within the switch structure and not just the single-line statements shown here. You don't need to enclose them in braces. If the case matches, the JavaScript interpreter executes statements until it encounters a break or the next case.

One of the main benefits of using a `switch` statement instead of an `if...else` statement is readability: In one glance you know that all the conditional tests are for the same expression, and you can therefore focus on understanding the desired outcome of the conditional tests. But using a `switch` statement is purely optional; you might find that you prefer `if...else` statements, and there's nothing wrong with that. Any efficiency gains in using a `switch` statement instead of an `if...else` statement will not be noticeable to human eyes, if any is even present at all. The bottom line is this: Use what you like.

Using `for` Loops

The `for` keyword is the first tool to consider for creating loops, much as you saw in the preceding lesson, in the random number example. A `for` loop typically uses a variable (called a *counter* or an *index*) to keep track of how many times the loop has executed, and it stops when the counter reaches a certain number. A basic `for` statement looks like this:

```
for (var = 1; var < 10; var++) {
    // more code
}
```

There are three parameters in the `for` loop, each separated by semicolons:

- ▶ **Initial expression**—The first parameter (`var = 1` in the example) specifies a variable and assigns an initial value to it. This is called the *initial expression* because it sets up the initial state for the loop.

- ▶ **Condition**—The second parameter (`var < 10` in the example) is a condition that must remain true to keep the loop running. This is called the *condition* of the loop.

- ▶ **Increment expression**—The third parameter (`var++` in the example) is a statement that executes with each iteration of the loop. This is called the *increment expression* because it is typically used to increment the counter. The increment expression executes at the end of each loop iteration.

After the three parameters are specified, a left brace (`{`) is used to signal the beginning of a block. A right brace (`}`) is used at the end of the block. All the statements between the braces will be executed with each iteration of the loop.

The parameters for a `for` loop might sound a bit confusing, but when you're used to `for`, you'll use `for` loops frequently. Here is a simple example of this type of loop:

```
for (i=0; i<10; i++) {
    document.write("This is line " + i + "<br>");
}
```

These statements define a loop that uses the variable i, initializes it with the value 0, and loops as long as the value of i is less than 10. The increment expression, i++, adds 1 to the value of i with each iteration of the loop. Because this happens at the end of the loop, the output will be nine lines of text.

When a loop includes only a single statement between the braces, as in this example, you can omit the braces if you want. The following statement defines the same loop without braces:

```
for (i=0; i<10; i++)
   document.write("This is line " + i + "<br>");
```

NOTE

It's a good style convention to use braces with every loop, whether it contains one statement or many statements. This makes it easy to add statements to the loop later, without causing syntax errors.

The loop in this example contains a document.write statement that will be repeatedly executed. To see what this loop does, you can add it to a <script> section of an HTML document, as shown in Listing 23.3.

LISTING 23.3   A Loop Using the for Keyword

```html
<!doctype html>
<html lang="en">
  <head>
    <meta charset="utf-8">
    <title>Using a for Loop</title>
    <meta name="viewport"
          content="width=device-width, initial-scale=1">
  </head>
  <body>
    <h1>Using a for Loop</h1>
    <p>The following is the output of the <strong>for</strong> loop:</p>
    <script>
      for (i=1;i<10;i++) {
         document.write("This is line " + i + "<br>");
      }
    </script>
  </body>
</html>
```

This example displays a message containing the current value of the loop's counter during each iteration. The output of Listing 23.3 is shown in Figure 23.2.

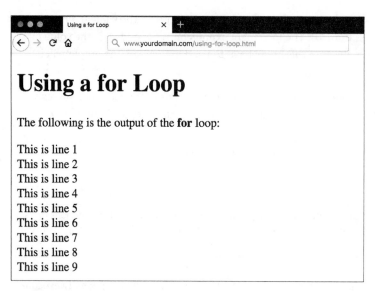

FIGURE 23.2
The results of the for loop example.

Notice that the loop was executed only nine times. This is because the conditional is i<10—that is, i is less than 10. When the counter (i) is incremented to 10, the expression is no longer true. If you want the loop to count to 10, you have to change the conditional; either i<=10 or i<11 will work fine.

The for loop is traditionally used to count from one number to another, but you can use just about any statement for the initialization, condition, and increment. However, there's usually a better way to do other types of loops with the while keyword, as described in the next section.

Using while Loops

Another keyword for loops in JavaScript is while. Unlike for loops, while loops don't necessarily use a variable to count. Instead, they continue to execute as long as a condition is true. In fact, if the condition starts out as false, the statements won't execute at all.

The while statement includes the condition in parentheses, and it is followed by a block of statements within braces, just like a for loop. Here is a simple while loop:

```
while (total < 10) {
    n++;
    total += values[n];
}
```

This loop uses a counter, n, to iterate through the values array. Rather than stopping at a certain count, however, it stops when the total of the values reaches 10.

You might have thought that you could have done the same thing with a `for` loop, and you'd be correct:

```
for (n=0;total < 10; n++) {
    total += values[n];
}
```

As a matter of fact, the `for` loop is nothing more than a special kind of `while` loop that handles an initialization and an increment for you, all in one line. You can generally use `while` for any loop. However, it's best to choose whichever type of loop makes the most sense for the job or takes the least amount of typing.

Using `do...while` Loops

JavaScript, like many other programming languages, includes a third type of loop: the `do...while` loop. This type of loop is similar to an ordinary `while` loop, with one difference: The condition is tested at the *end* of the loop rather than the beginning, so the commands inside the loop will always execute at least one time. Here is a typical `do...while` loop:

```
do {
    n++;
    total += values[n];
}
while (total < 10);
```

As you've probably noticed, this is basically an upside-down version of the previous `while` example. There is one difference: With the `do` loop, the condition is tested at the *end* of the loop. This means that the statements in the loop will always be executed at least once, even if the condition is never true.

NOTE

As with the `for` and `while` loops, the `do ... while` can include a single statement without braces or a number of statements enclosed in braces.

Working with Loops

Although you can use simple `for` and `while` loops for straightforward tasks, there are some considerations you should make when using more complicated loops. In the next sections, you'll look at infinite loops (to be avoided!) and the `break` and `continue` statements, which give you more control over the execution of your loops.

Creating an Infinite Loop

The `for` and `while` loops give you quite a bit of control over the loops. In some cases, this can cause problems if you're not careful. For example, look at the following loop code:

```
while (i < 10) {
    n++;
    values[n] = 0;
}
```

There's a mistake in this example. The condition of the `while` loop refers to the i variable, but that variable doesn't actually change during the loop; the n variable does. This creates an *infinite loop*, which means the loop will continue executing until the user stops it or until it generates an error of some kind—usually because the browser runs out of memory.

Infinite loops can't always be stopped by the user, except by quitting the browser—and some loops can even prevent the browser from quitting or may cause crashes.

Obviously, you should avoid infinite loops. They can be difficult to spot because JavaScript won't give you an error that actually tells you there is an infinite loop. Thus, each time you create a loop in a script, you should be careful to make sure there's a way out.

NOTE

Depending on the browser version in use, an infinite loop might even make the browser stop responding to the user because all the memory is used up. Be sure you provide an escape route from infinite loops and be sure to always test your work.

Occasionally, you might want to create a long-running and seemingly infinite loop deliberately. For example, you might want your program to execute until the user explicitly stops it or until you provide an escape route with the `break` statement, which is introduced in the next section. Here's an easy way to create an infinite loop:

```
while (true) {
    //more code
}
```

Because the value `true` is the conditional, this loop will always find its condition to be true.

Escaping from a Loop

There is a way out of a long-running and seemingly infinite loop. You can use the `break` statement at some point during the loop to exit immediately and continue with the first statement after the loop. Here is a simple example of the use of `break`:

```
while (true) {
    n++;
    if (values[n] == 1) break;
}
```

Although the while statement is set up as an infinite loop, the if statement checks the corresponding value of an array, and if it finds the value 1, it exits the loop.

When the JavaScript interpreter encounters a break statement, it skips the rest of the loop and continues the script with the first statement after the right brace at the loop's end. You can use the break statement in any type of loop, whether infinite or not. This provides an easy way to exit if an error occurs or if another condition is met.

Continuing a Loop

One more JavaScript statement is available to help you control the execution of a loop. The continue statement skips the rest of the loop but, unlike break, it continues with the next iteration of the loop. Here is a simple example:

```
for (i=1; i<21; i++) {
  if (score[i]==0) continue;
    document.write("Student number "+ i + ", Score: "
                   + score[i] + "<br>");
}
```

This script uses a for loop to print scores for 20 students, stored in the score array (not shown here). The if statement is used to check for scores with a value of 0. The script assumes that a score of 0 means that the student didn't take the test, so it continues the loop without printing that score.

Looping Through Object Properties

Yet another type of loop is available in JavaScript. The for...in loop is not as flexible as an ordinary for or while loop, but it is specifically designed to perform an operation on each property of an object.

For example, the built-in navigator object contains properties that describe the user's browser. You can use for...in to display this object's properties:

```
for (i in navigator) {
    document.write("<p>Property: " + i + "<br>");
    document.write("Value: " + navigator[i] + "</p>");
}
```

Like an ordinary for loop, this type of loop uses an index variable (i in the example). For each iteration of the loop, the variable is set to the next property of the object. This makes it easy when you need to check or modify each of an object's properties.

One common use of loops is to work with arrays. Without loops, it can be very difficult to initialize arrays. The following script will prompt the user for a series of names. After all the names have been entered, it will display the list of names in a numbered list. First, initialize some variables:

```
names = new Array();
var i = 0;
```

The `names` array will store the names the user enters. You don't know how many names will be entered, so you don't need to specify a dimension for the array. The `i` variable will be used as a counter in the loops.

Next, use the `prompt` statement to prompt the user for a series of names. The `prompt` statement acts like `alert`, only it asks for user input rather than just displaying a message. Use a loop to repeat the prompt for each name. You want the user to enter at least one name, so a `do . . . while` loop is ideal:

```
do {
    next = prompt("Enter the Next Name", "");
    if (next > " ") names[i] = next;
    i = i + 1;
} while (next > " ");
```

NOTE

If you're interested in making your scripts as short as possible, remember that you could use the increment (++) operator to combine the `i = i + 1` statement with the preceding statement, like so:

```
names[i++]=1
```

This loop prompts for a string called `next`. If a name was entered and isn't blank, it's stored as the next entry in the `names` array. The `i` counter is then incremented. The loop repeats until the user doesn't enter a name or clicks Cancel in the prompt dialog.

Next, your script can display the number of names entered:

```
document.write("<h2>" + (names.length) + " names entered.</h2>");
```

This statement displays the `length` property of the `names` array, surrounded by level 2 heading tags for emphasis.

Next, the script should display all the names in the order in which they were entered. Because the names are in an array, the `for . . . in` loop is a good choice:

```
document.write("<ol>");
for (i in names) {
    document.write("<li>" + names[i] + "</li>");
}
document.write("</ol>");
```

Here you have a `for...in` loop that loops through the `names` array, assigning the counter `i` to each index in turn. The script then prints the name between opening and closing `<li>` tags as an item in an ordered list. Before and after the loop, the script prints beginning and ending `<ol>` tags.

You now have everything you need for a working script. Listing 23.4 shows the HTML file for this example, and Listing 23.5 shows the JavaScript file.

LISTING 23.4   HTML to Prompt for Names and Display Them

```html
<!doctype html>
<html lang="en">
  <head>
    <meta charset="utf-8">
    <title>Loops Example</title>
    <meta name="viewport"
          content="width=device-width, initial-scale=1">
  </head>
  <body>
    <h1>Loops Example</h1>
    <p>Enter a series of names and JavaScript will display them
    in a numbered list.</p>
    <script src="loops.js"></script>
  </body>
</html>
```

LISTING 23.5   JavaScript to Prompt for Names and Display Them

```javascript
// create the array
names = new Array();
var i = 0;

// loop and prompt for names
do {
  next = window.prompt("Enter the Next Name", "");
  if (next > " ") names[i] = next;
  i = i + 1;
} while (next > " ");

document.write("<h2>" + (names.length) + " names entered.</h2>");

// display all of the names
document.write("<ol>");
for (i in names) {
  document.write("<li>" + names[i] + "</li>");
}
// close the list
document.write("</ol>");
```

To try this example, save the JavaScript file as `loops.js` and then load the HTML document into a browser. You'll be prompted for one name at a time. Enter several names and then click Cancel to indicate that you're finished. Figure 23.3 shows what the final results should look like in a browser.

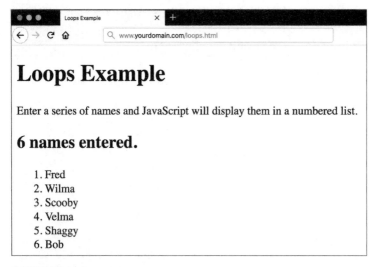

FIGURE 23.3
The output of the names example.

Summary

In this lesson, you've learned two ways to control the flow of your scripts. First, you learned how to use the `if` statement to evaluate conditional expressions and react to them. You also learned a shorthand form of conditional expression using the `?` operator and the `switch` statement for working with multiple conditions.

You also learned about JavaScript's looping capabilities using `for`, `while`, and the `do...while` loops, and how to control loops further by using the `break` and `continue` statements. Finally, you looked at the `for...in` loop for working with each property of an object.

Q&A

Q. What happens if I compare two items of different data types (for example, a number and a string) in a conditional expression?

A. The JavaScript interpreter does its best to make the values a common format and compare them. In this case, it would convert them both to strings before comparing. You can use the special equality operator `===` to compare two values and their types. Using this operator, the expression will be true only if the expressions have the same value *and* the same data type.

Q. Why don't I get a friendly error message if I accidentally use = instead of ==?

A. In some cases, using = does result in an error. However, the incorrect version often appears to be a correct statement. For example, in the statement if (a=1), the variable a is assigned the value 1. The if statement is considered true, and the value of a is lost.

Workshop

The Workshop contains quiz questions and activities to help you solidify your understanding of the material covered. Try to answer all questions before looking at the "Answers" section that follows.

Quiz

1. Which of the following operators means "is not equal to" in JavaScript?

    a. !

    b. !=

    c. <>

2. What does the switch statement do?

    a. Tests a variable or expression for a number of different values

    b. Turns a variable on or off

    c. Makes ordinary if statements longer and more confusing

3. Which type of JavaScript loop checks the condition at the *end* of the loop?

    a. for

    b. while

    c. do...while

4. Within a loop, what does the break statement do?

    a. Crashes the browser

    b. Starts the loop over

    c. Escapes the loop entirely

5. The statement while (3==3) is an example of which of the following?

    a. A typographical error

    b. An infinite loop

    c. An illegal JavaScript statement

6. How would you write the statement "if J is 10, then M is 40" in JavaScript?

   a. if (j == 10) m = 40;

   b. if (j == 10) then m = 40;

   c. if (j equals 10) m = 40;

   d. if (j equals 10) then m = 40;

7. Which of these is a logical operator?

   a. $$

   b. &*

   c. =

   d. !

8. What does the following statement say in English?

   ```
   Wilma = (Barney == 50) ? 44 : 29;
   ```

   a. Wilma is 44 and Barney is 50 if Wilma is 29

   b. Wilma is 44 if Barney is 50; otherwise, Wilma is 29

   c. Wilma is 29 if Barny is 50, otherwise Wilma is 44.

   d. Wilma is 29 less than Barney if Barney is 50; otherwise Wilma is 44.

9. What does the statement scooby++ mean in JavaScript?

   a. The function scooby subtracts 1 from the argument.

   b. The function scooby adds 1 to the argument.

   c. The variable scooby has 1 subtracted from its value.

   d. The variable scooby has 1 added to its value.

10. Why would you want to create an infinite loop?

   a. To let the script run until the user stops it.

   b. To let the script run until the computer ends it.

   c. To let the script run until the server stops it.

   d. You would never want to create an infinite loop.

NOTE

Just a reminder for those of you reading these words in the print or e-book edition of this book: If you go to **www.informit.com/register** and register this book (using ISBN 9780672338083), you can receive free access to an online Web Edition that not only contains the complete text of this book but also features an interactive version of this quiz.

Answers

1. b. The != operator means *is not equal to*.

2. a. The switch statement can test the same variable or expression for a number of different values.

3. c. The do...while loop uses a condition at the end of the loop.

4. c. The break statement escapes the loop.

5. b. Because the condition (3==3) will always be true, this statement creates an infinite loop.

6. a. The statement would be written as follows:

```
if (j == 10)
   m = 40;
```

7. d. JavaScript has the logical operators AND, OR, and NOT, written as &&, ||, and !.

8. b. The statement says that Wilma is 44 if Barney is 50; otherwise, Wilma is 29.

9. d. This is an increment expression, and it means that scooby will have 1 added to its value.

10. a. An infinite or long-running loop is usually created to let the script run until the user explicitly stops it or until a break or continue statement occurs.

Exercises

▶ Modify Listing 23.4 to sort the names in alphabetical order before displaying them. You can use the sort method of the Array object, described in Lesson 22, "Using JavaScript Variables, Strings, and Arrays."

▶ Modify Listing 23.4 to prompt for exactly 10 names. What happens if you click the Cancel button instead of entering a name?

Responding to Events and Using Windows

- ▶ How event handlers work
- ▶ How event handlers relate to objects
- ▶ How to create an event handler
- ▶ How to detect mouse and keyboard actions
- ▶ How to use `onclick` to change the appearance of `<div>`
- ▶ How to access and use the `window` object hierarchy with JavaScript
- ▶ How to delay a script's actions by using timeouts
- ▶ How to display alerts, confirmations, and prompts

In your experience with JavaScript so far, most of the scripts you've written have executed in a calm, orderly fashion, quietly and methodically moving from the first statement to the last. You've seen a few event handlers used in sample scripts and it is likely that you have noticed that the event handler names provide clues to their meaning. For example, `onclick` means "when a click happens." That alone speaks to the relative ease and simplicity of using JavaScript event handlers within your HTML.

In this lesson, you'll learn to use various event handlers supported by JavaScript. Rather than execute statements in a methodical order, a user can interact directly with different parts of your scripts by invoking an event handler. You'll use event handlers in just about every script you write throughout the rest of these lessons, and event handlers are likely to feature prominently in most scripts you will write, especially if you want to follow best practices and use unobtrusive JavaScript.

In this lesson we'll also return to some specific aspects of the Document Object Model (DOM). You'll learn more about some of the structural objects in the DOM—browser windows and dialog boxes—and how JavaScript can interact with them using events.

Understanding Event Handlers

As you learned in Lesson 20, "Getting Started with JavaScript Programming," JavaScript programs don't have to execute in order. You also learned that JavaScript programs can detect *events* and react to them. Events are things that happen within the scope of the browser—the user clicks a button, the mouse pointer moves, or a web page finishes loading from the server (just to name a few). Various events enable your scripts to respond to the mouse, the keyboard, and other circumstances. Events are the key methods JavaScript uses to make web documents interactive.

A script that you create and use to detect and respond to an event is generally referred to as an *event handler*. Event handlers are among the most powerful features of JavaScript. Luckily, they're also among the easiest features to learn and use; often, a useful event handler requires only a single statement.

Objects and Events

As you learned in Lesson 21, "Working with the Document Object Model (DOM)," JavaScript uses a set of objects to store information about the various parts of a web page—buttons, links, images, windows, and so on. An event can often happen in more than one place (for example, the user could click any one of the links on a page), and each event is associated with an object.

Each event has a name. For example, the onmouseover event occurs when the mouse pointer moves over an object on the page. When the pointer moves over a particular link, the onmouseover event is sent to that link's event handler, if it has one. In the next few sections you'll learn more about creating and using event handlers in your own code.

Creating an Event Handler

You don't need the <script> tag to invoke an event handler. Instead, you use the event name and code to invoke the event handler as an attribute of an individual HTML tag. For example, here is a link that invokes an event handler script when a mouse-over occurs on a link:

```
<a href="http://www.google.com/"
   onmouseover="alert('You moved over the link.');">
   This is a link.</a>
```

Note that this snippet is all one <a> element, although it's split into multiple lines for readability here. In this example, the onmouseover attribute specifies a JavaScript statement to invoke—namely, an alert message that is displayed when the user's mouse moves over the link.

NOTE

The previous example uses single quotation marks to surround the text. This is necessary in an event handler because double quotation marks are used to surround the event handler itself. You can also use single quotation marks to surround the event handler and double quotes within the script statements. Just don't use the same type of quotation marks because that is a JavaScript syntax error.

You can invoke JavaScript statements like the preceding one in response to an event, but if you need to invoke more than one statement, it's a good idea to use a function instead. Just define the function elsewhere in the document or in a referenced document and then call the function as the event handler, like this:

```
<a href="#bottom" onmouseover="doIt();">Move the mouse over this link.</a>
```

This example calls a function called doIt() when the user moves the mouse over the link. Using a function in this type of situation is convenient because you can use longer, more readable JavaScript routines as event handlers—and you can also reuse the function elsewhere without duplicating all of its code.

NOTE

For simple event handlers, you can use two statements if you separate them with a semicolon. However, in most cases it's easier and more maintainable to use a function to perform multiple statements.

Defining Event Handlers with JavaScript

Rather than specify an event handling script each time you want to invoke it, you can use JavaScript to assign a specific function as the default event handler for an event. This enables you to set event handlers conditionally, turn them on and off, and dynamically change the function that handles an event.

NOTE

Setting up event handlers this way enables you to use an external JavaScript file to define the function and set up the event, keeping the JavaScript code completely separate from the HTML file.

To define an event handler in this way, first define a function and then assign the function as an event handler. Event handlers are stored as properties of the document object or another object that can receive an event. For example, these statements define a function called mousealert and then assign it as the event handler for all instances of onmousedown in the current document:

```
function mousealert() {
  alert("You clicked the mouse!");
}
document.onmousedown = mousealert;
```

You can use this technique to set up an event handler for only a specific HTML element, but an additional step is required to achieve that goal: You must first find the object corresponding to the element. To do this, use the document.getElementById function.

First, define an element in the HTML document and specify an id attribute:

```
<a href="http://www.google.com/" id="link1">
```

Next, in the JavaScript code, find the object and apply the event handler:

```
var link1_obj = document.getElementById("link1");
link1_obj.onclick = myCustomFunction;
```

You can do this for any object as long as you've defined it and therefore can reference it by a unique id attribute in the HTML file. Using this technique, you can easily assign the same function to handle events for multiple objects without adding clutter to your HTML code.

Supporting Multiple Event Handlers

What if you want more than one thing to happen when you click on an element? For example, suppose you want two functions, called update and display, to both execute when a button is clicked. It's very easy to run into syntax errors or logic errors such that two functions assigned to the same event won't work as expected. One solution for clean separation and execution is to define a single function that calls both functions:

```
function updateThenDisplay() {
    update();
    display();
}
```

This isn't always the ideal way to do things. For example, if you're using two third-party scripts and both of them want to add an onload event to the page, there should be a way to add both events. The W3C DOM standard defines a function, addEventListener, for this purpose. This function defines a *listener* for a particular event and object, and you can add as many listener functions as you need.

There are many events you can listen for. These are some of the most commonly used ones:

- ▶ **focus**—When the element is focused on with a mouse or keyboard (tab)
- ▶ **blur**—When the element loses focus
- ▶ **click**—When the element is clicked
- ▶ **dblclick**—When the element is clicked twice
- ▶ **keydown**—When a key is pressed down
- ▶ **keyup**—When a key is released

- ▶ **keypress**—When a key is pressed, relaying the key value

- ▶ **mouseover**—When the mouse pointer is over the element

- ▶ **mouseout**—When the mouse pointer is moved off an element after hovering

- ▶ **mousemove**—When the mouse moves

- ▶ **mousedown**—When the mouse button is pressed over an element

- ▶ **mouseup**—When the mouse button is released over an element

- ▶ **load**—When the element has fully loaded

There are many more events you can listen for. You can learn more about them at https://developer.mozilla.org/en-US/docs/Web/Events#Standard_events. To listen for an event, you simply attach the event listener to the element you want to listen for. For example, to apply the `mousealert` function when a user clicks a link with the `link1 id`, you would write the following:

```
document.getElementById("link1").addEventListener("click",
  mousealert);
```

You can also remove event listeners when you're done with them: Simply use the `removeEventListener` method. As with the `addEventListener` method, simply attach it to the element you want to stop listening to.

NOTE

Remember that you can attach event listeners to any element in the DOM, including the document itself. When you write `document.addEventListener("click", myFunction);` you tell the browser to run the function `myFunction` whenever someone clicks anywhere on the document.

The `addEventListener` method is well supported in modern browsers, but if you have to support extremely old versions of Internet Explorer, you have to use a different function, `attachEvent`, to support them. In Lesson 25, "JavaScript Best Practices," you'll create a function that combines these two for a cross-browser event-adding script.

Using the event Object

When an event occurs, you might want or need to know more about the event in order for your script to perform different actions; for example, for a keyboard event, you might want to know which key was pressed, especially if your script performs different actions depending on whether the **j** key or the **l** key was pressed. The DOM includes an event object that provides this type of granular information.

CAUTION

Don't include the on prefix on your listeners when using addEventListener. Instead just use the event itself. For example, use click rather than onclick. This is a common error, especially if you're used to using HTML attributes rather than listeners.

To use the event object, you can pass it on to your event handler function. For example, this statement defines a keypress event that automatically passes the event object to the getKey function:

```
document.addEventListener("keypress", getKey);
```

You then define your function to accept the event as a parameter:

```
function getKey(e) {
    // more code
}
```

In modern browsers, an event object is automatically passed to the event handler function. This is why you don't need to define the parameter in your function.

NOTE

Internet Explorer 8 and below handle events differently. If you must support these older versions, you need to check the window object for the event properties. One way to do this is to check whether the properties exist inside your function. For example, you could add the line
if (!e) var e = window.event; to your function.

The following are some of the commonly used properties of the event object for modern browsers:

▶ **event.modifiers**—A flag that indicates which modifier keys (Shift, Ctrl, Alt, and so on) were held down during the event. This value is an integer that combines binary values representing the different keys.

▶ **event.pageX**—The x coordinate of the event within the web page.

▶ **event.pageY**—The y coordinate of the event within the web page.

▶ **event.which**—The key code for keyboard events (in Unicode) or the button that was pressed for mouse events.

▶ **event.button**—The mouse button that was pressed. The left button's value is 0, and the right button's value is 2. If the mouse has a middle button, the value is 1.

▶ **event.target**—The object where the element occurred.

NOTE

The event.pageX and event.pageY properties are based on the top-left corner of the element where the event occurred, not always the exact position of the mouse pointer.

Using Mouse Events

The DOM includes a number of event handlers for detecting mouse actions. Your script can detect the movement of the mouse pointer and when a button is clicked, released, or both. Some of these events will be familiar to you already because you have seen them in action in previous lessons.

Over and Out

You've already seen the first and most common event handler, mouseover, which is called when a user's mouse pointer moves over a link or another object. Note that mouseout is the opposite: It is called when the user's mouse pointer moves out of the object's border. Unless something strange happens and the user's mouse never moves again while the viewer is viewing the particular document, you can count on mouseout happening sometime after mouseover.

mouseout is particularly useful if your script has made a visual change within the document when the user's mouse pointer moved over the object—for example, displaying a message in the status line or changing an image. You can use a mouseout event handler to undo the action when the pointer moves away.

NOTE

One of the most common uses for the mouseover and mouseout event handlers is to create rollovers—images that change when the mouse moves over them. You'll learn how to create these later in the lesson.

Ups and Downs (and Clicks)

You can also use events to detect when the mouse button is clicked. The basic event handler for this is onclick. This event handler is called when the mouse button is clicked while positioned over the appropriate object.

For example, you can use the following event handler to display an alert when a link is clicked:

```
<a href="http://www.google.com/"
   onclick="alert('You are about to leave this site.');">
   Go Away</a>
```

Or you can do it unobtrusively by giving the link the id goAway and this script:

```
function goAway(e) {
  alert('You are about to leave this site.');
}
document.getElementById("goAway").addEventListener("click", goAway);
```

In this case, the click event handler invokes the JavaScript alert before the linked page is loaded into the browser. This is useful for making links conditional or displaying a disclaimer before sending the user away to the linked page.

If your click event handler returns the false value, the link will not be followed. For example, the following is a link that displays a confirmation dialog. If you click Cancel, the link is not followed; if you click OK, the new page is loaded:

```
function goAway(e) {
  if (!confirm('Are you sure?'))
    e.preventDefault();
}
document.getElementById("goAway").addEventListener("click", goAway);
```

This example uses the confirm method to display a modal dialog box. Then if the user chooses Cancel, it adds the preventDefault property to the event. This stops the link from being followed.

The dblclick event handler is similar but is used only if the user double-clicks on an object. Because links usually require only a single click, you could use this to make a link do two different things, depending on the number of clicks. (Needless to say, this could be confusing to the user, but it *is* technically possible.) You can also detect double-clicks on images and other objects.

To give you even more control of what happens when the mouse button is pressed, two more events are included:

▶ **mousedown**—Used when the user presses the mouse button

▶ **mouseup**—Used when the user releases the mouse button

These two events are the two halves of a mouse click. If you want to detect an entire click, use click, but you can use mouseup and mousedown to detect just one part or the other.

To detect which mouse button is pressed, you can use the `button` property of the `event` object. This property is assigned the value 0 for the left button or 2 for the right button. This property is assigned for `click`, `dblclick`, `mouseup`, and `mousedown` events.

CAUTION

Browsers don't normally detect `click` or `dblclick` events for the right mouse button. If you want to detect the right button, using `mousedown` is the most reliable way.

As an example of these event handlers, you can create a script that displays information about mouse button events and determines which button is pressed. Listing 24.1 shows a script that handles some mouse events.

LISTING 24.1 The JavaScript File for the Mouse Click Example

```
function mousestatus(e) {
  if (!e) e = window.event;
  btn = e.button;
  switch(btn) {
    case 0:
      whichone = "Left";
      break;
    case 1:
      whichone = "Middle";
      break;
    case 2:
      whichone = "Right";
      break;
    default:
      whichone = "UNKNOWN";
  }
  message=e.type + " : " + whichone + "<br>";
  document.getElementById('testarea').innerHTML += message;
  e.preventDefault();
}
obj=document.getElementById('testlink');

obj.addEventListener("click", mousestatus);
obj.addEventListener("mousedown", mousestatus);
obj.addEventListener("mouseup", mousestatus);
obj.addEventListener("dblclick", mousestatus);
```

This script includes a function, `mouseStatus`, that detects mouse events. This function uses the `button` property of the `event` object to determine which button was pressed. It also uses the `type` property to display the type of event, since the function will be used to handle multiple event types.

After the function, the script finds the object for a link with the `id` attribute `testlink` and assigns its `mousedown`, `mouseup`, `click`, and `dblclick` events to the `mousestatus` function. The `mousestatus` function uses a `switch` statement to determine if the left, center, or right mouse button was clicked and then writes that information to the `testarea` `<div>`.

Save this script as `click.js`. Next, you need an HTML document to work with the script; this is shown in Listing 24.2.

LISTING 24.2   The HTML File for the Mouse Click Example

```
<!doctype html>
<html lang="en">
  <head>
    <meta charset="utf-8">
    <title>Mouse Click Test</title>
    <meta name="viewport"
          content="width=device-width, initial-scale=1">
  </head>
  <body>
    <h1>Mouse Click Test</h1>
    <p>
      Click the mouse on the test link below. A message will
      indicate which button was clicked.
    </p>
    <h2><a href="#" id="testlink">Test Link</a></h2>
    <div id="testarea"></div>

    <script src="click.js"></script>
  </body>
</html>
```

This file defines a test link with the `id` property `testlink`, which is used in the script to assign event handlers. It also defines a `<div>` with an `id` of `testarea`, which is used by the script to display the message regarding the events. To test this document, save it in the same folder as the JavaScript file you created previously and load the HTML document into a browser. Some sample results are shown in Figure 24.1.

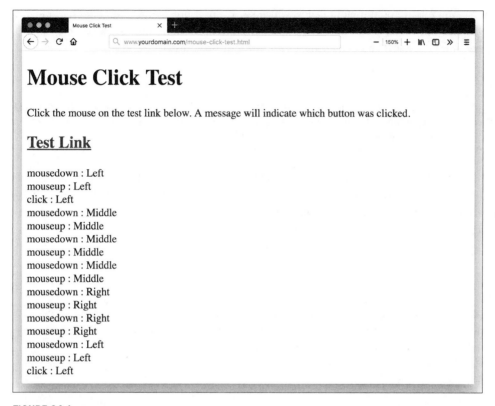

FIGURE 24.1
The mouse click example in action.

NOTE

Notice that a single click of the left mouse button triggers three events: mousedown, mouseup, and then click, whereas clicking the right mouse button triggers only two events.

Using Keyboard Events

JavaScript can also detect keyboard actions. The main event handler for this purpose is keypress, which occurs when a key is pressed and released or held down. As with mouse buttons, you can detect the down and up parts of a keypress with the keydown and keyup event handlers.

NOTE

The keypress and keydown events may seem to be the same thing, but they are subtly different. The keydown event references the exact moment that the key is moving down, while the keypress event references the key being pressed and sends the value of that key back to the script. The keydown event does not relay which key was pressed.

Of course, you might find it useful to know which key the user pressed. You can find this out with the event object, which is sent to your event handler when the event occurs. The event.which property stores the ASCII character code for the key that was pressed.

NOTE

ASCII (American Standard Code for Information Interchange) is the standard numeric code used by most computers to represent characters. It assigns the numbers 0 to 128 to various characters. For example, the capital letters A through Z are ASCII values 65 to 90.

If you'd rather deal with actual characters than key codes, you can use the fromCharCode String method to convert them. This method converts a numeric ASCII code to its corresponding string character. For example, the following statement converts the event.which property to a character and stores it in the key variable:

```
var key = String.fromCharCode(event.which);
```

NOTE

In older versions of Internet Explorer, event.keyCode stores the ASCII character code for the key that was pressed rather than event.which. If you must support Internet Explorer 8 or earlier, you should include a check for the e.keyCode property, like so:

```
if (e.keyCode) {
  var keycode = e.keyCode;
} else {
  var keycode = e.which;
}
```

The following function displays each key as it is typed:

```
function displayKey(e) {
  // which key was pressed?
  var keycode=e.which;
  character=String.fromCharCode(keycode);

  // find the object for the destination paragraph
  var keys_paragraph = document.getElementById('keys');

  // add the character to the paragraph
  keys_paragraph.innerHTML += character;
}
```

The `displayKey` function receives the `event` object from the event handler and stores it in the variable e. It assigns keycode to the `e.which` property. Then the remaining lines of the function convert the key code to a character and add it to the paragraph in the document with the `id` attribute `keys`. Listing 24.3 shows a complete example using this function.

NOTE

The final lines in the `displayKey` function use the `getElementById` function and the `innerHTML` attribute to display the keys you type within a paragraph on the page—in this case, a paragraph with an `id` of `keys`.

LISTING 24.3   Displaying Typed Characters

```
<!doctype html>
<html lang="en">
  <head>
    <meta charset="utf-8">
    <title>Displaying Keypresses</title>
    <meta name="viewport"
          content="width=device-width, initial-scale=1">
  </head>
  <body>
    <h1>Displaying Typed Characters</h1>
    <p>
      This document includes a simple script that displays the keys
      you type as a new paragraph below. Type a few keys to try it.
    </p>
    <p id="keys"></p>

    <script>
    function displayKey(e) {
      // which key was pressed?
      var keycode=e.which;
      character=String.fromCharCode(keycode);

      // find the object for the destination paragraph
      var keys_paragraph = document.getElementById('keys');

      // add the character to the paragraph
      keys_paragraph.innerHTML += character;
    }
    document.addEventListener("keypress",displayKey);
    </script>
  </body>
</html>
```

When you load this example, you can type and then watch the characters you've typed appear in a paragraph of the document. Figure 24.2 shows the result of some typing, but you should try it yourself to see the full effect!

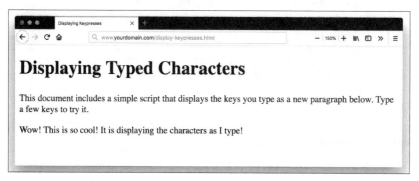

FIGURE 24.2
Displaying the output of the keys that were pressed.

Using the `load` and `unload` Events

Another event you are likely to use often is `load`. This event occurs when the current page (including all of its images) finishes loading from the server.

The `load` event is related to the `window` object, and to define it you use an event handler in the `<body>` tag. For example, the following is a `<body>` element that uses a simple event handler to display an alert when the page finishes loading:

```
window.addEventListener("load", function() {
  alert("Loading complete");
});
```

This event handler uses an *anonymous function* to display the alert. An anonymous function is typically used when the functionality of the function doesn't have a long-term use or doesn't need to be used in several locations.

CAUTION

Because the `load` event occurs after the HTML document has finished loading and displaying, you should not use the `document.write` or `document.open` statements within a `load` event handler because it would overwrite the current document.

An image can also have a `load` event handler. When you define a `load` event handler for an `<img>` element, it is triggered as soon as the specified image has completely loaded.

You can also specify an `unload` event for the `<body>` element. This event will be triggered whenever the browser unloads the current document—which occurs when another page is loaded or when the browser window is closed.

Using `click` to Change the Appearance of a `<div>`

As you've learned already in this lesson, the `click` event can be used to invoke all sorts of actions. You might think of a mouse click as a way to submit a form by clicking on a button, but you can capture this event and use it to provide interactivity within your pages as well. In the example that follows, you will see how you can use the `click` event to show or hide information contained in a `<div>` element.

In this case, you will be adding interactivity to a web page by allowing the user to show previously hidden information by clicking on a piece of text. I refer to it as a *piece of text* because, strictly speaking, the text is not a link. Although to the user it will look like a link and act like a link, it will not be marked up within an `<a>` tag.

Listing 24.4 provides the complete code for this example, which we'll walk through momentarily.

LISTING 24.4   Using `click` to Show or Hide Content

```
<!doctype html>
<html lang="en">
  <head>
    <meta charset="utf-8">
    <title>Steptoe Butte</title>
    <style>
    a {
       text-decoration: none;
       font-weight: bold;
    }
    img {
       margin-right: 12px;
       margin-bottom: 6px;
       border: 1px solid #000;
    }
```

```
    .mainimg {
       float: left;
       max-width: 35%;
       height: auto;
    }
    #eHide, #pHide, #elevation, #photos  {
       display: none;
    }
    #eShow, #pShow {
       display: block;
    }
    #photos {
      clear: both;
    }
    #photos img { max-width: 20%; height: auto; clear: left; }
    .fakelink {
       cursor: pointer;
       text-decoration: none;
       font-weight: bold;
       color: #E03A3E;
    }
    section {
       margin-bottom: 6px;
    }
    </style>
    <meta name="viewport"
          content="width=device-width, initial-scale=1">
</head>
<body>
   <header>
     <h1>Steptoe Butte</h1>
   </header>

   <section>
     <p>
       <img src="images/steptoe-butte.jpg" class="mainimg"
       alt="View from Steptoe Butte">Steptoe Butte is a quartzite
       island jutting out of the silty loess of the <a
       href="http://en.wikipedia.org/wiki/Palouse">Palouse</a>
       hills in Whitman County, Washington. The rock that forms
       the butte is over 400 million years old, in contrast with
       the 15-7 million year old <a
       href="http://en.wikipedia.org/wiki/Columbia_River">Columbia
```

```
      River</a> basalts that underlie the rest of the Palouse
      (such "islands" of ancient rock have come to be called
      buttes, a butte being defined as a small hill with a flat
      top, whose width at top does not exceed its height).
    </p>
    <p>
      A hotel built by Cashup Davis stood atop Steptoe Butte from
      1888 to 1908, burning down several years after it closed.
      In 1946, Virgil McCroskey donated 120 acres (0.49 km2) of
      land to form Steptoe Butte State Park, which was later
      increased to over 150 acres (0.61 km2). Steptoe Butte is
      currently recognized as a National Natural Landmark because
      of its unique geological value. It is named in honor of <a
      href="http://en.wikipedia.org/wiki/Colonel_Edward_Steptoe">
      Colonel Edward Steptoe</a>.
    </p>
</section>

<section>
    <button class="fakelink" id="eShow">
      &raquo; Show Elevation
    </button>
    <button class="fakelink" id="eHide">
      &laquo; Hide Elevation
    </button>
    <div id="elevation">
      3,612 feet (1,101 m), approximately 1,000 feet (300 m)
      above the surrounding countryside.
    </div>
</section>

<section>
    <button class="fakelink" id="pShow">
      &raquo; Show Photos from the Top of Steptoe Butte
    </button>
    <button class="fakelink" id="pHide">
      &laquo; Hide Photos from the Top of Steptoe Butte
    </button>

    <div id="photos">
      <img src="images/sb-top1.jpg" alt="View from Steptoe Butte">
      <img src="images/sb-top2.jpg" alt="View from Steptoe Butte">
      <img src="images/sb-top3.jpg" alt="View from Steptoe Butte">
    </div>
</section>
```

```
    <footer>
      <p>
        <em>Text from
        <a href="http://en.wikipedia.org/wiki/Steptoe_Butte">
        Wikipedia</a>, photos by Julie C. Meloni.</em>
      </p>
    </footer>

    <script>
document.getElementById("eShow").addEventListener("click", function() {
  this.style.display = 'none';
  document.getElementById("eHide").style.display='block';
  document.getElementById("elevation").style.display='block';
});
document.getElementById("eHide").addEventListener("click", function() {
  this.style.display = 'none';
  document.getElementById("eShow").style.display='block';
  document.getElementById("elevation").style.display='none';
});
document.getElementById("pShow").addEventListener("click", function() {
  this.style.display = 'none';
  document.getElementById("pHide").style.display='block';
  document.getElementById("photos").style.display='block';
});
document.getElementById("pHide").addEventListener("click", function() {
  this.style.display = 'none';
  document.getElementById("pShow").style.display='block';
  document.getElementById("photos").style.display='none';
});
    </script>
  </body>
</html>
```

Figure 24.3 shows how this code renders in a browser.

To begin, look at the entries in the style sheet. The first entry simply styles links that are surrounded by the <a></a> tag pair; these links display as non-underlined, bold, blue links. You can see these regular links in the two paragraphs of text in Figure 24.3 (and in the line at the bottom of the page). The next two entries make sure that the images used in the page have appropriate margins; the entry for <img> element sets some margins and a border, and the .mainimg class enables you to apply a style to the main image on the page but not the set of three images at the bottom of the page.

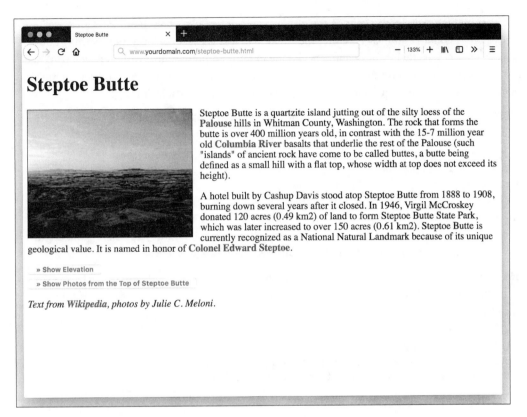

FIGURE 24.3
The initial display of Listing 24.4. Although you can't see it here, the mouse pointer changes to a hand when you hover over the buttons.

The next entry is for specific IDs, and those IDs are all set to be invisible (`display: none;`) when the page initially loads. In contrast, the two IDs that follow are set to display as block elements when the page initially loads. Again, strictly speaking, these two IDs do not have to be defined as block elements because that is the default display. However, this style sheet includes these entries to illustrate the differences between the two sets of elements. If you count the number of `<button>` elements in Listing 24.4, you will find four in the code: two that are invisible and two that are visible upon page load. There are also two `<div>` elements that are not visible when the page loads: the ones with the IDs `elevation` and `photos`.

The goal in this example is to change the display value of two IDs when another ID is clicked. But first you have to make sure users realize that a piece of text is clickable, and that typically happens when users see their mouse pointers change to reflect a present link. Although you can't see it in Figure 24.3, if you load the sample code on your machine and view it in your browser, the mouse pointer changes to a hand with a finger pointing at a particular link.

This functionality is achieved by defining a class for this particular text; the class is called fakelink, as you can see in this snippet of code:

```
<button class="fakelink" id="eShow">
  &raquo; Show Elevation
</button>
```

The fakelink class ensures that the button is rendered as non-underlined, bold, and red; cursor: pointer; causes the mouse pointer to change in such a way that users think the text is a link of the type that would normally be enclosed in an <a> element.

But the really interesting stuff happens when we associate a click event with a <button>. To be unobtrusive, we do this with an event listener on the element, as you can see in this snippet of code:

```
document.getElementById("eShow").addEventListener("click", function() {
  this.style.display = 'none';
  document.getElementById("eHide").style.display='block';
  document.getElementById("elevation").style.display='block';
});
```

In the sample snippet just shown, when the click event is seen on the eShow element, a function runs a series of commands to change the current value of CSS elements. Let's look at them separately:

```
this.style.display = 'none';
document.getElementById("eHide").style.display='block';
document.getElementById("elevation").style.display='block';
```

In the first line of the snippet, the this keyword refers to the element itself. In other words, this refers to the <button> element (actually any element) with the ID eShow. The keyword style refers to the style object; the style object contains all the CSS styles that you assign to the element. In this case, we are most interested in the display style. Therefore, this.style.display means "the display style of the eShow ID," and we are setting the value of the display style to none when the button is clicked.

But three actions also occur within the click event. The other two actions begin with document.getElementById() and include a specific ID name within the parentheses. We use document.getElementById() instead of this because the second and third actions set CSS style properties for elements that are not the parent element. As you can see in the snippet, in the second and third actions, we are setting the display property values for the element IDs eHide and elevation. When users click the currently visible `<div>` called eShow, the following happens:

▶ The eShow `<div>` becomes invisible.

▶ The eHide `<div>` becomes visible and is displayed as a block.

▶ The elevation `<div>` becomes visible and is displayed as a block.

Figure 24.4 shows the result of these actions.

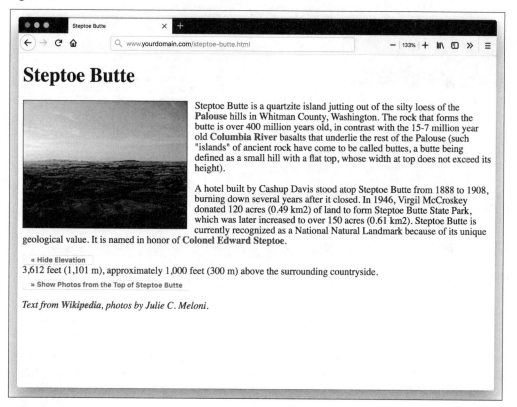

FIGURE 24.4
When Show Elevation is clicked, the visibility of it and other elements changes based on the commands in the `click` event listener function.

Another set of elements in the code in Listing 24.4 controls the visibility of the additional photos. These elements are not affected by the `click` events in the elevation-related elements. That is, when you click either Show Elevation or Hide Elevation, the photo-related `<div>` elements do not change. You can show the elevation and not the photos (as shown in Figure 24.4), the photos and not the elevation, or both the elevation and the photos at the same time (see Figure 24.5).

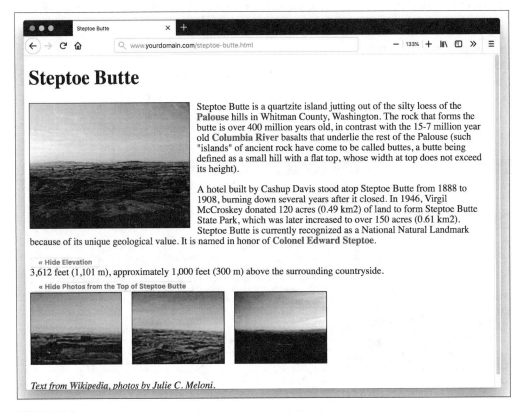

FIGURE 24.5
The page after both Show Elevation and Show Photos from the Top of Steptoe Butte have been clicked.

This brief example has shown you the very beginning of the layout and interaction possibilities that await you when you master CSS in conjunction with events. For example, you can code your pages so that your users can change elements of the style sheet or change to an entirely different style sheet, move blocks of text to other places in the layout, take quizzes or submit forms, and do much, much more.

Controlling Windows with Objects

In Lesson 21 you learned that you can use DOM objects to represent various parts of the browser window and the current HTML document. You also learned that the history, document, and location objects are all children of the window object.

Now we'll take a closer look at the window object itself. As you've probably guessed by now, this means you'll be dealing with browser windows.

The window object always refers to the current window (the one containing the script). The self keyword is also a synonym for the current window. As you'll learn in the next sections, you can have more than one window on the screen at the same time and can refer to these windows by using different names.

Properties of the window Object

Although there is normally a single window object available in a browser session, users might have more than one window object available in their browser session because they have multiple tabs open or a web page has opened a pop-up window. As you learned in Lesson 21, the document, history, and location objects are properties (or children) of the window object, and each open window object has these properties available for scripting purposes. In addition to these properties, each window object has the following useful properties:

▶ window.closed—Indicates whether the window has been closed. This makes sense only when you're working with multiple windows because the current window contains the script and cannot be closed without ending the script.

▶ window.name—Specifies the name for a window opened by a script.

▶ window.opener—In a new window opened by a script, provides a reference to the window containing the script that opened it.

▶ window.outerHeight and window.outerWidth—Specify the height and width, respectively, of the outside of a browser window.

▶ window.screen—Provides a child object that stores information about the screen the window is in—its resolution, color depth, and so on.

▶ window.self—Acts as a synonym for the current window object.

NOTE

The properties of the window.screen object include height, width, availHeight, and availWidth (the available height and width rather than the total), colorDepth (which indicates the color support of the monitor: 8 for 8-bit color, 32 for 32-bit color, and so on), and pixelDepth, which indicates the color resolution, in bits per pixel of the screen.

You can find a complete list of window properties (and methods) at https://developer.mozilla.org/en-US/docs/Web/API/Window.

Creating a New Window

One of the most convenient uses for the window object is to create a new window. You can do this to display a new document—for example, a pop-up advertisement or the instructions for a game—without clearing the current window. You can also create windows for specific purposes, such as navigation windows.

You can create a new browser window with the window.open method. A typical statement to open a new window looks like this:

```
myNewWindow=window.open("URL", "WindowName", "LIST_OF_FEATURES");
```

The following are the components of the window.open statement in this syntax:

▶ The myNewWindow variable is used to store the new window object. You can access methods and properties of the new object by using this name.

▶ The first parameter of the window.open method is a URL, which will be loaded into the new window. If URL is left blank, no web page will be loaded. In this case, you could use JavaScript to fill the window with content.

▶ The second parameter, WindowName, specifies a window name. This is assigned to the window object's name property and is used to refer to the window.

▶ The third parameter, LIST_OF_FEATURES, is a list of optional features, separated by commas. You can customize the new window by choosing whether to include the toolbar, status line, and other features. This enables you to create various "floating" windows, which might look nothing like a typical browser window.

The features available in the third parameter of the window.open() method include width and height, to set the size of the window in pixels; left and top, to set the distance in pixels of the new window from the left side and top of the user's desktop, respectively; and several features that can be set to either yes (1) or no (0): toolbar, location, status, menubar, personalbar, scrollbars, and resizable, among a few others. You list only the features you want to use.

This example creates a small window with no toolbar or status bar:

```
newSmallWin = window.open("","small", "width=300,height=220,toolbar=0,status=0");
```

Opening and Closing Windows

Of course, if you can open a window, you can use JavaScript to close windows as well. The window.close method closes a window. Browsers don't normally allow you to close the main browser window without the user's permission; this method's main purpose is for closing windows you have created. For example, this statement closes a window called `updateWindow`:

```
updateWindow.close();
```

As another example, Listing 24.5 shows an HTML document that enables you to open a small new window by clicking a button. You can then click another button to close the new window. The third button attempts to close the current window, and you'll see how well that works out later in this lesson.

LISTING 24.5 An HTML Document That Uses JavaScript to Enable You to Create and Close Windows

```
<!doctype html>
<html lang="en">
  <head>
    <meta charset="utf-8">
    <title>Create a New Window</title>
    <meta name="viewport"
          content="width=device-width, initial-scale=1">
  </head>
  <body>
    <h1>Create a New Window</h1>
    <p>
      Use the buttons below to open and close windows using
      JavaScript.
    </p>
    <button type="button" id="openNew">Open New Window</button>

    <button type="button" id="closeNew">Close New Window</button>

    <button type="button" id="closeSelf">Close Main Window</button>

    <script>
      document.getElementById("openNew").addEventListener("click", function() {
        newWin = window.open("", "NewWin", "toolbar=no,status=no,width=200,
                             height=100");
      });

      document.getElementById("closeNew").addEventListener("click", function() {
        newWin.close();
      });
```

```
    document.getElementById("closeSelf").addEventListener("click", function() {
      window.self.close();
    });
  </script>

  </body>
</html>
```

This example uses simple event handlers to do its work by providing a different listener for each of the buttons. Figure 24.6 shows the result of clicking the Open New Window button: It opens a small new window on top of the main browser window.

FIGURE 24.6
A new browser window opened with JavaScript.

However, notice the error message shown in the JavaScript console in Figure 24.7. This error message appears after an attempt is made to close the main browser window from this script. As you can see, modern web browsers do not allow JavaScript to close the entire browser window because JavaScript did not originally open the window.

FIGURE 24.7
The console appropriately displays an error when JavaScript tries to close a window it did not open.

Moving and Resizing Windows

The DOM enables you to move or resize windows that your scripts have created. You can do this by using the following methods for a `window` object:

- `window.moveTo(x, y)`—Moves the window to a new position. The parameters specify the x (column) and y (row) position.

- `window.moveBy(numX, numY)`—Moves the window relative to its current position, by numX or numY pixels. The numX and numY parameters can be positive or negative and are added to the current values to reach the new position.

- `window.resizeTo(width, height)`—Resizes the window to the width and height specified as parameters.

- `window.resizeBy(numX, numY)`—Resizes the window relative to its current size, by numX or numY pixels. The parameters are used to modify the current width and height.

As an example, Listing 24.6 shows an HTML document with a simple script that enables you to resize and move a new window you've created based on values entered in a form.

LISTING 24.6   Moving and Resizing a New Window

```
<!doctype html>
<html lang="en">
  <head>
    <meta charset="utf-8">
    <title>Moving and Resizing Windows</title>
    <meta name="viewport"
          content="width=device-width, initial-scale=1">
  </head>
  <body>

   <h1>Moving and Resizing Windows</h1>

   <form name="changeform">
     <p>
       <strong>Resize to:</strong> <br>
       <input size="5" type="text" name="w"> pixels wide and
       <input size="5" type="text" name="h"> pixels high
     </p>
     <p><strong>-- AND/OR --</strong></p>
     <p>
       <strong>Move to:</strong> <br>
       X-position: <input size="5" type="text" name="x">
       Y-position: <input size="5" type="text" name="y">
     </p>
     <p><input type="button" value="Change Window" id="doIt"></p>
   </form>

   <script>
     function doIt() {
       if ((document.changeform.w.value) &&
           (document.changeform.h.value)) {
         NewWin.resizeTo(document.changeform.w.value,
                      document.changeform.h.value);
       }
       if ((document.changeform.x.value) &&
           (document.changeform.y.value)) {
         NewWin.moveTo(document.changeform.x.value,
                      document.changeform.y.value);
       }
     }
```

```
    window.addEventListener("load", function() {
      NewWin=window.open('','NewWin', 'width=200,height=100');
    });

    document.getElementById("doIt").addEventListener("click", doIt);
  </script>
  </body>
</html>
```

In this example, the doIt function is called as an event handler when you click the Change Window button. This function checks whether you have specified width and height values. If you have, the function uses the self.resizeTo method to resize the current window. Similarly, if you have specified x and y values, it uses NewWin.moveTo to move the window. If you have set both pairs of values, the script both resizes and moves your window. Load up this code in a web browser and give it a try!

Using Timeouts

Sometimes the hardest thing to get a script to do is to do nothing at all—for a specific amount of time. Fortunately, JavaScript includes a built-in function to do this "nothing at all," which is also called "sleeping." The window.setTimeout method enables you to specify a time delay and a command that will execute after the delay passes.

NOTE

Timeouts don't make the browser stop what it's doing. Although the statement you specify in the setTimeout method won't be executed until the delay passes, the browser will continue to do other things while it waits (for example, acting on other event handlers and loading external content).

You begin a timeout with a call to the setTimeout method, which has two parameters. The first is a JavaScript statement, or group of statements, enclosed in quotation marks. The second parameter is the time to wait in milliseconds (thousandths of seconds). For example, the following statement displays an alert dialog box after 10 seconds:

```
timeoutID=window.setTimeout("alert('Time's up!')",10000);
```

CAUTION

Like an event handler, a timeout uses a JavaScript statement within quotation marks. Make sure that you use a single quote on each side of each string within the statement, as shown in the previous code snippet.

A variable (`timeoutID` in this example) stores an identifier for the timeout. This enables you to set multiple timeouts, each with its own identifier. Before a timeout has elapsed, you can stop by using the `clearTimeout` method and specifying the identifier of the timeout to stop:

```
window.clearTimeout(timeoutID);
```

Normally, a timeout happens only once because the statement you specify in the `setTimeout` statement is executed only once. But often you'll want a statement to execute over and over. For example, your script might be updating a clock or a countdown and might need to execute once per second.

You can make a timeout repeat by issuing the `setTimeout` method call again in the function called by the timeout. Listing 24.7 shows an HTML document that demonstrates a repeating timeout.

LISTING 24.7   Using Timeouts to Update a Page Every Two Seconds

```html
<!doctype html>
<html lang="en">
  <head>
    <meta charset="utf-8">
    <title>Timeout Example</title>
    <meta name="viewport"
        content="width=device-width, initial-scale=1">
  </head>
  <body>
    <h1>Timeout Example</h1>
    <p>The counter will update every two seconds.</p>
    <p>Press RESTART or STOP to restart or stop the count.</p>
    <p id="showText"></p>
    <section>
      <button type="button" id="restart">RESTART</button>
      <button type="button" id="stop">STOP</button>
    </section>

    <script>
      var counter = 0;

      // call Update function 2 seconds after first load
      timeoutID=window.setTimeout("Update();",2000);

      function Update() {
        counter++;
        var textField = document.getElementById("showText");
        textField.innerHTML = "The counter is now at " + counter;

        // set another timeout for the next count
        timeoutID=window.setTimeout("Update();",2000);
      }
```

```
    // set event listeners for the buttons
    document.getElementById("restart").addEventListener("click", function() {
        counter = 0;
        Update();
    });
    document.getElementById("stop").addEventListener("click", function() {
        window.clearTimeout(timeoutID);
    });
    </script>
  </body>
</html>
```

This script displays a message inside a specially named <p> element every two seconds, and it includes an incrementing counter that displays as part of that message. The specific <p> tag has an id value of showText, and the Update function includes two lines that tell the script that the text should be placed between these two tags:

```
textField = document.getElementById("showText");
textField.innerHTML = "The counter is now at " + counter;
```

The first line creates a variable called textField that holds the value of the element, given the id value of showText. The second line says that, given that value, the text message about the counter and the counter number should be placed inside the starting and ending tags of the element with the id value of showText; that is the purpose of the innerHTML method, as you learned previously.

This script calls the setTimeout method when the page loads and again at each update. The Update function performs the update, adding one to the counter and setting the next timeout. Clicking the RESTART button sets the counter to zero and reasserts the Update function, and clicking the STOP button demonstrates the clearTimeout method. Figure 24.8 shows the display of the timeout example after the counter has been running for a while.

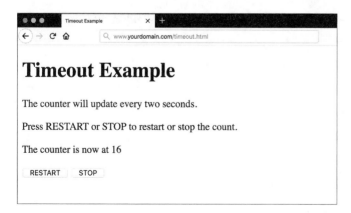

FIGURE 24.8
The output of the timeout example, after it has been running for some time.

Displaying Dialog Boxes

The window object includes three methods that are useful for displaying messages and interacting with the user. You've already used them in some of your scripts. Here's a summary:

- ▶ window.alert(message)—Displays an alert dialog box. This dialog box simply gives the user a message.

- ▶ window.confirm(message)—Displays a confirmation dialog box that displays a message and includes OK and Cancel buttons. This method returns true if OK is pressed and false if Cancel is pressed.

- ▶ window.prompt(message,default)—Displays a message and prompts the user for input. It returns the text entered by the user. If the user does not enter anything, the default value is used.

When using the confirm and prompt methods, you should use a variable to receive the user's response. For example, this statement displays a prompt and stores the text the user enters in the text variable:

```
text = window.prompt("Enter some text","Default value");
```

NOTE

You can usually omit the explicit reference to the window object when referring to these methods because it is the default context of a script. For example, you can use alert("text") instead of window.alert("text").

As a further illustration of these types of dialog boxes, Listing 24.8 shows an HTML document that includes buttons and event handlers to enable you to test dialog boxes.

LISTING 24.8 An HTML Document That Uses JavaScript to Display Alerts, Confirmations, and Prompts

```
<!doctype html>
<html lang="en">
  <head>
    <meta charset="utf-8">
    <title>Alerts, Confirmations, and Prompts</title>
    <meta name="viewport"
          content="width=device-width, initial-scale=1">
  </head>
  <body>
    <h1>Alerts, Confirmations, and Prompts</h1>
    <p>
      Use the buttons below to test dialogs in JavaScript.
    </p>
```

```
<button type="button" id="alert">
  Display an Alert
</button>

<button type="button" id="confirm">
  Display a Confirmation
</button>

<button type="button" id="prompt">
  Display a Prompt
</button>

<script>
  document.getElementById("alert").addEventListener("click",
                                    function() {
    alertVal = window.alert("This is a test alert.");
  });
  document.getElementById("confirm").addEventListener("click",
                                      function() {
    confirmVal = window.confirm("Would you like to confirm?");
  });
  document.getElementById("prompt").addEventListener("click",
                                     function() {
    promptVal = window.prompt("Enter Text:","This is the default.");
  });
</script>
</body>
</html>
```

This document displays three buttons, and each button uses an event handler to display one of the three types of dialog boxes.

Figure 24.9 shows the Listing 24.8 script in action, with the prompt dialog box currently displayed and showing the default value.

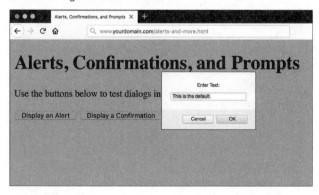

FIGURE 24.9
Showing a prompt dialog box as a result of clicking a button.

Summary

In this lesson, you learned to use events to detect mouse actions, keyboard actions, and other events, such as the loading of the page. You can use event handlers to perform a simple JavaScript statement when an event occurs or to call a more complicated function. In learning this, you learned how to make nearly every JavaScript script you write unobtrusive. By listening for events, you can place the script last in the HTML document so that it doesn't disrupt the loading of the rest of the page.

JavaScript includes various events. Many of them are related to forms, which you'll learn more about in Lesson 27, "Working with Web-Based Forms." In a longer example in this chapter, you saw how to use `click` to show or hide text in a page with some design elements in it. Some new CSS was introduced: the use of the `cursor` property. Assigning a `cursor` property of `pointer` enabled you to indicate to users that particular text or an HTML element was acting as a link even though it was not enclosed in `<a></a>` tags, as you are used to seeing.

In this lesson, you learned how to use the `window` object to work with browser windows and used its properties and methods to set timeouts and display dialog boxes. You also worked through several examples in which you put together all the pieces of the puzzle from the previous several lessons: working with the Document Object Model to change content and window display, creating new functions, and invoking those new functions through events.

Q&A

Q. Can you capture mouse or keyboard events on elements other than text, such as images?

A. Yes, these types of events can be applied to actions related to clicking on or rolling over images as well as text. However, some multimedia objects, such as embedded YouTube videos or Flash files, are not used in the same way, because those objects are played via additional software for which other mouse or keyboard actions are applicable. For instance, if a user clicks on a YouTube video that is embedded in your web page, he or she is interacting with the YouTube player and no longer your actual web page; that action cannot be captured in the same way.

Q. What happens if I define both `keydown` and `keypress` event handlers? Will they both be called when a key is pressed?

A. The `keydown` event handler is called first. If it returns `true`, the `keypress` event is called. Otherwise, no `keypress` event is generated.

Q. When a script is running in a window created by another script, how can it refer to the original window?

A. JavaScript includes the `window.opener` property, which lets you refer to the window that opened the current window.

Q. What are some examples of using timeouts in JavaScript? I'm not sure why I would want code to go to sleep.

A. Ideally, you want your code to execute all the time, but sometimes you need to wait for user input, or for long processes to finish, or even to ensure that users are not overloading your system by clicking on elements too often. In such cases, you can include a timeout that effectively disables certain buttons for a certain amount of time, such as to limit voting or "liking" something more than once every second.

Workshop

The Workshop contains quiz questions and activities to help you solidify your understanding of the material covered. Try to answer all questions before looking at the "Answers" section that follows.

Quiz

1. Which of the following is the correct event handler for detecting a mouse click on a link?

   a. `mouseup`

   b. `link`

   c. `click`

2. When does the `load` event handler for the <body> element execute?

   a. When an image is finished loading

   b. When the entire page is finished loading

   c. When the user attempts to load another page

3. Which of the following `event` object properties indicates which key was pressed for a `keypress` event?

   a. `event.which`

   b. `event.keyCode`

   c. `event.onKeyPress`

4. Which of the following methods displays a dialog box with OK and Cancel buttons and waits for a response?

    a. `window.alert`

    b. `window.confirm`

    c. `window.prompt`

5. What does the `window.setTimeout` method do?

    a. Executes a JavaScript statement after a delay

    b. Locks up the browser for the specified amount of time

    c. Sets the amount of time before the browser exits automatically

6. True or False: JavaScript can take control of a browser window and resize it, even if the script did not open it.

    a. True

    b. False

7. What is an anonymous function?

    a. A function that only runs when other functions cannot.

    b. A function with no name that is used as a default value.

    c. A function that takes the place of other functions.

    d. A function that has no name and doesn't need to be used anywhere except the one location.

8. How do you write an event that happens when the user leaves the page?

    a. `window.addListener("unload", function() { });`

    b. `window.addEvent("unload", function() { });`

    c. `window.addEventListener("unload", function() { });`

    d. `window.addEventListener("leave", function() { });`

9. What does the `resizeBy` method do, and what arguments does it use?

    a. Resizes the window relative to its current size with two arguments: numX and numY

    b. Resizes the window relative to the browser's current size with the arguments: numX and numY

    c. Resizes the current element using the arguments: numX and numY

    d. Resizes the current element using the arguments: numX, numY, and numZ

10. What does `window.self` do?

    a. A synonym for the current window object

    b. Reloads the current window

    c. Sends the link to the current open window

    d. Opens the link in a new window

NOTE

Just a reminder for those of you reading these words in the print or e-book edition of this book: If you go to **www.informit.com/register** and register this book (using ISBN 9780672338083), you can receive free access to an online Web Edition that not only contains the complete text of this book but also features an interactive version of this quiz.

Answers

1. c. The event handler for a mouse click is `click`.

2. b. The `<body>` element's `load` handler executes when the page and all its images are finished loading.

3. b. The `event.which` property stores the character code for each keypress.

4. b. The `window.confirm` method displays a dialog box with OK and Cancel buttons and waits for a response.

5. a. The `window.setTimeout` method executes a JavaScript statement after a delay.

6. b. False. Only windows created by a script can be manipulated by the script.

7. d. An anonymous function is a function that has no name and doesn't need to be used anywhere except the one location.

8. c. These lines will do something when the user leaves the page:

```
window.addEventListener("unload", function() {
   // add statements here
});
```

9. a. The `window.resizeBy` method resizes the window relative to its current size. It takes two arguments: `numX` and `numY`.

10. a. The `window.self` property is a synonym for the current window object.

Exercises

To gain more experience using event handlers and controlling windows in JavaScript, try the following exercises:

▶ Extend any (or all!) of the sample scripts in this lesson to check for specific values of keypress actions before continuing on to execute the underlying JavaScript statements within their associated functions.

▶ Add commands to the `click` attributes in Listing 24.4 such that only one of the elements—the elevation or photos—is visible at a time.

▶ Using timeouts and JavaScript to display date and time (which you learned earlier in these lessons), create a script to display a "live" clock with hours, minutes, and seconds shown.

▶ Modify Listing 24.9 to do something with the results of the `window.prompt()` dialog box—print the text, perform another action depending on specific text, or do something that combines the two.

LESSON 25
JavaScript Best Practices

What You'll Learn in This Lesson:

▸ Best practices for creating unobtrusive scripts

▸ The importance of separating content, presentation, and behavior

▸ The importance of following web standards to create cross-browser scripts

▸ How to read and display browser information

▸ How to use feature sensing to avoid errors

▸ How to support older, less compliant browser versions

▸ How to support non-JavaScript browsers

In this lesson, you'll learn some guidelines for *unobtrusive scripting*—creating scripts and pages that are easy to maintain and easy to use and that follow web standards. Unobtrusive scripting adds features without getting in the way of the user, the developer maintaining the code, or the designer building the layout of the site. You'll also learn how to make sure your scripts will work in multiple browsers and won't stop working when a new browser comes along. In addition, and perhaps most importantly, these practices will help you become a better developer and a better member of the overall JavaScript developer community.

Scripting Best Practices

As you start to develop more complex scripts, it's important to know some scripting *best practices*. These are guidelines for using JavaScript that more experienced programmers have learned the hard way. Here are a few of the benefits of following these best practices:

▸ Your code will be readable and easy to maintain, whether you're turning the page over to someone else or just trying to remember what you did a year ago.

▸ You'll create code that follows standards and won't be crippled when a new version of a browser is released.

▸ You'll create pages that work even without JavaScript.

- ▶ It will be easy to adapt code you create for one site to another site or project.

- ▶ Your users will thank you for creating a site that is easy to use and easy to fix when things go wrong.

Whether you're writing an entire AJAX web application or simply enhancing a page with a three-line script, it's useful to know some of the concepts that are regularly considered by those who write complex scripts for a living. The following sections introduce some of these best practices.

Avoid Overusing JavaScript

An important best practice is to avoid overusing JavaScript. This might seem counterintuitive in lessons teaching you to become a competent developer using JavaScript, but it's true. Because HTML5 and CSS3 have matured, and so has browser support for these advanced standards, there's now much less reason to use JavaScript for some of the enhanced interactions that required it even just a few years ago. For example, some developers spent years crafting useful JavaScript-based form validation scripts, all of which have been rendered moot by the inclusion of native HTML5 form field validation. So, as you're thinking about what to build with JavaScript, keep the following in mind:

- ▶ Many of the visual effects that once needed to be coded in JavaScript can now be achieved perfectly well using CSS. When both approaches are possible (for example, with image rollovers, animations, and some types of menus), CSS is usually preferable. It's well supported across browsers. In the rare case that CSS isn't supported, the page is rendered as standard HTML, usually creating a page that's at least perfectly functional, even if it's not so pretty.

- ▶ Users are likely to spend a lot of their Internet time on sites other than yours. Experienced Internet users become accustomed to popular interface components such as menus, bread-crumb trails, and tabbed browsing. These elements are popular, in general, because they work well, can be made to look good, and don't require the user to read a manual first. Familiarity with a site's operation will likely increase a user's productivity more than the potential benefits of your all-new JavaScript-heavy whizz-bang design. And if users are more productive, they will be happier with your site and stay longer.

- ▶ Users in many areas of the world are still using outdated, underpowered, hand-me-down computers and might also have slow and/or unreliable Internet access and old versions of web browsers. The CPU cycles taken up by unnecessary JavaScript code might be precious to them.

- ▶ In some cases you might cost yourself a degree of search engine page rank because the search engines' spiders don't always correctly index content that's been generated by JavaScript or designs that require it for navigation. Plus, if the JavaScript makes the page less mobile friendly, you will definitely get penalized by search engines.

Used carefully and with forethought, JavaScript can be a great tool, but sometimes there is such a thing as too much of a good thing.

Content, Presentation, and Behavior

When you create a web page, or especially an entire site or application, you need to deal with three key areas, *content*, *presentation*, and *behavior*, all of which you've learned about in the previous lessons:

▶ *Content* consists of the words that a visitor can read on your pages. You create the content as text and mark it up with HTML to define different classes of content—headings, paragraphs, links, and so on.

▶ *Presentation* is the appearance and layout of the words, images, and other elements on each page—text formatting, fonts, colors, and graphics. This is where the power of CSS comes into play.

▶ *Behavior* is what happens when you interact with a page—items that highlight when you move over them, forms you can submit, and so on. This is where JavaScript enters into the picture for enhanced front-end interactivity, along with server-side languages such as PHP and Ruby.

It's a good idea to keep these three areas in mind, especially as you create larger sites. It's also a good idea to keep content, presentation, and behavior separated as much as possible. One good way to do this is to create an external CSS file for the presentation and an external JavaScript file for the behavior and link them to the HTML document.

Keeping things separated like this makes it easier to maintain a large site. If you need to change the color of the headings, for example, you can make a quick edit to the CSS file without having to look through all the HTML markup to find the right place to edit. This separation also makes it easy for you to reuse the same CSS and JavaScript on multiple pages of a site. Last but not least, this separation encourages you to use each language where its strengths lie, which ultimately makes your job easier.

Speed and Web Page Loading

JavaScript can be a huge drain on a web page because it is downloaded all by itself. The browser cannot download anything else while the script is loading. This means that if there are other page elements to download that come after the script or scripts on your page, they will not begin downloading until the scripts are done.

There are two techniques to remedy this: Use only one external JavaScript file and place the `<script>` tag last in the HTML. By placing the `<script>` tag last—right before the closing `</body>` tag—you ensure that the entire page will render and be visible even as the script is loading. And putting all your scripts together in one JavaScript file ensures that the browser has to make only one call to the server for those scripts. This isn't always possible—sometimes you need to load things like libraries that are housed on other servers—but any scripts you write should all be contained in the same file as much as possible.

Graceful Degradation

Some of the earliest web browsers didn't even support the inclusion of images in HTML. As the `<img>` element and other tags were introduced, it became important for those text-only browsers to present something helpful to the user whenever an unsupported tag was encountered. In the case of the `<img>` tag, that facility was provided by the `alt` attribute. Web designers could assign a string of text to `alt`, and text-only browsers would display that text to the user instead of showing the image. At the whim of the page designer, the `alt` text might be simply a title for the image, a description of what the picture would have displayed, or a suggestion for an alternative source of the information that would have been carried in the graphic.

This was an early example of *graceful degradation*—the process by which a user whose browser lacks the required technical features to make full use of a web page's design (or has those features disabled) can still benefit from the site's content.

Let's take JavaScript itself as another example. Virtually every browser supports JavaScript, and only a small percentage of users turn it off. So, do you really need to worry about that 1% of possible visitors who don't have JavaScript enabled? The answer is probably yes. One type of frequent visitor to your site will no doubt be the spider programs from search engines, busy indexing the pages of the Web. A spider attempts to follow all the navigation links on your pages to build a full index of your site's content; if such navigation requires the services of JavaScript, you might find some parts of your site not being indexed. Your search ranking will probably suffer as a result.

Another important example lies in the realm of accessibility. No matter how capable a browser program is, there are some users who will access your site with other limitations, such as the inability to use a traditional mouse or the necessity to use screen-reading software. You probably want your site to be accessible to this part of your audience, and that may mean doing without all your JavaScript bells and whistles.

Many mobile devices also have limitations compared to traditional desktop computers. The obvious limitation is the small screen size. In addition, mobile devices don't have a mouse or other pointer device, so click and hover events don't work on them. Mobile devices are becoming an increasingly large portion of the web browsing audience, and ignoring them is a really bad idea.

Progressive Enhancement

The counterpart of graceful degradation is *progressive enhancement*, in which the primary development principle is to keep HTML documents as simple as possible so that they'll definitely work in even the most primitive browsers. After you've tested that and made sure that the basic functionality is always available, you can dynamically add features that make the site easier to use or better looking for those with new browsers. If you add these features unobtrusively, they have little chance of preventing the site from working in its primitive HTML form.

Here are some guidelines for progressive enhancement:

- Enhance your site's presentation by adding style rules to a separate CSS file. Try to avoid using HTML tags for presentation only, such as <b> for boldface or <blockquote> for an indented section.

- Enhance behavior by adding scripts to an external JavaScript file.

- Add events without using inline event handlers, as described later in this lesson and in Lesson 24, "Responding to Events and Using Windows."

- Use feature sensing, described later in this lesson, to ensure that JavaScript code executes only on browsers that support the features it requires.

Adding Event Handlers

In Lesson 24, you learned that there is more than one way to set up event handlers. The simplest way is to add them directly to an HTML tag. For example, this <body> tag has an event handler that calls a function called Startup:

```
<body onload="Startup();">
```

This method works, but it does involve putting JavaScript code in the HTML page, which means you haven't fully separated content and behavior. To keep things entirely separate, you can set up the event handler in the JavaScript file instead, like this:

```
window.onload=Startup;
```

This is an acceptable way to set up events: It keeps JavaScript out of the HTML file, and it works in all modern browsers. However, it does involve one problem: You can't attach more than one event to the same element of a page. For example, you can't have two different load event handlers that both execute when the page loads.

When you're the only one writing scripts, this is no big deal; you can combine the two into one function. But when you're trying to use two or three third-party scripts on a page, and all of them want to add a load event handler to the body, you have a problem.

The W3C Event Model

To solve this problem and standardize event handling, the W3C created an event model as part of the DOM Level 2 standard. It uses a method, addEventListener, to attach a handler to any event on any element. For example, the following uses the W3C model to set up the same `load` event handler as the previous examples:

```
window.addEventListener('load', Startup, false);
```

The first parameter of `addEventListener` is the event name, without the `on` prefix—`load`, `click`, `mouseover`, and so on. The second parameter specifies the function to handle the event, and the third is an advanced flag that indicates how multiple events should be handled (`false` works for most purposes).

Any number of functions can be attached to an event in this way. Because one event handler doesn't replace another, you use a separate function, `removeEventListener`, which uses the same parameters:

```
window.removeEventListener('load', Startup, false);
```

One problem with the W3C model is that although Internet Explorer 9 supports it, Internet Explorer 8 does not. Instead, Internet Explorer 8 supports a proprietary method, `attachEvent`, that does much the same thing. Here's the `Startup` event handler defined Microsoft-style:

```
window.attachEvent('onload', Startup);
```

The `attachEvent` method has two parameters. The first is the event, with the `on` prefix—`onload`, `onclick`, `onmouseover`, and so on. The second is the function that will handle the event. Internet Explorer also supports the `detachEvent` method, which has the same parameters, for removing an event handler.

Attaching Events the Cross-Browser Way

As you can see, attaching events in this new way is complex and requires different code for different browsers. In most cases, you're better off using the traditional method to attach events, and that method is used in most of the examples in these lessons. However, if you really need to support multiple event handlers, you can use some `if` statements to use either the W3C method or Microsoft's method. For example, the following code adds the `ClickMe` function as an event for the element with the `id` attribute `btn`:

```
obj = document.getElementById("btn");
if (obj.addEventListener) {
   obj.addEventListener('click',ClickMe,false);
} else if (obj.attachEvent) {
   obj.attachEvent('onclick',ClickMe);
} else {
   obj.onclick=ClickMe;
}
```

This checks for the `addEventListener` method and uses it if it's found. Otherwise, it checks for the `attachEvent` method and uses that. If neither is found, it uses the traditional method to attach the event handler. This technique, called *feature sensing*, is explained in detail later in this lesson.

Many universal functions are available to compensate for the lack of a consistent way to attach events. If you are using a third-party library, there's a good chance it includes an event function that can simplify this process for you.

NOTE

The YUI library, like many other third-party libraries, includes an event-handling function that can attach events in any browser, attach the same event handler to many objects at once, and perform other nice functions. See https://yuilibrary.com for details, and see Lesson 26, "Using Third-Party JavaScript Libraries and Frameworks," for information about using various other available libraries. Be aware that the YUI library is no longer being maintained, but you can still use the scripts and styles in it.

Web Standards: Avoiding Being Browser Specific

The Web was built on standards, such as the HTML standard developed by the W3C. Now there are a lot of standards involved with JavaScript—CSS, the W3C DOM, and the ECMAScript standard that defines JavaScript's syntax.

Microsoft, the Mozilla Project, Google, and other browser developers such as Opera Software continually improve their browsers' support for web standards, but there are always going to be some browser-specific, nonstandard features, and some parts of the newest standards won't be consistently supported between browsers.

Although it's perfectly fine to test your code in multiple browsers and do whatever it takes to get it working, it's a good idea to follow the standards rather than browser-specific techniques when possible. This ensures that your code will work on future browsers that improve their standards support, whereas browser-specific features might disappear in new versions.

NOTE

One reason to make sure you follow standards is that your pages can be better interpreted by search engines, which often helps your site get search traffic. Separating content, presentation, and behavior is also good for search engines because they can focus on the HTML content of your site without having to skip over JavaScript or CSS.

One place you can go to find out what features are supported by which browsers and browser versions is Can I Use: www.caniuse.com. This site provides up-to-date information on both desktop and mobile browsers and what features of JavaScript, HTML, CSS, and other web technologies they support.

Handling Errors Well

No matter how good your development skills are or might become, your code will have errors. All code has errors at some point, and handling errors well is a sign of a careful developer. When your JavaScript program encounters an error of some sort, a warning or an error will be created inside the JavaScript interpreter and displayed in the JavaScript console of your web browser. Whether and how this is displayed to the user depends on the browser in use and the user's settings; the user might see some form of error message, or the failed program might simply remain silent but inactive.

Neither situation is good for the user; he or she is likely to have no idea what has gone wrong or what to do about it. As you try to write your code to handle a wide range of browsers and circumstances, it's possible to foresee some areas in which errors might be generated. Examples include the following:

▶ The uncertainty about whether a browser fully supports a certain object and whether that support is standards compliant

▶ Whether an independent procedure has completed its execution, such as an external file being loaded

A useful way to try to intercept potential errors and deal with them cleanly is by using the `try` and `catch` statements. The `try` statement enables you to attempt to run a piece of code. If the code runs without errors, all is well; however, if an error occurs, you can use the `catch` statement to intervene before an error message is sent to the user and determine what the program should then do about the error. The syntax looks like this:

```
try {
    doSomething();
}
catch(identifier) {
    doSomethingElse();
}
```

Here, *identifier* is an object created when an error is caught. It contains information about the error. For instance, if you wanted to alert the user to the nature of a JavaScript runtime error, you could use a code construct like this to open a dialog containing details about the error:

```
catch(err) {
    alert(err.description);
}
```

Documenting Your Code

As you create more complex scripts, don't forget to include comments in your code to document what it does, especially when some of the code seems confusing or is difficult to get working. It's also a good idea to document all the data structures, variables, and function arguments used in a larger script.

Using comments is a good way to organize code and will help you work on the script in the future. If you're creating websites for a living, you'll definitely need to use comments so that others can work on your code as easily as you can. The following are some examples of how to use comments:

▶ Using comments as a prologue to any object or function that contains more than a few lines of simple code:

```
function calculateGroundAngle(x1, y1, z1, x2, y2, z2) {
/**
 * Calculates the angle in radians at which
 * a line between two points intersects the
 * ground plane.
 * @author Jane Doe you@yourdomain.com
 */
if(x1 > 0) {
.... more statements
```

▶ Using inline comments wherever the code would otherwise be confusing or prone to misinterpretation:

```
// need to use our custom sort method for performance reasons
var finalArray = rapidSort(allNodes, byAngle) {
.... more statements
```

▶ Using a comment wherever the original author can pass on specialist knowledge that the reader is unlikely to know:

```
// workaround for image onload bug in browser X version Y
if(!loaded(image1)) {
.... more statements
```

▶ Using comments as instructions for commonly used code modifications:

```
// You can change the following dimensions to your preference:
var height = 400px;
```

Ensuring Usability

While you're adding cool features to your site, don't forget about *usability*—making things as easy, logical, and convenient as possible for users of your site. Although there are many books and websites devoted to usability information, a bit of common sense goes a long way.

For example, suppose you provide a drop-down list as the only way to navigate between pages of your site. This is a common interface element, and it works well, but do your users find it usable?

Try comparing it to using a simple set of links across the top of a page, and you might find that the following is true:

▶ The list of links lets you see at a glance what the site contains; the drop-down list requires you to click to see the same list.

▶ Users expect links and can spot them quickly; a drop-down list is more likely to be part of a form than a navigation tool, and thus it won't be the first thing users look for when they want to navigate your site.

▶ Navigating with a link takes a single click, whereas navigating with a drop-down list takes at least two clicks.

Remember to consider the user's point of view whenever you add any functionality—and especially potentially intrusive JavaScript functionality—to a site. Ensure that you're making the site easier to use—or at least not harder to use. Also make sure that the site is easy to use without JavaScript; although this might apply to only a small percentage of your users, that percentage is likely to include users of screen readers or other software packages necessary for people with visual impairments.

Ensuring Accessibility

As a developer you must consider *accessibility*—making your site as accessible as possible for all users, including disabled users. For example, blind users might use a text-reading program that will ignore images and most scripts on your site. Accessibility is more than just good manners; it is mandated by law in some countries.

The subject of accessibility is complex, but you can provide most what is needed by following the philosophy of progressive enhancement: Keep the HTML as simple as possible, keep JavaScript and CSS separate, and make JavaScript an enhancement rather than a requirement for using your site.

NOTE

Ensuring that a site functions without JavaScript is one of the first steps toward accessibility compliance. For more information on accessibility, see www.w3.org/WAI/.

Benefitting from Design Patterns

If you learn more about usability, you'll undoubtedly see *design patterns* mentioned. In computer science, a design pattern is an optimal solution to a common problem. In web development, you use design patterns to design and implement part of a site that you run into over and over.

For example, if you have a site that displays multiple pages of data, you'll have Next Page and Previous Page links, and perhaps numeric links for each page. This is a common design pattern—a problem many web designers have had to solve, and one with a generally agreed-on solution.

Other common web design patterns include a login form, a search engine, and a list of navigation links for a site.

Of course, you can be completely original and make a search engine, a shopping cart, or a login form that looks nothing like any other, but unless you have a way of making them even easier to use, you're better off following the pattern and giving your users an experience that matches their expectations.

Although you can find some common design patterns just by browsing sites similar to yours and noticing how they have solved particular problems, there are also sites that specialize in documenting these patterns, and they're a good place to find ideas on how to make your site work.

NOTE

Google Developers offers a number of tools web designers can use to create more effective sites. For a bunch of responsive design patterns, visit https://developers.google.com/web/fundamentals/design-and-ux/responsive/patterns.

Reusing Code Where You Can

Now that you have all this JavaScript code sitting around, remember that the more you can modularize your code and make it reusable, the better. Take a look at this function:

```
function getElementArea() {
    var high = document.getElementById("id1").style.height;
    var wide = document.getElementById("id1").style.width;
    return high * wide;
}
```

This function attempts to return the area of screen covered by a particular HTML element. Unfortunately, it can work only with an element that has an id with the value id1, which is really not very helpful at all: It eliminates the possibility for you to use this code anywhere else, and if you want to do something similar, you're going to have to duplicate around 98% of this function elsewhere.

Collecting your code into modules such as functions and objects that you can use and reuse throughout your code is a process known as *abstraction*. You can give the preceding function a higher level of abstraction to make its use more general by passing as an argument the id of the element to which the operation should be applied:

```
function getElementArea(elementId) {
    var element = document.getElementById(elementId);
    var high = element.style.height;
    var wide = element.style.width;
    return parseInt(high) * parseInt(wide);
}
```

You can now call this function into action for any element that has an `id`, by passing the value of `id` as a parameter when the function is called:

```
var area1 = getElementArea("id1");
var area2 = getElementArea("id2");
```

Reading Browser Information

In Lesson 21, "Working with the Document Object Model (DOM)," you learned about the various objects (such as `window` and `document`) that represent portions of the browser window and the current web document. JavaScript also includes an object called `navigator` that you can use to read information about the user's browser. Knowing more about the browser can help your scripts determine whether to use certain elements of JavaScript—for example, if your script can tell that an older browser like Internet Explorer 8 is in use, it might try to implement code written specifically for that browser rather than generic code that might fail.

The `navigator` object isn't part of the DOM, so you can refer to it directly. It includes several properties, each of which tells you something about the browser:

- ▶ `navigator.appCodeName`—Specifies the browser's internal code name, such as `Mozilla`. You should be aware that all modern browsers will return `Mozilla` for this property, regardless of whether they are a Mozilla-based browser or not.

- ▶ `navigator.appName`—Specifies the browser's name, such as `Firefox` or `Microsoft Edge`.

- ▶ `navigator.appVersion`—Specifies the version of the browser being used—for example, `5.0 (Windows)`.

- ▶ `navigator.userAgent`—Specifies the user agent header, a string that the browser sends to the web server when requesting a web page. It includes all of the version information—for example, `Mozilla/5.0 (Macintosh; Intel Mac OS X 10.13; rv:59.0) Gecko/20100101 Firefox/59.0`.

- ▶ `navigator.language`—Specifies the language (such as English or Spanish) of the browser. This is stored as a code, such as `en-US` for U.S. English.

- ▶ `navigator.platform`—Specifies the computer platform of the current browser. This is a short string, such as `Linux i686`, `Win32`, and `MacIntel`. You can use this to enable any platform-specific features—for example, ActiveX components for Internet Explorer on Windows machines.

NOTE
_____

The `navigator` object is named after Netscape Navigator, the browser that originally supported JavaScript. Fortunately, this object is also supported by all modern browsers, despite its name.

Many other properties of the `navigator` object can be useful. You can learn more about the
`navigator` object at https://developer.mozilla.org/en-US/docs/Web/API/Navigator.

Displaying Browser Information

As an example of how to read the `navigator` object's properties, Listing 25.1 shows a script that
displays a list of the properties and their values for the current browser.

LISTING 25.1   A Script to Display Information About the Browser

```html
<!doctype html>
<html lang="en">
  <head>
    <meta charset="utf-8">
    <title>Browser Information</title>
    <meta name="viewport"
          content="width=device-width, initial-scale=1">
  </head>
  <body>
    <h1>Browser Information</h1>
    <p>
      The <strong>navigator</strong> object contains the
      following information about the browser you are using:
    </p>
    <ul id="info"></ul>

    <script>
    var txt = "";
    txt += "<li><strong>Code Name:</strong> " + navigator.appCodeName;
    txt += "<li><strong>App Name:</strong> " + navigator.appName;
    txt += "<li><strong>App Version:</strong> " + navigator.appVersion;
    txt += "<li><strong>User Agent:</strong> " + navigator.userAgent;
    txt += "<li><strong>Language:</strong> " + navigator.language;
    txt += "<li><strong>Platform:</strong> " + navigator.platform;

    document.getElementById("info").innerHTML = txt;
    </script>
  </body>
</html>
```

This script is wrapped inside a basic HTML document. JavaScript is used to display each of
the properties of the `navigator` object with the `innerHTML` property of the element with the
`id` `info`.

To try this script, load it into the browser of your choice. If you have more than one browser or
browser version handy, try it in each one. Firefox's display of the script is shown in Figure 25.1.

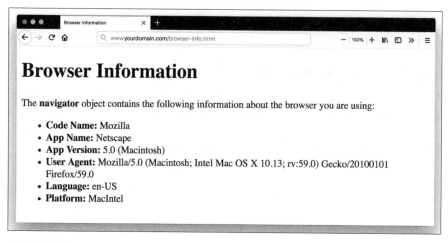

FIGURE 25.1
Firefox displays the browser information script.

Dealing with Dishonest Browsers

If you tried the browser information script in Listing 25.1 using certain versions of Internet Explorer, you probably got a surprise. Figure 25.2 shows how Internet Explorer 6.0 displays the script.

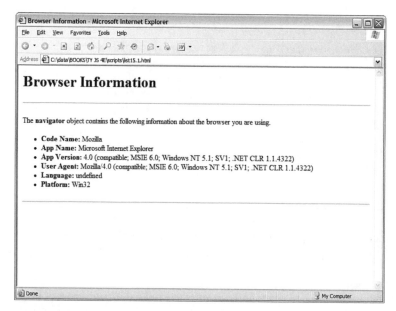

FIGURE 25.2
How Internet Explorer 6 displays the browser information script.

There are several unexpected things about this display. First, the `navigator.language` property is listed as undefined. This isn't much of a surprise because this property isn't supported by Internet Explorer.

More importantly, notice that the word `Mozilla` appears in the Code Name and User Agent fields. The full user agent string reads as follows:

```
Mozilla/4.0 (compatible; MSIE 6.0; Windows 98)
```

Believe it or not, Microsoft did have a good reason for this. At the height of the browser wars, about the time Netscape 3.0 and Internet Explorer 3.0 came out, it was becoming common to see "Netscape only" pages. Some webmasters who used features such as frames and JavaScript set their servers to turn away browsers without `Mozilla` in their user agent string. The problem with this was that most of these features were also supported by Internet Explorer.

Microsoft solved this problem in Internet Explorer 4.0 by making Internet Explorer's user agent read `Mozilla`, with the word `compatible` in parentheses. This allowed Internet Explorer users to view those pages and still included enough details to tell web servers which browser was in use.

You've probably already noticed the other problem with Internet Explorer 6.0's user agent string: the portion reading `Mozilla/4.0`. Not only is Internet Explorer claiming to be Netscape, but it's also masquerading as version 4.0. Why?

As it turns out, this was another effort by Microsoft to stay one step ahead of the browser wars, although this one doesn't make quite as much sense. Because poorly written scripts were checking specifically for "Mozilla/4" for dynamic HTML pages, Microsoft was concerned that its 5.0 version would fail to run these pages. Because changing it later on would only create more confusion, this tradition continued with Internet Explorer 6.0.

These are two interesting episodes in the annals of the browser wars, but what does all this mean to you? Well, you'll need to be careful when your scripts are trying to differentiate between Internet Explorer and Netscape and between different versions. You'll need to check for specific combinations instead of merely checking the `navigator.appVersion` value. Fortunately, there's a better way to handle this situation, as you'll learn in the next section.

Cross-Browser Scripting

If all the details about detecting different browser versions seem confusing, here's some good news: In most cases, you can write cross-browser scripts without referring to the `navigator` object at all. This is not only easier but better because browser-checking code is often confused by new browser versions and has to be updated each time a new browser is released.

Feature Sensing

Checking browser versions is sometimes called *browser sensing*. A better way of dealing with multiple browsers is called *feature sensing*. In feature sensing, rather than check for a specific browser, you check for a specific feature. For example, suppose your script needs to use the `document.getElementById` function. You can begin a script with an `if` statement that checks for the existence of this function:

```
if (document.getElementById) {
    // do stuff
}
```

If the `getElementById` function exists, the block of code between the brackets is executed. Another common way to use feature sensing is at the beginning of a function that makes use of a feature:

```
function changeText() {
    if (!document.getElementById) return;
    // the rest of the function executes if the feature is supported
}
```

NOTE

The `getElementById` method is widely supported by all modern browsers. You need to set up feature sensing for it only if your scripts are breaking and you've investigated every other possibility.

You don't need to check for *every* feature before you use it—for example, there's not much point in verifying that the `window` object exists in most cases. You can also assume that the existence of one feature means others are supported: If `getElementById` is supported, chances are the rest of the W3C DOM functions are supported.

Feature sensing is a very reliable method of keeping your JavaScript unobtrusive: If a browser supports the feature, it works, and if the browser doesn't, your script stays out of the way. It's also much easier than trying to keep track of hundreds of different browser versions and what they support.

NOTE

Feature sensing is also handy when you're working with third-party libraries, as discussed in Lesson 26. You can check for the existence of an object or a function belonging to a library to verify that the library file has been loaded before your script uses its features.

Dealing with Browser Quirks

So if feature sensing is better than browser sensing, why do you still need to know about the `navigator` object? There's one situation in which it still comes in handy, although if you're lucky you won't find yourself in that situation.

As you develop a complex script and test it in multiple browsers, you might run across a situation in which your perfectly standard code works as it should in one browser and fails to work in another. Assuming that you've eliminated the possibility of a problem with your script, you've probably run into a browser bug or a difference in features between browsers at the very least. Here are some tips for this situation:

▶ Double-check for a bug in your own code.

▶ If the problem is that a feature is missing in one browser, use feature sensing to check for that feature.

▶ When all else fails, use the `navigator` object to detect a particular browser and substitute some code that works in that browser. This should be your last resort.

NOTE

Peter-Paul Koch's QuirksMode, at www.quirksmode.org, is a good place to start when you're looking for specific information about browser bugs.

Supporting Non-JavaScript-Enabled Browsers

Some visitors to your site will be using browsers that don't support JavaScript at all. As hinted a few times in this lesson, these aren't just a few holdouts using ancient browsers. Actually, there are more non-JavaScript browsers than you might think:

▶ Most modern browsers, such as Safari, Firefox, and Chrome, include an option to turn off JavaScript, and some users do so. More often, the browser might have been set up by the user's ISP or employer with JavaScript turned off by default, usually in a misguided attempt to increase security.

▶ Some corporate firewalls and personal antivirus software block JavaScript.

▶ Some ad-blocking software mistakenly prevents scripts from working even if they aren't related to advertising.

▶ Some older mobile phones support little to no JavaScript.

▶ Some visually impaired users use special-purpose browsers or text-only browsers that do not support JavaScript.

As you can see, it would be foolish to assume that all your visitors will support JavaScript even though 99% of traffic is through JavaScript-enabled devices. Two techniques you can use to make sure these users can still use your site are discussed in the following sections.

NOTE

Search engines are another "browser" that will visit your site frequently, and they usually don't pay any attention to JavaScript. If you want search engines to fully index your site, it's critical that you avoid making JavaScript a requirement to navigate the site.

Using the `<noscript>` Tag

One way to be friendly to non-JavaScript browsers is to use the `<noscript>` tag. Supported in all modern browsers, this tag displays a message to non-JavaScript browsers. Browsers that support JavaScript ignore the text between the `<noscript>` tags, whereas others display it. Here is a simple example:

```
<noscript>
This page requires JavaScript. You can either switch to a browser
that supports JavaScript, turn your browser's script support on,
or switch to the <a href="nojs.html">Non-JavaScript</a> version of
this page.
</noscript>
```

Some older browsers don't support `<noscript>`. An alternative to using `<noscript>` is to send users with JavaScript support to another page. This can be accomplished with a single JavaScript statement:

```
<script>
window.location="JavaScript.html";
</script>
```

This script redirects the user to a different page. If the browser doesn't support JavaScript, of course, the script won't be executed, and the rest of the page can display a warning message to explain the situation. This is a pretty drastic option, so you should avoid using it unless you absolutely have to.

Keeping JavaScript Optional

Although you can detect JavaScript browsers and display a message to non-JavaScript-enabled browsers, the best choice is to simply make your scripts unobtrusive. This means using JavaScript to enhance rather than as an essential feature: If you keep JavaScript in separate files and assign event handlers in the JavaScript file rather than in the HTML, browsers that don't support JavaScript will simply ignore your script.

In rare cases when you absolutely need JavaScript—for example, with a JavaScript game—you can warn users that JavaScript is required. However, it's a good idea to offer an alternative, JavaScript-free, way to use your site, especially if it's an e-commerce or business site that your business relies on. Don't turn away customers by succumbing to lazy programming.

One place you should definitely *not* require JavaScript is in the navigation of your site. Although you can create drop-down menus and other fancy navigation tools using JavaScript, they prevent users' non-JavaScript browsers from viewing all of your site's pages. They also prevent search engines from viewing the entire site, which compromises your chances of getting search traffic.

NOTE

Google's Gmail application (https://mail.google.com), requires JavaScript for its elegant interface. However, Google offers a Basic HTML View that can be used without JavaScript. This enables Google to support older browsers and mobile phones without compromising the user experience for those with modern browsers.

Avoiding Errors

If you've made sure that JavaScript is only an enhancement to your site, rather than a requirement, those with browsers that don't support JavaScript for whatever reason will still be able to navigate your site. One last thing to worry about: It's possible for JavaScript to cause an error or confuse these browsers into displaying your page incorrectly. This is a particular concern with browsers that partially support JavaScript, such as older mobile phone browsers. They might interpret a `<script>` tag and start the script but might not support the full JavaScript language or DOM.

Here are some guidelines for avoiding errors:

- Use a separate JavaScript file for each script. This is the best way to guarantee that a browser will ignore a script completely if it does not have JavaScript support.

- Use feature sensing whenever your script tries to use the newer DOM features.

- Test your pages with your browser's JavaScript support turned off. Make sure nothing looks strange and make sure you can still navigate the site.

NOTE

The developer's toolbars for Firefox and Chrome include a convenient way to turn off JavaScript for testing.

Creating an Unobtrusive Script

As an example of unobtrusive scripting, you can create a script that adds functionality to a page with JavaScript without compromising its performance in older browsers—in this case, a script that creates graphic check boxes as an alternative to regular check boxes.

Let's start with the final result: Figure 25.3 shows this example as it appears in Chrome. The first check box is an ordinary HTML one, and the second is a graphic check box managed by JavaScript.

FIGURE 25.3
The graphic check box example in action, with the graphic check box checked.

The graphic check box is just a larger graphic that you can click on to display the checked or unchecked version of the graphic. Although this could just be a simple JavaScript simulation that acts like a check box, the implementation here is a bit more sophisticated. Take a look at the HTML for this example in Listing 25.2.

LISTING 25.2 The HTML File for the Graphic Check Box Example

```
<!doctype html>
<html lang="en">
  <head>
    <meta charset="utf-8">
    <title>Graphic Checkboxes</title>
    <meta name="viewport"
        content="width=device-width, initial-scale=1">
  </head>
  <body>
    <h1>Graphic Checkbox Example</h1>
    <form name="form1">
      <p>
        <input type="checkbox" name="check1" id="check1">
        An ordinary checkbox.
      </p>
```

```
    <p>
      <input type="checkbox" name="check2" id="check2">
      A graphic checkbox, created with unobtrusive JavaScript.
    </p>
  </form>

  <script src="checkbox.js"></script>
</body>
</html>
```

If you look closely at the HTML, you'll see that the two check boxes are defined in exactly the same way, using a standard <input> element. Rather than substitute for a check box, this script actually replaces the regular check box with the graphic version. The script for this example is shown in Listing 25.3.

LISTING 25.3   The JavaScript File for the Graphic Check Box Example

```
function graphicBox(box) {
    // be unobtrusive
    if (!document.getElementById) return;

    // find the object and its parent
    obj = document.getElementById(box);
    parentobj = obj.parentNode;

    // hide the regular checkbox
    obj.style.display = "none";

    // create the image element and set its onclick event
    img = document.createElement("img");
    img.addEventListener("click", Toggle);
    img.src = "images/unchecked.png";

    // save the checkbox id within the image ID
    img.id = "img" + box;

    // display the graphic checkbox
    parentobj.insertBefore(img,obj);
}

function Toggle(e) {
    if (!e) var e=window.event;

    // find the image ID
    img = (e.target) ? e.target : e.srcElement;
```

```
// find the checkbox by removing "img" from the image ID
checkid = img.id.substring(3);
checkbox = document.getElementById(checkid);

// "click" the checkbox
checkbox.click();

// display the right image for the clicked or unclicked state
if (checkbox.checked) {
   file = "images/checked.png";
} else {
   file="images/unchecked.png";
}
img.src=file;
}

// replace the second checkbox with a graphic
graphicBox("check2");
```

This script has three main components:

- ▶ The graphicBox function converts a regular check box to a graphic one. It starts by hiding the existing check box by changing its style.display property and then creates a new image node containing the unchecked.png graphic and inserts it into the DOM next to the original check box. It gives the image an id attribute containing the text img plus the check box's id attribute to make it easier to find the check box later.

- ▶ The Toggle function is specified by graphicBox as the event handler for the new image's click event. This function removes the text img from the image's id attribute to find the id of the real check box. It executes the click method on the check box, toggling its value. Finally, it changes the image to unchecked.gif or checked.gif, depending on the state of the real check box.

- ▶ The last line of the script file runs the graphicBox function to replace the second check box with the id attribute check2.

Using this technique has three important advantages. First, it's an unobtrusive script, in that the HTML has been kept simple, and browsers that don't support JavaScript will simply display the ordinary check box. Second, because the real check box is still on the page but hidden, it will work correctly when the form is submitted to a server-side script. Last but not least, you can use it to create any number of graphic check boxes simply by defining regular ones in the HTML file and adding a call to graphicBox to transform each one.

To try this example, save the JavaScript file as checkbox.js and ensure that the HTML file is in the same folder. You also need to have two graphics the same size, unchecked.gif and checked.gif, in the same folder.

Summary

In this lesson, you learned many guidelines for creating scripts that work in as many browsers as possible and learned how to avoid errors and headaches when working with different browsers. Most importantly, you learned how you can use JavaScript while keeping your pages small, efficient, and valid by using web standards.

Q&A

Q. Is it possible to create 100% unobtrusive JavaScript that can enhance a page without causing any trouble for anyone?

A. Not quite. For example, the unobtrusive script in the last section of this lesson is close: It will work in the latest browsers, and the regular check box will display and work fine in even ancient browsers. However, it can still fail if someone with a modern browser has images turned off: The script will hide the check box because JavaScript is supported, but the image won't be there. This is a rare circumstance, but it's an example of how any feature you add can potentially cause a problem for some small percentage of your users.

Q. Can I detect the user's email address by using the navigator object or another technique?

A. No. There is no reliable way to detect users' email addresses by using JavaScript. (If there were, you would get hundreds of advertisements in your mailbox every day from companies that detected your address as you browsed their pages.)

Workshop

The Workshop contains quiz questions and activities to help you solidify your understanding of the material covered. Try to answer all questions before looking at the "Answers" section that follows.

Quiz

1. Which of the following is the best place to put JavaScript code?

    a. In an HTML file

    b. In a JavaScript file

    c. In a CSS file

2. Which of the following is something you *can't* do with JavaScript?

   a. Send browsers that don't support a feature to a different page

   b. Send users of Internet Explorer to a different page

   c. Send users of non-JavaScript browsers to a different page

3. What is the term for modularization of code into reusable blocks for more general use?

   a. Abstraction

   b. Inheritance

   c. Unobtrusive JavaScript

4. Where is the best place to call a script in your HTML?

   a. In the <head> element

   b. At the top of the <body> element

   c. At the bottom of the <body> element

   d. It doesn't matter where you call your scripts

5. If you can either build something as a script or with CSS or HTML, which is the better choice?

   a. HTML first then add CSS

   b. HTML alone

   c. JavaScript

   d. There is no difference

6. Which is better: graceful degradation or progressive enhancement?

   a. Graceful degradation

   b. Progressive enhancement

   c. Use both

   d. Use neither

7. Why is attaching events like this: `window.onload=start;` less effective than using event listeners?

   a. These events are slower than event listeners.

   b. You can add only one event to the element, which can get in the way if other libraries need to attach events too.

   c. Not all browsers can understand event listeners.

   d. It's not less effective. This is how you should attach events.

8. Is doing browser detection with the `navigator` object a good idea?

  a. Yes, it is very effective.

  b. No. It's too slow to be effective.

  c. No. Some modern browsers don't support it.

  d. No. Browsers all send the same value.

9. What is a better way to solve the cross-browser scripting problem than using the `navigator` object?

  a. Feature detection

  b. Method detection

  c. Object detection

  d. There is no better way

10. Why should you test your pages with JavaScript turned off?

  a. Because many customers don't use JavaScript

  b. Because mobile browsers don't use JavaScript

  c. To ensure JavaScript isn't required

  d. You don't need to do this.

NOTE

Just a reminder for those of you reading these words in the print or e-book edition of this book: If you go to **www.informit.com/register** and register this book (using ISBN 9780672338083), you can receive free access to an online Web Edition that not only contains the complete text of this book but also features an interactive version of this quiz.

Answers

1. b. The best place for JavaScript is in a separate JavaScript file.

2. c. You can't use JavaScript to send users of non-JavaScript browsers to a different page because the script won't be executed at all.

3. a. Abstraction.

4. c. You should place all scripts last in the HTML document to ensure that the page is fully loaded before the scripts start.

5. a. You should try to create as much as possible with basic HTML and then use CSS. JavaScript should be a last resort.

6. **c.** People who use the Mobile First technique would claim that progressive enhancement is better, but both progressive enhancement and graceful degradation make your web pages more usable, so you should use both where it makes sense.

7. **b.** You can add only one event to the element, and if you're using multiple third-party scripts along with your own, this will become a problem.

8. **d.** This is not a good idea because while all modern browsers support the `navigator` object, they support the object by returning the same value ("Mozilla"), regardless of the browser being used.

9. **a.** A better way to deal with multiple browsers is to do feature detection. If a feature doesn't work on the browser, the script will fail gracefully, and the user will be left with the fallback option or with just HTML and CSS.

10. **c.** You should test your pages with JavaScript turned off to ensure that the pages don't require JavaScript to work.

Exercises

▶ Add several check boxes to the HTML document in Listing 25.2 and add the corresponding function calls to the script in Listing 25.3 to replace all of those check boxes with graphic check boxes.

▶ Modify the script in Listing 25.3 to convert all check boxes with a `class` value of `graphic` into graphic check boxes. You can use `getElementsByTagName` and then check each item for the right `className` property. You can also use `getElementsByClassName` and then step through the array, as you learned to do in Lesson 23, "Controlling Flow with Conditions and Loops."

LESSON 26

Using Third-Party JavaScript Libraries and Frameworks

What You'll Learn in This Lesson:

▶ Why you might use a third-party JavaScript library or framework

▶ The differences between libraries and frameworks

▶ How and when you might use Angular, jQuery, React, and other third-party libraries

▶ How to download and use a popular third-party JavaScript library in your applications

▶ The benefits of JavaScript frameworks

Third-party JavaScript libraries—that is, code libraries written and maintained by another party for easy implementation in your own code—offer many advantages over always writing your own code. First and foremost, using these libraries enables you to avoid reinventing the wheel for common tasks. In addition, these libraries allow you to implement cross-browser scripting and sophisticated user interface elements without first having to become an expert in JavaScript.

There are many third-party JavaScript libraries out there, and this lesson provides a brief introduction to a few popular ones. In addition, you'll learn a little about JavaScript frameworks, which—as the name suggests—provide you with some underlying structure for your development, as opposed to just building your own structure and using pieces (libraries) from elsewhere.

Using Third-Party JavaScript Libraries

When you use JavaScript's built-in and often-used `Math` and `Date` functions, JavaScript does most of the work; you don't have to figure out how to convert dates between formats or calculate a cosine but can just use the function that JavaScript provides. Third-party libraries are libraries that are not directly included with JavaScript, but they serve a similar purpose: They enable you to do complicated things with only a small amount of code because that small amount of code refers to something bigger under the hood that someone else has already created.

Although in general most people are big fans of third-party libraries, you should be aware of some of the common objections:

▶ You won't ever really know how the code works because you're simply employing someone else's algorithms and functions.

▶ JavaScript libraries contain a lot of code you'll never use but that the browser has to download anyway.

Blindly implementing code is never a good thing. You should endeavor to understand what is happening behind the scenes when you use any library. But that understanding could be limited to knowing that someone else wrote a complicated algorithm that you could not write; it's fine if that's all you know, as long as you implement it appropriately and understand the possible weaknesses.

The fact that libraries contain a lot of extraneous code should be a consideration if you know that your target users have bandwidth limitations or if the size of the library is disproportionate to the feature you're using from it. For example, if your code requires the browser to load a 1MB library just to use one function, you should look into ways to fork the library (if it is open source) so you can use just the sections you need, find other features of the library you can use to make it worthwhile, or just look for another library that does what you want but with less overhead.

However, regardless of the objections, there are numerous good reasons for using third-party JavaScript libraries, which in our opinion outweigh the negative objections:

▶ Using a well-written library can really take away some of the headaches of writing cross-browser JavaScript. You won't have every browser always at your disposal, but the library writers—and their communities of users—will have tested using several versions of all major browsers, both modern and older.

▶ Why invent code that somebody else has already written? Popular JavaScript libraries tend to contain the sorts of abstractions that programmers often need to use—which means you'll likely need those functions too from time to time. The thousands of downloads and pages of online documentation and commentary generated by the most-used libraries pretty much guarantee that the code these libraries contain will be more thoroughly tested and debugged than the ordinary user's home-cooked code would be.

▶ Advanced functionality like drag and drop and JavaScript-based animation is, well, really advanced. Truly cross-browser solutions for this type of functionality have always been among the trickiest effects to code for all browsers, and well-developed and -tested libraries to achieve these types of features are incredibly valuable in terms of the time and effort they can save you.

Using a third-party JavaScript library is usually as simple as copying one or more files to your server (or linking to an external but incredibly stable location) and including a `<script>` tag in your document to load the library, thus making its code available to your own scripts. Several popular JavaScript libraries are introduced in the following sections.

jQuery

jQuery was introduced in 2006 and has grown from an easy, cross-browser means of DOM manipulation to a stable, powerful library. This library contains not just DOM manipulation tools but many additional features that make cross-browser JavaScript coding much more straightforward and productive. In fact, many JavaScript frameworks, which you'll learn about later in this lesson, rely on the jQuery library for their functionality.

The current version (at this writing) is 3.3.1, and jQuery also has an advanced user interface extensions library, called jQuery UI, that can be used alongside the existing library to rapidly build and deploy rich user interfaces or to add various attractive effects to existing components. In addition, jQuery Mobile is a touch-optimized mobile framework that helps designers make responsive apps and websites that work on mobile devices as well as laptops and desktops.

NOTE
_____
At jQuery's home page, http://jquery.com, you can not only download the latest version but also gain access to extensive documentation and sample code. The companion UI library can be found at http://jqueryui.com, and jQuery Mobile is at https://jquerymobile.com.
_____

If you don't want to download and store the jQuery library on your own local development machine or production server, you can use a remotely hosted version from a content delivery network (CDN), such as the one hosted by Google. Instead of referring to a locally hosted `.js` file in your HTML files, use the following code to link to a stable and minified version of the code:

```
<script
src="https://ajax.googleapis.com/ajax/libs/jquery/3.3.1/jquery.min.js">
</script>
```

In many cases, this provides better performance than hosting your own version because Google's servers are optimized for low-latency, massively parallel content delivery. In addition, anyone visiting your page who has also visited another page that references this same file will have the file cached in his or her browser and will not need to download it again. Many of the libraries and frameworks you might want to use are hosted on the Google CDN and other such networks.

jQuery has at its heart a sophisticated, cross-browser method for selection of page elements. The selectors used to obtain elements are based on a combination of simple CSS-like selector styles, so with the CSS techniques you learned in Part III, "Advanced Web Page Design with CSS," you should have no problem getting up to speed with jQuery. Following are a few brief examples of jQuery code to illustrate this point.

If you want to get an element that has an `id` of `someElement`, you simply use the following:

```
$("#someElement")
```

You use the pound sign (#) to select for a specific ID, just as with CSS.

To return a collection of elements that have the `someClass` class name, you can simply use this:

```
$(".someClass")
```

You use the period (.) to indicate that you're selecting elements with a specific class.

You can very simply get or set values associated with selected elements. Suppose, for example, that you want to hide all elements having the class name `hideMe`. You can do that, in a fully cross-browser manner, with just one line of code:

```
$(".hideMe").hide();
```

Manipulating HTML and CSS properties is just as straightforward. To append the phrase "powered by jQuery" to all paragraph elements, for example, you would simply write the following:

```
$("p").append(" powered by jQuery");
```

To then change the background color of those same elements, you can manipulate their CSS properties directly, like so:

```
$("p").css("background-color","yellow");
```

In addition, jQuery includes simple cross-browser methods for determining whether an element has a class, adding and removing classes, getting and setting the text or `innerHTML` of an element, navigating the DOM, getting and setting CSS properties, and easily handling events in a cross-browser way.

The associated UI library adds a huge range of UI widgets (such as date pickers, sliders, dialogs, and progress bars), animation tools, drag-and-drop capabilities, and much more.

NOTE

You can even extend jQuery yourself by writing further plug-ins, or you can use the thousands already submitted by other developers. Browse http://plugins.jquery.com to see lots of examples in searchable categories.

Prototype

Prototype, created by Sam Stephenson, is a JavaScript library that simplifies tasks such as working with DOM objects, dealing with data in forms, and remote scripting (AJAX). By including a single `prototype.js` file in your document, you have access to many improvements over basic JavaScript.

For example, in other sections of these lessons, you've used the `getElementById` JavaScript method to obtain the DOM object for an element within a web page. Prototype includes an improved version of this: the $ function. Not only is the Prototype function easier to type, but it also is more sophisticated than the built-in function and supports multiple objects.

Adding Prototype to your pages requires only one file, `prototype.js`, and one `<script>` tag, such as the following:

```
<script src="prototype.js"></script>
```

Alternatively, you can get Prototype from a CDN and refer to it, just as in the jQuery example in the preceding section.

NOTE

Prototype is free, open-source software. You can download it from its official website at www.prototypejs.org. Prototype is also built into the Ruby on Rails framework for the server-side language Ruby; see https://rubyonrails.org for more information.

script.aculo.us

By the end of these lessons, you will have learned to do some useful things with JavaScript, often involving complex code. But you can also include impressive effects in your pages by using a prebuilt library and only a few lines of code.

script.aculo.us by Thomas Fuchs is one such library. It includes functions to simplify drag-and-drop tasks, such as rearranging lists of items. It also includes a number of combination effects, which enable you to use highlighting and animated transitions within your pages. For example, a new section of the page can be briefly highlighted in yellow to get the user's attention, or a portion of the page can fade out or slide off the screen.

CAUTION

While script.aculo.us is still widely used by many designers, it has not been updated since 2010 and may not have all the modern features you want.

After you've included the appropriate files, using effects is as easy as using any of JavaScript's built-in methods. For example, the following statements use script.aculo.us to fade out an element of the page with the `id` value `test`:

```
obj = document.getElementById("test");
new Effect.Fade(obj);
```

script.aculo.us is built on the Prototype framework, described earlier in this lesson, and it includes all the functions of Prototype; therefore, you could also simplify the preceding example further by using the $ function, like so:

```
new Effect.Fade($("test"));
```

The library's name, script.aculo.us, is also the URL where you get it.

NOTE

The next section shows a script that demonstrates several script.aculo.us effects.

Other Popular JavaScript Libraries

There are many more JavaScript libraries out there, and more are appearing all the time as JavaScript is taken more seriously as an application development language. Here are two more libraries you might want to explore:

▶ **Dojo** (www.dojotoolkit.org)—This is an open-source toolkit that adds power to JavaScript to simplify building applications and user interfaces. It adds features ranging from extra string and math functions to animation and AJAX.

▶ **MooTools** (https://mootools.net)—This is an open-source object-oriented JavaScript library. Its focus is on reusability and modularity.

Adding JavaScript Effects by Using a Third-Party Library

To see how simple it is to use an external library, in this section you'll create a sample script that includes the script.aculo.us library and uses event handlers to demonstrate several of the available effects.

CAUTION

This example was created using version 1.9.0 of script.aculo.us and version 1.7.3.0 of Prototype. The script should work with later versions because developers tend to ensure backward compatibility, but the underlying code might have changed since this lesson was written. If you have trouble, you might need to use these specific versions.

This example shows how to include script.aculo.us and Prototype in an HTML document by leveraging the Google CDN. To do this, simply use `<script>` tags to reference the code:

```
<script
    src="http://ajax.googleapis.com/ajax/libs/prototype/1.7.2.0/prototype.js">
</script>
<script
    src="http://ajax.googleapis.com/ajax/libs/scriptaculous/1.9.0/scriptaculous.js">
</script>
```

NOTE

Of course, you could download script.aculo.us and Prototype to your local development machine or web server and reference it accordingly. If you go down that path, try to keep all your assets in separate directories, such as a `js` folder that contains all JavaScript libraries, and ensure that your `<script>` tag references the path accordingly.

If you include these statements in the `<head>` section of your document, the library functions will be available to other scripts or event handlers anywhere in the page. But remember that when you place the scripts first, the browser won't load anything until those scripts are loaded—one at a time. Most developers include libraries in the `<head>` of their documents but place them last. But it's not required to place them there. As long as the link to the library is placed above any scripts that use it, you can place it below all your HTML, just as you would any other script.

After you have included the external code, you simply need to include a bit of JavaScript to trigger the effects. This section uses a section of the page wrapped in a `<p>` tag with the `id` value `testarea` to demonstrate some of the effects that script.aculo.us makes possible. Each effect is triggered by a simple event handler on a button. For example, this code defines the Fade Out button:

```
<button onclick="new Effect.Fade($('testarea'))">Fade Out</button>
```

This code uses the $ function that is built in to Prototype to obtain the object for the element with the `id` value `testarea` and then passes it to the `Effect.Fade` function that is built in to script.aculo.us.

NOTE

This example demonstrates 6 effects: `Fade`, `Appear`, `SlideUp`, `SlideDown`, `Highlight`, and `Shake`. There are more than 16 effects in the library, plus methods for supporting drag-and-drop and other features. See script.aculo.us for details.

Once you have included the script.aculo.us library, you can combine effects with event handlers and some sample text to see a complete demonstration of script.aculo.us effects. The complete HTML document for this example is shown in Listing 26.1.

LISTING 26.1   The Complete Library Effects Example

```html
<!doctype html>
<html lang="en">
  <head>
    <meta charset="utf-8">
    <title>Testing script.aculo.us effects</title>
    <style>
      #testarea {
        background-color:#CCC; margin:20px; padding:10px;
      }
    </style>
    <meta name="viewport"
          content="width=device-width, initial-scale=1">
    <script
src="https://ajax.googleapis.com/ajax/libs/prototype/1.7.3.0/prototype.js">
    </script>
    <script
src="https://ajax.googleapis.com/ajax/libs/scriptaculous/1.9.0/scriptaculous.js">
    </script>
  </head>
  <body>
    <h1>Testing script.aculo.us Effects</h1>
    <button onclick="new Effect.Fade($('testarea'))">Fade Out</button>
    <button onclick="new Effect.Appear($('testarea'))">Fade In</button>
    <button onclick="new Effect.SlideUp($('testarea'))">Slide Up</button>
    <button onclick="new Effect.SlideDown($('testarea'))">Slide Down</button>
    <button onclick="new Effect.Highlight($('testarea'))">Highlight
       </button>
    <button onclick="new Effect.Shake($('testarea'))">Shake</button>
    <hr>
    <h2>Testing Effects</h2>
    <p id="testarea">
    This section of the document is within a &lt;p&gt; element with
    the <strong>id</strong> value of <strong>testarea</strong>. The
    event handlers on the buttons above send this object to the
    <a href="http://script.aculo.us/">script.aculo.us</a> library
    to perform effects. Click the buttons to see the effects in action.
    </p>
  </body>
</html>
```

This document starts with two `<script>` tags to include the third-party files that contain the JavaScript code that your own scripts will reference. The effects themselves are triggered by the event handlers defined for each of the six buttons. The <p> section at the end defines the `testarea` element that will be used to demonstrate the effects.

When you load this script in your web browser, the display should look as shown in Figure 26.1. After it has been loaded, you should be able to click on any of the six buttons at the top of the page to trigger the effects provided by the script.aculo.us JavaScript library.

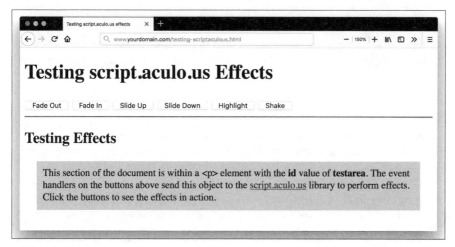

FIGURE 26.1
The JavaScript effects example, ready for action.

Using JavaScript Frameworks

There's a big difference between JavaScript libraries and JavaScript frameworks: Simple libraries tend to be smaller and provide ready-made pieces of code that provide functionality meant to enhance your custom architecture, and frameworks are larger, are more complicated, and impose an architectural pattern upon your application, such as the *model-view-controller* (MVC) pattern. In an MVC pattern, an application is conceived of as having three interconnected components:

▶ **Model**—Acts as the central component, even though it's listed first in the name, holding application data, business rules, functions, and other logical elements

▶ **View**—Requests information from the model to show to the user

▶ **Controller**—Sends information to the model for processing through user interactions

You can think of it this way: In a web-based application, the user interacts with a controller that manipulates the underlying model, which updates the view, which the user then sees in the web browser.

In a traditional web-based application, you will likely have experienced it this way: Both the model and the controller components sit on the back end, away from the browser, and are invoked through form elements or other interactions by the user that say, "Hey, back-end script, go do something with logic and data based on this input I'm giving you, and send the result back to the screen." The screen, in this case, would contain dynamically generated HTML (the view).

In a JavaScript-based MVC application, which most likely has been developed using one of the frameworks you'll learn about in a moment, all three components can sit on the client side; that is to say, a user can interact with data that is stored and manipulated entirely within the front end, never touching a back-end script or database. Or *most* of the three components can sit on the front end and use AJAX requests to invoke a script on the back end, which then sends results back into the view.

NOTE

AJAX (Asynchronous JavaScript and XML), also known as remote scripting, enables JavaScript to communicate with a program running on the web server. This means JavaScript can do things that were traditionally not possible, such as dynamically loading information from a database or storing data on a server without refreshing a page.

AJAX requires some complex scripting, particularly because the methods you use to communicate with the server vary depending on the browser in use. Fortunately, many libraries have been created to fill the need for a simple way to use AJAX.

By the end of these introductory lessons in HTML, CSS, and JavaScript, we wouldn't expect you or anyone else to be prepared to create a JavaScript framework of your very own—and please don't, because there are already 30 or more competing frameworks out there in the wild! But we would expect you to be able to start thinking about how a framework might be helpful in your work and to be able to begin understanding one or more of the major frameworks in use today.

If you are building a predominantly read-only website and using a little JavaScript or jQuery for some display features, a framework would be considerable overkill. But if you begin to think about ways to extend that website to include user interactivity, you might think about laying a framework in to handle that work for you. Following are some major JavaScript frameworks in use today, all of which would be fine starting points for further exploration:

- ▶ **Angular** (https://angular.io)—This is a very powerful and flexible framework, but it involves a steep learning curve. However, it has a very active user community that is ready to help new developers understand the framework. It is a complete makeover of the equally popular original framework, AngularJS (https://angularjs.org).

- ▶ **Backbone.js** (backbonejs.org)—This framework has been around for quite some time (relatively speaking) and served as the inspiration for many other frameworks. It enables a new developer to get started quickly, but the downside of that, for some, is that the applications will contain a lot of unused templating code.

▶ **Ember** (https://emberjs.com)—Like Backbone.js, Ember enables a new developer to get started quickly. Although it appears "too magical" to some, Ember's strong adherence to common programming idioms can be a benefit to new developers.

▶ **Knockout** (knockoutjs.com)—Less popular than the frameworks previously listed, Knockout nonetheless provides a strong alternative as well as several nice tutorials for new developers.

▶ **React** (https://reactjs.org)—There is some debate over whether React is a library or a framework, but whatever it is, it's a popular tool for creating interactive web pages and applications, and it has been growing in popularity.

There are many more than these few JavaScript frameworks out there at the time of this writing, and we fully expect that there will be more in years to come. To stay up to date or to get an overview of the core features of JavaScript frameworks and libraries, you can start by bookmarking and revisiting JavaScripting (www.javascripting.com).

Summary

In this lesson, you learned about some of the many third-party libraries available for JavaScript, which offer many advantages, including easy cross-browser scripting, selection and editing of HTML and CSS values, animation, and more sophisticated user-interface tools, such as drag-and-drop. You used the script.aculo.us and Prototype libraries to put some basic JavaScript effects like this into action.

In addition, you learned about some of the popular JavaScript frameworks, and how you can take advantage of them to develop feature-rich web applications following standard software architecture patterns such as the model-view-controller (MVC) pattern.

Q&A

Q. Can I use more than one third-party library in the same script?

A. Yes, in theory: If the libraries are well written and designed not to interfere with each other, there should be no problem with using them both in the same script. In practice, this will depend on the libraries you need and how they were written, but many JavaScript libraries can be used together or will include a warning about incompatibilities.

Q. Can I build my own library to simplify scripting?

A. Yes. As you deal with more complicated scripts, you'll find yourself using the same functions over and over, and if they're functions you have created, then storing them in a separate library file may be a good idea. This process is as simple as creating a `.js` file with your code, placing it on your server, and referencing it in a `<script>` tag as you would any other library.

Workshop

The Workshop contains quiz questions and activities to help you solidify your understanding of the material covered. Try to answer all questions before looking at the "Answers" section that follows.

Quiz

1. Which of the following objects *is not* a JavaScript library?

   a. script.aculo.us

   b. Yahoo! UI

   c. AJAX

2. How can you extend jQuery yourself?

   a. jQuery can't be extended.

   b. You can write server-side scripts.

   c. You can write a plug-in or use a prewritten one.

3. What other JavaScript third-party library does script.aculo.us employ?

   a. Prototype

   b. Dojo

   c. jQuery

4. What is a drawback to using JavaScript libraries?

   a. You don't know how the code works because you didn't write it.

   b. The code often has more in it than you need, bloating your pages.

   c. Many libraries have malicious code in them.

   d. Both A and B

5. What is your option if you don't want to download and store a library on your own server?

   a. Use a CDN

   b. Use a hosting provider

   c. Use another library

   d. Use PHP

6. What does the following jQuery snippet do?

```
$("em.bright").css("background-color","pink");
```

   a. Select all elements with the em and bright classes and change their background colors to pink.

   b. Select all <em> elements with the class bright and change their background color to pink.

   c. Select all elements with the bright class and make them <em> elements with a pink background.

   d. Select the first <em> element with the class bright and change its background color to pink.

7. What Prototype function replaces getElementById?

   a. There is no Prototype function that replaces getElementById.

   b. The getElement function

   c. The byId function

   d. The $ function

8. Why do you include script libraries in the <head> of your documents?

   a. Then they can be accessed by any script on the page.

   b. This is where they are required to be.

   c. Libraries load asynchronously, so they can be placed first.

   d. You should never include them in the <head>.

9. What does MVC stand for in programming architecture?

   a. Massive version change

   b. Multiuse-view-controller

   c. Model-view-controller

   d. Mobile-view-controller

10. What are three popular JavaScript frameworks in use today?

   a. Angular, JSEmber, and React

   b. AngularJS, Ember, and React

   c. AngularJS, Backbone.js, and Knockact

   d. Backbone.js, Ember, and Knockact

NOTE

Just a reminder for those of you reading these words in the print or e-book edition of this book: If you go to **www.informit.com/register** and register this book (using ISBN 9780672338083), you can receive free access to an online Web Edition that not only contains the complete text of this book but also features an interactive version of this quiz.

Answers

1. **c.** AJAX is a programming technique that enables your scripts to use resources hosted on your server. There are many libraries to help you employ AJAX functionality, but AJAX itself is not a library.

2. **c.** jQuery has a well-documented method for writing and using plug-ins.

3. **a.** script.aculo.us uses the Prototype library.

4. **d.** You don't know how the code works because you didn't write it, and libraries often contain a lot of extra code that you don't need but that the browser has to download anyway.

5. **a.** You can use a content delivery network (CDN).

6. **b.** This snippet selects all the <em> tags with the class `bright` and gives them the background color `pink`.

7. **d.** The $ function is an improved version in Prototype.

8. **a.** Most designers include them there because then they can be accessed by any script.

9. **c.** MVC is the model-view-controller pattern.

10. **b.** Some popular frameworks include Angular (and AngularJS), Backbone.js, Ember, Knockout, and React.

Exercises

▶ Visit the script.aculo.us website at script.aculo.us to find the complete list of effects and then modify Listing 26.1 to add buttons for one or more of these additional effects.

▶ Much as you practiced in this lesson using script.aculo.us, pick another third-party JavaScript library such as Dojo or MooTools and implement one or more of the library's custom features on your own. If you don't want to use either of those, you can pick one from the list at www.javascripting.com.

Working with Web-Based Forms

To this point, pretty much everything in these lessons has focused on getting information out to others. But you can also use your web pages to gather information from the people who read and interact with them.

Web forms enable you to receive feedback, orders, and other information from the users who visit your web pages. If you've ever used a search engine such as Google or Bing, you're familiar with HTML forms—those single-field entry forms, each with a single button that, when clicked, gives you all the information you are looking for and then some. Product order forms are also an extremely popular use of forms; if you've ordered anything from Amazon.com or purchased something from an eBay seller, you've used forms. In this lesson, you'll learn how to create your own forms, but you'll learn only how to create the front end of those forms. Working with the server-side handling of forms requires knowledge of a programming language and is beyond the scope of these lessons.

How HTML Forms Work

An HTML form is part of a web page that includes areas where users can enter information to be sent back to you, to another email address that you specify, to a database that you manage, or to another system altogether, such as a third-party management system for your company's lead generation forms, such as Salesforce.com.

Before you learn the HTML elements that are used to make your own forms, you should at least conceptually understand how the information from those forms makes its way back to you. The actual behind-the-scenes (the *server-side* or *back-end*) process requires knowledge of at least one programming language—or at least the ability to follow specific instructions when using someone else's server-side script to handle the form input. At that point in the process, you should either work with someone who has the technical knowledge or learn the basics on your own. Simple form processing is not difficult, and your web hosting provider likely has several back-end scripts that you can use with minimal customization.

NOTE

PHP is the most popular server-side programming language, and it is supported by any web hosting provider that's worth its salt. You can learn more about PHP at www.php.net, or you can just dive right in to learning this programming language (plus database interactivity) from the ground up in *Sams Teach Yourself PHP, MySQL, and JavaScript All in One* (ISBN: 978-0-672-33770-3). It is geared toward absolute beginners with PHP or any other programming language.

A form includes a button for the user to submit the form; that button can be an image that you create yourself or a standard HTML form button that is created when a form `<input>` element is created and given a `type` value of `submit`. When someone clicks a form submission button, all the information typed in the form is sent to a URL specified in the `action` attribute of the `<form>` element. That URL should point to a specific script that will process your form, sending the form contents via email or performing another step in an interactive process (such as requesting results from a search engine or placing items in an online shopping cart).

When you start thinking about doing more with form content than simply emailing results to yourself, you need additional technical knowledge. For example, if you want to create an online store that accepts credit cards and processes transactions, there are some well-established practices for doing so, all geared toward ensuring the security of your customers' data. That is not an operation that you'll want to enter into lightly; you'll need more knowledge than these lessons provide.

Before you put a form online, you should look in the user guide for your web hosting provider to see what it offers in the way of form-processing scripts. You are likely to find a readily available Perl or PHP script that you can use with only minimal configuration.

Creating a Form

Every form must begin with an opening `<form>` tag, which can be located anywhere in the body of the HTML document. The `<form>` tag typically has three attributes, `name`, `method`, and `action`:

```
<form name="my_form" method="post" action="myprocessingscript.php">
```

The most common `method` is `post`, which sends the form entry results as a document. In some situations, you need to use `method="get"`, which submits the results as part of the URL query string instead. For example, `get` is sometimes used when queries are submitted to search engines from a web form. Because you're not yet an expert on forms, just use `post` unless your web hosting provider's documentation tells you to do otherwise.

NOTE

The URL query string is the part of the URL after a question mark (?). It is made up of *name=value* pairs, separated by an ampersand (&) character, as in this example:

`https://www.yourdomain.com/path/to/page.html?this=that&a=anything`

The `action` attribute specifies the address for sending the form data. You have two options here:

▶ You can type the location of a form-processing program or script on a web server, and the form data will then be sent to that program. This is by far the most common scenario.

▶ You can type `mailto:` followed by your email address, and the form data will be sent directly to you whenever someone fills out the form. Here's an example:

```
<form name="my_form" method="post" action="mailto:me@mysite.com">
```

However, this approach is completely dependent on the user's computer being properly configured with an email client. People accessing your site from a public computer without an email client will be left out in the cold.

The form created in Listing 27.1 and shown in Figure 27.1 includes just about every type of user input component you can currently use in HTML forms in modern browsers. Refer to this listing and figure as you read the following explanations of the types of input element.

LISTING 27.1   A Form with Various User-Input Components

```
<!doctype html>
<html lang="en">
  <head>
    <meta charset="utf-8">
    <title>Guest Book</title>
    <meta name="viewport"
          content="width=device-width, initial-scale=1">
    <style>
      fieldset {
        width: 75%;
        border: 2px solid #9435d4;
      }
      legend {
        font-weight: bold;
        font-size: 125%;
      }
```

```
    label.question  {
        width: 225px;
        float: left;
        text-align: left;
        font-weight: bold;
    }
    span.question  {
        font-weight: bold;
    }
    input, textarea, select, button {
        border: 1px solid #000;
        padding: 3px;
    }
    #buttons {
        margin-top: 12px;
    }
    #errors {
        color: red;
        font-weight: bold;
        font-size: larger;
    }
  </style>
</head>
<body>
  <h1>My Guest Book</h1>
  <form name="gbForm" method="post" action="URL_to_script">
    <output id="errors"></output>
    <fieldset>
      <legend>Personal Information</legend>
      <p>
        <label class="question" for="the_name">
        What is your name?</label>
        <input type="text" id="the_name" name="the_name"
               placeholder="Enter your full name."
               size="50" required autofocus>
      </p>
      <p>
        <label class="question" for="the_email">What is your email
        address?</label>
        <input type="email" id="the_email" name="the_email"
               placeholder="Please use a real one!"
               size="50" required>
      </p>
    </fieldset>
    <fieldset>
      <legend>Survey Questions</legend>
      <p>
        <span class="question">Please check all that apply:</span><br>
```

```
    <input type="checkbox" id="like_it" name="some_statements[]"
           value="I really like your web site.">
    <label for="like_it">I really like your web site.</label><br>
    <input type="checkbox" id="the_best" name="some_statements[]"
           value="It's one of the best sites I've ever seen">
    <label for="the_best">It's one of the  best sites I've ever
    seen.</label><br>
    <input type="checkbox" id="jealous" name="some_statements[]"
           value="I sure wish my site looked as good as yours.">
    <label for="jealous">I sure wish my site looked as good as
    yours.</label><br>
    <input type="checkbox" id="no_taste" name="some_statements[]"
           value="I have no taste and I'm pretty dense, so your
    site didn't do much for me.">
    <label for="no_taste">I have no taste and I'm pretty dense, so
    your site didn't do much for me.</label>
</p>
<p>
    <label for="choose_scale"><span class="question">Please
    rate my site on a scale of 1 (poor) to 10
    (awesome):</span></label>
    <input type="number" id="choose_scale" name="choose_scale"
    min="1" max="10" step="1" value="5">
</p>
<p>
    <span class="question">Please choose the one thing you love
    Best about my web site:</span><br>
    <input type="radio" id="the_picture" name="best_thing"
           value="me">
    <label for="the_picture">That amazing picture of you</label><br>
    <input type="radio" id="the_animals" name="best_thing"
           value="animals">
    <label for="the_animals">All the animal photos, of course</label><br>
    <input type="radio" id="the_dandelions" name="best_thing"
           value="dandelions">
    <label for="the_dandelions">The comprehensive dandelion
    facts, by far</label><br>
    <input type="radio" id="the_story" name="best_thing"
           value="childhood story">
    <label for="the_story">The inspiring recap of your suburban
    childhood</label><br>
    <input type="radio" id="the_treasures" name="best_thing"
           value="Elvis treasures">
    <label for="the_treasures">The detailed list of all your Elvis
    memorabilia</label>
</p>
```

```
<p>
  <label for="the_worst"><span class="question">
  Please indicate the one thing I could improve about my web site:
  </span></label><br>
  <input type="text" id="the_worst" name="the_worst"
         placeholder="There's nothing bad, is there?"
         list="listOfBadChoices" size="50">
</p>
<p>
  <label for="how_improve"><span class="question">What else
  would you like to see on my web site?</span></label><br>
  <select id="how_improve" name="how_improve" size="4" multiple>
    <optgroup label="Preferred">
      <option value="Nothing. It's perfect.">Nothing. It's
      perfect.</option>
    </optgroup>
    <optgroup label="Likely">
      <option value="More about the animals.">More about the
      animals.</option>
      <option value="More about the dandelions.">More about the
      dandelions.</option>
    </optgroup>
    <optgroup label="Unlikely">
      <option value="More about Elvis.">More about Elvis.
      </option>
    </optgroup>
  </select>
</p>
</fieldset>
<fieldset>
  <legend>Free for All!</legend>
  <p>
    <label for="message"><span class="question">Feel free to send
    more praise, gift offers, etc.:</span></label>
    <textarea id="message" name="message" rows="7" cols="55">
    </textarea>
  </p>
</fieldset>
<div id="buttons">
<input type="submit" value="Click Here to Submit"> or
<input type="reset" value="Erase and Start Over"> or
<button type="button" id="standardValues">Fill in Standard
Values</button>
</div>
</form>
<datalist id="listOfBadChoices">
  <option value="nothing"></option>
  <option value="nada"></option>
  <option value="zip"></option>
```

```
      <option value="zilch"></option>
      <option value="I can't think of anything"></option>
    </datalist>
  </body>
</html>
```

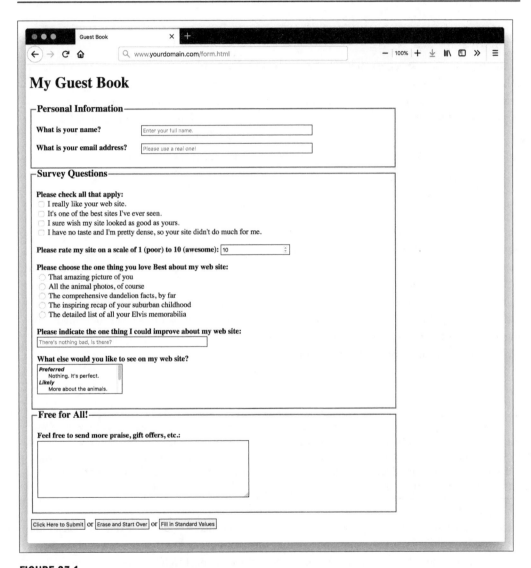

FIGURE 27.1
The code in Listing 27.1 uses many common HTML form elements.

The code in Listing 27.1 uses a `<form>` element that contains quite a few `<input>` tags. Each `<input>` tag corresponds to a specific user input component, such as a check box or radio button.

The input, select, text area, and button elements contain borders in the stylesheet, so it is easy to see the outline of each element in the form. Keep in mind that you can apply all sorts of CSS to those elements.

The next few sections dig into the details of the `<input>` tag and other form-related tags.

Accepting Text Input

To ask the user for a specific piece of information within a form, use the `<input>` tag. Although this tag does not explicitly need to appear between the `<form>` and `</form>` tags, putting it there is good practice and makes your code easier to follow. You can place `<input>` elements anywhere on the page alongside text, images, and other HTML tags. For example, to ask for someone's name, you could type the following text followed immediately by an `<input>` field:

```
<p><label class="question" for="the_name">What is your name?</label>
<input type="text" id="the_name" name="the_name"
       placeholder="Enter your full name."
       size="50" required autofocus></p>
```

The `type` attribute indicates what type of form element to display—in this case a simple, one-line text entry box. (Each element type is discussed individually in this lesson.) In this example, note the use of the `placeholder`, `required`, and `autofocus` attributes. You'll learn about the `required` attribute later in this lesson; the `autofocus` attribute automatically focuses the user's cursor in this text field as soon as the browser renders the form. A form can have only one `autofocus` field. The `placeholder` attribute enables you to define some text that appears in the text box but disappears when you begin to type. Using this attribute, you can give the user a bit more guidance in completing your form.

NOTE

If you want the user to enter text without having the text displayed on the screen, you can use `<input type="password">` instead of `<input type="text">`. Asterisks (***) are then displayed in place of the text the user types. The `size`, `maxlength`, and `name` attributes work exactly the same for `type="password"` as they do for `type="text"`. Keep in mind that this technique of hiding a password provides only minimal protection against people reading the screen; no encryption or other protection is associated with the password being transmitted.

The `size` attribute indicates approximately how many characters wide the text input box should be. If you are using a proportionally spaced font, the width of the input will vary depending on what the user enters. If the input is too long to fit in the box, most web browsers automatically scroll the text to the left. This attribute is often left off of most modern forms, as designers define the width and height of the boxes in the CSS.

The `maxlength` attribute determines the number of characters the user is allowed to type into the text box. If a user tries to type beyond the specified length, the extra characters won't appear. You can specify a length that is longer, shorter, or the same as the physical size of the text box. The `size` and `maxlength` attributes are used only for the input fields meant for text values, such as `type="text"`, `type="email"`, `type="URL"`, and `type="tel"`, but not check boxes and radio buttons since those have fixed sizes.

Naming Each Piece of Form Data

No matter what type an input element is, you must give a name to the data it gathers. You can use any name you like for each input item, as long as each one on the form is different (except in the case of radio buttons and check boxes, discussed later in this lesson). When the form is processed by a back-end script, each data item is identified by name. This name becomes a variable, which is filled with a value. The value is either what the user typed in the form or the value associated with the element the user selected.

For example, if a user enters **Jane Doe** in the text box defined previously, a variable is sent to the form-processing script; the variable is `user_name`, and the value of the variable is Jane Doe. Form-processing scripts work with these types of variable names and values.

NOTE

Form-processing scripts are oversimplified here for the sake of explanation within the scope of these lessons. The exact appearance (or name) of the variables made available to your processing script depends on the programming language of that script. But conceptually, it's valid to say that the name of the input element becomes the name of the variable, and the value of the input element becomes the value of that variable on the back end.

To use this text field (or others) in JavaScript, remember that the text object uses the `name` attribute; you refer to the value of the field in the previous snippet like this:

```
document.formname.user_name.value
```

Labeling Each Piece of Form Data

Labeling your form data is not the same as using a `name` or `id` attribute to identify the form element for later use. Instead, the `<label></label>` tag pair surrounds text that acts as a sort of caption for a form element. A form element `<label>` provides additional context for the element, which is especially important for screen-reader software.

You can see two different examples in Listing 27.1. First, you can see the `<label>` surrounding the first question a user is asked (**What is your name?**). The use of the `for` attribute ties this label to the `<input>` element with the same `id` (in this case, the_name):

```
<p><label class="question" for="the_name">What is your name?</label>
<input type="text" id="the_name" name="the_name"
       placeholder="Enter your full name."
       size="50" required autofocus></p>
```

NOTE

The `<label>` element is used for more than just screen readers. It makes form fields more usable because when the user clicks the label, the focus is moved to that form field.

A screen reader would read to the user, "What is your name?" and then also say "text box" to alert the user to complete the text field with the appropriate information. In another example from Listing 27.1, you see the use of `<label>` to surround different options in a check box list (and also a list of radio buttons, later in the listing):

```
<p><span class="question">Please check all that apply:</span><br>
<input type="checkbox" id="like_it" name="some_statements[]"
       value="I really like your web site.">
<label for="like_it">I really like your web site.</label><br>
<input type="checkbox" id="the_best" name="some_statements[]"
       value="It's one of the best sites I've ever seen">
<label for="the_best">It's one of the best sites I've ever
       seen.</label><br>
<input type="checkbox" id="jealous" name="some_statements[]"
       value="I sure wish my site looked as good as yours.">
<label for="jealous">I sure wish my site looked as good as
       yours.</label><b>
<input type="checkbox" id="no_taste" name="some_statements[]"
       value="I have no taste and I'm pretty dense, so your site
       didn't do much for me.">
<label for="no_taste">I have no taste and I'm pretty dense, so your
       site didn't do much for me.</label></p>
```

In this situation, the screen reader would read the text surrounded by the `<label>` tag, followed by "check box," to alert the user to choose one of the given options. Labels should be used for all form elements and can be styled using CSS in the same manner as other container elements; the styling does not affect the screen reader, but it does help with layout aesthetics and readability.

Grouping Form Elements

In Listing 27.1, you can see the use of the `<fieldset>` and `<legend>` elements three different times, to create three different groups of form fields. The `<fieldset>` element surrounds groups of form elements to provide additional context for the user, whether the user is accessing the form directly in a web browser or with the aid of screen-reader software. The `<fieldset>` element just defines the grouping; the `<legend>` element contains the text that will display or be read aloud to describe this grouping, such as the following from Listing 27.1:

```
<fieldset>
  <legend>Personal Information</legend>
    <p>
      <label class="question" for="the_name">
        What is your name?</label>
        <input type="text" id="the_name" name="the_name"
               placeholder="Enter your full name."
               size="50" required autofocus>
...
</fieldset>
```

In this situation, when the screen reader reads the `<label>` associated with a form element, as you learned in the preceding section, it also appends the `<legend>` text. In the example above, it would be read as "Personal Information. What is your name? Text box." The `<fieldset>` and `<legend>` elements can be styled using CSS, so the visual cue of the grouped elements can easily be made visible in a web browser (as you saw previously in Figure 27.1).

Including Hidden Data in Forms

Want to send certain data items to the server script that processes a form, but don't want the user to see those data items? Use an `<input>` tag with a `type="hidden"` attribute. This attribute has no effect on the display; it just adds any name and value you specify to the form results when they are submitted.

If you are using a form-processing script provided by your web hosting provider, you might be directed to use this attribute to tell a script where to email the form results. For example, including the following code causes the results to be emailed to `me@mysite.com` after the form is submitted:

```
<input type="hidden" name="mailto" value="me@mysite.com">
```

You sometimes see scripts using hidden input elements to carry additional data that might be useful when you receive the results of the form submission; some examples of hidden form fields include an email address and a subject for the email. If you are using a script provided by your web hosting provider, consult the documentation provided with that script for additional details about potential required hidden fields.

Exploring Form Input Controls

Various input controls are available for retrieving information from the user. You've already seen one text-entry option; the next few sections introduce you to most of the remaining form-input options you can use to design forms.

Check Boxes

Besides the text field, one of the simplest input types is the *check box*, which appears as a small square. Users can click check boxes to select or deselect one or more items in a group. For example, the check boxes in Listing 27.1 display after text that reads "Please check all that apply," implying that the user could indeed check all that apply.

The HTML for the check boxes in Listing 27.1 shows that the value of the name attribute is the same for all of them:

```
<span class="question">Please check all that apply:</span><br>
<input type="checkbox" id="like_it" name="some_statements[]"
       value="I really like your web site.">
<label for="like_it">I really like your web site.</label><br>
<input type="checkbox" id="the_best" name="some_statements[]"
       value="It's one of the best sites I've ever seen">
<label for="the_best">It's one of the best sites I've ever
seen.</label><br>
<input type="checkbox" id="jealous" name="some_statements[]"
       value="I sure wish my site looked as good as yours.">
<label for="jealous">I sure wish my site looked as good as
yours.</label><br>
<input type="checkbox" id="no_taste" name="some_statements[]"
       value="I have no taste and I'm pretty dense, so your
site didn't do much for me.">
<label for="no_taste">I have no taste and I'm pretty dense, so
your site didn't do much for me.</label>
</p>
```

The use of the brackets ([]) in the name attribute indicates to the back-end processing script that a series of values will be placed into this one variable instead of using just one value. (Well, it might be just one value if the user selects only one check box.) If a user selects the first check box, the text string I really like your web site. is placed in the website_response[] bucket. If the user selects the third check box, the text string I sure wish my site looked as good as yours. also is put into the website_response[] bucket. The processing script then works with that variable as an array of data rather just a single entry.

NOTE

If you find that the label for an input element is displayed too close to the element, just add a space between the close of the <input> tag and the start of the label text, like this:

```
<input type="checkbox" name="mini">
<label>Mini Piano Stool</label>
```

However, you might see groups of check boxes that do use individual names for the variables in the group. For example, the following is another way of writing the check box group:

```
<p>
  <span class="question">Please check all that apply:</span><br>
  <input type="checkbox" id="like_it" name="liked_site" value="yes"
      value="I really like your web site.">
  <label for="like_it">I really like your web site.</label><br>
  <input type="checkbox" id="the_best" name="best_site" value="yes"
      value="It's one of the best sites I've ever seen">
  <label for="the_best">It's one of the  best sites I've ever
seen.</label><br>
  <input type="checkbox" id="jealous" name="my_site_sucks" value="yes"
      value="I sure wish my site looked as good as yours.">
  <label for="jealous">I sure wish my site looked as good as
yours.</label><br>
  <input type="checkbox" id="no_taste" name="am_dense" value="yes"
      value="I have no taste and I'm pretty dense, so your site
              didn't do much for me.">
  <label for="no_taste">I have no taste and I'm pretty dense, so your
site didn't do much for me.</label>
</p>
```

In this second list of check boxes, the variable name of the first check box is "liked_site", and the value (if checked) is "yes" when handled by a back-end processing script.

If you want a check box to be checked by default when the web browser renders the form, include the checked attribute. For example, the following code creates two check boxes, and the first one is checked by default:

```
<input type="checkbox" id="like_it" name="liked_site" value="yes"
      value="I really like your web site." checked>
<label for="like_it">I really like your web site.</label><br>
<input type="checkbox" id="the_best" name="best_site" value="yes"
      value="It's one of the best sites I've ever seen">
<label for="the_best">It's one of the best sites I've ever
seen.</label><br>
```

The check box labeled `I really like your web site.` is checked by default in this example. The user must click the check box to uncheck it and thus indicate that he or she has another opinion of your site. The check box marked `It's one of the best sites I've ever seen.` is unchecked to begin with, so the user must click it to select it. Check boxes that are not selected do not appear in the form output.

To handle values from the `checkbox` object in JavaScript, you can use the following four properties:

- ▶ **name**—Specifies the name of the check box and also the object name.

- ▶ **value**—Specifies the "true" value for the check box—usually `on`. This value is used by server-side programs to indicate whether the check box was checked or unchecked. In JavaScript, you should use the `checked` property instead.

- ▶ **defaultChecked**—Specifies the default status of the check box, assigned by the `checked` attribute in HTML.

- ▶ **checked**—Specifies the current value. This is a Boolean value: `true` for checked and `false` for unchecked.

To manipulate the check box or use its value, you use the `checked` property. For example, this statement turns on a check box called `same_address` in a form named `order`:

```
document.order.same_address.checked = true;
```

The check box has a single method: `click`. This method simulates a click on the box. It also has a single event, `onClick`, that occurs whenever the check box is clicked. This happens whether the box was turned on or off, so you need to examine the `checked` property via JavaScript to see what action really happened.

Radio Buttons

Radio buttons, for which only one choice can be selected at a time, are almost as simple to implement as check boxes. The simplest use of a radio button is for yes/no questions or for voting when only one candidate can be selected.

To create a radio button, use `type="radio"` and give each option its own `<input>` tag. You use the same `name` for all the radio buttons in a group, but you don't use the `[]` as you do with the check boxes because you don't have to accommodate multiple answers:

```
<input type="radio" id="vote_yes" name="vote" value="yes" checked>
<label for="vote_yes">Yes</label><br>
<input type="radio" id="vote_no" name="vote" value="no">
<label for="vote_no">No</label>
```

The value attribute can be any name or code you choose. If you include the checked attribute, that button is selected by default. No more than one radio button with the same name can be checked.

When designing your form and choosing between check boxes and radio buttons, determine whether the question being asked or implied could be answered in only one way. If so, use a radio button.

NOTE

Radio buttons are named for their similarity to the buttons on old push-button radios. Those buttons used a mechanical arrangement so that when you pushed one button in, any other pressed button popped out.

In terms of scripting, radio buttons are similar to check boxes, except that an entire group of them shares a single name and a single object. You can refer to the following properties of the radio object:

- **name**—Specifies the name common to the radio buttons
- **length**—Specifies the number of radio buttons in the group

To access the individual buttons in JavaScript, you treat the radio object as an array. The buttons are indexed, starting with 0. Each individual button has the following properties:

- **value**—Specifies the value assigned to the button
- **defaultChecked**—Indicates the value of the checked attribute and the default state of the button
- **checked**—Specifies the current state.

For example, you can select the first radio button in the radio1 group on the form1 form with this statement:

```
document.form1.radio1[0].checked = true;
```

However, if you do this, be sure you set the other values to false as needed. This is not done automatically. You can use the click method to do both of these actions in one step.

Like a check box, a radio button has a click method and an onClick event handler. Each radio button can have a separate statement for this event.

Selection Lists

You can create both *scrolling lists* and *pull-down pick lists* with the `<select>` tag. You use this tag together with the `<option>` tag, as shown in the following example (taken from Listing 27.1):

```
<p>
  <label for="how_improve"><span class="question">What else
  would you like to see on my web site?</span></label><br>
  <select id="how_improve" name="how_improve" size="4" multiple>
    <optgroup label="Preferred">
      <option value="Nothing. It's perfect.">Nothing. It's
      perfect.</option>
    </optgroup>
    <optgroup label="Likely">
      <option value="More about the animals.">More about the
      animals.</option>
      <option value="More about the dandelions.">More about the
      dandelions.</option>
    </optgroup>
    <optgroup label="Unlikely">
      <option value="More about Elvis.">More about Elvis.
      </option>
    </optgroup>
  </select>
</p>
```

Unlike the `text` input type that you learned about briefly in a previous section, the `size` attribute here determines how many items show at once on the selection list. If `size="2"` were used in the preceding code, only the first two options would be visible, and a scrollbar would appear next to the list so the user could scroll down to see the third and fourth options.

Including the `multiple` attribute enables users to select more than one option at a time; the `selected` attribute makes an option initially selected by default. When the form is submitted, the text specified in the `value` attribute for each option accompanies the selected option.

NOTE

If you leave out the `size` attribute or specify `size="1"`, the list creates a simple drop-down pick list. A pick list doesn't allow for multiple choices; it is logically equivalent to a group of radio buttons. The following example shows another way to choose `yes` or no for a question:

```
<select name="vote">
  <option value="yes">Yes</option>
  <option value="no">No</option>
</select>
```

The object for selection lists is the `select` object. This object has the following properties:

- ▶ **name**—Specifies the name of the selection list.

- ▶ **length**—Specifies the number of options in the list.

- ▶ **options**—Specifies the array of options. Each selectable option has an entry in this array.

- ▶ **selectedIndex**—Returns the index value of the currently selected item. You can use this to check the value easily. In a multiple-selection list, this indicates the first selected item.

The `options` array has a single property of its own, `length`, which indicates the number of selections. In addition, each item in the `options` array has the following properties:

- ▶ **index**—Specifies the index of the array.

- ▶ **defaultSelected**—Indicates the state of the `selected` attribute.

- ▶ **selected**—Specifies the current state of the option. Setting this property to `true` selects the option. The user can select multiple options if the `multiple` attribute is included in the `<select>` tag.

- ▶ **name**—Specifies the value of the `name` attribute. This is used by the server.

- ▶ **text**—Specifies the text that is displayed in the option.

The `select` object has two methods—`blur` and `focus`—that perform the same purposes as the corresponding methods for `text` objects. The event handlers are onBlur, onFocus, and onChange, also similar to the event handlers of other objects.

NOTE

You can change selection lists dynamically; for example, choosing a product in one list could determine which options are available in another list. You can also add and delete options from the list.

Reading the value of a selected item is a two-step process. You first use the `selectedIndex` property and then use the `value` property to find the value of the selected choice. Here's an example:

```
ind = document.myform.choice.selectedIndex;
val = document.myform.choice.options[ind].value;
```

This example uses the `ind` variable to store the selected index and then assigns the `val` variable to the value of the selected choice. Things are a bit more complicated with a multiple selection: You have to test each option's `selected` attribute separately.

No HTML elements other than `<option>` and `<optgroup>` should appear between the `<select>` and `</select>` tags. The use of `<optgroup>`, as in the following snippet, enables you to create a group of options with a label that shows up in the list but can't be selected as an "answer" to the form field:

```
<select name="grades" size="8">
  <optgroup label="Good Grades">
    <option value="A">A</option>
    <option value="B">B</option>
  </optgroup>
    <optgroup label="Average Grades">
    <option value="C">C</option>
  </optgroup>
  <optgroup label="Bad Grades">
    <option value="D">D</option>
    <option value="F">F</option>
  </optgroup>
</select>
```

This snippet produces a drop-down list that looks like the example in Figure 27.2.

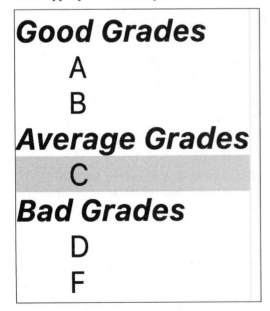

FIGURE 27.2
A drop-down list with options separated by the `<optgroup>` element.

In this situation, only A, B, C, D, and F are selectable, but the `<optgroup>` labels are visible.

Text Fields, Text Areas, and Other Input Types

The `<input type="text">` attribute mentioned earlier in this lesson allows the user to enter only a single line of text. When you want to allow multiple lines of text in a single input item, use the `<textarea>` and `</textarea>` tags to create a text area instead of just a text field. Any text you include between these two tags is displayed as the default entry in that box. Here's the example from Listing 27.1:

```
<textarea id="message" name="message" rows="7" cols="55">
</textarea>
```

NOTE

If you're adding a text input element, you don't need the `type="text"` attribute. If you leave it off, web browsers will by default assume that it's a text field.

As you have probably guessed, the `rows` and `cols` attributes control the number of rows and columns of text that fit in the input box. The `cols` attribute is a little less exact than `rows` and approximates the number of characters that fit in a row of text. Text area boxes do have a scrollbar, however, so the user can enter more text than can fit in the display area.

The `text` and `textarea` objects also have a few JavaScript methods you can use:

- **focus**—Sets the focus to the field. This positions the cursor in the field and makes it the current field.

- **blur**—Removes the focus from the field; the opposite of `focus`.

- **select**—Selects the text in the field, just as a user can do with the mouse. All the text is selected; there is no way to select only part of the text.

You can also use event handlers to detect when the value of a text field changes. The `text` and `textarea` objects support the following event handlers:

- **onFocus**—Occurs when the text field gains focus.

- **onBlur**—Occurs when the text field loses focus.

- **onChange**—Occurs when the user changes the text in the field and then moves out of it.

- **onSelect**—Occurs when the user selects some or all of the text in the field. Unfortunately, there's no way to tell exactly which part of the text was selected. (If the text is selected with the `select` method described previously, this event is not triggered.)

If these event handlers are used, they should be included in the `<input>` tag declaration. For example, the following is a text field including an `onChange` event that displays an alert:

```
<input type="text" name="text1" onChange="window.alert('Changed.');">
```

Let's turn back to the basic `<input>` element for a minute, however, because HTML5 provides many more `type` options for input than simply `"text"`, such as built-in date pickers. Here are a few of the different input types (some new, some not) that *are* fully supported but that we haven't discussed in any detail in this lesson:

▶ `type="email"`—This appears as a regular text field, but when form validation is used, the built-in validator checks that it is a well-formed email address. Some mobile devices display relevant keys (the @ sign, for example) by default instead of requiring additional user interactions.

▶ `type="file"`—This input type opens a dialog box to enable you to search for a file on your computer to upload.

▶ `type="number"`—Instead of creating a `<select>` list with `<option>` tags for each number, this type enables you to specify `min` and `max` values and the `step` between numbers to automatically generate a list on the browser side. You can see this in use in Listing 27.1.

▶ `type="range"`—Much like the `number` type just covered, this type enables you to specify `min` and `max` values and the `step` between numbers, but in this case, it appears as a horizontal slider.

▶ `type="search"`—This appears as a regular text field, but with additional controls that are sometimes displayed to allow the user to clear the search box such as an x or a similar character.

▶ `type="url"`—This input type appears as a regular text field, but when form validation is used, the built-in validator checks that it is a well-formed URL. Some mobile devices display relevant keys (the `.com` virtual key, for instance) by default instead of requiring additional user interactions.

You can stay up to date with the status of these and other `<input>` types by using the chart at https://developer.mozilla.org/en-US/docs/Web/HTML/Element/input.

Adding Data to Text Fields

Once you have a text field, you can add data to that field to provide customers with a list of suggested values. They can fill in the field with their own value instead, but either way, it gives them options.

To add data, you need to add a `<datalist>` to the page and then link to that list with the `list` attribute in the field where you want the data to appear. Here's how it is done in Listing 27.1:

```
<p>
  <label for="the_worst"><span class="question">
  Please indicate the one thing I could improve about my web site:
  </span></label><br>
  <input type="text" id="the_worst" name="the_worst"
         placeholder="There's nothing bad, is there?"
         list="listOfBadChoices" size="50">
</p>
...
<datalist id="listOfBadChoices">
  <option value="nothing"></option>
  <option value="nada"></option>
  <option value="zip"></option>
  <option value="zilch"></option>
  <option value="I can't think of anything"></option>
</datalist>
```

`<datalist>` is made up of a list of `<option>` elements. The `<option>` elements are a list of values that could be used in the input field. The `id` of the `<datalist>` matches the list value in the `<input>` field.

When the user gets to that `<input>` field, supporting browsers will show a drop-down of the options, as in Figure 27.3. The beauty of the `<datalist>` element is that browsers that don't support it simply display a text field as usual.

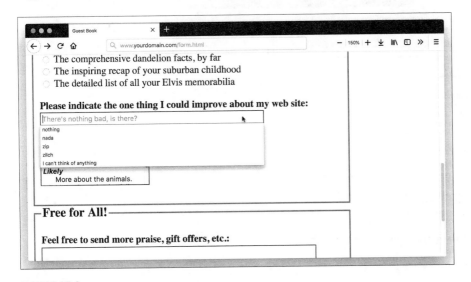

FIGURE 27.3
A drop-down list appears on an element with `<datalist>` applied to it.

Using HTML5 Form Validation

Many features in HTML5 have made web developers very happy people. One of the simplest yet most life-changing might be the inclusion of form validation. Before HTML5 form validation existed, we had to create convoluted JavaScript-based form validation, which caused headaches for everyone involved.

But no more! HTML5 validates forms by default, unless you use the `novalidate` attribute in the `<form>` element. Of course, if you do not use the `required` attribute in any form fields themselves or if you don't use specific input `type` options, like `email` or `url`, there's nothing to validate. As you learned in a previous section, not only are fields validated for content (any content at all), they are validated according to the type that they are. For example, Listing 27.1 includes a required field for an email address:

```
<p>
  <label class="question" for="the_email">What is your email
  address?</label>
  <input type="email" id="the_email" name="the_email"
         placeholder="Please use a real one!"
         size="50" required>
</p>
```

In Figures 27.4 and 27.5, you can see that the form automatically validates for the presence of content but then also slaps you on the wrist when you try to enter a junk string in the field instead of an email address.

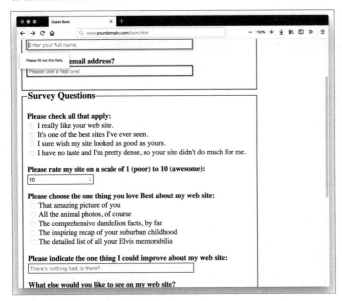

FIGURE 27.4
Attempting to submit a form with no content in a required field causes a validation error.

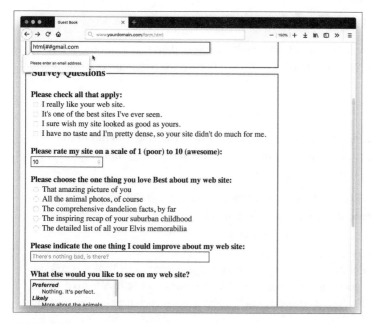

FIGURE 27.5
Attempting to submit a form with badly formed content in a field expecting an email address causes a validation error.

NOTE

Validation of email addresses begins and ends with the entry simply looking like an email address. This sort of pattern matching is really the only type of "validation" that you can do with email addresses, short of a time-consuming back-end processing script.

You can use the `pattern` attribute of the `<input>` field to specify your own pattern-matching requirements. The `pattern` attribute uses regular expressions, which is a large enough topic to warrant its own book, but here we consider a basic example. If you want to ensure that your `<input>` element contains only numbers and letters (no special characters), you could use the following:

```
<input type="text" id="the_text" name="the_text"
    placeholder="Please enter only letters and numbers!"
    size="50" pattern="[a-z,A-Z,0-9]" required>
```

The pattern here says that if the field contains any letter between a and z, letter between A and Z (case matters), and number between 0 and 9, it's valid. To learn more about regular expressions without buying an entire book, take a look at the online tutorial at http://regexone.com.

Submitting Form Data

It is common for a form to include a button that submits the form data to a script on the server or invokes a JavaScript action. You can use the `value` attribute to put any label you like on the Submit button:

```
<input type="submit" value="Place My Order Now!">
```

Unless you change the style using CSS, a gray button is sized to fit the label you put in the `value` attribute. When the user clicks it, all data items on the form are sent to the email address or script specified in the form's `action` attribute.

You can also include a Reset button that clears all entries on the form so that users can start over if they change their minds or make mistakes. Use the following:

```
<input type="reset" value="Clear This Form and Start Over">
```

If the standard Submit and Reset buttons look a little bland to you, remember that you can use CSS to style them. If that's not good enough, you'll be glad to know that there's an easy way to substitute your own graphics for these buttons. To use an image of your choice for a Submit button, use the following:

```
<input type="image" src="button.gif" alt="Order Now!">
```

The `button.gif` image displays on the page, and the form is submitted when a user clicks the `button.gif` image. You can include any attributes normally used with the `<img>` tag, such as `alt` and `style`.

Another form element is a generic button type. When using `type="button"` in the `<input>` tag, you get a button that performs no action on its own but can have an action assigned to it by a JavaScript event handler (such as `onclick`).

Understanding the `<button>` Element

When working with forms, you can use the HTML `<button></button>` element to create a clickable button on the page that includes whatever content is inside the element. The `<button>` can have any of three `type` values: `button`, `reset`, or `submit`. The `reset` and `submit` values make the button work like the corresponding values for `<input type="reset">` and `<input type="submit">` elements. And the `type="button"` value is used to create stand-alone buttons that work with JavaScript. The button in Listing 27.1 looks like this:

```
<button type="button" id="standardValues">Fill in Standard Values</button>
```

This creates a button with the text `Fill in Standard Values`. If you leave it like this, it does nothing when it's clicked, but you can add JavaScript to have the form filled in with the values you'd prefer, and then all the user has to do is submit the form. Listing 27.2 shows the JavaScript for this.

LISTING 27.2   Populate the Form with Values

```
document.getElementById("standardValues").addEventListener("click",
                                        function() {
  document.getElementById("the_name").value = "Your Name";
  document.getElementById("the_email").value= "you@yourdomain.com";
  document.gbForm.like_it.checked = true;
  document.gbForm.choose_scale.value = "10";
  document.gbForm.the_best.checked = true;
  document.gbForm.best_thing[2].checked = true;
  document.getElementById("the_worst").value = "Nothing";
  document.gbForm.how_improve.value = "More about the dandelions."
  document.getElementById("errors").innerHTML =
          "<p>Don't forget to give your feedback and submit the form.</p>";
document.gbForm.message.focus();
});
```

This script tells the browser that when the `standardValues` button is clicked, it should change the values of the various form fields. The last line places the cursor in the `message` field so the user can fill in a personal message and then submit the form.

You may also notice that this form attaches content to the `errors` field. This field is an `<output></output>` element, and it is intended to describe the output of forms. Error messages might not seem like an *output* of a form, exactly, but if you have something you'd like to add to a form dynamically, this is the element you should use. In Listing 27.1, the `<output>` element is at the top of the form, but you can place it anyplace you'd like the information to display.

CAUTION

Internet Explorer and Edge browsers do not support the `<output>` element. So, to use this most effectively, you should add a `<div>` or other element inside it and place your output inside that.

Using JavaScript for Form Events

The `form` object has two methods: `submit` and `reset`. You can use these methods to submit data or reset the form yourself, without requiring the user to click a button. You might want to do this, for example, to submit the form when the user clicks an image or performs another action that would not usually submit the form.

CAUTION

If you use the submit method to send data to a server or by email, most browsers will prompt the user to verify that he or she wants to submit the information. There's no way to do this behind the user's back.

The form object has two event handlers, onSubmit and onReset. You can specify a group of JavaScript statements or a function call for these events within the <form> tag that defines the form.

If you specify a statement or a function for the onSubmit event, the statement is called before the data is submitted to the server-side script. You can prevent the submission from happening by returning the value false from the onSubmit event handler. If the statement returns true, the data will be submitted. In the same fashion, you can prevent a Reset button from working with an onReset event handler.

Accessing Form Elements with JavaScript

The most important property of the form object is the elements array, which contains an object for each of the form elements. You can refer to an element by its own name or by its index in the array. For example, the following two expressions both refer to the first element in the form shown in Listing 27.1:

```
document.gbForm.elements[0]
document.gbForm.the_name
```

NOTE

Both forms and elements can be referred to by their own names or as indices in the forms and elements arrays. For clarity, the examples in this lesson use individual form and element names rather than array references. You'll also find it easier to use names in your own scripts.

If you do refer to forms and elements as arrays, you can use the length property to determine the number of objects in the array: document.forms.length is the number of forms in a document, and document.gbForm.elements.length is the number of elements in the gbForm form.

You can also access form elements by using the W3C DOM. In this case, you use an id attribute on the form element in the HTML document and use the document.getElementById method to find the object for the form. For example, this statement finds the object for the text field called the_name and stores it in the name variable:

```
name = document.getElementById("the_name");
```

This enables you to quickly access a form element without first finding the `form` object. You can assign an `id` to the `<form>` tag and find the corresponding object if you need to work with the form's properties and methods.

Displaying Data from a Form

As a simple example of interacting with forms purely on the client side, Listing 27.3 shows a form with name, address, and phone number fields, as well as a JavaScript function that displays the data from the form in a pop-up window.

LISTING 27.3   A Form That Displays Data in a Pop-up Window

```
<!doctype html>
<html lang="en">
  <head>
    <meta charset="utf-8">
    <title>Form Display Example</title>
    <meta name="viewport"
          content="width=device-width, initial-scale=1">
  </head>
  <body>
    <h1>Form Display Example</h1>
    <p>
      Enter the following information. When you press the Display
      button, the data you entered will be displayed in a pop-up.
    </p>
    <form name="form1" method="get" action="">
      <p>NAME: <input name="name" size="50"></p>
      <p>ADDRESS: <input name="address" size="50"></p>
      <p>PHONE: <input name="phone" size="50"></p>
      <p><input type="button" value="Display" id="display"></p>
    </form>
    <script>
    function display() {
      dispWin = window.open('','NewWin',
      'menubar=no,toolbar=no,status=no,width=400,height=100');

      message = "<ul><li>NAME:" +
      document.form1.name.value;
      message += "<li>ADDRESS:" +
      document.form1.address.value;
      message += "<li>PHONE:" +
      document.form1.phone.value;
      message += "</ul>";
      dispWin.document.write(message);
    }
```

```
    document.getElementById("display").addEventListener("click", display);
    </script>
  </body>
</html>
```

Here is a breakdown of how this simple HTML document and script work:

▶ The `<script>` section at the bottom of the document defines a function called `display` that opens a new window and displays the information from the form. It also includes the event listener on the `display` element to run the `display` function when it's clicked.

▶ The `<form>` tag begins the form. Because this form is handled entirely by JavaScript, the form `action` has no value. The `method` is `post` to ensure that no data is added to the URL.

▶ The `<input>` tags define the form's three fields: `yourname`, `address`, and `phone`. The last `<input>` tag defines the Display button, which is set to run the `display` function in the event listener in the script.

Figure 27.6 shows this form in action. The Display button has been clicked, and the pop-up window shows the results. Although this is not the most exciting example of client-side form interaction, it clearly shows the basics that provide a foundation for later work.

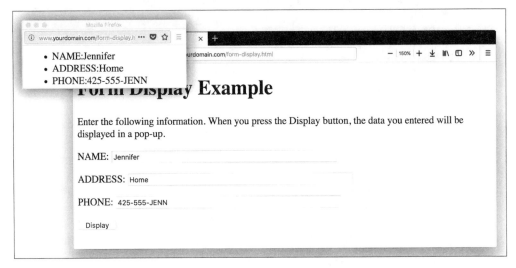

FIGURE 27.6
Displaying data from a form in a pop-up window.

Summary

In this lesson you learned how to create HTML forms in which visitors can provide information that is sent to you when the forms are hooked up to a back-end processing script (which is beyond the scope of these lessons).

You learned about all the major form elements, including a little about how form-processing scripts interpret the names and value attributes of those elements. When you are ready to try a back-end form-processing script, you'll be well versed in the front-end details, including how to access the form object in JavaScript.

This lesson stopped short of covering back-end form processing because server-side form handling requires an external script to process a form. However, there is plenty to do to set up a form that looks and acts just the way you want it to, including form validation, so you have a lot to practice before taking that next step into form interactivity.

Table 27.1 summarizes the HTML tags and attributes covered in this lesson.

TABLE 27.1   HTML Tags and Attributes Covered in Lesson 27

Tag/Attribute	Function
`<form>...</form>`	Indicates an input form.
Attribute	*Function*
`action="scripturl"`	Gives the address of the script to process this form input.
`method="post/get"`	Indicates how the form input will be sent to the server. Normally set to `post` rather than `get`.
`<label>...</label>`	Provides information for the form element to which it is associated.
`<fieldset>...</fieldset>`	Groups a set of related form elements.
`<legend>...</legend>`	Provides a label to a set of related form elements.
`<input>`	Indicates an input element for a form.
Attribute	*Function*
`type="controltype"`	Gives the type for this input widget. Some possible values are `checkbox`, `hidden`, `radio`, `reset`, `submit`, `text`, and `image`, among others.
`name="name"`	Gives the unique name of this item, as passed to the script.
`value="value"`	Gives the default value for a text or hidden item. For a check box or radio button, it's the value to be submitted with the form. For Reset or Submit buttons, it's the label for the button.
`src="imageurl"`	Shows the source file for an image.

Tag/Attribute	Function
Attribute	*Function*
checked	Is used for check boxes and radio buttons. Indicates that this item is checked.
autofocus	Puts focus on the element when the form is loaded.
required	Indicates that the field should be validated for content, according to type (where appropriate).
pattern="*pattern*"	Indicates that the content of this field should be validated against this regular expression.
size="*width*"	Specifies the width, in characters, of a text input region.
maxlength="*maxlength*"	Specifies the maximum number of characters that can be entered into a text region.
<textarea>...</textarea>	Indicates a multiline text entry form element. Default text can be included.
Attribute	*Function*
name="*name*"	Specifies the name to be passed to the script.
rows="*numrows*"	Specifies the number of rows this text area displays.
cols="*numchars*"	Specifies the number of columns (characters) this text area displays.
autofocus	Puts focus on the element when the form is loaded.
required	Indicates that the field should be validated for content according to type (where appropriate).
pattern="*pattern*"	Indicates that the content of this field should be validated against this regular expression.
<select>...</select>	Creates a menu or scrolling list of possible items.
Attribute	*Function*
name="*name*"	Shows the name that is passed to the script.
size="*numelements*"	Indicates the number of elements to display. If size is indicated, the selection becomes a scrolling list. If no size is given, the selection is a drop-down pick list.
multiple	Allows multiple selections from the list.
required	Indicates that the field should be validated for a selection.
<optgroup>...</optgroup>	Indicates a grouping of <option> elements.
Attribute	*Function*
label="*label*"	Provides a label for the group.
<option>...</option>	Indicates a possible item within a <select> element.

Tag/Attribute	Function
Attribute	*Function*
selected	Selects the <option> by default in the list when this attribute is included.
value="*value*"	Specifies the value to submit if this <option> is selected when the form is submitted.
<button>...</button>	Creates a clickable button in the form.
Attribute	*Function*
name="*name*"	Gives the unique name of this item, as passed to the script.
<output>...</output>	Represents the output or results of a form.

Q&A

Q. Is there any way to create a large number of text fields without dealing with different names for all of them?

A. Yes. If you use the same name for several elements in the form, their objects form an array. For example, if you defined 20 text fields with the name member, you could refer to them as member[0] through member[19]. This also works with other types of form elements.

Q. Since HTML5 contains form validation, do I ever have to worry about validation again?

A. Yes, you do. Although HTML5 form validation is awesome, you should still validate the form information that is sent to you on the back end. Back-end processing is beyond the scope of these lessons, but as a rule, you should never trust any user input; always check it before performing an action that uses it (especially when interacting with a database).

Workshop

The Workshop contains quiz questions and activities to help you solidify your understanding of the material covered. Try to answer all questions before looking at the "Answers" section that follows.

Quiz

1. What HTML elements do you use to create a guestbook form that asks someone for his or her name and gender?

  a. <input type=name> for the name and <input type=gender> for the gender

  b. <input type=text> for the name and <input type=radio> for the gender

  c. <input type=name> for the name and <input type=radio> for the gender

  d. <input type=text> for the name and <input type=gender> for the gender

2. If you created an image named `submit.gif`, how would you use it as the Submit button for a form?

   a. `<input type="button" src="submit.gif">`

   b. `<input type="image" src="submit.gif">`

   c. `<img type="submit" src="submit.gif">`

   d. `<submit type="submit" src="submit.gif">`

3. Which of these attributes of a `<form>` tag determines where the data will be sent?

   a. `action`

   b. `method`

   c. `name`

4. What are the two possible values of the `method` attribute of a form?

   a. `action` and `get`

   b. `action` and `post`

   c. `post` and `get`

   d. `get` and `action`

5. Is the following a valid input field?

   `<input name="thisField">`

   a. Yes.

   b. No. It needs a `type` attribute.

   c. No. It needs a `value` attribute.

   d. No. It needs a `width` attribute.

6. What does the `novalidate` attribute of a form do?

   a. Indicates there are no valid form fields

   b. Directs the browser to not validate the HTML of the form

   c. Directs the browser to not validate the HTML of the page

   d. Directs the browser to not validate the form fields

7. What is the `<label>` element used for?

   a. Creates a label style

   b. Indicates where the form field starts

   c. Indicates where the form field ends

   d. Defines the text to be read aloud by screen readers

8. Why are there brackets in the `name` of this form field?

```
<input type="checkbox" id="cb1" name="answers[]" value="one">
```

  a. Indicates that the field will take multiple values

  b. Indicates that the field is a required field

  c. Indicates that the field should be validated with an external regular expression

  d. No reason other than that the designer wanted to name the field with brackets.

9. What does the following JavaScript do?

```
document.entries.homeAddress.checked = true;
```

  a. Checks the box called `entries` in the `homeAddress` form

  b. Checks the box called `homeAddress` in the `entries` form

  c. Makes the element `entries` in the `homeAddress` form a checkbox

  d. Makes the element `homeAddress` in the `entries` form a checkbox

10. How do you write a field that will collect a lot of text and is 10 rows high and 60 columns wide?

  a.
```
<textarea id="text" name="text" rows="10" columns="60">
</textarea>
```

  b.
```
<textarea id="text" name="text" rows="10" cols="60"></textarea>
```

  c.
```
<input type="text" id="text" name="text" rows="10" columns="60">
</input>
```

  d.
```
<text id="text" name="text" rows="10" cols="60"></text>
```

NOTE

Just a reminder for those of you reading these words in the print or e-book edition of this book: If you go to **www.informit.com/register** and register this book (using ISBN 9780672338083), you can receive free access to an online Web Edition that not only contains the complete text of this book but also features an interactive version of this quiz.

Answers

  1. b. You use a text field for the name and radio buttons for the gender. The HTML code for the whole form would be similar to the following (with the appropriate `doctype` and other structural markup, of course):

```
<form name="form1" method="post" action="/scripts/formscript">
<input type="hidden" name="mailto" value="you@yoursite.com">
<p><label for="name">Your Name:</label>
```

```
<input type="text" id="name" name="name" size="50"></p>
<p>Your Gender:
<input type="radio" id="male" name="gender"
    value="male"> <label for="male">male</label>
<input type="radio" id="female" name="gender"
    value="female"> <label for="female">female</label>
<input type="radio" id="go_away" name="gender"
    value="mind your business"><label for="go_away">
    mind your business</label></p>
<p><input type="submit" value="Submit Form"></p>
</form>
```

2. b. Use this code:

```
<input type="image" src="submit.gif">
```

3. a. The `action` attribute determines where the data is sent.

4. c. They are `post` and `get`.

5. a. Yes, it's valid. If the `<input>` tag has no `type`, it defaults to `text`.

6. d. It tells the browser not to perform any validation actions.

7. d. It defines the text read aloud by screen readers and gives users a larger area to click to focus on the form field.

8. a. The brackets tell the processing script that a series of values will be placed in this value rather than just one.

9. b. It checks the box called `homeAddress` in the `entries` form.

10. b. Write the following:

```
<textarea id="text" name="text" rows="10" cols="60"></textarea>
```

Exercises

▶ Create a form using all the different types of input elements and selection lists to make sure you understand how each of them works.

▶ Learn a little bit about regular expressions and implement some custom validation by using the `pattern` attribute.

▶ Investigate the form-handling options at your web hosting provider and use a script that the web hosting provider made available to you to process the form you created in the first exercise.

LESSON 28
Organizing and Managing a Website

What You'll Learn in This Lesson:

▶ How to determine whether one page is enough to handle all your content

▶ How to organize a simple site

▶ How to organize a larger site

▶ How to write maintainable code

▶ How to optimize your site for search engines

▶ How to get started with version control

The bulk of these lessons have led you through the design and creation of static and dynamic web content, from text to graphics and multimedia, with a little JavaScript interactivity thrown in for good measure. Along the way, we've noted some of the ways you can think about the life cycle of that content. In this lesson, you'll learn how to look at your work as a whole.

This lesson shows you how to think about organizing and presenting multiple web pages so that visitors will be able to navigate among them without confusion. You'll also learn ways to make your website memorable enough to visit again and again. Web developers use the term *sticky* to describe pages that people don't want to leave. Hopefully this lesson will help you make your websites downright gooey! You'll also learn techniques to give your pages better exposure in search engine results so that your visitors can find your pages in the first place.

Because websites can be (and usually should be) updated frequently, it's essential to create pages that can be easily maintained. This lesson shows you how to add comments and other documentation to your pages so that you—or anyone else on your staff—can understand and modify your pages. It also introduces you to version control so that you can innovate individually or as part of a team without overwriting work that you might want to have saved.

By this point in the lessons, you should have enough HTML and CSS knowledge to produce most of your website. You have probably created a number of pages already, and perhaps you have even published them online.

As you proceed through this lesson, think about how your pages are organized now and how you can improve that organization. Have you used comments in your HTML or created a document for future website maintainers regarding your content organization? If not, now is a good time to start. Along the way, don't be surprised if you decide to do a redesign that involves changing almost all your pages. The results are likely to be well worth the effort!

When One Page Is Enough

Building and organizing an attractive and effective website doesn't always need to be a complex task. If you are creating a web presence for a single entity (such as a local event) that requires only a small amount of very specific information, you can effectively present that information on a single page with or without a lot of flashy graphics and interactivity. In fact, there are several positive features to a single-page web presence:

▶ All the information on the site downloads more quickly than on more extensive sites.

▶ The whole site can be printed on paper with a single print command, even if it is several paper pages long.

▶ Visitors can easily save the site on their hard drives for future reference, especially if it uses a minimum of graphics.

▶ Links between different parts of the same page usually respond more quickly than links to other pages.

Figure 28.1 shows the first part of a web page that serves its intended audience better as a single lengthy page than it would as a multipage site. The page begins, as most introductory pages should, with a succinct explanation of what the page is about and who would want to read it. A detailed table of contents enables visitors to skip directly to the section containing the material they find most interesting. If this "page" were printed, it would contain about six paper pages' worth of text about driving traffic to websites—something a visitor might think about printing and reading later, perhaps while also taking notes.

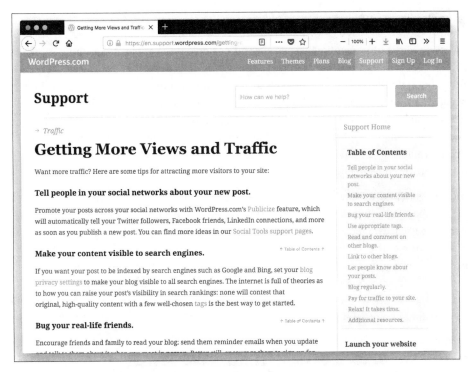

FIGURE 28.1
A good table of contents can make long pages easier to navigate.

When pages contain a table of contents to separate sections of information, it is also common for each short section to contain a link back up to the table of contents so that navigating around the page feels much the same as navigating around a multipage site. Because the contents of these types of longer pages are intended as a handy reference, visitors will definitely prefer the convenience of bookmarking or saving a single page over having to save 8 or 10 separate pages. The most common examples of single-page information websites are encompassed within Wikipedia, at www.wikipedia.org. If you consider each entry full of rich content to be its own "site," the single-page sites within Wikipedia—with their own tables of contents—represent millions of printed pages.

Having experienced many beautiful and effective graphical layouts online, you might be tempted to forget that using a good, old-fashioned outline is often the clearest and most efficient way to organize long web pages full of text-based content within a site. This is especially true with the influx of single-page interfaces (also called single-page *applications*) that attempt to bring all the interactivity of desktop applications into a web browsing experience. These applications are often built using HTML and JavaScript frameworks and include significant visual design elements; in fact, these sites are often used to publish design portfolios rather than the type of text-based content you see here.

Organizing a Simple Site

With the exception of the aforementioned special cases of single-page applications and portfolio sites, single-page websites tend to serve merely "coming soon" or placeholder purposes. If you spend any time at all on the Web, you'll quickly learn that most companies and individuals best serve their readers by dividing their sites into short, quickly-read pages surrounded by graphical navigation that enables them to gather almost all the information they could want within a few clicks. Furthermore, using multiple pages instead of a series of very long pages minimizes scrolling on the page, which can be especially bothersome for visitors who are using mobile devices to view the full site or who have relatively low-resolution monitors (less than 800×600).

The fundamental goal of a website is to make the individual or organization visible on the Internet, but another important—and more important—goal is to act as a portal to the information within the site itself. The main page of a site should give the user enough information to provide a clear picture of the organization, as well as traditional contact information and an email address to submit questions or feedback. It should also provide clear pathways into the highly structured information within other pages in the site. The main page shown in Figure 28.2 provides examples of all these good features: basic information, contact information, and paths to information for multiple audiences.

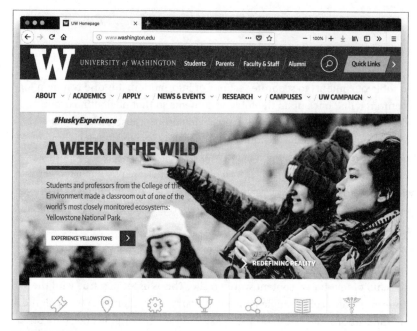

FIGURE 28.2
This university main page uses a basic design, minimal but useful graphics, and a clear structure to entice users to explore for more information.

NOTE

Regardless of how large your site is, it's a good idea to carefully organize your resources. For example, placing the images for your web pages in a separate folder named `images` is one step toward organization. Similarly, if you have files that are available for download, place them in a folder called `downloads`. This makes it much easier to keep track of web page resources based on their particular types (HTML pages, PNG images, and so on). In addition, if you organize your site into sections, such as Company, Products, and Press, put the individual pages into similarly named directories (`company`, `products`, `press`, and so on)—for the same organizational reasons.

One of the most common mistakes beginning website developers make is creating pages that look fundamentally different from other pages on the site. An equally serious mistake is using the same publicly available clip art that thousands of other web authors are also using. Remember that, on the Internet, one click can take you around the world. The only way to make your pages memorable and recognizable as a cohesive site is to have all your pages adhere to a unique, unmistakable visual theme. In other words, strive for uniqueness compared to other websites yet uniformity within the site itself.

As an example of how uniformity can help make a site more cohesive, think about large, popular sites you might have visited, such as ESPN.com. If you visit the MLB section at ESPN.com (see Figure 28.3) and then visit the NFL section (see Figure 28.4), you'll notice a very similar structure.

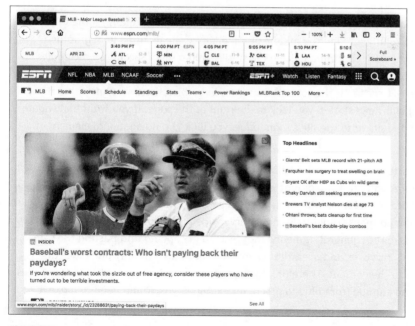

FIGURE 28.3
The MLB section at ESPN.com.

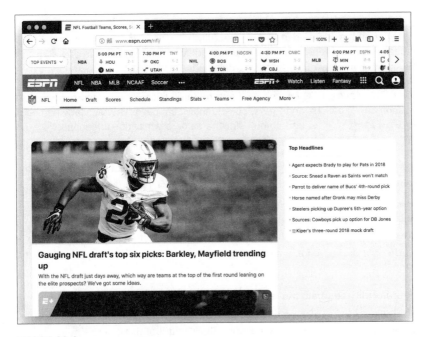

FIGURE 28.4
The NFL section at ESPN.com.

In both examples, you see navigation elements at the top of the page (including some sub-navigation elements), a large area in the middle of the page for the featured item graphic, a rectangle on the right side containing links to top stories, and a set of secondary rectangles under the primary image, leading readers to additional stories. The only difference between the MLB section and the NFL section is the content. However, in both sections, you know that if you want to read the popular news stories, you look to the right of the page. If you want to navigate to another section in the site or to the site's main page, you look to a navigational element at the top of the page.

The presence of consistent design and organizational elements helps ensure that your users will be able to navigate throughout your content with confidence. From a maintenance perspective, the consistent structural template enables you to reuse pieces of the underlying code. This type of code reuse typically happens through dynamic server-side programming that is beyond the scope of these lessons, but in general, it means that instead of copying and pasting the same HTML, CSS, and JavaScript over and over, that client-side code exists in only one place and is applied dynamically to the content. Therefore, instead of making changes to thousands of files to make a background change from blue to green, for example, you would need to make a change only once.

Organizing a Larger Site

For a more complex site, sophisticated layout and graphics can help organize and improve the looks of the site when used consistently throughout all your pages. To see how you can make aesthetics and organization work hand in hand, let's look at examples of navigation (and, thus, underlying organization) for a few sites that present a large volume of information to several different audiences.

Figure 28.5 shows the main page of Amazon.com, specifically with the navigation selected. Amazon is in the business of selling products, plain and simple. Therefore, it makes sense for Amazon to show product categories as the main navigational elements.

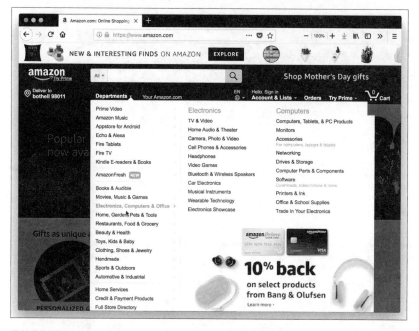

FIGURE 28.5
Amazon.com shows product categories as primary navigation elements.

Although Amazon is in the business of selling products, it also has to provide information regarding who it is, how to contact it, and other ancillary yet important information to enhance the business-to-consumer relationship. Links to this sort of information appear in the footer, or bottom portion, of the Amazon.com website—outside the viewing area of this screenshot. When creating your site template, you must determine the most important content areas and how to organize that content; also remember to provide users with basic information—especially if that information will enhance your image and make users feel as if you value what they have to say.

The next example is of a secondary page within the Peet's Coffee website (www.peets.com). All the pages in the Peet's website follow one of the common types of presenting navigation and sub-navigation: a horizontal strip for main navigation, with secondary elements for that section placed in a vertical column on the left. As Figure 28.6 shows, the secondary navigation changes depending upon what page the user visits—and it disappears completely in some cases. These types of visual indicators help users orient themselves within the site. Using a visual indicator like a color change or change in content is a useful tactic because your users might arrive at a page via a search engine or by a link from another website. After your users arrive, you want them to feel at home—or at least feel as if they know where they are in relationship to your site.

FIGURE 28.6
This Peet's Coffee secondary page shows a main navigation element with different secondary navigation on the left side of the page.

As you can see from the different main navigation elements—Craft, Coffee, Tea, Cold Brew, Gear, Gifts, Subscriptions, and Coffeebars—the Peet's website has to serve the needs of many different types of people who come to the website for many different reasons. As you organize your own site content, determine the information that is most important to you, as well as the information that is most important to your users, and create a navigation scheme that finds a happy medium between the two.

Figure 28.7 shows another example of a navigation style, this time with a twist on the standard top navigation/left-side navigation scheme. In this example, the left-side navigation (the secondary navigation, in this case) also appears in a drop-down menu under the main navigation (refer to Lesson 11, "Using CSS to Do More with Lists, Text, and Navigation," for information on how to do something like this). Hovering the mouse over any of the other main navigation elements brings up similar menus. This scheme gives users an entire site map at their fingertips because they can reach any part of the site within one click of any other page.

FIGURE 28.7
The BAWSI.org website shows sub-navigation attached to each main navigation element.

Also notice that the About Us link in the navigation is styled differently—with bright orange text—from the other links on the page, indicating to visitors which page they are on. This visual detail is an unobtrusive way to give users a sense of where they are within the current navigational scheme. You can also use other style features, like background colors, changing font sizes, or even using different font families. Some sites also use icons to indicate the location on the site.

You can choose among many types of navigation styles and ways of indicating to users where they are and where they might want to go next. Keep in mind the following fact: Studies have repeatedly shown that people become confused and annoyed when presented with more than seven choices at a time, and people feel most comfortable with five or fewer choices. Therefore, you should avoid presenting more than five links (either in a list or as graphical icons) next to one another, if at all possible—and you should definitely avoid presenting more than seven at once. Amazon.com gets a pass here because it is an Internet superstore, and users expect a lot of "departments" in which to shop when they get there. But when you need to present more than seven links in a navigation list, break them into multiple lists with a separate heading for each of the five to seven items.

It will also help your readers navigate your site without confusion if you avoid putting any page more than two (or, at most, three) links away from the main page. You should also always send readers back to a main category page (or the home page) after they've read a subsidiary page. In other words, try to design a somewhat flat link structure in which most pages are no more than one or two links deep. You don't want visitors to have to rely heavily, if at all, on their browser's Back button to navigate your site.

Optimizing Your Site for Search Engines

One major part of managing a website is getting it search engine ready. While not all sites rely on search engines for traffic, the majority do, so it's a good idea to understand the basics of *search engine optimization (SEO)* so you don't make mistakes that will hurt your traffic.

What you need to do is make sure that your site provides the information that both your customers and search engines can use to find your site.

There are dozens of search engines out there, and they all use a different method for determining what sites show up first in the results. But there are a few things you can do that will help improve your site rankings no matter what search engine your customers use:

- ▶ **Interesting content**—This is the most important feature of a search engine–friendly site. You need to have text, multimedia, and images that people want to read and view.

- ▶ **Easy-to-use navigation**—You want visitors to your site to stay as long as they want, no matter what page they end up on.

- ▶ **Mobile friendliness**—Mobile-friendly sites are critical for search engine placement. More and more people use mobile devices, and Google and other search engines are switching to an index that prioritizes mobile-friendly designs.

Creating Interesting Content

It used to be that to get good placement in search engines, your content had to be full of keywords. While keywords have some importance, they are not as important as the content itself. The content needs to be interesting, easy to read, and comprehensive. You can't get by with short, dull articles on your site. You need to write fully formed documents that cover whatever topic you're writing about in depth.

CAUTION

Not all your pages need to be optimized for search or have long form content on them. Pages like your home page and navigation pages can be short and provide links and information to other parts of your site. Focus your SEO efforts on the actual content articles (and videos and images) that you post on the site.

The following are some tips for making sure your pages have enough in-depth content:

▶ Write long articles—2000 words or more.

▶ Use headings like <h2>, <h3>, and <h4> with the correct numbered level to create a document outline.

▶ Include good internal navigation.

▶ Don't forget tables, figures, and graphs.

If you are determined to use keywords in your documents, focus on latent semantic indexing (LSI) keywords. These are keyword phrases that tend to have the same meaning in different contexts. If that sounds too technical, don't worry too much about it: Just write your articles. But if you really want to make sure you're covering it, you can use a tool like LSIGraph (https://lsigraph.com) to generate keywords for you.

Keeping Your Navigation Usable

Search engines navigate your site very much like human users (although they are often much faster). So, you need to make sure that your site navigation works and can get users to any page available. Don't ever use JavaScript as the only way to get to navigation on your site—especially the primary navigation.

But don't forget about internal navigation. Since you're writing long, in-depth articles, you should have a form of navigation within the document. This could be a table of contents or just extra links to other parts of the page. If you don't remember how to do that, now is a good time to go back and review Lesson 7, "Using External and Internal Links."

Writing for Mobile Devices

Google and other search engines are prioritizing mobile devices and mobile-friendly pages more and more. If your pages break, are hard to read, or look bad on mobile devices, then you're not going to rank well in search engines. More and more people use mobile devices either first or as their only access to the web; by making your site mobile friendly, you will get better ranking and have happier customers.

If you've been following the instructions in previous lessons about how to write for mobile, and especially the Mobile First information from Lesson 17, "Designing for Mobile Devices," then you are well on your way to creating a site that works for mobile and for search engines. But keep in mind these key tips:

- ▶ Write valid HTML, CSS, and JavaScript.

- ▶ Make your pages responsive.

- ▶ Remember that download speeds matter a lot, so keep your pages as small as possible—but no smaller.

- ▶ Never hide content from mobile users. It's fine to change how things are displayed, but content should be available no matter what device your customer uses.

- ▶ Use the Mobile-Friendly Test tool from Google (https://search.google.com/test/ mobile-friendly) to see how easy your site is for a mobile customer to use.

Writing Maintainable Code

If you've done any coding before reading these lessons, you already know how important it is to write code that can be maintained—that is, you or someone else should be able to look at your code later and not be utterly confused by it. The challenge is to make your code as immediately understandable as possible. A time will come when you'll look back on a page that you wrote, and you won't have a clue what you were thinking or why you wrote the code the way you did. Fortunately, there is a way to combat this problem of apparent memory loss.

Documenting Code with Comments

Whenever you develop an HTML page, CSS snippet, or JavaScript function, keep in mind that you or someone else will almost certainly need to make changes to it someday. Simple text web pages are usually easy to read and revise, but complex pages with graphics, tables, and other layout tricks can be quite difficult to decipher.

NOTE

To include comments in a style sheet, begin comments with /* and end them with */ (with your commented code between these characters).

The HTML <!-- and --> comment syntax does not work in style sheets.

To see what I'm talking about, visit just about any page in a web browser and view its source code. Using Microsoft Edge, right-click a page and select View Source. Using Chrome or Firefox, right-click a page and select View Page Source. In Safari, right-click a page and select Show Page Source. You might see a jumbled bunch of code that is as tough to decipher as pure HTML. This might be because content management software systems have generated the markup dynamically, or it might be because its human maintainer has not paid attention to structure, ease of reading, code commenting, and other methods for making the code readable by humans. For the sake of maintaining your own pages, I encourage you to impose a little more order on your HTML markup, style sheet entries, and JavaScript code. And remember: Proper indentation is your (and your future development partner's) friend.

NOTE

Some designers use minify programs to compress their HTML, CSS, and JavaScript to make sure that it's as small as possible. These speed up download for pages, but can make the code difficult to read. One solution is to use a tool like CodeKit (https://codekitapp.com) to minify your code after you've written it, immediately before delivering it to the live site. CodeKit is for Mac only. If you're looking for a Windows alternative, one possibility is Prepros (https://prepros.io). You minify your code to make the pages faster, but you only do it once you're done developing and ready to publish.

As you have seen in several of these lessons, you can enclose comments to yourself or your coauthors by using the HTML beginning and ending comment syntax: <!-- and -->. These comments will not appear on the web page when viewed with a browser but can be read by anyone who examines the HTML code in a text editor or via the web browser's View Source (or View Page Source or Show Page Source) function. The following example provides a little refresher of how a comment is coded:

```
<!-- This image needs to be updated daily. -->
<img src="headline.jpg" alt="Today's Headline">
```

NOTE

One handy use of comments is to hide parts of a web page that are currently under construction. Instead of making the text and graphics visible and explaining that they're under construction, you can hide them from view entirely with some carefully placed opening and closing comment indicators around the HTML that you do not want to appear. This is a great way to work on portions of a page gradually and show only the end result to the world when you're finished.

As this code reveals, the comment just before the <img> tag provides a clue to how the image is used. Anyone who reads this code knows immediately that this is an image that must be updated every day. Web browsers completely ignore the text in the comment.

▼ TRY IT YOURSELF

Commenting Your Code

It will be well worth your time now to go through all the web pages and style sheets you've created so far and add any comments that you or others might find helpful when revising them in the future. Here's what to do:

1. Insert a comment explaining any fancy formatting or layout technique before the tags that make it happen.

2. Use a comment just before an `<img>` tag to briefly describe any important graphic whose function isn't obvious from the `alt` message.

3. Consider using a comment (or several comments) to summarize how the cells of a `<table>` are supposed to align.

4. If you use hexadecimal color codes (such as `<div style="color: #8040B0;">`), insert a comment indicating what the color actually is (bluish-purple).

5. Indent your comments to help them stand out and make both the comments and the HTML or CSS easier to read. Don't forget to use indentation in the HTML, CSS, or JavaScript itself to make it more readable, too, as discussed in the next section.

You can also comment your CSS and JavaScript in a similar fashion. This is a CSS comment:

```
/* these are the main reset styles */
```

And this is a JavaScript comment:

```
# This line is commented out
```

Indenting Code for Clarity

We have to make a confession. Throughout these lessons, we've been carefully indoctrinating you into an HTML code development style without really letting on. It's time to spill the beans. You've no doubt noticed a consistent pattern with respect to the indentation of all the HTML code in the lessons. More specifically, each child tag is indented to the right two spaces from its parent tag. Furthermore, content within a tag that spans more than one line is indented within the tag.

The best way to learn the value of indentation is to see some HTML code without it. You know how the song goes—"You don't know what you've got 'til it's gone." Anyway, here's a very simple table coded without any indentation:

```
<table><tr><td>Cell One</td><td>Cell Two</td></tr>
<tr><td>Cell Three</td><td>Cell Four</td></tr></table>
```

Not only is there no indentation, but there is also no space between rows and columns within the table. Now compare the code above code with the following code, which describes the same table:

```
<table>
  <tr>
    <td>Cell One</td>
    <td>Cell Two</td>
  </tr>
  <tr>
    <td>Cell Three</td>
    <td>Cell Four</td>
  </tr>
</table>
```

This heavily indented code makes it plainly obvious how the rows and columns are divided up via `<tr>` and `<td>` tags.

Consistent indentation might even be more important than comments when it comes to making your HTML code understandable and maintainable. And you don't have to buy into this specific indentation strategy. If you'd rather use three or four spaces instead of two, that's fine. And if you want to tighten things up a bit and not indent content within a tag, that also works. The main point to take from this section is that it's important to develop a coding style of your own (or your team's own) and then ruthlessly stick to it.

NOTE

If you work with other people (or plan to) in developing a website or a web-based application, consider getting together as a group to formulate a consistent coding style. That way, everyone is on the same page—pun intended.

Thinking About Version Control

If you've ever used Google Docs, you have encountered a form of version control; when you're using Google Docs, Google automatically saves revisions of your work as you are typing. This is different from simply automatically saving your work (although it does that, too) because you can revert to any revision along the way. You might have encountered this concept when using popular blog-authoring software such as Blogger or WordPress, or even when editing wikis—both of these types of applications also enable users to revise their work without overwriting, and thus deleting for all time, their previous work.

You might be wondering, "Well, what does that have to do with developing HTML, CSS, or JavaScript? You're just talking about documents." The answer is simple: Just as you might want to revert to a previous edition of an article or a letter, you might want to revert to a previous edition of your HTML, CSS, or JavaScript code. This could be because you followed a good idea to the end, but your markup just proved untenable and you don't want to start over entirely—you just want to back up to a certain point along your revision path. Or, let's say you developed a particularly involved bit of JavaScript and discovered that something in the middle of it just doesn't work with some browsers; you'll want to build on and extend the work you did, not throw it away completely, and knowing what you did in the past will help you in the future. We use version control for every website we manage and every book or lesson we write.

Version control involves more than just revision history. When you start using version control systems to maintain your code, you will hear terms like these:

▶ **Commit/check in and check out**—When you put an object into the code repository, you are *committing* that file; when you *check out* a file, you are grabbing it from the repository (where all the current and historical versions are stored) and working on it until you are ready to *commit* or *check in* the file again.

▶ **Branch or fork**—The files you have under version control can *branch* or *fork* at any point, thus creating two or more development paths. Suppose you want to try some new display layouts or form interactivity, but you don't want an existing site to appear to be modified in any way. You might have started with one master set of files but then forked that set of files for the new site, continuing to develop them independently. If you continued developing the original set of files, that would be working with the *trunk*.

▶ **Change or diff**—The terms *change* and *diff* both refer to a modification made under version control. You might also hear *diff* used as a verb, as in "I diffed the files," to refer to the action of comparing two versions of an object (and there is an underlying UNIX command called `diff`).

▶ **Fork, push, pull, and fetch**—When you find an open-source GitHub repository that you want to use as the basis for your own work (or that you want to contribute to), you *fork* the repository to then create a copy of it that you can work on at your own pace. From the forked repository, you can *push* commits to your own version, *fetch* changes from the original repository, and issue *pull requests* to the owner of the original if you would like to contribute your changes to the original repository that you forked.

You will hear many more terms than just the few listed here, but if you can conceptualize the repository, the (local) working copy, and the process of checking in and checking out files, you are well on your way to implementing version control for your digital objects.

Using a Version Control System

Several version control systems are available for use, some free and open source, and some proprietary. Some popular systems are Subversion (subversion.apache.org), Mercurial (www.mercurial-scm.org), and Git (www.git-scm.com). If you have a web hosting service that enables you to install any of these tools, you could create your own repository and use a GUI or command-line client to connect to it. However, for users who want to get started with a repository but don't necessarily want, need, or understand all the extra installation and maintenance overhead that goes with it, there are plenty of hosted version control systems that can even be used free for personal and open-source projects. These hosted solutions aren't just for individuals; all sorts of companies and organizations both big and small use hosted version control systems, such as GitHub (www.github.com) or Bitbucket (www.bitbucket.org). For a few dollars, you can turn your free, public account into a private account and keep your code to yourself.

For anyone wanting to get started with version control, I highly recommend GitHub for relative ease of use and free, cross-platform tools. The GitHub Help site is a great place to start: See http://help.github.com. An added benefit of the already-free GitHub account is the capability to use Gist (gist.github.com) to share code snippets (or whole pages) with others (those snippets themselves are Git repositories and, thus, are versioned and forkable in their own right). Using GitHub repositories, including Gists, is also an excellent way to get started with version control of your work.

Using HTML and CSS Frameworks

If you use a content management system (CMS) such as WordPress (www.wordpress.org) or Drupal (www.drupal.org) to power your website, you will end up using a presentation template designed for one of those systems. But what if you do *not* want to use a CMS but *would* like a starting point for an advanced HTML and CSS presentation? Over the past few years, the web development world has seen the rise of HTML and CSS (or "front-end") frameworks that can help solve this problem. Many of these frameworks are open source and available for download or forking from GitHub repositories. These frameworks often also include advanced JavaScript libraries, like the ones you learned about in Lesson 26, "Using Third-Party JavaScript Libraries and Frameworks."

I recommend three popular HTML and CSS frameworks:

▶ **Bootstrap**—Developed internally by engineers at Twitter, this framework is open-source software for anyone who wants to use it to get started with modern design elements. Learn more at http://getbootstrap.com, which includes a simple "Get Started" section that explains what is included and how to use it. Or you can get Jennifer's book *Sams Teach Yourself Bootstrap in 24 Hours*.

▶ **Foundation**—Another open-source framework, Foundation emphasizes responsive design so that people with all kinds of devices, from desktops to phones, can enjoy and use your website. Learn more at http://foundation.zurb.com, which includes an extensive "Getting Started" section that details the components of the display templates you can use.

▶ **HTML5 Boilerplate**—One of the leanest frameworks out there, this might be the most useful for beginners because it provides the basics of what you need without overwhelming you with the possibilities. Learn more at http://html5boilerplate.com and see the documentation maintained within the GitHub repository.

Although front-end frameworks can be incredibly useful for speeding up some of the foundational work of web development, you run the risk of falling into the "cookie cutter" trap, in which your site looks like all the others out there (at least the ones using the same framework). However, with a little creativity, you can avoid that trap.

Summary

This lesson gave you examples and explanations to help you organize your web pages into a coherent site that is informative, attractive, easy to find in search engines, and easy to navigate. Web users have become quite savvy and expect well-designed websites, and they will quickly abandon your site if they experience a poor design that is difficult to navigate.

This lesson also discussed the importance of making your code easy to maintain by making liberal use of comments and indentation. Comments are important not only as a reminder for you when you revisit code later but also as instructions for someone who someday inherits your code. Indentation might seem like a minor aesthetic issue, but it can help you quickly analyze and understand the structure of a web page at a glance.

Because you likely will soon need code-management tools either for yourself or for yourself and other developers in your group, this lesson introduced you to a few version control concepts. Version control enables you to innovate without losing your solid, production-quality work and also provides more opportunities for other developers to work within your code base.

Finally, you learned a little bit about HTML and CSS frameworks, of which there are many. These frameworks can help you speed up your web development project by giving you templates that already contain modern and validated markup.

Q&A

Q. Won't adding a lot of comments and spaces make my pages load more slowly when someone views them?

A. The short answer is not really because text is small and doesn't add much to the file size. But you should still think about this because it is something that search engines consider when evaluating a page. If your site is 1/10 of a second slower than another, equally ranked site, that other site will be given precedence over yours in the search engine index. One thing you can do is minify your code by removing all the comments and extraneous spaces before you publish. You can learn more about the concept of minifying your HTML, CSS, and JavaScript at https://developers.google.com/speed/docs/insights/MinifyResources.

Q. Using version control seems like overkill for my tiny personal website. Do I have to use it?

A. Of course not. Websites of any type, personal or otherwise, are not required to be under version control or other backup systems. However, most people have experienced some data loss or a website crash, so if you don't use version control, I highly recommend at least performing some sort of automated backup of your files to an external system. By "external system," I mean any external drive, whether a physical drive attached to your computer or a cloud-based backup service such as Google Drive (https://drive.google.com), Microsoft OneDrive (https://onedrive.live.com), or Apple iCloud (https://www.apple.com/icloud/).

Workshop

The Workshop contains quiz questions and activities to help you solidify your understanding of the material covered. Try to answer all questions before looking at the "Answers" section that follows.

Quiz

1. How can you ensure that all your pages form a single cohesive website?

  a. Use consistent backgrounds, colors, and fonts.

  b. Repeat words or graphics at the top of your pages.

  c. Avoid repeating images.

  d. Both A and B

2. What types of information should you always include in your home page?

  a. Site name and descriptive information

  b. Site name and contact form

  c. Contact form and product list

  d. Both A and C

3. You want to say to future editors of a web page, "Don't change this image of me. It's my only chance at immortality." But you don't want users who view the page to see that message. How can you do this?

  a. Put the message in CSS

  b. Put the message in JavaScript

  c. Put the message in a comment

  d. You can't. Everything you post will appear on the page.

4. What is a benefit of a single-page website?

    a. More mobile friendly

    b. Downloads quickly

    c. People prefer to link to them

    d. Both A and B

5. What is the largest number of links you should have in a navigation bar for maximum usability?

    a. Seven

    b. Six

    c. Five

    d. Four

6. What is an important aspect of SEO?

    a. Interesting content

    b. Easy-to-use navigation

    c. Mobile friendly

    d. All of the above

7. What is a way to write maintainable code?

    a. Use comments

    b. Use a code template

    c. Use user-friendly tags

    d. Both A and B

8. What does it mean to *diff a version-controlled file*?

    a. Add a new version to the repository

    b. Compare the version to the copy in the repository

    c. Modify the version in the repository

    d. Roll back to a previous version

9. How can you write mobile-friendly websites?

    a. Make pages as large as needed.

    b. Write valid HTML.

    c. Optimize images for quality over speed.

    d. Both B and C

10. Why use an HTML framework like Bootstrap?

    a. To speed up page loading.

    b. To make your code easier to read.

    c. To take advantage of a system for writing advanced designs.

    d. Both A and B

NOTE

Just a reminder for those of you reading these words in the print or e-book edition of this book: If you go to **www.informit.com/register** and register this book (using ISBN 9780672338083), you can receive free access to an online Web Edition that not only contains the complete text of this book but also features an interactive version of this quiz.

Answers

  1. **d.** Use consistent background, colors, fonts, and styles. Repeat the same link words or graphics on the top of the page that the link leads to. Repeat the same small header, buttons, or other elements on every page of the site.

  2. **a.** Use enough identifying information that users can immediately see the name of the site and understand what it is about. Also, whatever is the most important message that you want to convey to your intended audience, state it directly and concisely. Whether it's your mission statement or a trademarked marketing slogan, make sure it is in plain view here.

  3. **c.** Put the following comment immediately before the `<img>` tag:

```
<!-- Don't change this image of me.
     It's my only chance at immortality. -->
```

  4. **b.** A single-page website downloads quickly, it can be fully printed, it can be saved on a hard drive, and internal links tend to respond more quickly than external links.

  5. **a.** Most people struggle if there are more than seven links in the main navigation, and they prefer to see five or fewer.

  6. **d.** Your site should have interesting content, implement easy-to-use navigation, and be mobile friendly.

  7. **d.** Use comments to document the code and use a code template (indenting) to format the code for easier reading.

8. b. It means that you're comparing it to the version in the repository or another version.

9. b. Write valid code (HTML, CSS, and JavaScript). Create responsive pages. Make the pages as small as possible. Never hide content from mobile users just because they are on a mobile device. Test your pages in the Mobile-Friendly Test tool.

10. c. HTML frameworks are great when you don't want to use a full CMS but you do want a system for writing advanced HTML and CSS presentation.

Exercises

▶ Open the HTML, CSS, and JavaScript files that make up your current website and check them all for comments and code indentation. Are there areas in which the code needs to be explained to anyone who might look at it in the future? If so, add explanatory comments. Is it difficult for you to tell the hierarchy of your code; that is, is it difficult to see headings and sections? If so, indent your code so that the structure matches the hierarchy and thus enables you to jump quickly to the section you need to edit.

▶ Create an account at GitHub and create a repository for your personal website or other code-based project. From this point forward, keep your repository in sync with your work on your personal computer by committing your changes to the GitHub repository.

Index

N

O

P

X-Y-Z